WORKING FOR BETTER TIMES

DISPOSED OF
BY LIBRARY
HOUSE OF LORDS

WORKING FOR BETTER TIMES

Rethinking work for the 21st century

Edited by

Jean-Michel Servais, Patrick Bollé, Mark Lansky
and Christine L. Smith

INTERNATIONAL LABOUR OFFICE GENEVA

Copyright © International Labour Organization 2007
First published 2007

Publications of the International Labour Office enjoy copyright under Protocol 2 of the Universal Copyright Convention. Nevertheless, short excerpts from them may be reproduced without authorization, on condition that the source is indicated. For rights of reproduction or translation, application should be made to ILO Publications (Rights and Permissions), International Labour Office, CH-1211 Geneva 22, Switzerland, or by email: pubdroit@ilo.org. The International Labour Office welcomes such applications.

Libraries, institutions and other users registered in the United Kingdom with the Copyright Licensing Agency, 90 Tottenham Court Road, London W1T 4LP [Fax: (+44) (0)20 7631 5500; email: cla@cla.co.uk], in the United States with the Copyright Clearance Center, 222 Rosewood Drive, Danvers, MA 01923 [Fax: (+1) (978) 750 4470; email: info@copyright.com] or in other countries with associated Reproduction Rights Organizations, may make photocopies in accordance with the licences issued to them for this purpose.

J.-M. Servais, P. Bollé, M. Lansky, C. Smith (eds.)
Working for better times: Rethinking work for the 21st century
Geneva, International Labour Office, 2007

ISBN 978-92-2-117956-6

Work, decent work, employment, quality of working life, work-life balance, future of work, developed countries, developing countries. 13.01.1

Also available in French: *Travail et temps au XXIe siècle* (ISBN 978-92-2-217956-5; 92-2-217956-0), Geneva, 2006

ILO Cataloguing in Publication Data

The designations employed in ILO publications, which are in conformity with United Nations practice, and the presentation of material therein do not imply the expression of any opinion whatsoever on the part of the International Labour Office concerning the legal status of any country, area or territory or of its authorities, or concerning the delimitation of its frontiers.

The responsibility for opinions expressed in signed articles, studies and other contributions rests solely with their authors, and publication does not constitute an endorsement by the International Labour Office of the opinions expressed in them.

Reference to names of firms and commercial products and processes does not imply their endorsement by the International Labour Office, and any failure to mention a particular firm, commercial product or process is not a sign of disapproval.

ILO publications can be obtained through major booksellers or ILO local offices in many countries, or direct from ILO Publications, International Labour Office, CH-1211 Geneva 22, Switzerland. Catalogues or lists of new publications are available free of charge from the above address, or by email: pubvente@ilo.org.

Visit our website: www.ilo.org/publns.

Photocomposed by the International Labour Office, Geneva, Switzerland
Printed in Switzerland

DTP
SRO

The first thematic compilation of articles from the *International Labour Review* dates back to the publication of *Women, gender and work* in 2001.[1] This successful precedent alone might have been sufficient to justify a follow-up compilation on a different theme. But there are at least two other reasons why we felt that this new selection of articles might make a useful addition to the literature at this juncture. The first is strictly a matter of quality of content and the enduring – not to say increasing – relevance of the contributions it contains. On these points, readers are of course invited to judge for themselves by reading on. Suffice it to say that *Working for better times* is – as its subtitle suggests – a deliberately visionary venture because vision is badly needed at a time when familiar bearings are lost, and new ones so hard to find.

To most people, work is indeed the mainstay of livelihood, social integration and identity. But the 20th-century meanings of "work" can no longer be taken for granted. Nor, therefore, can the ways in which work traditionally shaped those interrelated spheres of human existence. Thus, as patterns of work continue to shift in response to the demands of production and trade in the global economy, huge challenges have arisen – not only in the lives of individual workers and their families, but also for employers engaged in global competition, and for the makers of national and international policy and law. At the heart of the debate lies the complex challenge of reframing the concepts and rules whereby people's socio-economic security and the human dimensions of work can be reconciled with the global market's growing need for competitive labour flexibility.

Because of the multiplicity of real-life situations both within and across countries, there obviously is no clear-cut policy prescription on offer – only

---

[1] *Women, gender and work: What is equality and how do we get there?* (edited by Martha Fetherolf Loutfi) was awarded the distinction of "Notable Document" by the American Library Association.

trade-offs that can be improved upon. The ILO's Decent Work Agenda provides a broad conceptual framework within which this can be done in a joint effort by government policy-makers and employers' and workers' organizations. As Amartya Sen explains in one of his contributions to this volume, the concept of decent work implies rights, and also tangible socio-economic security. But perhaps above all, it is an affirmation that whatever a country's level of economic development, the right policy framework can bring about qualitative improvement in the work/life experiences of the millions worldwide who are left to make what cynical sense they can out of the connection between what they do for a living and the constantly evolving global environment that ultimately determines their worth and the very life they lead.

Clearly, no single academic discipline or field of research has the wherewithal to produce the right mix of policies for every situation. Only multidisciplinary analysis can provide a satisfactory understanding of the underlying trade-offs and identify the options for improving their terms. Hence the second reason for publishing this book: the list of contributors features economists, sociologists, lawyers, social philosophers, government policy-makers and an international trade unionist – because the *International Labour Review* is multidisciplinary by nature. Being multilingual as well, the *Review* also serves as a channel of communication between researchers who do not share a common culture or common academic traditions but whose perspectives on the globalizing world of work are all the more mutually enriching when they are brought together.

In particular, the selection of articles reproduced in this volume includes contributions by some of continental Europe's most distinguished thinkers on the nature and future of work. Their academic background is often legal, as are their basic analytical frameworks. But the way in which they approach their subject can be strongly reminiscent of what the English literature calls "employment theory". This label has no real equivalent in, say, the French literature. And in the common-law countries, it applies to a field of investigation more typically dominated by social scientists. As French lawyer Alain Supiot points out, the law is merely a reflection of what society aspires to be, not a reflection of what it is. In a very broad sense, however, the interplay of academic disciplines and traditions featured in this book is aimed precisely at exploring and, where possible, bridging that gap.

Jean-Michel Servais introduces the selection with an overview of the issues and a special focus on the increasingly time-constrained relationship between "work" (broadly defined) and the other pursuits which – out of necessity or choice – make up a fully human life. The following chapters are divided into three main parts. The first – "Policy challenges in a changing environment" – offers a wide-ranging selection that explores some of the policy implications of today's changing patterns of work – from William Milberg's searing critique of the win-win mantra of comparative advantage to Hilary Silver's conceptual investigation of the workings of social exclusion, or

Bob Hepple's challenge to current policies for promoting "equality". The second part of the book looks at different aspects of the work-life balance from a broad policy perspective, while the third part consists of an extensive collection of contributions that have been grouped under the self-explanatory heading of "Fresh perspectives, new ideas".

In a sense, an editor's job consists in tuning into, clarifying and amplifying the message from a researcher's findings and arguments. The contributions assembled in this book were selected in that spirit: over the past decade or so, the *Review* team has repeatedly picked up strong consonant signals from research carried out in different countries and different disciplines. Given the nature and clarity of the overall message that has emerged over time, we felt that it deserved to be "amplified" and relayed in its own right, by bringing together in a single volume the works of these outstanding scholars on different aspects of a common concern that has tentatively been summed up in terms of *Rethinking work for the 21st century*. On behalf of Jean-Michel Servais and the entire team of the *International Labour Review*, I hope you agree the message is worth tuning into.

Mark Lansky

CONTENTS

ACKNOWLEDGEMENTS

Special thanks are due to the authors, in universities and institutes and in the International Labour Office, who kindly and voluntarily contributed this material to the *International Labour Review*. Their contributions were checked, carefully edited and revised by the staff of the *ILR* – Patrick Bollé, Monique Grimaud, Mark Lansky, Luis Lázaro Martínez, Martha Fetherolf Loutfi, Marie-Christine Nallet, Kate Pfeiffenberger and Christine L. Smith. They were turned into publishable form by staff in the Document and Publications Production, Printing and Distribution Branch.

The preparation and finalization of this volume owe a great deal to an ILO official in the Book Production Unit, May Hofman Öjermark. The support of the Director of the Department of Communication and Public Information, Zohreh Tabatabai, was indispensable to its publication.

INTRODUCTION

WORKING FOR BETTER TIMES*

Jean-Michel SERVAIS**

1

The steady pace of change in production, communication and information technology has no doubt greatly contributed to the disruption of the employment relationship over the past 20 to 25 years.[1] Capital mobility, more so than labour mobility, has limited what governments can do to attract foreign investment, often prompting them to relax not just fiscal constraints but also social and labour regulations. The shift towards globalized markets has heightened competition between private firms, increased downward pressure on wages and social benefits, and undermined collective bargaining positions because of the possibilities for relocating production. The social partners, notably the trade unions, have been landed in an increasingly awkward position.

In an article that appeared in the *International Labour Review* in 2004, William Milberg examines the extent to which the structures of today's international trade and production – particularly the increased trade in intermediate products associated with the break-up and relocation of production – have led to qualitative changes whose impact is much stronger than that of quantitative developments.[2] He argues that a new approach is needed, one that analyses today's fierce competition in terms of absolute advantages and externalization rather than comparative advantages and reciprocal benefits. This, obviously, has clear policy implications for developing countries, in particular as concerns the imperative need to ensure that the changes under way are accompanied by social measures. Another area of rapid change, particularly in industrialized countries, is the composition of the labour force, which is made up increasingly of service-sector and knowledge workers, with a dwindling proportion of manufacturing labour. Some industries, like the coal industry, have declined; others, like the new technologies, are growing.

---

* In this introduction, references to *ILR* articles in the compilation are indicated in notes. Other works cited are identified in the reference list at the end of the introduction.

** Visiting Professor, Universities of Gerona and Liège; Honorary President of the Société internationale du Droit du Travail et de la Sécurité sociale; former official of the ILO.

These transformations have led to changes in the way work is organized, involving a flattening of management hierarchies and the promotion of decentralized team work. The key word is flexibility, not only in workforce size, but also in working methods and conditions of employment, including wages.[3] Reconciling these imperatives with adequate labour protection is the daunting challenge summed up as "decent work" – the stated goal of the International Labour Organization (ILO).[4]

The changes taking place rob a large part of the labour force of security. As always in a period of transition, some adapt immediately, or at least quickly, while others take longer or simply do not make it. Young people, who inevitably have little work experience, face a protracted up-hill struggle to enter the labour market. A growing number of people work part time, on a temporary or casual basis, or on call. Meanwhile, the proportion of unemployed has not declined. Numerous studies have been conducted on the so-called "social" exclusion of all these groups, on its causes and possible remedies (see Rodgers, Gore and Figueiredo, 1995); Figueiredo and de Haan, 1998).[5]

The "dualization" of societies due to labour market segmentation is particularly obvious in many developing countries,[6] where the informal economy is burgeoning and wages are going down. According to the United Nations' *Report on the World Social Situation 2005: The inequality predicament*, this trend is inducing a "human capital" crisis and undermining efforts to bring about a lasting reduction in poverty. As stressed by the World Bank in its *World Development Report 2006: Equity and development*, the problem is everywhere traceable to unacceptable and widening inequality.[7]

Many of the articles recently published in the *International Labour Review* share this anxious concern about the impact of globalization on people's lives, particularly their ability to earn a living. While many have focused on labour market reform or poverty-reduction policies, this book reproduces a selection of the *Review*'s contributions to the debate that highlight a different perspective, one more sharply focused on women and men at work, on their lives and on the way in which their lives are shaped by their work.

Working time has taken the brunt of the disruption caused by the above developments, including – and perhaps especially – in the poorest countries. In some parts of the world, such as east and south-east Asia, workers are having to agree to substantial increases in their working time in exchange for job security. Elsewhere, as in south Asia and Latin America, every conceivable form of outsourcing is flourishing. Everywhere, new arrangements are emerging, and reconfiguring conventional patterns of shift work. Work done on call or in a call centre eludes government regulations on effective working time.

Research by Alain Supiot and other scholars in France and by Vittorio Valli in Italy has shown the extent to which working-time issues have transcended not only the enterprise level, but also national systems of industrial relations, and in fact relate to how societies are organized. The point, obviously, is not only the numbers of hours spent at work, but all the time that a man or a woman spends working to earn a living, compared with the amount of time he or she devotes to family and the household, rest, social or political activities, volunteer work ... or looking for a paid job. Taken together, the resulting patterns of time use point to new experiences and propositions that were felt to deserve consideration in the context of this book (Supiot, 1995).

Much interest has been shown in new working time arrangements that balance private and professional lives, and thus provide men and women with true equality of opportunity and treatment (Anxo, 2004; Fagan, 2004; Méda, 2001; and Pocock and Clarke, 2005, for an analysis of implications for children). This does not alter the fact that changes in workplace organization brought about by the revolution in production and communication technology have already had a considerable impact on the way in which family and social relations are structured (Carnoy, 2001).

If a society's overall patterns of time use are to be organized rationally, account must be taken both of working time and of time set aside for the other activities, including daily social and cultural life. Such a policy framework is ambitious but not unrealistic, as revealed by several successful experiences in Italy and elsewhere.[8]

WORKING TIME IN CONTEXT

Working time and social policy

Working time raises a great many questions. These relate inter alia to matters of concern to wage earners or employers, the broader interests of the social partners, and urban scheduling problems that governments can no longer ignore.

The societal setting of work

In a typical life cycle, engagement in paid activity – i.e. work as it is commonly understood – starts with an apprenticeship or some form of occupational activity. The break between schooling and working life is not one that everyone finds easy to handle. Hence the concern of States to link the school-leaving age to the minimum age for employment (and individual responsibility for social security contributions, i.e. the end of dependency). Hence also the spread, especially in western Europe, of work experience and training schemes that guarantee a smoother transition to working life, both in terms of adjustment and in terms of finding a job. Yet the need to coordinate policies so as to enhance occupational skills and fight unemployment is a concern that relates to people's entire working lives. The policies pursued to that end often involve adjustments in working time, e.g. reduced hours, paid leave for training purposes, sabbaticals, the management of working time within more flexible weekly limits, job-sharing, etc.

At the other end of a working life, retirement age is also a focus of social policy. Many governments have encouraged early retirement in the hope of creating jobs for younger people – a target rarely met. This policy, however, has sent occupational pension funds deeper into the red. Flexible retirement schemes are more attractive and meet many people's aspirations. They establish no fixed age for termination of the employment relationship; rather, they provide a legal framework for bringing forward or putting off that moment through definitive or gradual retirement. But obviously, whatever the public policy adopted, the decision to retire or to continue working depends on the parties to the employment relationship, notably the employer.

The initial and final periods of a working life raise different but related issues in regard to occupational health and safety. Accident prevention and protection against occupational illnesses indeed are two other mainstays of social policy; they involve preventive measures such as periods of rest and leisure, including the option of practising sports.

After the Second World War, there was a gradual, but marked reduction in working time for all wage earners in all industrialized countries. Initially, this was done for health-related reasons, particularly in dangerous or arduous occupations, but later on the underlying rationale shifted to include other reasons, such as a fair distribution of the fruits of economic progress,[9] or the promotion of family-friendly or equal opportunity policies. A number of governments thus hoped to ease the endemic problem of unemployment. Others, by contrast, resisted the trend, as did many employers, citing the need to remain competitive. At issue is not so much the reduction of extremely long working hours – the positive impact of which appears to be widely recognized – as the effect of shorter hours on productivity (see ILO, 1988, pp. 30-40).

Increasingly, the way in which people balance their working and private lives appears to be a key factor in their physical and psychological well-being. The solution is to rearrange schedules, including those of public transport, to meet the needs of people in their daily roles as parents, customers, consumers or users. Some even argue that time should be set aside for voluntary work, for involvement in clubs and associations, and for public debate.[10]

Moreover, the modern organization of companies and services, the use of new production and communication technologies and the gradual disappearance of economic boundaries have had a strong impact on people's working hours. Internet workers in particular have to adapt their lives to the demands of globalized markets and the need to stay in contact with correspondents living in other time zones.

Working time and industrial relations

This is a familiar topic. Wages and hours of work are the central issues in collective bargaining. Employers, especially in small or medium-sized enterprises,[11] typically prefer to pay overtime than to hire extra staff. And, if they do hire anybody, they tend to do so for a limited period (which can now be extremely short), hiring workers on a casual or on-call basis. For workers who become technically self-employed or "parasubordinate",[12] working hours no longer fall within the scope of their legal relationship, with the employer whose interests are to increase productivity and amortize investment in equipment that can be very costly. Thus, employers often require discontinuous, semi-continuous or continuous shift work in order to optimize capacity utilization. They hire cautiously, as and when orders come in. What they want is flexibility in contractual relations and work organization, so that they can react swiftly to international competition, economic developments and scientific and technological advances.

Such constraints on the duration of employment destabilize wage earners. What they want is protection against material insecurity – through contracts without limit of time – and against accidents and illness by means of rest periods appropriate to the laboriousness of the work they perform. They also want free time to perform household tasks, bring up their children, engage in sports or social activities, or even hold public office. They want the choice of full- or part-time work (Messenger, 2004a, pp. 7-8). In the Netherlands, legislation promoting part-time work has indeed met with great success. All these questions were discussed in depth at a symposium organized jointly by the ILO and the French Government in 2001.[13]

The individualization of working time

For a policy on working time to be successful, it needs to take account of considerations of public interest and of the respective interests of employers and workers. Individual concerns are also becoming increasingly diverse (Messenger, 2004b; Camos Victoria and Rojo Torrecilla, 2002; Lallement, 2003; Daugareilh and Iriart, 2004; Favennec-Héry, 2005). Among wage earners, this is not only because some have stable jobs while others do not.[14] All of them have a wider range of aspirations than they did in the past, with variations depending on their sector of activity, occupation, qualifications, age, sex and family situation. Such diversity calls for more individualized responses that take account of workers as a heterogeneous group, of their daily routines and individual constraints.

From the employers' point of view too, each firm has its own culture, and employers tend to be reluctant to adopt standardized measures.[15]

THE LAW OF WORKING TIME

The options

Whether the regulation of working time is statutory or contractual is a matter of policy, not to say one of doctrine: the choice is between state intervention and allowing the parties to a contract or collective agreement to reach their own terms. Comparative law offers solutions that tend to reflect the dominant culture and ideology,[16] but which typically steer clear of extreme positions. That being said, state regulation, in which labour law is grounded, used to be the general rule, but clearly that trend is now being reversed by globalization.

The current consensus is that the open-ended, full-time contract of employment is no longer the archetype it used to be: it is giving way to fixed-term contracts which can hardly be called "atypical" anymore. Indeed, such contractual arrangements can no longer be conceptualized in terms of exceptions to a common law of unlimited employment relationships. This pattern now survives only in legal systems that explicitly provide so – as the French Labour Code does.

At all events, the principle of freedom of contract allows the parties to specify all manner of provisions for termination of their relationship, subject to statutory exceptions. Such provisions may include a specific date (which may be near or distant), the completion of a particular task (e.g. a harvest or a project abroad), the end of a period of replacement (e.g. of a sick colleague, a woman on maternity leave or, in the United States, a striking worker), or the end of a season. Some agreements may also provide for a trial period. In the absence of any such provision for termination, the law in many European countries still presumes – as does the French Labour Code – that the intention of the parties to the contract was to enter into an employment relationship of unlimited duration. Work may also be performed on call.

Part-time work arrangements are proliferating, inter alia in the context of job-sharing and phased retirement (Favennec-Héry, 1997; Sciarra, Davies and Freedland, 2004). And many workers now have more than one job.

The precarious nature of contractual relationships frequently translates into equally precarious working conditions, because fear of job-loss deters workers from standing up for their rights, even on such basic issues as occupational health. A further source of instability is that, where the law so permits, employment relationships are often intermediated by private employment agencies or firms that "lend" or subcontract labour – to the point where it may become difficult to establish who the employer is.[17]

Freedom of contract works to the wage earners' advantage if they are in demand. But, more often than not, the balance of power favours the employer. The latter's position of strength does not mean that she/he can unilaterally modify basic terms of the contract on, say, working time or termination,[18] but it may be enough to pressure the worker into accepting such changes. Significantly, the domestic legislation of several countries (e.g. Belgium, France and Italy) and European law have for several years authorized departures from statutory rules on working time by collective agreement (Lyon-Caen, 1995, pp. 41 et seq.; Jamoulle et al., 1997, pp. 500 et seq.; Bocquillon, 2005, pp. 803-808)[19] and, exceptionally, by individual agreement.[20]

The ILO and working time

Comparative law on working time is still much influenced by its origins. Recent developments are the outcome of occasional "social truces", rather than consensus. The ILO's Conventions and Recommendations reflect the underlying tensions.

The *limitation of working time* was originally prompted by concern for the physical health of workers, including children. Scientists and people of good will (including many senior civil servants), together with enlightened employers and the leaders of nascent labour movements called for and secured a reduction in hours of work. Ever since its inception, the ILO has been an active proponent of this cause: the preamble to its Constitution – Part XIII of the Treaty of Versailles, which established the Organization – underscored the need to regulate working time and to set upper daily and weekly limits. Article 427 established the principle of the eight-hour day and 48-hour week, with a weekly rest of at least 24 hours, usually on Sunday.[21]

The first Convention adopted by the new Organization – the Hours of Work (Industry) Convention, 1919 (No. 1) – set the standard of eight hours per day and 48 hours per week in industry, specifying permissible exceptions and the rules governing overtime. This standard was then extended to work in commerce and offices by the somewhat more detailed Hours of Work (Commerce and Offices) Convention, 1930 (No. 30). These Conventions had a lasting impact on domestic labour legislation and many collective agreements. One of their merits was to rationalize the issue of working time and show to what extent it all boiled down to a matter of proper organization of work (Servais, 2005, pp. 184 et seq.).

The outlook changed with the Forty-Hour Week Convention, 1935 (No. 47), which was adopted at the end of the long depression experienced by the industrialized countries between the two world wars. Its aim was to combat unemployment by reducing working time. It was followed by several sectoral instruments, some of which lowered the weekly limit to 40 hours, and the Reduction of Hours of Work Recommendation, 1962 (No. 116), which the ILO still considers the reference text.

The ILO's constituents have not yet been able to reach agreement on a more modern Convention integrating the many demands for more flexible working-time arrangements. Particularly contentious are the effects of reduced working hours on job creation, and the cost – and for whom? – of a more flexible approach.

Meanwhile, the Organization has adopted instruments specific to certain forms of work and to *part-time work*. This type of employment has recently been encouraged in the obvious hope that it will help to curb unemployment. Adopted in 1994, Convention No. 175 and Recommendation No. 182 set out the principle of equal protection for part-time and full-time wage earners. Several of their provisions aim to facilitate access to part-time work – if necessary, through reconsideration of any legislative impediments thereto – and transitions between full-time and part-time employment.

Changes in the regulatory approach to *night work* illustrate two trends. The first has consisted in giving precedence to equality between women and men rather than to specific "protection" for women. The second has been a tendency to eliminate certain safeguards, considered superfluous, in order to relax the legal constraints on employers. Both trends have their justifications, and both have their supporters.[22] But they are not to be confused. Moreover, there continues to be widespread acceptance of the prohibition of night work for adolescents under 18 years of age; the Minimum Age Recommendation, 1973 (No. 146), which upholds that principle, is considered a priority instrument within the Organization.[23]

The international prohibition of night work for women in industry dates back to 1906, before the ILO was founded, when a conference in Bern adopted a convention on this subject (Valticos, 1983, para. 32, note 73). Upon its establishment in 1919, the ILO endorsed that convention and expanded on it: the Night Work (Women) Convention, 1919 (No. 4), defined "night" as "a period of at least eleven consecutive hours, including the interval between ten o'clock in the evening and five o'clock in the morning" (Article 2, para. 1).

Successive revisions[24] allowed greater leeway in the calculation of the night period and authorized more exceptions for given categories of female workers. The same trend emerged in the domestic legislation of various countries, though the latter proved quicker to respond to the equality argument and were the first to overturn the prohibition. At the ILO, a Protocol added in 1990 to Convention No. 89 authorized night work for women in industry provided, in principle, that the employers' and workers' organizations concerned agreed. Noteworthy here is the role given to the social partners in providing for an exception to a general prohibition.

Concomitantly, the Organization adopted Convention No. 171 and Recommendation No. 178 to improve the night work conditions of both men and women. The Convention calls for the adoption of such specific measures as the nature of night work may require to protect workers' safety and health (including in respect of maternity), help them meet their family and social obligations, provide them with opportunities for occupational advancement, and compensate them in terms of working time, pay and additional benefits. This Convention also calls for appropriate social services to be provided for night workers. It further stipulates that before introducing work schedules requiring the services of night workers, the employer must consult the workers' representatives concerned on the details of those schedules, the organization of the night work, and the occupational health measures and social services required. Such consultation is to take place regularly – another example of the responsibility given to workers' and employers' organizations.

National and international labour standards authorize *absence from work* for a variety of reasons: physical constraints (ill health, maternity), moral obligations (parental leave) or civic duties (military service, jury duty). Workers may also be allowed to take limited periods of leave in order to further their general, social, civic, trade union or above all vocational education and training. The Paid Educational Leave Convention, 1974 (No. 140), and its accompanying Recommendation No. 148, adopted by the ILO in 1974, specify that such leave must be paid. The Termination of Employment Recommendation, 1982 (No. 166), suggests that workers who have been served notice of dismissal should, during the period of notice, be entitled to a reasonable amount of time off without loss of pay, taken at times that are convenient to both parties, for the purpose of seeking other employment (paragraph 16).

Current usage of the word "leave", however, still usually evokes a day of rest. Such rest can be taken to compensate for work performed outside normal hours, say, at night. Official holidays – which vary from one country to another and over time – are also days of rest. The ILO does not deal with this question directly, but the United Nations International Covenant on Economic, Social and Cultural Rights stipulates that days of rest must be paid (Article 7).

The ILO has, however, drawn up instruments on weekly rest and paid leave. The basic standards governing the former are the Weekly Rest (Industry) Convention, 1921 (No. 14) and the Weekly Rest (Commerce and Offices) Convention, 1957 (No. 106).[25] They provide for a period of rest comprising at least 24 consecutive hours in every seven-day period, if possible to be granted the same day of the week to the entire workforce in keeping with local tradition or custom. Both Conventions authorize exceptions for humanitarian or economic reasons (i.e. actual or threatened accident, *force majeure*, urgent work on premises or equipment, abnormal pressure of work, to prevent the loss of perishable goods). The terms and conditions of such exceptions and compensatory leave arrangements are to be set down in domestic legislation.

Convention No. 132, of 1970, and Recommendation No. 98, of 1954, deal with paid holidays, to which all wage earners are entitled (three weeks at least for one year of service, and pro rata for a shorter period of employment). Special rules may apply to employees who, during their paid holidays, carry out a paid activity incompatible with the purpose of the holidays.

The Minimum Age Convention, 1973 (No. 138), prohibits the *employment of adolescents* under the age of 15 (or 14 in countries whose economies and educational facilities are insufficiently developed). It provides for two types of exception. The first relates to developing countries, which are allowed various forms of flexibility. The second pertains to physically or morally hazardous work – in which case the minimum age is raised to 18 years – and, conversely, "light work", in which case it is lowered to 13 or even 12 years.

Looking at the other end of a working life, experts have been questioning the advisability of imposing a compulsory *retirement age*. The argument is that prolonging people's working lives reduces social security costs, while benefits from the experience of more senior workers usually more than compensate the firm for the disadvantages of old age (ILO, 1995, pp. 30 et seq.). Accordingly, the ILO's Older Workers Recommendation, 1980 (No. 162), proposes that retirement should be voluntary within a framework allowing for "a gradual transition from working life to freedom of activity". It also recommends flexibility in regard to the rules on the qualifying age for old-age benefits and on the mandatory termination of the employment relationship at a specific age.

This Recommendation calls on States to examine the matter in depth: to identify the types of activity likely to hasten the ageing process or in which older workers encounter difficulties in adapting to the demands of their work, to determine why this happens, and to devise appropriate solutions. The proposed responses include:

- modifying the forms of work organization and working time which lead to stress or to an excessive pace of work, in particular by limiting overtime;

- adapting the job and its content to the worker by recourse to ergonomic principles;

- systematic supervision of the workers' state of health and supervision on the job as is appropriate for preserving the workers' safety and health.

In Japan, for example, older workers are eligible for a special pay scheme and employment opportunities where their skills can be used to best effect. Such a policy, however, implies providing information not only to the workers concerned, but also to employment and training officers and to the public at large.

A NEW APPROACH IN THE MAKING

Success stories and untested ideas

The political parties represented in national parliaments rarely find common ground.[26] Compromise is the order of the day, but latent conflicts remain. Rather than giving expression to a genuine labour policy, legislation tends to be "adjusted".[27]

And yet numerous proposals have been made and tried out. What they have in common is the will to break away from the dilemma of (contractual) freedom vs. (regulated) protection, to broaden the debate into taking a comprehensive life-cycle approach, and to come up with a framework for achieving a more satisfactory balance between individual needs.[28] Legal scholars, economists and sociologists are having to become more pragmatic and innovative.[29] Such thinking is not entirely new, however. As regards working time, issues such as shop opening hours, staggered working times, flexitime, and a compressed working week have been debated for years (ILO, 1988, pp. 44-46 and 49-50; ILO, 1985, pp. 69-70).

Nevertheless, recent experiences have opened up new avenues. For example, legislation passed in Japan in 1987 introduced performance-based management of working time at the enterprise level: if the workers concerned – particularly those in highly specialized jobs – agree with their supervisors on the targets and deadlines to be met, they are allowed to fix their work schedule as they see fit within those limits (Inagami, 1999, pp. 695-696; Messenger, 2004b, pp. 181-182; Le Goff, 2005, pp. 155-156).

Elsewhere, legislation allowed reduced working hours for workers with dependants (Austria, Denmark, Sweden). A more radical approach is reflected in the Dutch law on working-time arrangements of 19 February 2000, which introduced truly individualized hours of work: it gives wage earners the right to ask for a reduction, an extension or a redistribution of their working hours; management must agree if there is no good reason to object (the law lists a number of possible objections). Germany has adopted similar provisions, as has, to a certain extent, the United Kingdom (McCann, 2004, pp. 21-23).

Meanwhile, some researchers observed that new institutional arrangements increasingly made allowance for vocational training, that the wide variety of individual needs required greater flexibility in the organization of work, and that non-traditional forms of employment called for rethinking the relationship between work and other socially useful activities (European Academy of the Urban Environment, 1998; Gazier and Schmid, 2002). What they came up with was the concept of a "transitional labour market" as the broad framework within which the new arrangements were being implemented (in terms of organization, incomes policies, social policies and their fiscal effects). The subject was debated at length at another symposium organized by the ILO and the French Government, in 2002.[30]

Another group of researchers, headed by Alain Supiot, sought an alternative to this conceptual approach to the labour market.[31] They observed that people could be active in a number of ways in the course of their working lives, e.g. wage employment, self-employment, public service employment,[32] training or internship,[33] vocational retraining, sabbatical leave, household work, public office, civic duties (military or civil service), etc. (Supiot, 1998).

Following this line of thought, some have proposed to construct working-life scenarios made up of interlocking modules that alternate working time, training and paid leave, e.g. maternity leave, parental leave, leave for military service, etc. (see Boissonnat, 1995; Valli, 1988, pp. 13-38, and 177-197; Ladear, 1995, p. 145).[34] Improved skills and greater independence (the latter depends on the former) would allow for more satisfactory coordination of the various activities – work, training and retraining, leave for a specific purpose, voluntary or low-paid tasks that have a high social value, such as caring for children or the elderly, assistance to the victims of violence, etc.[35] – and for the planning of such activities over the course of a working life. Conflicts of interest – both in workers' personal lives and in their employment relationships – would thus be more easily resolved. In particular, this would also lead to a more satisfactory balance between private (family) life and working life.[36]

In practice, however, these proposals come up against major obstacles (Castel, 1999, pp. 438-442; Jacobs, 2000, pp. 55 et seq.). The foremost among them relates to the possibility of using such a framework to map out people's life-cycle and finance those periods during which they are not engaged in gainful activity. Indeed, the aim of social protection is to reassure workers and would-be workers about their lives, their health, their subsistence and that of their loved ones.[37] It is not intended to eliminate all uncertainties, to provide for every contingency, to organize every single aspect of people's lives. Besides, to the most dynamic people uncertainty is a spur to enterprise, innovation and creation, and hence a factor of progress.

Nevertheless these ideas offer a fresh perspective on the loss of meaning or centrality of work.[38] They are also helpful in understanding the many forms work can take, including in the informal economy of the developing countries. They furnish convincing arguments for a minimum guaranteed income or small loans for training (Supiot, 2001, pp. 56-57), the care of dependants, social work, etc.[39]

Italy has come up with the concept of *tempi della città* – "the times of the city" (Bonfiglioli and Mareggi, 1997; Belloni and Bimbi, 1997). This approach has been experimented in many towns in central Italy – but also in Milan and Rome – and replicated in Germany and France. It started with a group composed mainly of women reflecting on the quality of life in an urban environment and the possibility of arranging urban schedules more coherently. This grass-roots initiative sought the best fit between working times, the opening hours of shops and public and private services, and public transport timetables. City-dwellers were seen as consumers and users as well as workers, with a focus on their needs and expectations, their aspirations to lead fulfilling private, public and social lives. This approach required such a broad range of individual interests to be taken into account that it could not be implemented "from the top", say through state legislation. Hence the emergence in the mid-1980s of a new model of "collective bargaining" involving all sorts of local-level stakeholders. Organizations of women and public service users, trade unions, chambers of commerce and trade guilds, neighbourhood organizations and employers' associations thus met with the municipal authorities to agree on arrangements for better coordinating the times during which shops, offices and public services, schools, public transport and enterprises were to open for business.

Critics argued the process would be long and complicated, and they may have been right, but still the results have surpassed all expectations, including in terms of smoother traffic flows. This experience also offers an interesting example of how work and family responsibilities can be harmonized as provided for, inter alia, in the Workers with Family Responsibilities Convention, 1981 (No. 156) and its accompanying Recommendation No. 165. It demonstrates that the social actors can broaden their vision beyond an exclusive political focus on material interests in order to satisfy people's aspirations for richer social and private lives. It has also helped to widen the horizons of labour law. Initially protective, such legislation evolved into a law of mediation between the interests of employers and their employees; and it is now developing into a law of social cohesion and integration that clearly must take account of the times when people living in today's society are not at work.[40]

International perspectives

There has been much international debate about working time and its reduction, daily, monthly and annualized working-time arrangements, employment for limited or freely chosen periods, and early or phased retirement. More often than not, however, such debate has been polarized between the concerns of workers – their protection and sharing in productivity gains – and those of employers, notably their concern for production process efficiency in the face of globalized competition.

The authors of the articles reproduced in this book reconsider the very concept of work in terms of relationships,[41] market connections and instrumentality in economic security,[42] and as a typically crucial period of human activity. This is also the aim of the ILO's current programmes, summed up in the concept of decent work.[43]

The experiences and ideas mentioned above should help to find new ways of overcoming such conflicts as the controversy in France surrounding the 35-hour working week and to explore the options for better coordinating working time, social life and leisure for the benefit of all. In short, the point is to think of working-time issues as being societal, not as being narrowly confined to employment relationships. As the stakeholders in Italy's *tempi della città* have showed, employers and wage earners are also consumers, users, clients and taxpayers; they want to purchase the products and services they need at the lowest possible cost and at times that are convenient to them, i.e. outside their working hours. They want to have free time to care for their children or elderly parents, either together with their spouse or on the basis of some alternating arrangement with their spouse. Flexible working hours are indeed a sure means of equalizing opportunities for men and women. Lastly, some people may want to work shorter hours on account of their health, or to pursue training, or for other reasons.

Government policy-makers tend to link working time with employment, in order to prevent redundancies and to promote recruitment. In many cases, however, they have failed to take due account of the positive employment effects of keeping shops and offices open longer by rotating staff – not to mention the implications for economic growth. Like staggered school and working hours, such a policy would also ease traffic congestion and crowding on public transport. However. the mobilization of civil society organizations and other social institutions with a view to giving everyone a chance to participate in the determination of their own working time raises a number of questions.[44]

The first concerns the role of the State, which would have to furnish the legal framework required to promote private initiatives in this field. This would connect with the modern tendency for labour law to focus on procedures rather than substance. In this case, it would indeed fall to the law to encourage national, regional or local authorities to recognize truly representative social actors, to help them develop, to provide them with access to useful information, to recognize such organizations as they may establish (or even help establish them), and to foster relations between the various stakeholders. The law would have to provide for their incorporation into the bodies that plan and implement the systemic management of time in society. It must also broaden the scope for independent negotiations. The State would thus act more as a source of inspiration than as a guide, as a mediator ensuring a favourable climate for dialogue.

The second question concerns the kinds of legal rule that would encourage such interaction and coordination. Preference would of course have to be given to standards that allow the parties themselves to strike their own work-life balance, both individually and collectively – i.e. "programmatic standards" that set objectives and impose only the obligation to strive to attain them, without directly regulating the process. In several countries (including Belgium and France) and at the European level, the social partners have recently been empowered to negotiate collective agreements that liberalize regulatory frameworks or provide for exceptions to the principles laid down in the law, notably in regard to working-time arrangements (Lyon-Caen, 1995, pp. 41 et seq.; Revet, 1996, pp. 61 et seq.).[45] In some cases, they are given an even greater role: in principle, Italian legislation allows employers and nationally or locally representative trade unions to determine, by collective agreement, the grounds (relating to the organization of production) that justify recourse to casual labour.[46]

This approach could easily be taken one step further. Specifically, instead of restricting the social partners to negotiating exceptions to a common rule or safeguards against extreme precariousness, they could be empowered positively and freely to set the terms of the work-life balance within a more flexible and comprehensive regulatory framework than the current narrow focus on daily and weekly working time.

The third question concerns the actors who would be called upon to perform regulatory functions. In spite of the well-known difficulties they face, workers' organizations remain crucial to social policy-making in democratic societies. They are among the most representative bodies in civil society; few others can claim to have the same capacity to mobilize or as many long-standing members (ILO, 1997, especially pp. 31-55).[47] The same holds true for employers' organizations (ibid., pp. 57-67). However, other movements have also emerged in the recent past, and they have been instrumental more than once in seeing an initiative through to success (ibid., pp. 228-229).

Indeed, successful experiences owe much to the consideration of wider social concerns, such as the defence of a specific cause (human rights, the environment), of a minority (e.g. an ethnic minority), of an underprivileged category (women) or of more general interests (e.g. those of users or consumers). Like employers' and workers' federations, the coalitions that back these causes act as intermediaries between civil society and the public authorities.

Employers' and workers' organizations listen more willingly to some of these interest groups than to others. Nevertheless, if they take united action, as in the *tempi della città* project, they are more likely to obtain tangible results.

Notes

[1] See G.M. Kelly: *Employment and concepts of work in the new global economy* (Chapter 2 in this volume).

[2] See William Milberg: *The changing structure of trade linked to global production systems: What are the policy implications?* (Chapter 3 in this volume).

[3] See Tiziano Treu: *Labour flexibility in Europe* (Chapter 4 in this volume).

[4] See Robert B. Reich: *The challenge of decent work* (Chapter 5 in this volume).

[5] See Hilary Silver: *Social exclusion and social solidarity: Three paradigms* (Chapter 6 in this volume).

[6] See Henry Bruton and David Fairris: *Work and Development* (Chapter 7 in this volume).

[7] See Amartya Sen: *Inequality, unemployment and contemporary Europe* (Chapter 8 in this volume); and Bob Hepple: *Equality and empowerment for decent work* (Chapter 9 in this volume).

[8] See below. More generally, for an overview of work and time, see Supiot (2001).

[9] A shorter working week is in many cases an alternative to wage increases. See *European Industrial Relations Review* (2005); Morel (2005).

[10] See Virginie Pérotin: *The voluntary sector, job creation and social policy: Illusions and opportunities* (Chapter 10 in this volume).

[11] See Geraldo von Potobsky: *Small and medium-sized enterprises and labour law* (Chapter 11 in this volume).

[12] Workers who are legally independent but economically vulnerable (as in Germany or Italy, for example).

[13] See Patrick Bollé: *The future of work, employment and social protection (the Annecy Symposium, January 2001)* (Chapter 12 in this volume).

[14] See Joseph A. Ritter and Richard Anker: *Good jobs, bad jobs: Workers' evaluations in five countries* (Chapter 13 in this volume).

[15] See Marie-Laure Morin: *Labour law and new forms of corporate organization* (Chapter 14 in this volume).

[16] For an overview of the issues from the perspective of political economy, see Jacoby (2003).

[17] If domestic legislation does not stipulate whether it is the labour-supplying intermediary or the enterprise "using" the worker which is the true employer, this typically has to be decided by interpreting the content of the contract, the nature and conditions of the work and the intent of the parties. See ILO (2005a, pp. 42-52); and Siau (1996).

[18] Cassation française 17 novembre 2004, in *Droit social* (Paris), No. 2, February 2005, and note Ch. Rodé, pp. 227-228.

[19] On European law, see Directive 2003/88/CE of the European Parliament and of the Council of 4 November 2003 concerning certain aspects of the organization of working time, article 18, in *Official Journal of the European Union* (Luxembourg), 18 Nov. 2003, No. L299, pp. 9-19.

[20] See also the European Directive cited above, article 22. To date, the British Government is the only one to have availed itself of this option. On this point, see Kenner (2004).

[21] For more details, see Le Crom (2004); and ILO (2005b), paras. 3-8.

[22] See George P. Politakis: *Night work of women in industry: Standards and sensibility* (Chapter 15 in this volume).

[23] See Servais, *op. cit.*, para. 370.

[24] See the Night Work (Women) Convention (Revised), 1934 (No. 41), and the Night Work (Women) Convention (Revised), 1948 (No. 89).

[25] See also the Weekly Rest (Commerce and Offices) Recommendation, 1957 (No. 103), which supplements the Convention.

[26] See Joseph E. Stiglitz: *Employment, social justice and societal well-being* (Chapter 16 in this volume).

[27] See Pietro Ichino: *The labour market: A lawyer's view of economic arguments* (Chapter 17 in this volume).

[28] See Amartya Sen: *Work and rights* (Chapter 18 in this volume); and Martha Nussbaum: *Women and equality: The capabilities approach* (Chapter 19 in this volume).

[29] See Jean-Claude Javillier: *Pragmatism and daring in international labour law: Reflections of a labour lawyer* (Chapter 20 in this volume).

[30] See Patrick Bollé: *The dynamics of change and the protection of workers* (Chapter 21 in this volume).

[31] See Alain Supiot: *Perspectives on work: Introduction* (Chapter 22 in this volume); and Dominique Méda: *New perspectives on work as value* (Chapter 23 in this volume).

[32] See Alain Supiot: *Work and the public/private dichotomy* (Chapter 24 in this volume).

[33] See Françoise Favennec-Héry: *Work and training: A blurring of the edges* (Chapter 25 in this volume).

[34] See Jean Boissonnat: *Combating unemployment, restructuring work: Reflections on a French study* (Chapter 26 in this volume); and Patrick Bollé: *What is the future of work? Ideas from a French report* (Chapter 27 in this volume).

[35] See Raymond Le Guidec: *Decline and resurgence of unremunerated work* (Chapter 28 in this volume).

[36] See Gérard Lyon-Caen: *By way of conclusion: Labour law and employment transitions* (Chapter 29 in this volume).

[37] See Jean-Baptiste de Foucauld: *Post-industrial society and economic security* (Chapter 30 in this volume).

[38] See Robert Castel: *Work and usefulness to the world* (Chapter 31 in this volume).

[39] See Alain Supiot: *The transformation of work and the future of labour law in Europe: A multidisciplinary perspective* (Chapter 32 in this volume).

[40] This perspective is naturally also to be found in international labour law. See Servais (2005, paras. 6-8).

[41] See Ulrich Mückenberger: *Towards a new definition of the employment relationship* (Chapter 33 in this volume).

[42] See Bernd von Maydell: *Perspectives on the future of social security* (Chapter 34 in this volume).

[43] See Philippe Egger: *Towards a policy framework for decent work* (Chapter 35 in this volume).

[44] See Jean-Michel Servais: *Globalization and decent work policy: Reflections upon a new legal approach* (Chapter 36 in this volume).

[45] See also Directive 2003/88/CE of the European Parliament and of the Council of 4 November 2003, *op. cit.,* article 18; cf. article 22.

[46] Article 34 of Legislative Decree No. 276 of 2003, as amended.

[47] See Andreas Breitenfellner: *Global unionism: A potential player* (Chapter 37 in this volume).

References

Anxo, Dominique. 2004. "Working time patterns among industrialized countries: A household perspective", in Messenger, 2004a, pp. 60-107.

Belloni, M.C.; Bimbi, F. (eds.). 1997. *Microfisica della cittadinanza. Città, genere, politiche dei tempi.* Milan, Franco Agneli.

Bocquillon, Fabrice. 2005. "Loi susceptible de dérogation et loi supplétive: les enjeux de la distinction en droit du travail", in *Recueil Dalloz* (Paris), No. 12/7197, 24 Mar., pp. 803-808.

Boissonnat, Jean. 1995. *Le travail dans vingt ans.* Paris, Odile Jacob/La documentation française.

Bonfiglioli, Sandra; Mareggi, Marco (eds.). 1997. "Il tempo della città fra natura e storia. Atlante di progetti sui tempi della città", in *Urbanística Quaderni* (Rome), No. 12 (May).

Camos Victoria, Ignacio; Rojo Torrecilla, Eduardo. 2002. "A propos du rapport Supiot: réflexions sur les changements dans le monde du travail et en droit du travail", in *Les cahiers de droit* (Quebec), Vol. 43, No. 3 (Sep.), pp. 562-564.

Carnoy, Martin. 2001. "The family, flexible work and social cohesion at risk", in Martha Fetherolf Loutfi (ed.): *Women, gender and work.* Geneva, ILO, pp. 305-325.

Castel, Robert. 1999. "Droit du travail, redéploiement ou refondation", in *Droit Social* (Paris), No. 5 (May), pp. 438-442.

Daugareilh, Isabelle; Iriart, Pierre (eds.). 2004. *Leçons d'une réduction de la durée du travail.* Bordeaux, Maison des Sciences de l'homme d'Aquitaine.

European Academy of the Urban Environment. 1998. *New institutional arrangements in the labour market: Transitional labour markets as a new full employment concept.* Berlin.

European Industrial Relations Review (London). 2005. "Sweden: Reducing working time", Apr., pp. 22-25.

Fagan, Colette. 2004. "Gender and working time in industrialized countries", in Messenger, 2004a, pp. 108-145.

Favennec-Héry, Françoise. 2005. "Vers l'autoréglementation du temps de travail dans l'entreprise", in *Droit Social* (Paris), July-Aug., pp. 794-802.

—.1997. *Le travail à temps partiel.* Paris, Litec.

Figueiredo, José B.; de Haan, Arjan. 1998. *Social exclusion: An ILO perspective.* Geneva, ILO/International Institute for Labour Studies.

Gazier, Bernard; Schmid, Gunther (eds.). 2002. *The dynamics of full employment. Social integration by transitional labour markets.* Cheltenham, Edward Elgar.

ILO. 2005a. *The employment relationship.* Report V (1), International Labour Conference, 95th Session, 2006. Geneva.

—.2005b. *Hours of work: From fixed to flexible?* Report III (Part 1B), International Labour Conference, 93rd Session, 2005. Geneva.

—.1997. *World Labour Report 1997-98: Industrial relations, democracy and social unity.* Geneva.

—.1995. *World Labour Report.* Geneva.

—.1988. *Working time issues in industrialized countries.* Geneva, ILO.

—.1985. *Problems specific to employees in commerce and offices.* Advisory Committee on Salaried Employees and Professional Workers, 9th Session. Geneva.

Inagami, Takeshi. 1999. "The end of classic model of labor law and post-Fordism", in *Comparative Labor Law and Policy Journal* (Champaign, IL), Vol. 20, No. 4 (Summer), pp. 691-701.

Jacobs, A. 2000. "Critique du rapport du Groupe de Madrid sur la transformation du travail", in *Semaine sociale Lamy* (Paris), Supplement No. 997, 2 Oct., p. 55.

Jacoby, Sanford M. 2003. "Economic ideas and the labor market: Origins of the Anglo-American model and prospects for global diffusion", in *Comparative Labor Law and Policy Journal* (Champaign, IL), Vol. 25, No. 1 (Fall), pp. 43-78.

Jamoulle, Micheline; Geerkens, Eric; Foxhal, Gaëtane; Kefer, Fabienne; Bredael, Sylvie. 1997. *Le temps de travail: Transformation du droit et des relations collectives de travail.* Brussels, CRISP.

Kenner, Jeff. 2004. "Re-evaluating the concept of working time: An analysis of recent case law", in *Industrial Relations Journal* (Oxford), Vol. 35, No. 6 (Nov.), pp. 588-602.

Ladear, K.L. 1995. "Social risks, welfare rights and the paradigms of proceduralisation: The combining of the liberal constitutional State and the social State", in Jean de Munck, Jacques Lenoble and M. Molitor (eds.): *L'avenir de la concertation sociale en Europe.* Louvain, Centre for Philosophy of Law, Catholic University of Louvain.

Lallement, Michel. 2003. *Temps, travail et modes de vie.* Paris, PUF (Sciences sociales et sociétés).

Le Crom, Jean-Pierre (ed.). 2004. *Les acteurs de l'histoire du droit du travail.* Rennes, Presses universitaires de Rennes.

Le Goff, Jacques. 2005. "Faire autorité? Nouveaux modes de subordination dans le travail", in *Esprit* (Paris) Mar.-Apr., pp. 143-157.

Lyon-Caen, Gérard. 1995. *Le droit du travail. Une technique réversible.* Paris, Dalloz.

McCann, Deirdre. 2004. "Regulating working time needs and preferences", in Messenger, 2004a, pp. 10-28.

Méda, Dominique. 2001. *Le temps des femmes. Pour un nouveau partage des rôles.* Paris, Flammarion.

Messenger, Jon C. (ed.). 2004a. *Working time and workers' preferences in industrialized countries.* London, Routledge.

—.2004b. "Working time at the enterprise level: Business objectives, firms' practices and workers' preferences", in Messenger, 2004a, pp. 147-194.

Morel, Franck. 2005. "Repos ou argent? Un arbitrage variable dans le droit de la durée du travail", in *Droit Social* (Paris), No. 6 (June), pp. 625-633.

Pocock, Barbara; Clarke, Jane. 2005. "Time, money and job spillover: How parents' jobs affect young people", in *Journal of Industrial Relations* (Sydney), Vol. 47, No. 1 (Mar.), pp. 62-76.

Revet, Thierry. 1996. "L'ordre public dans les relations de travail", in Thierry Revet (ed.): *L'ordre public à la fin du XXe siècle.* Paris, Dalloz.

Rodgers, Gerry; Gore, Charles; Figueiredo, José B. (eds.). 1995. *Social exclusion: Rhetoric, reality, responses.* Geneva, ILO/International Institute for Labour Studies.

Sciarra, Silvana; Davies, Paul; Freedland, Mark (eds.). 2004. *Employment policy and the regulation of part-time work in the European Union: A comparative analysis.* Cambridge, Cambridge University Press.

Servais, Jean-Michel. 2005. *International labour law.* The Hague, Kluwer Law International.

Siau, Bruno. 1996. *Le travail temporaire en droit comparé européen et international.* Paris, LGDJ.

Supiot, Alain (rapporteur). 2001. *Beyond employment: Changes in work and the future of labour law in Europe.* Report for the European Commission. Oxford, Oxford University Press.

— (ed.). 1998. *Le travail en perspective.* Paris, LGDJ.

—.1995. "Temps de travail: pour une concordance des temps", in *Droit Social* (Paris), No. 12 (Dec.), pp. 947-954.

Valli, Vittorio (ed.). 1988. *Tempo di lavoro ed occupazione: Il caso italiano.* Rome, La Nuova Italia Scientifica.

Valticos, Nicolas. 1983. *Droit international du travail.* Second edition. Paris, Dalloz.

PART I

POLICY CHALLENGES IN A CHANGING ENVIRONMENT

EMPLOYMENT AND CONCEPTS OF WORK IN THE NEW GLOBAL ECONOMY

2

G. M. KELLY *

We approach the end of a century of upheaval whose beginning is extraordinarily remote. Amid conditions of total war and mass horror, the nineteenth-century political firmament was smashed and new paradigms emerged. Concurrent transformation took place in the circumstances of daily life. At least in the developed world, technical innovation in the household liberated women from culturally determined domestic drudgery and fostered their integration into the world of men. That world – beginning with the transatlantic community – was also revolutionized. Mechanization engineered a human desertification of the countryside. The Industrial Revolution had already given momentum to that transition, and created the iron cage of regimented employment, as Taylorism structured the lives and blunted the sensibilities of factory workers. Ultimately, capitalism became less oppressive, until sanguine observers spoke of the century of the common man. But advanced technology now assumed the role of an industrial proletariat in a post-industrial world; human labour was being ousted from industry even as new, uncertain avenues of employment began to emerge. And the ways that were first Europe's became the ways of the world. Technology globalized its consequences, with startling reductionist effects. The twentieth century was a century of surprise.

This inquiry looks toward the future from the vantage point of the twentieth-century experience. The shock of the past forewarns against confidence in extrapolation, but it is important to make the attempt. The focus of attention may be identified by two questions:

(a) on the basis that technological and structural dynamism are likely to be sustained, at very least, at the pace set during the past century, what is in prospect for the conventional world of work; and

Originally published in *International Labour Review*, Vol. 139 (2000), No. 1.

* Barrister and Solicitor, High Courts of Australia and New Zealand. Assistance was provided by the National Library of Australia (Canberra), the Faculty of Law and Burgmann College (Australian National University) and Raymond S. Milne (formerly an ILO official).

(b) if the indications are that human labour may have a dramatically shrinking role as a factor of production, what are the implications for contemporary concepts of work – the accumulated baggage of work-related beliefs?

The inquiry is necessarily speculative but is not intended as polemical. There is no ideological assumption for or against the existence of a fundamental personal, social or religious value in respect of work.

The argument begins by noting the historical development of contemporary concepts of work. Attention then turns to assessment of global employment prospects – is orthodox confidence in the possibility of full employment (however defined) still justified or does emerging evidence suggest the probability of an employment collapse? Finally, the article considers the erosive implications for present-day concepts of work if, as a secular trend, a large proportion of available and intending workers can no longer be absorbed in the labour market.

There is a threshold question of definition. Within its generic meaning, "work" has many connotations. Some are far removed from understandings of the kind of work known as "employment" – the focus for present purposes. The narrower term raises its own difficulties. It is normally associated with work that is essentially contractual and has an essential purpose of reward. But how does that sit, for instance, with self-employment that is wholly or substantially indifferent to market criteria? Except as is otherwise apparent in the text, the dilemmas are evaded by reading down "work" as "employment" in its ordinary meaning and ignoring the debatable margins.

CONCEPTS OF WORK

The concept of work developed into modern times by way of a long march from the presumed original role of ensuring subsistence. But an assumption in those terms is itself hazardous, since play – the essential verve of *homo ludens* – coloured the labour of primitive societies and assimilation into religious ritual was quite general. Rarely in human experience has work been understood as confined within purely instrumental objectives.

Greek civilization is said to be an example of escape from the instrumental approach – by way of semantic sleight of hand. Work needed for the satisfaction of material needs was held to be degrading and largely left to slaves. Higher callings such as philosophy and politics were not classified as work (Méda, 1995; Piore, 1995). The pertinent point is that work as a concept was limited in ambit, pejorative in usage and without claims to central ideological value (Lyon-Caen, 1996).

That approach made some contribution to the doctrinal confusions of early Christianity. Key texts such as St. Paul's *First Epistle to the Corinthians* and the *De civitate Dei* of St. Augustine contain quite powerful vindications of work but were doubtfully compatible with an ascetic and intellectual monastic tradition that set the tone. That tradition resisted legitimation of work for gain. Such attitudes broke down gradually; certain occupations were accepted as meritorious and St. Thomas pronounced the overarching test of community value.

In mediaeval Europe, notwithstanding, the spiritual element was fundamental; economic motives were subordinate and suspect (Tawney, 1926). Populist ideas of the dignity and humanizing ministry of work that lurked in Christian doctrine were stifled by the institutional inclinations of the Church. But theocratic hegemony and the feudal order that gave it special strength were soon shattered by forces of social change.

The most representative was the Reformation. Luther sanctioned worldly labour, now invested with a certain nobility and a spiritual aspect as the will of God. That was a solvent of mediaeval assumptions, but not a prescription for individual assertion. Socially, Lutheran doctrine was rooted in the status quo (Weber, 1976). Work within traditional society would ensure the salvation of souls.

Calvinism collected a more potent following and had a greater role in creative destruction. It also reconstructed Christian religion to admit an audaciously encompassing ideology of work. Luther's distrust of acquisition was replaced by the notion of gainful employment as a fundamental life purpose. The doctrine of predestination, which might have seemed to invite fatalism, became an engine of assertion. Industry and success in dignified accumulation served to demonstrate inclusion in the ranks of the elect. The more abundant the fruits of enterprise, the more conclusive the proof. "God's stewards" deployed explosive energies for which the comparatively static conditions of the mediaeval world did not provide as good an outlet (Weber, 1976; but see Fanfani, 1935).

Thus the concept of work was transformed: work was now regarded both as an economic means and as a spiritual end (Tawney, 1926; Furnham, 1990). There were rather different long-term implications. Calvin's theocracy and its offspring struck a special chord with solid middle-class burghers of self-reliant and utilitarian inclinations. Individualism filtered out some of the original religious and ethical essence of Calvinism. Social morality and religion ultimately became less determinant of economic conduct.

The movement of philosophical fashion strengthened these tendencies. The European Enlightenment sanctified reason at the expense of religious faith and institutions. In England, Hobbes asserted a secular individualism but found individual destiny so wretched as to need the refuge of a sovereign. Without such reservations, John Locke proclaimed an insistent credo of individual liberty. Emphasis on the rational also derived from the mechanistic model – and retreat from religion – proclaimed by Descartes. That was antecedent to Political Arithmetic and also to the partly veiled economic materialism of Adam Smith.

These developments culminated in the secularization of work as a factor of production in the industrial machine. That did much more than simply validate individual assertion. Because of the historical legacy, work was still equated with righteousness. It was an easy step to the proposition that lack of work involved a fecklessness and turpitude which society should not indulge. In this way, the work ethic was distorted into a bleak prescription for social control which dragooned the poorer classes into submission to commodification of labour and the dark satanic mills of the factory system. More generally, it landed up as a weapon to blackguard the poor (Bauman, 1998; and see Silver, 1994).

While the poor laboured under a goad, the rich and upwardly mobile were presented with an open sesame for the worship of mammon. To the extent that ethical foundations had been removed, the work ethic was threatened with debasement as an ideology of greed. But here again the historical legacy worked its magic. The pursuit of wealth was still affirmed as a moral imperative, although progressively divorced from public as well as ethical purposes. To speak generally, ends were taken to justify means. Money-making was endorsed as a fundamental preoccupation of Western culture. In the industrial age, work came to be venerated – and enjoined – as instrumental to acquisition.

Idealism, notwithstanding, recovered a place on the agenda by way of the "oracular philosophy" of Hegel (Popper, 1966). Work was ennobled as the essence of human existence and as a means of connecting with the Universal Spirit. Hegel's system had a collectivist emphasis but also envisaged an ultimate consummation of joyful and self-directed labour effected by historical evolution.

Marx took over this historical determinism, including the utopian element, but brought it down to earth. In his dialectic, primacy belonged to economic forces, and that gave a more practical twist to the concept of work. Marx regarded work as a fundamental and inherently fulfilling human function. In capitalist society, however, utopian possibilities were blocked by the alienating conditions of wage slavery (Méda, 1995). Revolution and the final withering away of the State would alone make possible the flowering of human capacity. This paradigm owed a debt to contemporary French socialists such as Louis Blanc – whose main contribution was to launch into history the pregnant concept of the right to work (Gray, 1946).

As industrialism gathered momentum, the scales tipped toward urban living and structured employment. Idealism faded in face of the extreme instrumentalism of the labour market and workplace brutalities exemplified by Taylorism.[1] These trends were mitigated by the new collective solidarity of organized labour and a public conscience that gave rise to labour reform. A further consequence was another paradigm shift in the role and meaning of work. Employment became the conventional indicator for the allocation of national welfare and for assessment of the public liabilities of the citizen.

To speak generally, work in industry lost the factor of aspiration and was deprived of ethical sanction.

The change was never complete. Because a civilization of work had emerged (Castel, 1995 and 1996), however, work was sanctified as the touchstone of citizenship as well as economic utility. The concept of work as a human imperative took on greater importance as work became the most significant channel to social affiliation and relationships and defined community standing. These trends reflected the new primacy of economic considerations in the ideology of the state. The citizen was valued, first and foremost, as economic man.

The purpose of peeling off all these archaeological layers becomes apparent. In the evolution of Western societies, so many concepts of work have emerged. None was completely dropped off at the gate of the Industrial Revolution; at the threshold of the post-industrial order, none has been completely abandoned. In the result, "work" now bears an oppressive overload of semantic significance and conceptual implication. The key ingredients may be suggested as follows:

(1) instrumental/utilitarian
   work for survival or subsistence;
>   for personal enrichment;
>   for community security and abundance;
>   as a factor of production.

(2) individual
   work as a psychological imperative, intrinsic to human nature;
>   as an expression of creativity;
>   as personal affirmation or validation;
>   as a path to power;
>   as a defence against idleness, boredom or temptation.

(3) ethical
   work as a spiritual calling and source of redemption;
>   as testifying to divine selection;
>   as sacramental obedience to the will of God;
>   as a means of entry into a Universal Ideal.

(4) social
   work as an implied contract of social obligation;
>   as a process of socialization;
>   to establish social identity;
>   to maintain social solidarity and cohesion.

(5) institutional
   work as a lever of authority and control;
>   as the conventional mechanism of distribution;
>   as the touchstone of liability for public contribution.

THE ECONOMIC CIVILIZATION AND ITS PROSPECTS

Discussion of the complex evolution of the European concept of work should not evade the difficulty that non-European societies have followed different paths. Some primitive societies would seem to have had no ideology of work at all. In other communities, the background is more compatible. Within the "social familism" of Japan, for example, a congruence of individual and collective objectives fostered an ethic of strong group loyalty and effort and of inter-group competitiveness (Kubota, 1983; Sampson, 1989). That ethic was apt for remoulding into the civilization of work (Lyon-Caen, 1996). The result was a certain convergence but not uniformity. The economic civilization is a Western invention, and is not identical even within its own orbit, since Anglo-American and Rhenish capitalism diverge. Capitalist institutions and attitudes still exhibit their separate cultural legacies.[2]

As the assimilative influences of industrialization, corporate organization and advanced technology penetrate ubiquitously, however, it is not so important to stress unique characteristics deriving from local tradition. For present purposes, developed countries that are now entering upon the post-industrial era may be dealt with as an entity and their global model is being substantially followed elsewhere.

There is abundant evidence of convergence in the elaboration of fundamental principles. In international converse and compacts, two matters stand out: the right to work and the objective of full employment. The Constitution of the International Labour Organization (1919), as amplified by the Declaration of Philadelphia (1944) and the Employment Policy Convention, 1964 (No. 122), entrenches the goal of securing "full, productive and freely chosen employment" (Article 1, C. 122). From Bretton Woods (1944) to the Universal Declaration of Human Rights (1948), the European Social Charter (1996) and the Copenhagen World Summit for Social Development (1995), the same issues are addressed. It is a fair question, however, whether approaches reflecting the prevailing multi-layered ideology of work are still realistic. Are post-industrial conditions creating a fundamental disjunction between labour market supply and demand?

Factors of reassurance

Both in Keynesian and in neoclassical theory, there is no sympathy for the notion of an irretrievable employment collapse. Unemployment is regarded as a disease of the economic system which may be diagnosed and cured – though that process is not necessarily straightforward. The Keynesian view is that the market has a propensity to reach equilibrium below the point at which full employment is generated (see Moggridge, 1992; Soros, 1996). The gap may be closed by stimulating aggregate demand, most effectively and accurately by government measures of fiscal, monetary and structural manipulation. The regime implies a public sector of substantial size and responsibility (Galbraith, 1992). Neo-Keynesians, it should be added, have less confidence in this traditional nostrum, partly because it is nowadays unacceptable to financial markets. They prefer, or are impelled, to pin their faith to interest rate movements.

Neoclassical theory denies the effect of demand management and assumes full employment is attainable if conditions are created for clearing the market (see Singh, 1995). The emphasis is placed on supply-side factors such as labour market flexibility, training and the reduction of production costs. Since government activity is seen as "crowding out" investment in productive enterprise, there is much emphasis on slimming the State (Kelsey, 1997). In contrast to the Keynesians, neoclassical economists have supreme confidence in the unconstrained mechanisms of the market.

There is also an important difference in defining full employment. Keynesians adopt the conventional or Beveridge measure (accounting for frictional unemployment) of about 3 per cent (Beveridge, 1944). Neo-Keynesians acknowledge that, having regard to greater instability and "churning" in the labour market, a more elastic measure may now be appropriate (ILO, 1996b; Britton, 1997). Neoclassicists, perhaps mindful that the bogey of inflation latterly dogged the Keynesian consensus, postulate a "natural" rate of unemployment below which wage pressures generate inflation (Friedman, 1968). The rule of thumb for this equilibrium (the non-accelerating inflation rate of unemployment – NAIRU) was about 6 per cent, but recent realities have thrown the concept into some disarray because the relationship between inflation and unemployment appears to be asymmetrical (Baker, Epstein and Pollin, 1998; and see Krugman, 1998, p. 32). In the afterglow of the 30-year boom, neoclassical thresholds are bound to appear socially insensitive.

Technical unemployment, then, is thought to be logically impossible (Gruen, 1981). Demand management or correction of market failure and rigidities (as the respective allegiances prescribe) is said to be able to ensure a full employment equilibrium (ILO, 1994a). Irreconcilable differences as to means, moreover, still allow room for a measure of common ground. Prospects of a virtuously expanding circle of higher production > higher income > higher consumption and investment and increasing capital stock bewitch the imagination of economists generally (Lee, 1995; Krugman, 1997). On this showing, unemployment is not inevitable or irreversible.

These considerations take the discussion closer to the actualities of the labour market, where recent trends are confused. Some of the confusion relates to sharp shrinkage in important sectors. To generalize, advanced countries now manage agriculture with less than one-tenth of the post-Second World War labour requirement or about 3-5 per cent of the workforce (Wieczorek, 1995, p. 216; Brown, 1997b). Manufacturing employment has been similarly downsized to less than half that of 30 years ago, despite expansion of output. Much reliance is placed on the compensating effect of the move to services, which in some economies now absorb up to 75 per cent of workers. But hopes may be misplaced, because large activities such as banking, insurance and retailing have a capacity for concentration through technological and managerial innovation. Wholesale staff cuts result.

The services sector, notwithstanding, is said to be robust. The star performer may be health services, where explosive expansion is taking place. In the United States, they now assure about 8 per cent of total employment (see Britton, 1997, p. 303). Other emerging growth activities include hospitality (including tourism), security services, the sports industry and work relating to the environment, where expansion could be very substantial but for funding constraints. Domestic services, it should be recalled, formed about 20 per cent of the working population of England before the First World War. In recidivist economies pushing toward the hierarchical world of laissez-faire, large numbers of the losers could be impelled to domestic employment. Finally, very diverse recent growth gives some support to claims that the labour market future depends on smaller enterprises and occupational invention. Evidence from the United States is quite persuasive – between 1987 and 1991, corporations are estimated to have shed 2.4 million jobs, whereas enterprises employing fewer than 20 workers picked up 4.4 million (Boissonnat, 1996). Most of the increase is said to have been in low-paying industries such as services and retailing, but a high proportion of new work in those spheres was in comparatively senior positions (ILO, 1994c, p. 709). In the opinion of Paul Krugman, the possibilities for our grandchildren – and for us – are limited only by individual capacity for imagination (Krugman, 1994).

These anecdotal indications are compatible with ILO statistical analysis to the effect that there is not much evidence of labour market saturation. Fears of "jobless growth" and of the "inexorable disappearance" of jobs are not supported by analysis relating to the years 1960-95 – which indicate steady employment growth. Despite an acknowledged trend to non-standard and contingent employment, moreover, conventional job tenure during that period was holding up quite well. A large core of the workforce still had "stable and secure jobs" (ILO, 1996b, p. 25).[3]

That employment record does not support assertions as to chronic problems on the demand side, even though one of the very largest economies – Japan had plunged into a liquidity trap by the end of the stated period. It is not possible, however, to discern the momentum of an historical (Kondratieff) or technological (Schumpeter) long cycle. Information technology is identified in terms of some such impulse, but the evidence is not convincing. Production is not notably labour intensive, dramatic innovation is becoming less predictable and supply is already pressing upon effective demand.

The longer-term implications of IT usage are more complex and conjectural; labour market effects have been dramatic so far but there is no obvious net trend. The demand for operatives once seemed nearly insatiable but is now slackening; there is closer scrutiny of proposals for further intensive installation of IT equipment in view of suspicions – epitomized in Thomas Landauer's "productivity paradox" – that efficiency gains cannot be taken for granted (Landauer, 1995). If employment gains balance the losses, with lower-order processes directed increasingly to the huge industrial reserve army of the developing world, we shall probably be lucky (but see, for example, Freeman, Soete and Efendioglu, 1995; Zuckerman, 1998).

The total demand for working time also shows no clear overall trends. Especially in North America, skilled technical workers and those described by Robert Reich as "symbolic analysts" (Reich, 1992) have recently been working longer than in earlier years and are considered to be under serious pressure (Schor, 1991). Pleas to expand élite education are partly based on the proposition that suitable recruits are necessary to spread the load. But there is much variance between countries, regions and occupational groups and from time to time. Less skilled workers, in any event, are encountering problems in terms both of finding work and of the quality of employment available.

Institutional seers would find a remedy for that kind of shrinkage in a rationing regime, an approach that has the merits of gradualism and familiarity, since it continues broad contemporary trends. Especially in Europe, quite fruitful experiment is taking place with job-sharing, and there is significant movement toward a shorter working week. Some initiatives of this kind are alien to Anglo-American thinking. At rather different rates, notwithstanding, all industrialized economies are adopting flexible labour market regimes that imply rationed work. A shorter working week is consistent with *longer* term trends. The average working week in the United States and other advanced countries is now about half as long as it was before the twentieth century (Bosch, 1999).

There are other synergies. In developed countries, childhood is insulated from work. There are pressures to make that universal on human rights grounds. It is a long road, but child labour is in rapid retreat. Moreover, time spent in education and occupational formation has been increasing, and a greater proportion of that is full time. Theory and practice, formerly in double harness, do not function so compatibly together in a more sophisticated age. Especially in the case of higher-level cadres, gainful "lifetime" employment may begin only after an apprenticeship (including schooling) of at least 20 years.

By the same token, an employment lifetime is not what it once was. Although arbitrary retirement ages are being discarded as discriminatory, more older workers – especially men – are leaving their jobs early and not seeking, or not finding, re-employment. All too frequently, redundancies and departure packages speed them on their way. In France, only 40 per cent of men in late middle age are still in the labour force (Sennett, 1998). Japanese law enforces retirement at age 55. Thus, the conventional work profile of industrialism has been transformed in the developed world: employment starts later, finishes earlier and is restricted in between.

These trends might seem apt to relieve any prospective imbalance between the potential workforce (however identified) and the availability of jobs. So far, however, employment aggregates have not been substantially affected, because of the massive influx of women into paid work. Another qualification needs to be made. Comparison with earlier times is revealing, but also to an extent unrealistic. For most industrial workers in the nineteenth century, retirement had no practical meaning – they did not live long enough to get there.

Disabling factors

Some influences, while not fundamentally destructive, may militate against conditions of "sufficient work". A threshold matter which does not affect real employment should first be mentioned. From a world perspective, it is impossible to know what is happening in the labour market. Despite advanced statistical capacity, that is readily understandable for the developing world, where rural underemployment merges indistinctly with unemployment and uncertainties are inescapable in capturing the movement of urban migration. China is the classic example; implosion of the communes and recent restrictions on urban settlement appear to have left great numbers of peasants in a state of near vagrancy – not to mention a statistical limbo. Some estimates put the current level of "real" unemployment at more than 100 million.

The position for developed countries is also unsatisfactory. Hidden employment is an important reason. Pamela Meadows has fairly recently suggested that, despite an apparent economic revival in the United Kingdom during recent years, as many as 7 million people may recently have been out of work (Meadows, 1996). That would mean that official surveying methods are not getting to grips with realities. It is also true that, for political reasons, they incorporate dampening strategies – such as deleting from registers all those in certain older age-groups. Suggestions of underestimation in the United Kingdom are compatible with Ajit Singh's conclusion for the early 1990s that European unemployment may have been understated by as much 50 per cent (Singh, 1995).

The accepted international measure of employment creates further confusion and makes a near-nonsense of unrefined statistics. By ILO norms gainful work for more than one hour per week is counted as employment. Thus a person working eight hours weekly for the United States minimum wage of $5.15 an hour (from 1997, under the Fair Labor Standards Act 1938) ends up with $41.20 a week and is said to be employed. The measure appears to inflate assumptions as to real work in countries with radically rationalist regimes, substantial labour market flexibility and high levels of non-standard labour. In some advanced countries, about 45 per cent of total employment is not permanent and full time (Beynon, 1997). "Employment" ought to bear a reasonable relation to livelihood and the measure does not remotely do so.

To turn to substantive obstacles to employment, the first port of call is globalization, in this analysis taken to comprise trade liberalization, liberalization of capital flows and the dominance in world production and trade of transnational corporations. The rationale is comparative advantage, and implies mobility of resources. But practice falls well short of the ideal. In many corporate decisions, comparative advantage is a long way subordinate to short-term issues such as tax concessions, or even irrational choice, and all resources – especially labour – are not equally mobile. The discontinuance of activities that do not satisfy theoretical tests of viability may cause more economic disruption and social distress than integration into the international system is worth. Great instability has accompanied the evolution of the global economy (Haass and Litan, 1998). It has been usefully brought to attention that the massive employment dislocations brought about as that process advances can be more comfortably accommodated if economies are run at or near full employment – a condition rarely obtaining in today's world (Hutton, 1995). At this stage, detriment cannot be satisfactorily measured against present and foreseeable rewards (see Lee, 1996). Employment aspects of the process share that opacity to evaluation.

Structural and institutional inadequacies also endanger the stability on which employment in the global economy depends. The progress represented (for example) by the World Trade Organization (WTO) has to be acknowledged, but it falls well short of establishing comprehensive regulation of global commerce, and compliance machinery is likely to prove fragile. And the WTO is no more than one link in an incomplete chain. If finance rather than trade is in question, the salient feature is that Bretton Woods was never rebuilt with updated mechanisms and that its breakdown has never been repaired (ILO, 1994b; Hutton, 1995 and 1997).

International institutions and great power interventions have had some positive effects but also bear responsibility for spectacular setbacks. The draconian rationalism of the International Monetary Fund (IMF) since the 1980s was at first supported by economic orthodoxy, though always condemned by a distinguished professional fringe (see George, 1989). It now has few friends. So many programmes – Africa, Latin America, Asia – have turned out badly and so many conditionalities have proved ill advised. The current consensus is, on a charitable view, that IMF constraints and liberalization went much too fast and far too far (Feldstein, 1998 and 1999; Krugman, 1998; Garten, 1999). It is tenable that the key international institution in the development field has been more trouble to the developing world than it has been worth. If that standard of intervention is to remain the norm, the outlook for economic optimization – and dependent labour markets – is gloomy.

Great power impacts are usually less transparent and are not always direct. In some episodes, international relationships are an expedient screen for unilateral assertion. For assessment of the most important of these influences – that of the United States – these matters are an impediment. But case histories are not in short supply.

The classic example relates to the Volcker shock. At the beginning of the 1980s, following the Vietnam war, inflation was endemic in the United States and economic indicators were in disarray. The remedy chosen was severe and included a new approach to monetary management. The conspicuous feature was a sharp rise in interest rates. The measures taken were initiated not with an imperialist agenda but in order to rectify difficulties within the United States system. But the new interest rate regime was at once communicated to countries in the developing world which had been encouraged to borrow too heavily at moderate rates during the 1970s. That world was now expendable. A narrow national egotism produced severe economic dislocation and social distress (Emmerij, 1994; Singh, 1995). Latin America and Africa entered upon a lost decade.

The next question is a topical one: is it in prospect that the social consequences of economic rationalism and globalization will thwart optimum performance on the part of the economic machine? Certainly increasing attention is being paid to theories to the effect that markets are not perfect and governments are not necessarily malign. But, especially in the key Anglo-American sector, a paradigm shift is not in sight. Realities of polarization, trashing of the low-skilled workforce and exclusion are not unique to that sector but are most significant in it. Robert Reich's characterization of "two economies" (Reich, 1992) and Will Hutton's searing 40: 30: 30 formula – yielding the conclusion that one-half of the population of the United Kingdom lives in conditions of poverty or permanent stress and insecurity (Hutton, 1995) – recall the facts of present-day inequality. In quite dramatic statistical terms, Simon Head has identified how the ordinary American has been put on short commons – "for the bottom 80 per cent of the American working population, average weekly wages (adjusted for inflation) fell by 18 per cent between 1973 and 1995, while pay of the corporate élite rose 19 per cent before taxes and 66 per cent after the tax accountants had worked their magic" (Sennett, 1998, p. 54, quoting Head, 1996, p. 47).

Latter-day capitalism has disturbingly recidivist features, even in Europe. While great numbers are condemned to contingent and precarious employment, ordinary workers in "good" jobs and apparently most higher cadres typically endure long hours and an unrelenting sense of urgency. Insistent pressure for higher productivity, anxieties relating to workplace status and strong tendencies to wage compression negate the supposed advantages of any concurrent flexibility in working arrangements.

In all "advanced" societies, concepts such as the family wage and the 40-hour week, which once seemed to be engraved in stone, have been swept unceremoniously away. In most of those societies, most women of working age now work. In the United States, it is estimated that a working woman with a family may expect a total workload of not less than 80 hours weekly. The resultant psychological pressures are formidable. It is suggested that, in 1996, 46 per cent of workers in large American firms feared being laid off. This was twice the 1991 level – despite five years of expansion and a significantly lower unemployment rate. The psychological problem is that workers in this situation feel "their lives [are] buffeted by forces over which they have virtually no control" (Zuckerman, 1998, p. 30). In New Zealand, where a somewhat draconian form of radical capitalism has been imposed, more than 40 per cent of the labour force is said to be suffering from disturbing levels of stress (see *New Zealand Herald,* 24 Nov. 1998)

Japan and the newly industrializing countries have partly distinct arrangements but are scarcely more favoured. The strong work ethic of the former, and lifetime employment and corporate loyalty, are eroded by traumas of recession. Management approaches quite recently trumpeted as world best practice are threatened; insecurity has more than a foothold. Under compelling conditions of global competition, it is harder to hold out against a universal tempo and methods and the global vision of radical capitalism. Newly industrializing countries, including China, appear to have no escape. Wage slavery, entrepreneurial (and state) exploitation, managerial dictatorship and the insensitivities of laissez-faire are exhumed from their graveyard in the European past to find among abounding populations elsewhere a scarcely less heartless vitality.

Does this have implications for the "reputation" of work? To an extent not known since the worst decades of the European industrial revolution, the labour force everywhere is exposed to a work fatigue that is deeper than and different from mere physical or nervous exhaustion. Notions of work as fulfilment, as the expansion of individuality, as an enjoyable alternative to idleness, are retreating before the remorseless instrumentalism of global competition and rationalist ideology. And so is the work ethic which helped in the nineteenth century to lock the working poor into the "iron cage" of factory employment. That cohort had few other options. But what happens now if the generality of workers turns off work? What happens if deunionized workers elect to reorganize collectively to say so?

Since radical capitalism implies high profit levels, there is room for movement. In competitive conditions, however, it is not easy to accommodate demands for less work, or different work styles. And declining work commitment and vitality imply falling standards and output. Precarious employment already fosters those trends, partly because insecurity is not conducive to expertise. In short, hyper-competition exacts hyper-work and may bring hyper-profits, but the price cannot be ignored. Inferior performance through stress is the least of the hazards involved; disillusion and alienation are more fundamental, and there may be no cure.

The immediately preceding comments relate particularly to "lucky" workers who are overcommitted in jobs a traditional taxonomy would characterize as solid and respectable. As has been indicated, the numbers involved are still substantial but declining. By way of emphasis, an authority with practical experience in depressed areas may be heard in evidence – "the reorganization of work in late twentieth-century capitalist societies is forcing an increasingly large proportion of people to seek the means for their economic and social survival through various types of disorganized, insecure, risky, casualized and poor work" (MacDonald, 1997, p. 123). Even if the work available to those people may be frequently or mostly performed under pressure, they are essentially under-committed. In the Anglo-American sector, the realities of social exclusion, psychological deprivation and economic waste are pretty much swept under the carpet – even if the archetypal insider of that sector, Alan Greenspan, has suggested that such realities could become a major threat. Even more than those who are over-worked, the underworked have reason for alienation.

Another aspect of the matter has economic as well as social implications. With current settings, especially in deregulated economies following the radical capitalist road, dispersion of earnings has become very considerable and is still increasing (Bosch, 1999; Krugman, 1994, p. 131). That aggravates social inequality but may also threaten economic equilibrium. As has recently been recalled, authorities of great standing, including Keynes, J.K. Galbraith and Myrdal have linked unequal income distribution with crises of underconsumption (Hutton, 1995). A distinguished American voice echoes this apprehension – generally free markets, with all the benefits they bring, are unlikely to survive in a world where insufficient demand is a continual threat (Krugman, 1999, p. 157).

Unless we have indeed entered a new "consumer society" from which the spectre of lagging consumer demand has been banished for ever. In that event, the alternative would appear to be mountains of debt. As in much else, the United States may be showing the way. The sharp turnaround during the Reagan years and the subsequent record are certainly ominous portents. American external liabilities are now estimated to be more than $4 trillion and net foreign debt around $2 trillion (Bergsten, 1997, p. 93; 1999, p. 26). The implied dilemma is painful and serious (Krugman, 1996). One way or another, the survival of the "new" economy may be at stake.

As globalization proceeds, it is a further disabling influence that state action is out of favour. One fundamental reason is that it narrows the field of activity for the private sector and thus for the operation of the profit motive. Neoclassical theory also adopts the simplistic position (stoutly contested by James Tobin and others) that state activity is unproductive; slimming the State is necessary to avoid crowding out productive enterprise. On that ground and because public expenditure is so oddly regarded as alien to "public choice", minimum taxation is advocated. These features of the supply-side agenda have a facile popular appeal and are now conventional wisdom. As Galbraith and others have lamented, that deprives the public sector of much of its earlier capacity to act as a balancing force in the economy. In case of a setback, there is no immediately sufficient engine to stimulate aggregate demand and employment (Galbraith, 1992). That means sacking the fire service in a situation of unusual fire hazard. Moreover, the very large issue of environmental degradation is now an urgent item on the world agenda. Enterprises will bear mounting exogenous costs and public power is indispensable, not only as the presumed allocative agency for the attribution of charges but for direct rehabilitation.

Negative factors

The above-mentioned matters may prejudice the employment outlook by way of functional breakdown. But that is contingent only; effective policies may possibly avoid it. Are there factors with an ineradicable propensity to cause labour market deflation? Earlier discussion mentioned theoretical confidence that unemployment results only from inappropriate techniques, and also optimism as to the foreseeable prospect. Must those assumptions be treated as conclusive?

Current perceptions incorporate a distorted historical vision. In the afterglow of the 30-year boom, unemployment is seen as an aberration. The record of capitalism since the industrial revolution proclaims otherwise; unemployment has been endemic and in some phases a scourge of the system. The 30-year boom is the aberration (Singh, 1995). Some time earlier, even before the Depression of the 1930s, underconsumption theories and theories of the mature economy proliferated. As in the nervous 1990s, work-sharing and work-shortening schemes were legion. In 1933, the United States Congress very nearly enacted the Black Bill, which would have conferred on American labour a 30-hour week (Rifkin, 1995).

Widespread opinion to the effect that there was a gremlin in the works thwarting the functioning of the economy appeared to be vindicated by Roosevelt's pragmatic reflation and Keynesian theory. The gremlin was that the process of production did not necessarily generate *and make available* the means to buy the product back. Provided that was identified, the difficulties could be overcome. Even during the Keynesian consensus, however, significant questions on the demand side were unresolved. And then the consensus broke down. In two respects, that was the story of the Emperor's clothes: confidence in the consensus had apparently been misplaced – and no consensus could be found on the reasons for the failure. These developments painfully exposed the limits of economic understanding.

Neoclassical, supply-side thinking muscled out the enfeebled Keynesian system and purported to establish the Washington consensus on theoretical foundations that were this time secure. Application in the developing world – where advanced economies would have no trouble bearing the political costs of experiment – gave early indications that all was not well (George, 1989). To speak generally, material instability actually grew and theoretical bewilderment did not cease. In the United States, Ronald Reagan, the political figurehead and popular icon of the new secular religion, led the country from being the largest creditor to being the largest debtor in the world. During his terms, United States citizens formed the bad habit of borrowing 20 per cent of the world's savings (Sampson, 1989).

In other respects, the analytical reliability of neoclassical policy proved lamentable. Nobody knew certainly why some economies collapsed so badly and unexpectedly (Mexico, South-east Asia, Brazil), why they stubbornly resisted revival (Japan), or why they should suddenly seem to become successful (as latterly, the United States). The extreme distributive polarization produced by the system was not foreseen and has not been adequately explained. Important weapons in the neoclassical armoury, such as the NAIRU, failed to fire as intended. A fresh aim was taken on capacity utilization. Small wonder that this latter-day subspecies of general equilibrium theory provoked a substantial neo-Keynesian counter-revolution. These developments painfully exposed the limits of economic understanding.

Little confidence remained in the idea of the market economy as a mechanism which, as Fourier said of his phalanstère, "une fois montée, elle marchera d'elle-même" [once set up, it will function automatically] (see Soros in Schlesinger, 1997, p. 8; Garten, 1999). The cognoscenti were reminded that macroeconomics rests on value judgments – and of Karl Polanyi's prescient condemnation of "the utopian endeavour to establish a system of self-regulating markets" (Polanyi, 1944). The huge confusion, overload and contradictions of current data compound the difficulties of using judgment to arrive at workable basic principles – and some principles whose validity seemed settled are now shown to be precarious. Does the assumed correlation exist between output and employment? Is the consumer society governed by rational choice and expectation? (see Krugman, 1994; Greider, 1997; Soros, 1998). Is some degree of indifference now appropriate in respect of indifference curve techniques and elasticity of demand? In the post-industrial world, what is the role of a calculus relating to economies of scale? In the rush to labour market deregulation, is it forgotten that such a measure cannot of itself create aggregate demand (ILO, 1994b)? The conclusion to be stressed is straightforward. In face of the current crisis of macroeconomic theory, reliance on mainstream confidence in long-term employment prospects would be culpably imprudent.

To make these points is not to disparage all theoretical inquiry or to deny the certainty of new and fruitful insights. Theory and policy, notwithstanding, are shrouded in mystery. Economic planning in the broadest sense is planning for the unknown. With that caveat, it is agreeable to return to practical discussion of the likely employment consequences of globalization and advancing technology.

The glut of low-skilled workers in Europe is a good starting-point. Three distinct causes are identified – labour displacement by the development of newly industrializing countries, technological displacement and internal problems of structural mismatch or policy mismanagement. The first two invite comment here. In the prevailing view, the foreign trade of Europe – relevant imports amount to only about 1.5 per cent of GDP – is too insignificant to be responsible for mass unemployment and steep income inequality (Appelbaum and Schettkat, 1995; Lawrence, 1996; Krugman, 1996; Lee, 1996, pp. 487-488). But that conclusion is controversially challenged. Adrian Wood concludes that the pertinent calculations may understate the true position by as much as a factor of ten (Wood, 1994). By focusing on commodity exchange, moreover, the calculations appear to leave a yawning gap. What industries might have been established or maintained in Europe – irrespective of production *for* Europe – if they had not been captured elsewhere? (see Freeman, Soete and Efendioglu, 1995).

Globalization is dictating relocation from the developed world and the preferential siting of much new enterprise in the newly industrializing countries (NICs). No end to that process is in sight and the employment consequences are incalculable. Much higher productivity per worker and technical sophistication have been the standard advantages of the developed world, but the gap is closing. Cheap infrastructure and labour costs are the historical attractions of the NICs, but that logic is losing its force. Both in industry and in services, state-of-the-art enterprise places more reliance on compatible conditions and reliability than on cost. And the vision of a Taylorism of huge congregations of low skilled non-European operatives is out of date. The favourable labour costs on which transnational corporations prefer to rely relate increasingly to highly trained technicians, computer operators and engineers. The bad news for the developed world is the prospect of continuing *relative* decline. The bad news elsewhere is the dwindling expectation that very large numbers of prospective workers, typically drawn from underemployment in the countryside, can be taken up. In the People's Republic of China, a quasi-official estimate foreshadows unemployment exceeding 250 millions within ten years (see Greider, 1997, p. 70).

If technological displacement is important, why are employment outcomes perverse? Recent indications are an enigma. During the 1960s and 1970s, the rate of technological innovation in both Anglo-American and Rhenish capitalism was higher than in the 1980s, yet employment depression was avoided. That occurred despite good productivity gains and substantial entry of women into the workforce. A productivity effect does appear to have been significant in the 1980s. The American productivity record was flat and employment remained fairly robust. European productivity gains were substantial and employment began to fall away (ILO, 1996b, p. 31; and see Wieczorek, 1995, pp. 220-221).

Were European problems the bitter fruit of productivity success? Was American stability the anomalous reward of comparatively static performance? Different adaptation rates of technological innovation were an implausible explanation of the difference. And how does the recent leap in American productivity fit in? One theory is that a long time lag occurred before the benefits of recent innovation were captured. But the relevant investment (as far as identifiable) did not occur in a similar surge. Nor has the predictable adverse pressure on employment eventuated. Has this apparently favourable outcome occurred not because of technological change *per se* but because the labour market has developed a better structural fit?

Latterly, confident assertions about different economic outcomes and employment regimes in the United States and Europe have been fashionable. This comparative commentary should now be noticed. Some analysis focuses on allegations of Eurosclerosis and approaches the American record with more than a tinge of triumphalism. European persistence in sustaining decent wage levels is contrasted unfavourably with severe wage depression in the Anglo-American sector – widely identified as a major engine of recovery for employment and activity. That calculus, typically, does not dwell on the exigencies of the working poor who are supposed to have made it all possible. True to the tenets of radical capitalism, moreover, European social protection is presented as a crippling public burden that crowds out the development of enterprise.

More fundamentally, it is contended that, since about 1980, OECD countries have been hit by a major shift in the occupational structure of labour demand toward a managerially and technically superior workforce (Heylen, Goubert and Omey, 1996). Europe has reacted comparatively sluggishly. Structural and operational flexibility in the United States has fostered a more rapid and successful adjustment. Flexibility is a sacred cow of radical capitalism – which is far from ensuring consensus about its value as a workplace expedient. The distinguished American observer Richard Freeman has argued that its only significant effect is redistributive – in favour of employers – with no appreciable effect on output and no favourable implications for levels of employment (see ILO, 1996a, p. 110). Flexible work arrangements are gaining ground rapidly, notwithstanding. In the lower reaches of the hierarchy of work, conventional full-time jobs may be almost on the way out. In terms of *overall* statistics, it should be conceded, full-time employment is not yet in that degree of crisis.

It is true that European capitalism is more protective of the citizen. There is a greater propensity to uphold public systems of welfare and to sustain as a public good provision for education and health. Minimum wage levels are comparatively high and higher unemployment is tolerated. The

Anglo-American approach is less sensitive to community values, venerates self-reliance and includes the historical obsession with the work ethic. Unsurprisingly, therefore, authorities in that camp criticize "smug" European persistence with "generous" social security benefits and urge market-clearing flexibility in wage rates – adoption of the Washington consensus or *pensée unique*. Amartya Sen has recently offered a doleful but persuasive taxonomy of the psychological and social ills attendant upon unemployment (Sen, 1997).

Other approaches suggest greater flexibility in Europe than that kind of commentary would admit and throw much doubt on the likelihood of appreciable employment growth from further deregulation (Appelbaum and Schettkat, 1995; Judt, 1997). There is good evidence that wage flexibility in Europe improved during the 1980s and that real wage rigidities are not higher in Europe than in the United States (ILO, 1996b, pp. 39-40). And why should neoclassical thunderbolts be launched as if the Washington consensus constituted an ideal model? Since it has been shown to be theoretically fragile and a social disaster for disadvantaged groups, it obviously does not. Real alarm is justified where workers are commodified and factors of human fairness and feeling become irrelevant. A political rather than economic paradigm might imply that there is a basic immorality and irrationality in imposing employment at any level below a "sufficient wage" – and would sustain the hoary dictum that the labourer is worthy of his hire.

As between the situation of psychological insecurities and material humiliations of Americans locked into an undercaste of precarious employment and the socially adequate security of jobless Europeans, the balance of misery does not necessarily fall on the European side. It is simply not true that any job is necessarily better than no job. That thought would appear to be inherent in references under the Universal Declaration of Human Rights to "lust and favourable remuneration" and "an existence worthy of human dignity" (Art. 23).

The argument can be taken further. Within assumptions unwelcome to Anglo-American ideology, Rhenish capitalism is rational and viable – and also successful. France and (usually) Germany record healthy current account surpluses, as against massive American deficits (see Bergsten, 1999). The scale of financial wealth in relation to the underlying economy is large. With acquired prosperity, static populations and correspondingly modest growth, there is no need for the aggressive expansionary impulse and obsessively mean human perspectives which unconstrained capitalism tends to. Moreover, there is no clear empirical evidence that high non-wage costs hamper the totality of economic performance (ILO, 1996b, pp. 92-94). Unemployment that constitutes a "waste" – and even something of a personal crime – for transatlantic critics tends to be regarded neutrally in Europe. For reasons that are historical and cultural, in any case, the United States model "causes quivers of distaste and anxiety" in Europe (Judt, 1997,

p. 106) and is not likely to gain a secure foothold. Because the social will and financial means exist, non-workers can be adequately maintained.

Two conclusions emerge. In the long run, but long before all of us are dead, the market-clearing orientation is likely to be seen more clearly as offensive to human rights and dignity and thus found unsustainable. Secondly, European unemployment rates, which the conventional wisdom prefers to regard as temporary, are likely to be the heralds of a permanent trend. As the work ethic attenuates and new paradigms evolve, European arrangements, not those of the Americans, are likely to prefigure the future of work.

Environmental concerns are likely to cause further employment problems because of the potential to inhibit growth. Under traditional relativities, GDP growth is taken to stimulate employment. Okun's Law placed the growth threshold where employment creation begins at about 2.5 per cent. It is now apparent, however, that the GDP-employment nexus is not consistent. (Appelbaum and Schettkat, 1995; Freeman, Soete and Efendioglu, 1995). Much lower estimates have been made for some countries – 0.6 per cent for the United States and 2 per cent for Europe (ILO, 1996b, p. 17). More recently, figures much closer to Okun have been confidently advanced (Krugman, 1998, pp. 34-36). Especially in relation to developing countries, then, the equation of lower growth = higher unemployment may still be relied on as a significant rule of thumb.

That is ominous in relation to the emerging need to attend to environmental degradation. The case is familiar. Global warming – whose existence is not now much contested – is simply the best advertised illustration. Production and use of many accessories of the modern industrial State will have to be curbed. Modernization programmes in populous regions such as South and East Asia may appear as threatening prospectively as are present indulgent levels of consumption in the United States. Nil growth advocates are finally getting a hearing. On present indications, their objective seems unrealistic. But even if present growth rates were merely moderated sufficiently to avert impending crisis, current employment levels would be unsustainable. Environmentally induced contraction would contribute a significant multiplier effect to factors already conducing to employment collapse.

It is important, however, that focused argument should not exclude conjecture as to the grand sweep of historical trends. Beginning in Europe, the industrial revolution fostered urban migration and expansion, continuing technological innovation, regimented employment and profound social change. Nearly concurrently, village-centred rural societies based on status and intensive farming were mortally wounded by agricultural transition. That dual upheaval was communicated to the rest of the world. Similar dramatic contraction is now taking place in factory industrialism as the labour requirement per unit of output rapidly diminishes. The impact, likewise, is global, but much more sudden in its incidence. The implications are portentous because industrial civilization in its universalizing form has been a civilization of work. There is no certainty that employment shrinkage of the industrial State will be balanced by the universal unfolding of new spheres of gainful activity. Humanity is once more venturing over the edge of the familiar into uneasy continents of the unknown.

A WORLD WITHOUT WORK

The preceding safari through the debatable domain of radical capitalism and the slough of despond of present-day economic arrangements ends, appropriately, close to its starting-point – in the shifting sands of concepts of work. On the arguments presented, it is clearly conceivable that such influences as technological and organizational change, globalization and persistence with faulty policy settings may finally precipitate an employment collapse – of just what magnitude it is unnecessary to speculate. In terms of regular, lifelong, full-time work, such a process is already well under way. What are the implications for the complex of work-related beliefs visited in the opening stage of our journey? The concluding commentary takes up that question.

Work in the widest generic sense will always be with us. About work as employment, we cannot be sure. A distinction between these two terms is fundamental to this article and has been suggested by way of introduction. The doubt is whether enough employment can, or will, be generated for all the populations of what is now considered working age. The indications are that society may be dividing into Spartans and Helots – the former an elite of Robert Reich's "symbolic analysts" locked into onerous responsibilities and work pressures, the latter surplus to requirements in part because of intrinsic incapacity for the requisite conceptual and technical mastery (Rifkin, 1995). Does it appear so heinous that they might as well be pensioned off at the beach? Not all, it must be interposed, for even in a brave new world of automation and robotics, somebody may have to do some dirty jobs. But the essential thing is the trend – and a trend toward employment collapse is postulated.

Political implications should first be quarantined. If the contraction should come about by attrition, protective mechanisms would presumably have time to develop. But political or economic shock could initiate more violently what longer trends were preparing. And globalization implies universal effects. The large issue put aside for present purposes is conjecture as to the political consequences if an employment debacle seriously threatened domestic cohesion and international stability.

Instrumental assumptions are a convenient starting-point. The immemorial assumption is entrenched that every man must earn his daily bread. Emancipated women have succumbed to the contagion. Even in times of occupational specialization, work is conceived as obliquely fulfilling requirements of subsistence and is also regarded in terms of social obligation. That is endorsed institutionally. The conventional mechanism for the distribution of welfare is work. It follows that contemporary societies and international conventions treat access to work as a basic human right and proclaim the objective of full employment. How else could the existing system function? These matters are not pronounced in the language of aspiration but as undertakings of a social contract.

Assertions in international instruments in relation to full employment and the right to work imply a human right to subsistence. Such "rights" are statements of principle, expressed at large; no agency (or method) is identifiable with a correlative duty of enforcement. But the world must have aspirations and it is right to embed them by collegiate processes. Does that hold, however, if the gap between aspiration and reality is so large that credibility is destroyed? Not much is to be said for undertakings that are essentially deceptive and foster illusory expectations. The implied contradiction is a reminder of the hazards of setting up ethical absolutes. Even "rights" that are apparently indefeasible may owe their sanctity only to the circumstances of a particular era.

It is awkward, however, that adoption of work-related principles came as the culmination of a protracted struggle; their emotional weight is substantial. Understandably, resistance to their removal from codes, or even modification, might be stubborn. Could related and more pertinent guarantees be substituted? It is certainly arguable that the fundamental purpose is not so much to establish a universal claim to employment as to secure distributional equity of welfare by the medium of work. If work is no longer the standard distributional mechanism, work-related "rights" will appear in a different perspective. Attention will necessarily focus directly on the conditions for sharing wealth within whatever political entity is relevant, not on the conventional intermediary device of employment. The "right to work", in that event, will lapse from the social agenda as a slogan of exhausted purpose.

At the individual level, problems of cultural adjustment would seem formidable. What is to become of economic man when he (or she) can no longer live to and for work? How is the void of time to be filled without access to work? That was less of an issue in the pre-industrial age because needs of subsistence and obligations of status imposed a menu of activity, and because personal culture was possibly more expansive and unhurried and less confined. It may well be true that humanity generally led a life described by Hobbes as nasty, brutish and short, but much of that life would appear to have been less concentrated and channelled, and much less driven by the clock.

Almost universally, of course, public and private entities are nowadays quite heavily involved in promoting and providing activity and education for those who do not work – not simply by way of training to resume employment but also to enable greater satisfaction in the pursuit of leisure. Movements such as the University of the Third Age readily come to mind. As long as historical attitudes to work persist, however, such initiatives do not intend or effect a basic remoulding of the public mind. Frequently, indeed, work is there in the background as a kind of passport to entry – in terms of expectation or voluntary (or involuntary) release. Modern man would lose important psychological moorings without the looming presence of conventional understandings of work.

Employment, moreover, confers identity and status. How is a person to establish identity, how is a person to be placed by others, without the measuring rod of work? As authorities have been at pains to tell us, workers in the industrial age of contractual employment have been beneficiaries as well as victims, because liberated by the system from traditional tyrannies of status. Would new principles of status emerge to answer to apparent human imperatives of precedence?

No ethic, it has been said, is as ethical as the work ethic. Whether or not attributed to the Protestant Reformation, a Western work ethic is still a significant impulse of the civilization of work, and is still loaded with religious connotation (Furnham, 1990). Sacralization of work as a calling, the belief in fulfilling the divine will through work, survives. And a great many people who have no religious affiliation or conscious religious inclination still have ethical beliefs about work. Puritan beginnings and the frontier experience gave those beliefs much greater currency in the United States than they have in the old Catholic culture in Europe, or even in European areas where reformed churches have been influential. In a world of vanishing work, such convictions would lack a field of operation – "we have based our social structures on the work ethic and now it would appear that it is to become redundant with millions of people" (Jenkins and Sherman, quoted in Furnham, 1990, p. 235). How could the beliefs remain credible? Unless an ethical or more broadly cultural revolution eventuated, the implied contradiction would result in considerable individual crisis.

A civilization of work readily absorbed the secular concept that work is a fundamental human impulse and psychological imperative (see Supiot, 1996). That approach was called in aid to validate Taylorism and the shabbier aspects of industrialism. The idea of work as an expression of creativity was swept in also, even though the creative or inspirational ministry of factory labour would have been difficult to identify. But decoupling of work from creative activity does not present difficulties, since there is no necessary connection. In an evolution Marx would have applauded, the withering-away of structured jobs could open the way to a free and imaginative release of individual capacities.

It is rather less hopeful that all this seems doubtfully compatible with the conventional function of work as a distributional mechanism. If work rationing schemes (and implied distributional constraints) are left aside, the puzzle is to ensure the subsistence of those who have no work. If the commodification of people must be abandoned and employment is no longer the touchstone of distribution, what mechanisms will be feasible? That question must be asked in the climate of a prevailing ideology that resists state intervention, opposes the growth of a "culture of dependence", has a doctrinaire obsession with the supposed benefits of a very low tax regime and rests on individualist concepts that subordinate motives of community solidarity.

It is possible to keep calm. Paradoxically, the historical position of women is the joker in the pack. It demonstrates that, where the social will exists, very significant groups may be supported in disconnection from the market. In relation to women, the traditional expedient in many societies has been to throw responsibility upon the private sector – a breadwinner husband was expected to keep his wife. The responsibility extended to children of the union, themselves dissociated from the market until an age at which they might be employed. This precedent was created in the straitened world of the economics of scarcity. In modern-day communities of abundance (to take a cue from the developed world), how could a corresponding obligation be found unrealistic?

As women have entered the workforce, the traditional paradigm dissolves and the breadwinner worker is, in a sense, off the hook. Even the nurture of children may become a shared expense. Gender dependence is vestigial, up to a point. Whether that brings satisfactory financial relief is conjectural, for the modern style is a lifestyle entailing great expense. The point to emphasize is that dependence has not been eliminated – its incidence and implications have simply been changed. Care of the aged, for example, used to be an obligation with which families were burdened. Contraction to the nuclear family and evolving social expectations mean that such a view of the matter is now widely regarded as inappropriate. The burden is evaded or, more accurately, displaced.

Voluntary agencies are prominent as a substitute source of support. Some who fear for the future of market-related employment, such as Jeremy Rifkin, are optimistic that activities of that kind will take up much of the slack. Social upheaval and employment volatility are certainly giving them an expanded role. But there appear to be limits: most such entities operate under financial strain and many depend to a greater or lesser extent on state funding. Under conditions of economic rationalism, needs are becoming too large and urgent for dispersed and partly uncoordinated assistance. That implies state intervention, with some loss of autonomy. Insulation from market criteria is precarious.

As the welfare state generations supposed, social protection is best assured, and human dignity maintained, by using public power. On that assumption, the world of less work is bound to impose substantial demands, probably in the well-canvassed form of a universal "dividend" or wage. There is nothing new, of course, about redistributive assistance with a large field of operation; in numbers of countries in the developed world, more than one-third of the population draws some state benefit (Boissonnat, 1996). The difference envisaged may be just a matter of scale. Because habits of individualism die hard, however, there would be an expectation of resistance if state aid crossed perceived boundaries of social deprivation. In conventional language, why should the working segment of the population "support" another segment that is perceived to be idle, has no shame about it and is cosseted in a culture of dependence?

There are persuasive answers. First of all, the concept of lifetime employment is already fading in face of the imperatives of competitive markets and restless structural change. The typical worker at any level may expect to hold successive jobs, with intermissions of no work when social insurance is important. State responsibility for education and for age assistance is still considered to be an implied term of the social contract, and health care may be an additional part of the package. Thus every citizen is a contingent beneficiary. The social budget is not an infliction upon the reputable to indulge the laggards, but a public good involving contribution according to capacity and distribution according to need. Radical market liberalism has obscured the credibility of this paradigm, but its essential cogency is untouched. In a world of less work, well-embedded impulses of mutuality and community would have to be reanimated.

The basic recidivism of the neo-liberal credo has revived assumptions of the laissez-faire era. Entitlement is in retreat and charity is in vogue. The practical limitations of charitable provision have been outlined. It has no prospect of providing a sufficient response if an employment collapse comes about. Charity, moreover, is identified with an ethic of individualism and invested with class connotations of good works for the deserving poor. Condescension is inherent. The point is disingenuously disregarded, but that is fundamentally at variance with modern community beliefs. The contradiction of charity within equality would soon be exposed in conditions of disappearing work.

There are formidable obstacles on the road back from radical individualism, the sovereignty of greed and the ambiguities of charitable aid. The ancient concept of the citizen deriving aspiration from and finding personal validity within the political community has fallen into discredit. Collectivist ideologies spawned the totalitarian aberration of the 1930s. Once it was over, influential theorists such as von Hayek and Popper nailed down the beast's coffin with a powerful individualist message (von Hayek, 1946; Popper, 1966). Scared out of their wits by the Nazi perversion, democratic communities and their spokesmen recoiled from the idea of the Gemeinschaft – of the community as a closely knit unit. For purposes of political discourse, the Volksgeist had been done to death. In the eyes of Margaret Thatcher and her ideological associates, for example, there was no such thing as society.

The neo-liberal credo takes that orientation from the realm of political ideas and applies it to the realities of governance. The resultant extremism is a curious image of totalitarian excess, crowding out ancient and benign habits of the European home. Globalization of that credo erodes belief in the generally more collectivist values of non-European countries. An ideology of extravagant individualism now ranks as a worldwide problem.

A possible outcome is an ideologically unified global society purporting to operate as a market-powered machine. The pretension of economics to act as a value-free calculus with application over the whole range of human activity (Méda, 1995) would to that extent be satisfied. The historical priority of political and ethical standards would be subverted. Under the new ethos of egotism, commodification of labour and market-clearing mechanisms, values of human dignity, group solidarity, social compassion – and ultimately personal individuality – would be lost. Under a radically instrumental approach, the worker as factor of production would be exposed to obsessive efficiency and reductionism. That prescription would be calamitous for civilized society, not to mention for the future of work.

A cultural counter-revolution could mitigate these trends. The first step would be in the field of ideas. Vilification of European collectivism after the totalitarian years was an over-reaction to a political deviation caused by singular circumstances. Even if individualism is cultivated, moreover, any regime in the complex modern world must impose far-reaching limitations on liberty. Greater acknowledgment of that truth would allow renewed confidence in concerted action pursuant to the popular will. There is no reason why a society building on democratic trust in the mandate of the state should turn to oppression or be more alien to legitimate freedoms than any other.

A necessary parallel measure would be to dethrone economics from pretensions to be the overarching regulator of human organization. That usurpation stands the logic of history on its head. It forestalls concern with political and ethical issues which, because they are truly fundamental, any society should be thrashing out. Economic considerations ought to be instrumental only. That point is the more easily appreciated once conceptual foundations of economics that purport to be mechanistic are revealed as a camouflage for value judgments.

Is an ideological reorientation possible? For Europe, the portents are favourable; statist doctrine still strongly influences France and communal inclinations in Germany were not extinguished by the Nazi disgrace (see Judt, 1997). Hegel's idealist collectivism was a representative local emanation. In Anglo-American capitalism, by contrast, political and economic individualism has the powerful sanction of centuries of dominance. In the United Kingdom, that has now turned to a cruder conditioning with an extreme economic bias. Self-reliance is the watchword of the United States, but there an odd equilibrium may be perceived. The American experience also instilled the lesson of community dependence. Two credos blend in a manner Americans find compatible – macropolitical (and macroeconomic) individualism beside micropolitical (or microsocial) collectivism. Big government is disfavoured; the authority of church council and town council is indulged with deference. Beyond the transatlantic heartlands, detoxification from the *pensée unique* of societies in which principles of social solidarity once had prior importance is unlikely to be excessively traumatic.

As well as ideological and individual problems, the twilight of the civilization of work would impose difficulties affecting the practical affairs of society. That civilization is based on hyper-competitive national and regional entities that fear the consequences of relaxation of effort. So far, globalization has intensified the spirit of international competition. If income is delinked from work, how is the effort to be sustained? Without the goad of work as the mechanism of welfare distribution, what other incentives can be imagined? There is no guarantee that societies will spawn enough workaholics to continue the momentum on a basis of work for work's sake (see ILO, 1996b, esp. p. 21).

It is germane to the present argument, however, that there are additional compelling reasons for a slackening of the insensate frenzy latter-day capitalism is developing. Sadly, moves toward remodelling of the basic architecture of the world economy are so far concerned only with functional management, transparency and disciplined regulation (Haass and Litan, 1998). It is scarcely within contemplation that nations at different levels of development would be ready to accept economic speed limits. In principle, notwithstanding, that would be a splendid alternative to the "race to the bottom" which is a possible issue of current trends.

Uncertainty is the inseparable henchman of the new millennium. Destructive forces are felling the protective barriers of established ways. With the advent of neo-industrial conditions and globalization, a convulsion comparable in its implications to the agricultural and industrial revolutions is eventuating. A consequential collapse of traditional modes of employment cannot be excluded. For present purposes, that is taken to be more likely to occur than not. The burden of analysis is that prevailing neo-liberal policies which are colonizing the whole world are peculiarly unfitted to deal with the resultant exigencies. As long as ideological remoulding is resisted, there can be no adequate adjustment to a world of vanishing work. The concept of the political community will have to be revived. Once policies focus on the citizen rather than on economic man, on common purpose and a decent dignity for all, advanced technology and globalization will no longer be demons for the fearful, but will take their place as instruments for the pursuit of happiness in a less fraught, more leisured and more equitable world.

Notes

[1] This label is generally preferred to "Fordism", presumably because Taylor is remembered as the *theoretical* architect of the "secular theology of technology". The constituents of the theory have been well characterized as: (i) division of tasks; (ii) standardization of tasks; and (iii) organization by managers (Lansbury, 1981).

[2] "Rhenish capitalism" is useful as a distinguishing generic term (see p. 41), but the European "nations" certainly retain distinct cultural characteristics that influence governance. The following

identikit sketches illustrate succinctly: Italy – feudal/paternalistic structures and relationships; France – elitist/hierarchical; Germany – corporatist structures and beliefs; Sweden – individualism balanced with welfarism in an outward-looking enterprise economy (Raymond S. Milne, private communication).

[3] The significance of such findings is hotly debated, especially on the ground that global statistics do not capture social deficits and realities of deprivation among substantial sectors of the population that are losers in the transition to radical capitalism; see, for example, MacDonald, 1997; Sennett, 1998; Applebaum, 1998 and the discussion commencing at p. 34.

References

Appelbaum, Eileen; Schettkat, Ronald. 1995. "Employment and productivity in industrialized economies", in *International Labour Review* (Geneva), Vol. 134, No. 4/5, pp. 605-623.

Applebaum, Herbert. 1998. *The American work ethic and the changing work force.* Westport, CT, Greenwood Press.

Baker, Dean; Epstein, Gerald; Pollin, Robert (eds.). 1998. *Globalization and progressive economic policy.* Cambridge, Cambridge University Press.

Bauman, Zygmunt. 1998. *Work, consumerism and the new poor.* Buckingham, Open University Press.

Bergsten, C. Fred. 1999. "America and Europe: Clash of the titans?", in *Foreign Affairs* (New York, NY), Vol. 78, No. 2 (Mar.-Apr.), pp. 20-34.

—.1997. "The dollar and the euro", in *Foreign Affairs* (New York, NY), Vol. 76, No. 4 (July-Aug.), pp. 83-95.

Beveridge, Sir William. 1944. *Full employment in a free society.* London, Allen and Unwin.

Beynon, Huw. 1997. "The changing practices of work", in Brown (ed.), pp. 20-53.

Boissonnat, Jean. 1996. "Combating unemployment, restructuring work: Reflections on a French study", in *International Labour Review* (Geneva), Vol. 135, No. 1, pp. 5-15.

Bosch, Gerhard. 1999. "Working time: Tendencies and emerging issues", in *International Labour Review* (Geneva), Vol. 138, No. 2, pp. 131-149.

Britton, Andrew. 1997. "Full employment in the industrialized countries", in *International Labour Review* (Geneva), Vol. 136, No. 3, pp. 293-314.

Brown, Richard K. (ed). 1997a. *The changing shape of work.* London, St. Martin's Press.

—.1997b. "Introduction: Work and employment in the 1990s", in Brown (ed.), pp. 1-19.

Castel, Robert. 1996. "Work and usefulness to the world", in *International Labour Review* (Geneva), Vol. 135, No. 6, pp. 615-622.

—.1995. *Les métamorphoses de la question sociale: Une chronique du salariat.* Paris, Fayard.

Emmerij, Louis. 1994. "The employment problem and the international economy", in *International Labour Review* (Geneva), Vol. 133, No. 4, pp. 449-466.

Fanfani, Amintore. 1935. *Catholicism, protestantism, capitalism.* London, Sheed and Ward.

Feldstein, Martin. 1999. "A self-help guide for emerging markets", in *Foreign Affairs* (New York, NY), Vol. 78, No. 2 (Mar.- Apr.), pp. 93-109.

—.1998. "Refocusing the IMF", in *Foreign Affairs* (New York, NY), Vol. 77, No. 2 (Mar.-Apr.), pp. 20-33.

Freeman, Chris; Soete, Luc; Efendioglu, Umit. 1995. "Diffusion and the employment effects of information and communication technology", in *International Labour Review* (Geneva), Vol. 134, No. 4/5, pp. 587-604.

Friedman, Milton. 1968. "The role of monetary policy", in *American Economic Review* (Menasha, WI), Vol. 68, No. 1 (Mar.), pp. 1-17.

Furnham, Adrian. 1990. *The Protestant work ethic: The psychology of work-related beliefs and behaviours.* London, Routledge.

Galbraith, John Kenneth. 1992. *The culture of contentment.* Boston, MA, Houghton Mifflin.

Garten, Jeffrey E. 1999. "Lessons for the next financial crisis", in *Foreign Affairs* (New York, NY), Vol. 78, No. 2, (Mar.- Apr.), pp. 76-92.

George, Susan. 1989. *A fate worse than debt.* London, Penguin.

Gray, Sir Alexander. 1946. *The socialist tradition: Moses to Lenin.* London, Longmans.

Greider, William. 1997. *One world, ready or not: The manic logic of global capitalism.* New York, NY, Simon and Schuster.

Gruen, Fred H. 1981. "The economic perspective", in Wilkes, pp. 1-20.

Haass, Richard W.; Litan, Robert E. 1998. "Globalization and its discontents", in *Foreign Affairs* (New York, NY), Vol. 77, No. 3, (May-June), pp. 2-6.

Hayek, Friedrich A. von. 1946. *The road to serfdom.* London, Routledge.

Head, Simon. 1996. "The new, ruthless economy", in *New York Review of Books* (New York, NY), 29 Feb.

Heylen, Freddy; Goubert, Lucia; Omey, Eddy. 1996. "Unemployment in Europe: A problem of relative or aggregate demand for labour?", in *International Labour Review* (Geneva), Vol. 135, No. 1, pp. 17-36.

Hutton, Will. 1997. *The state to come.* London, Vintage.

—.1995. *The state we're in.* London, Jonathan Cape.

ILO. 1996a. "What is the future of work? Ideas from a French report", in *International Labour Review* (Geneva), Vol. 135, No. 1, Perspectives, pp. 93-110.

—.1996b. *Employment policies in a global context.* Report V to the 83rd Session of the International Labour Conference. Geneva.

—.1994a. "Towards full employment: An ILO view", in *International Labour Review* (Geneva), Vol. 133, No. 3, Perspectives, pp. 401-415.

—.1994b. "The ILO and Bretton Woods: A common vision?", in *International Labour Review* (Geneva), Vol. 133, No. 5/6, Perspectives, pp. 695-700.

—.1994c. "Service sector employment and the productivity challenge", in *International Labour Review* (Geneva), Vol. 133, No. 5/6, Perspectives, pp. 707-713.

Jenkins, Clive; Sherman, Barrie. 1979. *The collapse of work.* London, Eyre Methuen.

Judt, Tony. 1997. "The social question redivivus", in *Foreign Affairs* (New York, NY), Vol. 76, No. 5 (Sept.-Oct.), pp. 95-117.

Kelsey, Jane. 1997. *The New Zealand experiment.* Auckland, Auckland University Press/Bridget Williams.

Krugman, Paul. 1999. *The return of depression economics.* New York, NY, W. W. Norton.

—.1998. "America the boastful", in *Foreign Affairs* (New York, NY), Vol. 77, No. 3 (May-June), pp. 32-45.

—.1997. "Is capitalism too productive?", in *Foreign Affairs* (New York, NY), Vol. 76, No. 5 (Sept.-Oct.), pp. 79-94.

—.1996. "First, do no harm" (Replies to Kapstein), in *Foreign Affairs* (New York, NY), Vol. 75, No. 4 (July-Aug.), pp. 164-170.

—.1994. *Peddling prosperity: Economic sense and nonsense in the age of diminished expectations.* New York, NY, W. W. Norton.

Kubota, Akira. 1983. "Japan: Social structure and work ethic" in Vol. 20 *Asia Pacific Community.* Spring, pp. 35-65.

Landauer, Thomas K. 1995. *The trouble with computers, usefulness, usability and productivity.* Cambridge, MA, MIT Press.

Lansbury, Russell D. 1981. "Structural and institutional barriers to change", in Wilkes, pp. 110-125.

Lawrence, Robert Z. 1996. "Resist the binge" (Replies to Kapstein), in *Foreign Affairs* (New York, NY), Vol. 75, No. 4 (July-Aug.), pp. 170-173.

Lee, Eddy. 1996. "Globalization and employment: Is anxiety justified?", in *International Labour Review* (Geneva), Vol. 135, No. 5, pp. 485-497.

—.1995. "Overview", in *International Labour Review* (Geneva), Vol. 134, No. 4/5, pp. 441-450.

Lyon-Caen, Gérard. 1996. "Labour law and employment transitions", in *International Labour Review* (Geneva), Vol. 135, No. 6, pp. 697- 702.

MacDonald, Robert. 1997. "Informal work, survival strategies and the idea of an 'underclass'", in Brown (ed.), pp. 103-124.

Meadows, Pamela (ed). 1996. *Work out or work in: Contributions to the debate on the future of work.* York, Rowntree Foundation.

Méda, Dominique. 1995. *Le travail, une valeur en voie de disparition.* Paris, Aubier.

Moggridge, D.E. 1992. *Maynard Keynes: An economist's biography.* London, Routledge.

Piore, Michael. 1995. *Beyond individualism.* Cambridge, MA, Harvard University Press.

Polanyi, Karl. 1944. *The Great Transformation: The political and economic origins of our time.* New York, NY, Rinehart.

Popper, Karl R. 1966. *The Open Society and its enemies.* London, Routledge and Kegan Paul.

Reich, Robert B. 1992. *The work of nations: Preparing ourselves for 21st century capitalism.* New York, NY, Vintage Books.

Rifkin, Jeremy. 1995. *The end of work: The decline of the global labor force and the dawn of the post-market era.* New York, NY, G.P. Putnam's Sons.

Sampson, Anthony. 1989. *The Midas touch.* London, Hodder and Stoughton.

Schlesinger, Arthur, Jr. 1997. "Has democracy a future?", in *Foreign Affairs* (New York, NY), Vol. 76, No. 5 (Sept.-Oct.), pp. 2-12.

Schor, Juliet B. 1991. *The overworked American: The unexpected decline of leisure.* New York, NY, Basic Books.

Sen, Amartya. 1997. "Inequality, unemployment and contemporary Europe" in *International Labour Review* (Geneva), Vol. 136, No. 2, pp. 155-172.

Sennett, Richard. 1998. *The corrosion of character: The personal consequences of work in the new capitalism.* New York, NY, W.W. Norton.

Silver, Hilary. 1994. "Social exclusion and social solidarity: Three paradigms", in *International Labour Review* (Geneva), Vol. 133, No. 5/6, pp. 531-578.

Singh, Ajit. 1995. "Institutional requirements for full employment in advanced economies" in *International Labour Review* (Geneva), Vol. 134, No. 4/5, pp. 471-496.

Soros, George. 1998. *The crisis of global capitalism.* New York, NY, Public Affairs.

—. 1996. "Can Europe work? A plan to rescue the Union", in *Foreign Affairs* (New York, NY), Vol. 75, No. 5 (Sept.-Oct.), pp. 8-14.

Supiot, Alain. 1996. "Perspectives on work: Introduction" in *International Labour Review* (Geneva), Vol. 135, No. 6, pp. 603-613.

Tawney, R.H. 1926. *Religion and the rise of capitalism.* London, John Murray.

Weber, Max. 1976. *The protestant ethic and the spirit of capitalism* (transl. Talcott Parsons). Second edition. London, George Allen and Unwin.

Wieczorek, Jaroslaw. 1995. "Sectoral trends in world employment and the shift toward services", in *International Labour Review* (Geneva), Vol. 134, No. 2, pp. 205-226.

Wilkes, John (ed). 1981. *The future of work.* Sydney, George Allen and Unwin.

Wood, Adrian. 1994. *North-South trade, employment and inequality: Changing fortunes in a skill-driven world.* Oxford, Clarendon Press.

Zuckerman, Mortimer B. 1998. "A second American century", in *Foreign Affairs* (New York, NY), Vol. 77, No. 3, (May-June), pp. 18-31.

THE CHANGING STRUCTURE OF TRADE LINKED TO GLOBAL PRODUCTION SYSTEMS: WHAT ARE THE POLICY IMPLICATIONS?

3

William MILBERG *

Most studies of economic globalization emphasize the rise in the degree of world trade openness since 1980, as measured in terms of the *amount of trade* in relation to overall economic activity. This quantitative rise, however, may be less significant than the qualitatitive change in the structure of world trade that has occurred over the same period, specifically the trade associated with the international "disintegration" of production, i.e. breaking up the production process into different parts and locating these parts in different countries. This article examines the extent of that structural change, its causes and its significance in the context of economic development.

The shift in the structure of international trade – both to more intermediate goods and increasingly outside the confines of the multinational enterprise – poses challenges to both theory and policy. The theoretical challenge is to the traditional theories of international trade and foreign direct investment (FDI). With the rise of international capital mobility and trade in intermediate goods, the theoretically harmonious world of comparative advantage gives way to a competitive struggle of absolute advantage and the relative desirability of a location for producing a particular input used in the overall production process. With respect to foreign investment, the internalization theory diminishes in importance, creating the need for an economic theory of externalization.

The policy challenge arises out of the fact that while global production sharing has apparently helped developing countries expand export-oriented manufacturing activity, the value added from that activity has not increased

Originally published in *International Labour Review*, Vol. 143 (2004), No. 1-2.

* New School University. This article is based on a background paper prepared for the World Commission on the Social Dimension of Globalization, ILO. Email address: milbergw@newschool.edu. I am grateful to Codrina Rada for excellent research assistance, to Jorg Mayer for providing the data used in the section on competition and spatial dispersion, and to Gary Gereffi, Peter Gibbon, Susan Hayter, John Humphrey, Dave Kucera, Katherine McFate and Tim Sturgeon for useful comments on the first draft.

markedly over previous, commodity-based export regimes. This is because lead firms in global production networks outsource lower value-added activities, retaining control over production in the higher value-added areas of their "core competency". These areas are often characterized by higher technological and skill requirements, but they are also commonly oligopolistic and subject to significant barriers to entry. The lower value-added portions of many global production networks have low entry barriers and are characterized by ongoing entry by firms into countries that previously did not produce. Competition at this level can be so intense as to make it difficult to raise profits and wages. While wage stagnation affects the standard of living today, it is the difficulty of capturing rents for reinvestment that poses the greatest challenge to longer-term economic development.

The growth of FDI in developing countries does not solve the problem because most profits are repatriated, and FDI tends to lag rather than lead economic development. Countries should not make major concessions to attract FDI. Instead, to achieve the goal of skill and infrastructure development – crucial for successful managerial capitalism (and likely to attract FDI) – countries should devise industrial and competition policies aimed at meeting their specific needs and at expanding rents from productive activity. It is on the socially productive reinvestment of these rents that economic development crucially hinges.

This article is divided into eight sections. The first presents an overview of world trends in trade and FDI, with an emphasis on explaining the driving forces for FDI, and the slow growth in vertical as opposed to horizontal FDI. The second considers global production sharing generally, stressing the growing importance of arm's-length and other external forms of outsourcing. The third and fourth sections analyse the implications of global production systems for the theories of foreign trade and investment, respectively. The fifth section reviews the evidence on market structure across global commodity chains. The sixth section then looks at the consequences of globalized production for labour and capital, including wage and employment implications, and for international profit flows. The seventh section takes up some policy issues of direct relevance to the challenge of economic development resulting from globalized production. These relate to industrial policy, competition policy, policy towards inward FDI and labour market policies within the global production system. A final section offers brief concluding remarks.

THE GLOBALIZATION OF PRODUCTION: TRADE AND FDI

Economic globalization is a two-pronged process: the globalization of finance and the globalization of production. The common feature of these two components is heightened international capital mobility. With the widespread liberalization and computerization of financial markets, gross international capital flows have skyrocketed over the past 20 years. Consider the market for foreign exchange: in 1977, annual transactions in foreign exchange totalled US$4.6 trillion. By 2001, transactions were running at a *daily* rate of US$1,210 billion, equivalent to the annual value of world trade.[1]

Trade

While the globalization of finance has increased dramatically, the globalization of production has grown significantly too. The globalization of production comprises both international trade and FDI. Since the mid-1980s, the global volume of FDI has grown more than that of international trade, which, in turn, has grown more than world output (see IMF, 2001; UNCTAD, 2001).

The globalization of production comes with great promise of a new phase of export growth from developing countries, whose inclusion in the process opens new markets and introduces new technologies. As world trade has expanded, both in absolute terms and in relation to world output, developing countries have maintained their share of world exports and significantly expanded their share of world exports of manufactured goods. At just over 33 per cent, the developing countries' share of world exports was the same in 2001 as it was in 1963. But the composition of their exports shows a dramatic expansion in the share of manufactured goods, from around 10 per cent in 1975 to almost 75 per cent in 1996 (WTO, 2002).

Foreign direct investment

The multinational enterprise is often viewed as a key driver of the process of the globalization of production. This is understandable, since the existence of the multinational enterprise is, by definition, premised on some previous and significant (controlling) foreign investment.[2] Moreover, the past 20 years have seen an explosive rise in the activities of multinational enterprises.

Recent estimates suggest there are about 65,000 TNCs today, with about 850,000 foreign affiliates across the globe. Their economic impact can be measured in different ways. In 2001, foreign affiliates accounted for 54 million employees compared to 24 million in 1990; their sales of almost $19 trillion were more than twice as high as world exports in 2001, compared to 1990 when both were roughly equal; and the stock of outward foreign direct investment (FDI) increased from $1.7 trillion to $6.6 trillion over the same period.... Foreign affiliates now account for one-tenth of world GDP and one-third of world exports (UNCTAD, 2002a, p. 1).

The share of FDI in world gross capital formation rose by two-thirds between the early 1980s and the early 1990s; for developing countries, the increase was by three-quarters. Globally, FDI skyrocketed in the 1990s, although it dipped suddenly in 2001 as a result of world recession, asset deflation (especially stock market declines) and a consequent decline in the value of a number of large mergers, mainly in Europe. Thus the decline in FDI flows was skewed toward developed countries. FDI to developing countries rose from US$8.4 billion in 1980 to US$205 billion in 2001, and the developing country share of global FDI rose from 15 per cent in 1980 to 22 per cent in 1999-2001. This has not been enough of an increase, however, to make a change in the developing countries' share of the world stock of foreign investment, which has fluctuated around 35 per cent for the past 20 years (UNCTAD, 2002b).

While the developing country share of world FDI flows has increased slightly, the role of FDI in the total inflow of foreign capital to developing countries has expanded dramatically. Since the debt crises of the 1980s, direct investment has supplanted private debt or equity as well as government grants as the major channel of foreign capital inflows into developing countries. Over the period 1999-2001, FDI accounted, on average, for 86 per cent of private foreign capital inflow and 71 per cent of total capital inflow into developing countries (World Bank, 2000, 2001 and 2002). Relative reliance on FDI to meet foreign capital needs could hardly be higher.

What drives foreign direct investment?

The picture described above suggests that FDI by multinational enterprises has become one of the true driving forces of globalization. What is motivating such high levels of FDI? There have been hundreds of empirical studies of the locational "determinants" of FDI. A typical econometric model regresses FDI on measures of economic activity, population, distance (both geographical and cultural, the latter using a language variable) and then adds a variable to capture human capital and perhaps, in the more recent versions, labour standards and political stability. Regulations on labour standards and tax concessions are often found to be insignificant. Kucera (2002) finds a significant negative effect of higher manufacturing wages/value added for a sample of 100 less developed countries. However, he does not find a negative effect of stronger union rights. This suggests the greater importance of non-cost effects of union rights on FDI, perhaps resulting from greater political and social stability.[3]

This result is less surprising when placed in the context of the traditional distinction between horizontal and vertical FDI. Horizontal FDI is also called "market-seeking" in that it involves a replication of productive capacity in the foreign location, presumably for sales there. Two conditions are necessary to induce such FDI. First, the foreign market must already exist or be about to develop. Second, replication of production on foreign soil must be preferable to export from home. Typically, this second condition depends on an absence of significant economies of scale and the presence of high tariffs in the foreign market, and for this reason such horizontal FDI is often termed "tariff hopping". Certainly most FDI to developed countries is aimed at better serving host markets, and some FDI in developing countries is driven by similar reasoning – Brazil being a well-documented example (see Evans, 1995; on China, see Braunstein and Epstein, 2002). Thus, econometric studies looking at *all* FDI are likely to find host market GDP to be the most significant determinant.

Vertical FDI involves capital movement aimed at more efficient backward linkages, either in production or in natural resources. "Efficiency-seeking" vertical FDI is the movement abroad of productive resources with the aim of lowering costs. It can be driven by a variety of factors, including lower labour costs, lower taxes on profits, low or lax standards on labour or the environment. These advantages must more than offset the tariffs and transportation costs incurred as a result of the international movement of any parts, components or assembled goods. Efficiency-seeking FDI is typically viewed as investment in low-wage countries, but it is not exclusively so. Considerable direct investment from the United States in Canada, for example, serves to produce or assemble parts used in goods sold in the United States. And Japanese direct investment in Ireland, for example, has been understood to be driven by that country's relatively efficient labour force and proximity to the major markets of the European Union.

"Resource-seeking" vertical FDI is driven by the desire of lead firms to control supplies of natural resources or primary commodities used in the production of other goods. This is what motivated the traditional structure of colonial and neocolonial foreign investment, led by the United Kingdom in the 1870-1913 period and by the United States after the Second World War, and it continues to be a factor in FDI today for sectors which are resource-intensive, such as steel or fabricated metal products. Some analysts have recently added "strategic-asset seeking" as an additional motive for FDI, referring to cases such as European investment in Silicon Valley. Such investment is vertical, though it tends to focus on forward linkages rather than on the backward linkages typically associated with vertical FDI (Dunning, 2000).

Globally, the accumulated *stock* of vertical FDI has increased gradually over time, though it has done so at approximately the same rate as that of horizontal FDI in the 1990s, leaving their relative shares unchanged at about 33 and 67 per cent, respectively (UNCTAD, 2002b).[4] The dominance of horizontal FDI would explain why horizontal investment swamps the dynamics of vertical investment in most econometric studies. Another reason these studies have often not found cost differences to be a significant driver of globalized production is that movements in relative costs may trigger production sharing through external rather than intra-firm channels, an issue considered in detail below.[5]

Internalization

There is a commonality across the three motives for FDI in the traditional taxonomy. In all cases, firms have decided to maintain the foreign operation within the firm. This is the process of *internalization*, according to which firms will expand their own operations when they control an asset – often an intangible or knowledge-based asset – that allows them to earn above-normal profits rather than seek another firm to supply the downstream, upstream or horizontally located product or service.

The rationale for internalization is rooted in the very logic of the capitalist firm itself: firms are organizations that exist as distinct from markets precisely because they can organize production at a lower cost than would be incurred if all aspects of their production process took place separately in markets. In a classical article on "the nature of the firm", Coase (1937) identified lower transaction costs as the source of the advantage of firm-based rather than market-based organization of production. This rationale for the existence of the firm was then extended to explain FDI, in terms of the simultaneous desire of firms to expand their markets and retain the benefits of intra-firm organization.

Coase's insights have formed the basis for the theory of the multinational enterprise for the past three decades. Hymer (1976) and, later, others have described the transnational firm as a non-market institution in the Coasian sense: the international extension of the firm reflects its apparent organizational superiority, perhaps because of the transaction-cost savings it brings compared to the costs that would be incurred through market transactions. Such savings, or rents, could result from the firm's intangible assets related to technology, production process, product design, management, labour relations, marketing, service or any other dimension of the production or delivery of a good or service. While the internalization of international operations through foreign investment is a result of the relative inefficiency of the market, the protection of such knowledge-based assets by keeping them internal to the firm is widely recognized as the prime reason why firms invest abroad rather than serve foreign markets in other ways, such as exports or even licensing or subcontracting. Today, the advantages of internalization are still seen as the key explanation of FDI.[6]

GLOBAL PRODUCTION SHARING

Given the sheer magnitude of their operations, multinational enterprises are, not surprisingly, at the centre of current discussions of globalization. Their ability to break up the production process into parts and integrate this process across many countries has come to be the symbol of globalization itself. Ford's "world car", for example, has parts produced in 14 countries and assembly operations in nine countries (UNCTAD, 1993). Such increased verticality may account for the fact that international trade and FDI, once seen as mutually substitutable means of serving foreign markets, are now complementary, with FDI often resulting in more imports and exports.

Ironically, because FDI is measured so precisely and for so many countries, analysts tend to see globalization through an FDI lens. Like the proverbial drunk who searches for his lost keys under the streetlight only because that is where she/he can see best, economists have overemphasized the relevance of FDI for economic development – in terms of both its direct role in developing country production processes and its distinctiveness from the process of international trade.

A different picture emerges if we focus more generally on the change in the structure of international trade over the past 20 years and, in particular, on the rise in the share of intermediate goods in overall international trade, whether it is intra-firm trade resulting from FDI or trade resulting from "arm's-length" subcontracting. Having risen more rapidly than trade in final goods, trade in intermediate goods is the defining manifestation of globalized production or what has variously been termed "outsourcing", "the international disintegration of production" (Feenstra, 1998), "the slicing up of the value chain" (Krugman, 1995), "global production sharing" (Yeats, 2001), "the international integration of production" (UNCTAD, 1993), "vertical integration", "vertical specialization" (Hummels, Rapoport and Yi, 1998), "fragmentation" (Arndt and Kierzkowski, 2001), "intra-product specialization" (Arndt, 1997) and "the rise of global production networks" (Ernst, Fagerberg and Hildrum, 2002) or "global value chains" (Sturgeon, 2001). We begin by evaluating the extent of the process, and then turn to an analysis of its causes and consequences.

Extent of global production sharing

Because international production sharing is not measured explicitly in the international trade data (with one exception discussed below), economists have applied a variety of techniques to measure its extent. All studies support the same general conclusion: such processes have become more prevalent over the past decade and they have reached significant levels in relation to industrial production. A narrower measure of outsourcing, which considers only those inputs that are purchased from the same two-digit SIC industry as the good being produced, shows a similar acceleration between 1972 and 1990 (see Feenstra and Hanson, 1999).[7]

Campa and Goldberg (1997) provide slightly more recent evidence and look at two-digit manufacturing sectors for Canada, Japan, the United Kingdom and the United States in the mid-1970s, mid-1980s and mid-1990s. They measure imported inputs as a share of total inputs using input-output data. They find a monotonic increase across industries in all countries. Moreover, the rate of increase in the use of imported inputs across industries was relatively constant, implying that "industries with relatively high levels of import penetration or imported input use in the early 1970s retained their relatively high reliance on imported inputs through the mid-1990s" (Campa and Goldberg, 1997, p. 4).

A detailed study of the machinery and transportation equipment sector (SITC 7), found very striking patterns in the globalization of production (Yeats, 2001). Machinery and transportation equipment accounts for about 50 per cent of global trade in manufactures, and is used by the author because under SITC revision 2 (implemented by most countries in the early 1980s), it is the only industrial category for which trade in parts and components is distinguished from trade in assembled goods. Since the early 1980s, trade in parts and components in this sector has increased more rapidly than trade in finished goods. By 1995, trade in parts and components accounted for 30 per cent of overall SITC 7 trade, up from 26.1 per cent in 1978. As a share of total trade in machinery and transportation equipment, exports of parts and components increased across the industrialized countries between 1978 and 1995, but they did so most dramatically in Japan, which greatly expanded its global production system in developing Asia (Yeats, 2001). This trend was accompanied by a shift in the destination of OECD exports of parts and components, with less going to Europe and more going to developing countries – presumably for assembly and re-export (ibid.). China and the rest of east Asia in particular experienced large increases in the share of imports received, reflecting their huge role in the production of machinery and transportation equipment. In the area of telecommunications equipment, almost three-quarters of Asian imports now consist of components for further processing and subsequent export.

Other studies use a more trade-oriented measure of production sharing. One measure is "processing trade", i.e. the amount of imports of intermediates that are processed and re-exported. Feenstra and Hanson (2001) report that such imports from China and the United States rose dramatically in the 1990s to countries of the European Union's periphery, namely Greece, Ireland, Portugal and Spain. Hummels, Rapoport and Yi (1998) define "vertical specialization" as "the amount of imports embodied in goods that are exported", and find an average increase of 20 per cent in this measure for OECD countries between the 1960s and 1990s. Specific industries showed huge increases: vertical specialization in Japanese-Asian trade in electronics increased nine-fold between 1986 and 1995.

Although the available trade data permit a precise measure only for a few industries, there is now massive evidence that global production sharing is being undertaken in a wide variety of sectors, including textiles and apparel, consumer electronics, transportation and machinery, light consumer goods industries such as toys, and even services as diverse as sales and finance (see Feenstra, 1998, p. 7, for a concrete example).

But there may be limits to the degree to which production processes can be dispersed across the globe. The opposite of such dispersion, so-called "spatial clustering" or "agglomeration", has been observed as the result of scale economies, high transportation costs and preferential trade arrangements. According to Venables, "vertical specialisation is extremely transport-intensive. Products cross borders many times, so small transport costs and trade frictions cumulate into large overall effects. This suggests that trade will develop primarily between clusters of countries with good communication and transport links" (2002, p. 3). That is, dispersion of production networks is more likely when transport costs are low, and clustering more likely when transport costs are high. Venables hypothesizes that clustering may increase in the future as new technologies promote the spread of "just-in-time" production processes. In addition to these technical factors limiting dispersion, organizational considerations have certainly confined the process for those aspects of corporate activity associated with R&D, finance, and strategic and market planning (Doremus et al., 1998).

Foreign direct investment and global production sharing

Because of the simultaneous expansion of the activities of transnational corporations and of trade in intermediates, one might assume that the latter is driven by the former. One might also assume that the growing share of intermediate goods in total world trade is largely the result of growth in intra-firm trade, i.e. international trade that takes place within multinational enterprises. Surprisingly, however, the share of trade that is intra-firm has been relatively constant for the past 25 years, implying that it has grown at the same rate as the overall volume of trade. For example, while the share of intra-firm trade in total United States trade is high, it has remained remarkably constant for over 20 years, at around 35 per cent for exports and 42 per cent for imports over the period 1977-1998 (Bureau of Economic Analysis, 2002). In fact, intra-firm trade constituted a smaller share of the United States' exports and imports in 1998 than it did in 1984. A similar pattern is found in the intra-firm trade from Japan and Sweden, the only other countries on which reliable intra-firm trade data exist (see Milberg, 1999, for details).

The high but constant share of intra-firm trade in the total trade of the United States, Japan and Sweden indicates that despite the stunning increase in the transnational activity of large firms – measured by employment, production or sales – such firms find it increasingly desirable to outsource internationally in an arm's-length relationship rather than expand their own (intra-firm) production capacity abroad. In other words, with the share of intermediate goods trade increasing and the share of intra-firm trade constant, the rise in the share of trade in intermediates must be the result of arm's-length transactions, i.e. international outsourcing outside the confines of the multinational enterprise. This suggests that another reason why econometric analyses of the determinants of FDI tend to find an insignificant relation between production costs and capital movements is that arm's-length subcontracting is increasingly being substituted for efficiency-seeking FDI.

Coordination of global production systems

The dichotomy between arm's-length outsourcing and intra-firm production sharing by multinational enterprises fails to capture the variety of organizational forms that link lead and supplier firms in a "network" or "quasi-hierarchy". These relations mix elements of intra-firm hierarchy and arm's-length, market-based relations. A key to the hierarchical form of components supply is the trust established across divisions of the firm over time. Such trust is important in guaranteeing both reliability of supply and flexibility in responding to exogenous shocks, such as shifts in demand or design. Within the global production system, trust is sometimes established through personal contacts. According to one study of the apparel industry:

> Pre-existing social relationships facilitate global production networks by reducing the risks of misunderstanding and opportunism. In the global apparel industry, ethnic ties appear to do just that, as Asian entrepreneurs based in the United States are linking up to factories in Asia at a much higher rate than other ethnicities, and are more able to establish the necessary connections required to ensure reliable transactions and to reduce quality and delivery risks (Christerson and Appelbaum, 1995, p. 1371).

There is a combination of factors driving this growth in global production systems. The shift from hierarchy to market or quasi-market is driven by the efforts of lead firms to lower costs, raise efficiency and speed of delivery, increase flexibility and risk sharing, and "improve the incentive and control structure of hierarchical organization" (Semlinger, 1991, p. 105) The relative gain from vertical disintegration makes apparent some limitations of the vertical organization that characterized successful firms for the entire twentieth century. Powell mentions three weaknesses of vertically integrated firms: "an inability to respond quickly to competitive changes in international markets; resistance to process innovations that alter the relationships between different stages of the production process; and systematic resistance to the introduction of new products" (Powell, 1990, pp. 318-319).

Table 1 presents a simple taxonomy of forms of international outsourcing, differentiated by the degree of coordination between lead and supplier firms. There is a rich literature analysing the global production networks, but the focus here is on how this form of industrial organization is captured in the analysis of trade and investment. From the perspective of international trade statistics, the network form is most like a market, since international trade along such a network is considered an arm's-length exchange. In addition to arm's-length international outsourcing of intermediate goods, there has been a rise in trade in final goods at the wholesale level, i.e. goods whose production is complete except for marketing and retailing. These goods are imported by large retailers (e.g. Wal Mart, Gap) or by so-called "manufactures without factories" or "fab-less" firms, such as Nike, Calvin Klein or Fischer-Price, which import goods fully assembled – but containing the lead firm label or package – from a foreign producer or intermediary. In these

Table 1. Coordination in global production systems

Coordination	Type of goods flow	Type of capital flow	Type of industry
None (market)	Arm's-length trade	None	Low design, specification requirement (e.g. standard apparel, electronics, toys)
Some (network or quasi-hierarchy)	Arm's-length trade	Some, mainly technological or knowledge-based	Low technological requirement, high design requirement (e.g. non-standard apparel, footwear, electronics)
Complete (firm or hierarchy)	Intra-firm trade	Foreign direct investment	High technological and design requirement (e.g. autos)

cases the value added by the lead firm comes in the areas of design, marketing or retailing.

In other respects, the relation among firms in networks or quasi-hierarchies is closer to that of a single firm and its majority-owned affiliate. Information may be shared between lead and supplier firms that traditionally would be kept within the firm. Technical and communications support might be provided by the lead firm in order to smooth the delivery of supplies. Production blueprints may even be provided to developing country supplier firms (Tybout, 2000, p. 36). Japanese subcontractors, for example, use "long-term close relations with suppliers" including "rich information sharing" (Holmstrom and Roberts, 1998, pp. 80-82, cited in Williamson, 2002, p. 190). Nolan, Sutherland and Zhang (2002) describe such suppliers as "the external firm of the large global corporations", an ambiguous term that reflects precisely this organizational arrangement between market and hierarchy. This means that while there may be no measured FDI between lead and supplier firms in a network, there is possibly significant capital flow, be it of the tangible or intangible kind.

IMPLICATIONS OF GLOBAL PRODUCTION SYSTEMS FOR THE THEORY OF TRADE

The rise in trade in intermediate goods in manufacturing constitutes a fundamental shift in the structure of international trade and poses a challenge to economists' understanding of how countries fit into the international division of labour. In the traditional theory of international trade, the direction of trade (that is, which countries produce what goods for export) is determined by the principle of comparative advantage. According to this principle, a country will specialize in the production and export of the good or goods for which its relative productivity advantage exceeds that of the foreign country. Since, by definition, each country will always have a relative productivity advantage in at least one sector, the principle of comparative advantage generates the happy result that all countries will be able successfully to participate in international trade in the sense that they will benefit from such trade and be able to generate export revenue equal to the value of imports. In other words, free trade will be beneficial and balanced for all countries, even for those that have higher costs in all sectors. Paul Krugman sums up this view nicely:

International competition does not put countries out of business. There are strong equilibrating forces that normally ensure that any country remains able to sell a range of goods in world markets, and to balance its trade on average over the long run, even if its productivity, technology, and product quality are inferior to those of other nations... Both in theory and in practice, countries with lagging productivity are still able to balance their international trade, because what drives trade is comparative rather than absolute advantage (1991, pp. 811 and 814).

The "equilibrating forces" to which Krugman refers are the price adjustments that should occur in the event that trade is not balanced. These adjustments were originally described by David Hume in 1746 and are known today as Hume's "price-specie-flow mechanism". Under a gold standard, a country running, say, a trade deficit, will experience a net outflow of specie (gold), leading to a decline in the money supply and thus the price level. This lowering of prices improves the competitiveness of the country's goods, and the specie and price movements end when trade is balanced. Today, it is the exchange rate that is supposed to adjust, depreciating in the face of a trade deficit and appreciating to spur adjustment to a surplus.

But the globalization of production and finance has rendered irrelevant some of the key assumptions of the Ricardo-Hume model of trade. The following subsections focus briefly on three of these. The first is the assumption of no international movement of capital or input production. The second is the Humean adjustment process that converts comparative advantage into money cost differences that make international trade actually happen. The third is the non-uniform distribution of knowledge-based assets across firms and countries.

International capital mobility and footloose input production

The rise of capital mobility and the increased share of trade in intermediate goods imply that capital or, analogously, the production of the intermediate inputs can move to where it is most profitable. What determines the international division of labour and the direction of international trade will then depend not on comparative advantage, but on the desirability of a location.

Ricardo, writing in the early nineteenth century, had been clear in his justification of the assumption of no international capital mobility. After stating the implications of full capital mobility for the location of production – that all factors of production would move from England to Portugal in his famous example – Ricardo then asserts that the assumption of no international capital mobility is reasonable because:

...the natural disinclination which every man has to quit the country of his birth and con-nections, and intrust himself with all his habits fixed, to a strange government and new laws, check the emigration of capital. These feelings, which I should be sorry to see weakened, induce most men of property to be satisfied with a low rate of profits in their own country, rather than seek a more advantageous employment for their wealth in for-eign nations (1817, pp. 136-137).

In the twenty-first century, the assumption of no international capital mobility and no international movement in the location of the production of inputs is at odds with the undeniable forces of globalization described in this article.[8] The introduction of an internationally mobile factor of production into the theory of trade reduces the relevance of comparative advantage in the determination of trade patterns. With free capital mobility, a good will be produced only where it is most profitable, typically where unit labour costs are the lowest. At the extreme, that is if one country has an absolute advan-tage in all goods (i.e. if unit costs are lower in the production of all goods), this country will attract foreign capital, reducing foreign production and employ-ment to zero in equilibrium. Caves describes the implications of such a situa-tion: "In general, the more mobile are factors of production, the less does comparative advantage have to do with patterns of production. If all factors are more productive in the United States than in Iceland and nothing im-peded their international mobility, all economic activity would be located in the United States" (1982, p. 55). Ronald Jones makes a similar point:

Although each nation can, by the law of comparative advantage, find something to pro-duce, it may end up empty-handed in its pursuit of industries requiring footloose factors. Once trade theorists pay proper attention to the significance of these internationally mobile productive factors, the doctrine of comparative advantage must find room as well for the doctrine of "relative attractiveness" where it is not necessarily the technical requirements of one industry versus another that loom important, it is the overall appraisal of one country versus another as a safe, comfortable, and rewarding location for residence of footloose factors (1980, p. 258).

Relative productivities or costs will not necessarily play a determining role, and in this sense the operative principle will be absolute advantage, not comparative advantage. In his 2000 Ohlin Lectures, Jones went on to explain:

The idea of comparative advantage is linked to the notion that inputs are trapped by national boundaries, so that the only decision that needs to be made concerns the alloca-tion within the country of these inputs... [A] world in which some inputs are inter-nationally mobile or tradeable is a world in which... the doctrine of comparative advantage, with its emphasis on the question of what a factor *does* within the country, needs to share pride of place with the doctrine of absolute advantage guiding the question of where an internationally mobile factor *goes* ... [O]nce international mobility in an input is allowed, *absolute* advantage becomes a concept that takes its rightful place alongside *comparative* advantage in explaining the direction of international commerce (2000, p. 7).

The price (exchange rate) adjustment process

The second fundamental weakness of the theory of comparative advantage in the twenty-first century is its presumption of a well-functioning Hume price adjustment mechanism. As financial markets, including foreign exchange markets, have been liberalized, exchange rates have increasingly been driven by financial market fluctuations, and certainly have not responded to "fundamentals" like the balance of trade. The delinking of exchange rates from the trade balance has led to persistent trade imbalances and the unlikelihood that comparative cost differences will be transformed into a situation of absolute money cost and price differences across countries.

A country running a trade deficit as a result of high labour standards and costs, for example, cannot expect a market-driven depreciation in the medium run. Since 1980, trade imbalances among the major OECD countries have been larger and more persistent than earlier in the post-war era. Yet these are the countries with the most highly developed and liberal financial markets, and therefore those where current account adjustment would be expected to be most efficient. In every case except Canada, the magnitude (in relation to GDP) and the persistence of these countries' current account imbalances were greater in the 1992-2001 period than they were in the 1972-1981 span (see OECD, 1999 and subsequent updates).[9]

Technology gaps

In addition to the issues of international capital mobility, footloose input production and financial market liberalization, the growing role of non-price competition – particularly competition over new products or processes – has further reduced the effectiveness of the Hume mechanism in balancing trade and thus the relevance of comparative advantage. With persistent differences in technology or knowledge across firms and countries, writes Alice Amsden:

The price of land, labor and capital no longer uniquely determines competitiveness. The market mechanism loses status as its sole arbiter, deferring instead to institutions that nurture productivity. Because a poor country's lower wages may prove inadequate against a rich country's higher productivity, the model of 'comparative advantage' no longer behaves predictably: latecomers cannot necessarily industrialize simply by specializing in a low-technology industry. Even in such an industry, demand may favor skilled incumbents (2001, pp. 5-6).[10]

Firms seek profits and growth by creating and protecting a knowledge advantage over rivals, be it through innovation, FDI, international outsourcing, inter-firm cooperation or state subsidies. International differences in social institutions – from systems of innovation and finance to tax treatment of corporate profits, to labour market regulations and even the scope of the welfare state – can affect both productivity and non-price dimensions of traded goods. This, in turn, affects the competitiveness of particular sectors and of the overall trading position of a national economy. A firm's export market share will depend on the overall pattern of these advantages. Market share adjustments lead to income changes and these, in turn, are likely to be more important for the evolution of trade than any cost-based changes, such as exchange rate adjustments. The Humean mechanism may be operative to some degree, but it is dominated by the absolute advantages resulting from knowledge-based differences in productivity. The diminished role of price competition due to the dominance of knowledge-based differences further raises the likelihood that trade imbalances will persist, as noted above.

IMPLICATIONS OF GLOBAL PRODUCTION SYSTEMS FOR THE THEORY OF FOREIGN INVESTMENT

Externalization and endogenous market structure

Trade patterns may be a function of the global production location strategies of firms. But does the ownership structure within these global production systems matter? I will argue that this structure is partly endogenous to the dynamics of international competition itself. Specifically, if intra-firm trade is the result of internalization strategies, then the observed rise in arm's-length subcontracting requires a theory of *externalization*.

Firms internalize an international production process to protect rents that accrue to their firm-specific (often knowledge-based) assets. Such rents are possible only in an oligopolistic industry, in which economies of scale and market power can both foster the development of such assets and permit their continued profitability. Conversely, firms will externalize a portion of the operation if the expected cost savings exceed the expected rent accrual. This is more likely to be the case when (intermediate) product markets are competitive.

If there is competition or if it is possible to create competitive conditions among suppliers, then the lead firm should externalize its sourcing. If oligopoly conditions can be maintained at the level of suppliers, then it is in the lead firm's interest to retain suppliers internally. In other words, firm strategy is to externalize whenever downstream markets are competitive. If externalization itself fosters downstream competition, the asymmetry of market structures along the global commodity chain can be considered endogenous to lead firms' competitive strategies.

To the extent that the asymmetry in market structures is endogenous, then by the same reasoning so is the rising incidence of externalization. Competition among suppliers is beneficial to lead firms not only because of its cost implications, but also because it enhances the flexibility of lead firm supply conditions.[11] Lead firms can set relatively short-term subcontracts, allowing for more rapid responses to changes in final-good demand conditions or supply-side changes, on issues ranging from product design to wages, exchange rates or policies in the countries where suppliers or potential suppliers are located.

Many management experts have remarked on the increasing tendency of firms to focus on "core competence" and otherwise to rely on arm's-length outsourcing. This shift permits firms to focus on aspects of the production process in respect of which entry is difficult, mainly because of the skill and technology they require. Firms reduce their scope to their core competence not only for the obvious reason that this is what they are best at, but also because this is the aspect of the integrated production process that generates rents and maximizes the possibility of retaining those rents over time. Thus core competence is difficult to isolate from market power.

Another factor driving such externalization is policy, in both the developed and the developing countries, in particular the establishment of export processing zones (EPZs), i.e. special areas into which goods may be imported duty-free and most output is for export. EPZs are most common in east Asia and Latin America and are largely concentrated in just two sectors: apparel and electronics. Electronics is considerably more capital-intensive than apparel. The degree of foreign ownership of EPZ-based firms varies across regions, and is much higher in Latin America than in east Asia. In a study of Central American EPZs, for example, Jenkins, Esquivel and Larrain (1998) find local ownership of 11 per cent of firms in Honduras and Nicaragua, about 20 per cent in Costa Rica and El Salvador, and 43 per cent in Guatemala. Another study of global patterns finds that "much of the offshore assembly processing activity is by locally owned producers rather than with foreign-owned manufacturing activities" (Yeats, 2001, p. 33, box 2).

Global commodity chains

In sum, globalized production will be increasingly coordinated externally rather than within firms if external sourcing can create competition among suppliers, thereby reducing costs and raising flexibility beyond what could be accomplished within the realm of internal operations. The resulting competitive pressure on suppliers could also translate into pressure on labour costs or on labour standards.[12] Such endogeneity of market structure among subcontractors can be illustrated with the concept of the global commodity chain, defined by Sturgeon as "the sequence of productive (i.e. value added) activities leading to and supporting end use" (2001, p. 11). The notion of the global commodity chain is similar to that of the column vector of an input-output table, but whereas input-output analysis emphasizes the volume of inputs per unit of output, the global commodity chain emphasizes the ownership and power structure within each link and across links in the process of commodity production (e.g. between lead firms and supplier firms, or between first-tier supplier firms and smaller – even home-based – subcontractors).

The lead firm typically controls the global commodity chain. Gereffi (1994) distinguishes between buyer-driven and producer-driven value chains, the distinction depending on the nature of the lead firm in the chain. A producer-driven chain is typical in industries characterized by scale economies and driven by multinational firms which may outsource production but which keep R&D and final-good production within the firm. Automobiles, computers and aircraft are examples of goods produced in this way. Buyer-driven commodity chains occur mainly in industries producing consumer durables such as apparel, footwear and toys. In this case the global commodity chain is driven by large retailers (e.g. Wal-Mart, Gap). Such firms do no manufacturing themselves: they may do design and marketing, but they subcontract the actual production of the good.

While the distinction between the producer-led and consumer-led chains may be useful for some purposes, the emphasis here will be on differences in market structure and thus firm power along the global commodity chain. Some hypothetical patterns of ownership and power among lead and supplier firms in the global commodity chain are summarized in figure 1. This is a highly simplified depiction, especially because at the lower end of the value chain there are likely to be multiple suppliers, possibly reflecting great variation in organization, from assembly-line factories, to agglomerations of craft-like production, to small-scale, home-based work. The point of the stylized representation in figure 1 is to illustrate varieties of vertical arrangements and their implications for pricing and income distribution. Each box in the diagram represents the possibility of a different owner and a different location from the other boxes in the chain.

The four hypothetical cases illustrated are distinguished by the markup over costs and the share of value added at different points in the chain. Case I in the figure is labelled "vertical competition" because it depicts that of uniform markups at each point in the chain. The standard view that "moving up the value chain" implies moving into higher value-added activities is illustrated by Case II, entitled "Pressure on subcontractors". This shows declining markups and declining value-added shares at lower points in the commodity chain, indicating both the possible motivation for outsourcing (less value added) and the ability to squeeze suppliers (lower markups over costs). Case II describes an oligopolistic market structure at the top of the chain and a highly competitive structure at the bottom. This case most clearly reflects the asymmetry identified above with the increasing volume of arm's-length outsourcing.

Case III is that of the strong first-tier supplier, typically in a developed or newly industrialized country, for example car parts producers in Brazil, semiconductor firms in the Republic of Korea or even some apparel producers in Mexico (see, for example, Bair and Gereffi, 2001; Sturgeon, 2002). Case IV is titled "Strong middleman", reflecting a bloated markup in the middle of the chain, resulting from the ability of traders both to squeeze suppliers below them and to retain proprietary advantages not appropriable by those to whom they sell. Examples of this are the cut-flower industry, the Hong Kong apparel trade and the cocoa and coffee trades.[13]

Figure 1.   Cost markups and value added in the global commodity chain:
Four hypothetical cases

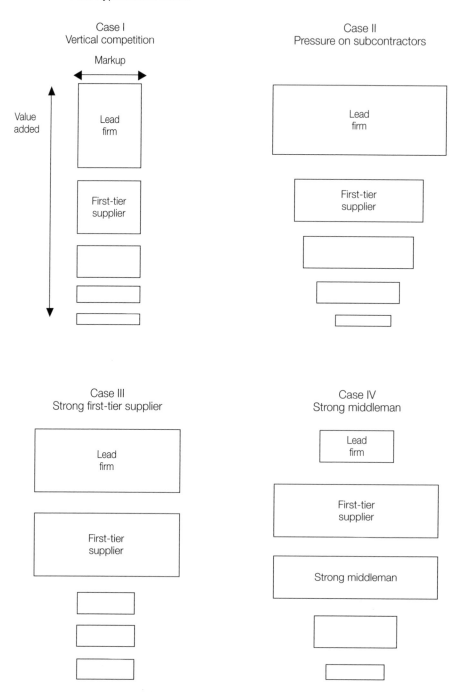

ENDOGENOUS ASYMMETRY OF MARKET STRUCTURE
AND ITS CONSEQUENCES

Oligopoly competition among lead firms

The surge of cross-border mergers and acquisitions over the past ten years indicates that there is a global consolidation of industry under way. This tendency to greater concentration has been documented in some detail at the industry level. There is a prevalence of market concentration across manufacturing sectors. Firms with large market shares are exclusively firms based in developed countries. Specifically, in the face of considerable economic integration over the past 25 years, oligopoly continues to be the dominant market structure in manufacturing, agriculture and mining. Nolan, Sutherland and Zhang (2002) characterize the situation as a "global business revolution", though they provide no time series evidence. This revolution, they write, "produced an unprecedented concentration of business power in large corporations headquartered in the high-income countries" (op. cit., p. 1). They identify a broad range of industries with high degrees of concentration as measured by market share, including commercial aircraft, automobiles, gas turbines, microprocessors, computer software, electronic games and even consumer goods, including soft drinks, ice cream, tampons, film and cigarettes, and services such as brokerage for mergers and acquisitions and insurance (see also Oliveira Martins and Scarpetta, 1999).

Competition and spatial dispersion among supplier firms

There is less evidence available on markups and market structure at the lower levels of global commodity chains. Certainly most of the world's largest firms are based in developed countries. In 2000, a mere 5 per cent of "Fortune Five Hundred Companies" and 3 per cent of "Financial Times 500" companies were based in low-income countries. Of the 27 developing country firms on the Financial Times 500 list, 24 were from Asia and only three were from Latin America. Of the 100 largest non-financial multinational enterprises in the world in 2000 (ranked by foreign assets), just five were from developing countries and two of these were petroleum producers: Petroleos Venezuela and Petronas of Malaysia (*Fortune Magazine*, 2000; *Financial Times*, 2000; UNCTAD, 2002b). To the extent that they are associated with firm size, markups can be expected to be smaller among developing country firms.

While size no doubt matters, it is the structure of markets and the investment strategies of firms that will determine markups. At the low end of the global commodity chain, low entry barriers are the norm. More and more countries are establishing production capability in manufacturing sectors. Most of this spatial dispersion of production is occurring in low value-added niches of markets. Though this pattern has often been documented in the textiles and apparel sector and in consumer electronics, the phenomenon of more countries entering production in low value-added sectors over time has been identified much more broadly across manufacturing.[14] Mayer, Butkevicius and Kadri (2002) measure industry concentration in terms of the number of countries involved in production. They use a standard measure of concentration, the Herfindahl-Hirschman index, substituting the number of countries for the number of firms in an industry. Of the 149 sectors (at the three-digit SITC level) in their data set, 119 experienced a decrease in concentration over the period 1980-1998. In non-manufacturing sectors, 50 out of 76 experienced decreased concentration. The trend decrease in concentration is also reflected in patterns across manufacturing, as shown by these authors' data on industries as diverse as dyeing and colouring materials, iron and steel, office machines and telecommunications equipment.

This direct evidence of greater dispersion of production across a wide variety of generally low value-added manufacturing sectors is consistent with a number of recent econometric studies of competition in developing countries. Roberts and Tybout (1996) present a series of country studies that focus on entry and exit conditions, with evidence on Chile, Colombia, Mexico, Morocco and Turkey for the 1970s and 1980s. Summarizing the studies, they write that "entry and exit rates are substantial... Despite the popular perception that entry and the associated competitive pressures are relatively limited in developing countries, these entry figures *exceed* the comparable figures for industrial countries" (op. cit., p. 191). Another study – by Glen, Lee and Singh (2002) – focuses on profitability and its persistence in seven developing countries, namely Brazil, India, Jordan, Korea, Malaysia, Mexico and Zimbabwe. The authors compare their findings to estimates for industrialized countries: "Surprisingly, both short- and long-term persistence of profitability for developing countries are found to be lower than those for advanced countries" (op. cit., p. 1). Finally, a study from the labour market perspective also confirms the competitive picture in developing countries. Brainard and Riker (1997) estimate the wage elasticity of labour demand across affiliates of United States multinational enterprises. A drop in the wage in a low-wage affiliate has little effect on employment in the home operation, but a large and significant effect on employment in other low-wage affiliates of the same firm.

In sum, there are two, seemingly incongruous, tendencies that can be discerned in the evolving structure of global industry. On the one hand, and despite the popular association of globalization with greater competition, there is a strong tendency towards greater concentration of industry globally. On the other hand, there is evidence that more and more developing countries are entering manufacturing industries at the low end of the value chain. This constitutes the asymmetry of market structures in global commodity chains.

At least three factors make this asymmetry sustainable over time. The first of these is the existence of entry barriers at the high end of the value chain and their absence at the low end. Entry barriers exist both for lead firms and many first-tier suppliers. At these two levels of the global commodity chain, scale economies may deter entry (see Palpaceur, 2002, p. 5). In addition to the technological issues mentioned above, brand loyalty makes market access difficult at the top of the supply chain. Even fab-less firms limit market access by innovative product design and marketing activity. In this environment, it is difficult for developing country firms to develop their own brands.

A second factor is capital mobility, which affects the low value-added operations much more significantly than the high value-added ones (Gereffi, 1999). Also suggesting that capital mobility creates competition among low-wage locations, Brainard and Riker's (1997) finding that the elasticity of labour demand is much greater for low-wage affiliates of multinational enterprises with respect to other low-wage operations than it is between a high-wage and low-wage location.

A third factor is political. Tariffs have fallen most in low value-added sectors (Hanson and Harrison, 1999). This is true generally, but it has also been an explicit policy goal, as seen in the tariff policies that promote low-wage offshore assembly operations, such as the "8208 program" of the United States, European provisions evolving from the Lomé Convention, and the establishment of EPZs in many developing countries. These programmes are highly concentrated in the garment and electronics sectors. Textiles and apparel are traditionally one of the lowest value-added sectors in manufacturing. And the electronics parts and components that dominate in EPZs are at the low end of the spectrum of value added for electronics goods.

CONSEQUENCES FOR LABOUR AND CAPITAL

Wages, wage inequality and employment

According to the standard theory of international trade, trade liberalization brings welfare gains to each country and globally, though not to each individual or group in every country. The widely-held belief in the beneficence of free trade results from the view that "winners" in a given country can potentially compensate "losers" and still be better off than before the liberalization of trade.[15] Specifically, the Stolper-Samuelson theorem of the factor endowments model predicts that trade liberalization will lead to gains for each country's relatively abundant factor of production. Recent research on trade liberalization and income distribution has focused on the fate of high-skill and low-skill labour. The model predicts that industrialized countries, since they are abundant in high-skill labour, will experience a relative rise in

77

the wage of high-skill labour relative to that of low-skill labour as trade liberalization leads to a relative increase in demand for skilled labour. Developing countries, abundant in low-skill labour, should experience the opposite, i.e. a narrowing of the gap between high- and low-skill labour as the relative demand for low-skill labour increases.

Economic models of trade in intermediate goods hypothesize that such trade follows the same pattern in terms of its effect on relative labour demand and thus relative wages (e.g. Deardorff, 2001). Feenstra and Hanson (2001) argue that the greater the share of intermediate goods trade, the stronger the effect of trade on wages. This is because such trade affects both the labour demand in import competing sectors (in the traditional fashion) and the labour demand for users of the imported input. Thus, they write, "trade in intermediate inputs can have an impact on wages and employment that is much greater than for trade in final consumer goods" (op. cit., p. 1). A separate, but related, area of research centres on the effect of FDI on employment and wages. Theoretical models again hypothesize that capital movement by firms will alter relative demand for labour in the same way as trade liberalization does. Capital should thus move from where it is abundant ("the North") to where it is scarce ("the South"), leading to a rise in its return in the North and a fall in its return in the South, and thus an international equalization.

The prediction of the Stolper-Samuelson theory is consistent with the pattern of income inequality – particularly that of wage inequality – observed in many industrialized countries. This has resuscitated interest in the factor endowments model of trade, and led to a debate over the relative importance of technological change versus international trade in explaining the rise in the wage of skilled workers relative to unskilled workers. Estimates of the effect of trade range from 5 to 20 per cent of the total increase in wage inequality in the United States.

The prediction of Stolper-Samuelson for developing countries runs counter to their observed experience. Most studies show that developing countries have also experienced a rise in wage inequality. A cross-country study covering Argentina, Chile, Colombia, Costa Rica, Malaysia, Mexico, Philippines, Taiwan (China) and Uruguay found that after netting out labour supply changes, trade liberalization was associated with a widening wage differential between skilled and unskilled workers in all cases, except during Argentina's second liberalization episode (1989-1993), when relative wages were stable (Robbins, 1996). In separate studies, it was found that in Mexico the ratio of average hourly compensation between skilled and unskilled workers rose over 25 per cent between 1984 and 1990; and in Chile between 1980 and 1990, the pay of university graduates increased by 56.4 per cent over that of non-graduates.[16]

What are the reasons for the failure of Stolper-Samuelson to predict the effect of trade and investment liberalization on income distribution in developing countries? In the mid-1990s, international trade economists developed the notion of "skill-enhancing trade", according to which increasing specialization in low-skill-intensive sectors still constituted an increase in the demand for skills in these markets, mainly as a result of the requirements of work with more high-technology, imported inputs. But skill-enhancing trade was more of an *ex-post* rationale than a full-blown theory, and other factors are also at work.

It is hard to disentangle the apparently simultaneous forces of technical change, globalization, and policy or institutional reform that have occurred over the past 25 years. A number of authors have questioned the importance of skill-biased technical change, even in the industrialized countries where it was alleged to be most evident (see Howell, Houston and Milberg, 2001, and references therein). The problem is that much of the rise in wage inequality occurred before the great wave of workplace computerization. But few studies have considered the timing of such changes in developing countries.

A second factor is FDI. Since trade and FDI are increasingly complementary, it is perhaps not surprising that their labour market effects in developing countries appear to be mutually reinforcing. Most studies of the effect of FDI on wages find that multinational enterprises pay above-market wages, ranging from 8 per cent higher in Cameroon to 29 per cent higher in Venezuela (Te Velde and Morrissey, 2001). In every comparative study of high-skilled and low-skilled workers, the wage premium – i.e. the amount above the market wage – is greater for the high-skilled workers. This may be due to the differential effect of FDI demand for labour (see the review in Te Velde and Morrissey, 2001). Slaughter (2002), for example, finds that labour demand generated by United States FDI in developing countries is biased toward more high-skilled labour. Non-technological factors, perhaps related to efficiency wages, are also likely in the case of multinational employment.

Feenstra and Hanson (1997) claim that it is the increase in FDI and foreign outsourcing by developed-country multinationals – rather than trade liberalization *per se* – that is behind the rising wage inequality in developing countries. Using regional data from Mexico, they find that in regions where FDI is concentrated, over half the rise in the wage share of skilled labour in the 1980s was associated with foreign outsourcing. In other words, with FDI, production became more skill-intensive both in the high-skill-abundant and in the low-skill-abundant regions. More recent research shows foreign outsourcing to have a statistically significant association with the rise in wages of skilled workers in the United States, Japan, Hong Kong (China) and Mexico (Feenstra and Hanson, 2001). As mentioned above, Brainard and Riker (1997) find that wage declines in low-wage locations have no measurable effect on employment in parent multinationals, although they do have a fairly large impact on employment in affiliates in other low-wage locations. Finally, economists have just begun to consider the indirect effects of trade and investment liberalization resulting from their effects on the bargaining power of labour (see Epstein and Burke, 2001, for a review of the issues and evidence).

The endogenous asymmetry of market structures provides an additional explanation, since it posits that external sourcing will increase competitive pressure on developing country firms in global production systems. There are at least two channels through which wages are affected. One is the neoclassical channel whereby product prices affect factor prices. Thus as suppliers are pressured to lower their prices, they will in turn reduce wages. The other is the institutional channel whereby competitive pressure on suppliers and their host countries leads to deregulation or circumvention of existing labour market regulation and pressure on workers to accept wage declines.[17] Endogenous asymmetry of market structures does not necessarily imply growing wage inequality in developing countries, although low-skilled workers are typically in a weaker bargaining position than high-skilled workers. However, the endogenous asymmetry of market structures does imply a divergence in factor prices internationally, contrary to the prediction of the traditional theory.

The international flow of profits

In addition to its wage and employment effects, globalized production also has an impact on corporate profits and the flow of profits internationally. This flow, in turn, has consequences for the balance of payments and, more importantly, for the ability of developing countries to invest and grow. Profit on FDI is either repatriated or reinvested in the host country. As shown above, global production systems are increasingly based on arm's-length or quasi-arm's-length arrangements. This growing tendency towards externalization implies that the return on external outsourcing – implied by the cost reduction it brings to the buyer firm – must exceed that on internal vertical operations. Indeed, the asymmetry of lead and supplier market structures, I have argued, created the conditions for greater returns from externalization than internalization. The return on vertical FDI suggests a lower bound on cost saving from external outsourcing. And these cost savings constitute rents accruing abroad in the same sense that internal profit generation does for a multinational enterprise.

To get a crude measure of implicit profit flows from external outsourcing, we can apply the return on foreign assets to all trade in intermediate goods. As a first pass, the *ex-post* rate of return on the operations of United States corporations abroad are calculated by dividing foreign income by the corresponding accumulated stock of foreign investment in various countries. The results are presented in table 2. For the aggregate of United States investment abroad in 2000, the return was 9.32 per cent on a foreign capital stock of US$1.3 trillion.[18] The average return on assets in developed countries was 9.1 per cent against 9.82 per cent in developing countries. But when vertical and horizontal investment are disaggregated, the gap widens further, at 10.96 per cent for vertical and 8.45 per cent for horizontal. And since the return on external outsourcing must exceed that on vertical FDI, this implies considerable cost savings from externalization.

Given the limited time-series evidence available on the return on assets in foreign investment (the data go back to 1994), we cannot say anything about whether the return on verticalization has increased either absolutely or relative to horizontal investment over time. However, we do have evidence over time generally on the growth in outsourcing and profits by sector of the United States economy. Here we find a shift in the relation between profits growth and international outsourcing by sector over time (shown in table 3). The correlation between outsourcing and the growth of profits was statistically insignificant in the period 1975-1985. In the period 1985-1995, outsourcing and profits growth were positively and significantly correlated (see bottom of table 3).

This evidence of a correlation between outsourcing and profits growth is consistent with the findings of a variety of studies of outsourcing in the business and economics literature. Frohlich and Westbrook (2001) find firm success to be more common among firms with a wider network of supplier relations, what they term a wider "arc of integration". In sum, international outsourcing is increasingly associated with profits growth, and the "return" on outsourcing is above 11 per cent. While such cost reductions (greater than 10.9 per cent) constitute a welfare gain for the United States in the same way that repatriated profits on FDI are a benefit, the rents from externalization will be shared among stockholders, employees and consumers. In theory, the degree to which the cost saving from international outsourcing translates into lower consumer prices will depend on domestic product-market structure. Thus, in industries typically considered more competitive in the developed countries – such as textiles and apparel, toys and footwear – more international outsourcing would be expected to bring lower consumer prices. By contrast, in industries known for their oligopolistic structure, such as steel and automobiles, markups would be likely to rise in the presence of cost-reducing international outsourcing. In the case of intra-firm trade, a third possibility arises: transfer pricing aimed at raising profits in subsidiary firms.

The cases of apparel and electronics have been the most widely studied and the price effects of outsourcing have been noted even in the popular press. A December 2002 article in The *New York Times* noted that: "Even intrepid bargain hunters are shocked by the prices they are seeing in the stores this holiday season" (Day, 2002). Noting that prices in apparel and electronics have dropped for over a decade because of low-wage outsourcing, the article pointed out that the price pressures on producers were particularly effective that year because of the decline in demand following the terrorist attacks of 11 September 2001 and the excess capacity in place. In the same article, one Hong Kong-based manufacturer is quoted as saying

Table 2.   Return on foreign assets (ROFA) United States vis-à-vis selected countries, 2000 (millions of US dollars)

Average ROFA	FDI in US			US FDI abroad				
Developed countries	3.38			9.10				
Developing countries	2.04			9.82				
Horizontal	3.70			8.45				
Vertical	0.25			10.96				
Countries	FDI stocks	FDI flows	Income	FDI stocks	FDI flows	Income	ROFA In US	Abroad
All countries	**1 163 681**	**236 241**	**38 272**	**1 282 742**	**151 174**	**119 519**	**3.29**	**9.32**
Canada	**104 586**	**19 010**	**−1 488**	**126 531**	**17 171**	**12 855**	**−1.42**	**10.16**
Europe	**807 273**	**193 402**	**34 769**	**672 403**	**82 595**	**59 965**	**4.31**	**8.92**
Austria	3 229	171	120	3 243	−85	359	3.72	11.06
Belgium	13 439	1 577	378	20 010	601	1 620	2.82	8.09
Denmark	3 911	22	−12	5 104	893	459	−0.30	8.99
Finland	7 562	1 869	186	1 174	110	198	2.46	16.89
France	122 879	31 315	4 849	39 056	1 059	1 903	3.95	4.87
Germany	129 908	21 928	747	53 615	6 242	3 966	0.57	7.40
Ireland	22 227	2 037	949	624	32	109	4.27	17.52
Italy	5 451	794	123	31 420	4 738	4 443	2.26	14.14
Netherlands	143 174	29 820	6 886	119 921	9 088	12 624	4.81	10.53
Norway	2 457	−494	−32	6 046	605	1 381	−1.30	22.84
Spain	4 433	2 093	43	19 300	2 597	1 341	0.97	6.95
Sweden	21 560	3 090	1 455	16 833	4 993	931	6.75	5.53
Switzerland	82 578	23 720	2 924	54 417	8 332	7 233	3.54	13.29
United Kingdom	195 121	66 149	12 589	239 813	32 278	15 874	6.45	6.62
Other	5 892	3 224	216	12 329	1 193	1 215	3.67	9.85
Latin America	**51 372**	**10 045**	**1 135**	**253 056**	**28 076**	**19 019**	**2.21**	**7.52**
Brazil	733	−17	69	37 578	2 186	1 282	9.46	3.41
Mexico	5 750	2 152	−321	40 796	5 640	4 409	−5.58	10.81
Panama	4 400	−418	626	29 252	1 414	1 106	14.23	3.78
Venezuela	1 820	454	49	8 786	2 059	948	2.69	10.79
Other	1 873	635	115	769	−45	24	6.16	3.12
Africa	**2 460**	**494**	**−84**	**14 637**	**816**	**2 205**	**−3.43**	**15.06**
South Africa	1 107	381	−22	3 068	453	152	−1.99	4.94
Other	1 353	113	−62	7 719	−3	966	−4.61	12.52
Middle East	**5 530**	**786**	**242**	**11 481**	**970**	**1 583**	**4.38**	**13.79**
Israel	2 684	357	53	3 813	652	241	1.96	6.31
Saudi Arabia	945	−325	0	4 085	−77	223.7	0.00	5.47
United Arab Emirates	18	−21	0	757	63	205	0.00	27.08
Other	71	2	34	2 825	332	913	47.89	32.33
Asia and Pacific	**192 460**	**12 504**	**3 699**	**202 044**	**21 412**	**23 688**	**1.92**	**11.72**
Australia	19 935	4 602	266	34 716	1 747	2 583	1.34	7.44
Hong Kong (China)	1 327	138	60	25 901	4 075	4 144	4.52	16.00

Table 2.   Return on foreign assets (ROFA) United States vis-à-vis selected
            countries, 2000 (millions of US dollars) *(cont.)*

Average ROFA	*FDI in US*			*US FDI abroad*				
Developed countries	*3.38*			*9.10*				
Developing countries	*2.04*			*9.82*				
Horizontal	*3.70*			*8.45*				
Vertical	*0.25*			*10.96*				
Countries	**FDI stocks**	**FDI flows**	**Income**	**FDI stocks**	**FDI flows**	**Income**	**ROFA**	
							In US	**Abroad**
Asia and Pacific **(cont.)**								
Japan	158 793	5 926	3 333	59 979	7 067	6 079	2.10	10.14
Korea, Republic of	3 033	463	56	8 632	1 595	1 045	1.85	12.11
Malaysia	61	−40	−21	6 718	161	1 307	−34.78	19.46
New Zealand	425	81	29	4 079	−132	277	6.82	6.80
Philippines	51	−27	5	2 881	−88	416	9.80	14.45
Singapore	5 206	1 491	69	24 502	3 235	2 823	1.33	11.52
Taiwan (China)	2 901	−200	−111	7 715	923	1 169	−3.83	15.15
Other	728	70	12	1 108	−9	84	1.65	7.58

Notes: FDI Stocks Flows and Income are calculated as 1999-2001 average. Horizontal group consists of all of the developed countries and Brazil but without Canada and Ireland. Vertical group consists of developing countries without Brazil but with Canada and Ireland added.

Source: United States Department of Commerce (2002).

that: "Other factories, other countries are lowering their prices, so I can't keep my price" (op. cit.).

The flow of profits and rents to developed-country firms that results from asymmetric market structure constitutes a loss of capital for investment in developing countries and a drain on the balance of payments. Developing countries have successfully shifted out of commodity exports and into the export of manufactured goods. Still, most studies find that the terms of trade for developing countries have not improved and may even have deteriorated over the past 20 years.[19] Once again, I would look to the nature of global production systems in explaining this. Developing countries have specialized in low value-added products and parts, partly because of their skills and partly because of barriers to entry in the higher value-added segments. Moreover, competition is intense among producers of these goods, generating enormous excess capacity globally, which places even more downward pressure on prices.

In sum, many developing countries, having successfully followed the strategy of moving away from reliance on the export of commodities and natural resources and into the export of manufactures, have found themselves in a modern-day Prebisch-Singer trap (see Bacha, 1978, for a formalized restatement). With the change in the structure of international production and

Table 3.   Growth in outsourcing and profits by sector: United States, 1975-1995
(percentage change over the indicated period)

Industry	1975-1985		1985-1995	
	Profits	Outsourcing	Profits	Outsourcing
Food and kindred products	−43.0	25.4	246.0	16.6
Tobacco products	53.1	8.3	−65.0	34.4
Textiles mill products	−0.8	80.9	46.5	34.2
Apparel and other textiles	−23.8	82.7	58.5	39.7
Lumber and wood products	−22.9	59.1	102.6	21.4
Furniture and fixtures	103.1	47.1	76.3	8.4
Paper and allied products	−14.2	22.1	98.5	23.4
Printing and publishing	42.0	11.7	24.0	19.2
Chemical and allied products	−58.7	49.5	278.3	41.8
Petroleum and coal products	−66.8	0.3	−60.3	−21.7
Rubber and miscellaneous products	30.2	43.3	91.7	34.0
Leather and leather products	−44.6	179.9	−35.7	30.1
Stone, clay and glass products	11.1	68.5	59.7	31.5
Primary metal products	−117.9	86.1	−503.6	15.3
Fabricated metal products	−25.3	63.4	220.3	11.6
Industrial machinery and equipment	−87.4	73.9	533.8	52.5
Electronic and other electric equipment	−58.9	50.4	1 002.1	72.9
Transportation equipment	140.2	66.6	−61.2	47.3
Instruments and related products	−56.7	42.1	241.8	17.3
Miscellaneous manufacturing	−34.0	87.0	279.4	15.9
Total manufacturing	−43.9	53.0	85.7	32.0
Wholesale trade	−33.1		13.2	
Retail trade	3.8%		60.9%	
Total corporate profits	−16.5%		115.1%	

Addendum:	1975-1985	1985-1995	Total
Corr. coeff.	*−0.194*	*0.539*	*0.012*
Two-tailed *t*	5E-05	0.10	0.66

Sources: Campa and Goldberg, 1997; Bureau of Economic Analysis, 2002.

trade, promotion of manufacturing has not been sufficient to improve the barter or factoral terms of trade. The rents earned by oligopolistic firms in developed countries could, under a different constellation of market structure, be redistributed to developing countries, boosting their ability to invest and grow. The final section of this article considers some policies that might improve developing country prospects within the system of global production.

POLICY IMPLICATIONS OF GLOBAL PRODUCTION SYSTEMS

Industrial policy

The distributional consequences of globalized production discussed in the previous section are static effects. However, it is the dynamics of industrialization and economic development that are the focus of governments and international policy-makers. Because of the globalization of production, industrialization today is different from the final-goods-oriented, export-led process of just 20 years ago. Now, the issue facing firms and governments is less that of finding new, more capital-intensive goods to sell to consumers in foreign countries. Instead, it seems to require moving up through the chain of production of a particular commodity or set of commodities, so-called "industrial upgrading", into higher value-added activities. This involves fitting into the existing corporate strategies of a potentially wide array of firms, within the confines of a broadly liberal international trade and investment environment.

Industrial upgrading requires productive reinvestment of profits, i.e. the establishment of a nexus between profits and investment.[20] This, in turn, requires, first, the market conditions to generate such profits in the first place and, second, the institutions and regulations that induce the investment of those profits into productive channels. Regarding market conditions, we have seen that oligopoly firms are by definition more able to generate the necessary rents compared to competitive firms. Market demand is also crucial, as firms typically learn not just by "doing", but also by selling.[21] Regarding institutions and regulations, there are two levels: the first is the protection of rents, through clearly defined property rights and a rule of law to enforce those rights; and the second is the ability to channel profit income into productive investment. These conditions are necessary regardless of whether the rents are generated by private or public enterprise.

Added to these "apparent" requirements are the structural obstacles to upgrading, which are closely related to the persistence of the asymmetry of market structure discussed above. Moving into higher value-added activities may be difficult because of barriers to entry. First, many studies show that there are limits to the international shifting of multinational enterprise operations. Such high value-added functions as financial management, R&D, product design and even marketing are maintained in the parent country (UNCTAD, 1993; Doremus et al., 1998). Second, global production networks are driven and in many cases designed by lead firms, the focus being on the profitability and flexibility of the lead firm. The profitability or even efficiency of the supplier is not necessarily a consideration in the construction of the global production network (Semlinger, 1991). Third, industrial upgrading requires capital investment that is usually generated from oligopoly profits, not the competitive conditions that increasingly characterize supplier markets, as we saw above. Finally, excessive protection from competition can foster inefficiency and unproductive rent seeking.

Despite these obstacles, a number of countries have achieved widespread industrial upgrading, the most prominent examples being the Republic of Korea and other "newly industrialized countries" of east Asia. Significant pockets of upgrading have also occurred in Latin America, especially Argentina, Brazil, Chile and Mexico. In most cases, the effort was underpinned by an industrial policy which, on the basis of prior industrial experience, selectively targeted and subsidized certain sectors and activities, building up a base of technology, labour skills and management that led to a slow climb up the global commodity chain. In the Korean case, for example, industrial policy included export subsidies, import and foreign-investment controls, production targets, low-interest credit and technical support, in order to generate the long-run efficiency defined above (see Amsden, 1989). This was supplemented by a growing educational system that raised the average skill-level of the workforce.

The common theme behind such industrial policies was what Amsden (2001) calls "reciprocal control": aid to firms was contingent on firm performance, be it in terms of output, production or exports. Because industrial upgrading (and international competitiveness generally) requires unique knowledge-based assets, successful industrialization has required state intervention where free and competitive markets were inadequate. Enforcement of such a regime of state-industry relations requires a particular commitment to development on the part of the State; and the reciprocity in "reciprocal control" involves an assurance to the private sector that the State will effectively deliver its developmentalist channelling of the social surplus. Evans (1995) characterizes such interventionist but independent state action as "embedded autonomy", and finds it particularly important in cases where countries developed knowledge-based assets, such as the software industry in India, the semiconductor industry in the Republic of Korea and the computer sector in Brazil.

Amsden (2001) identifies aspects of reciprocal control in all successful late-industrializing countries, from Japan and the Republic of Korea to Argentina, Brazil, Chile, China, India, Malaysia, Mexico, Taiwan (China), Thailand and Turkey. Despite these successes with reciprocal control and industrial policy, the industrial upgrading model is a difficult and risky path. Mexico, for all its links to multinational enterprises and to the United States market through geographic proximity and preferential trading relations under the North American Free Trade Agreement, has achieved only minimal gains in terms of real wages and economic growth. After their transition to capitalism, a number of eastern European countries, for all their skill accumulation and proximity to the rich market of the European Union, saw their presence across commodity chains reduced to the low end.[22] Global integration, for which there is really no viable alternative, thus brings a risk of industrial "downgrading".

Policies to attract foreign direct investment

In the 1990s, FDI came increasingly to be viewed as the panacea for economic development ills, providing a non-volatile source of capital that required neither a fixed interest payment nor a repayment of principal at a specified date. Accordingly, developing countries have relied increasingly on FDI to meet their need for foreign capital; and the developing country share of world FDI has grown (albeit slightly) over the past ten years. In terms of their direct effect on host developing countries, multinational enterprises have been found to pay above-market wages and to demand relatively more skilled labour than unskilled labour. Employment by affiliates of multinational enterprises operating in developing countries has risen steadily since 1990.

These promising developments veil a more mixed picture at the level of specific countries. First of all, FDI in developing countries is highly skewed. Most of it has gone to a single country – China – which accounts for 23 per cent of the global total (34 per cent if Hong Kong is included). The remainder has gone mostly to a small handful of other countries, most significantly Mexico and Brazil, which, together, account roughly for a further 20 per cent of the total (see UNCTAD, 2002b). This skewed distribution implies that most countries have not received much FDI at all. Moreover, FDI continues to represent only a small percentage of gross fixed capital formation in developing countries, ranging from 8 per cent in Africa and 12 per cent in Asia to just over 20 per cent in Latin America and Central Asia (see UNCTAD, 1998, table B.5, and 2002b, table B.5). Though these figures may seem impressive, almost half (42 per cent) of FDI in Latin America is "brownfield" – i.e. the result of international mergers and acquisitions – rather than "greenfield" investment (see UNCTAD, 2002b; IMF, 2001). Overall, it is thus more likely that inward FDI lags rather than leads indicators of long-term economic growth. Certainly this was the experience of the most successful cases of industrialization in the last part of the twentieth century in east Asia (see Amsden, 1992).

These points about the relation between FDI and economic development are well known. In fact, the debate over FDI and economic development has largely shifted away from discussion of the static issues of effective demand and employment towards issues of "externalities", broadly understood as the indirect effects of multinational enterprise activity on labour through their impact on host country competition and productivity. Foreign investment may enhance or diminish the degree of competition in host country markets. Agosin and Mayer (2000) find that over the period 1970-1996, FDI tended to crowd out or have no effect on domestic investment in Latin

America and Africa, and to crowd in or have no effect on investment in east Asia. Braunstein and Epstein (2002) find crowding out in the case of FDI in China.

Indirect productivity effects of FDI are said to occur through technological spillovers. If technology spillovers from the activities of multinationals raise domestic productivity in other firms or sectors, then both wages and, possibly, employment will be positively influenced. But here too the evidence is mixed at best. Most studies have found no measurable effects of new technologies on domestic firms' ability to upgrade and raise productivity (see Gorg and Greenaway, 2001; Rodrik, 1999).

The establishment of EPZs has become an important policy for attracting FDI. There is an ongoing theoretical debate over the merits of EPZs for countries that maintain them (see Chaudhuri and Adhikari, 1993, for a review). In practice, EPZ activities are concentrated in only two sectors, textiles/apparel and electronics, the latter being considerably more capital-intensive than the former. They are most prominent in east Asia and Latin America, and in both cases they employ mainly young women. Wages in EPZs are found to be about the same as in the rest of the local manufacturing sector, although there is variation by country. In sum, the direct effect of EPZs is positive for employment and the trade balance. In some cases, they also exert significant attraction on foreign investors. In Costa Rica, for example, over half of inward FDI is located in EPZs.

The effect of EPZs on economic development depends on the backward linkages they create, i.e. connections with the rest of the domestic economy. These linkages are often measured by the share of locally produced inputs they use. Here, the east Asian and Latin American experiences have been quite different. In east Asia, the use of domestically produced inputs has typically grown after an initial period. In Latin America, this has not been the case: EPZs in Latin America have produced a greater share of total exports than has been the case in East Asia, but this may also reflect east Asian countries' greater success in diversification and upgrading. The main success stories in the promotion of backward linkages from EPZs are Ireland, Republic of Korea and Taiwan (China). These countries used policy to link EPZ activity to domestic producers in an effort to create a broader base of strength in exports. These are the exceptions, however. In Central America, a region where EPZs are widespread, EPZs "have been seen mostly as mechanisms to create employment and generate foreign exchange, but not as drivers of an export-led growth strategy. Consequently, the creation of linkages has not been a priority in the policy agenda of most of the region" (Jenkins, Esquivel and Larrain, 1998, p. 45).

In sum, FDI has not tended to spur economic development. In most cases, even for developing countries, FDI has been a lagging phenomenon, growing most when a strong domestic market existed already or when infrastructure and political stability were in place to guarantee adequate returns.

Indeed, capturing the potential positive technological spillovers from FDI presupposes the attainment of a certain level of absorptive capacity in terms of infrastructure and human capital. Moreover, incentives to attract FDI – including tax breaks, tariff reductions, promises of lax labour or environmental standards – have generally not been very successful (Wheeler and Mody, 1992; Kucera, 2002). A detailed study of the incentives granted by Costa Rica to the semiconductor producer Intel finds that these were probably not necessary to attract the investment in the first place, but they certainly have diminished the host country's benefits from the investment (Hanson, 2001). Besides, FDI concentrated in EPZs has not generated significant backward linkages.

As with many other aspects of globalization, inward FDI is neither "good" nor "bad" for developing countries in any *a priori* sense. Its effects vary over time, by country and by industry. FDI should be understood as a source of capital, technology and market access that must be managed to be most effective. While domestic protection for the affiliates of multinationals will promote anti-competitive outcomes, at the same time, competition to attract multinational enterprises by offering tax concessions and lax labour standards works against the strategy of industrial upgrading.

Policy-makers must realize that the attraction of FDI is not an end in itself. Though some countries and industries may be exceptions, policies designed to attract FDI should not be the centrepiece of any development strategy if the aim is to promote sustainable economic growth. According to Rodrik:

Gearing economic policy toward performance in the external sectors of the economy, at the expense of other objectives, amounts to mixing up the ends and the means of economic policy. Furthermore, there is nothing more conducive to trade and DFI than strong economic growth itself. Foreign investors care little about Botswana's huge public sector, and neither are they much deterred by Chinese-style socialism. Policies that are successful in igniting growth are also likely to pay off in terms of "international competitiveness" (1999, p. 147).

Competition policy

Industrial upgrading is a new paradigm of industrialization. Its attainment requires not just overcoming the asymmetry of market structure in global production systems, but also the attainment of dynamic efficiency, i.e. the maximization of long-run productivity growth. This is different from static or "allocative" efficiency, a condition whereby productive resources move to where the returns are greatest and sovereign consumers demand goods at their lowest possible prices. Monopoly competition creates a deviation from this welfare optimum, often resulting in less output of a good and at a higher price than would be the case under competitive conditions. Competition policy is aimed at limiting monopoly in order to encourage competition and its beneficial welfare effects. Any country may unilaterally adopt a domestic competition policy. And most countries have done so. Today there are more than 90 countries with competition laws. Still, about one-third of WTO members do not currently have such laws.

There are reasons why an internationally standardized competition policy enforced by the WTO – as currently on the agenda in the Doha Round of WTO trade negotiations – might not serve the interests of economic development. Since each country has unique considerations with respect to its sectoral strengths, labour relations and social policy institutions, and place in the world economy, it is hard to imagine that a uniform competition policy could serve the economic development strategies of all developing country members of the WTO. Most of these unique features relate to the underlying need of every developing country for room to manoeuvre economically and politically in order to establish dynamic, rather than static, efficiency.

Competition policy in the industrialized countries arrived late relative to their level of economic development; and even then, it has varied considerably across countries and been applied very selectively across sectors and interest groups in each country. This should not be surprising, since all of these countries pursued economic development strategies that included considerable protectionist and anti-competitive behaviour in their efforts to promote the development of domestic industrial capacity and to attain dynamic efficiency in the form of technological progress or the potential therefor. As they formulate and revise their competition policies, developing countries today should draw from the lessons of the countries that have already achieved industrialization.

More competition is not always better, especially when the objectives are technological progress, capital accumulation, economic growth and sustainable development. Technological innovation hinges on innovative effort, and such effort requires resources. In a perfectly competitive environment, firms break even by powerlessly charging the "going price". To charge a higher price is to risk collapse, hence the economic term "ruinous competition". According to Singh and Dhumale, "unfettered competition may lead to price wars and ruinous rivalry and therefore may be inimical to future investment: from this perspective too much competition can be as harmful as too little" (1999, p. 12). Rather than pursue a maximum degree of competition, countries should seek the *optimum* degree: that amount of rivalry among firms which still generates profits such that firms are able to invest in innovation and other non-price dimensions of success. Oligopoly firms are able to price at a markup over costs, and this markup can be determined, in part, by the investment needs of the firm, including those related to technological innovation. Furthermore, competition policy should not limit the State's ability to use industrial policy as described above.

Developing countries should continue to construct their own domestic competition policies, both to regulate domestic monopoly and to control the possible anti-competitive behaviour of transnational corporations. These same countries should enter discussions of a WTO-based international competition policy with much caution, as the potential costs of such an agreement are likely to outweigh its potential benefits. The benefits of a WTO-based agreement would possibly lie in the ability of any signatory to temper the anti-competitive effects of affiliates of multinationals. The costs will result from likely restrictions on countries' freedom to run targeted industrial policies and to nurture domestic producers as they seek to move up the value chain of global production. There is a risk that the Doha Round of trade negotiations will lead to an agreement that will mainly serve the developed countries which want market access, particularly where there are large private or state enterprises controlling an industry. According to Hoekman and Holmes, a WTO-based agreement is unlikely to be helpful since, "the agenda is likely to be dominated by market access issues more than international antitrust... [T]he WTO process is driven by export interests (market access), not national welfare considerations, and there is no assurance that the rules that will be proposed or agreed will be welfare enhancing" (1999, p. 16).

Development experience suggests that a WTO-enforced agreement on competition policy will be in the interest of developing countries only if:

(a)   it allows exemption for the least developed countries;

(b)   it allows for a variety of domestic competition policy regimes like those the developed countries themselves have maintained over the past 50 years;

(c)   it allows adequate flexibility with respect to sectoral coverage and enforcement.

Because such contingency and flexibility are almost impossible to negotiate and enforce at the level of the WTO, developing countries must be very careful not to sacrifice the tools for the attainment of dynamic efficiency for the sake of furthering the goal of static or allocative efficiency.

Raising labour standards

The "vertical disintegration" of production and its internationalization has made the location of production increasingly sensitive to labour cost differentials. According to Krugman:

It is often said that labor costs are now such a low share of total costs that low wages cannot be a significant competitive advantage. But when businesspeople say this, they do not mean that labor costs have declined as a share of value added: on the contrary, the division of value added between capital and labor has been impressively stable over time. What they mean, instead, is that because of the growing vertical disintegration of industry the value added by a given manufacturing facility is likely to be only a small fraction of the value of its shipments; and thus the labor share of that value added is also a small fraction of costs, which are dominated by the cost of intermediate inputs. But this vertical disintegration, or slicing up of the value chain, creates a greater, not smaller opportunity to relocate production to low-wage locations.

In such an environment, the level of wage and non-wage labor standards has become a source of competition among firms and countries (1995, pp. 336-337; see also Milberg and Elmslie, 1997).

The tying of minimum labour standards to market access or trade liberalization – through a WTO provision, for example – is a contentious issue for developing country governments, some of which see their interest in keeping labour standards low so as to be able to compete internationally. While a low-wage/low-productivity regime may become a difficult "trap" to get out of, it can also be a short-run solution to the problems of high unemployment and lack of connection to international markets.

The fact that jobs in developing countries are increasingly connected to global production systems is double-edged for those who advocate raising the level of labour standards globally. On the one hand, to the extent that global production systems can be traced – say, from the small, home-based producer up to the large, lead-firm subcontractor – firms at the high end of the value chain could in principle be held accountable for labour conditions throughout the global value chain. On the other hand, to the extent that global value chains are increasingly organized using arm's-length or quasi-arm's-length relations across firms in a given chain, lead firms or top-tier supplier firms can more easily disclaim responsibility for labour conditions at the lower end of the value chain. Even opponents of the linking of trade liberalization to enforcement of a code of labour standards have tended to support the idea that countries might want to impose minimum labour or environmental standards on their own firms, even when those firms are operating abroad. Thus, to the extent that global production systems work through arm's-length rather than intra-firm relations, the regulation of a minimum set of labour standards would be outside the realm of control of any single firm or set of leading firms.

One way around this problem would be to enforce an expanded code of conduct on buyers at different levels of the value chain. Current voluntary codes of conduct generally call for the monitoring of supplier employment conditions. An extended code would not just require monitoring but would also impose specific conditions on those firms from which inputs are purchased. In this way, responsibility for labour standards cannot simply be passed down through the value chain and ultimately ignored at low levels of the chain. Lead firms and first-tier supplier firms could be held responsible for labour standards among the producers from which they buy inputs, even if the sellers are completely independent in terms of ownership rights. Moreover, if firms are made accountable for conditions of work and employment among their suppliers, lead firms would be unable to circumvent higher-cost production because of higher standards adopted by one producer simply by moving to a lower-cost and lower-standard producer. A system encouraging lead firms and/or first-tier supplier firms to purchase from firms satisfying minimum standards would, if adopted across a wide array of sectors, also put a brake on any "race to the bottom" of global labour standards.

CONCLUDING REMARKS

In this paper I have argued that it is the change in the structure of trade – with more trade in intermediate as opposed to final goods – rather than the growth in trade volume that makes globalization an important phenomenon when it comes to the formulation of policies for economic development. This structural change in trade is the result of the emergence of global production systems, whereby parts and components of a good are produced in different locations around the globe. Of equal significance are the ownership characteristics of this structural change. While trade in intermediate goods constitutes a rising share of world trade, intra-firm trade appears to make up a constant or falling portion of trade. Thus global production systems are increasingly characterized by arm's-length relations between lead and supplier firms.

I have argued that this shifting ownership pattern in global production systems is the result of the logic of lead firm competitive strategies. Lead firms outsource externally (i.e. outside the firm) those aspects of the production process which do not contribute to the firms' rents. These rents are typically associated with returns from proprietary, usually knowledge-based, assets, but they may also arise from entry barriers and market power. The end result of such externalization is the establishment of an asymmetry of market structures across the global production system – oligopolistic at the top and more competitive at the lower end. I have argued that the theoretical implications of these changes call for an abandonment of the theory of comparative advantage in favour of a theory of trade based on absolute advantage. Moreover, the focus of international production theory should shift from internalization toward an understanding of externalization.

Given the prominence of global production systems, the policy challenge is then how best to build economic and political institutions that can promote industrial upgrading and higher labour standards. The pursuit of these objectives calls for measures to build large firms with the capacity to generate rents and investment in knowledge-based assets, while remaining subject to some competitive pressure, through the market or the mechanisms of reciprocal control. This, in turn, will require an industrial policy to promote R&D and skill development in production and management. It will also be facilitated by a very specific competition policy, which may sacrifice some allocative efficiency in order to attain dynamic efficiency. Moreover, multinational enterprises have generally not been associated with the reinvestment of rents locally and the development of indigenous knowledge-based assets. Thus, special treatment for multinational enterprises does not usually promote dynamic efficiency. Nor, most studies find, is it effective in attracting inward foreign investment.

Notes

[1] Net capital flows (as opposed to gross flows) have arguably been inadequate or, worse, perverse, in the sense that debt repayment and profit repatriation by multinational enterprises have generated a flow from the developing to the developed countries.

[2] The convention for measurement purposes continues to be greater than 10 per cent ownership in a foreign asset. With the growth of stock markets even in many developing countries in the 1990s, the liquidity of FDI was raised, further blurring the distinction between portfolio and direct foreign investment. See Milberg (1999) for a more detailed discussion.

[3] On tax concessions, see Wheeler and Mody (1992). See also Hanson (2001) for case studies that support the Wheeler and Mody results.

[4] Hanson, Mataloni and Slaughter (2001) find evidence of increased verticality in outward FDI from the United States in the 1990s compared to the 1980s.

[5] For example, Brainard and Riker (1997) find little substitution of foreign for domestic labour by multinational enterprises when foreign labour costs fall. They consider only multinational enterprises and their affiliates, thus leaving out any "arm's-length" international outsourcing. See Feenstra (1998) for a similar criticism of studies of outsourcing that only include foreign investment data (i.e. excluding arm's-length subcontracting).

[6] Dunning (2000) has for many years embellished the internalization theory with two other types of advantages that would explain FDI: ownership and location.

[7] Where imported inputs $= \sum_j$ [inputs purchases of good j by industry i]*[imports of good j/consumption of good j].

[8] Twentieth-century trade theorists were able to avoid the issue of international capital mobility because of Samuelson's (1949) development of the factor price equalization theorem, which implied that even in the absence of international movements of factors of production, free trade in *goods* will bring about an equalization in the remuneration of productive factors. Thus all the welfare benefits of international exchange could be gained without any international capital (or labour) mobility.

[9] Supporting this result, empirical studies find that the Marshall-Lerner conditions – the conditions required if devaluation is to bring a trade balance improvement – are often not satisfied for the industrialized countries or the developing countries. See, for example, Rose (1991).

[10] An important exposition of the technology-gap model of trade is Dosi, Pavitt and Soete (1991). For a survey of empirical studies of price versus non-price competition, see Fagerberg (1996).

[11] In a study of the domestic operations of United States firms, Harrison and Kelly (1993) found that outsourcing was driven more by a concern with flexibility than with cost reduction *per se*.

[12] Similarly, arm's-length relations with suppliers reduces the buyer firm's responsibility for standards in the supplying firm. A company is less likely to be held accountable for standards if the supplier is independently owned than if it is an affiliate of the buyer firm.

[13] On cut flowers, see Ziegler (2001). On the Hong Kong apparel trade, see Feenstra et al. (1998). Regarding coffee, see Fitter and Kaplinsky (2001), and on cocoa, see Cowell (2002). One problem with using the global commodity chain for understanding the generation of value and its distribution is that there is very little data on wages, markups and value added along particular chains. In some cases there is even difficulty tracing the chain, either because home-based production is largely unregulated and unaccountable or because the push for monitoring of labour standards by NGOs has provided an incentive for suppliers simply to hide the identity of the firms to which they subcontract (Balakrishnan, 2002). A potentially fruitful area for future research is to assess empirically the incidence of each of these (and other) forms across sectors, regions and over time. Such research could help provide a better understanding of the role of power relations in global produc-

tion systems and, more important for policy purposes, the patterns of industrial upgrading and downgrading that have occurred.

[14] See Gereffi (1999) on apparel, and Ng and Yeats (1999) on electronics. These two sectors are also highlighted in UNCTAD (2002c).

[15] A number of observers have remarked that the potential Pareto criterion is misleading because in fact compensation almost never occurs.

[16] See Robbins (1996) for a survey of the cross-country evidence and original estimates. Note that this period in Argentina was also the only case in the study in which trade liberalization reduced trade openness (as measured by exports plus imports as a share of GDP). This was largely due to an overvalued exchange rate that dampened exports. Moreover, even this result is overturned when we consider a longer time period: between 1986 and 1994 there was an increase in the return on investment in college education and a decline in the return on investment in less-than-college education. See Pessino (1997) and Amadeo (1998).

[17] The Stolper-Samuleson theory used above as a benchmark assumes full employment. But changes in trade and investment patterns can of course have considerable net employment effects. Of particular concern among developed country workers is the erosion of jobs in manufacturing relative to non-manufacturing employment, a process otherwise termed deindustrialization. To what extent has foreign trade and investment contributed to the process of deindustrialization? Kucera and Milberg (2003) find that of the 6.2 million decline in OECD manufacturing employment between 1978 and 1995, more than half can be associated with changes in the OECD trade pattern, especially trade with developing countries. They conclude, however, that what is driving this result is the drop in developing country imports from the OECD following the debt crises of the 1980s. They do not separate the effects of final goods and intermediate goods trade.

[18] Note that for foreign investment in the United States, the return on assets was only 3.29 per cent. This difference has been attributed to a variety of factors, including age of investment and firms' concern with United States market share. See Mataloni (2000) for a detailed study.

[19] See UNCTAD (2002c) for a review of recent evidence. Kaplinsky's (1993) study of EPZs in the Dominican Republic provides a clear example of how the switch to manufacturers can fail to stem the decline in the terms of trade.

[20] This terminology is borrowed from Akyuz and Gore (1996).

[21] This point is emphasized by Porter (1990).

[22] This was the case of the garment sector in Romania, for example.

References

Agosin, Manuel R.; Mayer, Ricardo. 2000. *Foreign investment in developing countries: Does it crowd in domestic investment?* Discussion Paper No. 146 (UNCTAD/OSG/DP/146). Geneva, UNCTAD. Feb.

Akyuz, Yilmaz; Gore, Charles. 1996. "The investment-profits nexus in east Asian industrialization", in *World Development* (Oxford), Vol. 24, No. 3, pp. 461-470.

Amadeo, Edward J. 1998. "International trade, outsourcing and labour: A view from the developing countries", in Richard Kozul-Wright and Robert Rowthorn (eds.): *Transnational corporations and the global economy*. Basingstoke, Palgrave, pp. 373-401.

Amsden, Alice H. 2001. *The rise of "the rest": Challenges to the West from the late-industrializing economies*. Oxford, Oxford University Press.

—.1992. "A descriptive theory of government intervention in late industrialization", in Louis G. Putterman and Dietrich Rueschemeyer (eds.): *State and market in development: Synergy or rivalry?* Boulder, CO, Lynne Rienner, pp. 53-84.

—.1989. *Asia's next giant: South Korea and late industrialization*. New York, NY, Oxford University Press.

Arndt, Sven W. 1997. "Globalization and the open economy", in *North American Journal of Economics and Finance* (Greenwich, CT), Vol. 8, No. 1, pp. 71-79.

—; Kierzkowski, Henryk (eds.). 2001. *Fragmentation: New production patterns in the world economy*. Oxford, Oxford University Press.

Bacha, Edmar L. 1978. "An interpretation of unequal exchange from Prebisch-Singer to Emmanuel", in *Journal of Development Economics* (Amsterdam), Vol. 5, No. 4 (Dec.), pp. 319-330.

Bair, Jennifer; Gereffi, Gary. 2001. "Local clusters in global chains: The causes and consequences of export dynamism in Torreon's blue jeans industry", in *World Development* (Oxford), Vol. 29, No. 11, pp. 1885-1903.

Balakrishnan, Radhika (ed.). 2002. *The hidden assembly line: Gender dynamics of subcontracted work in a global economy*. Bloomfield, CT, Kumarian Press.

Brainard, S. Lael; Riker, David A. 1997. *Are U.S. multinationals exporting U.S. jobs?* NBER Working Paper No. 5958. Cambridge, MA, National Bureau of Economic Research. Mar.

Braunstein, Elissa; Epstein, Gerald. 2002. *Bargaining power and foreign direct investment in China: Can 1.3 billion consumers tame the multinationals?* Paper presented at New School University's CEPA Conference on "Labor and the Globalization of Production", New School University, New York, NY. Mar.

Bureau of Economic Analysis. 2002. *National income and product accounts tables*. Washington, DC, United States Department of Commerce. [available online at: www.bea.gov/bea/ai/iidguide.htm]

Campa, José Manuel; Goldberg, Linda S. 1997. *The evolving export orientation of manufacturing industries: Evidence from four countries*. NBER Working Paper No. 5919. Cambridge, MA, National Bureau of Economic Research. Feb.

Caves, Richard E. 1982. *Multinational enterprise and economic analysis*. Cambridge, Cambridge University Press.

Chaudhuri, T. Datta; Adhikari, Smita. 1993. "Free trade zones with Harris-Todaro unemployment: A note on Young-Miyagiwa", in *Journal of Development Economics* (Amsterdam), Vol. 41, No. 1 (June), pp. 157-162.

Christerson, Brad; Appelbaum, Richard P. 1995. "Global and local subcontracting: Space, ethnicity, and the organization of apparel production", in *World Development* (Oxford), Vol. 23, No. 8, pp. 1363-1374.

Coase, R.H. 1937. "The nature of the firm", in *Economica* (London), Vol. 4, No. 16 (Nov.), pp. 386-405.

Cowell, Alan. 2002. "War inflates cocoa prices but leaves Africans poor", in *New York Times* (New York, NY), 31 Oct., Section C, p. 1.

Day, Sherri. 2002. "Bargains are plentiful for shoppers this season", in *New York Times* (New York, NY), 21 Dec., Business section, p. 1.

Deardorff, Alan V. 2001. "Fragmentation across cones", in Arndt and Kierzkowski, pp. 35-51.

Doremus, Paul N.; Keller, William W.; Pauly, Louis W.; Reich, Simon. 1998. *The myth of the global corporation*. Princeton, NJ, Princeton University Press.

Dosi, Giovanni; Pavitt, Keith; Soete, Luc. 1991. *The economics of technical change and international trade*. New York, NY, New York University Press.

Dunning, John H. 2000. "The eclectic paradigm as an envelope for economic and business theories of MNE activity", in *International Business Review* (Oxford), Vol. 9, No. 2, pp. 163-190.

Epstein, Gerald; Burke, James. 2001. *Globalization and labor bargaining power: A survey.* Unpublished mimeo. Amherst, MA, Political Economy Research Institute (PERI), University of Massachussetts-Amherst.

Ernst, Dieter; Fagerberg, Jan; Hildrum, Jarle. 2002. *Do global production networks and digital information systems make knowledge spatially fluid?* TIK Working Paper No. 13. Oslo, University of Oslo.

Evans, Peter. 1995. *Embedded autonomy: States and industrial transformation.* Princeton, NJ, Princeton University Press.

Fagerberg, Jan. 1996. "Technology and competitiveness", in *Oxford Review of Economic Policy* (Oxford), Vol. 12, No. 3, pp. 39-51.

Feenstra, Robert C. 1998. "Integration of trade and disintegration of production", in *Journal of Economic Perspectives* (Nashville, TN), Vol. 12, Fall, pp. 31-50.

—; Hai, Wen; Woo, Wing T.; Yao, Shunli. 1998. *The US-China bilateral trade balance: Its size and determinants.* NBER Working Paper No. 6598. Cambridge, MA, National Bureau of Economic Research.

—; Hanson, Gordon H. 2001. *Global production sharing and rising wage inequality: A survey of trade and wages.* Unpublished mimeo. Davis, CA, University of California-Davis. [available online at: www.econ.ucdavis.edu/faculty/fzfeens]

—; —.1999. "The impact of outsourcing and high-technology capital on wages: Estimates for the United States, 1979-1990", in *Quarterly Journal of Economics* (Cambridge, MA), Vol. 114, No. 3 (Aug.), pp. 907-940.

—; —.1997. "Foreign direct investment and relative wages: Evidence from Mexico's maquiladoras", in *Journal of International Economics* (Amsterdam), Vol. 42, No.3/4 (May), pp. 371-393.

Financial Times (London). 2000. "FT500", 4 May.

Fitter, Robert; Kaplinsky, Raphael. 2001. "Who gains from product rents as the coffee market becomes more differentiated? A value chain analysis", in *IDS Bulletin* (Brighton), Vol. 32, No. 3 (July), pp. 69-82.

Fortune Magazine (New York, NY). 2000. "The fortune 500" (annual issue).

Frohlich, Markham T.; Westbrook, Roy. 2001. "Arcs of integration: An international study of supply chain strategies", in *Journal of Operations Management* (Amsterdam), Vol. 19, No. 2, pp. 185-200.

Gereffi, Gary. 1999. "International trade and industrial upgrading in the apparel commodity chain", in *Journal of International Economics* (Amsterdam), Vol. 48, No. 1 (June), pp. 37-70.

—.1994. "The organization of buyer-driven global commodity chains: How U.S. retailers shape overseas production networks", in Gary Gereffi and Miguel Korzeniewicz (eds.): *Commodity chains and global capitalism.* Westport, CT, Greenwood Press, pp. 95-122.

Glen, Jack; Lee, Kevin; Singh, Ajit. 2002. *Corporate profitability and the dynamics of competition in emerging markets: A time series analysis.* Working Paper No. 248. ESRC Centre for Business Research, University of Cambridge. Dec.

Gorg, Holger; Greenaway, David. 2001. *Foreign direct investment and intra-industry spillovers*. Paper presented to the UNECE/EBRD Regional Expert Meeting on Finance for Development, Geneva, United Nations Economic Commission for Europe. Dec.

Hanson, Gordon H. 2001. *Should countries promote foreign direct investment?* G-24 Discussion Paper Series (Research papers for the Intergovernmental Group of Twenty-Four on International Monetary Affairs), No. 9, UNCTAD/GDS/MDPB/G24/9. Geneva, UNCTAD. Feb.

—; Harrison, A. 1999. "Trade, technology and wage inequality", in *Industrial and Labor Relations Review* (Ithaca, NY), Vol. 52, No. 2 (Jan.), pp. 271-288.

—; Mataloni, Raymond J.; Slaughter, Matthew J. 2001. *Expansion strategies of US multinational firms*. NBER Working Paper No. 8433. Cambridge, MA, National Bureau of Economic Research.

Harrison, Bennett; Kelley, Maryellen. 1993. "Outsourcing and the search for flexibility", in *Work, Employment and Society* (Durham), Vol. 7, No. 2 (June), pp. 213-235.

Hoekman, Bernard; Holmes, Peter M. 1999. *Competition policy, developing countries and the WTO*. World Bank Working Paper No. 2211. Washington, DC, World Bank. Oct.

Holmstrom, Bengt; Roberts, John. 1998. "The boundaries of the firm revisited", in *Journal of Economic Perspectives* (Nashville, TN), Vol. 12, No. 4 (Fall), pp. 73-94.

Howell, David R.; Houston, Ellen; Milberg, William. 2001. "Skill mismatch, bureaucratic burden, and rising earnings inequality in the U.S.: What do hours and earnings trends by occupation show?", in Jim Stanford, Lance Taylor and Ellen Houston (eds.): *Power, employment and accumulation: Social structures in economic theory and practice*. Armonk, NY, ME Sharpe, pp. 23-65.

Hummels, David; Rapoport, Dana; Yi, Kei-Mu. 1998. "Vertical specialization and the changing nature of world trade", in *FRBNY Economic Review* (New York, NY), June, pp. 79-99.

Hymer, Stephen Herbert. 1976. *The international operations of national firms: A study of direct foreign investment*. Cambridge, MA, MIT Press.

IMF. 2001. *World Economic Outlook database*. Washington, DC. [available online at: www.imf.org/external/pubs/ft/weo/2001/01/data]

Jenkins, Mauricio; Esquivel, Gerardo; Larrain, Felipe. 1998. *Export processing zones in Central America*. Development Discussion Paper No. 646. Cambridge, MA, Harvard Institute for International Development. Aug.

Jones, Ronald W. 2000. *Globalization and the theory of input trade*. Cambridge, MA, MIT Press.

—. 1980. "Comparative and absolute advantage", in *Schweizerische Zeitschrift für Volkswirtschaft und Statistik* (Basel). Sep., pp. 235-260.

Kaplinsky, Raphael. 1993. "Export processing zones in the Dominican Republic: Transforming manufactures into commodities", in *World Development* (Oxford), Vol. 21, No. 11, pp. 1851-1865.

Krugman, Paul. 1995. "Growth in world trade: Causes and consequences", in *Brookings Papers on Economic Activity* (Washington, DC), No. 1, pp. 327-377.

—. 1991. "Myths and realities of US competitiveness", in *Science* (Washington, DC), No. 254, 8 Nov., pp. 811-815.

Kucera, David. 2002. "Core labour standards and foreign direct investment", in *International Labour Review* (Geneva), Vol. 141, No. 1-2, pp. 31-69.

—; Milberg, William. 2003. "Deindustrialization and changes in manufacturing trade: Factor content calculations for 1978-1995", in *Weltwirtschaftliches Archiv* (Kiel), Vol. 139, No. 4, pp. 601-624.

Mataloni, Raymond J. 2000. "An examination of the low rates of return of foreign-owned US companies", in *Survey of Current Business* (Washington, DC), Vol. 80, Mar., pp. 55-73.

Mayer, Jörg; Butkevicius, Arunas; Kadri, Ali. 2002. *Dynamic products in world exports.* UNCTAD Discussion Paper No. 159. Geneva, United Nations.

Milberg, William. 1999. "Foreign direct investment and development: Balancing costs and benefits", in UNCTAD (ed.): *International monetary and financial issues for the 1990s.* Geneva, United Nations, Vol. XI, pp. 99-116.

—; Elmslie, Bruce. 1997. "Harder than you think: Free trade and international labor standards", in *New Labor Forum* (New York, NY), Vol. 1, No. 1 (Fall), pp. 69-80.

Ng, Francis; Yeats, Alexander. 1999. *Production sharing in East Asia: Who does what for whom and why?* World Bank Working Paper No. 2197. Washington, DC, World Bank.

Nolan, Peter; Sutherland, Dylan; Zhang, Jin. 2002. "The challenge of the global business revolution", in *Contributions to Political Economy* (London), Vol. 21, No. 1, pp. 91-110.

OECD. 1999. *Economic Outlook.* No. 66. Paris.

Oliveira Martins, Joaquim; Scarpetta, Stefano. 1999. *The levels and cyclical behaviour of mark-ups across countries and market structures.* Economics Department Working Papers, No. 213. Paris, OECD.

Palpaceur, Florence. 2002. *Global value chains: Note for discussion.* Unpublished mimeo. Geneva, ILO. Sep.

Pessino, Carola. 1997. "Argentina: The labour market during the economic transition", in Sebastian Edwards and Nora Claudia Lustig (eds.): *Labor markets in Latin America: Combining social protection with market flexibility.* Washington, DC, Brookings Institution, pp. 151-200.

Porter, Michael E. 1990. *The competitive advantage of nations.* New York, NY, The Free Press.

Powell, Walter. 1990. "Neither market nor hierarchy: Network forms of organization", in Barry M. Straw and Larry L. Cummings (eds.): *Research in organizational behavior.* Greenwich, CT, JAI Press, Vol. 12, pp. 295-336.

Ricardo, David. 1817. *The principles of political economy and taxation.* [Quotation from *The collected works of David Ricardo*, edited by Piero Sraffa, Cambridge, Cambridge University Press, Vol. 1, 1951.]

Robbins, Donald J. 1996. *Evidence on trade and wages in the developing world.* OECD Development Centre, Technical Papers Series, No. 119, OECD/GD(96)182. Paris, OECD. Dec.

Roberts, Mark J.; Tybout, James R. 1996. "A preview of the country studies", in Mark J. Roberts and James R. Tybout (eds.): *Industrial evolution in developing countries: Micro patterns of turnover, productivity and market structure.* New York, NY, Oxford University Press, pp. 188-199.

Rodrik, Dani. 1999. *Making openness work*. Washington, DC, Overseas Development Council.

Rose, Andrew K. 1991. "The role of exchange rates in a popular model of international trade: Does the 'Marshall-Lerner' condition hold?", in *Journal of International Economics* (Amsterdam), Vol. 30, pp. 301-316.

Samuelson, Paul. 1949. "International factor-price equalization once again", in *Economic Journal* (Oxford), Vol. 59, June, pp. 181-197.

Semlinger, Klaus. 1991. "New developments in subcontracting: Mixing market and hierarchy", in Ash Amin and Michael Dietrich (eds.): *Towards a new Europe? Structural change in the European economy*. Aldershot, Edward Elgar, pp. 96-115.

Singh, Ajit; Dhumale, Rahul. 1999. *Competition policy, development and developing countries*. South Centre Working Paper No. 7. Geneva, South Centre.

Slaughter, Matthew J. 2002. *Does inward foreign direct investment contribute to skill-upgrading in developing countries?* Paper presented at New School University's CEPA Conference on "Labor and the Globalization of Production", New School University, New York, NY, Mar. (June revision).

Sturgeon, Timothy J. 2002. "Modular production networks: An American model of industrial organization", in *Industrial and corporate change* (Oxford), Vol. 11, No. 3, pp. 451-496.

—.2001. "How do we define value chains and production networks?", in *IDS Bulletin* (Brighton), Vol. 32, No. 3 (July), pp. 9-18.

Te Velde, Dirk Willem; Morrissey, Oliver. 2001. *Foreign ownership and wages: Evidence from five African countries*. CREDIT Research Paper No. 01/19. Nottingham, Centre for Research in Economic Development and International Trade, University of Nottingham. [available online at: www.nottingham.ac.uk/economics/research/credit]

Tybout, James R. 2000. "Manufacturing firms in developing countries: How well do they do, and why?", in *Journal of Economic Literature* (Nashville, TN), Vol. 38, No. 1 (Mar.), pp. 11-44.

UNCTAD. 2002a. *World Investment Report 2002: Transnational corporations and export competitiveness – Overview*. [available online at: www.unctad.org/en/docs/wir2002 overview_en.pdf]

—.2002b. *World Investment Report 2002: Transnational corporations and export competitiveness*. Geneva.

—.2002c. *Trade and Development Report*. Geneva.

—.2001. *World Investment Report 2001*. Geneva.

—.1998. *World Investment Report 1998*. Geneva.

—.1993. *World Investment Report 1993*. Geneva.

United States Department of Commerce. 2002. *Survey of Current Business*. Bureau of Economic Analysis, Washington, DC.

Venables, Anthony J. 2002. *Vertical specialization*. Unpublished mimeo. Geneva, ILO.

Wheeler, David; Mody, Ashoka. 1992. "International investment location decisions: The case of US firms", in *Journal of International Economics* (Amsterdam), Vol. 33, No. 1, pp. 57-76.

Williamson, Oliver E. 2002. "The theory of the firm as governance structure: From choice to contract", in *Journal of Economic Perspectives* (Nashville, TN), Vol. 16, No. 3 (Summer), pp. 171-195.

World Bank. 2002. *A new database on foreign direct investment.* [available online at: www 1.worldbank.org/economicpolicy/globalization/data.html]

—.2001 and 2000. *Global Development Finance Database Online.* [accessible via the above address]

WTO. 2002. *International trade statistics 2002.* [available online at: www.wto.org/english/ res _e/statis_e/its2002_e/its02_longterm_e.htm]

Yeats, Alexander J. 2001. *Just how big is global production sharing?* Unpublished mimeo. Washington, DC, World Bank.

Ziegler, C. 2001. *The global garden.* Unpublished mimeo. New York, NY, Department of Anthropology, Graduate Faculty, New School University.

LABOUR FLEXIBILITY IN EUROPE

Tiziano TREU *

4

THE ORIGINS OF THE DEBATE

Labour flexibility[1] first became a focus of attention in Europe[2] around the mid-1970s as a result of the economic crisis sparked off by the massive oil price increases of 1973.

While the immediate cause of the crisis was clear, opinion on where ultimate responsibility lay was divided. The controversy extended to the role played by labour issues, and the debate over the rights and wrongs of labour flexibility soon took on ideological overtones. One widely shared view attributed the poor performance of European firms to a set of institutional rigidities which greatly reduced the ability of enterprises to adapt to increasingly turbulent market conditions. The "Eurosclerosis" due to these rigidities was held to be a major obstacle to the international competitiveness of European economies and to the optimal use of the opportunities for innovation offered by new information technologies. This inability to adapt was seen as a structural and not merely a transitory problem. In the early 1980s the political initiative was largely in the hands of proponents of such views, who were particularly well represented in European employer and government circles (Boyer, 1988, 1990).

The counter-argument ran that the economic crisis could not be attributed solely to institutional rigidities. The rigidities themselves stemmed not just from the need to regulate labour relations but were linked to the organizational structures and management methods typifying the Fordist mode of production. Indeed the rigidities were to be considered more a *result* of the crisis of Fordism and its production-line techniques than the *origin* of the European "disease" (Boyer, 1990).

Originally published in *International Labour Review*, Vol. 131 (1992), No. 4-5.

* Professor of Labour Law, Catholic University of Milan, Italy.

At the beginning of the 1990s the controversy over the economic consequences of institutional rigidities is still not settled but it has lost much of its bitterness and ideological divisiveness. The experience of the 1980s has shown that a pragmatic approach to labour flexibility is possible and that acceptable compromises can be found among the parties on ways and means of achieving it. The relative improvement in the economic and employment performance of European Community (EC) countries has facilitated this more cooperative approach.

For their part, the unions underwent a marked decline in most EC countries as a result of the economic crisis of the 1970s and were clearly on the defensive as regards all aspects of labour relations (Kochan, 1988). High levels of unemployment were a major factor in this decline, but it was also due to the profound changes taking place in the structure of all advanced economies (the increasing importance of the tertiary sector and the trend towards economic decentralization) and to parallel changes in the composition and attitudes of the workforce (greater participation of women and higher educational levels). Despite the decline in unionization, labour-management relations have begun to achieve a new equilibrium, and the extreme prospect of a deunionized and deregulated Europe has not materialized (Baglioni and Crouch, 1990).

NUMERICAL FLEXIBILITY

Numerical or external flexibility – the employers' ability to alter the size of their workforce – has been the most controversial form of labour flexibility.

Restrictions on the hiring of workers

The freedom of the employer to hire has been the subject of debate in several countries, particularly in Italy which used to have a uniquely rigid recruitment system. Not only were Italian employers obliged to use public employment offices for all recruitment but (especially with the less skilled) they were not entitled to select the particular workers they wanted and could only specify the number of employees they wished to hire in a given occupational category; these were then drawn from a list of employees prepared according to seniority by the public employment offices. The absolute rigidity of this system, a survival from a time when Italy was an agricultural country hit by heavy unemployment, has been gradually broken down by law (Acts 863/1984, 56/1987 and 223/1991) and bypassed in various other ways (Treu, 1991).

Other and no less controversial limitations on the freedom of employers to hire labour are to be found in the legal quotas for physically and socially disadvantaged groups (here again, in Italy the quotas are higher than the European average).

Protection against dismissal

The issue of employment protection, in particular the regulation of dismissals, has been widely discussed. The European labour relations systems, which all have some institutionalized system of protection against dismissal provided both by law and by collective agreement, have been contrasted at length with the extreme models presented by the United States, traditionally characterized by the legal freedom to dismiss (Grenig, 1991), and Japan, well known for its practice of lifetime employment, at least for the core labour force (Dercksen, 1989). At the beginning of the 1990s one can say that the pressures for deregulation and increased numerical flexibility have had only a limited impact on the European systems.

As far as individual dismissals are concerned, the basic principle remains that the employer's decision is subject to various limitations: prior notice must be given to the interested party (as a minimum) and, in most countries, a valid reason must be shown, connected with the capacity or conduct of the worker or based on the operational requirements of the enterprise (to use the words of the ILO Termination of Employment Convention, 1982 (No. 158)). The validity of the reason may have to be justified in court after the discharge, and sometimes also earlier, at public hearings (the Netherlands) or through a procedure established by collective agreement (Germany).

The consequences of the reason being found invalid vary considerably. In most countries the employer is financially penalized but does not have to reinstate the employee. The applicability of such legislation also varies. In some countries the smallest production units, which are by definition the most "flexible" part of the economy, are exempt from these legal controls. The issue remains a controversial one. A recent Italian law has gone against the stream and extended employees' protection against unfair dismissal to all production units, regardless of their size, though with different consequences: in units of up to 15 employees the remedy is purely financial compensation, in larger units it may be reinstatement.

The regulations concerning collective or mass dismissals tend to be more complex. Changes have been introduced in some countries making the law less favourable to employees (Buechtemann, 1989). In France, under strong pressure from employers, the Chirac Government of 1986-87 abolished the traditional requirement for an administrative authorization by a labour inspector prior to collective dismissals.[3] A similar change has been introduced in Spain. In the Netherlands authorization by the public employment offices remains necessary in all cases of dismissal, but the procedure has been simplified.

In general, collective dismissals remain a matter of serious concern both to the social partners and to governments in most European countries. EC Directive 1975/129 was intended to harmonize the regulations of member

States in this respect. It requires employers to consult the representatives of employees in order to reach agreement on either the prevention of the dismissals or the numbers of employees involved or the measures to be taken to mitigate the consequences of the dismissals; they must also inform the competent government authority, which may take action to find a solution to the problem.

Countries have implemented this directive in various ways, but the general direction taken is similar. The law does not prevent employment adjustment but it does specify certain conditions: in the case of collective dismissals it requires both sides of industry to search for alternative solutions wherever possible, dismissal being seen as a last resort because of the social and economic costs involved.

Regulating redundancies and finding viable alternatives to dismissal have not been easy, particularly during the periods of severe economic crisis following the oil shocks of the 1970s. This has particularly been the case in France, Italy and the United Kingdom where the tradition of industrial relations – adversarial attitudes and lack of trust between the social partners – does not favour consensual, collaborative solutions. Over time, however, collective bargaining has produced successful solutions in many cases: even in the countries mentioned the unions have come to accept a complex trade-off between reduced unemployment and increased labour market flexibility.[4]

Measures that have been used as alternatives to mass dismissals include internal and external mobility; short-time working on a rota system instead of total lay-off, even with temporary wage reductions; recruitment freezes; overtime reductions; and early retirement. This kind of trade-off has been easier to achieve in countries such as Germany which have a tradition of collaborative or participative labour relations.

Other measures to help the social partners achieve accommodations of this sort have often been introduced by public bodies. The Italian Wages Guarantee Fund (Cassa Integrazione Guadagni), for example, has played a major role (notably by encouraging so-called solidarity contracts[5]) in alleviating the impact of short-time working or temporary lay-offs on the working population, thereby allowing large sectors of Italian industry to adjust to changed economic circumstances with relatively low social and economic costs.

Active manpower policies have also been used to help find jobs for employees whose redeployment appears inevitable. In some countries (Belgium, France, Italy) the implementation of such policies (like other flexibility measures) is possible only if the industrial adjustment is effected through a process of concertation and bargaining between the two sides of industry, usually with some intervention from public bodies.[6]

In conclusion, most European governments (with the major exception of the United Kingdom) have not adopted a policy of outright deregulation but have promoted concerted measures to increase the flexibility of the labour market.[7] Indeed, the legislation introducing the various forms of flexibility is usually itself the result of tripartite consultation (Treu, 1990).

The peripheral labour force

The level of employment protection and the forms of negotiated flexibility described so far refer to the permanent labour force. This picture would be misleading if we failed to consider the various forms and growing incidence of "atypical" or "peripheral" employment. The introduction of different types of employment contract has probably been the major development in European law and practice in the labour field during the past 15 years and has played a leading role in increasing labour market flexibility (Kravaritou-Manitakis, 1988).

Until the mid-1970s the basic legal instrument for regulating the employment relationship in most EC countries was the full-time employment contract concluded for an indefinite period. The employment relationship for life typical of the public service was proposed as a model for the private sector too. Fixed-term contracts were permitted in most countries but were subject to fairly stringent legal restrictions. Temporary work organized through special agencies was also strictly controlled, and indeed was outlawed in some countries (such as Greece, Italy and Spain). There was little recourse to part-time employment, which was often actively discouraged, largely because of the indirect and social security costs involved.

This situation has now changed drastically. Different forms of employment have proliferated to such an extent that the attribute "atypical" has become inappropriate for most of them. "Precarious" would be the more accurate term. The main trend has been the spread of temporary forms of employment. This has been promoted by legislation, mainly through a gradual widening of the range of acceptable reasons justifying the use of fixed-term contracts beyond the original cases to which they applied (special projects, seasonal work, sickness of a permanent employee, etc.).

Young workers have been the first and main beneficiaries of this policy, which coincided with a period of increasing youth unemployment (up to the mid-1980s). Not only has temporary work for young people been legally permitted, it has also received public subsidies and in some cases has been made more attractive to employers by reductions in minimum standards of employment, particularly wage levels, which have usually been justified by the special mix of training and work these contracts involve. This combination, which was typical of the old apprenticeship contract, has been applied in varying degrees to different kinds of employment training contract, the intention being to familiarize young people with the work environment.

The routine use of temporary employment contracts was subsequently extended beyond the original age bracket. In Germany fixed-term contracts have been allowed in all hiring of first-time jobseekers, regardless of age (Act of 26 April 1985). Special temporary contracts are also being offered to other workers, the main aim being to allow occupational adjustment to technological change (Ojeda Avilés, 1989).

This less restrictive attitude towards temporary work has indirectly promoted the spread of agencies that specialize in leasing manpower to meet employers' short-term needs. Even in countries where such agencies remain prohibited by law for historical reasons, the pressure to remove the ban is growing: in Italy, for example, a recent Bill prepared by the Government allows their operation under public control, in accordance with a draft EC directive.

Here too the methods followed by most European legislators have not been purely deregulatory, the main exception again being the United Kingdom. While removing pre-existing legal obstacles to temporary work, in most cases the legislators have required the use of fixed-term contracts to be agreed upon by both sides of industry. In Italy Act 56/87 contains a general provision whereby the collective bargaining partners can determine how many employees can be hired on fixed-term contracts and in what circumstances. Similarly, the criteria and conditions for hiring young workers on training contracts are now also to be determined by collective agreements in France (since 17 June 1986) and again in Italy.

Other examples of the complex range of measures adopted include laws under which employers have been given greater freedom to adapt their temporary workforce to meet changing demand, while at the same time new working patterns and employment opportunities, particularly for specific groups of disadvantaged employees, have been promoted. Moreover, incentives have often been provided not only for the initial hiring of young workers under employment training contracts, but also for the conversion of these contracts into regular ones; this has been a common procedure in various Italian regional administrations, for example.

All these policies have been quite effective in helping to increase the number of temporary workers, particularly among first-time jobseekers; in recent years this has almost become the normal mode of entry into the labour market for young workers.[8]

This enlarged segment of the peripheral workforce, then, has become a stable part of an officially authorized dual labour market. Consequently the relationship between core and periphery of the labour market has become a critical issue – particularly in those increasingly grey areas where employment begins to merge into self-employment. A variety of intermediate types of semi-independent work is now emerging and being recognized and even encouraged by the courts, inasmuch as such employment needs less protection and is by definition flexible, precisely because of the "autonomy" of the parties involved.

An even broader trend should be mentioned here: the increased use of various forms of external collaboration such as subcontracting, outworking, telework and just-in-time methods of supply. This trend should greatly contribute to increasing numerical flexibility, particularly around the "periphery" of enterprises.

WORKING TIME FLEXIBILITY

Working time was another important and controversial testing ground for flexibility, particularly in the late 1970s. Far-reaching changes have taken place in this area, possibly even greater than those in respect of employment protection (Treu, 1989).

The initiative for change came mostly from the employers. Although the trade unions initially reacted defensively, there did emerge the outlines of a consensus on the needs and values of a workforce that now contained more women and more people working in the tertiary sector. However, the trend towards more flexible working patterns was also influenced by union pressure for reduced working hours, which met with considerable (and continuing) success in a number of countries.

The search for flexibility was not merely a tactical move on the part of employers. It had to do with strategic factors such as the need to adapt the organization of work to the increasingly variable needs of production and with welfare issues relating to the quality of working life and changing lifestyles. Nevertheless, the *quid pro quo* element was important. Faced with union pressure to reduce the working week, employers found that a counter-demand for flexibility in working schedules proved a more effective way of achieving cost reductions than either a purely negative stand or insistence on compensating wage reductions. Moreover, this type of trade-off has been looked upon favourably by European governments as being more socially acceptable than any other solution.

As in the area of numerical flexibility, some of the rigidities in traditional labour legislation (which were much more extensive in Europe than elsewhere) have been removed. Among the most relevant examples of this legislative liberalization of working time may be mentioned the reduction of restrictions on part-time work (Italy); the easing of standards concerning daily and weekly maximum work hours; allowing employers greater flexibility in organizing working time over the year (Spain) or in individualizing work schedules (France); and the abolition or relaxation of restrictions on night work and compulsory rest periods for women workers (Italy, Act 903/1977; France, Act of 19 June 1987) (Blanpain and Köhler, 1988).

In quite a number of cases deregulatory and promotional objectives have coincided: the clearest case, though it was not particularly successful, was the French legislation of 1982 whereby, contrary to previous practice, flexible working time arrangements were permissible provided working time reductions were also adopted. The Belgian Act of 17 March 1987 on the adaptation of working time permitted the adoption of flexible working time and the extension of working hours on condition that the measures had positive employment effects. And most countries have introduced legislation encouraging working time reductions over a lifetime, such as early or phased retirement.

As in the case of fixed-term contracts, collective bargaining has played a major role in introducing and/or implementing flexibility in this area. The result has been such legislation as the Italian Act 863/1984 on solidarity contracts and Act 903/1977 on night work for women; the French law of 19 June 1987 on the duration and arrangement of working time; and the Belgian Act of 17 March 1987 on the adaptation of working time.

There has been more bargaining here than in other spheres, and mostly at decentralized levels (enterprise, plant or workshop). The trend towards decentralization in collective bargaining over working time arrangements is reported even in traditionally centralized systems such as those of the Nordic countries, the Netherlands and Germany, although centrally negotiated collective agreements have continued to set the guidelines on the extent and limits of flexibility and reductions in working time, and on implementation procedures.

By the end of the 1980s the variety of working time arrangements had increased more than was originally envisaged by the social partners themselves, and this development contributed further to the diversification of employment patterns noted above – indeed it is part of the same continuum. It is now open to employers to distribute hours over the week, or longer periods, with fewer constraints than before and without having to pay overtime bonuses. Such arrangements are usually negotiated in conjunction with reductions in total working time (in Germany, for example, from 37 to 35 hours a week). Employees are allowed to work an increased amount of overtime, and employers have more discretion in assigning it, often even for work on Saturday and Sunday. There are also more possibilities for shift-work and part-time arrangements, including weekend working, for new formulas such as job-sharing and for the non-standard distribution of working time over longer periods, with more scope for granting sabbaticals and occasional leaves of absence, introducing phased retirement, etc.

One major implication of this multiplication of working arrangements is the "personalization" of working time: for the first time there is a clear distinction between the working time of the individual employee and the operating hours of a production unit. The effects on employment and productivity, however, are difficult to evaluate (Hart, 1987). Most of the new patterns are tentative; and so, as in other areas, a trial-and-error approach seems to prevail on both sides of industry.

FUNCTIONAL FLEXIBILITY

Functional flexibility is distinguished from and sometimes opposed to numerical or external flexibility because it concerns an enterprise's own internal organization of labour.

Broadly, it involves a reversal of the division of labour and the fragmentation of work organization which were typical of the traditional production-line model; this is achieved both by extending the range of tasks and skills involved in a job and by increasing internal mobility.

The traditional rigidities attributed to European labour relations in this area derive not so much from legal restrictions as from management and union practices, which reflect the basic nature of labour-management relations in Europe and of company strategy and organization. For this reason they have been called "built-in rigidities" (Boyer, 1990; Dore, 1986, 1987). This is not to play down the importance of legal deregulation, but it must be said that the latter has on the whole come about indirectly through the deregulation of product and financial markets and the removal of obstacles in specific fields of labour organization, such as those mentioned above concerning working time arrangements and employment patterns.

In a few countries functional mobility is limited by the legal principle that the tasks required by a job cannot be downgraded to less skilled ones. In recent years, however, this principle has been interpreted less rigidly by both courts and unions so as to allow work redesign and job reassignment, temporary or permanent, to less skilled tasks, provided that it does not result in a net deskilling of the employee concerned.

Functional flexibility has come to be widely accepted and practised throughout the European Community. The forms it takes have been largely determined by the strategies adopted by the social partners, particularly the employers, given that implementation is their direct responsibility. Generalizations are difficult, but on the whole employers have come to assume a somewhat proactive role in this area. Research evidence suggests that there was a significant trend towards greater functional flexibility throughout the 1980s (Bamber, 1989).

It has been suggested (Boyer, 1990) that the very persistence of employment protection in most European countries, underpinned as it is by legislation and industrial relations practice, has induced employers to look for internal flexibility, that is, to adopt innovative forms of work organization in order to achieve optimal use of the various factors of production. Such innovations have taken many forms: the relaxation or abolition of restrictive work practices, as in the United Kingdom; the reduction of job demarcation and the number of grades; job enlargement and enrichment (so far as is compatible with efficiency); experiments with team-work, coupled with job and organization redesign; and the introduction of other new human resource management practices such as sophisticated selection, training and performance appraisal techniques, communication programmes and quality circles.[9]

The implementation of functional flexibility has often given employers an opportunity to bypass the unions. Innovations in this field, as in working time practices, have given them an ideal opportunity to introduce participative management practices and establish direct relations with employees outside union channels. Such practices have gained ground, particularly where they enjoy government approval, as in the United Kingdom, and in weakly unionized areas (the tertiary sector, high-tech firms, etc.).

The unions have reacted in various ways, but in those sectors and countries where they are more solidly entrenched (Belgium, Germany, Italy) they have met the challenge: in return for greater internal flexibility, as indicated above, they have obtained guarantees of employment security, at least for the core workforce, and possibly closer involvement in company-level decision-making. Indeed, this kind of experiment has even encouraged trade union negotiators in countries with a tradition of conflictual pluralism (Italy and the United Kingdom) to move towards the participative practices typical of central European systems (most notably Germany).

A significant volume of comparative research emanating from both Europe and Japan seems to suggest that flexibility and innovation in labour relations practices are more likely to succeed where labour relations and management styles are participative (Bamber, 1989).

PAY FLEXIBILITY

Wages have not remained untouched by the pressures for greater flexibility. Indeed, the failure of companies to adjust to turbulent markets has repeatedly been blamed on the complexity and rigidity of wage structures. The need for change has been widely recognized.

In Europe wages are determined mainly through collective agreements, so here too the introduction of flexibility has been a major task for the social partners. However, legislation has also played some part in reducing certain forms of automatic wage increases, particularly indexation. During the 1980s indexation came under attack as a major factor contributing to inflation, and in most countries its use was gradually reduced, if not abolished, under the combined influence of legislation and collective bargaining.[10] Where indexation does still exist (Belgium, Italy), it only provides compensation up to a given ceiling. Thus it ensures not so much an automatic adjustment of the total wage to the cost of living as the protection of a basic portion of that wage from inflation.

The retreat from indexation has become a general trend; pay differentials, on the other hand, have received varying treatment. They have been increased in those countries where the combined effects of indexing and the egalitarian wage policies pursued by the unions during the 1970s had compressed them to the point where they were considered "punitive" for the skilled segment of the workforce (Italy and the United Kingdom). But it is a slow process, largely controlled by the unions, except at the most senior levels where wage increases are unilaterally decided by the employer. Conversely, however, it is worth noting that during the 1980s Germany, a country with a great commitment to productivity and to a skilled labour force, did not experience any significant change in occupational pay differentials. This seems to imply that widening differentials is not necessarily the way to enhance skill and performance.

The link between wages and productivity or performance is a controversial one in view of the macro-economic implications bound up with the general question of incomes policy. It would take us beyond the limits of the present article to discuss this problem here. Suffice it to say that the very idea of incomes policy was largely discredited in the 1980s by the rise of neo-liberalism and the polemics surrounding tripartism and government intervention. In the early 1990s, however, the need is again being felt for some generally agreed criteria of wage regulation at the macro level that will keep sectoral and national wage trends in line with economic performance, although this point is still widely contested (Dell'Aringa and Samek, 1992; Treu, 1992; Soskice, 1990). European unions have strongly resisted the idea, having less inclination than, for example, their Japanese counterparts to moderate their wage demands in accordance with the economic cycle and the need to protect employment.

The need for such responsiveness is particularly pressing at enterprise level and indeed has been partially met. The movement in this direction has occurred simultaneously with a (controlled) decentralization of collective bargaining and thus with a greater share of gross earnings being determined at enterprise or plant level, either collectively or unilaterally by the employer (Treu, 1987). Considerable attention has been devoted to the need to make wages more flexible, in the sense of being more closely correlated with various indicators of organizational and individual performance. Here again the initiative has been taken mainly by employers, as a possible way of reducing that part of the wage bill that is not based on merit or performance.

The actual impact of these trends varies considerably from one national system of industrial relations to another. One particularly important factor is the collective bargaining structure, which in Europe ranges from extreme decentralization in the United Kingdom to bipolarism in Italy and balanced centralization in Germany. On the whole, however, existing research indicates that so far this kind of wage flexibility has been limited in scope; and this applies to most of the various forms of flexible pay. Merit pay and productivity-related wages, for example, even when applied to large numbers of employees (as in France and the United Kingdom), have never amounted to more than a small proportion of gross earnings; in part this is due to the growth of other "indirect" or variable components of labour costs, notably social security payments, holiday pay (often linked to length of service), and occasional bonus payments.[11] Profit-related pay has also experienced some growth in most countries and has received explicit legal sanction in some (especially France). This seems to be related to the (limited) objective of making employees more aware of the economic performance of their firm, but here again the impact appears to have been relatively modest (Della Rocca and Prosperetti, 1991).

The growth in indirect forms of pay negotiated between individual firms and their employees has been seen as significant evidence of the increasing importance of the company-employee relationship and of the declining influence of local labour markets on employers' behaviour.

Such factors may also explain some of the difficulties experienced when firms seek to introduce or expand performance pay schemes in response to external labour market pressures, as a substitute for existing payment systems. Some observers believe that this difficulty is caused by firms having to pay workers – notably skilled workers – at rates reflecting conditions on the internal labour market (seniority entitlements etc.), rather than being free to respond to external factors (such as market supply and demand). This highlights the critical importance of labour and wage stability within the firm, as opposed to external flexibility, and is very much in line with the Japanese model.

CONCLUDING REMARKS

Our review indicates that there has been considerable movement towards flexibility, affecting most aspects of the employment relationship.

The factors underlying this trend have been the focus of much attention. On the employers' side, the main reason for seeking flexibility is the need to be able to adapt more speedily to turbulent and competitive international markets. On the employees' side, the issues are less clear-cut, but there is certainly a feeling that some form of flexibility might meet the needs of new patterns of living and working, as well as favouring greater security of employment.

Since the beginning of the 1980s, both the social partners and the public authorities have been committed to reaching an acceptable compromise over flexibility. This presents problems all round. For the employers the difficulty is that their pursuit of flexibility must take into account not only traditional "objective" factors related to international competitiveness but also the need for a more educated workforce.

The challenge is even greater for the unions, which have simultaneously to take account of the employers' arguments on efficiency – backed by their superior power – and pressure from their members for greater individualization of employment conditions, without losing sight of collective goals such as maintaining common minimum standards and promoting employment.

The search for flexibility in Europe has two main characteristics: first, the significant role played by legislation, which is largely directed at removing traditional rigidities in the regulation of certain areas of the employment relationship (working time and employment patterns, although not employment protection); second, a basically consensual approach to seeking a solution, whereby the various forms of flexibility are subject to collective negotiation, often with government participation. The actual form such tripartite action has taken has been influenced both by labour market conditions and by employers' and unions' strategies, so the outcomes are anything but uniform.

The impact of flexibility in its various forms on the performance of enterprises and on other economic indicators, including employment, has yet to be fully evaluated using convincing comparative evidence.

It is probably going too far to say that the phase of "defensive" flexibility (which is based on "easier firings and lower wages") is over (Boyer, 1990); but certainly employers now place less emphasis on external flexibility and on outright reductions in employment protection.

Greater flexibility may in fact form part of opposing management strategies as regards labour relations: one strategy relies heavily on the external labour market and gives priority to low employee involvement in the life of the enterprise, whereas the other favours internal mobility and the promotion of polyvalent skills amongst existing employees. This helps to explain why deregulation has lost its urgency in labour relations policies,[12] and in fact it was never fully put into practice in most countries.

So in most cases policy-makers have not pursued flexibility – least of all external flexibility – at all costs, at any rate where the official labour market is concerned. Here the social partners, with the support of government, have agreed on regulated internal flexibility in return for external stability. This compromise has been easier to reach where labour-management relations are less conflictual and more cooperative, which is increasingly the case in many European countries (Bamber, 1989). Indeed, such flexibility and productivity agreements – which have proved an ideal testing ground for cooperative labour relations – appear to have worked, probably to the benefit of both parties.

Many policy-makers and observers have come to believe that profitable and acceptable flexibility involves more than mere deregulation. It comes about as the result of a complex set of measures covering many aspects of work and enterprise organization: a strong emphasis on the skill requirements and education of the workforce and on high-quality work, but at the same time closer employee involvement in the enterprise and, at the collective level, the enhancement of long-term cooperative relations between employers and employee representatives.[13]

However, the implementation of these policies remains uneven in the various areas and sectors of the labour market, often pulling in opposite directions in response to differing needs and demands. This unevenness is apparent as between the North and the South – economically strong and weak areas; as between the private and public sectors (the latter being usually much more rigid than the former); and, above all, as between the core and the periphery of the labour force, as this article has tried to show. Some analysts suggest that the persistence of peripheral work in depressed areas of the labour market is the price that must be paid for successfully linking internal flexibility with external employment security in the more prosperous core segments of the labour market. But the question remains whether it is a fair price. How large a periphery is needed for a stable core? How much disparity in working conditions and job security may be tolerated?

These are critical issues for the future, in Europe and elsewhere. If Europe is to be a social as well as an economic community, some sort of harmonization or convergence between the various areas and segments of the labour market must be sought, even if it will be difficult to achieve (Treu, 1990; Streeck, 1991; Blanpain, 1990).

Notes

[1] This term has a wide range of applications. In what follows we consider numerical (or external) flexibility, i.e. the freedom employers enjoy to expand or contract their workforce as they wish and to employ workers on a temporary or part-time basis; working time flexibility; functional flexibility; and pay flexibility. A further and essential form of flexibility, but one that cannot be explored here, is managerial flexibility (see the analysis by Koshiro, 1989).

[2] Throughout this article "Europe" means the countries forming the European Community.

[3] The effect of this deregulation has apparently been less than expected. Overmanning was quickly reduced, but the reduction in total employment was insignificant.

[4] The results are uneven and depend heavily on the relative position and strength of the social partners. Success stories are found mainly in large enterprises with participative labour relations, while they are rare in depressed segments of the labour market and in small firms.

[5] Solidarity contracts are company-level agreements which provide for a reduction in the working hours and pay of all employees, in order either to avoid collective dismissals due to overstaffing or to permit the hiring of new personnel. In Italy a solidarity contract concluded to avoid staff cuts – known as a "defensive" agreement – attracts assistance from the Wages Guarantee Fund equivalent to 50 per cent of the total pay forgone, for a maximum period of 24 months. If, however, the purpose is to permit the hiring of new personnel – an "offensive" solidarity contract – the employer is paid a contribution for each new employee hired (Act 863/1984) (Treu, 1991).

[6] According to Dercksen (1989), a weak system of employment protection together with an active labour market policy gives workers more protection against the capriciousness of the labour market than a high degree of employment protection coupled with a passive labour market policy. Moreover, the incentive to deregulate employment protection diminishes as labour market policy becomes increasingly effective. National labour law, as well as European labour law, provides only minimum standards for employment protection. For this reason collective bargaining is, and will remain, an important source of employment protection.

[7] Permanent wage reductions in return for job security are exceptional in Europe, being limited to extreme cases of enterprises in crisis. The general link between wage flexibility (wage moderation) and employment protection has been widely discussed but its mechanisms have still not been clearly identified.

[8] In Italy between 1985 and 1988, for example, over 1.2 million young workers were hired on employment training contracts. The large majority (75 per cent according to employer sources) have subsequently been given regular (i.e. indefinite) employment contracts.

[9] The development of appropriate skills has been considered a cornerstone of job flexibility. Education and training shape the attitudes and behaviour of managers and other employees. As the Dahrendorf report observed, "the rigidities of the educational system and the constraints of public finance are, if anything, greater obstacles to change than the rigidities of labour markets" (OECD, 1986, para. 42).

[10] Wage increases for length of service have also come under attack, but have been left basically unchanged (Marsden, 1991).

[11] The small contribution that merit- and performance-related payments make to employees' gross earnings and their small increase relative to other components of earnings lead one to conclude they have had little effect on increasing flexibility in reward systems or employers' labour costs, or in encouraging greater flexibility of work practices or improved motivation (Marsden, 1988 and 1991).

[12] In quite a few countries the critical issue has become the search for possible alternatives to the rigid models of management and enterprise organization derived from Fordism; the solution is being sought not in market deregulation but in flexible forms of enterprise organization supported by labour-management cooperation at micro level and, possibly, tripartite consultation and agreement at a higher level.

[13] However, that there is a dilemma over job security cannot be denied. On the one hand, complete immobility of labour within and outside firms would inhibit adjustment to changing international conditions and to technological and organizational innovation. Moreover, statistical evidence suggests that some employment regulations have induced long-term unemployment and labour market segmentation in Europe, and may have exacerbated mass unemployment. On the other hand, the absence of any constraints on hiring may reduce pressure for product and process innovations (Boyer, 1990).

References

Baglioni, G.; Crouch, C. 1990. *European industrial relations. The challenge of flexibility.* London, Sage.

Bamber, G. J. 1989. *Job flexibility: Some international comparisons and hypotheses about the dynamics of work organisation.* Paper for the 8th World Congress of the International Industrial Relations Association, Brussels, 4-7 September 1989.

Blanpain, R. 1990. "1992 and beyond: The impact of the European Community on the labour law systems of the member countries", in *Comparative Labor Law Journal* (Philadelphia), Vol. 11, No. 4, pp. 403-410.

—; Köhler, E. (eds.). 1988. *Legal and contractual limitations to working-time in the European Community member States.* European Foundation for the Improvement of Living and Working Conditions. Deventer, Kluwer.

Boyer, R. (ed). 1988. *The search for labour market flexibility. The European economies in transition.* Oxford, Clarendon Press.

—.1990. *The economics of job participation and emerging capital-labour relations.* Paper for an international conference at the Wissenschaftszentrum Berlin für Sozialforschung (WZB), Berlin, 16-18 May 1990.

Buechtemann, C. F. 1989. "More jobs through less employment protection? Evidence for West Germany", in *Labour* (Rome), Vol. 3, No. 3, pp. 23-56.

Dell'Aringa, C.; Samek, M. 1992. "Industrial relations and economic performance", in Treu, 1992.

Della Rocca, G.; Prosperetti, L. (eds.). 1991. *Salari e produttività: Esperienze internazionali e italiane.* Milan, Franco Angeli.

Dercksen, W. 1989. *Employment protection and flexibility in Western Europe.* Paper for the 8th World Congress of the IIRA, Brussels, 4-7 September 1989.

Dore, R. 1986. *Flexible rigidities: Industrial policy and structural adjustment in the Japanese economy 1970-80.* London, Athione Press.

—.1987. *Taking Japan seriously. A Confucian perspective on leading economic issues.* London, Athione Press.

Grenig, J.E. 1991. "The dismissal of employees in the United States", in *International Labour Review,* Vol. 130, No. 5-6, pp. 569-581.

Hart, R.A. 1987. *Working time and employment.* Boston, Allen & Unwin.

Kochan, T.A. 1988. "The future of worker representation: An American perspective", in *Labour and Society* (Geneva), Vol. 13, No. 2, pp. 183-201.

Koshiro, K. 1989. *Labour market flexibility and new employment patterns in Japan.* Paper for the 8th World Congress of the IIRA, Brussels, 4-7 September 1989.

Kravaritou-Manitakis, Y. 1988. *New forms of work: Labour law and social security aspects in the European Community.* Dublin, European Foundation for the Improvement of Living and Working Conditions.

Marsden, D. 1988. "Short-run wage flexibility and labour market adaptation in western Europe", in *Labour,* Vol. 2, No. 1, pp. 31-54.

—.1991. "Le politiche retributive aziendali. Il ruolo e la diffusione del 'merit pay'", in Asap Unità Studi: *1990. Rapporto sui salari.* Milan, Franco Angeli.

OECD. 1986. *Flexibility in the labour market: The current debate. A technical report.* Paris.

Ojeda Avilés, A. 1989. *Flexibilidad laboral y contratos de trabajo: Tendencias recientes en Europa Occidental.* Paper for the 8th World Congress of the IIRA, Brussels, 4-7 September 1989.

Soskice, D. 1990. "Reinterpreting corporatism and explaining unemployment: Co-ordinated and non-co-ordinated market economies", in R. Brunetta and C. Dell'Aringa (eds.): *Labour relations and economic performance.* London, Macmillan.

Streeck, W. 1991. *Industrial relations in a changing western Europe.* Paper for the 3rd European Regional Congress of the IIRA, Bari/Naples, 23-26 September 1991.

Treu, T. 1987. "Centralisation and decentralisation in collective bargaining ", in *Labour,* Vol. 1, No. 1, p. 147.

—.1989. "Introduction: New trends in working time arrangements", in A. Gladstone et al. (eds.): *Current issues in labour relations: An international perspective.* Berlin and New York, de Gruyter.

—.1990. "European unification and Italian labor relations", in *Comparative Labor Law Journal,* Vol. 11, No. 4, pp. 441-461.

—.1991. "Italy", in R. Blanpain (ed.): *International encyclopaedia for labour law and industrial relations.* Deventer, Kluwer.

— (ed). 1992. *Participation in public policy-making.* Berlin and New York, de Gruyter.

Visser, J. 1990. "In search of inclusive unionism", in *Bulletin of Comparative Labour Relations* (Deventer), No. 18.

THE CHALLENGE OF DECENT WORK

Robert B. REICH*

5

Even before the terrorist attacks of 11 September 2001 the United States' economy may technically have been in recession. Consumers were worried about the future. Their savings had reached a 70-year low. Businesses had stopped spending and investing, and unemployment was starting to rise. The value of stock portfolios had already dropped sharply, and the value of housing – the nest egg that most American households depend on for their retirement savings – was beginning to falter.

A similar slowdown was affecting the rest of the global economy as well. Even before 11 September 2001 Germany too was heading for recession, and dragging much of the rest of Europe with it. Japan, the world's second-largest economy, has been in recession for several years; more lately, it has faced the spectre of deflation – falling prices, which further deter spending because consumers anticipate that prices will continue to fall and because their loans are more difficult to repay. East-Asian economies were hit hard by the bursting of the technology bubble; they had relied on exports of technological components to the United States. Argentina was already teetering on the edge of financial difficulty, and thus threatening much of the rest of South America.

Economics is not a physical science. It is not a natural science. It is a social science. It is intimately connected to the hopes and the fears of populations. It is more akin to social psychology than to any other discipline. As consumers in the United States became more fearful, that country's economy began to slow considerably. Even spendthrift Americans will save for a rainy day when they see a storm cloud on the horizon. And 11 September

Originally published in *International Labour Review*, Vol. 141 (2002), No. 1-2.

* University Professor, Brandeis University; Hexter Professor of Social and Economic Policy at Brandeis's Heller School. Robert B. Reich was the 22nd Secretary of Labor of the United States. This article is based on an address given at the International Labour Office on the occasion of the Global Employment Forum, held in Geneva from 1 to 3 November 2001.

2001 brought more than a storm cloud. Fear, moreover, is infectious: global information and communication technologies carry it to all corners of the world at the speed of electronic impulses. The combination of an already-slowing global economy with new fears of global terrorism have taken a severe toll.

Against this background, the challenge of decent work is both short term and long term. In the short term, we face rising unemployment because the global economy is heading toward recession.

THE SHORT TERM: EXPANSIONARY FISCAL AND MONETARY POLICIES

There is no easy formula for restarting the global economy, but a first step must be expansionary fiscal and monetary policies. As Secretary of Labor of the United States, I never had an opportunity to talk publicly about fiscal and monetary policies. The assumption was that fiscal and monetary policies were none of the business of a labour secretary. But this assumption was wrong: fiscal and monetary policies are very much the business of people who are concerned about employment. Such policies should not be solely the responsibility of finance ministers and central bankers. Fiscal and monetary policies are among the most important levers of social policy in the advanced industrialized countries – and they should be treated as such.

When national economies slow, and the global economy begins to contract, the people who are likely to be hurt most are those at the end of the employment line. These are the people who are likely to lose their jobs first. They have the weakest connection to the labour market. Their skills are often the least developed. In short, the people who are the first to be drafted into the fight against inflation by losing their jobs are among the most vulnerable members of society.

This does not mean we should retreat from fighting inflation. Chronic inflation hurts everyone. But it is important to remember that the finance ministers and central bankers who have direct responsibility for fiscal and monetary policy necessarily have some discretion. They cannot predict precisely how their policies will affect inflation or employment. So the question is whether they err on the side of fighting inflation or err on the side of fighting joblessness. Because the social costs of unemployment are so high, and the social benefits of an abundance of decent jobs so significant, they should err on the side of fighting joblessness.

Now that the global economy is in danger of recession, central bankers should continue to reduce short-term interest rates and pilot their economies toward as tight a labour market as possible. Their goal must be full employment consistent with the avoidance of accelerating inflation. To achieve that goal may entail some experimentation, because from one time to the next there is no way of knowing what the correct monetary policy is. Technologies are constantly changing, as are the terms of competition. A level of employment that sparked accelerating inflation in the 1980s or 1990s may not spark it today.

When I became Secretary of Labor in 1993, another assumption among economists was that the so-called natural rate of unemployment – the rate below which you could not go without risking accelerating inflation – was 6 per cent in the United States, as we measure unemployment. But it turned out that because of technological changes and globalization it was possible to achieve levels of unemployment substantially below 6 per cent without igniting accelerating inflation.

All of the old economic rules had changed for several reasons. Companies were much more competitive with one another, and competition overall was much more intense than it had been even a decade before. Information and communication technologies had made it easier for consumers and investors to find better deals. Production and transportation technologies had made it easier for new producers to enter markets and take on large, established companies. As a result of this intensifying competition, companies found it more difficult in the 1990s than in previous decades.

In addition, trade unions in the United States were less powerful than they had been. Again, technologies of information, communication and transportation enabled consumers to get lower-cost products and services. In many cases, the lower-cost products were those produced by lower-wage workers, and often those lower-wage workers were not union members. In the 1950s, unionized workers comprised more than 35 per cent of the American workforce, and their wage agreements established the prevailing wages for over 60 per cent of the workforce. But by the 1990s, less than 10 per cent of private-sector workers were unionized, and collective agreements had relatively little effect on overall wage levels. As a result, wage gains were harder to come by.

For these reasons, it was possible to run the United States economy, not at 6 per cent, but at 5.5 per cent, at 5 per cent, some would say even at 4.5 per cent unemployment, without risking accelerated inflation. Alan Greenspan, the Chairman of the United States Federal Reserve, deserves credit for understanding the new economy of the 1990s and its influence on that supposed putative trade-off between inflation and unemployment. As unemployment dipped much lower than its presumed "natural" rate, Greenspan reassured the sceptics that the new economy ran by different rules.

The Federal Reserve has continued to reduce short-term interest rates, in light of the global contraction. It is important for other central banks to reduce short-term rates as well. The European Central Bank and the Bank of England have been reluctant to cut rates as aggressively as the Fed has. Partly this is due to the structure of labour markets in Europe, which are still "stickier" than America's. The "natural" rate of unemployment in Europe may well be higher than it is in the United States.

Yet central bankers have a social responsibility to do some experimenting. Inflation is not a genie that, once out of the bottle, is let loose and cannot thereafter be put back inside. That is a false and dangerous metaphor, which may have had an empirical basis in the old mass-production economy in which wages and prices sometimes spiralled out of control. But it does not fit the new realities of the new economy. Now, if inflation begins to accelerate, it can be stopped. Central bankers should reduce rates until they reach the point where inflation is accelerating.

As to fiscal policy, the overall approach should be similarly expansionary, especially in times like the present, when the global economy is teetering. It is well to remember that government budget deficits are not necessarily bad. To be sure, in 1993 when President Clinton took over in the United States, we found ourselves with a fiscal mess on our hands. Budget deficits of US$300 billion or more per year were forecast "as far as the eye can see". We had no choice but to reduce the budget deficit. Indeed, that was a precondition for persuading the Federal Reserve Board that it could comfortably reduce short-term interest rates without risking inflation.

John Maynard Keynes' insight is still valid, nonetheless: if consumers and businesses are not spending or investing enough to maintain adequate aggregate demand for all the goods and services the economy is capable of producing, government must step in. In a situation such as that we are now facing – an impending global recession accompanied by vast overcapacity in many industries around the world – it is entirely appropriate for governments to run deficits.

Governments in the Euro zone are handicapped in this regard. They have agreed with one another to place strict limits on their fiscal deficits. This is an understandable condition for entering into a currency agreement, but Europe must be careful that this stricture does not prevent it from adopting an adequately expansive fiscal policy. Sizeable deficits may be necessary in order to counteract the effects of businesses and consumers reducing their demand for goods and services.

THE LONG TERM: EDUCATION, "GOOD FLEXIBILITY" AND GLOBALIZATION

Over the longer term, even expansionary fiscal and monetary policies are not enough to assure decent work. In the long run, we need microeconomic policies that enable people to add more value to the global economy. Among the most important of such policies is the provision of adequate education and training, because of the central importance of human capital in the emerging global economy. Terms of competition are rapidly shifting from high-volume, stable, standard mass production to high-value production based on continuous innovation. People able to identify and solve new problems are critical to competitive success.

There must also be some degree of labour market flexibility, though one needs to be very careful with that term "flexibility". If flexibility simply means that employers have the right to fire workers at will and set whatever wage they wish, the result may be low unemployment but also very low wages and chronic job insecurity. The best kind of "labour market flexibility" is that which allows workers to move easily into new and better jobs. Lifelong education and training systems are necessary in this regard, but so are good systems of transportation so that workers can easily commute to new jobs, and also insurance schemes to cover the cost of moving from one location to another.

The goal of decent work also depends on continuing efforts to integrate the global economy in ways that generate better jobs for more people, while not imposing inordinate burdens on a few. In this connection, let us hope that what occurred on 11 September 2001 does not cause nations to seek to withdraw from the rest of the world, tightly protect their borders, cut back on immigration, or erect other barriers to trade and investment.

The experience of the United States is instructive, and disturbing. Even during 1999 and 2000, when the American economy was soaring, a number of polls asked Americans whether they believed global integration was good, whether further liberalization of trade and immigration were in the best interest of the United States. A significant number of those polled – in some polls a majority – said no. In follow-up interviews they expressed fear of further global integration.

Where did this fear come from? In 1999 and 2000, unemployment in the United States reached its lowest level in 30 years. Indeed, the American economy between 1993 and the year 2000 generated a record number of net new jobs – 23 million.

The fear stemmed not so much from a fear of being unemployed for a long period of time as from fear of losing one's income, one's livelihood. If one lost a job, it was relatively easy to find a new one. But there was a high likelihood that the new job would pay less than the old. The rate of job loss remained higher through the 1990s than it had been in the 1980s, and the median wage hardly increased at all. Americans lacking any formal education beyond the age of 17 or 18 were particularly hard hit. They had work, but their jobs paid less and less, and whatever benefits were attached to those jobs at the start of the decade were likely to have disappeared by the end.

It was easy for many Americans to blame trade and immigration for this. Yet technology has been at least as great a cause of job loss and earnings insecurity. Many jobs became obsolete or lost value because of new technologies. If people do not have the right education and skills, they are likely to lose ground in the new economy. Even if a country were to erect a wall around itself and secede from the global economy – a step which I do not recommend, by the way – many jobs would still disappear, and the people who once performed them would be likely to find themselves in new jobs paying less than the old, especially if they lack the skills for the new. Just look at what happened to elevator operators, to many routine manufacturing jobs, garage attendants, gas station attendants, telephone operators, bank tellers, and so on.

Nevertheless, globalization is an easy target. In order to avoid a backlash against globalization, we must understand that decent work – that is, a decently paying job with some degree of job or wage security attached to it – is an important condition for achieving a political consensus in favour of opening national borders.

GLOBAL SOCIAL JUSTICE, TRADE AND LABOUR STANDARDS

The events of 11 September 2001 should also remind us of another aspect of globalization. In raising this final point, I do not want to be understood to justify terrorism. There is no justification for what occurred on that day. But I think it is very important for the advanced industrialized countries to acknowledge the context in which terrorism thrives, the soil in which violence takes root, and the circumstances in which demagogues can find a following. I am referring to global poverty and the widening gap between the global "have mores" and the global "have lesses".

Over the past 30 years, the global economy has grown by an average of 2.3 per cent a year. That is a respectable rate of growth. Yet, over the same three decades, the gap between the richest and poorest countries has widened tenfold. And far greater numbers of people are living in abject poverty, some barely managing to have enough food for themselves and their families.

Certain steps must be taken. A globally coordinated move toward expansionary fiscal and monetary policies constitutes one small piece of the puzzle. An expanding global economy can help poorer countries move upward. It is also important that the advanced industrialized countries provide debt relief to poorer countries now struggling under a great debt load. I understand the worries about "moral hazard" – that is, that debt relief will necessarily cause some debtors and creditors to take risks in the future on the assumption that governments will bail them out eventually. But such a concern must be balanced against the significant human cost of this debt load. The steps that developed countries have already taken in regard to debt relief are commendable, but not nearly adequate.

In addition, developed countries should open their borders to agricultural products coming from developing countries. When Europe, Japan and the United States subsidize or otherwise protect their farmers, they make it difficult for people in developing countries to gain their first foothold on the ladder to decent work. This is, of course, a difficult political question in the industrialized countries. Given the distribution of political power, farmers and agricultural interests are disproportionately represented. And yet, we must understand that farm subsidies and protections have a direct negative impact on developing countries that depend on agricultural exports for decent work.

The same is true of the barriers advanced industrialized countries impose on the export of textiles, steel and other commodities from poor countries. Efforts by advanced countries to bar imports of goods produced in developing countries under the pretext of "unfair competition", must also be understood to impoverish many workers in developing countries. "Anti-dumping" laws are politically popular in the United States, especially among middle- and lower-middle-income blue-collar workers who are understandably fearful that they will lose their jobs and their livelihoods if lower-cost commodities are allowed in from developing countries. But there is no internationally agreed definition of a "dumped" good. In the United States, a good is called "dumped" if it is sold in the United States at less than "fair market value". But again, there is no internationally agreed definition of what fair market value is. Consumers have a different word to describe "dumped" goods: they call them "bargains".

I am an advocate of labour standards. As Secretary of Labor of the United States, I addressed the International Labour Conference on the importance of all countries adhering to core labour standards barring forced labour, slave labour and the employment of young children, insisting that all countries respect freedom of association so that workers may form unions. But we also must understand that other labour standards, involving wages and working conditions, cannot be applied uniformly because not all countries are rich enough and sufficiently developed to apply them.

Wages and working conditions are expected to improve as a country becomes wealthier. Such "developmental" standards must therefore not be used as back doors to protectionism, whereby rich countries prevent poor countries from exporting their production to them. In other words, developmental standards must be variable, appropriate to a country's stage of development.

For example, rather than consider a fixed minimum wage that would be applicable around the world, a more useful approach might be to ask that all countries strive for a minimum wage between 40 and 50 per cent of the value of their national median wage. Such a standard would not only respect differences among countries' capacities to pay their workers, it would also acknowledge that the world community has an interest in the development of strong middle classes to which the poor in every country can aspire.

We all have a stake in widening the circles of prosperity within every country in terms of democratic stability and social justice – and this includes the United States, where the minimum wage has declined as a percentage of the median. Indeed, the United States has a serious problem of widening inequality: it has the most unequal distribution of earnings and wealth of all the advanced industrialized countries. The gap between the have-mores and the have-lesses is wider in the United States now than it has ever been since the 1920s.

Many readers may already have been in agreement with the points I have made. Yet there is some utility in reaffirming that the ideas and ideals for which they have worked so hard continue to be worth fighting for: I know that the fight can sometimes be lonely. To be an agent of change, to be an advocate for what may not be popular but what, over the long term, must be done, can be a difficult job. Many will understand how critically important it is to fight for decent work that gives people the possibility for better lives.

There is no silver lining to what happened on 11 September 2001. But I do know that the only way terrorism wins is if we collaborate psychologically with it, if we give in to the impulses that terrorism tries to generate. If we fight for fuller employment and economic justice, for better jobs, decent work, and fight against poverty, we will be fighting the circumstances in which terrorism can flourish.

SOCIAL EXCLUSION AND SOCIAL SOLIDARITY: THREE PARADIGMS

6

Hilary SILVER *

> The changes affecting the poor were changes in kind as well as degree, in quantity, in ideas, attitudes, beliefs, perceptions, values. They were changes in what may be called the "moral imagination". (Gertrude Himmelfarb, referring to England circa 1760, in *The idea of poverty: England in the early industrial age*, pp. 18-19.)

Since the mid-1970s, the advanced capitalist democracies have been undergoing a process of profound economic restructuring. As a consequence, new social problems have emerged that appear to challenge the assumptions underlying Western welfare states. While universal social policies still insure against risks predictable from a shared life-cycle, career pattern, and family structure, a standardized life course can no longer be assumed. More and more people suffer insecurity, are dependent upon "residual" means-tested programmes, or are without any form of social protection. In the countries of the European Union, 50 million people live below a poverty line set at one-half the national median income; 16 million people (10.5 per cent of the workforce) are officially registered as unemployed, of whom more than half have been unemployed for over a year (EC Commission, 1994).

How are we to understand these developments? As Himmelfarb noted, earlier economic and social upheavals brought about a shift in the "moral imagination", giving us the concepts of "poverty" and "unemployment". Similarly, today's transformations are giving rise to new conceptions of social disadvantage: the "underclass", the "new poverty", and "social exclusion". This article traces the evolution of the term "exclusion" over time, notably but not exclusively in France. It focuses on definitions of the term indicating its numerous connotations, and distinguishes three paradigms within which social exclusion is embedded (solidarity, specialization and monopoly), presenting the theory underlying each, with clarificatory remarks. Finally,

---

Originally published in *International Labour Review*, Vol. 133, 1994/5-6.

* Department of Sociology, Brown University, USA. This article is based on a longer discussion paper with the same title, prepared in 1994 for the Labour Institutions and Economic Development Programme of the ILO's International Institute for Labour Studies.

the economic dimensions of the three paradigms are discussed. In conclusion, questions regarding the significance of exclusion in politics and social policy are raised.

THE EXCLUSION DISCOURSE

Exclusion became the subject of debate in France during the 1960s. Politicians, activists, officials, journalists and academics made vague and ideological references to the poor as *les exclus* (e.g. Klanfer, 1965). However, the exclusion discourse did not become widespread until the economic crisis. As successive social and political crises erupted in France during the 1980s, exclusion came to be applied to more and more types of social disadvantage (Paugam, 1993; Nasse, 1992) and the continual redefinition of the term to encompass new social groups and problems gave rise to its diffuse connotations.

The identification of exclusion as a social problem occurred just as France was belatedly completing its system of standard social provision and as postwar economic growth was slowing down. The coining of the term is generally attributed to René Lenoir (1974), who was then Secretary of State for Social Action in the (Gaullist) Chirac Government. He estimated that "the excluded" made up one-tenth of the French population: the mentally and the physically handicapped, suicidal people, aged invalids, abused children, drug addicts, delinquents, single parents, multi-problem households, marginal, asocial persons, and other "social misfits". All were social categories unprotected under social insurance. Since the mid-1970s, France has introduced numerous policies designed explicitly to combat exclusion of these sorts so that today, the handicapped and single mothers, for example, tend to fall outside both the rhetoric of exclusion and the purview of commissions on "integration" and "insertion".

During the 1970s, the French Left also began to distinguish between objective and subjective exclusion. The latter, drawing upon the existentialism of Jean-Paul Sartre and the participatory ideology of Catholic social action, referred to alienation and the loss of personal autonomy under advanced capitalism. In stressing subjective exclusion, the discourse moved away from political expressions of class conflict towards the struggles of mass urban and social movements. Exclusion meant being treated as an object – a condition which could apply to virtually any individual or group (Verdes-Leroux, 1978).

If exclusion and "insertion" were used as ideological terms during the 1970s (Paugam, 1993), economic recovery from the oil crisis soon made it clear to the public that some were being excluded from economic growth. As Lionel Stoléru (1977) observed, poverty was a problem that economic growth could not resolve. Thus, during the late 1970s, the excluded referred to "the ones that economic growth forgot" (Donzelot and Roman, 1991). By the early 1980s, the use of the term "insertion" in political discourse shifted from a focus on the handicapped to young people leaving school without the adequate skills to obtain a job (Paugam, 1993). Bertrand Schwartz, who wrote a report, *L'insertion professionnelle et sociale des jeunes*, for Prime Minister Pierre Mauroy in 1981, headed a new policy for locally based programmes for the "insertion" of young people into employment. Over the next decade and a half, and after street demonstrations by young people protesting against reforms of church schools and education (1984), universities (late 1986), and minimum wages (1994), the State instituted a wide variety of "insertion" policies to help young people in difficulty.

By the mid-1980s, both the Right and the Communist opposition were blaming the Socialist Government for rising unemployment and what was being called "the new poverty" (Paugam, 1993). In symbolic politics, the power to name a social problem has vast implications for the policies considered suitable to address it. Thus, in response to the opposition's emphasis on the new poverty and inequality, the Government took to speaking of "exclusion". The term referred not only to the rise in long-term and recurrent unemployment, but also to the growing instability of social bonds: family instability, single-member households, social isolation, and the decline of class solidarity based on unions, the labour market, and the working-class neighbourhood and social networks. There were not only material but also spiritual and symbolic aspects to this phenomenon. As I will show, this exclusion discourse drew upon the rich Republican rhetorical tradition of France to describe the difficulty of establishing solidarity between individuals and groups and the larger society. The prototypical definitions of social exclusion can be found in the publications of the Commissariat Général du Plan (CGP) [general planning commission] which has recognized the State's responsibility to nourish "social cohesion" (Fragonard, 1993). The current Planning Commissioner, Jean-Baptiste de Foucauld (1992a, b), argues that preventing exclusion requires a conception of social justice different from the one underlying the postwar social consensus which simply insured the population against predictable risks. The welfare state must bind itself to the ethical and cultural values that define citizenship not only in the form of rights, but as a particular relation to "the other". A more personalized, participatory welfare state should rest on new principles of social cohesion, sharing, and integration. This new citizenship "enables us to reconcile our tradition of solidarity with the rise of individualism" (pp. 264-265). In another CGP account (Nasse, 1992), exclusion is used as a metaphor for the "social polyphony of postmodern society", for the lack of communication between individuals and groups or for their mutual incomprehension which prevent them from negotiating on mutual recognition and a sense of belonging.

The long review by Martine Xiberras (1993) of the sociological literature upon which this diagnosis was based defined exclusion as the result of a gradual breakdown of the social and symbolic bonds – economic, institutional, and individually significant – that normally tie the individual to society.

Exclusion entails a risk for each individual in terms of material and symbolic exchange with the larger society. In the terms of Durkheimian rhetoric, exclusion threatens society as whole with the loss of collective values and the destruction of the social fabric.

So in this particular case, integration means solidarity, that is, the ability to re-establish mutual recognition by all parties in society. For the regulating State, this would mean the ability to handle the expression of a multitude of beliefs and values (Xiberras, 1993, p. 196).

The emphasis on "insertion" and integration as the appropriate responses to exclusion is reflected in the titles of a wide variety of new social programmes introduced in France during the 1980s. For example, the social activists who advocated the *revenu minimum d'insertion* (RMI) [minimum income for social integration] adopted the Republican rhetoric of "solidarity", "cohesion", "social bonds", and a "new social contract" in Jean-Jacques Rousseau's sense. One analyst, after claiming to strip away the multiple and ideological meanings of "insertion", then went on to define it as a form of regulation of the social bond and a response to a perceived threat to social cohesion (Paugam, 1993). The discourse was so compelling that, by the 1988 presidential campaign, the electoral manifestos of both Right and Left included proposals for a minimum income to promote "insertion".

However, subsequent political crises served to expand the meanings of exclusion and "insertion". Since in Republican France the Nation and the State are one, *les exclus* came to mean the "pariahs of the nation", in the words of Paul-Marie de la Gorce. Political and social developments in the 1980s in which the term exclusion came to acquire further nuances of meaning include the rise of xenophobia, open political attacks on immigrants and restrictions on their rights; the consequent emergence of new anti-racist movements like SOS-Racisme and France-Plus, which mobilized mass demonstrations; and the ongoing public debate about integration and Republican values occasioned by some Muslim girls wearing headscarves at their state, non-denominational schools. In January 1990 came the establishment of the Secrétariat Général à l'Intégration [general secretariat for integration], an indication of the sense of crisis in French Republican values.

Finally, exclusion encompassed the issue of the *banlieues,* the deprived outer suburbs. It became possible to associate the related rhetorics of integration of immigrants, youth problems, and economic exclusion in a spatial sense after a series of violent incidents in suburban housing estates during the 1980s and early 1990s. Residents of these deprived suburbs were increasingly described as "excluded". Through ongoing state decentralization and reform of social and housing services, policies to combat juvenile delinquency, the neighbourhood social development programme (DSQ), and the creation in 1991 of a fully-fledged Ministry for Urban Affairs, the State sought to combat "urban exclusion" (see Linhart, 1992). Again, programmes were couched in Republican terms: *prêts locatifs aidés d'insertion* [housing loans to assist integration], *fonds de solidarité logement* [solidarity housing funds], and *programme développement-solidarité* [solidarity and development programme], to name but a few.

From France, the discourse of exclusion rapidly spread across the rest of Europe. In 1989, the Council of Ministers of Social Affairs of the then European Community passed a resolution to fight "social exclusion" and to foster integration and a "Europe of Solidarity". The European Commission's 1994 White Paper, *Growth, competitiveness, employment*, called for fighting exclusion and "the poverty which so degrades men and women and splits society in two". Today, Denmark, Germany, Italy, Portugal, France and Belgium in particular, have introduced new institutions to take action on social exclusion (Kronauer, 1993; Kronauer, Vogel, and Gerlach, 1993; Yépez del Castillo, 1993; EC Commission, 1994, 1992, 1991; Room et al., 1992, p. 32; Carton, 1993).

US President Clinton himself took up the rhetoric of exclusion in late 1993 when, speaking of inner city problems, he remarked, "It's not an underclass any more. It's an outer class." But an attentive ear discerns some differences of meaning across the Atlantic. In October 1994, the President remarked, "to rebuild a society that has been pressured both in our inner cities [and] our isolated rural areas is going to take a concerted effort that starts with parents, churches and community groups and private business people and people at the local level. The Federal Government cannot be the salvation of that. We have to rebuild the bonds of society."

Defining exclusion

Given the varied usages of the term, one might justifiably ask what precisely is meant by exclusion? The remainder of this paper seeks to answer this question by distinguishing three paradigms within which the notion of exclusion is embedded.

By all accounts, defining exclusion is not an easy task. One European Union document conceded that "it is difficult to come up with a simple definition" (EC Commission, 1992, p. 10). Similarly, a recent review of sociological theories of exclusion concluded:

In fact, observers agree on only one point: the impossibility of having a single, simple criterion with which to define exclusion. The numerous surveys and reports on exclusion all reveal the profound helplessness of the experts and responsible officials (Weinberg and Ruano-Borbalan, 1993).

Indeed, the CGP in France, although responsible for designing and evaluating policies to combat exclusion, also recognized how difficult it is to define the term and to synthesize existing theories (Nasse, 1992). The CGP'S Commission on Social Cohesion and the Prevention of Exclusion concluded that:

Every attempt at establishing typology is inevitably reductionist, and all the more so in cases of excluded population groups or those facing exclusion. The factors bringing about exclusion – whether originating in individual, family or socio-economic circumstances – are numerous, fluctuate and interact in such a way that, often, they end up by reinforcing each other (Fragonard, 1993).

Thus, exclusion appears to be a vague term (Mongin, 1992, p. 8), loaded with numerous economic, social, political, and cultural connotations and dimensions. Despite attempts at official definitions,

... in the end, the notion of exclusion is permeated with both sense and nonsense and is liable to misinterpretation; after all the concept can be made to express pretty well anything, including even the pique of someone who cannot get everything he wants (Julien Freund, in Xiberras, 1993, p. 11).

Clearly, the expression is so evocative, ambiguous, multidimensional and elastic that it can be defined in many different ways.

Yet the difficulty of defining exclusion and the fact that it is interpreted differently according to context and time also can be seen as an opportunity. The discourse of exclusion may serve as a window through which to view political cultures. This paper argues that exclusion is polysemic, i.e. it has multiple meanings and therefore requires extensive semantic definition (Riggs, 1988). The different meanings of social exclusion and the uses to which the term is put are embedded in conflicting social science paradigms and political ideologies.

Thomas Kuhn describes a paradigm as "a constellation of beliefs, values, techniques and so on shared by the members of a given community" (1970, p. 175).[1] Paradigms "specify not only what sorts of entities the universe does contain but also, by implication, those that it does not" (p. 7). In effect, they are ontologies that render reality comprehensible and that mingle elements of what "is" and what "ought to be". When paradigms conflict, practitioners speak from incommensurable viewpoints using the same language to mean different things.

In what follows, I introduce three paradigms of social exclusion and indicate how each accounts for economic disadvantages like poverty and long-term unemployment.

Exclusion in French Republicanism

Whereas poverty and inequality have become accepted concepts in social science, it is more accurate to consider the term "exclusion" as a "keyword", in Raymond Williams' sense (1985), in French Republican discourse. It not only originated in France, but is deeply anchored in a particular interpretation of French revolutionary history and Republican thought. From this perspective, "exclusion" is conceived not simply as an economic or political phenomenon, but as a deficiency of "solidarity", a break in the social fabric (CGP, 1992).

The moral discourse of "social solidarity" rejected both liberal individualism[2] and political representation (or citizenship) as sufficient bases for defining social integration. Rather, it sought a "third way" that would reconcile individual rights with state responsibility and socialist rejection of exploitation (Procacci, 1993; Ruano-Borbalan, 1993; Berstein and Rudelle, 1992). The concept of "poverty" which originated in the United Kingdom was discredited in France by its association with Christian charity, the *ancien régime,* and utilitarian liberalism. Socialists incorporated "poverty" into the broader category of "inequality", making it a labour issue. Republicans, however, rejected both liberal individualism and socialism in favour of the distinctively "social" idea of "solidarity", which legitimized the Third Republic.

Seeing the State as the embodiment of the General Will of the Nation and the moral duties of citizens, Republican solidarity justified the establishment of public institutions to further social integration. Under that banner, French "social policies became parts of a more general rationalization of collective authority" (Ashford, p. 48). In France, social security did not result from working-class struggles or from the overwhelming rise in poverty and urban misery, as it did in the United Kingdom (Hatzfeld, 1971). Rather, social reform expressed the perfection of Republican democracy and the collective responsibility for any citizen suffering from the failures of the State. The idea of social solidarity allowed the State to assume responsibility for social aid. In the Revolutionary rhetoric, equality meant that the Republic must promise citizens subsistence or assure them a right to work. In return, assisted citizens have a duty to work and to participate in public life.

Solidarity mingled notions of Catholic charity with Revolutionary rhetoric on fraternity and nineteenth-century working-class mutual aid. In contrast to traditional Christian charity, solidarity had a philanthropic or humanist element based on compassion, equality, and a more secular morality. Coined by Pierre Leroux and propagated by Léon Bourgeois, the term solidarity was more humanist than it was organic in its reconciliation of the feeling of belonging to the collectivity with the demand for individual fulfilment. Thus, solidarity had both a subjective aspect in individual experience, borrowed from liberalism, and an objective component, grounded in socialism and expressed in principles of social and political organization. The mutual aid movement contributed the notion that solidarity comes from the society, justifying social protection policies. From the sentimental vision of the social bond as sympathy, solidarity developed into a logical, secular moral system of rights and duties underlying future social policies. The work of Emile Durkheim was "the climax of a long intellectual struggle to demonstrate the interdependence of social solidarity" (Chevallier et al., 1992, p. 39).

Indeed, reconciling the needs of State and society was a constant preoccupation of nineteenth-century French political philosophers (Ashford, 1986). Since that time, the Republic sought to create a "social bond" (*lien social*) with the poor, a bond which is central to the Republican concept of solidarity. In Revolutionary thought, the social bond created a "quasi-contract uniting the individual to the species and to the collectivity of his peers" (see Berstein and Rudelle, 1992, p. 193). Rousseau, who coined the term *lien social* in Chapter 5 of the *Manuscrit de Genève,* saw the social bond as natural and, hence, communitarian. The Law and the General Will would bring about a distinctively "social" conviviality that went beyond formal, civil or legal equality (Farrugia, 1993). As Rousseau argued in *The social contract,* the State is composed "of morality, of custom, above all, of public opinion". Over time, Republican solidarity came to encompass cultural as well as political criteria of citizenship (Nicolet, 1982; Berstein and Rudelle, 1992; Roy, 1991).

Indeed, the State defends the superior interests of the Nation – the General Will – over those of the communes and ethnic groups (Nicolet, 1982). According to Republican values, *les mœurs républicaines,* individual citizens are less bearers of rights than participants in a communal civil life, a public life of fraternity (Rosanvallon, 1992). Such moral unity and equality demanded abolition of feudal representative bodies that competed with the State for citizens' loyalty and in fact oppressed individuals. Throughout the nineteenth century, the laws on association were a major preoccupation in France until the passage in 1901 of the law on associations which created public bodies that shared the legal and moral authority of the State in return for registering and then submitting to state regulation (Ashford, 1986). The law officially recognized religious and voluntary associations partly in order to control and relegate them to the private sphere. Whereas social integration under the old regime rested on the Estates *(les états),* the State *(l'Etat)* became the new basis for social integration (Nicolet, 1982). This "Jacobin" State – strong, unitary, centralized, egalitarian, universalist, and secular – actively sought to assimilate regional, national, and religious cultures into a single, distinctive conception of citizenship and national civilization. The State incorporated mediating institutions in order to reconcile and synthesize separate interests and memberships (Rosanvallon, 1992).

The term "social bond" is most fully discussed in Durkheim's *Division of labour in society* where the term "solidarity" specified two sorts of social bond, the organic and the mechanical, that morally regulated individual behaviour. Solidarity referred to distinctively "social" relations, in contrast to political or market relations. Thus, Durkheim rejected liberal, individualist, utilitarian, or "Anglo-Saxon" notions of the social contract, in which social relations are economically motivated, commercial, and competitive, the State is minimal, and interested free exchange and cultural and political pluralism are valued (Farrugia, 1993).

Three paradigms

In contrast with these distinctive French Republican conceptions, challenges to Republican ideology and the adoption of exclusion discourse in other

Table 1. Three paradigms of social exclusion

	Solidarity	Specialization	Monopoly
Conception of integration	Group solidarity/ cultural boundaries	Specialization/ separate spheres/ interdependence	Monopoly/social closure
Source of integration	Moral integration	Exchange	Citizenship rights
Ideology	Republicanism	Liberalism	Social democracy
Discourse	Exclusion	Discrimination, underclass	New poverty, inequality, underclass
Seminal thinkers	Rousseau, Durkheim	Locke, Madison, utilitarians	Marx, Weber, Marshall
Exemplars	de Foucauld	Stoléru, Lenoir	Room
	Xiberras	Shklar	Townsend
	Schnapper	Allport, pluralism	Balibar, Silverman
	Costa-Lascoux	Chicago School	
	Douglas, Mead	Murray	Gobelot, Bourdieu
Model of the new political economy	Flexible production	Skills	Labour market segmentation
		Work disincentives	
		Networks	
		Social capital	

national contexts imparted meanings to the term more properly considered within other paradigms of social disadvantage. For example, liberal reconstructions of exclusion concentrate on various forms of discrimination, isolation, and the cross-cutting or cumulative personal characteristics of excluded individuals which are often generalized into the idea of an "underclass". The European Union increasingly uses an evolving, social democratic notion of exclusion based on T.H. Marshall's idea of social citizenship, recementing the term to notions of inequality and the discourse of social rights.

For this reason, the threefold typology of the multiple meanings of exclusion presented here distinguishes between different theoretical perspectives, political ideologies, and national discourses (see table 1). Based on different notions of social integration, I call these types the *solidarity*, *specialization*, and *monopoly* paradigms. Each paradigm attributes exclusion to a different cause and is grounded in a different political philosophy: Republicanism, liberalism, and social democracy. Each provides an explanation of multiple forms of social disadvantage – economic, social, political, and cultural – and thus encompasses theories of citizenship and racial-ethnic inequality as well as poverty and long-term unemployment. All three paradigms are cast into relief when contrasted with conservative notions that present social integration in organic, racial, or corporatist terms and with neo-Marxist conceptions of the capitalist social order which deny the possibility of social integration to begin with.

Exclusion not only varies in meaning according to national and ideological contexts. Another reason it is difficult to define is that the empirical referents of the idea of exclusion are not always discussed in that terminology. The concept – if often conflated with the new poverty and inequality, discrimination and the underclass – is also expressed in such terms as superfluity, irrelevance, marginality, foreignness, alterity, closure, disaffiliation, dispossession, deprivation, and destitution. This means that exclusion must also be analysed "onomasiologically", defining the same concept with reference to more than one term (Riggs, 1988). Identifying the many synonyms of exclusion makes it possible to delimit the term conceptually and empirically.

The multiple, often contradictory, connotations and synonyms of exclusion transform it into an "essentially contested concept", in that the proper use of it "inevitably involves endless disputes" (Gallie, 1956). Essentially contested concepts are usually appraisive, complex, open in meaning, and explicable in terms of their parts, so that selecting from among the mutually exclusive meanings of exclusion necessarily entails the adoption of particular values and world views. Prior to recasting social exclusion as a general phenomenon or a scientific concept transcending national and political contexts, the values underlying its usage should be made explicit in order to clarify the implicit objectives of anti-exclusion policies.

Indeed, the use of the term exclusion to denote the changing nature of social disadvantage in the West may have important political implications. On the one hand, by highlighting the generalized nature of the problem, the idea of exclusion could be useful in building new broad-based coalitions to reform European welfare states. On the other hand, exclusion discourse may also ghettoize risk categories under a new label and publicize the more spectacular forms of cumulative disadvantage, distracting attention from the general rise in inequality, unemployment, and family dissolution that is affecting all social classes. In fact, by recasting the rationale for social solidarity, it may inadvertently undermine consensual support for older welfare state schemes, much as distinguishing the unemployed from the poor created two-tiered welfare states in the United Kingdom and the United States. Thus, just as the idea of exclusion reflects different notions of social integration, solidarity, and citizenship, it can also serve a variety of political purposes.

Exclusion and integration

Those unfamiliar with the term exclusion often ask the question "exclusion from what?" since virtually any social distinction or affiliation excludes somebody. In the United States, for example, the term calls to mind exclusionary immigration policy, exclusionary zoning, and exclusionary social clubs. But, by comparison with France, the English-speaking countries use the rhetoric of exclusion relatively rarely. Yet consider just a few of the things the literature says people may be excluded from: a livelihood; secure, permanent employment; earnings; property, credit, or land; housing; the minimal or prevailing consumption level; education, skills, and cultural capital; the benefits provided by the welfare state; citizenship and equality before the law; participation in the democratic process; public goods; the nation or the dominant race; the family and sociability; humane treatment, respect, personal fulfilment, understanding.

At the heart of the question "exclusion from what?" lies a more basic one, the problem of social order during times of profound social change in society.[3] Just as the ideas of poverty and unemployment emerged from the great transformations of earlier centuries as did the first sociological accounts of social order to address them, so under contemporary conditions the notion of exclusion calls for an account of social inclusion. In this case, theories of "insertion", "integration", "citizenship", or "solidarity" provide points of reference, making it possible to identify three paradigmatic approaches to exclusion: solidarity, specialization, and monopoly.

Solidarity

In French Republican thought, as mentioned, exclusion occurs when the social bond between the individual and society known as social solidarity breaks down. Adumbrated by Rousseau and exemplified by Durkheimian sociology, the "social" order is conceived as external, moral, and normative, rather than grounded in individual, group, or class interests. A national consensus, collective conscience, or general will ties the individual to the larger society through vertically interrelated mediating institutions. The approach lays heavy emphasis on the ways in which cultural or moral boundaries between groups socially construct dualistic categories for ordering the world.

Like deviance or anomie, exclusion both threatens and reinforces social cohesion. The inverse of exclusion is thus "integration" and the process of attaining it, "insertion".[4] In a Durkheimian sense, this implies assimilation into the dominant culture; however, most recent uses of the term are postmodernist in that they incorporate multicultural notions about how the basis of solidarity is reconfigured, as the dominant culture adjusts to the minority culture as well as the reverse (Haut Conseil à l'Intégration, 1992, 1991).

This paradigm draws heavily on anthropology, sociology, ethnography, and cultural studies generally. It focuses attention on the exclusion inherent in the solidarity of nation, race, ethnicity, locality, and other cultural or primordial ties that delimit boundaries between groups. Yet applications go beyond analyses of Republican citizenship, ethnic conflicts, and deviance to include discussion of cultures of poverty and long-term unemployment and of trends toward "flexible specialization" in political economy.

Specialization

In Anglo-American liberalism, exclusion is considered a consequence of *specialization*: of social differentiation, the economic division of labour, and the separation of spheres. It assumes that individuals differ, giving rise to specialization in the market and in social groups. It is thus individualist in method, although causation is situated not simply in individual preference but also in the structures created by cooperating and competing individuals – markets, associations, and the like. Liberalism thus conceives of the social order, like the economy and politics, as networks of voluntary exchanges between autonomous individuals with their own interests and motivations.

Specialized social structures are comprised of separate, competing, but not necessarily unequal spheres, which leads to exchange and interdependence between them. Social groups are voluntarily constituted by their members, and shifting alliances between them reflect their various interests and wishes. This gives rise to cultural and political pluralism. Liberal models of citizenship emphasize the contractual exchange of rights and obligations and the separation of spheres in social life. Thus, exclusion results from an inadequate separation of social spheres, from the application of rules inappropriate to a given sphere, or from barriers to free movement and exchange between spheres.

Because of the existence of separate social spheres, exclusion may have multiple causes and dimensions. The same individual may not be excluded in every sphere. Nor are social spheres and categories necessarily ordered hierarchically in terms of resources or value. Specialization protects liberties and may be efficient, as long as excluded individuals have the right to move across boundaries. Individual freedom of choice based on diverse personal values and psychological motives for engaging in social relations should give rise to cross-cutting group affiliations and loyalties contributing to the integration of society. To the extent that group boundaries impede individual freedom to participate in social exchanges, exclusion is a form of "discrimination". However, group and market competition and the liberal State's protection of individual rights impede the operation of this form of exclusion.

In social science, liberal individualism is often reflected in methodological individualism which treats group characteristics as individual attributes. Liberal individualism underlies neo-classical economics, theories of political pluralism, rational and public choice theories, and mainstream sociology. It encompasses two streams of thought: libertarian or neo-liberalism and social or communitarian liberalism.

Monopoly

Finally, the third paradigm, influential on the European Left, sees exclusion as a consequence of the formation of group monopoly. Drawing heavily on Weber and, to a lesser extent, Marx, it views the social order as coercive, imposed through a set of hierarchical power relations. In this social democratic or conflict theory, exclusion arises from the interplay of class, status, and political power and serves the interests of the included. Social "closure" is achieved when institutions and cultural distinctions not only create boundaries that keep others out against their will, but are also used to perpetuate inequality. Those within delimited social entities enjoy a monopoly over scarce resources. The monopoly creates a bond of common interest between otherwise unequal insiders. The excluded are therefore simultaneously outsiders and dominated. Exclusion is combated through citizenship, and the extension of equal membership and full participation in the community to outsiders.

These processes of social closure are evident in labour market segmentation. The particular boundaries of exclusion may be drawn within or between nation-states, localities, firms, or social groups. Whatever the nature of the boundary, the overlap or coincidence of group distinctions with inequality – "the barrier and the level", to adopt Gobelot's (1925) terms – is at the heart of the *problématique* of this paradigm.

Clarification

A number of remarks are in order, before applying these paradigms to the question of economic exclusion set in the context of these paradigms. The paradigms are, of course, ideal types – in reality, different societies and cultures define "belonging" in their respective ways. For this reason, defining exclusion with reference to its opposite can pose its own problems. This is not simply because social integration necessarily coexists with exclusion, both being relative concepts (Xiberras, 1993, p. 25). If this were the only issue at stake, the relationship between exclusion and integration might seem to be zero-sum, by definition. In fact, only the monopoly paradigm posits that integration makes it easier to exclude others – through greater social control or state power (Touraine, 1992). Rather, the problem with considering the reverse of exclusion is that such a concept implies that a clear political consensus exists within nation-states as to the nature and bases of citizenship, integration, and membership of society.

I wish to argue, on the contrary, that fighting exclusion means different things to different people. Moreover, at various times, national debates have emphasized some aspects of exclusion and not others:

Sometimes the emphasis is on migration and refugees (e.g. Belgium, Germany), sometimes on long-term or extremely long-term unemployment and exclusion from the labour market (e.g. Denmark, France, the Netherlands); or on the problem of low income (Portugal). Discussion is sometimes directly linked to specific policy-making, as is the case with the guaranteed minimum income (France, Spain) or it can be part of a more general consideration of the functions of the welfare state (United Kingdom: Citizens' Charter) or be used in policies discouraging the passivity engendered by certain forms of social protection (Denmark, the Netherlands, United Kingdom). It is sometimes fuelled by campaigns run by associations or the media, which focus on particularly visible problems or those which in any case catch the public eye, such as the homeless (France, United Kingdom), drugs (Italy), child labour (Portugal), and inner-city crisis (France) (EC Commission, 1992, p. 32).

Although the cultural embeddedness of the concept of exclusion makes the development of legitimate cross-national indicators more difficult than those of the development of similar indicators for measuring poverty or unemployment, the paradigms do illuminate the reasons underlying the contested and selective meanings of the term. Choosing one definition means accepting the theoretical and ideological "baggage" associated with it.

Second, as is appropriate for a sociological analysis, each of these paradigms presents exclusion as a social relationship between the included and the excluded. That relationship may derive from social action, from the activity of excluding, thereby calling attention to the actors responsible. But does exclusion refer only to a change in the condition of those who were integrated, or can it refer to the constant condition of excluded people who wish to be included? In so far as exclusion is a process, analysts should specify its beginning as well as its end.

Observers who insist that exclusion is only a dynamic process (rather than an identity or a condition) miss the structural outcome of the process.[5] The institutionalization of exclusion may create a social boundary or a permanent division between the "ins" and the "outs". It may take the form of social distancing over time or of social distance at any one point in time. The action of exclusion becomes structural when it is repeatedly confirmed through social relations and practices. Turnover among the individuals who are excluded does not alter the structural existence of the social boundary. Indeed, its social reality is confirmed when movement across the boundary provokes reactions like distancing, fear, or new legal barriers. Collective reactions like these properly belong in any study of exclusion. To be sure, the excluded themselves need not constitute a social group with common consciousness, goals and activities. In fact, the very differentiation and isolation of the excluded may be responsible for their collective inability to demand inclusion on their own. In this respect, as in others, social exclusion can also be a condition.

Nevertheless, exclusion should not be confused with social differentiation *per se*. If the existence of social groups necessarily implies the existence of boundaries, it is less clear that every difference or distinction implies exclusion. Exclusion may be based on virtually any social difference, but the extent to which differences produce exclusion depends on such issues as the permeability of boundaries, the extent to which membership is freely chosen, and whether, as in John Rawls's principle of difference or Adam Smith's division of labour, distinctions have any social benefits (Wolfe, 1992). Indeed, some marginal or deviant individuals may not want to be included; they can deliberately choose to be social drop-outs (Room, 1992; Xiberras, 1993). These issues should be explored rather than defined out of the scope of scrutiny.

Third, exclusion can be viewed macro-sociologically or micro-sociologically. Achille Weinberg and Jean-Claude Ruano-Borbalan (1993) distinguish between macro and micro causes in contrasting exclusion from "above" and "below". "Top-down" perspectives may view exclusion as an employment crisis, or as a crisis of ineffective immigration and social policies, or as a crisis in the integrative social institutions of the nation generally. They emphasize macro-sociological phenomenona like modernity, cosmopolitanism, and individualism, or increasingly global, mobile labour markets, and technological innovation. In contrast, local and communitarian "grass-roots" perspectives cast exclusion as a crisis of community solidarity and social regulation, with micro-sociological processes of assimilation, downward mobility, or social isolation as a person is gradually excluded from a job and other social relations.

Fourth, the distinctions between paradigms should not be confused with institutional classifications, like types of welfare state. Institutions are historical accretions that bear the imprint of past conflicts between ideologies and paradigms. To say, for example, that the French Republic institutionalized Republican ideas implies that during a given period of institution-building a popular coalition was formed around a particular ideological consensus. However, other coalitions contested these ideas and, to the extent that they too had influence, the law, the welfare state, and other social institutions incorporated their different ideas as well.

Fifth, all three paradigms must be distinguished from organic approaches to social integration. The solidarity, specialization, and monopoly paradigms of social integration fall within the spectrum of mainstream sociological thought which attributes greater scope and autonomy to civil society relative to the State and market than do other paradigms. Indeed, the discipline of sociology (and its central concern with integration) developed to provide an alternative explanation of the social changes brought about by the democratic and industrial revolutions to those offered by utilitarian liberalism and socialism, as well as reactionary thought. However, where democracy and industrialization came late, as in Germany, Italy, the Iberian Peninsula, and many less developed countries, other less sociological conceptions of social integration took hold. In some places, traditional conservative, pre-industrial, and corporatist notions of integration degenerated into justifications of authoritarianism and fascism. In the postwar era in particular, Christian Democracy and societal corporatism tempered organicist thought with a recognition of individual rights and tolerance of ideological and religious rivals. Indeed, some analysts classify France in this category, merging Republican ideology with Christian Democratic or neo-corporatist thought (Esping-Andersen, 1991). Finally, some "plural societies" developed a form of stable consociational democracy in which élites compromise and check one another's power on behalf of distinct social segments. These alternative notions of social integration took hold in both European and Third World contexts.

Organic models of social integration are often contrasted with liberal and Marxist paradigms, whose pitfalls – extreme individualism or extreme collectivism – they seek to avoid. Yet, like those paradigms, organic models are empirical, normative, and methodological; they describe social reality, provide conceptions of what a good society should be, and offer a selective strategy of analysis (Stepan, 1978; Lijphart, 1977). Although organicism is often considered conservative, these paradigms may in fact call for state intervention to restructure the established society and institute changes in the pursuit of social justice. Thus, organicism and Catholicism in a context of entrenched privilege may actually be radical.

What most distinguishes organic approaches is less their politically con-servative or centrist tendencies than their seeking to construct a social order based on groups, be they functional, regional, or primordial (on ethnic, reli-gious or linguistic bases). Within this broad range of thought, three streams can be identified: Christian Democratic (societal or neo-corporatist); state corporatist; and consociational. Although they differ in the emphasis they accord to individual rights and group autonomy, all reflect to some degree the principles of "community" and "subsidiarity".

The vision of a harmonious community is classically expressed in Leo XIII's encyclical, *Rerum Novarum* (1891), in which it is denied that class conflict is necessary. Liberalism and capitalism encourage class struggle because of insufficient state intervention, while socialism entails an over-reaching of the State into autonomous spheres. Subsidiarity is the term used in Catholic social thought for the notion that "it is an injustice, a grave evil, and a disturbance of right order for a larger and higher organization to arro-gate to itself functions which can be performed efficiently by smaller and lower bodies" (Pius XI, *Quadragesimo Anno*, 1931). While Protestant Reform churches speak of "sovereignty in one's own circle", thereby empha-sizing the separate and exclusive (if limited) responsibility of the individual and small group, the Catholic formulation stresses "the inclusion of these small units of society in greater wholes, within which, however, they have a sphere of autonomy on which they have a right to insist. The responsibility for what can be done at lower levels must not be allowed to gravitate to the top" (Fogarty, 1957, p. 41).

Christian principles of social integration imply a particular perspective on the issue of exclusion. On the one hand, the State has the responsibility to ensure personal development and thus social, political, and civil rights for all. On the other hand, the inequality inherent in horizontal pluralism is also jus-tified. Thus, if the pre-labour-commodification "corporatist-statist legacy" – feudal paternalism, patronage, and clientelism; corporativism of cities, guilds, and friendly societies; and Bismarckian statism – justified the earliest welfare states, it also shaped the tendency of Christian Democratic welfare states to preserve differentials between social classes, occupations, and sta-tus groups as well as to support the traditional family (Esping-Andersen, 1991). Thus, this paradigm recognizes the exclusion of those not organically integrated into the various smaller, autonomous units of society that make up the greater whole – families, communities, classes, nation-states, and so on – but is less cognizant of gender and economic inequality as causes of exclusion.

By contrast, Roman law recognized no individual freedom of association. The only legal organizations were those officially recognized by the State on the basis of *lex specialis*, or "privilege" (Stepan, 1978, p. 38). Thus, the State legitimately shapes the structure of civil society so that functional parts are integrated into an organic whole. In return for a corporate charter, associations have an obligation to the State to perform a public service. In this, organic statism differs from Republicanism. Indeed, in the second preface to *The division of labour in society*, Durkheim rejected state corporatism because controls on worker and other associations made them part of the official administration, restricted meaningful participation, and implied coerced integration rather than integration through the collective conscience.

Several weaknesses in the organic-statist model produce what might be called "social exclusion". First, there is no clear justification for recognizing some groups rather than others. For example, the paradigm privileges functional groups over groups based on primordial (e.g. ethnic, religious, regional, or linguistic) identities, which are thus excluded. Second, it is unclear why vertical functional associations, with élite representatives, are privileged over horizontal, decentralized, participatory and membership organizations, like community groups, which can be considered as excluded. Third, if functional groups are indeed granted autonomy, there is little to prevent some groups – particularly those with the initial hold on power – from gaining control over others, thus undermining the presumption of organic harmony. This inequality in civil society can also produce social exclusion. Finally, while the State's concern with the integration of parts of society can lead to top-down control of functional groupings, undermining their autonomy, dependent States may find it difficult to integrate multinational capital within national corporatist structures. In such a case, workers in the export sector would be "excluded" from bargaining rights.

In sum, unlike liberalism, Christian Democracy is "personalist" rather than individualist and, unlike socialism, is "pluralist" rather than collectivist. Similarly, consociationalism, by checking the power of majorities, guarantees groups the autonomy to run their internal affairs within nation-states. And corporatism (organic statism, to use Stepan's terminology), rests upon official state recognition or "chartering" of mediating associations which are thus centrally coordinated and controlled for the public good, which contrasts strongly with their free, competitive, interest-based operation in liberal pluralism or their suppression under command socialism.

Finally, each paradigm addresses more than one dimension or aspect of exclusion: economic, sociological and interactional, cultural and political. Thus, the paradigms cut across the social sciences. This interdisciplinary approach differs from prior classifications of theories of exclusion, which focus on conditions in one country, usually France, or on one discipline, especially sociology (Nasse, 1992; Xiberras, 1993; Weinberg and Ruano-Borbalan, 1993). Although each paradigm includes theories drawn from economics, political science, and anthropology, I also stress sociological theories because the concepts of exclusion and integration are central to that discipline.

Even when social exclusion is defined in global terms, research tends to be more sectoral, focusing on a specific population identified as being at risk of exclusion. Thus, empirical studies of exclusion may draw on more than one paradigm, although they tend to emphasize one over the others. The research literature on exclusion includes studies of the following specific social categories: the long-term or recurrently unemployed; those employed in precarious and unskilled jobs, especially older workers or those unprotected by labour regulations; the low paid and the poor; the landless; the unskilled, the illiterate, and school drop-outs; the mentally and physically handicapped and disabled; addicts; delinquents, prison inmates, and persons with criminal records; single parents; battered or sexually abused children, those who grew up in problem households; young people, those lacking work experience or qualifications; child workers; women; foreigners, refugees, immigrants; racial, religious, and ethnic minorities; the disenfranchised; beneficiaries of social assistance; those in need, but ineligible for social assistance; residents of rundown housing or disreputable neighbourhoods; those with consumption levels below subsistence (the hungry, the homeless, the Fourth World); those whose consumption, leisure, or other practices (drug or alcohol abuse, delinquency, dress, speech, mannerisms) are stigmatized or labelled as deviant; the downwardly mobile; the socially isolated without friends or family.

These absolute and relative social disadvantages may occur simultaneously. Indeed, the extent to which these dimensions overlap is a frequent subject of research on exclusion. Some find very weak correlations between the types of exclusion (Wuhl, 1992). But others conceive of exclusion as the accumulation of such disadvantages, as the last stage in a process of social disqualification (Paugam, 1993). For example, those born into certain groups, with a particular upbringing, education, family or work history may in a sense be doubly or triply excluded. However, the disproportionate representation of people with these social characteristics among the "excluded" does not imply that these characteristics determine whether any given individual is excluded. One needs to examine the incidence of these attributes in the included population as well. Some individuals with such characteristics do make their way into secure, well-paid employment, stable families, political participation, and the like. Provided turnover is ensured, there need be no "hard-core" group of excluded people.

ECONOMIC EXCLUSION

The three paradigms may be illustrated with theories addressing the economic dimension of exclusion. Although the discipline of economics is less prone to paradigm conflicts than the other social sciences, it still has a number of "schools" which differ along the lines already delineated. In so far as economists address "social exclusion", as distinct from poverty, inequality, or unemployment *per se*, it is probably more precise to say these are schools of *political* economy.

Readily available quantitative indicators of poverty and unemployment, and job statistics are often used in discussions of economic exclusion. In the United States, where there has been low-wage job growth, the focus has been on poverty and the underclass, whereas Europe has emphasized long-term unemployment. But on both sides of the Atlantic, the development of new socio-economic indicators has highlighted the novelty of the concept of social exclusion. The new measures not only offer insight into new thinking, but reflect existing paradigm assumptions as well.

Because the paradigms provide three different ways of linking economic and social concerns, social scientists other than economists have addressed the economic dimensions of exclusion. Thus, one can also glean analyses of economic exclusion from the literature on the underclass, the culture of poverty, and informal economies.

Solidarity

As mentioned, the French idea of solidarity drew upon the nineteenth-century working-class mutual aid movement and syndicalism. Through this influence, assumptions central to the solidarity paradigm can be found in the flexible specialization school of political economy. In addition, the French regulation school shares with the flexibilization school several important components of Republican and Durkheimian thought, especially the role of institutional, legal and normative regulation. However, I shall show that regulation theory more properly belongs in the monopoly paradigm, which treats exclusion more narrowly as either a social control mechanism or a barrier to competition. In any case, both schools of contemporary political economy depart from the liberal specialization paradigm's assumption of self-regulating markets.

As is typical of the solidarity paradigm, the "flexible specialization" approach rejects the assumption of classical political economy that the economy is separate from society. Flexible specialization rests upon "micro-regulation" – compatible institutions that instigate and coordinate innovation – in which family, school, and community ties are tightly intertwined with economic organization. Flexibility refers to the continual reshaping and rearranging of the components of the productive process, while specialization reflects limitations on the possible rearrangements and the ends to which they are put. Unlike liberal specialization that does not recognize constraints on economic organization beyond those of markets (e.g. transaction costs), flexible specialization is grounded in social solidarities. Productive decentralization and the "reinvigoration of affiliations that are associated with the pre-industrial past" (Piore and Sabel, 1984, p. 275) enable relatively autonomous, skilled workers to deploy modern technology successfully. However, organizations and communities of flexible specialization have boundaries that limit entry, and "outsiders... cannot be permitted to lay claim" to local public services or the system will be overburdened (p. 270). Relationships fostering cooperation and coordination beyond the workplace wed politics to markets. A system based on honour and pervasive trust is the foundation of community institutions that temper but do not eliminate economic competition. "The recognition of common interests and mutual obligations does not guarantee that all members of the community are treated equally" (p. 270). Indeed, limited competition on the basis of products rather than labour costs promotes innovation, productive flexibility and, thereby, economic growth. Thus, the approach differs from the liberal specialization paradigm in restricting competition and from the monopoly paradigm in promoting group boundaries and accepting moderate inequality.

Because it focuses on the advanced industrialized countries, the implications of flexible specialization for Third World economic development are ambiguous. On the one hand, developing countries may be specializing in mass production, while the advanced countries shift to flexible specialization. However, small-scale enterprises, community norms, and informal economies might provide the basis of flexible specialization in the Third World, as well (Hirst and Zeitlin, 1991; Putnam, 1993).

Despite its strong Marxist orientation, the French regulation school contains elements that recall the solidarity paradigm. Key to the regulation school is the concept of "regimes of accumulation", stable configurations that wed economic institutions to social regulations and norms. Such regimes are governed by institutionalized rules and social conventions which constrain collective and individual behaviour. Regulation adjusts production to social demand so that there develops a relative compatibility between income distribution and growth in the means of production and consumption. Another key concept for this school is the *rapport salarial,* one that also recalls the solidarity paradigm's social bond: this refers to the legal and institutional conditions regulating the use and reproduction of wage labour under capitalism. Wage relations differ according to the production norm, labour process, organization, consumption norm or way of life (Boyer, 1987, pp. 17-18).

For example, the Fordist regime of the post-war Golden Age was based on a social pact which gave corporations control of mass production in return for high wages to fuel mass consumption. Unlike an earlier regime of competitive capitalism, Fordism administered the economy through Keynesian economic policy, collective bargaining, Taylorism, and economies of scale. However, there are differences of opinion within the school as to the likely course of global capitalism since the crisis. It is not clear whether the emerging regime will pursue high-quality employment in a post-Fordist regime of flexible regulation or revert to a competitive strategy of externalizing market uncertainties through low-quality, low-wage jobs subject to numerical flexibility. Most regulation theorists do support the further development of a social pact within the European Union.

Regulation theory has also influenced post-Marxist thinkers like André Gorz (1989), who advocate worksharing and the development of socially productive and democratic activities outside the capitalist workplace. French "insertion" policies, however, epitomize the solidarity approach. The minimum income for social integration (RMI) was based on the idea that "insertion" is a form of regulation of the social bond and a response to a perceived threat to social cohesion (Paugam, 1993). Thus, in return for a minimum income, beneficiaries must sign a contract agreeing to pursue either a "social" or an "employment" activity, be it a subsidized job, training, community activity, or a personal project that enhances the ability to form social relationships and function in society. These functions are also the aim of French schemes for deprived young people as well as many urban revitalization schemes. Even schemes officially directed at "insertion" through economic activity combine social and business rationales. The *entreprises d'insertion* (enterprises established for the purpose of helping the excluded to rejoin society through work), for example, draw upon an older tradition of the crafts guilds and conceive of the work group as a community with social as well as economic functions (Hatzfeld, 1993; Delahaye, 1994).

Although the flexible specialization and regulation schools both emphasize historical contingency, national variation, and institutional and normative regulation, there remain important differences between them (Hirst and Zeitlin, 1991). Regulation theory tends to emphasize macroeconomic phenomena, the form of competition, and employment or class relations, which the flexible specialization school considers too deterministic. Rather than seek a new international economic regime, the latter school emphasizes the microeconomic and holds that many different types of political economy may coexist.

Moreover, a careful reading of the regulation school indicates that it is best classified under the monopoly paradigm, especially when the framework is applied to developing countries. For example, Alain Lipietz (1986, p. 26) argues that Fordism, the postwar intensive regime of accumulation based on mass consumption, rested upon a "monopolistic mode of regulation". A network of institutions stabilized the growth in workers' income and created "monopolies in a productive structure that allows the big firms of leading sectors to administer their prices independently of fluctuations in demand". By exporting mass production goods, the regime also "excluded" less developed countries from capital accumulation. However, the contradictions setting off the crisis of Fordism produced a series of changes in the developing world. First, "bloody Taylorization" integrated Third World labour into competitive, exploitative mass production. Then, in the 1970s, attempts at import substitution and the growth of internal markets allowed a form of "peripheral Fordism" to take hold, especially in the newly industrialized countries. However, the collapse of Fordism and Keynesianism encouraged monetarist policies that withdrew investment capital and exacerbated the indebtedness of less developed countries. In sum, Western advantages in the world economy were preserved by maintaining forms of monopolistic regulation.

As the discussion of the monopoly paradigm will show, the regulation school's approach dovetails with labour market segmentation approaches to productive flexibility. However, economists are not the only ones to address the issue of economic exclusion from the perspective of the solidarity paradigm.

Recall that the solidarity paradigm sees exclusion as a necessary by-product of group solidarity, cultural cohesion, and hence, social ties. It draws upon Durkheimian thought in which Republican concepts like social bond, organic solidarity, moral density, and collective conscience play a central role. The Durkheimian school of sociology concentrates on the problem of human solidarity, particularly moral and normative integration, that entails classification of people and ideas into sacred and profane, conforming or deviant. This tradition influenced cultural anthropologists who emphasize the binary oppositions or dualisms inherent in symbolic representations. For example, in *Natural symbols*, Mary Douglas introduced a distinction to explain how cultural codes control individual behaviour and social organization. "Group" refers to the external boundaries that differentiate collectivities from "the outside world". "Grid" refers to the other internal distinctions and delegations of authority used to limit social interaction. Cross-classifying these two dimensions provides a classification of individual behaviour in daily interaction and the ways in which social institutions constrain and channel individual behaviour. In this view, the moral order divides the world into categories which are continually recreated by primordial sentiments, essential identities, and institutional enforcement of the norms and values that define group boundaries.

The cultural solidarity approach to exclusion is based upon *primordialist/essentialist*, rather than constructivist, instrumentalist, or materialist approaches to culture (see Young, 1993). The primordialist school maintains that, unlike class and interest group conflicts, cultural conflicts have a peculiarly intensive, affective or emotional nature because they touch on primordial identity. Cultural boundaries enclose a social space behind walls where social life is orderly and people feel they "belong" and are "safe". Outsiders thus threaten this social order. They may provoke a reaffirmation of in-group solidarity or, if the bases of group solidarity expand to encompass those once considered as outsiders, inclusion and integration can be achieved. Essentialism may also underlie the cultural solidarity of excluded or minority groups who demand self-determination, cultural autonomy, separatism, political decentralization, or multiculturalism.

While the essentialist approach is most frequently used to analyse ethnic, racial, linguistic, religious, and other forms of cultural exclusion, it can also be applied to those excluded for economic reasons. For example, Godfried Engbersen et al. (1993) applied Mary Douglas's (1966) group/grid framework to the question of whether the long-term unemployed in the Netherlands have developed a monolithic culture. Cross-classifying cultures by group and grid, they arrive at five ways of life among the unemployed: egalitarian, hierarchical, individualistic, fatalistic, and autonomous. Hence, Engbersen et al. conclude there are in fact multiple cultures of unemployment and not a monolithic Dutch "underclass."

Exclusion was most evident in the fatalistic culture of unemployment, which Engbersen et al. consider a sort of "culture of poverty". Older, poorly educated persons were more likely to experience an isolated, dependent existence – a "shrinking of the social and geographic world they lived in". Long-term unemployment led to:

...exclusion from social institutions and networks and had made them completely dependent on the Government... The negligible success on the labour market, the high social costs that continual job-seeking behaviour entails and the reduction or disappearance of social frameworks can all serve to account for this shift from conformist to retreatist behaviour, and the longer the unemployment lasts, the more this is the case (1993, p. 178).

It is important to note that proponents of the solidarity paradigm often reject the term underclass.[6] For example, one CGP publication explicitly translates *les exclus* as *outsiders* in Howard Becker's (1963) sense of deviants, rather than as underclass (Nasse, 1992). Nevertheless, as the Dutch study illustrates, the literature on the underclass does touch upon the issue of exclusion.

It might appear that some "conservative" theories of the underclass fall within the solidarity paradigm, given their strong emphasis on the deviant behaviour of the poor and their use of dominant consensual values as a point of reference. Empirical studies that use single motherhood, school-leaving, or welfare receipt as "behavioural" indicators of the United States underclass essentially treat the poor as deviants. For example, Ken Auletta (1982, p. xiii) says the underclass "generally feels excluded from society, rejects commonly accepted values, suffers from behavioural as well as income deficiencies. They don't just tend to be poor; to most Americans their behaviour seems aberrant."

The reference to mainstream culture is also found in the work of David Ellwood (1988), a major proponent of American welfare reform in the Clinton administration. He has argued that the proposed reform embodies the contradictory American values of individual autonomy, the virtue of work, the primacy of family, and community. Because Americans want all of these, policy has reflected the trade-offs found in three "helping conundrums": security vs. work, assistance vs. family structure, and targeting vs. isolation. Ellwood finds exclusion in the third conundrum – the more services are targeted at the most needy,

...the more you tend to isolate the people who receive the services from the economic and political mainstream... Targeting can label and stigmatize people... When people see the most support and services going to those who are doing worst, it appears to the non-poor and possibly to the poor that the needy live by different rules than does everyone else... Targeting tends to isolate politically the "truly needy" from the rest of society (pp. 23-25).

This implies that welfare reform should reflect the consensual values underpinning social solidarity.

However, truly conservative underclass theories more appropriately fall within the *organic* paradigm of social integration. They assume that preserving the moral order is a state responsibility and that policy should coerce people into appropriate behaviour. Just as some members of the British Conservative Party have recently been proposing a "Back to Basics" ethic, American neo-conservatives have been insisting on "family values", sexual probity, and the individual responsibility to work. For example, Lawrence Mead (1986) argues that the idleness of the underclass reflects moral failure, not insufficient job creation, so the State should force able-bodied citizens to participate in workfare programmes. To become full citizens, the poor must balance their entitlement to social support with the exercise of moral obligations.

In contrast, Charles Murray (1984), who is conventionally considered a conservative, more properly belongs in the specialization paradigm because he views joblessness as a rational, self-interested reaction to the work disincentives in welfare policies. As the next section indicates, liberal theories of the underclass attribute persistent poverty and unemployment to perverse welfare state effects, market imperfections, or supply-side and human capital variables. These concerns differ from the moral emphases in the organic and solidarity paradigms.

Specialization

It is banal to note that liberalism underpins neo-classical economics. In the specialization paradigm of separate spheres, markets work best when States and institutions intervene least. Generous government income supports create perverse work disincentives that engender long-term dependency. The traditional solution to poverty and unemployment is to create jobs and raise productivity by lowering wages and eliminating rigid employment regulations.

It is no accident that both liberal political economy and the idea of "poverty" emerged from the Great Transformations of late eighteenth-century Britain. Just as exclusion is now being distinguished from poverty, so during this earlier period of dramatic social change did new distinctions set the poor apart from the rest of society. This new concept of poverty, culminating in the Poor Law reforms and exemplified by the workhouse spread quickly, especially to the United States. It is the origin of the principle of "least eligibility" in means-tested schemes, one which continues to stigmatize recipients as undeserving or morally unworthy.

These early liberal assumptions are also reflected in measures of poverty as such. The narrow conception of poverty is reflected in the myriad thresholds of absolute poverty used by Western governments to determine eligibility for means-tested schemes. Not only are poverty lines often pegged to subsistence levels, but income support levels are pegged to minimum wages so as to eliminate work disincentives and preserve union-negotiated wage standards.[7]

While the distinction between the undeserving and the industrious poor persisted, over time further distinctions were refined with which to measure the poor (Himmelfarb, 1984, p. 21). By the end of the nineteenth century, persons suffering from the effects of economic dislocation came to be distinguished from undeserving paupers who rarely (if ever) worked, lived on alms, and lacked direction and self-respect (Patterson, 1981; Katz, 1989, p. 13). The "respectable poor" were distinguished from the "residuum" (Morris, 1994, p. 21). During the 1880s in the United Kingdom:

For the first time unemployment became a political issue, perceived as a problem distinct from poverty, caused by factors other than moral failings, deserving of public sympathy and remedial action by the State… Much attention was subsequently focused on the need to separate the efficient unemployed, who could and should be helped into the labour market, from the "unemployables" or "inefficients" who should be removed from it (Burnett, 1994, pp. 145-8).

If early mutual aid associations and social insurance schemes served the "aristocracy of labour" and excluded the unskilled and casual worker (Stedman-Jones, 1984; Morris, 1994), workers of all kinds were soon covered by universal welfare state schemes.

With the rise of this Anglo-American "social liberalism", rights to social insurance were legitimated on the basis of contributions made during employment. Unlike means-tested schemes, insurance implied an obligation of the able-bodied to work when economic conditions allowed. Thus, liberals still insist that even contributory unemployment coverage be accompanied by job search requirements and policing against fraud (Morris, 1994). Pauperism was slowly restricted to a small segment of the poor unable to work – the Fourth World, as Father Wresinski, a French activist priest, has called them. Since the poverty addressed by means-tested benefit schemes came to be regarded as a residual problem, its meaning gradually narrowed to denote simply an insufficiency of income.

Yet, the liberal conception of exclusion does not reduce it to an economic phenomenon any more than do the other paradigms. Because individuals have diverse personal values and psychological motives for engaging in social relations, specialization arises not only in the market but also among social groups. Specialized social structures are comprised of separate, competing, but not necessarily unequal spheres which lead to exchanges and interdependence between them. Much as market competition erodes discriminatory practices, individual freedom to choose group affiliations and competition between groups for members create cross-cutting loyalties that break down tendencies toward social closure. Conversely, exclusion results from "discrimination", that is, from the inappropriate exercise of personal tastes or the enforcement of group boundaries that individuals are not free to cross. Thus, it may have multiple causes and dimensions, depending upon the social sphere in question.

Yet not all social differences are the consequence of deliberate exclusion or discrimination. Unlike organic models reliant on a strong State, liberalism allows for voluntary deprivation. Simply granting rights to assistance does not mean that free individuals will choose to accept it. As long as there is free access to information and people are not shamed, stigmatized or coerced, the take-up rates of welfare benefits may vary widely. The liberal State is under no obligation to bring the excluded in.

Nor do specialization and interdependence of separate social spheres necessarily imply social inequality. Liberalism considers social differentiation to be a horizontal dimension of social structures, rather than a vertical one. Like the division of labour, specialization may have positive outcomes: economies of scale, skill enhancement, reduced transaction costs, diversification of choice, and the preservation of liberty. On the grounds of efficiency or freedom, liberals may justify social distinctions that the other paradigms may consider exclusionary.

For example, efficiency wage models assume that some firms find it profitable to pay above-market wages because they raise worker productivity more than enough to offset additional labour costs (for a review see Katz, 1989). If higher wages increase the cost of losing a job and lower the costs of supervision, recruitment, and training new workers, then shirking and turnover can be reduced and work effort increased (Bulow and Summers, 1986). Thus, firms with high monitoring costs (such as large corporations) might find it easier to trust their workers when they reward them amply. Efficiency wages may also improve workers' morale and loyalty to the firm because they are perceived to be "fairer" than market wages. Indeed, industrial wage differentials are related to job tenure and quit probabilities (Krueger and Summers, 1988).

To some, this may suggest workers in high-wage industries are earning rents that they do not want to lose. Indeed, inter-industry wage dispersion rose between 1970 and 1987, partly because workers in more productive industries enjoyed increased rents (Bell and Freeman, 1991). Thus, from a monopoly perspective, exclusion would appear to benefit "insiders". Yet, efficiency wage models also show how excess labour supply can become a structural feature of the labour market in equilibrium. Over and above the wage effects of union threats, minimum wage laws, large firms' internal labour markets, or "imperfect" competition produced by other institutions, long-term structural unemployment may be consistent with market efficiency.

In so far as exclusion constitutes "discrimination" – the drawing of inappropriate group distinctions between free and equal individuals which deny access to or participation in exchange or interaction – it is construed as an individual experience. In social science, liberal individualism is often reflected in methodological individualism which treats group memberships as individual attributes. In contrast to the solidarity paradigm, these studies do not emphasize the dualism between insiders and the excluded but, rather, perceive the latter in all their rich diversity.

Neo-classical labour economists often associate the duration of poverty, dependency on welfare, and unemployment with the personal characteristics of the poor, rather than with economic or political conditions (e.g. Duncan, 1984). These "supply-side" studies, based on survey analysis, usually find that the poor, unemployed, or underclass population is socially heterogeneous (Wuhl, 1991; Jencks, 1991). For example, the Centre for the Study of Costs and Income (CERC) found that no single characteristic (e.g. difficulty in childhood, living in a single-parent household) could be identified as the principal cause of poverty or receipt of RMI in France.

Most scholarly research in the United States (Schlozman and Verba, 1979), United Kingdom (Morris, 1990), the Netherlands (Engbersen et al., 1993) and Germany (Kronauer, 1993) reports that those unemployed for at least a year are also socially heterogeneous. Because there is so much turnover among the unemployed over time, long-term unemployment affects virtually all categories of French workers (Reynaud, 1993). The National Institute of Statistics and Economic Studies (INSEE) found that those unemployed for under a year are no different socially from newly hired workers. While those unemployed on the way to becoming excluded tend to be older, to lack qualifications, skills, or experience, and to be more likely to have an immigrant background or handicap, even these individual characteristics do not predict well who will regain employment. Sometimes, even school-leavers are hired in preference to their experienced and educated elders. An additional reason why some categories of worker remain unemployed longer is that hiring is based not only on whether the worker's skill fits the job, but also on whether the worker will integrate into the work group (Vincens, 1993). Indeed, a wide range of social characteristics may be hindrances to regaining employment. In addition to cyclical and seemingly permanent unemployment, France faces a problem of recurrent unemployment – *chômage d'exclusion* – in which many move back and forth between idleness, internships, training courses, and short-term jobs (Wuhl, 1991, 1992).

In contrast to labour economists, sociologists have a long research tradition on the social psychology and behaviour of the unemployed on which to draw (Jahoda, Lazarsfeld, and Zeisel, 1971; Bakke, 1940; Komarovsky, 1940). These micro-sociologists found that unemployment is usually experienced as humiliating, causing the jobless to withdraw from friends and family. For example, Newman's (1988) study of downwardly mobile Americans identified both general and particular responses to unemployment. Most workers felt anger, dismay, and a sense of injustice, as if a social contract had been broken. Unemployment challenged personal identities, disrupted the life trajectories of entire families, and undermined cultural values, like loyalty and the work ethic. Managers, with their individualist, meritocratic creed, tended to blame themselves, whereas workers who share their sense of identity with others in a union or a community, tended to blame outside forces for unemployment. Groups based on a shared experience of unemployment helped the unemployed retain some dignity, as well as providing an explanation for their fate. Nevertheless, a common sense of victimization did not overcome feelings of helplessness.

Even French sociologists who use solidarity rhetoric have treated exclusion as a process of individual disaffiliation (Castel, 1991) or disqualification (Paugam, 1991, 1993). The longer people are unemployed, the more personal problems they develop, the more they appear unemployable to potential employers, and the more discouraged and isolated they become. *The* defining characteristic of exclusion is thus gradual withdrawal from face-to-face social relations. The micro-sociological causes of exclusion are located in the individual's immediate social environment, life course, or personal attributes. One sees in these studies an emphasis on individual characteristics, micro-sociological interaction, and psychological effects, even if they are considered as outcomes of economic restructuring. Indeed, it is no accident that micro-sociology and "the curious importance of small groups" (Silver, 1990) arose in liberal America.

In these studies, exclusion is neither a problem of macro-social integration nor an absolute categorical condition resulting from having crossed over some boundary line. Rather, it is a multidimensional process that individuals undergo. In a person's life trajectory, exclusion occurs at different paces and in different social spheres. For example, Serge Paugam (1993, 1991) defines exclusion as a process of "social disqualification" that occurs in three consecutive stages: fragility (under/unemployed but retaining links with society), dependence on social aid (discouraged from working but filling other social roles), and then complete breakdown of social bonds. At each stage, people renegotiate their identities and may find a way of regaining their previous status. But if individuals travel the full course of disaffiliation, they lose most of their social ties – job, housing, relations with the social support system, and the most elementary form of solidarity, a stable family. Accumulating handicaps and failures, they come to feel useless, uncared for, hopeless, and may turn to drugs or alcohol or become hostile to the welfare system. Without social relations of any kind, they lack the resources to find a way back into society.

Robert Castel (1991) also argues that there is a dynamic, three-stage process running from full integration through precarious, vulnerable employment and fragile relations to disaffiliation or exclusion. Castel argues that although the new poor are socially heterogeneous, the overrepresented social categories share a particular mode of dissociation of the social bond that he calls "disaffiliation". It is an effect of the conjuncture of two vectors, one economic, the other social. The first axis runs from integration (stable employment) through forms of precarious, intermittent, or seasonal occupations to the complete loss of work which he calls "exclusion". The second axis runs from "insertion" in stable socio-familial networks of sociability to total "isolation". When cross-classified, these dimensions identify a zone of integration (guaranteed permanent work and solid relational support) which assures social cohesion, and a zone of disaffiliation (the absence of work and social isolation) which provides little or no cohesion. Between the two extremes is a zone of vulnerability in which work is precarious and relations are fragile. Although integration in one sphere may compensate for exclusion in another, vulnerability puts one at risk of both kinds of exclusion. For example, 77 per cent of RMI beneficiaries lack jobs and 76 per cent lack a stable marital relationship. Thus, "insertion" measures must go beyond distributing aid to filling the social void caused by disaffiliation.

Apart from changes in the structure of employment, changes in other institutional spheres socially isolate the economically excluded. First, losing a job or re-employment on a temporary, short-term basis means losing job-related social insurance coverage. Receiving means-tested assistance that was formerly reserved for the permanently excluded entails a loss of status as well as of income (Castel, 1991). Second, the decline of organized labour, ideological politics, and the break-up of working-class neighbourhoods have eroded class solidarity. In deprived outer suburbs, many young people do not form stable relationships and immigrants cannot assimilate (Dubet, 1987); in the ghettos, the young have no positive role models, clubs or centres of their own (Wilson, 1987). The decline of shared values and practices in daily life also weakens financial and social support from neighbours. Third, while school should he a vector of social cohesion, many young people drop out of school because they feel excluded. One's own home can amount to a ghetto if the family has no money. Indeed, job and family instability have led to more single-parent families and to more people living alone (Daugareilh and Laborde, 1993). In sum, exclusion is a series of breaks in the web of belonging that leave individuals stranded in a "social no-man's-land" (Castel, 1991).

As in the other paradigms, these French sociological studies consider exclusion to be a process both economic and social. However, they focus on the individual's experience. The analysis posits the existence of separate spheres, and individuals are located along multiple dimensions which do not necessarily intersect. A similar approach was used by Jencks (1991) who rejected the idea of the existence of an American underclass, arguing that because trends in various social indicators have moved in different directions over time, disadvantages do not cluster in the same group of people. New and increasingly multi-dimensional ways of measuring the underclass consistently show that single parents, ghetto residents, school drop-outs and people dependent on transfers constitute only a subset of the poor. Findings like these are moving social policy in an increasingly individualistic direction. Since each individual has a different combination of problems, assistance must be personalized and rendered comprehensively. Income support, medical and housing assistance, social services, training, and subsidized employment are increasingly "packaged" to fit each individual's or household's needs.

The specialization paradigm does not emphasize the individual and micro-sociological causes of economic exclusion only. Social liberals are cognizant of the effects of structural changes in labour demand on individuals' immediate social environments, and thus on their opportunities for social affiliation in a variety of separate spheres. The split between supply-side and demand-side theories parallels the division between classical and social liberalism. The latter is concerned with maintaining boundaries between separate spheres, including that between politics (with its equality of citizenship) and the market (with its inequality of resources).

In contrast to supply-side theoreticians who attribute poverty or unemployment to individual failings, most sociologists now accept that the new poverty and long-term unemployment have demand-side or structural causes, perhaps exacerbated by liberal economic and social policies (Wilson, 1987: Jencks and Peterson, 1991). The educational level of the Western labour force continues to rise, suggesting that supply-side policies will be ineffective in addressing these problems (Jencks, 1991; Wuhl, 1991). Evaluations of French training schemes, for example, report that they do little to improve the job prospects of the trainees unless they are tied to enterprises (Delahaye, 1994; CGP, 1993; Paugam, 1993). Even when the unemployed re-enter the labour market, new openings are almost all to jobs of short duration. About half the figures of newly registered unemployed in France concern lost "precarious jobs" (Paugam, 1993; Wuhl, 1992). The trend is for jobs at all skill levels to offer little security.

However, different social spheres offer different affiliations and resources. Family and community ties may replace income for the long-term structurally unemployed. With access to productive assets (land, capital, credit), self-employment and self-support/sufficiency in food may be possible, incorporating the excluded into direct market exchanges, barter, and informal economies. The West has seen a rise in self-employment, self-help strategies, and household economies among the poor, a phenomenon once confined to developing countries (Pahl, 1984; Morris, 1990; Esping-Anderson, 1994).

One illustration of the liberal approach to informal economies weds network theories to the concept of "social capital". It builds on rational choice theory but rejects its extreme, individualistic premises of utility maximization by assuming that individuals are socialized in micro-sociological settings. For example, James Coleman (1988) views the various forms of social capital – obligations and expectations, information channels, and social norms – as resources for action, increasing human and financial capital. Networks that attain social structural "closure" enhance the positive effects of particularistic obligations, expectations, and norms. Larger households and residents of tightly-knit local communities have an advantage in maintaining consumption on these bases. By contrast, informal economies are less likely to work among the socially disaffiliated and the State may he the only recourse to the latter.

Such attention to the various institutions, groups, and spheres in civil society is characteristic of liberal paradigms in sociology and political science. Unlike the monopoly paradigm, these approaches do not privilege the market. Like the solidarity paradigm, they highlight the social embeddedness of economic activity, but do not assume that rank in one social sphere is always consonant with rank in the others. Indeed, social liberalism finds the roots of exclusion in the inadequate separation of spheres, unenforced rights, or market failures, which justify state intervention.

Monopoly and labour market segmentation

The monopoly paradigm treats exclusion and unemployment as symptoms of group monopolies which generate inequality and severe economic exploitation. As Joan Robinson put it, "the only thing that is worse than being exploited is not being exploited" (cited in Streeten, 1993, p. 2).[8] Powerful "status groups" with distinctive cultural identities and institutions use social closure to restrict the access of outsiders to valued resources. The overlap of group distinctions and inequality is at the heart of the *problématique* of this paradigm.

Theories of labour market segmentation epitomize the paradigm's link between social closure and economic exclusion. Segmentation occurs wherever there are barriers to free competition between workers and/or firms. Many labour market barriers – from regulations to credentials – operate simultaneously. Like social closure in a more general way, labour market segmentation results in poverty and economic inequality.

Two theories dominated the first wave of segmentation research. First, in institutional economics, Peter Doeringer and Michael Piore (1971) identified the "dual labour market", which distinguished between primary and secondary labour markets based on both job quality and worker characteristics. To explain why some groups could not gain access to highly paid, secure employment, they proposed the notion of the "internal labour market" that insulates primary workers from external market competition. Early dual labour market theories assumed that the secondary labour market operates like a classic competitive market, but that non-price criteria, such as the racial origin of workers, ration good jobs in the primary labour market (Lang and Dickens, 1988). Similarly, some firms can use union membership, promotion from within, and other institutional restrictions on mobility to limit access to in-house jobs. Second, complementing the neo-institutional approach, neo-Marxist economists portrayed the segmentation and stratification of labour markets as mechanisms to divide and control labour under conditions of partial unionization. Worker power produces higher wages in unionized segments, while the disproportionately female and minority secondary and subordinate labour markets serve as a reserve army of labour (Gordon, Reich, and Edwards, 1982).

Although these early studies were criticized on theoretical, methodological, and empirical grounds,[9] they shared the assumption that, contrary to competitive or human capital theories of wages, jobs vary in the compensation they offer to equally productive workers. Compensation of all kinds – wages, promotion opportunities, fringe benefits, or risks of unemployment – can serve as monopolized resources. Since the supply side is controlled, these theories reason, a persisting differential must result from the rationality of firms. If wages remain higher, there must be institutional or "non-price" barriers to mobility, access, and competition from unemployed or otherwise employed workers. Such exclusion rations jobs and creates queues. Thus, high unemployment may in fact be compatible with productivity and economic growth.

The second round of labour market segmentation studies improved upon methodology and provided strong evidence for the theory (Dickens and Lang, 1988).[10] Some of the most compelling empirical substantiation for the theory was the evidence provided by some American economists of large and enduring inter-industry wage differentials between equally productive workers (Krueger and Summers, 1988; Bulow and Summers, 1986). Yet, current economic segmentation theories differ as to the particular mechanisms responsible. For example, "insider-outsider" models start from the same premise as efficiency wage models. However, reasoning from union behaviour, they argue that the turnover costs of replacing incumbent workers with the unemployed increase the bargaining power of organized insiders who, by threatening to quit, can demand higher wages. Since insiders can cost employers more than they would gain by hiring outsiders, the acceptance of lower wages by outsiders is insufficient to give them access to good jobs. Both the erosion of skills and the stigma employers attach to "outsiders" make it more difficult to re-enter the labour market after a spell of unemployment, particularly if it is a long one. The empirical support for this model is that high-wage industries have lower quit rates (Lindbeck and Snower, 1986).

Where monitoring and turnover costs are more important in some sectors, industries or firms than in others, one would expect to find labour market segmentation. Some jobs will pay higher wages to increase productivity and will be rationed. Occupants of "good jobs" who do not need added incentives will still collect "rents" because those jobs will be scarce relative to the number of workers wanting them. In neo-classical theory, this excess labour supply for good jobs should drive down primary sector wages, enabling workers to attain access through intersectoral mobility. Instead, it produces a labour queue of either the unemployed or workers in "bad" jobs. Labour market queues also support the theory of statistical discrimination (Thurow, 1975).

In sum, labour market institutions and institutional demand-side variables can be seen as the source of group monopolies and social exclusion, which in turn cause wage inequality. Because of non-universal coverage, attempts to reduce inequality through collective bargaining and labour legislation may have inadvertently created new bases of exclusion. For example, there is an incentive to shift work to small firms, the self-employed, or part-time and temporary employees who evade or are exempted from compulsory welfare contributions and taxes, paying compulsory benefits, or respecting standards on hours and safety. Rules on length of service also restrict the access of new labour market entrants to well-paid, protected jobs. There may also be trade-offs between redistributive equity, in the form of social security contributions, and economic efficiency. Although negative income tax experiments suggest that substitution effects (that reduce effort) may be outweighed or at least offset by income effects (that increase effort), marginal (rather than proportional) taxation may exacerbate the trade-off. Assumptions about a decent family wage that underlie much labour legislation and collective bargaining may also have contributed to exclusion on the basis of sex and of household structure. The labour force influx of working women partly accounts for growth in part-time employment (Godbout, 1993).

The European Union appears to have accepted the existence of these trade-offs. The Commission's 1994 White Paper, *Growth, competitiveness, employment*, proposed collective mechanisms of "solidarity" between those with and without jobs, rich and poor, men and women, generations, regions, and neighbours:

Social protection schemes have – in part at least – had a negative impact on employment in that they have, in the main, tended to protect people already in work, making their situation more secure and consolidating certain advantages. They have in effect proved to be an obstacle to the recruitment of jobseekers or of new entrants to the labour market (p. 124).

In addition to this "dual standard of treatment working to the detriment of the jobless," the Commission deemed labour market rigidity to be "the root cause of what are relatively high labour costs". Those in employment have enjoyed the fruits of economic growth while the unemployed are excluded. Of the 10 million new jobs in the European Union created between 1990 and 1993, only 3 million were taken by the registered unemployed; the rest absorbed new entrants or re-entrants (p. 141). In countries where a large youth cohort has bloated the labour supply, there may indeed be a trade-off between wages and employment (Bloom, Freeman, and Korenman, 1988; OECD, 1993).

Yet, the higher wages produced by group monopolies may also have created incentives to shift employment to more competitive sectors. Indeed, these processes underlie some theories of the informal economy (Portes, Castells, and Benton, 1989). In both developed and developing countries, employers and the self-employed evade legal regulations in order to lower the cost of production. This makes them attractive as subcontractors for larger, even multinational, corporations. Obviously, differential sectoral labour costs are only one reason for the rise of precarious informal employment and subcontracting. Others are greater market uncertainty and the economies of scale derived from specialization. Nevertheless, the monopoly paradigm emphasizes the contribution of regulatory barriers to sectoral segmentation and, thus, economic exploitation and exclusion.

As the French regulation school points out, similar processes may account for the increasing "numerical" flexibility in Western labour markets (OECD, 1989, 1986; Boyer, 1987; Tarling, 1987; Rodgers and Rodgers, 1989). Global competition has increased the pressure to cut labour costs through quantitative flexibility, hiring and firing workers with fluctuations in demand. Indeed, in OECD countries like France and Germany, growth was almost exclusively in part-time employment (Godbout, 1993). As good jobs in high-wage sectors are automated or subdivided into more low-wage jobs in less regulated, more competitive sectors, employment growth may he decoupled from its historic association with rising wages and greater income equality.

The problem is not only a consequence of low-wage job growth, however. With technological innovation, the relative wage return to higher education has been rising in most advanced countries, resulting in greater income inequality (Davis 1993; Katz, Loveman, and Blanchflower, 1994; OECD, 1993). Differential access to firms, or jobs within firms introducing internal, "qualitative" flexibility – where jobs and profits are more tied to capital investment, reorganization, teamwork, and retraining than to the cost of labour inputs – may itself generate a new basis for labour market segmentation and exclusion in the future. Job security and benefits as well as wages may be traded off for employment. In sum, there is a tendency towards dualism among those who do have jobs, as well as between those in and those out of work.

This example of "dual closure" (Parkin, 1974; Murphy, 1988) illustrates how segmentation theories account for economic exclusion within the framework of the monopoly paradigm. Any labour market barriers to or shelters from competition that persistently raise wages for some workers at the expense of others effectively exclude the latter from access to some forms of compensation or employment conditions. Whether justified on grounds of efficiency, merit or for political or institutional reasons, exclusion may result from differential access to high-wage countries, high-wage industries, or firms and jobs with internal labour markets and "flexible specialization".

Since informal social contacts and place of residence often channel some groups into such firms and industries, socially isolated or minority groups may find themselves at a disadvantage. Thus, not only material and legal, but also cultural and geographic boundaries restrict access to valued resources, giving insiders a form of monopoly and power over outsiders. The monopoly paradigm sees culture as a form of domination: by including some, it necessarily excludes others. While the solidarity paradigm stresses culture's essentialism and the specialization paradigm sees culture as an autonomous sphere of valued beliefs and practices, the monopoly paradigm's deconstructivism sees culture as "interested", i.e. protecting material advantages. Any form of exclusion necessarily entails inequality. For this reason, perhaps, British writers' discussions of economic post-Fordism often conflate it with cultural post-modernism: both advocate relaxing rigid social boundaries.

The monopoly paradigm treats the subject of informal economies as another aspect of sectoral segmentation. The formal/informal split is yet another expression of exploitative core/periphery relations. Although social contacts and community ties, coupled with free time, may help all the economically inactive to enlarge their social world through participation in the "household economy" and local voluntary activities, the opportunity to engage in informal economic activities is differentially distributed among the unemployed (Pahl, 1984; Morris, 1994).

In the monopoly paradigm, the unequal power underlying group monopolies can be mitigated, if not eliminated, by inclusive citizenship or social rights. The social democratic formulation of citizenship as "full and equal participation in the community" draws explicitly upon Marshall's (1950) classic formulation. The gradual extension of civil, then political and, finally, social rights bestows an equal status and the equal rights and duties with which that status is endowed. Although capitalist societies are inherently unequal and conflictual, social citizenship in a redistributive welfare state and "a direct sense of community membership based on loyalty to a civilization which is a common possession" would "abate" economic inequality. Over time, European social democrats adopted Marshall's rhetoric of citizenship to support an egalitarian programme of decommodification, class compromise, and material redistribution through the expansion of universalist welfare states

(Esping-Andersen, 1991; Klausen, 1995). They contrasted citizenship with inequality.

The distinction between the monopoly and solidarity paradigms is clearly illustrated by the European Union's shifting discourse of exclusion. Initial discussions used the French Republican sense of the term. For example, the Community Charter of the Fundamental Social Rights of Workers adopted by the (then) European Community's Heads of State declares that "... in a spirit of solidarity, it is important to combat social exclusion" (Room et al., 1992, p. 11). However, the European Commission's report, *Towards a Europe of solidarity*, already shifted towards a rhetoric of social rights:

... social exclusion refers, in particular, to inability to enjoy social rights without help, suffering from low self-esteem, inadequacy in their [sic] capacity to meet their obligations, the risk of long-term relegation to the ranks of those on social benefits, and stigmatization which, particularly in the urban environment, extends to the areas in which they live (1992, p. 10).

The subsequent European Commission report on the subject explicitly used Marshall's notion of social citizenship:

Here we define social exclusion first and foremost in relation to the social rights of citizens... to a certain basic standard of living and to participation in the major social and occupational opportunities of the society (Room et al., 1992 p. 14).

The Final Poverty 3 Programme report also noted this passage and itself concluded that exclusion "implies the denial (or non-realization) of *social rights*" (Andersen et al., 1994).

Many European social scientists are now analysing the underclass in terms of a Marshallian understanding of exclusion (Schmitter Heisler, 1991; Dahrendorf, 1985). In the rare cases in which the term exclusion is used in this context in the United Kingdom, reference is usually made to Marshall's three-pronged conception of citizenship and its role in combating inequality. For example, the Child Poverty Action Group used the rhetoric of exclusion to argue that the poor are excluded from full citizenship and participation in the society and, thus, are often excluded from public consciousness as well (Lister, 1990; Golding, 1986).

A contrast with the liberal perspective highlights the monopoly paradigm's incorporation of inequality into the notion of exclusion. In line with Marshall, the monopoly perspective defines the underclass as "that group of people who are not fully citizens because they are not able to participate in certain basic social activities" and "are excluded from the mainstream of society... Against this, it can be argued that members of the underclass exclude themselves by refusing to make the best of their opportunities" (Smith, 1992, p. 7). The paradigms thus differ on the question of who is responsible for exclusion.

Most British thinkers on the question argue along the lines that "the idea of an underclass is a counterpart to the idea of social classes, and acquires its meaning within that same framework of analysis... they belong to family units having no stable relationship at all with the 'mode of production' – with legitimate gainful employment" (Smith, 1992, p. 4). Like poverty and the underclass, exclusion has class-based connotations in the United Kingdom. For example, Peter Townsend (1979) maintained that the poor "are, in effect, excluded from ordinary living patterns, customs, and activities". Frank Field (1989, p. 4) noted that "the very poorest are separated, not only from other groups on low income, but, more importantly, from the working class". The underclass is situated below the working classes, because their "roles place them more or less permanently at the economic level where benefits are paid by the State to those unable to participate in the labour market at all" (Runciman, 1990).

Slowly, the monopoly model of citizenship is expanding beyond social class questions. Social democratic thought is just beginning to adjust to increasing diversity in styles of life and cultural values and to the political challenges posed by immigrant minorities, environmental movements, and long-term unemployment. British multiculturalist and post-modernist thinkers are increasingly using the notion of citizenship and equality of status to encompass the recognition of diversity, the inclusion of all groups, and the protection from stigma (e.g. Harris, 1987). Weberian references consonant with the monopoly paradigm can also be found: Lydia Morris (1994), for example, concluded that the British underclass consists of those suffering from "status exclusion".

Even some American social democrats have adopted the monopoly paradigm's exclusion discourse. Lee Rainwater (1974, p. 135) has argued that "the person living in poverty is not the Middle American: he has passed over an invisible border". Michael Harrington (1962, p. 18) asserted that *The Other America* is invisible: "to be impoverished is to be an internal alien [without] links with the great world". Michael Katz provides an excellent example. First, he deconstructs the solidarity approach to exclusion in terms reminiscent of Marshall:

We can think about poor people as "them" or as "us". For the most part, Americans have talked about "them". Even in the language of social science, as well as in ordinary conversation and political rhetoric, poor people usually remain outsiders, strangers to be pitied or despised, helped or punished, ignored or studied, but rarely full citizens, members of a larger community on the same terms as the rest of us (1989, p. 236).

Then he deconstructs liberal discourse: "Poverty in America is profoundly individual; like popular economics, it is supply side" (p. 237). Lastly, he casts exclusion and citizenship as issues of monopoly and inequality:

For finally, the politics of poverty are about the processes of inclusion and exclusion in American life: who, to put the question crudely, gets what? How are goods distributed? As such, it is a question of race, class, gender, and the bases of power... Europeans today write about the "new poverty", which they understand in a similar way. They do not write very much about the underclass, which highlights the peculiarly American tendency to transform poverty from a product of politics and economics into a matter of individual behaviour (p. 237).

He blames the economic, spatial, social and cultural isolation of the inner-city black poor on exclusionary laws and practices of private employers, unions, and white workers. And like Marshall and social democrats, Katz calls for "finding ways to talk about poor people as 'us' that expand ideas of citizenship" (p. 239).

The dominance of the monopoly perspective on the Continent is also reflected in methodology. The European Union's statistical service, Eurostat, and the Luxembourg Income Survey adopted standardized comparative methods to measure poverty *relative* to average national income (equivalent expenditure). Relative poverty lines simultaneously incorporate absolute deprivation and inequality, "a barrier and a level". Moreover, many justify these measures with reference to Marshall's definition of citizenship, arguing that poverty must be measured relative to a society's normative standards of living (Fuchs, 1967; EC Commission, 1992) or consumption levels (Townsend, 1987, 1979; Mayer and Jencks, 1989). "Without a requisite level of goods and services, ... individuals cannot participate as full members of their society" (Rainwater, 1992, p. 5). Similarly, poverty may be considered in subjective terms, based on what most people in a society regard as the "decent" or "adequate" income necessary to "get by" (Rainwater, 1992; van Praag et al., 1980; Danziger et al., 1984).

Relative poverty lines have been used for decades, but the term "new poverty" was introduced to maintain the distinction between those populations traditionally considered as the poor and those displaced by economic change (Room, 1990; Donzelot and Roman, 1991; Paugam, 1991). Unlike the old poverty which reflected cyclical downturns, the new poverty, especially in the United Kingdom, was considered structural, grounded in a new economy that subjects all social classes to employment insecurity. This vulnerability to downward mobility created a relative poverty of deprivation, as many lose what they expected to have – a socially accepted or customary style of life (Townsend, 1993, 1987, 1979; Rainwater, 1992, 1990, 1974). The term "new poverty" encompassed many of the same empirical realities as those that the French labelled "exclusion" phenomena.

Yet French observers insist on the distinction between "exclusion" and "inequality". For example, Touraine (1991, 1992) argues that the two phenomena follow different types of logic. Inequality occurs in an industrial society of production in which opposing classes are "integrated" because they confront each other face to face; whereas exclusion is a symptom of economic growth and social change in which social actors contesting the dominant power structure and culture are divorced from the economic and political system. In the emerging postindustrial society, the social problem is no longer inequality, but justice and the rules of the game. Jean-Baptiste de Foucauld (1992a, b) also argues that inequalities and exclusions are not the same, although both are rising and may have cumulative effects. Unlike inequality, exclusion is associated with rising individualism and a changing market society which is divorcing actors from the system and separating productive and social demands. De Foucauld still sees inequality and exclusion through Republican eyes: despite their differences they are joined through the perspective of the need for social cohesion in a dynamic society. Thus, it is necessary to encourage both equality and justice, rather than trade one off against the other.

Finally, it is worth noting that while participatory democracy is an essential part of the social democratic vision of citizenship, it is not directed towards a form of solidarity based on national consensus. Rather than stressing participation as a duty of citizenship or integration in the republic or nation, both the Catholic and the Socialist Left advocate direct participation in local associations and social movements as a means of connecting the excluded to the larger society through organized opposition and challenges to powerful interests. Decentralizing power to localities and workplaces permits the excluded, whatever their group background, to pursue their common interests in inclusion and redistribution. Locally based "insertion" and integration policies should create "a political space of belonging". Integration is a project seeking to reconstruct an active citizenship. Participation in public life makes the struggle against exclusion political and launches a debate over the nature of new forms of solidarity and the terms of a new social contract (Donzelot and Roman, 1991; Mongin, 1992). State intervention might thereby be legitimated.

CONCLUSION: EXCLUSION, POLITICS, AND SOCIAL POLICY

In this paper I have presented three major paradigms of exclusion, each grounded in a different conception of integration and citizenship. In the solidarity paradigm dominant in France, exclusion is the breakdown of a social bond between the individual and society that is cultural and moral, rather than economically interested. Cultural boundaries give rise to socially constructed dualistic categories for ordering the world, defining the poor, the unemployed, and ethnic minorities as deviant outsiders. However, by tying national solidarity to political rights and duties, Republican citizenship imposes an obligation on the State to aid in the inclusion of the excluded. By presenting itself as a "third way" between liberalism and socialism, Republican thought weds economic to social concerns through the notion of solidarity. Similar emphases can be found in new schools of political economy.

In the specialization paradigm, exclusion reflects discrimination. Social differentiation, economic divisions of labour, and the separation of spheres should not produce hierarchically ordered social categories if excluded individuals are free to move across boundaries and if spheres of social life governed by different principles are kept legally separate. Cultural pluralism, like political pluralism, rests upon voluntary membership and group competition. Liberal models of citizenship emphasize the contractual exchange between individual rights and obligations and the tensions between the sphere of civil society based on liberty and a public sphere based on equality and democracy. Liberal assumptions are rooted in micro-sociology, which emphasizes small groups, and in neo-classical economics and other social sciences which are characterized by methodological individualism.

Finally, the third paradigm sees exclusion as a consequence of the formation of group monopolies. Powerful groups, often displaying distinctive cultural identities and institutions, restrict the access of outsiders to valued resources through a process of "social closure". The same process is evident in labour market and enterprise segmentation which draws exclusive boundaries between and within firms. At the heart of this paradigm is the necessary overlap of group distinctions and inequality, "the barrier and the level". Inequality is mitigated by social democratic citizenship which, in Marshall's formulation, entails full participation in the community.

However they are conceived, the empirical manifestations of rising deprivation in the advanced countries call into question the adequacy of existing welfare arrangements. The numbers of means-tested schemes designed to serve small constituencies are growing rapidly. The assumption underlying post-war social insurance schemes of a uniform life-cycle, career pattern, and family structure applies to a shrinking number of people. "New" types of social disadvantage are increasingly emerging as are demands that these newly identified social problems be addressed.

Once-quiescent beneficiaries are organizing politically under the banners of their various "demographic identities", are forming lobby groups, and are pressuring local government in the areas where they are concentrated. This "politics of consumption" is concerned less with transfers than with unpopular and residual social services (e.g., drug rehabilitation, assistance for refugees or immigrants, urban renewal programmes); as such it introduces distributive conflicts not only between productive and unproductive citizens, but between cultural groups as well. The demand for individualized, differentiated services for socially marginal groups also challenges the principle of universalism that once legitimated the postwar welfare states (Immergut, 1993). This crisis in social policy requires a rethinking of the notions of citizenship and solidarity.

Although these manifestations of the phenomenon of "exclusion" have led to new social policy approaches, especially in France, any large-scale recasting of welfare state institutions will require a broad political consensus. It is useful to recall that the initial establishment of national welfare states was a process of "institutional searching" for political compromise (Ashford, 1986). To achieve such compromises, it was necessary to formulate political ideas that blended pre-existing nation-specific norms and practices. As the paradigms illustrate, such ideas are still reflected in existing welfare state institutions. Today, as new social problems call for major social policy reforms, the importance of new ideas to forge political consensus appear to be just as important. Does the notion of exclusion offer a formula with which to achieve the political compromises necessary to meet these challenges?

As I have indicated, exclusion means different things to different people. Only at the extremes of the political spectrum is one likely to find people actually in favour of it. Given the multiple connotations of the term, it might provide a political opportunity to cement a broadly based alliance in favour of new social policies. For example, the importance that French observers attach to distinguishing exclusion from other terms denoting social disadvantage suggests that the concept does have political significance. If we define exclusion as a thoroughly new, multidimensional phenomenon touching people at all levels of the social hierarchy in some respects or at some point in their lives, large, cross-class coalitions to combat it may become easier to build. Most people have suffered from some kind of rejection or misery in their lives, and apprehension about being excluded has become widespread (see Bourdieu, 1993; Balibar, 1992). As the connotations of exclusion expand to encompass the dashing of extravagant aspirations, "in the end everyone will consider himself excluded from something" (Xiberras, 1993).

For example, a survey conducted in France in December 1993 by CSA/ La Rue, a newspaper sold by the homeless, found that 55 per cent of French adults and 69 per cent of young people aged 18-24 fear they will become "excluded" and three-quarters worried that someone close to them would (André, 1994). That feeling of vulnerability is not confined to France. The Families and Work Institute found that 42 per cent of American workers report their companies are reducing their workforces temporarily or permanently (Gans, 1993). That near-majorities of respondents perceive a clear threat of exclusion – in the broad sense of a loss of social status – may account for the term's wide appeal and its even wider application.

Recent inflammatory remarks about immigrants by certain French politicians are nothing if not divisive and have mobilized the opposition.

However, whether public apprehension and indignation will be sufficient to mobilize strong political support for new social policies in France remains to be seen. In the spring of 1994, demonstrations against inadequate provision for unemployed young people revealed a wide range of attitudes among the young – including a fear that their expectations of continuing a comfortable lifestyle acquired at home will not be fulfilled. If the common fear of exclusion may cement an alliance among those differentially placed in the social hierarchy, this may not prove sufficient to overcome other social cleavages.

Indeed, to the extent that exclusion is understood in the liberal, individualistic terms of the specialization paradigm, it may become a euphemism for stigmatized, isolated, or scapegoated groups. Its meaning may narrow to those with multiple disadvantages. From this perspective, the university student protests against declining employment prospects may simply reflect a defence of their traditional prerogatives and a demand for protection from increasing competition. By identifying the victims of economic restructuring and the end of full employment, terms like exclusion, the new poor, or the underclass may even serve to justify majority resistance to redistributive taxation and expenditures (Room, 1990). Targeted social policies will then entail no sacrifice by the privileged and dualism will be reinforced.

Thus, though the idea of exclusion could be useful to reformers who wish to point to the inadequacies of existing welfare states, conversely it may serve to distract attention from the overall rise in inequality, general unemployment, and family breakdown that is affecting all social classes. By ghettoizing risk categories under a new label and publicizing the more spectacular forms of poverty requiring emergency aid, policies to combat exclusion may make it easier to re-target money on smaller social categories, like the homeless or the long-term unemployed. It may even undermine the universal social insurance schemes that traditionally protected the working- and middle-classes. In sum, therefore, just as the idea of exclusion has many meanings, it can also serve a variety of political purposes.

Notes

[1] They also refer to "concrete puzzle-solutions which, when employed as models or examples, can replace explicit rules as a basis for the solution of the remaining puzzles of normal science" (Kuhn, 1970, p. 175). From such exemplary studies or scientific practices spring particular coherent traditions of scientific research. They are sufficiently unprecedented to attract an enduring group of adherents away from competing modes of scientific activity and sufficiently open-ended to leave all sorts of problems for the new group of practitioners to resolve (p. 10). Paradigms provide a criterion with which to select for consideration problems that, so long as the paradigm is taken for granted, can be assumed to have solutions (p. 37). In brief, they guide a scientific community's research.

[2] Individualism characterizes both neo-classical economics and liberal political doctrine. Just as Jean-Jacques Rousseau was a seminal Republican thinker, so John Locke and other liberal contract theorists made seminal contributions to liberalism. As I indicate below, "social liberalism" developed later in the nineteenth and early twentieth centuries and includes John Stuart Mill, L.T. Hobhouse and American Progressive thinkers among its early theorists.

[3] Conventionally, solutions to the problem of order come under one of two perspectives. In the first, social integration is externally imposed on individuals; in the second, social integration grows out of voluntary interaction between individuals. This distinction between the coercive and the voluntaristic nature of social integration corresponds to other dualisms in the social sciences (see Alexander, 1992; Lamont and Fournier, 1992). These basic dualisms are reflected in two of the paradigms I propose (exclusion as a basis of monopoly and as a basis of specialization); exclusion as a consequence of solidarity represents the French attempt to steer a "third course" between these two polarities.

[4] Nasse (1992) maintains that liberal individualist conceptions of society use "insertion" to mean making room beside others or placing them side by side, while Durkheimian cultural and normative conceptions use the term "integration" to mean "assimilation". However, a content analysis of ten years of the French press found that the term "integration" was used synonymously with "insertion" and "adaptation", with little reference to who was being integrated into what (Barou, 1993). "Insertion" also has multiple meanings (Paugam, 1993; Commissariat Général du Plan, 1993). For example, a CGP committee on "insertion", realizing that the term was never clearly defined in law, fell back on an admittedly unsystematic classification of a "pluridimensional concept" (Commissariat Général du Plan, 1993).

[5] For example, Jean-Baptiste de Foucauld, the current Planning Commissioner in France, argues that "being excluded is not a form of identity but the result of a process" (in Nasse, 1992, p. 6).

[6] For critical reviews of literature on the underclass, see Gans, 1991; Aponte, 1990; Katz, 1989; Stafford and Ladner, 1990; Jencks, 1991; Morris, 1994.

[7] Even measures of absolute poverty contain some acknowledgement of social relativity. Poverty levels are often adjusted for family size, inflation and geography. They may also reflect transfers in kind, changes in cost of living, and the duration of poverty (for a review, see Ruggles, 1990).

[8] Castel (1991) also cited the seventeenth-century *Traité des Ordres* as saying "il n'est certes pire profession que de ne pas avoir profession" [there is no worse occupation than to have none].

[9] These studies attracted criticism for various deficiencies, among the most important that the industrial characteristics defining sectors were not strongly correlated; that classifying workers into sectors by their earnings introduced circular reasoning and truncation bias in rates of return; and that individuals choose sectors for their differential characteristics, introducing heterogeneity and selectivity bias.

[10] Two techniques for testing the existence of labour market segmentation appear to pass muster. One uses "switching models" in which no assumptions are made as to which jobs are in which sectors: the other uses clustering techniques that split jobs at the mean to avoid truncation and estimates effects separately by race and gender to avoid heterogeneity bias.

References

Alexander, Jeffrey. 1992. "Citizen and enemy as symbolic classification: On the polarizing discourse of civil society", in Michele Lamont and Marcel Fournier (eds.): *Cultivating differences: Symbolic boundaries and the making of inequality.* Chicago, University of Chicago Press, pp. 29-30.

Andersen, John et al. 1994. *Contribution of Poverty 3 to the understanding of poverty, exclusion and integration.* Brussels, EEIG/Directorate General for Employment, Social Affairs and Industrial Relations.

André, Catherine. 1994. "La France des pauvres", in *Alternatives Economiques* (Dijon), 114 (Feb.), pp. 23-32.

Aponte, Robert. 1990. "Definitions of the underclass: A critical analysis", in Herbert Gans (ed.): *Sociology in America.* Newbury Park, Sage, pp. 117-138.

Ashford, Douglas. 1986. *The emergence of the Welfare States.* London, Basil Blackwell.

Auletta, Ken. 1982. *The underclass.* New York, Vintage.

Bakke, E.W. 1940. *The unemployed worker.* New Haven, Yale University Press.

Balibar, Etienne. 1992. "Inégalités, fractionnement social, exclusion: Nouvelles formes de l'antagonisme de classe?", in Joëlle Affichard and Jean-Baptiste de Foucauld (eds.): *Justice sociale et inégalités.* Paris, Editions Esprit, pp. 149-161.

Barou, Jacques. 1993. "Les paradoxes de l'intégration: De l'infortune des mots à la vertu des concepts", in *Ethnologie Française* (Paris), 23, 2 (Apr.-June), pp. 169-176.

Becker, Howard. 1963. *Outsiders.* New York, Free Press.

Bell, Linda; Freeman, Richard. 1991. "The causes of increasing interindustry wage dispersion in the United States", in *Industrial and Labour Relations Review* (Ithaca), 44, 2 (Jan.), p. 275.

Berstein, Serge; Rudelle, Odile. 1992. *Le modèle républicain.* Paris, Presses Universitaires de France.

Bloom, David; Freeman, Richard; Korenman, Sanders. 1988. "The labour-market consequences of generational crowding", in *European Journal of Population* (Amsterdam), 3, pp. 131-176.

Body-Gendrot, Sophie. 1993. "Migration and the racialization of the postmodern city in France", in M. Cross and M. Keith (eds.): *Racism, the city, and the State*. London, Routledge, pp. 77-93.

Bourdieu, Pierre (ed.). 1993. *La misère du monde*. Paris, Seuil.

Boyer, Robert (ed). 1987. *La flexibilité du travail en Europe*. Paris, Editions La Découverte.

Brubaker, Roger. 1992. *Citizenship and nationhood in France and Germany*. Cambridge, Harvard University Press.

Bulow, Jeremy; Summers, Lawrence. 1986. "A theory of dual labour markets with application to industrial policy, discrimination, and Keynesian unemployment", in *Journal of Labor Economics* (Chicago), 4, 3, part I, pp. 376-414.

Burnett, John. 1994. *Idle hands: The experience of unemployment, 1790-1990*. London, Routledge.

Carton, Luc. 1993. *Etat de la pauvreté dans la région de Bruxelles-Capitale*. 2 vols. Brussels, Fondation Travail-Université, Nov.

Castel, Robert. 1991. "De l'indigence à l'exclusion: la désaffiliation", in Jacques Donzelot (ed.): *Face à l'exclusion: Le modèle français*. Paris, Editions Esprit.

Chevalier, Jacques et al. 1992. *La solidarité: Un sentiment républicain?* Paris, Presses Universitaires de France.

Coleman, James. 1988. "Social capital in the creation of human capital", in *American Journal of Sociology* (Chicago), 94 (Supplement), pp. S95-120.

Commissariat Général du Plan (CGP). 1993. *L'insertion des adolescents en difficulté*. Paris, La Documentation Française.

—.1992. "L'exclusion, rupture du lien social", in *Problèmes économiques* (Paris), 2.252 (1 July), pp. 1-4.

Commission of the European Communities (EC Commission). 1993. *White Paper: Growth, competitiveness, employment*. Luxembourg.

—.1992. *Towards a Europe of solidarity: Intensifying the fight against social exclusion, fostering integration*. Brussels. Dec.

—.1991: *National policies to combat social exclusion, First Annual Report*. Edited by Graham Room. Brussels. Directorate General for Employment, Social Affairs and Industrial Relations.

Dahrendorf, Ralf. 1985. *The modern social conflict: An essay on the politics of liberty*. London, Weidenfeld and Nicolson.

—.1985. *Law and order*. Boulder, Colorado, Westview.

Danziger, Sheldon; Van der Gaag, Jacques; Taussig, Michael; Smolensky, Eugene. 1984. "The direct measurement of welfare levels: How much does it cost to make ends meet?", in *Review of Economics* (Amsterdam), 66, 3, pp. 500-505.

Daugareilh, Isabelle and Jean-Pierre Laborde (eds.). 1993. *Insertions et solitudes*. Bordeaux, Editions de la Maison des Sciences de l'Homme Aquitaine.

Davis, Steven. 1993. *Cross-country patterns of change in relative wages*. Cambridge, Massachusetts, National Bureau of Economic Research, Working Paper No. 4085.

Delahaye, Valérie. 1994. *Politiques de lutte contre le chômage et l'exclusion et mutation de l'action sociale*. Paris, Ecole nationale d'administration.

Dickens, William; Lang, Kevin. 1988. "The re-emergence of segmented labor market theory", in *American Economic Association Papers and Proceedings* (Nashville), May, pp. 129-134.

Doeringer, Peter; Piore, Michael. 1971. *Internal labor markets and manpower analysis.* Lexington, Massachusetts, D.C. Heath.

Donzelot, Jacques; Roman, Joel. 1991. "Le déplacement de la question sociale", in Jacques Donzelot (ed.): *Face à l'exclusion: Le modèle français,* Paris, Editions Esprit, pp. 5-11.

Douglas, Mary. 1966. *Purity and danger.* London, Routledge and Kegan Paul.

Dubet, François. 1987. *La galère: Jeunes en survie.* Paris, Fayard.

Duncan, Greg. 1984. *Years of poverty, years of plenty.* Ann Arbor, Michigan, Survey Research Center, University of Michigan.

EC Commission: see Commission of the European Communities.

Ellwood, David. 1988. *Poor support.* New York, Basic Books.

Engbersen, Godfried; Schuyt, Kees; Timmer, Jaap; Waarden, Van. 1993. *Cultures of unemployment.* Boulder, Colorado, Westview.

Esping-Andersen, Gosta. 1994: "The eclipse of the democratic class struggle? European class structures at *fin de siècle*". Paper presented at the Center for European Studies, Harvard University, Nov.

—.1991. *The three worlds of welfare capitalism.* Princeton, Princeton University Press.

Farrugia, Francis. 1993. *La crise du lien social: Essai de sociologie critique.* Paris, L'Harmattan.

Field, Frank. 1989. *Losing out: The emergence of Britain's underclass.* London, Basil Blackwell.

Fogarty, Michael. 1957. *Christian democracy in Western Europe 1820-1953.* Notre Dame, Notre Dame University Press.

de Foucauld, Jean-Baptiste. 1992a. "Exclusion, inégalités et justice sociale", in *Esprit* (Paris), No. 182 (June), pp. 47-57.

—.1992b. "Vouloir faire, savoir faire", in Joëlle Affichard and Jean-Baptiste de Foucauld (eds.): *Justice sociale et inégalités.* Paris, Editions Esprit, pp. 257-268.

Fragonard, Bertrand. 1993. *Cohésion sociale et prévention de l'exclusion.* Paris, Commissariat Général du Plan, Feb.

Fuchs, Victor. 1967. "Redefining poverty and redistributing income", in *Public interest* (Washington, DC), 8 (Summer), pp. 88-95.

Gallie, W. B. 1956. "Essentially contested concepts", in *Aristotelian Society Proceedings* (Oxford), 56, pp. 167-198.

Gans, Herbert J. 1993. "From 'underclass' to 'undercaste': Some observations about the future of the postindustrial economy and its major victims", in *International Journal of Urban and Regional Research* (Oxford), 17, 3, pp. 327-335.

—.1991. "The dangers of the underclass: Its harmfulness as a planning concept", in Herbert Gans (ed.): *People, plans, and policies.* New York, Columbia University Press, pp. 328-343.

Genestier, Philippe. 1991: "Pour une intégration communautaire", in *Esprit,* No. 169 (Feb.), pp. 48-59.

Gobelot, Edmond. 1925/1967. *La barrière et le niveau: Etude sociologique sur la bourgeoisie française moderne.* Paris, Presses Universitaires de France.

Godbout, Todd. 1993. "Employment change and sectoral distribution in 10 countries, 1970-90", in *Monthly Labor Review* (Washington, DC), (Oct.) pp. 3-20.

Golding, P. (ed). 1986. *Excluding the poor*. London, Child Poverty Action Group.

Gordon, David; Edwards, Richard; Reich, Michael. 1982. *Segmented work, divided workers: The historical transformation of labour in the United States*. Cambridge, UK, Cambridge University Press.

Gorz, André. 1989. *Critique of economic reason*. London, Verso.

Harrington, Michael. 1962. *The other America: Poverty in the United States*. Baltimore, Penguin.

Harris, David. 1987. *Justifying state welfare: The New Right vs. the Old Left*. London, Basil Blackwell.

Hatzfeld, Henri. 1971. *Du paupérisme à la sécurité sociale, 1850-1940*. Paris, Colin.

Hatzfeld, Marc. 1993. *L'insertion par l'activité économique: Des expériences, des pratiques, des acteurs*. Paris, Ministère du Travail, de l'Emploi et de la Formation Professionnelle/Syros.

Haut Conseil à l'intégration. 1992. *La connaissance de l'immigration et de l'intégration*. Paris, La Documentation Française.

—.1991. *Pour un modèle français d'intégration*. Paris, La Documentation Française.

Himmelfarb, Gertrude. 1984. *The idea of poverty: England in the early industrial age*. New York, Alfred A. Knopf.

Hirst, Paul; Zeitlin, Jonathan. 1991. "Flexible specialization versus post-Fordism: Theory, evidence and policy implications", in *Economy and Society* (London), 20, 1 (Feb.), pp. 1-54.

Hollifield, James. 1994. "Immigration and Republicanism in France: The hidden consensus". Paper presented at the International Conference of Europeanists, Council for European Studies, Chicago, Mar.

Immergut, Ellen. 1993. "Dilemmas of the welfare state in the current conjuncture". Paper presented to the Study Group on Citizenship and Social Policy, Center for European Studies, Harvard University.

Jahoda, Marie; Lazarsfeld, Paul; Zeisel, Hans. 1971. *Marienthal: The sociography of an unemployed community*. Chicago, Aldine.

Jencks, Christopher. 1991. "Is the American underclass growing?", in Christopher Jencks and Paul Peterson (eds.): *The urban underclass*. Washington, DC, The Brookings Institution, pp. 28-102.

—; Peterson, Paul (eds.). 1991. *The urban underclass*. Washington, DC, The Brookings Institution.

Katz, Lawrence. 1988. "Some recent developments in labour economics and their implications for macroeconomics", in *Journal of Money, Credit, and Banking* (Columbus), 20, 3 (Aug. Part 2), pp. 507-522.

—; Loveman, Gary; Blanchflower, David. 1994. "A comparison of changes in the structure of wages in four OECD countries", in Richard Freeman and Lawrence Katz (eds): *Differences and changes in wage structures*. Chicago, Chicago University Press for National Bureau for Economic Research.

Katz, Michael. 1989. *The undeserving poor*. New York, Pantheon.

Klanfer, Jules. 1965. *L'exclusion sociale*. Paris, Bureau de Recherches Sociales.

Klausen, Jytte. 1995. "Social rights advocacy and state-building: T.H. Marshall in the hands of social reformers", in *World Politics* (Baltimore) (Jan.).

Komarovsky, Mirra. 1940. *The unemployed worker and his family.* New York, Dryden Press.

Krueger, Alan; Summers, Lawrence. 1988. "Efficiency wages and the inter-industry wage structure", in *Econometrica* (Oxford), 56, 2 (Mar.), pp. 259-293.

Kronauer, Martin. 1993. "Unemployment in Western Europe: Individual and social consequences", in *International Journal of Political Economy* (Chicago), 23, 3 (Fall), pp. 3-13.

—; Vogel, Berthold; Gerlach, Frank. 1993. *Im Schatten der Arbeitsgesellschaft: Arbeitslose und die Dynamik sozialer Ausgrenzung.* Frankfurt, Campus Verlag.

Kuhn, Thomas. 1970. *The structure of scientific revolutions.* 2nd ed. Chicago, University of Chicago Press.

Lamont, Michele; Fournier, Marcel (eds.). 1992. *Cultivating differences: Symbolic boundaries and the making of inequality.* Chicago, University of Chicago Press.

Lang, Kevin; Dickens, William. 1988. "Neoclassical and sociological perspectives on segmented labour markets", in George Farkas and Paula England (eds.): *Industries, firms, and jobs: Sociological and economic approaches.* New York, Plenum, pp. 65-88.

Lenoir, René. 1974/1989. *Les exclus: Un Français sur dix.* 2nd ed. Paris, Seuil.

Lijphart, Arend. 1977. *Democracy in plural societies.* New Haven, Yale University Press.

Lindbeck, Assar; Snower, Dinnis. 1986. "Wage setting, unemployment, and insider-outsider relations", in *American Economic Review* (Nashville), 76 (May), pp. 235-239.

Linhart, Virginie. 1992. "Des Minguettes à Vaulx-en-Velin: Les réponses des pouvoirs publics aux violences urbaines", in *Revue française de Science Politique* (Paris), 3 (June), pp. 91-111.

Lipietz, Alain. 1986. "New tendencies in the international division of labor", in Alan Scott and Richard Storper (eds.): *Production, work, territory.* Boston, Allen and Unwin, pp. 16-40.

Lister, Ruth. 1990. *The exclusive society.* London, Child Poverty Action Group.

Marshall, T.H. 1950. *Citizenship and social class and other essays.* Cambridge, Cambridge University Press.

Mayer, Susan; Jencks, Christopher. 1989. "Poverty and the distribution of material hardships", in *Journal of Human Resources*, 24, 1, pp. 88-114.

Mead, Lawrence. 1986. *Beyond entitlement: The social obligations of citizenship.* New York, Free Press.

Mendras, Henri; with Alistair Cole. 1991. *Social change in modern France: Towards a cultural anthropology of the Fifth Republic.* Cambridge, Cambridge University Press and Editions de la Maison des Sciences de l'Homme. [Originally published as *La Seconde Révolution Française.* Paris, Gallimard].

Mongin, Olivier. 1992. "Le contrat social menacé?", in *Esprit*, No. 182 (June), pp. 5-11.

Morris, Lydia. 1994. *Dangerous classes: The underclass and social citizenship.* New York, Routledge.

—.1990. *The workings of the household: A US-UK comparison.* Cambridge, Polity.

Murphy, Raymond. 1988. *Social closure: The theory of monopolization and exclusion.* Oxford, Clarendon Press.

Murray, Charles. 1984. *Losing ground: American social policy 1950-1980.* New York, Basic.

Nasse, Philippe. 1992. *Exclus et exclusions: Connaître les populations, comprendre les processus.* Paris, Commissariat Général du Plan, Jan.

Newman, Katherine. 1988. *Falling from grace: The experience of downward mobility in the American middle class.* New York, Vintage.

Nicolet, Claude. 1982. *L'idée républicaine en France: Essai d'histoire critique.* Paris, Gallimard.

Organisation for Economic Co-operation and Development. 1993. *Employment Outlook.* Paris.

—.1989. *Labour market flexibility: Trends in enterprises.* Paris.

—.1986. *Flexibility in the labour market: The current debate.* Paris.

Pahl, R.E. 1984. *Divisions of labour.* Oxford, Blackwell.

Parkin, Frank. 1974. "Strategies of social closure in class formation", in Frank Parkin (ed.): *The social analysis of class structure.* London, Tavistock, pp. 1-18.

Patterson, James. 1981. *America's struggle against poverty 1900-1980.* Cambridge, Harvard University Press.

Paugam, Serge. 1993. *La société française et ses pauvres.* Paris, Presses Universitaires de France.

—.1991. *La disqualification sociale: essai sur la nouvelle pauvreté.* Paris, Presses Universitaires de France.

Piore, Michael; Sabel, Charles. 1984. *The second industrial divide.* New York, Basic Books.

Portes, Alejandro; Castells, Manuel; Benton, Lauren (eds.). 1989. *The informal economy: Studies in advanced and less developed countries.* Baltimore, Johns Hopkins University Press.

Procacci, Giovanna. 1993. *Gouverner la misère: La question sociale en France 1789-1848.* Paris, Seuil.

—.1989. "Sociology and its poor", in *Politics and Society* (Newbury Park), 17, 2 (June), pp. 163-187.

Putnam, Robert. 1993. "The prosperous community: Social capital and public life", in *American Prospect* (Cambridge, Massachusetts), Spring, pp. 35-42.

Rainwater, Lee. 1992. *Poverty in American eyes,* Luxembourg Income Study Working Paper No. 80. Luxembourg, CEPS/INSTEAD.

—.1990. *Poverty and equivalence as social constructions,* Luxembourg Income Study Working Paper No. 55. Luxembourg, CEPS/INSTEAD.

—.1974: *What money buys: Inequality and the social meanings of income.* New York, Basic Books.

Reynaud, Emmanuèle. 1993. "Le chômage de longue durée: la théorie et l'action", in *Revue française de sociologie* (Paris), 34, 2, pp. 271-291.

Riggs, Fred W. 1988. *The Intercocta Manual: Towards an international encyclopaedia of social science terms.* Paris, Unesco.

Rodgers, Gerry; Rodgers, Janine (eds.). 1989. *Precarious jobs in labour market regulation: The growth of atypical employment in Western Europe.* Geneva, International Labour Office.

Room, Graham et al. 1992. *Observatory on National Policies to Combat Social Exclusion, Second Annual Report*. Brussels, Directorate General for Employment, Social Affairs and Industrial Relations, Commission of the European Communities.

—.1990. *'New poverty' in the European Community*. London, St. Martin's.

Rosanvallon, Pierre. *1992. Le sacre du citoyen: Histoire du suffrage universel en France*. Paris, Gallimard.

Roy, Olivier. 1991. "Ethnicité, bandes et communautarisme", in *Esprit*, No. 169 (Feb.), pp. 37-47.

Ruano-Borbalan, Jean-Claude. 1993. "L'imaginaire de l'exclusion", in *Sciences Humaines* 28 (May), pp. 29-30.

Ruggles, Patricia. 1990. *Drawing the line: Alternative poverty measures and their implications for public* policy. Washington, DC, Urban Institute Press.

Runciman, W. G. 1990. "How many classes are there in contemporary British society?" in *Sociology* (Solihull), 24, 3, pp. 377-396.

Schlozman, Kay; Verba, Sidney. 1979. *Insult to injury*. Cambridge, Harvard University Press.

Schmitter Heisler, Barbara. 1991. "A comparative perspective on the underclass: Questions of urban poverty, race, and citizenship", in *Theory and Society* (Dordrecht), 20, 4 (Aug.), pp. 455-484.

Schnapper, Dominique. 1991. *La France de l'intégration: Sociologie de la nation en 1990*. Paris, Gallimard.

Silver, Allan. 1990. "The curious importance of small groups in American sociology", in Herbert J. Gans. (ed.): *Sociology in America*. Newbury Park, Sage, pp. 61-72.

Smith, David J. (ed.). 1992. *Understanding the underclass*. London, Policy Studies Institute.

Stafford, Walter; Ladner, Joyce. 1990. "Political dimensions of the underclass concept", in Herbert Gans (ed.): *Sociology in America*. Newbury Park, Sage, pp. 138-155.

Stedman-Jones, Gareth. 1984. *Outcast London*. London, Penguin.

Stepan, Alfred. 1978. *The State and society: Peru in comparative perspective*. Princeton, Princeton University Press.

Stoléru, Lionel. 1977. *Vaincre la pauvreté dans les pays riches*. Paris, Flammarion.

Streeten, Paul. 1993. "Comments on The 'Framework of ILO Action against Poverty'". Presented at the symposium on Poverty: New Approaches to Analysis and Policy, International Institute for Labour Studies, Geneva.

Taguieff, Pierre-André. 1991. *Face au racisme*. 2 vols. Paris, La Découverte.

—.1988. *La force du préjugé: Essai sur le racisme et ses doubles*. Paris, La Découverte.

Tarling, Roger (ed) 1987. *Flexibility in labour markets*. New York, Academic.

Thurow, Lester. 1975. *Generating inequality: Mechanisms of distribution in the US economy*. New York, Basic Books.

Touraine, Alain. 1992. "Inégalités de la société industrielle, exclusion du marché", in Joëlle Affichard and Jean-Baptiste de Foucauld (eds.): *Justice sociale et inegalités*, Paris, Editions Esprit, pp. 163-176.

—.1991. "Face à l'exclusion", in *Esprit*, No. 169 (Feb.), pp. 7-13.

Townsend, Peter. 1993. *The international analysis of poverty.* Milton Keynes, Harvester Wheatsheaf.

—.1987. "Deprivation", in *Journal of Social Policy* (Cambridge, UK), 16, 2, pp. 125-146.

—.1979. *Poverty in the United Kingdom.* Harmondsworth, Penguin.

van Praag, Bernard; Goedhart, Theo; Kapteyn, Arie. 1980. "The poverty line: A pilot survey in Europe", in *Review of Economics and Statistics*, 62, 3, pp. 461-465.

Verdes-Leroux, Jeannine. 1978. "Les 'exclus'", in *Actes de la Recherche en Sciences Sociales* (Paris), 19 (Jan.), pp. 61-66.

Vincens, Jean. 1993. "Réflexions sur le chômage de longue durée", in *Revue française de sociologie* (Paris), 34 (July-Sep.), pp. 327-344.

Weinberg, Achille; Ruano-Borbalan, Jean-Claude. 1993. "Comprendre l'exclusion", in *Sciences Humaines,* 28 (May), pp. 12-15.

Williams, Raymond. 1985. *Keywords.* New York, Oxford University Press.

Wilson, William Julius. 1987. *The truly disadvantaged.* Chicago, University of Chicago Press.

Wolfe, Alan. 1992. "Democracy versus sociology: Boundaries and their political consequences", in Michele Lamont and Marcel Fournier (eds.): *Cultivating differences: Symbolic boundaries and the making of inequality*, Chicago, University of Chicago Press.

Wuhl, Simon. 1992. "Chômage: de la longue durée à l'exclusion", in *Esprit,* No. 182 (June), pp. 12-22.

—.1991. *De chômage à l'exclusion.* Paris, Syros.

Xiberras, Martine. 1993. *Les théories de l'exclusion.* Paris, Meridiens Klincksieck.

Yépez del Castillo, Isabel. 1993. "Review of the French and Belgian literature on social exclusion: A Latin American perspective". Discussion paper for UNDP-IILS project on "Patterns and causes of social exclusion", International Labour Office, Geneva.

Young, Crawford (ed.). 1993. *The rising tide of cultural pluralism: The nation-state at bay?* Madison, University of Wisconsin Press.

WORK AND DEVELOPMENT

Henry BRUTON* and David FAIRRIS**

7

From the outset of interest in economic development in the late 1940s, great attention has been given to employment in low-income countries. In Arthur Lewis's early and influential article, a less developed country was defined as one in which there was a large pool of people who were either unemployed or whose productivity was low or even zero (Lewis, 1954). The great task of development was seen as that of creating a demand for labour such that its productivity would be positive and growing. This objective was to be accomplished primarily through capital formation in a modern, capitalist sector.

Since those early years, the labour issue in development has become more complex than that of simply creating jobs. Skills and the idea of human capital and its creation more generally, the institutions and norms of the labour market and labour practices in developing countries, the shadow wage notion, the role of unions, and labour/management relations in general are all now recognized as important. More recently, considerations with respect to labour have widened even more. The labour issue now includes a role for work not simply as a source of income but as a direct source of well-being and as an important factor in generating and maintaining growth.[1]

This article takes up three distinct, but related, aspects of the latter set of issues: efficiency and justice in the allocation of resources to working conditions quality; the role of the workplace, and labour's role in production in particular, in generating productivity and its growth; and the way that work fits in with and serves other social activities and thereby contributes to well-being beyond its purely financial rewards.[2]

The general point of departure is as follows. Because a person fortunate enough to have a full-time job will spend at least one half of his/her waking hours at work, it is incumbent on social scientists to investigate the

Originally published in *International Labour Review*, Vol. 138 (1999), No. 1.

* Department of Economics, Williams College, Williamstown, MA. ** Department of Economics, University of California, Riverside, CA.

conditions necessary for the maintenance of working conditions that are safe and pleasant, and for the creation of jobs that contribute to individual and social well-being. Based on that investigation, the question which then needs to be asked – and answered – is whether working conditions are currently "adequate" in developing countries.

This investigation begins by framing the issue in the context of neoclassical economic analysis. The question that economists usually ask is "does society allocate resources efficiently with regard to the stated demands of workers and employers concerning workplace conditions?" This article identifies circumstances under which the market will succeed in allocating resources efficiently, and circumstances under which it is likely to fail to do so. But it also moves beyond this narrow conception of the "adequacy" of working conditions. Indeed, there are at least three limitations to this neoclassical way of framing the issue. First, and most obvious perhaps, is that allocatively efficient arrangements can be – to paraphrase Amartya Sen (1970) – perfectly disgusting from a moral point of view. One might, thus, conclude that although allocatively efficient, the resources flowing to the provision of such things as workplace safety in developing countries are, by virtue of extreme inequalities in the distribution of wealth and income for example, suboptimal from the point of view of justice.

Second, and less obvious, is that neoclassical analysis typically views the quality of working conditions as the equivalent of a consumption good for workers and as a component of labour costs to firms – of a sort that is either direct (e.g. purchasing safety shoes for workers) or indirect (e.g. lost productivity due to a slower, but safer pace of production). This view, however, obscures the link between worker satisfaction and productivity. It will be argued here that the discretionary effort of workers in production is often contingent on their views of the justice and legitimacy of the conditions under which they labour. Moreover, for an economy to grow, labour must learn on the job, but learning by doing requires a work environment that is conducive to searching and learning by the workforce. This mutually constitutive aspect of worker satisfaction, autonomy and productivity is too seldom considered in the conventional neoclassical literature.

A final limitation of the conventional economic view of working conditions is that it is consequentialist – that is, it takes the self-reported goals of workers and employers in the economy, given the resource endowments and technologies of production available to them, as the sole basis for judging whether working conditions are optimal. There are reasons for concern with consequentialist notions of welfare, and an attempt is made here to clarify non-consequentialist notions of the meaningfulness of work. This approach takes explicit account of the endogeneity of interests; who we are determines the kind of work we wish to do, but the kind of work we do also determines who we are. In this view, work is seen as more integrated with culture, norms and a way of life, and "well-being" is a far more complex concept.

This article endeavours to put this set of issues into a general theoretical framework, to reflect empirically on some of the key points raised in the analysis, and to offer some general policy prescriptions for developing countries that follow therefrom. A preliminary point is appropriate before moving forward, however.

It is tempting to argue that in developing countries where per capita income and labour productivity are both extremely low and unemployment and underemployment extremely high, the overwhelmingly important objective is simply to create jobs that pay a living wage. The quality of work is often viewed as a luxury, to be sought only after incomes are much higher. This temptation must be rejected for two reasons.

First, there is substantial evidence to suggest that qualitative issues are as crucial at low incomes as at higher ones. Even at low incomes, workers value safety, relationships with management consistent with the prevailing norms and customs, and meaningful work. And second, at the outset of change there may be more freedom and more opportunity to introduce policies and practices that reflect the many sided nature of work and the workplace than after the industrialization process is well under way. If industrialization (and structural change in general) takes place in an environment where both the quality of working conditions and the meaning of work are ignored, it may be difficult later on to establish practices, policies and institutions that properly reflect the role of work in the overall search for well-being.

An analogy can be found in arguments to the effect that developing countries must achieve a much higher GDP before they take heed of environmental issues. Fortunately, this view has lost much ground, and it is increasingly appreciated that it is extremely helpful and usually much easier to get an environmental policy in place as growth begins, not after interests are created that will be penalized by such a policy. The same kind of argument applies to workplace norms and institutions. Indeed, over-emphasis on rates of growth of per capita output as the criterion of well-being is ill-advised and can lead to myopic policies.

THE ADEQUACY OF WORKING CONDITIONS: THEORETICAL REFLECTIONS

Working conditions and allocative efficiency

While modern-day economists rarely posit the importance of working conditions to workers, there is nothing in their analytical framework that rules out a consideration of these issues. Indeed, building on Adam Smith's analysis of wage differentials in his *An inquiry into the nature and causes of the wealth of nations* (1776), a small body of literature has emerged that models workers' preferences for working conditions and how these preferences influence economic outcomes via the market. This body of literature is identified with what has become known as the theory of compensating wage differentials (see, for example, Rosen, 1974).

Under certain circumstances, the labour market will serve as an efficient device for the allocation of resources to workplace quality. Jobs vary as to the degree of danger or tedium of the tasks involved, and workers vary as to the extent to which they value jobs that are free from these workplace "bads". Workers can "purchase" good working conditions by accepting a lower wage, and employers can attract workers to conditions that are "bad" by offering to pay more for labour. When the labour market comes into equilibrium, workers and employers will have "matched" in ways that best suit their preferences and technologies, backed of course by the purchasing power of the respective parties to meet their workplace goals. In equilibrium, the variation in wages paid to similarly skilled workers thus represents the compensating differential for the bundle of workplace "bads" workers experience.

If workers are fully informed of the psychological and other health-related consequences of their workplace choices, and labour mobility is costless, and employers and workers are price takers, and there is a healthy demand for labour leading to full employment, then workers sacrifice good working conditions only to the extent that doing so serves other, more highly-valued desires such as consumption. Working conditions outcomes are thereby allocatively efficient.

The requisites for optimality of working conditions in a dynamic context, with technological change and economic growth, raise a more difficult issue.[3]

Even here, though, because workplace "bads" require that employers pay compensating payments in the form of higher wages, it can be argued that new technologies will not be adopted by firms unless these new techniques reflect workers' preferences – that is, unless they leave the quality of working conditions unchanged or provide, through enhanced productivity, the compensation workers require to work under the new conditions. Indeed, the possibility of reducing wages through improved working conditions offers firms an incentive to adopt technologies that do just this.

Note that this analysis of working conditions points to an important deficiency in the use of productivity and its growth as measures of social welfare. Increased productivity may lead to reduced unit labour costs and increased wages and profits, but also to increased intensity of labour effort and perhaps reduced workplace health and safety. If there are net costs for workers, and these costs outweigh the gains to employers, an increase in productivity will not improve welfare in either a Pareto or Kaldor-Hicks sense.[4] Thus, social welfare cannot be measured by labour productivity alone, but rather requires a more complicated measure that takes into account shop-floor conditions as well. This result may obtain even when wage rates rise to the full extent of the productivity increase.

Some of the conditions which are necessary for the labour market to serve as an allocative device for working conditions may fail to hold, in which case the labour market fails to generate efficient outcomes. Workers are seldom fully aware of the health-related consequences of working conditions choices, or of alternative job prospects. Moreover, various impediments exist to the mobility of labour, from macroeconomically generated unemployment to job-specific skills with the present employer which may lower wage expectations from the next best alternative. Under such circumstances, workers would be discouraged from quitting their present job even though they deemed the current sacrifice of workplace quality to be undesirable.

Other conditions may prevent the labour market from serving as an adequate mechanism for the revelation of worker preferences over working conditions, but most of these can be fully mitigated by perfect information and costless mobility. It can be claimed, for example, that many workplace "bads" are collective in nature, and that their improvement thereby constitutes a public good, with all the attendant market failures that have come to be associated with that term. For example, the speed of the assembly line is experienced equally by all who are a part of its rhythms, and a reduction in its speed would redound to all in a non-rival and non-excludable form. However, with ease of mobility and an abundance of alternative jobs, the existence of local public goods poses no particular problem for the labour market; workers will simply locate in firms that offer the optimal wage/working conditions mix for them.[5]

Labour markets will indeed fail to serve as an adequate allocative device for working conditions if labour mobility is impaired and workers are uninformed of the consequences of their choices. In this case, alternative institutional arrangements, in the form of unions or government regulation, may be required to ensure that optimal resources are allocated to working conditions (e.g. safety goggles and reduced speed in production). Collective bodies such as unions or works councils may facilitate collective decision-making over local public goods when labour mobility is impeded, and address workers' imperfect knowledge with respect to working conditions consequences. Government regulation may force firms to devote more nearly optimal resources to the provision of better quality working conditions.

Union, however, may cause misallocation of labour, and it is easy to argue that government failure is so rampant and so intractable that any approach that calls for an active role by the government is doomed to failure. Yet, neither the presence of a monopoly side to union activity nor government failure means that unrestricted markets work better. Markets may fail abysmally, and in many cases there will be powerful non-governmental agencies that can exploit the market for their own gain. Thus, the problem centres on how to proceed in the presence of various market and government failures.

Working conditions and justice in the distribution of rewards

A basic criticism of the neoclassical economic approach to working conditions is that it ignores issues of distributive justice. Indeed, the primary objection to the quality of working conditions in many societies today arguably rests on the issue of distributive justice, not allocative inefficiency. Thus, health and safety regulation typically emerges out of a concern for the unfair treatment of workers, not because workers are unable to reach mutually advantageous arrangements with employers to improve workplace safety in exchange for lower wages.

Justice and fairness are difficult concepts in any context, but especially so when examining the role of the workplace in well-being and its enhancement over time in a developing country. Economists typically abstract from these concerns by taking the distribution of income and wealth as given, and then asking whether resources flow to their highest valued use – where "value" reflects both preference satisfaction and ability to pay. The fact that work in coal mines significantly reduces both the quality of life and the life expectancy of workers need not indicate an inefficient allocation of resources to safety in mines. It simply means that workers do not possess sufficient purchasing power (i.e. income and wealth) to entice employers to provide better mine safety.

To see how purchasing power, and thus the distribution of income and wealth, matters in the case of working conditions, conduct the following thought experiment: what would happen to mine safety if the distribution of income and wealth were equalized tomorrow and safety were a normal good? It is pretty clear that labour supply to the mines in most countries would be substantially reduced, and that in order to attract workers to the mining sector employers would have to raise the compensating wage payment and/or improve safety. In other words, the increased purchasing power of workers would allow them to "purchase" improved safety by forgoing dangerous jobs, which, in turn, would force employers with dangerous working conditions to improve those conditions (or pay dramatically increased wages) in order to maintain a sufficient labour supply.

It might be argued that there are inevitably trade-offs, and that producing more output generally requires that the quality of working conditions be sacrificed. According to this view, the only important question is whether workers are sacrificing an inefficient amount of workplace quality in the process of production. However, the criticism introduced in this section suggests that, even if efficient, the sacrifice might be too great to the extent that workers possess an unjust share of the income/wealth pie. If workers value workplace quality, and it exhibits a positive income elasticity of demand, and workers do not possess their fair share of the income and wealth of a society, then they sacrifice too much workplace quality for output and its growth.

Worker satisfaction, autonomy, and productivity

Thus far it has been assumed that workers care about the conditions under which they work, but, beyond that, working conditions have not been treated differently from any other "good" produced in society. To be sure, this particular "good" is a joint product of the production process of more ordinary goods and services, but it is no different from other goods and services in the sense that it yields satisfaction and requires resources to produce (e.g. the forgone output associated with reduced physical exertion). This section of the article challenges this view of the workplace by arguing that the work environment may itself be an "input" of sorts into productivity and its growth.

Put somewhat differently, the analyses of the last two sections assumed that in the absence of market failures, society would be on its production frontier, and that the choice must then be made between greater output of goods and services and better working conditions. This section examines the possibility that the work environment experience of workers may play a role in shifting that frontier outward, and thus that there need not always exist a trade-off of output for workplace quality even in the absence of market (as distinct from institutional) failures.

Offered below are two analyses that illustrate this point. Both rest on the simple and sensible proposition that no technique of production can be fully described by blueprints that spell out every step in the production process. Workers are therefore likely to have some discretion in how they do their work, and will be compelled to improvise and adapt to changing and unanticipated circumstances. Labour productivity, in turn, depends on how workers feel about the work they do and on the local and tacit knowledge (as distinct from schooling or skill requirements) they have acquired about production, typically by tinkering and experimenting.

Labour productivity, workplace justice and legitimacy

Recent contributions to the literature on the production process and the productive performance of labour emphasize the importance of workers' feelings about work. Akerlof (1982) has argued that workplace productivity might improve if employers were to offer their workers a "gift" of improved conditions, which would engender feelings of good will and reciprocity. Fairris (1997) has argued that the extent of workers' cooperation with management in production, and thus workplace productivity, depends on workers' sense that rewards are being distributed in a "just" manner and that managerial authority is "legitimate". Workers' discretionary effort is more forthcoming when trust, fairness and respect are components of workplace industrial relations.

The extent to which workers view their relationship with management as possessing these attributes is determined by the formal and informal institutional arrangements of the employment relationship. Cooperation – including such things as reduced absenteeism, greater care in work, and acceptance of new technologies – is fostered by improved communication between labour and management, an enhanced belief in the truth of that communication, and the belief of both parties that the structure of decision-making authority is legitimate and the distribution of rewards from production is just. Cooperation fosters efficiency in firm performance and its growth over time.[6]

Why might employers fail to establish institutional arrangements conducive to feelings of justice and legitimacy on the part of workers, and to the efficiency enhancement such feelings foster? One answer is that efficiency enhancement can have distributional consequences that employers wish to avoid (Marglin, 1974; Bowles, 1985). Suppose, for example, that granting workers greater power in shop-floor decision-making enhances efficiency by making shop-floor outcomes more just and by rendering managerial authority more legitimate, thereby improving labour's willingness to cooperate with management. But suppose that doing so also puts workers in a position to appropriate a larger share of the rewards from production, implying potential losses for employers. Moving to a more efficient level of firm performance does not necessarily leave all parties at least as well off as before.

The extent to which institutional and organizational changes that grant workers a greater role in production will in turn result – via a greater sense of justice and legitimacy – in increased productivity is likely to vary across firms. It seems quite clear that the "ethos" of a firm undergoing such changes would be affected, and that a firm's productivity is affected by its "ethos". Productivity can be affected both directly (more careful effort) and indirectly (by the greater willingness of workers to adapt to new routines and new technologies). Thus, changes of this sort are not always simply a matter of increased costs.

Productivity growth and worker learning

Labour productivity is low in developing countries. To eliminate widespread poverty requires that labour productivity rise. It is therefore necessary to distinguish between low productivity (currently the case) and rising productivity. Low and static productivity is a dead end, while low but rising productivity is an essential characteristic of a successful developing country. There is evidence that the activities of the workforce and the nature of the work environment are strategic to achieving sustained growth of labour productivity. In studying the role of labour in a developing country, therefore, one must ask about the kind of labour environment that helps to achieve this objective.

The bottom line is to establish a work environment which induces searching and learning as a routine part of working. A sentence by Joseph

Stiglitz makes the point: "The frame of mind which is associated with asking 'how can this task be performed better?' is fundamentally different from the frame of mind which is associated with asking 'how am I supposed to perform this task?'" (1987, p. 6). How then to create an environment in which the first question is constantly recognized? There are many aspects to this issue – including the proper incentives, especially price incentives – but the following discussion focuses on the nature of the knowledge accumulation process.

Although the origins and nature of productivity growth have been widely studied for several decades, generalization in this field still calls for great caution. Two points have emerged that have considerable empirical and theoretical justification and that are highly relevant to the present discussion:

- A great deal of the knowledge that is directly used and useable in production is local and tacit in contrast to generic and amenable to complete description. Such knowledge is necessarily created within the enterprise or the community in which it is used and cannot (by definition) be sold or transported to other firms or areas.[7]

- This accumulation of local and tacit knowledge occurs as production takes place – learning by doing, learning by using, by explicit searching and by tinkering. Such learning is in significant part what happens on the shop floor. It does not occur in just any work environment and does not occur automatically.

The question now is what kind of shop-floor situation and work environment more generally creates conditions that will result in the workforce contributing to this sort of learning and knowledge accumulation.

The above quotation from Stiglitz refers to "frame of mind", a notion different from incentives as usually defined. Frame of mind is partly a consequence of the prevailing attitudes and institutions in the community, and these in turn have effects on the kind of incentives that will have the desired result. The matter is especially complex in those countries (most of the developing countries) where much of the labour force engaged in industrial activity still has some links with more traditional activities, and with widespread and long-term poverty. Widespread, long-term poverty results in institutions and attitudes that help make poverty bearable, rather than in facilitating learning and change. Cultural and religious institutions in particular are safety oriented and, where prevalent, can significantly dampen activities that involve risks.[8] In such an environment, as several observers have noted, members of the labour force may have to learn how to learn or, more fundamentally, learn how to search in order to learn.

These arguments add major complications to understanding labour's role in the economy and to the design of policies that recognize these aspects of the role of work. Now it is not simply a matter of allocating resources given the state of knowledge, but a matter of allocating resources and creating institutional arrangements such that the role of labour as discretionary producer, searcher and learner can be fully recognized.

Non-consequentialist views: The intrinsic meaningfulness of work

That work possesses (or should possess) special meaning for workers is a belief held by many of the most important thinkers of the modern era. Marx was among the major proponents of this view, maintaining that the essence of human happiness is the freedom to be creative in work, actively to create the world around us according to our conception of how it should be. Marx's criticism of capitalism, in fact, rested fundamentally on its denial of precisely this freedom to all who laboured within its domain.[9]

Non-Marxist thinkers have held similar views. John Rawls' famous treatise on the just society, for example, while striving not to embrace any particular view of what constitutes human happiness, none the less expressly privileges the world of work. Rawls claims that the just society would maintain "fair equality of opportunity" for all in access to occupations. And in a discussion of the importance of a high standard of living, he states that: "What men want is meaningful work in free association with others... To achieve this state of things great wealth is not necessary. In fact, beyond some point it is more likely to be a positive hindrance, a meaningless distraction at best if not a temptation to indulgence and emptiness" (1971, p. 290).

Both Marx and Rawls, as well as many other important social analysts, hold what are called non-consequentialist views of social welfare. That is, they do not look to peoples' expressed interests as the sole criterion for judging what it is that constitutes human happiness. Marx, more than most, privileged the world of work in his conception of the good life – or, as he called it, the "true realm of freedom". However, similar positions on the importance of work can be found in the literature on developing countries. Here, the emphasis is on the degrading nature of much available work, its dissociation from the social life of the individual, and the general social transformation that accompanies the development process (Bruton, 1997).

One of the strongest reasons for embracing non-consequentialist views of human happiness is that preferences or interests are endogenous – they are formed by the social system in which we function. Economic theory, and consequentialism in particular, assume that preferences are "given" and ask no questions about their origins or their moral or ethical validity.[10] If preferences are in fact affected by economic activity, by policies and by the way the economy works – i.e. if preferences are deemed to be endogenous to the working of the system – then an argument can be made for abandoning consequentialism as a methodological approach for determining individual and social welfare.[11] In countries where industrialization is taking place at a rapid pace and where the content and demands of jobs, the organization and ethos of the workplace, the hierarchical relationships and so on are different from what obtained in the past and are being superimposed on a general social system that evolved over time with different arrangements, organized for different purposes, the "meaningfulness" of work may be in considerable jeopardy. This must be a matter of significance to the study of labour economics in developing countries.[12] It is also an important factor in achieving sustained, stable growth.

In the 1950s, for example, the view was widely held that in most developing countries – especially in rural areas – there was little or no differentiation of the economic as a distinct sector of social life. Wilbert Moore (1951) has an especially clear discussion of this notion. Moore argues that because of the absence of this sharp distinction, "reciprocity within an established organizational context is more highly valued than private gain". He adds that "the incentive offered to participate in any new productive activity must either fit the existing functional matrix, or else depend on such changes in the social structure as will make the incentive effective" (1951, p. 172).

Moore claims that any separation of work from the social context that gives work its meaning and that corresponds to "motives strongly instilled and accepted as natural requires a radical departure from traditional patterns" (1951, p. 172). He argues that people will work hard when the "productive activities fit a meaningful pattern of social existence", and adds that all workers everywhere are like this. The basic idea is that for work to be other than a source of disutility, it must be seen as an integral part of one's general social milieu, not outside of that milieu and not as something to be done simply to earn money.[13]

This strong position has changed over the decades. Workers, for example, have appeared to be much more responsive to wage incentives than the Moore argument implies. But the more general point surely remains: in some way or other, work should "fit" the larger social environment; it should be consistent with the values and institutions and "non-work" activities of the society. Sharp changes in work routines and practices and organizations impose costs that cannot be compensated for by money income.[14] The fact that workers join new activities voluntarily, of their own free will, does not mean that all costs are offset by the resulting income, or that their well-being is enhanced.

These arguments, though they are vague and lack rigour, are an important part of understanding how work contributes to well-being and its enhancement in countries that are rapidly changing. The essence is that a job that provides only income, but not recognition, not learning, not compatibility with the rest of the social environment, is a job that cannot do much to enhance the well-being of the worker.[15] Where changes in the institutions and other basic characteristics of a society are urged – or imposed – in order to achieve a higher level of output, these basic characteristics are being viewed as instruments for the achievement of economic objectives rather than as autonomous characteristics which, themselves, contribute to the well-being of individuals and society.[16]

THE ADEQUACY OF WORKING CONDITIONS: FURTHER REFLECTIONS AND EXAMPLES

In the preceding pages, it has been argued that the labour economics of developing countries should be widened and deepened compared to the treatment found in textbooks. It is necessary to do this because work and the workplace are a major source of the well-being of an individual and of a society. Workplace conditions, managerial practices, the extent of on-the-job learning, and the meaningfulness of work must be included in a study of labour in developing countries, alongside the more traditional topics, such as the determination of wages and the demand for labour. This section reflects upon empirical evidence that illustrates and further illuminates the foregoing arguments.

Allocative efficiency and the conditions of work

During the early stages of a successful industrialization process – especially one in which there is plenty of room for on-the-job learning and tinkering – tension may emerge between the conditions necessary for the efficiency of labour markets and those required for the establishment of practices and institutions and an "ethos" that will, over time, contribute to labour performing the roles examined in the preceding sections. This tension is not the result of misleading price signals, distorting policies or rent seeking. Rather, it is a consequence of the nature of the development process.

A tension of this very sort emerged, for example, during the period of rapid industrialization in the early 20th century in the United States (Fairris, 1997).[17] As discussed above, a well-functioning labour market can facilitate efficient matching of workers and employers and provide for the transmission of workers' workplace concerns through a process of labour quits or exits. Fishback and Kantor (1992) provide evidence that turn-of-the-century labour markets in the United States did function in this regard, at least to the extent that they forced employers to compensate employees for workplace "bads" through compensating payments.

However, labour mobility may be very costly to firms which, in order to economize on recruitment and training costs or ensure maximum opportunities for worker learning and tinkering, wish to maintain a stable workforce. And indeed, beginning in the 1910s, many progressive employers in the United States acted to reduce the very high rates of voluntary labour turnover existing at that time through the introduction of internal labour markets and benefits such as pension plans and paid vacations that were tied to an employee's length of service with the firm.

These efforts increased firm efficiency at the same time as they undercut the ability of the labour market to act as an efficient device for the regulation of shop-floor conditions. Stable employees were inhibited from using the market to resolve workplace discontents, but, due to the collective nature of many of their discontents, neither could they turn to individual contracting with employers. Instead, collective organizations emerged – first, in the form of independent unions in the late 1910s, followed by the so-called company unions of the 1920s – as voice mechanisms to replace the crippled exit option. Empirical evidence reveals that these were efficient institutional developments compared to reliance on the market mechanism (Fairris, 1997, Ch. 1).

Numerous examples exist in both developed and developing countries of mutually-advantageous adjustments to working conditions that the market mechanism, via quits and job changes, was apparently unable to bring about. Moreover, voluntary exits do not seem like the appropriate mechanism for regulating working conditions when the ideal is employment stability for the purpose of facilitating on-the-job learning and tinkering for heightened growth and development. Where exit, or threatened exit, cannot bring off the desired result, evidence suggests that some form of worker voice may prove necessary. This point is elaborated upon in the policy section that concludes this article.

Justice and fairness and the conditions of work

What is the appropriate means by which to improve the quality of working conditions in the name of justice and fairness? Although economists tend to be agnostics on what constitutes justice in the distribution of rewards, they typically possess strong views on the means by which justice should be brought about once society decides what precisely is meant by the term.

It is popular among economists to argue for monetary compensation (e.g. lump-sum taxes and transfers) in lieu of in-kind transfers or market regulation as redistributive measures to improve the well-being of the less fortunate. With money, in contrast to in-kind transfers, people can buy whatever they choose. Lump-sum transfers, in contrast to market regulation, allow for efficiency in the allocation of resources. This approach to justice appears never to have been put forth with regard to workplace conditions such as health and safety or the intensity of labour effort. However, it seems perfectly consistent with the market-oriented view of the determination of working conditions, which suggests that workers effectively "buy" the level of workplace safety that accords with their preferences and purchasing power.

Greater equality of purchasing power will generate improved workplace safety only if workers' preferences possess the appropriate characteristics (e.g. safety is a normal good) and the labour market acts as an efficient device by which workers can communicate those preferences to management. The sparse empirical evidence on the relation between increased income and improved workplace conditions provides no firm conclusions. Empirical analyses using cross-sectional data on individuals have found limited support for the notion that income effects are positive for workplace health and safety, *ceteris paribus* (Fairris, 1992; Garen, 1988).

Country-level empirical evidence – on workplace injury rates over time as per capita income grows – produces mixed results. Among the more developed economies, for example, Japan made significant progress in improving workplace health and safety in the period immediately following the Second World War, whereas the United States did not (see Fairris, 1997, Ch. 5). Indeed, it was during the 1960s, when real wages grew most rapidly for manufacturing workers in the United States, that manufacturing injury rates also rose very rapidly.

An important question in the interpretation of this evidence is whether the observed positive relationship between income and workplace quality was generated by the market, as opposed to, say, government regulation or private sector worker voice. The cross-sectional results of micro-surveys of workers yield little useful information in this regard. And the time-series findings on countries do not lend themselves to strong conclusions. Japan managed to improve workplace safety rather dramatically over the immediate post-war period, but the growing importance of lifetime employment during this period cautions against attributing these improvements to market forces.

There are two objections to using income redistribution in combination with the market mechanism for creating workplace justice and fairness, regardless of what the empirical evidence reveals on this matter. The first is that, even if markets worked efficiently with regard to the determination of workplace quality, a mechanism that relies on voluntary labour turnover may not meet workers' preferences regarding employment security, or may be very costly in terms of forgone opportunities for on-the-job learning and tinkering, which require employment stability in order to contribute significantly to growth and development.

The second objection, which has been put forward most eloquently by Michael Walzer (1983), is a moral one. Walzer argues that societies may desire different rules for the allocation of different kinds of goods. When a society comes to the conclusion that safe work, for example, is a precondition of justice, it is expressing the view that in the just society, safety should not be subject to purchase and sale. Safety should become, in effect, a right, much like the right to free speech or to be judged by a jury of one's peers when accused of a crime. To offer workers with unsafe working conditions more money in order that they may buy safety is to make safer work more accessible to the populace, perhaps, but not a bona fide right.

One suspects that it is both the larger inefficiency of the market mechanism and the ethical claim captured by Walzer's argument that has led most countries to reject income redistribution in combination with the labour market as the device for creating justice in the distribution of working conditions. Government regulation of workplace health and safety is the norm in many developed and developing countries. Typically, regulatory agencies set health and safety standards and then enforce those standards by means of on-site inspections and fines for violators. With regard to this regulatory approach, however, one must confront the real possibility of government failure.

While many developing countries possess numerous laws meant to regulate workplace conditions, these laws are often enforced in a hit-and-miss fashion, and usually apply only to foreign and large domestic firms. The evidence is fairly clear that governments in most developing countries cannot really ensure that the great mass of private firms obey the laws that are on the books. In Jamaica, for example, about 45 per cent of all firms disregard government regulations related to health and safety and minimum wages. About the same percentage of firms in Algeria ignore such regulations, while in Niger over 90 per cent of firms pay no heed (World Bank, 1995). Moreover, where enforcement is better, the process by which standards are set often is held hostage to the interests of employers.

If neither markets nor government regulation seem an appropriate device for creating workplace justice, what is an appropriate device? A form of decentralized worker voice, in combination with both market and government influence, might play a useful role in this area. The final, policy section of this article spells out that view in greater detail.

Worker satisfaction, autonomy and productivity

Evidence from developing country experience suggests that institutional factors – factors other than formal training, education, health, etc. – may affect the level of worker productivity while leaving workplace conditions largely unchanged. James C. Scott's (1985) penetrating study of how peasants protect themselves from the exercise of "unfair" advantage by landlords and others with economic power is an example of such evidence. Scott's case studies of rural Malaysia illustrate clearly how violations of norms and conventions can lead not only to abuses of power, but also to the penalization of growth through the creation of a strongly antagonistic atmosphere. The forms of protection that peasants invoke almost always have negative effects on productivity and its rate of growth.

Similar evidence can be found in the high performing economy of the Republic of Korea. Until recently, that country achieved remarkable rates of growth of GDP and exports, strong employment growth, considerable sharing of the growth, and a good macroeconomic balance. Yet the evidence is accumulating that labour is also increasingly discontented. There is little doubt that well-being of the community would have increased more rapidly had more resources been allocated to meeting workers' grievances, but there is also some evidence to suggest that productivity growth might have been greater as well.

David Lindauer, et al. (1997) found that long hours and hazardous workplaces were a major cause of labour grievances during the Republic of Korea's rapid development process over the past few decades. That well-being could have been improved is suggested by their study's conclusion that "although real wages rose dramatically, the increase was insufficient to compensate labor for the treatment they received or the independent representation labor desired but had long been deprived of" (1997, p. 160).

Recent evidence from the effects of mandatory works councils on firm productivity in the Republic of Korea suggests that productivity and its growth might have also been greater had labour's grievances been addressed. Works councils were initiated by the Korean Government in 1980 in response to militant demonstrations by trade unions. In 1987, the works council statute of 1980 was amended as part of the liberalization of labour market institutions "to promote the common interests of labour and management through their mutual understanding and cooperation; thereby seeking peace in industry and making a contribution to the development of the national economy" (Republic of Korea, 1991, p. 16, Art. 1).

A recent research paper by Kleiner and Lee (1997) explores the effect of both unions and works councils in the Republic of Korea. Their empirical results are illuminating. Kleiner and Lee find that, compared to unions, works councils are associated with both higher levels of worker satisfaction and higher levels of firm productivity. This is true despite the fact that, unlike unions, works councils have no effect on wages. Indeed the evidence suggests that a successful system of collective worker voice may shift outward the working conditions-productivity boundary.

There is also considerable evidence to suggest that this frontier might be shifted through learning by doing and tinkering. One of the earliest case studies offering evidence on this took place at the Horndal Iron Works in Sweden. In his study of that factory, Erik Lundberg found that over a period of some 15 years there was literally no change in any aspect of its operation or in its equipment, and yet labour productivity rose steadily (for a full discussion, see Lazonick and Brush, 1982). The experience of China's "Town and Village Enterprises" in the post-1970s period provides further evidence. These new, small firms set up in small towns and rural areas of China often achieved sustained rates of growth in productivity with little or no new physical capital (Byrd and Qingsong, 1990).

Rosenberg, Landau and Movery (1992) have evidence showing that certain activities, especially when threatened, find ways to increase productivity or improve their product through nothing more than tinkering. For example, they show that sailing ships competed well with steam ships well after steam seemed to be the most efficient. A similar story applies to steam and diesel locomotives.

A number of students of the history of technology distinguish between large-scale breakthroughs – Mokyr (1990), for example, calls them macro inventions – and small incremental changes made on the job and in consequence of learning about the process and the machinery by working with it. Evidence suggests that without the learning and tinkering, the macro inventions would rarely achieve levels of productivity that would make them competitive. Thus, while there are no data enabling one to say that learning by doing and tinkering resulted in productivity growing by a specific percentage over a given period, there appears to be abundant evidence that productivity growth cannot be sustained unless such learning exists.

The meaningfulness of work

For work to be meaningful, it must be chosen in an autonomous fashion by the people who do it.[18] They must know the immediate opportunity costs of the choices before them – in the form, particularly, of lost output and consumption – but they must also be aware of the type of people they are likely to become given the choices they make. Typically, work will be seen as more meaningful the more compatible it is with the prevailing culture and norms, and the more it fits in with the broader "way of being". Evidence is accumulating that meaningful work is greatly challenged in developing countries that strive for the abrupt adoption of modern manufacturing techniques as part of export-led growth strategies.

Compare, for example, the model of an abrupt shift to "modern" factory work characteristic of Thailand or Malaysia with a very different model based on small-scale firms that are tied closely to the home and the household routine in Japan or Taiwan (China). In Japan a large percentage – in some cities over one half – of firms are attached to the home or are on the same premises as the home, so that work and non-work are easily meshed.[19] In Taiwan (China) the development of small firms in rural areas supplied products primarily for local use, and often employed labour whose primary jobs were in agriculture. This practice helped to maintain the links between work and other activity that is so common in rural areas. It illustrates a development strategy in which work in new activities can be compatible with existing life styles and thus meet the needs of "meaningfulness".

Tessa Morris-Suzuki (1994) describes in rich detail how Japanese technology developed basically through indigenous firms, through what she calls the "social network of innovation". This latter notion refers to strictly Japanese organizations and institutions that prevailed over many decades and were the agencies through which the Japanese firms learned from abroad and used that learning plus purely local knowledge and local lore to put in place a genuinely Japanese-based knowledge accumulation process. Part of this network of innovation was the workforce and the workplace.

Morris-Suzuki makes clear that the role played by labour in this social network of innovation was crucial to its success. She also explains how this process occurred without destroying abruptly the link between work and the social framework that prevailed in Japan. The Japanese labour force has, over the decades, been a cooperative and independent factor in Japanese development. The development process in place in Japan has been such that work continued to be "meaningful", despite the fact that it produced many changes in routines, institutions and forms of organization. Japanese development has been genuinely endogenous, even as the economic actors learned from the rest of the world.[20]

Consider now Malaysia and Thailand. In these countries, where foreign direct investment (FDI) and foreign capital inflows have been rampant since the 1980s, work has often been incompatible with existing institutions, practices and routines, and ideas of what is legitimate. The strong demand for labour in both countries has been a great boon for many, but evidence suggests that much of the reward that can and should be associated with work has not been available to many Malaysian and Thai workers. Similarly the spillover of technical and administrative knowledge from foreign firms to domestic firms has been limited. A major source of the differences between these two countries and Japan is their greater openness to trade, FDI and foreign capital. There is little doubt, for example, that workers in the foreign firms in free-trade zones (especially in Malaysia) have little involvement with their work and little commitment to the company. "Meaningfulness" is thereby penalized.

SOME POLICY IMPLICATIONS

The achievement of "full employment" in safe and congenial workplaces at jobs that meet the needs of social meaningfulness and that create opportunities for searching and learning is perhaps the most fundamental criterion of development. It is a much more relevant measure of development than is per capita GDP, for example. Understanding of the process by which this objective can be met, however, remains extremely primitive.

Scepticism has been expressed here concerning the efficiency of the labour market as an allocative device for working conditions, especially given workers' preferences for employment security and the growth-enhancing effects of on-the-job learning and tinkering. It thus seems likely that the amount of resources devoted to the creation of "good" jobs is suboptimal in any developing country that relies solely on markets to generate such outcomes. Also expressed in the foregoing discussion is the belief that the predominant form of government regulation of working conditions in developing countries fails to generate working conditions whose quality accords with basic principles of justice, and indeed may fail as a mere corrective for the inefficiency of market outcomes.

But the difficulties in attaining the goal set out above go beyond mere market or government failures, as these notions are typically conceived. In sacrificing working conditions in the way that most developing countries appear to do, these countries forgo a development path that might possess even more rapid productivity growth. Furthermore, there seems to be little visible commitment in most developing countries to thinking through carefully what constitutes meaningful work, and how work should be structured so as to reflect and reproduce shared cultural values and normative virtues. These two concerns are not typically the assigned tasks of either market or government.

What kinds of policy prescriptions follow from this analysis? Two general points should guide prescriptions in this area. First, generalization across countries is dangerous. This is always true in cases where institutions are important, but especially so with respect to labour markets and labour practices as they vary so widely between countries. A study of the individual country over time is therefore necessary to give the analyst and policymaker the correct feel for the specific environment within which labour works. Second, it should be recognized explicitly that one is proceeding into areas in which ignorance is vast. This means many things, but the most immediate is that a pragmatic, trial-and-error approach is in order. Ideology and dogmatism are sure to be costly.

With this in mind, several prescriptions for improving work in developing countries are offered here, many of which can be viewed as bolstering the functioning of both markets and government in this important area of social welfare. For the labour market to be an effective device in allocating resources to working conditions, demand for labour must press strongly against supply. Policies to accomplish this should therefore be given greater weight than they are at present.

Economists are quick to point out two immediate problems with doing so. The first is that it may produce inflationary pressure which can easily get out of control, and ultimately require a labour policy package that holds in check continuing inflationary pressures.[21] However, the attention given by many analysts to preventing and eliminating inflation is misplaced. Attention should be given to ensuring that demand for labour is strong. The employment objectives take precedence over preventing inflation.

The second potential problem refers to labour's unwillingness to perform effectively when alternative jobs are available to fired workers. This issue has received recent theoretical (but much less empirical) attention in the burgeoning literature on efficiency wages. Managerial philosophies that strive to enforce standards of worker performance through close supervision and threat of job loss fail to acknowledge the ultimate discretion workers possess in production and the extent to which that discretion can be funnelled into either productive or unproductive activity. The problem of worker shirking appears to be greatest where the shop floor is unpleasant and unhealthy, where the worker feels exploited, and where the work has little or no meaning beyond serving as a source of income. The problem of inadequate worker effort is therefore less, the greater the extent to which the objectives discussed above are met.

It has been argued here, however, that in many contexts it may be inefficient to rely on the labour market to regulate working conditions, regardless of how strongly demand pushes against supply. Learning and tinkering, for example, require some permanency of employment, not immediate job search when working conditions turn sour. In these contexts, worker voice mechanisms can be effective substitutes for the labour market mechanism. The prescribed institutional form of worker voice is likely to differ across countries.[22] However, some form of plant-level voice is particularly important for co-determining with management the day-to-day operations of the plant. Plant-level entities can also act as an efficient conduit through which information flows from the collective of workers to management and vice-versa. Either works councils or local unions may play this role.[23]

Works councils seem particularly attractive as local voice mechanisms. Most prominent today in German industrial relations, works councils are democratic worker organizations that operate at the plant level and which are mandated by the State for firms above a certain size and endowed by the State with statutory rights of participation. German works councils, for example, are granted the right to consultation with management over a wide range of workplace issues (excluding wages) and co-determination rights over a more limited range of workplace issues. In addition to fostering communication and empowering labour, works councils can play an important role in government regulation of the workplace as well. There has recently been increasing interest in a system of statutory working conditions rights enforced by the mandatory presence of works councils as a way of bolstering government regulation of the workplace (see, for example, Rogers and Streeck, 1995). If properly empowered with the responsibility for enforcing such things as governmental safety standards, works councils could act as a more efficient form of enforcement than the occasional safety inspector. And where works councils are given strong rights of participation with management in determining workplace outcomes (e.g. the right to halt unsafe production) government standards could be stated in broad terms, thereby granting a degree of flexibility that is attractive given the fact that workers' preferences vary as do employers' costs of satisfying them.

Works councils have two important limitations, however. The first is that their reach is unlikely to extend to small-scale firms, a sector which is integral to the development process as envisaged here. The challenge, in this case, is to find mechanisms by which small firms can achieve their employment and productivity growth objectives while simultaneously meeting the other objectives emphasized above. While there are no easy answers to this challenge, a variety of measures hold considerable promise.

Fostering worker-owned firms, for example, would eliminate the conflict between owners and workers, and address the poor conditions that emanate from the power of capital over labour. Also worth encouraging are cooperative institutions through which small enterprises and micro-enterprises can share the costs of, say, gathering and distributing information on workplace hazards or training workers in healthy and safe workplace practices. Finally, the effectiveness of national and international standards, even if only through moral suasion, should not be forgotten.

The second limitation of works councils is that their power is localized. And so, for both the small- and large-enterprise sectors, there is a need for a collective worker voice operating at the national level, and perhaps at the industry and regional levels as well. Without these more aggregate mechanisms, competition between plants and firms might threaten hard-won working condition improvements. (Remember that firms influenced by a strong worker voice may be more efficient, and maybe even more productive, but they need not be more profitable.) A high-level collective mechanism must also be in place to represent workers' interests in the development of national policy regarding such things as workplace health and safety.

Democratic political institutions are an important part of the story here; but, with regard to workers' interests in the large-scale enterprise sector in particular, regional and national unions may also be part of the solution. It is often thought that works councils are substitutes for unions. This was the charge, for example, in the United States during the 1920s, when employers instituted local voice mechanisms to fend off the union organizing drives of the period. However, works councils and regional and national unions can be seen as complements rather than substitutes. Works councils help to focus the attention of unions on workplace concerns other than wages, while unions are able to ensure that the benefits from any productivity enhancement that works councils generate are shared with workers.[24]

What about the larger, more difficult-to-attain goal of creating efficient institutional arrangements for productivity growth? What particular policy concerns emerge from the foregoing analysis of this issue? While speculative, the following points should be emphasized.

There is much evidence to suggest that, in addition to greater efficiency in resource allocation, productivity growth is greater when workers view the rewards from production as justly distributed and the authority of management as legitimate. Thus, all that has been said above regarding the creation of worker voice institutions is equally important in this context as well.

Learning by tinkering is unquestionably another fundamental source of growing productivity, and yet it can best be done – indeed, maybe only be done – when the workforce is using technologies with which it has some familiarity. Technologies that are quite alien to the workforce are much more difficult to modify and improve, simply because they are alien. This has major implications for the role that multinational corporations can play in the development process.

Multinational corporations bring a technology that is "modern" but also alien to most of the domestic workforce of developing countries. Labour productivity is often higher in multinational firms, but the capacity of the workforce to tinker and hence learn and improve is less. Foreign firms may therefore create islands of static efficiency, but are much less successful in contributing to an economy-wide searching ethos.[25] Moreover, because multinationals offer opportunities for only a small part of the workforce (except in very small countries, e.g. Singapore) they have only a moderate impact on the overall level of productivity. It is the small indigenous firms that can play a key role in getting economy-wide, sustained productivity growth under way.[26]

About one quarter of the people of working age in developing countries work in very small firms, many of them one-person enterprises. There are many retail firms which serve mainly as a source of employment of last resort, but there are also manufacturing firms. The birth and death rates of these firms are high, but many of them do survive and grow, and in many instances these achieve impressive rates of productivity growth, almost all of which is due to tinkering and other forms of on-the-job learning.[27] A technique that is not the least costly today may well still be the right technique to choose because it offers more opportunities for learning. A very active small-scale manufacturing sector, especially in rural areas, is perhaps the single most effective means of ensuring economy-wide, indigenous productivity growth (see Jones and Sakong, 1980; Whittaker, 1997). An active small-scale enterprise sector provides opportunities for the workforce to gain experience in a variety of activities and work environments, helping to create a flexible, adaptable, learning labour force. The most important conditions for a dynamic small-scale enterprise sector to come into existence and thrive are strong demand for products that its firms can produce, and responsive credit markets. In almost all developing countries, this means a strongly growing agricultural sector – the largest sector of most developing economies – and the selective targeting of credit to small-scale producers. Some protection from imports is probably necessary as well.[28]

In those countries where the institutions and culture are uncongenial to searching, tinkering and risk taking in the constant pursuit of knowledge, the policy task involves deeper and more intractable issues than simply getting wage rates equal to the opportunity cost of labour.[29] The main point is to foster the notion that learning is feasible and that it can pay off in several ways. Currently popular development strategies often frustrate such notions. At present, numerous people and institutions are pushing a development strategy in which non-traditional exports and private foreign investment serve as "engines" of growth. Great emphasis is placed on new industries becoming "internationally competitive" more or less immediately upon their being established. However, for a new firm to be able to compete in world markets immediately upon beginning production, members of its workforce must be as effective as the workers of long-established firms. This is not possible except in simple, repetitive tasks.

Foreign firms, in particular, will therefore find it simpler and more economical to teach workers a concrete job that is so narrow and specific that it prevents them from being curious about how their tasks fit in with other tasks or about general principles. The job becomes one of rote and blind repetition; on-the-job learning is greatly dampened, and so too is the knowledge spillover on to indigenous firms. It is evident that where the technology and machinery are unfamiliar this problem is exacerbated. This kind of situation is especially true of foreign firms operating in free-trade zones. Even if exports grow in such an environment, long-run development objectives typically go unmet.

On the much more difficult issue of how to create "meaningful work", many of the above considerations are relevant as well. Ultimately, an "ethos" must be created that elevates this goal in the consciousness of the nation. A duly empowered collective worker voice mechanism, combined perhaps with a push towards worker ownership in the small-scale enterprise sector, can play a useful role in fostering the development of such an ethos. For workers to be offered a say in the design of the workplace is arguably the first step in the process of developing a collective notion of what constitutes "meaningful work".

Notes

[1] For recent contributions on this general theme, see for example Castel (1996) and Méda (1996).

[2] There are a great variety of firms in developing countries: large enterprises (both foreign and domestic) using modern equipment and organizational techniques; very small enterprises using modern equipment; traditional enterprises of the informal sector; enterprises in the rural sectors that have few links with other parts of the country; and agricultural units of all kinds. The ideas and arguments developed in this article apply to all of these units, as the intent is to examine the broad question of the role that all labour must play if the well-being of a country's population is to rise in a sustained way over extended periods. This position is even stronger when it is appreciated that the development objective for most countries must mean finding a way to get the traditional sectors to grow – to dynamize the traditional sectors – rather than to try to import growth from abroad.

[3] If one thinks of growth in the trivial sense of the optimal allocation of resources over time, things are easier. A time dimension can be added to the analysis above without much difficulty. With a system of complete forward markets, for example, workers' changing preferences for strenuous labour as they age, or their changing choices with respect to workplace quality as their income increases, can be adequately handled.

[4] That is, the winners would be unable to compensate the losers.

[5] This is the familiar Tiebout (1956) equilibrium for local public goods.

[6] Based on the discussion in the first section of this article, efficiency here refers to a combination of productivity and the quality of working conditions.

[7] For a good review of local versus generic knowledge issues and the notion of tacit knowledge, see Antonelli, 1995.

[8] This situation has been noted by a number of observers (see, for example, Dia, 1996). It is different from the notion, common in the 1950s and 1960s, that people in traditional societies were unresponsive to price incentives. The latter do matter, but how they matter depends very much on the existing institutions and ideas of a non-growing or slow-growing economy.

[9] Marx's position on this matter is expressed most clearly in his *Economic and Philosophic Manuscripts* (1992).

[10] See Hausman and McPherson (1996) for an exploration of some of the implications of this assumption.

[11] Bowles (1998) offers an illuminating review of the many aspects of this issue.

[12] In *An inquiry into the nature and causes of the wealth of nations,* Adam Smith expresses concern about the impact of dull jobs on the human spirit, and on the kinds of characteristics such work is likely to foster in workers (see Smith, 1776). Mundane labour, writes Smith, is likely to result in the "torpor of his mind" and to render him "not only incapable of relishing or bearing a part in any rational conversation, but of conceiving any generous, noble, or tender sentiment, and consequently of forming any just judgment concerning many of the ordinary duties of private life" (1776, p. 734).

[13] The argument here is similar to the argument that there is no such thing as "the economy" until people establish artificial boundaries around certain activities and define them as economic. The opening sentence of Schumpeter's *Theory of economic development* reflects this point of view: "The social process is really one indivisible whole." (1934, p. 3). Similarly, Louis Dumont considers that: "It should be evident that there doesn't exist anything in the outside reality that resembles an economy, until the moment we construct such an object." (1977, p. 77).

[14] This point differs from the issues discussed earlier with respect to safety and health standards in the factory. It is more akin to Amartya Sen's "recognition" aspect of labour (see Sen, 1975).

[15] Amartya Sen (1992, 1997) in his discussions of equality uses the notion of space. There are many spaces for equality, and income is only one, often not the most important.

[16] A rather common example may help make the argument clearer. It is now quite common for foreign consultants and employees of international organizations to urge countries to allow women to have greater role in the labour force as a means of raising output or output per capita. The role of women in many countries rests on deeply held values whose origins are often lost in history and surely need to be re-examined carefully and objectively. That women's role should be changed in order to raise output is another matter, and is not an argument that should be made by outsiders.

[17] This example is not intended to put forth the United States as the model of an ideal development process. Indeed, there was far too little energy devoted to establishing opportunities for on-the-job learning and tinkering in the mass-production industries of this period.

[18] See Connolly (1972) for an interesting approach to the concept of "autonomously chosen interests".

[19] See Whittaker (1997) and Allen (1983) for further details. Ronald Dore's numerous writings on Japan also make similar points (see, for example, Dore, 1986). Whittaker states that though the Japanese in such firms work many hours and often on weekends, they also take time off to run home and watch a favourite TV show or babysit for an hour.

[20] There were other issues with respect to labour in the early period of Japanese development that were considerably less desirable. See, for example, Landes (1998, Chs. 22 and 23).

[21] Less developed countries frequently experience inflation, and just as frequently are told to get rid of it. Where the inflation is due simply to government deficit spending to pay for unproductive activities, there is little to justify it. However, inflation produced by expenditures that add to capacity and create a robust demand for labour can be problem solving, rather than problem creating. Severe inflation is, it is safe to say, always harmful, but it is rarely the consequence simply of too high an investment rate. In most developing countries a moderate inflation is probably necessary to achieve a robust demand for labour, as well as other objectives.

[22] For example, union movements in some countries seem capable of acting as productive collective voice mechanisms, while others are simply rent-seeking monopolies. Pencavel (1997) offers a useful discussion of this issue.

[23] It may also be noted that where a national "ethos" qualifies the severe profit-seeking nature of firm activities, there may be less need for voice or it may not have to be so loud. Public firms were, in many instances, said to qualify their profit-seeking efforts in order to recognize this role of labour. In most instances, however, things have not worked this way. These firms are just inefficient without creating the environment that is necessary to meet the arguments made in this article.

[24] The view that works councils and unions are complementary institutions was voiced most clearly by Paul Douglas (1921).

[25] This argument is developed in detail in a number of books and articles. Sanjaya Lall (1996, Ch. 2) offers an especially illuminating discussion. The basic question to ask about foreign firms in developing countries is how and to what extent they contribute to the emergence of a genuine indigenous searching and learning ethos (Bruton, 1997).

[26] More generally, small-scale, indigenous firms that use a fairly simple technology should not be considered units to be eliminated or replaced by a modern (i.e. imported) technique as soon as possible. Such firms are rather to be considered the agency through which growth occurs. The point here is that the role of labour is crucial to the success of any such effort.

[27] For a recent study of small-scale firms in developing countries, see Mead and Liedholm (1998), from which some of the points made in this article are derived.

[28] This role of the small indigenous firm is one of several reasons why the current widespread emphasis on the necessity of exporting must be questioned.

[29] Culture and institutions refer to the middle ground between universal human characteristics and those that are peculiar to a sub-group. The terms include traits, preferences (baseball rather than cricket), modes of thinking and acting and responding, values and common sense which are shared by members of the group about whom one is speaking. Clearly, such features of a society emerge over time and link the present with the past. A good illustration is Joel Mokyr's (1990) statement that as the industrial revolution got underway in Britain, there was a "great thirst for knowledge". The existence of such a thirst would certainly induce efforts of all kinds to learn.

References

Akerlof, George A. 1982. "Labor contracts as partial gift exchange", in *Quarterly Journal of Economics* (Cambridge, MA), Vol. 97, No. 4 (Nov.), pp. 543-569.

Allen, G.C. 1983. *Appointment in Japan.* London, Athlone.

Antonelli, Cristiano. 1995. *The economics of localized technological change and industrial dynamics.* Economics of Science, Technology and Innovation Series, Volume 3. Dordrecht, Kluwer Academic Publishers.

Bowles, Samuel. 1998. "Endogenous preferences: The cultural consequences of markets and other economic institutions", in *Journal of Economic Literature* (Nashville, TN), Vol. 36, No. 1 (Mar.), pp. 75-111.

—.1985. "The production process in a competitive economy: Walrasian, Neo-Hobbesian and Marxian models", in *American Economic Review* (Menasha, WI), Vol. 75, No. 1 (Mar.), pp. 16-36.

Bruton, Henry J. 1997. *On the search for well-being.* Ann Arbor, MI, University of Michigan Press.

Byrd, William A.; Qingsong, Lin (eds.). 1990. *China's road to industry.* New York, NY, Oxford University Press.

Castel, Robert. 1996. "Work and usefulness to the world", in *International Labour Review* (Geneva), Vol. 135, No. 6, pp. 615-622.

Connolly, William. E. 1972. "On 'interests' in politics", in *Politics and Society* (Thousand Oaks, CA), Vol. 2, No. 4 (Summer), pp. 459-477.

Dia, Mamadou, 1996. *Africa's management in the 1990s and beyond.* Washington, DC, World Bank.

Dore, Ronald P. 1986. *Flexible rigidities: Industrial policy and structural adjustment in the Japanese economy, 1970-80.* Stanford, CA, Stanford University Press.

Douglas, Paul H. 1921. "Shop committees: Substitutes for, or supplement to, trades unions?", in *Journal of Political Economy* (Chicago, IL), Vol. 29, No. 2, pp. 89-107.

Dumont, Louis. 1977. *From Mandeville to Marx: The genesis and triumph of economic ideology.* Chicago, IL, University of Chicago Press.

Fairris, David. 1997. *Shopfloor matters.* London, Routledge.

—.1992. "Compensating payments and hazardous work in union and nonunion settings", in *Journal of Labor Research* (Fairfax, VA), Vol. 13, No. 2, pp. 205-221.

Fishback, Price V.; Kantor, Shawn Everett. 1992. "Square deal or raw deal? Market compensation for workplace disamenities, 1884-1903", in *Journal of Economic History* (Cambridge), Vol. 52, No. 4 (Dec.), pp. 826-848.

Garen, John. 1988. "Compensating wage differentials and the endogeneity of job riskiness", in *Review of Economics and Statistics* (Amsterdam), Vol. 70, No. 1, pp. 9-16.

Hausman, Daniel M.; McPherson, Michael S. 1996. *Economic analysis and moral philosophy.* London, Cambridge University Press.

Jones, Leroy P.; Sakong, Il. 1980. *Government, business, and entrepreneurship in economic development: The Korean case.* Cambridge, MA, Harvard University Council on East Asian Studies.

Kleiner, Morris M.; Lee, Young-Myon. 1997. "Works councils and unionization: Lessons from South Korea", in *Industrial Relations* (Cambridge, MA), Vol. 36, No. 1, pp. 1-16.

Labor-Management Council Law of South Korea, 1989, as amended.

Lall, Sanjaya. 1996. *Learning from the Asian Tigers.* New York, NY, St. Martin's Press.

Landes, David S. 1998. *The wealth and poverty of nations.* New York, NY, W.W. Norton.

Lazonick, William; Brush, Thomas. 1982. *The Horndal effects in early U.S. manufacturing.* Harvard Institute of Economic Research Discussion Paper No. 936. Cambridge, MA, Harvard University.

Lewis, W. Arthur. 1954. "Economic development with unlimited supplies of labour", in *Manchester School of Economic and Social Studies* (Oxford), Vol. 22, May, pp. 139-191.

Lindauer, David L.; Kim, Jong-gie; Lee, Jaung-Woo; Lim, Hy-Sop; Son, Jae-Young; Vogel, Ezra. 1997. *The strains of economic growth: Labor unrest and social dissatisfaction in Korea.* Cambridge, MA, Harvard Institute of International Development.

Marglin, Stephen. 1974. "What do bosses do? The origins and function of hierarchy in capitalist production", in *Review of Radical Political Economics* (Cambridge, MA), Vol. 6, Spring, pp. 60-112.

Marx, Karl. 1992. "The economic and philosophic manuscripts", in Penguin Classics (ed.): *Karl Marx: Early writings.* London, Penguin Classics.

Mead, Donald C.; Liedholm, Carl C. 1998. "The dynamics of micro and small enterprises in developing countries", in *World Development* (Oxford), Vol. 26, No. 1 (Jan.), pp. 61-74.

Méda, Dominique. 1996. "New perspectives on work and value", in *International Labour Review* (Geneva), Vol. 135, No. 6, pp. 633-651.

Mokyr, Joel. 1990. *The lever of riches.* Oxford, Oxford University Press.

Moore, Wilbert E. 1951. *Industrialization and labor.* Ithaca, NY, Cornell University Press.

Morris-Suzuki, Tessa. 1994. *The technological transformation of Japan.* Cambridge, MA, Cambridge University Press.

Pencavel, John. 1997. "The legal framework for collective bargaining in developing economies", in Sebastian Edwards and Nora Claudia Lustig (eds.): *Labor markets in Latin America: Combining social protection with market flexibility.* Washington, DC, Brookings Institution Press, pp. 27-61.

Rawls, John. 1971. *A theory of justice.* Cambridge, MA, Harvard University Press.

Republic of Korea (Government of the). 1991. "Labour-Management Council Law", in Ministry of Labour (ed.): *Labour laws of Korea.* Seoul, Ministry of Labour, pp. 16-21.

Rogers, Joel; Streeck, Wolfgang. 1995. *Works councils.* Chicago, IL, University of Chicago Press.

Rosen, Sherwin. 1974. "Hedonic prices and implicit markets", in *Journal of Political Economy* (Chicago, IL), Vol. 82, No. 1 (Jan.-Feb.), pp. 34-55.

Rosenberg, Nathan; Landau, Ralph; Movery, David C. (eds.). 1992. *Technology and the wealth of nations.* Stanford, CA, Stanford University Press.

Sen, Amartya. 1997. *Inequality, unemployment and contemporary Europe.* Development Economics Research Programme, No. 7. London, London School of Economics.

—.1992. *Inequality reexamined.* Oxford, Clarendon Press.

—.1975. *Employment and technology.* Oxford, Clarendon Press.

—.1970. *Collective choice and social welfare.* Mathematical Economics Texts Series, Volume 5. San Francisco, CA. Holden-Day/Edinburgh, Oliver & Boyd.

Schumpeter, Joseph A. 1934. *The theory of economic development.* Cambridge, MA, Harvard University Press.

Scott, James C. 1985. *Weapons of the weak: Everyday forms of peasant resistance.* New Haven, CT, Yale University Press.

Smith, Adam. 1776. *An inquiry into the nature and causes of the wealth of nations.* London, Strahan [textual quotation from: New York, NY, The Modern Library, 1937].

Stiglitz, Joseph E. 1987. *Learning to learn, localized learning and technological progress.* Department of Economics Reprint No. 7. Princeton, NJ, Princeton University.

Tiebout, Charles M. 1956. "A pure theory of local expenditures", in *Journal of Political Economy* (Chicago, IL), Vol. 64, No. 5 (Oct.), pp. 416-424.

Waizer, Michael. 1983. *Spheres of justice.* New York, NY, Basic Books.

Whittaker, D.H. 1997. *Small firms in the Japanese economy.* Cambridge, MA, Cambridge University Press.

World Bank. 1995. *World Development Report 1995: Workers in an integrating world.* New York, NY, Oxford University Press.

INEQUALITY, UNEMPLOYMENT AND CONTEMPORARY EUROPE

8

Amartya SEN *

John Dewey, the philosopher and educationist, has argued that serious decisional problems involve a kind of "struggle within oneself." "The struggle," Dewey explained, "is not between a good which is clear to him and something else which attracts him but which he knows to be wrong." Rather, "it is between values each of which is an undoubted good in its place but which now get in each other's way" (Dewey and Tufts, 1932, p. 175). If a private dilemma is a struggle within an individual, a social dilemma is one between different values each of which commands public concern and can reasonably compete for our respect and loyalty. The tension involves divergent demands made on the society by principles that cry out for our attention (with good reason), and yet conflict with each other in such a way that we cannot satisfy them all.

The subject of economic and social inequality involves many such dilemmas. The conflict that has received most attention concerns the contest between aggregative and distributive considerations. Substantial economic or social inequalities are not attractive, and many find severe inequalities to be downright barbaric. And yet attempts to eradicate inequality can, in many circumstances, lead to loss for most, or even for all. This kind of conflict can arise in mild or severe form, depending on particular circumstances.

This particular issue has received a fair amount of professional attention, and rightly so, since it is an important conflict. Many compromise formulae have been suggested to evaluate social achievements by taking note simultaneously of aggregative and distributive considerations. A good

Originally published in *International Labour Review*, Vol. 136 (1997), No. 2 (Summer).

* Professor of Economics and Philosophy, and Lamont University Professor, Harvard University. This article is a slightly shortened and edited version of a paper presented at the Lisbon conference on "Social Europe" of the Calouste Gulbenkian Foundation, May 5-7,1997. It is being published here with the kind permission of that Foundation.

example is Tony Atkinson's concept of "equally distributed equivalent income," which adjusts the aggregate income by reducing it in the light of the extent of inequality in income distribution, with the "trade-off" between aggregative and distributive concerns being given by the choice of a parameter that reflects our ethical judgment (Atkinson, 1970, 1983; see also Kolm, 1969; Sen, 1973; and the annex by Foster and Sen in Sen, 1997a). Despite its importance, however, that conflict is not the focus of this article, largely because the main issues are, by now, well understood and have been well seized in evaluative writings and in policy discussions.

A different type of conflict – a different class of "inner struggle" – will be considered here. This is the conflict between the different variables in terms of which inequality may be assessed. Inequality of incomes can differ substantially from inequality in several other "spaces" (that is, in terms of other relevant variables), such as well-being, freedom, and various aspects of the quality of life (including health and longevity). We may be interested in inequality in each of these variables, but their rankings can conflict with each other, and the policy implications they have may also be significantly different. It can, for this reason, be argued that the central issue in the study of inequality is not so much the value of equality in the abstract, but "equality of what?" (as argued in Sen 1980, 1992).

A person with high income but no opportunity of political participation is not poor in the usual sense, but still does lack an important freedom. Someone who is richer than most others, but suffers from an ailment that is very expensive to treat is clearly deprived in an important way, even though she would not be classified as poor in the usual statistics of income distribution. A person who is denied the opportunity of employment but given a hand-out from the State as "unemployment benefit" may look much less deprived in the space of incomes than in terms of the valuable – and valued – opportunity of having a fulfilling occupation. In fact, as the study of the Belgian unemployed by Schokkaert and Van Ootegem (1990) has shown, the unemployed may feel deprived because of the lack of freedom in their lives, and this goes well beyond just the lowness of incomes. There are other ways in which deprivation of different kinds requires that one look beyond the limits of income poverty.

The important issue to note here is not only the need to go beyond income poverty, but also the conflict between distinct inequalities judged in different spaces. For example, income inequality may substantially diverge from inequality of political freedoms, and health inequality can differ from both. We do have reason to attach importance to each. This kind of conflict is not between aggregative and distributive considerations; rather it is between different "spaces," in terms of which both aggregate achievements and inequalities are to be judged. The choice of the "evaluative space" is extremely important for normative judgments and can have much relevance for policy decisions (discussed in Sen, 1992).

RELEVANCE OF SPACE

There are three distinct reasons for concentrating on this type of "inner struggle." First, the conflict between inequality in different "spaces" has often been neglected in the academic as well as policy literature. Indeed, if you announce that you are working on economic inequality, it is quite commonly assumed that you are studying income distribution.[1] The fact that economics has much to say about factors other than income that influence people's wellbeing, or freedom or quality of life, is largely ignored in this narrowing of the understanding of economic inequality.

Second, in the context of European policy-making, this contrast can be quite significant. For one thing, the development of unemployment in Europe makes the perspective of income distribution rather limited, since unemployment causes deprivation in many other ways as well. The loss of income caused by unemployment could, to a considerable extent, be compensated, as far as the affected *individual* is concerned, by unemployment benefits and other forms of income support (though for the society, such compensation is achieved at considerable fiscal costs and possibly incentive effects). In terms of *income distribution,* an income received through a governmental transfer payment is much the same as an income earned through employment. But unemployment has many other serious effects even for the individual (on which more presently), and the identification of economic inequality with income inequality impoverishes the understanding and study of economic inequality.

Given the massive scale of unemployment in contemporary European economies, the concentration on income inequality alone can be particularly deceptive. Indeed, it can be argued that at this time the massive levels of European unemployment constitute at least as important an issue of inequality, in its own right, as income distribution itself. This question will be taken up later.

Health problems and inequality

The important issue of health care and medical insurance also takes us well beyond income inequality. Even when the two go together, which they may or may not do, health inequality raises issues of a very different kind from income inequality. For example, post-reform Russia has seen a sharp increase both in *income inequality* (along with a fall in average income) and also a sharp increase in *health inequality* (along with a fall in average longevity). These developments are not entirely unrelated, but they are not so closely linked as to be sensibly seen as two aspects of the same problem.

The health crisis in Russia, in particular, involves the breakdown of hospital systems and medical services, along with psychological dejection and alcoholism. Even when the economy picks up and average income goes up and income inequality falls, many of the causal antecedents of high morbidity and mortality will still survive in Russia, given the crisis in its medical system. The fact that Russian men have a substantially lower life expectancy at birth (now fallen to 57 years) than do, say, Indian men (61 years) is not primarily a matter of income poverty, since Russians are still substantially richer than the Indians. The answer involves organizational matters that require us to go beyond income considerations (on which see Drèze and Sen, 1989).

Inequality in Europe cannot be sensibly studied in terms of income distribution statistics, despite the importance they have. Since public expenditure patterns on health, education and other fields are undergoing serious re-examination at this time (along with scrutiny of cash transfers such as pensions and benefits), the importance of distributive and aggregative considerations in spaces other than income has to be kept firmly in view. These have to figure more explicitly in European public debates on inequality, which have tended to concentrate mostly on income distribution statistics.

Political disparities

The issue of political debate draws attention to an inequality of another kind, to wit, that of political participation. This is, of course, one of the central entitlements of individuals living in a democracy, and the "social choice" perspective would make us ask some very basic questions on the equality or inequality that obtains in this field. Barriers to participation are not only iniquitous in themselves, but they can have far-reaching effects on inequalities of other kinds, which are influenced by public policy and by the political process (on this, see Sen, 1995).

The extent of participation does vary between social and cultural groups, but on top of that there is also a peculiar anomaly in much of Europe whereby legally settled immigrants do not have the political right to vote because of the difficulties and delays in acquiring citizenship. This keeps them outside the political process in a systematic way. Not only does it reduce the political freedom of the settled immigrants (for example in a country like Germany, where acquiring citizenship is very difficult even for the legally settled long-run residents of Germany), it also makes social integration that much more difficult.

Largely through a historical accident, Britain has substantially escaped this problem. This is because the right to vote continues to be determined in the United Kingdom in terms of imperial connections (not British citizenship): any citizen of the Commonwealth immediately acquires voting rights in Britain on being accepted for settlement. Since most of the non-white immigrants to Britain have come from the Commonwealth countries (such as India, Pakistan, Bangladesh, the West Indies, Nigeria, Kenya, Uganda, etc.), they have had the right of political participation in Britain immediately on arrival on a permanent basis. This has made the political parties quite keen on wooing the immigrant vote, and this clearly acted as a brake on the early attempts at racist politics in Britain.

This is certainly among the reasons why Britain has, to a great extent, been able to avoid the persistence of racist extremism that one finds, for example, in Germany, despite the best efforts of many visionary political leaders and committed citizens. The political incentive to seek support from immigrant communities (rather than targeting them for attack) has been a factor of some importance both in the political freedom and in the social integration of immigrants in Britain. The French situation comes somewhere in between the British and the German. It is interesting to speculate whether making the entitlement to political rights easier would tend to make the immigrant communities in Germany and France less prone to systematic attack in electoral politics.

This is a hard subject to speculate on without further research, but it is mentioned here to illustrate how very different the considerations of inequality in the broader sense may be, compared with its being confined to the narrow box of income distribution. If we are really concerned with inequalities that matter, we have to take an interest in disparities in political and social position, in addition to other aspects of inequality, of which income distribution is a part.

Contrasting Europe and America

The third reason for emphasizing the need to focus on the "evaluative space" is the possibility of learning from comparative pictures of inequality in the United States and western Europe. An exclusive focus on income inequality tends to give the impression that western Europe has done very much better than the United States in keeping inequality down and in avoiding the kind of increase in income inequality that the United States has experienced. In the "space" of incomes, Europe does indeed have, on the whole, a better record in terms both of levels and of trends of inequality, as is brought out by the careful investigation reported in the OECD study, *Income distribution in OECD countries*, prepared by Tony Atkinson, Lee Rainwater and Timothy Smeeding (OECD, 1996). Not only are the usual measures of income inequality higher in the United States than is the case, by and large, on the European side of the Atlantic, but also income inequality has gone up in the United States in a way that has not happened in most countries in western Europe.

And yet if we shift our gaze from income to unemployment, the picture is very different. Unemployment has dramatically risen in much of western Europe, whereas there has been no such trend in the United States. For example, in the period 1965-73, the unemployment rate was 4.5 per cent in the United States, while Italy had 5.8 per cent, France 2.3 per cent, and West

Germany below 1 per cent. By now all three of these European countries – Italy, France and Germany – have unemployment rates around 12 per cent, whereas the US unemployment rate is still below 5 per cent. If unemployment batters lives, then that must somehow be taken into account in the analysis of economic inequality. The comparative trends in income inequality give Europe an excuse to be smug (an opportunity that seems to be too frequently seized in somewhat insular discussions in Europe), but that complacency can be deeply questioned if a broader view is taken of inequality.

The contrast between western Europe and the United States raises another interesting – and in some ways a more general – question. The American social ethics finds it possible to be very non-supportive of the indigent and the impoverished, in a way that a typical western European, reared in a welfare state, finds hard to accept. But the same American social ethics would find the double-digit levels of unemployment, common in Europe, to be quite intolerable. Europe has continued to accept worklessness – and its increase – with remarkable equanimity. Underlying this contrast is a difference in attitudes towards social and individual responsibilities – an issue that would call for some comment.

UNEMPLOYMENT AND ITS RELEVANCE

There are three further questions related specifically to unemployment – the central dilemma for some of the most prosperous countries in Europe. We have to ask, first, what exactly is so bad about unemployment? What are the ways in which it makes lives harder, aside from its association with low income? Second, how does the Euro-American contrast referred to here relate to the respective "social philosophies"? How do these attitudinal differences correspond to different views of individual responsibility and social support? Third, how should we evaluate the claims of these different and conflicting – approaches in terms of the needs of social policy in Europe at this time? What are the pros and cons of the divergent approaches to social and individual responsibility?

The joblessness that plagues Europe today inflicts damages in many different ways, and we have to differentiate between the different concerns. At the social level, the fiscal cost of unemployment benefits is one of the bigger burdens on European economies. But even at the individual level of the unemployed person, the penalties of unemployment can be enormously more serious than income distribution statistics may suggest. The analysis that follows draws on Sen, 1997b.

The separate problems are, of course, interrelated, but each is significant in its own way, and they have to be distinguished from one another. Their negative effects are cumulative, and they act individually and jointly to undermine and subvert personal and social life. The need to distinguish between the different ways in which joblessness causes problems is important not only for a better understanding of the nature and effects of unemployment, but also for devising an appropriate policy response.

What, then, are the diverse penalties of massive unemployment, other than its association with low income? The list would have to include at least the following distinct concerns.

(1) *Loss of current output and fiscal burden:* Unemployment involves wastage of productive power, since a part of the potential national output is not realized because of unemployment. Since this is such an obvious issue, it needs no elaborate discussion (but see Okun, 1962 and Gordon, 1984). But the point to be stressed is the need to look not only at the income loss of the unemployed, but also the impact that a lower volume of aggregate output has on others. Indeed, in so far as the unemployed and their families have to be supported by the State, the resources to be transferred have to come from slimmed-down aggregate production. So unemployment hits the incomes of others in two distinct and mutually reinforcing ways: it cuts down the national output and it increases the share of the output that has to be devoted to income transfers.

(2) *Loss of freedom and social exclusion:* Taking a broader view of poverty, the nature of the deprivation of the unemployed includes loss of freedom which goes well beyond the decline in income. A person stuck in a state of unemployment, even when materially supported by social insurance, does not get to exercise much freedom of decision. Attitudinal studies, for example by Schokkaert and Van Ootegem (1990) of the Belgian unemployed, have brought out the extent to which this loss of freedom is seen by many unemployed people as a crucial deprivation.

The recent interest in the notion of "social exclusion" has helped to highlight the absence of freedom of deprived people to enjoy opportunities that others can readily use. Unemployment can be a major causal factor predisposing people to social exclusion. The exclusion applies not only to economic opportunities, such as job-related insurance, and to pension and medical entitlements, but also to social activities, such as participation in the life of the community, which may be quite problematic for jobless people.

(3) *Skill loss and long-run damage:* Just as people "learn by doing," they also "unlearn" by "not doing" – by being out of work and out of practice. Also, in addition to the depreciation of skill through non-practice, unemployment may generate a loss of cognitive abilities as a result of the unemployed person's loss of confidence and sense of control. The relation between motivation and competence is not easy to quantify, but empirical studies (for example, by Lefcourt (1967) and Lefcourt, Gronnerud and McDonald (1973)) have shown how strong this effect can be in practice.

(4) *Psychological harm:* Unemployment can play havoc with the lives of the jobless, and cause intense suffering and mental agony. Empirical studies of unemployment, for example by Jahoda, Lazarsfeld and Zeisel (1933),

Eisenberg and Lazarsfeld (1938), Bakke (1940a, 1940b), and Hill (1977), have brought out how serious this effect can be. Indeed, high unemployment is often associated even with elevated rates of suicide, which is an indicator of the perception of unbearability that the victims experience (see, for example, Boor, 1980 and Platt, 1984). The effect of prolonged joblessness can be especially damaging for the morale (see, for example, Harrison, 1976). The connection between psychological suffering and motivational impairment has been illuminatingly – and movingly – analysed recently by Robert Solow (1995).

The suffering of the unemployed does, of course, relate inter alia to the economic hardship associated with it, although the force of that suffering has been to a considerable extent reduced since the bad old days of the 1930s, through the provision of unemployment benefits and other forms of social support. Had low income been the only reason for suffering as a result of unemployment, it could be claimed (as some European commentators do) that unemployment is no longer such an evil because of plentiful support by the State. Indeed, some even claim that the hard-working American poor person who accepts low-paid employment may have more reason for suffering on this count than the "generously provided for" European unemployed person who is well supported by the State.

This argument is not only rather smug and somewhat of an apologia for not trying to cure unemployment, it is also, in general, unconvincing because of the presumption that large transfers of income of this kind can be effected with relatively little cost and can be continued indefinitely without other damaging effects on the economy. More immediately in the present context, it is specifically unconvincing as a response to the issue of "psychological harm," because the suffering generated is not just a matter of low income, but also of other deprivations, including the loss of self-respect and the dejection associated with being dependent and feeling unwanted and unproductive.[2]

Youth unemployment can take a particularly high toll, leading to long-run loss of self-esteem among young workers and would-be workers (such as school-leavers) (see, for example, Gurney, 1980; Ellwood, 1982; Tiggemann and Winefield, 1984; and Winefield, Tiggemann and Goldney, 1988). There is some considerable evidence, based on American studies (for example, by Goldsmith, Veum and Darity 1996a, 1996b), that this damaging effect is particularly severe for young women (see also Corcoran, 1982). It has to be examined whether a comparable pattern applies to Europe as well. Youth unemployment has become a problem of increasing seriousness in Europe, and the present pattern of European joblessness is quite heavily biased in the direction of the young, including young women.

(5) *Ill health and mortality:* Unemployment can also lead to clinically identifiable illnesses and to higher rates of mortality (not just through more suicide). This can, to some extent, be the result of loss of income and material

means, but the connection also works through dejection and a lack of self-respect and a collapse of motivation generated by persistent unemployment (see, for example, Seligman, 1975; Smith, 1987; and Warr, 1987).

(6) *Motivational loss and future work:* The discouragement that is induced by unemployment can lead to a weakening of motivation and make the long-term unemployed more resigned and passive. Some have argued against this by suggesting that the unemployed may go into a more spirited response to overcome the problem (for example, under the theory of "react-ance" outlined by Brehm, 1966). There is, however, considerable evidence suggesting that the more typical effect, especially of long-term unemploy-ment, is one of motivational decline and resignation. This can yield a hard-ening of future poverty and further unemployment, as has been well illustrated by the investigations by Darity and Goldsmith (1993).

The motivational loss resulting from high levels of unemployment can be very detrimental to the search for future employment. On the basis of his pioneering study of unemployment in the Welsh coal mines in the 1930s, Eli Ginzberg noted that the "capacities and morale of the unemployed had been so greatly impaired by years of enforced idleness that the prospect of return-ing to work was frightening" (1942, p. 49). (On this issue, see also Solow, 1995.) Recent studies suggest that this motivational impact may be particu-larly significant for young women (see Goldsmith, Veum and Darity, 1996a, 1996b).

This general issue also relates to the composition and variation of what counts as the "labour force." The impact of prolonged unemployment can be severe in weakening the distinction for people of working age between being "in the labour force but unemployed" and being "out of the labour force". The empirical relevance of the distinction between these states (and possible transitions from the former state to the latter) can be important for the future of the economy as well as the predicaments of the particular persons involved.[3]

(7) *Loss of human relations and family life:* Unemployment can be very disruptive of social relations (see, for example, Jahoda, Lazarsfeld and Zei-sel, 1933; and Hill, 1977). It may also weaken the harmony and coherence within the family. To some extent these consequences relate to the decline of self-confidence (in addition to the drop in economic means), but the loss of an organized working life can itself be a serious deprivation. In addition, a crisis of identity can be involved in this kind of disruption (see, for example, Erikson, 1968).

(8) *Racial and gender inequality:* Unemployment can also be a signifi-cant causal influence in heightening ethnic tensions as well as gender divi-sions. When jobs are scarce, the groups most affected are often the minorities, especially parts of the immigrant communities. This worsens the prospects for easy integration of legal immigrants into the regular life of the mainstream of

society. Furthermore, since immigrants are often seen as people competing for employment (or "taking away" jobs from others), unemployment feeds the politics of intolerance and racism. This issue has figured prominently in recent elections in some European countries.

Gender divisions too are hardened by extensive unemployment, especially because the entry of women into the labour force is often particularly hindered in times of general unemployment. Also, as was mentioned earlier, the discouraging effects of youth unemployment has been found to be particularly serious for young girls, whose re-entry into the labour market after a substantial bout of unemployment may be seriously impeded by early experiences of joblessness.

(9) *Loss of social values and responsibility:* There is also evidence that large-scale unemployment has a tendency to weaken some social values. People in continued unemployment can develop cynicism about the fairness of social arrangements, and also a perception of dependence on others. These effects are not conducive to responsibility and self-reliance. The observed association of crimes with youth unemployment is, of course, substantially influenced by the material deprivation of the jobless, but a part is played in that connection also by psychological influences, including a sense of exclusion and a feeling of grievance against a world that does not give the jobless an opportunity to earn an honest living. In general, social cohesion faces many difficult problems in a society that is firmly divided between a majority of people with comfortable jobs and a minority – often a large minority – of unemployed and "rejected" human beings.

(10) *Organizational inflexibility and technical conservatism:* The possibility that the nature and form of technological change have greatly contributed to unemployment and its persistence in Europe has been analysed and investigated in the recent literature (for example, by Luigi Pasinetti, 1993). The impact of technology on unemployment is indeed important to investigate, but there is also a connection that goes the other way – the influence of unemployment in restricting the use of better technology. In a situation of widespread unemployment, when displacement from one's present job can lead to a long period of joblessness, the resistance to any economic reorganization involving job loss can be particularly strong. In contrast, when the general level of unemployment is quite low and displaced workers can expect to find other employment readily enough, reorganization may be less resisted.

It is possible to argue that the United States economy has benefited from its relatively high level of employment in making reorganization and rationalization easier than in Europe. While the workers in an enterprise may have good reason to prefer, in general, not to have to change employment, the penalty of losing one's job is enormously larger when the alternative is just unemployment, possibly for a long stretch of time. Unemployment can thus contribute to technological conservatism through organizational inflexibility, thereby reducing economic efficiency as well as international competitiveness. The same applies to other types of organizational changes, such as raising the retirement age because of an increasing span of healthy life, since any such change appears to be very threatening in an economy that already has much unemployment. This question of interdependence will be revisited below in connection with policy issues.

DIAGNOSIS AND POLICY

With the high levels of unemployment that have now become the standard state of affairs in Europe, the social costs of these penalties are indeed heavy. These costs diminish the lives of all, but are particularly harsh on the minority – a large minority – of families severely afflicted by persistent unemployment and its far-reaching damages.

This sad state of affairs calls for economic reasoning as well as political responsibility and leadership. On the economic side, there is need to consider employment policies in relation to different ends, including demand management and macroeconomic considerations but also going well beyond them. The market economy signals costs and benefits of different kinds, but does not adequately reflect all the costs of unemployment, which – as has just been discussed – arise in several different ways. There is thus a need for public policy that takes into account those burdens of unemployment which are not well reflected in market prices. This suggests the case for considering incentive schemes of various kinds that may increase the inclination to employ more people, as has been investigated recently by Phelps (1994a, 1994b, 1997), Fitoussi (1994), Fitoussi and Rosanvallon (1996), Lindbeck (1994) and Snower (1994), among others. Unemployment also calls for a scrutiny of the possible effectiveness of dedicated public action that operates not just by adjusting the effective prices, but by creating more opportunities for appropriate training and skill formation, for more research on labour-friendly technology, and for institutional reforms that make the labour market more flexible and less constrained.

The aged and the rising dependency ratio

Taking a compartmentalized view of problems of work, reward and security can produce social concerns that are artificially separated from each other. One example is the much-discussed problem of the rising ratio of older people in Europe as well as America, and indeed in much of the world. This is often seen as imposing an increasingly unbearable burden on the younger people who have to support the old. But a greater life span typically also goes with longer years of working ability and fitness, especially in less physically demanding jobs. One way of dealing with the rising age-composition problem, then, is to raise the retirement age, which would help to reduce the rise in the dependency ratio (the ratio of dependent people to those at work). But this may make it harder, it is thought, for younger people to have employment. Thus the employment problem is at the very root of the age composition issue as well.

For one thing, a fall in the rate of unemployment would immediately reduce the dependency ratio if that is calculated as the ratio of dependent people to those *at work* (rather than those *of working age*). But more substantially, an expansion of job opportunities can absorb not only the unemployed young, but also the able-bodied people who have been forced to retire prematurely.

These problems are thus interdependent. The interrelations involve both actual job opportunities and also social psychology. In a situation where unemployment is a constant threat that worries many people, any proposal to raise the retirement age appears to be threatening and regressive. But since there is no basic reason why employment opportunities should not adjust, when there is time and flexibility, to the size of a larger labour force (as the retiring age is raised), there is no immovable obstacle here. We do not tend to assume that a country with a larger population must, for that reason, have more unemployment since there are more people looking for work. Given the opportunity to adjust, availability of work can respond to the size of the working population. Unemployment arises from barriers to such adjustment, and must not end up "vetoing" the possibility of raising the retiring age and thereby increasing the work force.

The long-term structural problem of rising age-composition simply has become, to a considerable extent, a prisoner of the present circumstances of high levels of unemployment in Europe. Not surprisingly, there has been little difficulty in raising – indeed removing – the age of compulsory retirement in the United States, since it has so much lower levels of unemployment than Europe. This does not, in itself, eliminate all the problems of rising age composition (particularly the greater cost of medical care for aged people), but lifting the age of retirement can greatly help to reduce the burden of dependency. When the diverse effects of unemployment are considered, it can be seen how far-reaching its penalties are.

Taking note of different types of costs associated with unemployment is important in searching for proper economic responses to this large problem. This is because the enormity of the harm created by unemployment can be easily underestimated when many of its far-reaching effects are ignored.

Europe, America and the requisites of self-help

Given the serious and many-sided nature of the unemployment problem in Europe, the need for a political commitment to deal with this issue is particularly strong at this time. It is certainly a subject in which the European Union can provide a forum for commitment. There has recently been much discussion in Europe on the need for coordinated reductions in budget deficits and in public debts. The Maastricht Treaty has specified a particular requirement for the ratio of deficit to the gross national product (GNP), and a somewhat less strict norm for the ratio of public debt to GNP. The connection of these conditions with the announced plan to inaugurate a single European currency is easy to appreciate.

While there is no officially declared "event" that calls for an all-round reduction of unemployment in Europe, the social urgency of such a move would be hard to deny. The different penalties of unemployment bite hard into individual and social lives across Europe. Given the high magnitude of unemployment in virtually every country in the European Union, an appropriate response can sensibly be a European commitment, rather than a purely national one. Also, given the free movement of people between different countries in Europe, the employment policies certainly call for some coordination. There is, in fact, as yet no articulated commitment to reduce unemployment in the way that the resolve to reduce budget deficits has been affirmed. There is also relatively inadequate public discussion on the penalties of unemployment. The role of public dialogues on the formation of ethical and political commitments, especially dealing with deprivation, can be quite central (on this see Atkinson, 1996 and forthcoming).

It is interesting to contrast the types of political commitments that get priority in Europe with those that rule in the United States. On one side, there is little commitment in American official policies on providing basic health care for all, and it appears that more than 30 million people are, in fact, without any kind of medical coverage or insurance in that country. A comparable situation in Europe would be, I believe, politically intolerable. The limits on governmental support for the poor and the ill are too severe in the United States to be at all acceptable in Europe. On the other hand, in the United States double-digit unemployment rates would be political dynamite. I believe that no American government could emerge unscathed from doubling the present level of unemployment which, incidentally, would still keep the US unemployment ratio below what it currently is in Italy or France or Germany. The nature of the respective political commitments differs fundamentally.

The contrast may relate, to some extent, to the fact that the value of being able to help oneself is much higher in America than in Europe. This value does not translate into providing medical care or social insurance for all Americans; its domain is different. The tendency to ignore poverty and deprivation in public policy-making is peculiarly strong in American self-help culture. On the other hand, denying employment hits at the very root of having the opportunity of helping oneself, and there is much more public engagement on that issue in the United States. Thus the American self-help culture provides a much stronger commitment against unemployment than against being medically uninsured or against falling into deep poverty.

The contrast is worth examining at this time. Europe is increasingly being persuaded to put more emphasis on people's ability to help themselves, rather than on the State doing things for them. While this shift of emphasis can be overdone (it would be sad indeed for European civilization to lose the basic protections of the welfare state against deep poverty or the absence of medical care), a major rethinking on these lines is important, necessary and overdue. The need for greater emphasis on self-help will tend to receive more support in Europe in the years to come.

In examining the requirements of a greater role for self-help, nothing is as important as a big reduction in European unemployment from its enormously high level. Such unemployment does, of course, create a heavy burden of transfer payments on the State. In addition, a situation in which a person, especially a young person, has a high probability of being jobless is not the best preparation for a psychology of independence. A school-leaver who cannot find a job and falls immediately into the necessity of being supported by the State is not being particularly encouraged to think of being self-reliant.

There is, I would even argue, a basic political schizophrenia in wanting people to rely more on themselves and, at the same time, finding the present levels of European unemployment to be "regrettable but tolerable." When jobs are nearly impossible to get for particular groups of workers, to advise "self-help" can be both unhelpful and cruel. To be able to help oneself, anyone needs the hands of others in economic and social relationships (as Adam Smith (1776) noted more than two centuries ago). The opportunity of paid employment is among the simplest ways of escaping dependency.

In terms of public values and private virtues, Europe – like the rest of the world – is very much at the crossroads now. The old value of social support for people in adverse circumstances is weakening very fast – possibly too fast – with the growing insistence on the importance of self-help.[4] And yet the political and economic implications of having a society in which people can help themselves are not adequately seized. Employment opportunity is a crucial link in the chain.

It is not my contention that the American balance of social ethics is problem-free; far from it. The United States, in its turn, has to come to grips with the problem that the self-help philosophy has its serious limits, and that public support has an important role to play in providing, in particular, medical coverage and safety nets. The fact that some American jobs are low paid is often pointed out, and certainly things can be improved in that respect.[5] It can, however, be argued that a failing that is possibly even more important than low pay is the American neglect of the need to develop health care for all – rich and poor – and also better public education and the ingredients of a peaceful community life.

These neglects are among the factors responsible for high levels of mortality among socially deprived groups in the United States. For example, African-Americans – American blacks – have a lower chance of reaching a mature age than the people of China, or Sri Lanka, or the Indian state of Kerala (see Sen, 1993). The fact that these people from the Third World are so much poorer than the United States population (and also poorer than the American black population, who are more than 20 times richer in terms of per capita income than, say, Indians in Kerala), makes the comparative disadvantage of African-Americans in survival particularly disturbing.

Incidentally, the much higher death rates of American blacks compared with American whites can be statistically established even after correcting for income variations within the United States. The mortality differentials are not connected only with death from violence, which is the stereotype that the media often portray to explain the lower longevity of African-Americans. In fact, death from violence is a big factor only for younger black men, and that, again, is only a partial explanation of the higher mortality of that group. In fact, the severe mortality disadvantages of American blacks apply sharply also to women and to older men (35 and older).[6]

A CONCLUDING REMARK

The fact that America has skeletons in its cupboard is not a good reason for smugness in Europe, nor a good ground for ignoring the very important lessons that can be learned from the more robust respect for employment in American social ethics and its impact on pro-employment policies. Europe has to give more acknowledgement to the real requirements of the philosophy of self-help, to which it is increasingly attracted without seizing the social requirements associated with that approach. Tolerating enormously high levels of unemployment certainly goes against the foundations of a society in which self-help is possible. The penalties of unemployment include not only income loss, but also far-reaching effects on self-confidence, work motivation, basic competence, social integration, racial harmony, gender justice, and the appreciation and use of individual freedom and responsibility.

The big issue that has to be addressed is the possibility of combining the more successful features of each type of approach. For example, European experiences in health care have positive features from which the United States can learn (as indeed, it would appear, can contemporary, post-reform Russia). On the other hand, the respect for individual freedom and flexibility that are implicit in the positive American attitude towards employment has much to offer Europe. The fact that European policy leaders are increasingly attracted towards a self-help philosophy is understandable, since that philosophy has many fine features and can be very effective if suitably grounded on a social background that makes self-help possible. But that social grounding calls for special attention and a policy response. Increasing employment cannot but be at the very top of the list of things to do. It is amazing that so much unemployment is so easily tolerated in contemporary Europe.

Notes

[1] For example, when lecturing as a guest speaker at a university some years ago, I found that the title I had chosen for my talk, "Economic Inequality", had been changed to "Income Inequality." When I inquired about the reason for this shift, my host's response was, "What's the difference?".

[2] That the role of work in human life is not confined just to earning an income was extensively discussed by Marx (1844, 1845-46, 1875).

[3] See the studies presented by – and the debates between – Clark and Summers (1979), Heckman and Borjas (1980), Flinn and Heckman (1982, 1983), and Goldsmith, Veum and Darity (1996a, 1996b).

[4] For a reasoned critique of proposals to "roll back" the welfare state, see Atkinson, 1997; on related issues, see also Van Parijs, 1995.

[5] The need for simultaneously increasing employment and take-home pay has been addressed particularly by Fitoussi and Rosanvallon (1996) and Phelps (1997).

[6] On this see Sen, 1993, and the medical references cited therein.

References

Atkinson, Anthony B. Forthcoming. *The economic consequences of rolling back the welfare state.* Cambridge, MA, MIT Press.

—.1996. "Promise and performance: Why we need an official poverty report," in P. Barker (ed.): *Living as equals.* Oxford, Oxford University Press.

—.1983. *Social justice and public policy.* Brighton, Wheatsheaf, and Cambridge, MA, MIT Press.

—.1970. "On the measurement of inequality," in *Journal of Economic Theory* (San Diego, CA), Vol. 2; reprinted in Atkinson, 1983.

Bakke, E. Wight. 1940a. *Citizens without work: A study of the effects of unemployment upon the workers' social relations and practices.* New Haven, CT, Yale University Press.

—.1940b. *The unemployed worker: A study of the task of making a living without a job.* New Haven, CT, Yale University Press.

Boor, M. 1980. "Relationship between unemployment rates and suicide rates in eight countries, 1962-1979", in *Psychological Reports* (Missoula, MT), Vol. 47, pp. 1095-1101.

Brehm, J. W. 1966. *A theory of psychological reactance.* New York, Academic Press.

Clark, Kim B.; Summers, Lawrence H. 1979. "Labor market dynamics and unemployment: A reconsideration", in *Brookings Papers on Economic Activity* (Washington, DC), No. 1, pp. 13-72.

Corcoran, Mary. 1982. "The employment and wage consequences of teenage women's nonemployment", in Freeman and Wise (eds.), pp. 391-423.

Darity, William, Jr.; Goldsmith, Arthur H. 1993. "Unemployment, social psychology, and unemployment hysteresis", in *Journal of Post Keynesian Economics* (Armonk, NY), Vol. 16, No. 1, pp. 55-71.

Dewey, John; Tufts, J.H. 1932. *Ethics.* New York, Holt.

Drèze, Jean; Sen, Amartya. 1989. *Hunger and public action.* Oxford, Clarendon Press.

Eisenberg, P.; Lazarsfeld, Paul F. 1938. "The psychological effects of unemployment", in *Psychological Bulletin* (Washington, DC), Vol. 35, pp. 358-390.

Ellwood, D.T. 1982. "Teenage unemployment: Permanent scars or temporary blemishes?", in Freeman and Wise (eds.), pp. 349-385.

Erikson, E.H. 1968. *Identity: Youth and crisis.* London, Faber & Faber.

Fitoussi, Jean-Paul. 1994. "Wage distribution and unemployment: The French experience", in *American Economic Review* (Papers and Proceedings) (Nashville, TN), Vol. 84, No. 2 (May), pp. 59-64.

—; Rosanvallon, R. 1996. *Le Nouvel age des inégalites.* Paris, Seuil.

Flinn, Christopher J.; Heckman, James. 1983. "Are unemployment and out of the labor force behaviorally distinct labor force states?", in *Journal of Labor Economics* (Chicago), Vol. 1, No. 1 (Jan.), pp. 28-42.

—; —.1982. "Models for the analysis of labor force dynamics", in R.L. Basmann and George F. Rhodes, Jr. (eds.): *Advances in econometrics: A research annual.* Greenwich, CT and London, JAI Press, pp. 35-95.

Freeman, Richard B.; Wise, David A. (eds.). 1982. *The youth labor market problem: Its nature, causes, and consequences.* Chicago, University of Chicago Press.

Ginzberg, Eli. 1942. *Grass on the slag heaps.* New York, Harper.

Goldsmith, Arthur H.; Veum, Jonathan R.; Darity, William, Jr. 1996a. "The impact of labor force history on self-esteem and its component parts, anxiety, alienation and depression", in *Journal of Economic Psychology* (Amsterdam), Vol. 17, pp. 183-220.

—; —; —.1996b. "The psychological impact of unemployment and joblessness", in *Journal of Socio-Economics* (Greenwich, CT), Vol. 25, pp. 333-358.

Gordon, Robert J. 1984. "Unemployment and potential output in the 1980s", in *Brookings Papers on Economic Activity* (Washington, DC), No. 2, pp. 537-564.

Gurney, Ross M. 1980. "Does unemployment affect the self-esteem of school-leavers?", in *Australian Journal of Psychology*, Vol. 32, No. 3, pp. 175-182.

Harrison, Richard. 1976. "The demoralizing experience of prolonged unemployment", in *Department of Employment Gazette* (London), Vol. 84, No. 4 (Apr.), pp. 339-348.

Heckman, James J.; Borjas, George J. 1980. "Does unemployment cause future unemployment? Definitions, questions and answers from a continuous time model of heterogeneity and state dependence", in *Economica* (Oxford), Vol. 47, No. 187 (Aug.), pp. 247-283.

Hill, J.M.M. 1977. *The social and psychological impact of unemployment: A pilot study.* London, Tavistock.

Jahoda, Marie; Lazarsfeld, Paul F.; Zeisel, Hans. 1933. *Die Arbeitslosen von Marienthal.* Vienna. *(Marienthal: The sociography of an unemployed community.* Chicago, Aldine, 1971.)

Kolm, Serge Ch. 1969. "The optimum production of social justice", in J. Margolis and H. Guitton (eds.): *Public economics.* London, Macmillan, pp. 145-200.

Lefcourt, Herbert M. 1967. "Effects of cue explication upon persons maintaining external control expectancies", *in Journal of Personality and Social Psychology* (Washington, DC), Vol. 5, No. 3, pp. 372-378.

—; Gronnerud, Paul; McDonald, Peter. 1973. "Cognitive activity and hypothesis formation during a double entendre word association test as a function of locus of control and field dependence", in *Canadian Journal of Behavioural Science* (Quebec), Vol. 5, No. 2, pp. 161-173.

Lindbeck, Assar. 1994. "The welfare state and the employment problem", in *American Economic Review* (Papers and Proceedings) (Nashville, TN), Vol. 84, No. 2 (May), pp. 71-75.

Marx, Karl. 1875. *Critique of the Gotha Program.* English translation. New York, International Publishers, 1938.

—.1844. *The economic and philosophic manuscript of 1844.* English translation. London, Lawrence and Wishart.

Marx, Karl (with F. Engels) 1845-46. *The German ideology.* English translation. New York, International Publishers, 1947.

OECD. 1996. *Income distribution in OECD countries.* Social Policy Studies No. 18. Study prepared by Anthony B. Atkinson, Lee Rainwater and Timothy Smeeding. Paris.

Okun, Arthur M. 1962. "Potential GNP: Its measurement and significance", in American Statistical Association: *Proceedings of the Business and Economic Statistics Section,* Washington, DC, ASA, pp. 98-103; reprinted in Arthur M. Okun: *Economics for policymaking,* Cambridge, MA, MIT Press, 1983.

Pasinetti, Luigi L. 1993. *Structural economic dynamics: A theory of the economic consequences of human learning.* Cambridge, Cambridge University Press.

Phelps, Edmund S. 1997. *Rewarding work.* Cambridge, MA, Harvard University Press.

—.1994a. *Structural slumps: The modern equilibrium theory of unemployment, interest, and assets.* Cambridge, MA, Harvard University Press.

—.1994b. "Low-wage employment subsidies versus the welfare state", in *American Economic Review* (Papers and Proceedings) (Nashville, TN), Vol. 84, No. 2 (May), pp. 54-58.

Platt, S. 1984. "Unemployment and suicidal behavior: A review of the literature", in *Social Science and Medicine* (Tarrytown, NY), Vol. 19, pp. 93-115.

Schokkaert, E.; Van Ootegem, L. 1990. "Sen's concept of the living standard applied to the Belgian unemployed", in *Recherches Economiques de Louvain* (Louvain), Vol. 56.

Seligman, M.E.P. 1975. *Helplessness: On depression, development and death.* San Francisco, W.H. Freeman.

Sen, Amartya. 1997a. *On economic inequality.* Enlarged edition, Oxford, Clarendon Press, with an Annex by James Foster and Amartya Sen.

—.1997b. *The penalties of unemployment.* Paper for the Bank of Italy, 1997, mimeo.

—.1995. "Rationality and social choice", in *American Economic Review* (Nashville, TN), Vol. 85, No. 1 (Mar.), pp. 1-24.

—.1993. "The economics of life and death", in *Scientific American* (New York), May.

—.1992. *Inequality re-examined.* Oxford, Clarendon Press, and Cambridge, MA, Harvard University Press.

—.1980. "Equality of what?", in S. McMurrin (ed.): *Tanner Lectures on human values,* Vol. I. Cambridge, Cambridge University Press.

—.1975. *Employment, technology and development.* Oxford, Clarendon Press.

—.1973. *On economic inequality.* Oxford, Clarendon Press.

Smith, Adam. 1776. *An inquiry into the nature and causes of the wealth of nations.* Republished, Oxford, Clarendon Press, 1976.

Smith, R. 1987. *Unemployment and health.* Oxford, Oxford University Press.

Snower, Dennis. 1994. "Converting unemployment benefits into employment subsidies", in *American Economic Review* (Papers and Proceedings) (Nashville, TN), Vol. 84, No. 2 (May), pp. 65-70.

Solow, Robert M. 1995. "Mass unemployment as a social problem", in K. Basu, P. Pattanaik and K. Suzumura (eds.): *Choice, welfare, and development: A Festschrift in honour of Amartya K. Sen.* Oxford, Clarendon Press, pp. 313-322.

Tiggemann, Marika; Winefield, A.H. 1984. "The effects of unemployment on the mood, self-esteem, locus of control, and depressive affect of school-leavers", in *Journal of Occupational Psychology* (Leicester), Vol. 57, No. 1, pp. 33-42.

Van Parijs, P. 1995. *Real freedom for all: What (if anything) can justify capitalism?* Oxford, Clarendon Press.

Warr, Peter. 1987. *Work, unemployment, and mental health.* Oxford, Clarendon Press.

Winefield, A.H.; Tiggemann, Marika; Goldney, R.D. 1988. "Psychological concomitants of satisfactory employment and unemployment in young people", in *Social Psychiatry and Psychiatric Epidemiology* (Berlin), Vol. 23, pp. 149-157.

EQUALITY AND EMPOWERMENT FOR DECENT WORK

Bob HEPPLE*

9

Equality is at the heart of the notion of "decent work", the ILO's exciting new vision to promote "opportunities for women and men to obtain decent and productive work, in conditions of freedom, equity, security and human dignity" (ILO, 1999, p. 3). In this context – and with national and local action increasingly moving away from negative duties to avoid discrimination towards positive and inclusive duties to promote equality – this article argues that the best model of regulation is one which involves the empowerment or participation of the disadvantaged groups. To that end it begins by deconstructing the idea of equality and goes on to explore this idea in the context of other fundamental rights, explaining why positive duties to promote equality are needed. Finally, it examines some regulatory models for implementing duties to promote equality and how these can be used as vehicles of empowerment.

THE CONCEPT OF EQUALITY

The subject of equality is topical across the globe. The ILO's Discrimination (Employment and Occupation) Convention, 1958 (No.111), a remarkably far-sighted and comprehensive instrument, is one of the most widely ratified of all ILO Conventions, and one which continues to inspire national legislation and other measures. The ILO Declaration on Fundamental Principles and Rights at Work of 18 June 1998 declares that "the elimination of discrimination in respect of employment and occupation" is an obligation of all member States, whether or not they have ratified the relevant Conventions.[1]

Originally published in *International Labour Review*, Vol. 140 (2001), No. 1.

* Professor of Law and Master of Clare College, Cambridge, United Kingdom. This article is based on a public lecture given by the author on the occasion of the 40th anniversary of the International Institute for Labour Studies (IILS) at the ILO, Geneva, on 7 November 2000. For the verbatim text of the lecture published by the IILS, see Hepple (2001).

In the European Union, a comprehensive anti-discrimination directive addressed to the Member States under Article 13 of the Treaty establishing the European Community, as amended by the Treaty of Amsterdam, was adopted by the Council of Ministers in November 2000.[2] The European Union Charter of Fundamental Rights, which was adopted at Nice in December, has a separate chapter devoted to equality.[3] The Council of Europe, for its part, opened for signature on 4 November 2000 a new Protocol (No. 12) to the European Convention on Human Rights, which plugs a gap in that Convention. At present the Convention is breached only when there is discrimination in the enjoyment of a right it expressly protects. But because it makes no provision for the right to employment, for example, the Convention affords no protection in respect of discrimination in employment. The new Protocol provides a free-standing guarantee against discrimination, which is not dependent upon the breach of some other Convention right.

These instruments, and the provisions of national constitutions and legislation, provide a bewildering range of concepts of equality. It is, therefore, necessary to clarify how "equality" might be understood in the context of "decent work". This is not for any semantic or ideological reason, but because in fashioning a decent work programme, it is essential to have regard for the underlying principles from which legal and social concepts of equality derive.

Equality as consistency or formal equality

The concept of equality has two basic dimensions: equality as consistency – i.e. likes must be treated alike – and substantive or material equality.[4] The first of these is found in all anti-discrimination laws, and also in Article 1(1)(a) of ILO Convention No. 111.[5] It embodies a notion of procedural justice which does not guarantee any particular outcome. So there is no violation of this principle if an employer treats women and men equally badly, or sexually harasses women and men to the same extent. A claim to equal treatment in this sense can be satisfied by depriving both persons compared of a particular benefit (levelling down) as well as by conferring the benefit on them both (levelling up).

For example, in cases brought to the European Court of Justice under Article 141 EC (ex 119 of the EC Treaty), which follows ILO Convention No. 100 in guaranteeing equal remuneration for women and men doing work of equal value, employers have been allowed to raise women's pensionable age to the same as that applying to men, rather than lowering men's pensionable age.[6] The choice of comparators can also be determinative of a claim to equal treatment. For example, a railway company in the United Kingdom had a policy of granting travel concessions to its employees' spouses or unmarried partners of the opposite sex. A female employee with a same-sex partner claimed that this was unlawful sex discrimination, but the European Court of Justice made a comparison with the way in which the same-sex partner of a male employee would have been treated, and concluded that there was no sex discrimination.[7] A comparison with an unmarried heterosexual would have shown a clear breach of the principle of equal treatment.

Substantive equality

The limitations of the principle of formal or procedural equality have led to attempts to develop the concept of substantive or material equality. Here, three different, but overlapping, approaches can be identified. The first is equality of results.

Equality of results

Apparently consistent treatment infringes the goal of substantive equality if its results are unequal. Inequality of results itself can be understood in three senses. The first focuses on the impact of apparently equal treatment on the individual. The second is concerned with the impact on a group, e.g. women, ethnic groups, people with disabilities, etc. And the third demands an outcome which is equal, such as equal remuneration for women doing work of equal value to that of men, or equal representation of women and men in a given occupational grade.

The concept of indirect or adverse-impact discrimination is that an apparently neutral practice or criterion has an unjustifiable adverse impact upon the group to which an individual belongs. The best-known examples are selection criteria for recruitment, promotion or lay-offs with which it is significantly more difficult for members of a disadvantaged group to comply. This concept is thus results-oriented in the first sense – in that the treatment must be detrimental to an individual – but it also involves equality of results in the second sense. However, the concept of indirect discrimination is not redistributive in the third sense: if there is no exclusionary practice or criterion, or if no significant disparate impact can be shown, or yet if there is an objective business or administrative justification for the practice, then there is no violation. This concept is usually said to have its origins in case law of the 1960s under Title VII of the United States Civil Rights Act. In fact, its foundation was laid in 1958 in Article 1 of ILO Convention No. 111, which covers any "distinction, exclusion or preference ... which has the effect of nullifying or impairing equality of opportunity or treatment". But Article 1(2) of this Convention – like the later case law of the United States Supreme Court and the European Court of Justice – goes on to provide that: "Any distinction, exclusion or preference in respect of a particular job based on the inherent requirements thereof is not deemed to be discrimination".

An approach which is more results-oriented in a redistributive sense is to define equality in terms of "fair" (sometimes referred to as "full") participation of groups in the workforce, and fair access of groups to education and training, and to other facilities and services. This aims to overcome the under-representation of disadvantaged groups in the workplace and to ensure their fair participation in the distribution of benefits. This may involve special measures to overcome disadvantage. These measures are generally described as "affirmative action". Professor Faundez, in his useful ILO study, defines this as "treating a sub-class or a group of people differently in order to improve their chances of obtaining a particular good or to ensure that they obtain a proportion of certain goods" (Faundez, 1994, p. 3). Once again, it was the ILO's far-seeing Convention No. 111 which in its Article 5, was one of the first instruments to recognize that "special measures or protection or assistance" for disadvantaged groups should not be deemed to be "discrimination".

The term "affirmative action", however, is unfortunately tarnished by negative experiences with its use in some countries. For this reason, the notion of "employment equity" was coined in Canada, as was "fair participation" or "fair access" in Northern Ireland. Canada's Employment Equity Act 1995 uses "employment equity" to denote that equality "means more than treating persons in the same way but requires special measures and the accommodation of differences". South Africa's Employment Equity Act of 1998 treats affirmative action as the means of achieving employment equity. It provides that "affirmative action measures are measures designed to ensure that suitably qualified people from [disadvantaged] groups have equal employment opportunities and are equitably represented in all occupational categories and levels in the workforce".

Affirmative action in this sense is used as a tool of social policy in many countries and is endorsed in international human rights conventions, such as the International Convention on the Elimination of All Forms of Racial Discrimination of 21 December 1965[8] and the International Convention on the Elimination of All Forms of Discrimination against Women, of 18 December 1979.[9] Another example is the legislation in force in Northern Ireland since 1989, which aims to secure greater fairness in the distribution of jobs and opportunities and to reduce the relative segregation of the Catholic and Protestant communities in that part of the United Kingdom. A recent report on the impact of this legislation reveals that it has led to significant reductions in employment segregation, in the under-representation of the Catholic community overall and of Protestant and Catholic communities in specific areas, as well as reduction in the unemployment differential between the two communities (House of Commons, 1999, paras. 48 et seq.).

Equality of opportunity

A second way of characterizing substantive equality is in terms of equality of opportunity. Convention No. 111 uses this concept. It brings to mind "the graphic metaphor of competitors in a race" and "asserts that true equality cannot be achieved if individuals begin the race from different starting points. An equal opportunities approach therefore aims to equalise the starting points" (Fredman, 1999, para. 3.12).

However, the use of this concept does not make it clear whether the promotion of equality of opportunity is a narrow procedural obligation, or a broader substantive one. The procedural view involves the removal of barriers or obstacles, such as word-of-mouth recruitment or non-job-related selection criteria. This opens up more opportunities but "does not guarantee that more women or [members of ethnic minorities] will in fact be in a position to take advantage of those opportunities" (Fredman, 1999, para. 3.13). A more substantive approach would require affirmative action to compensate for disadvantages.

Equality of human dignity

A third approach to substantive equality is based on the broad values of the dignity, autonomy and worth of every individual. Such an approach is to be found in many national constitutions. In some there is emphasis on equality as the sharing of "common humanity", or "equal worth". One example is Article 23 of the Belgian Constitution which provides that "everyone has the right to lead a life worthy of human dignity". Another is Article 2 of the Greek Constitution which speaks of "respect and protection for the value of the human being" as the primary obligation of the State. In the field of labour law, this approach is reflected in the idea that "labour is not a commodity". The work of the ILO has been based on this principle ever since the Organization's very inception. Labour is "human flesh and blood". It is not a commodity to be exchanged because a person's working power cannot be separated from her or his existence as a human being.

A good illustration of the importance of human dignity as the starting point of an approach to equality is the judgment of 28 September 2000 of the South African Constitutional Court in the case of *Hoffmann v. South African Airways*. The practice of South African Airways (SAA) – like that of many other airlines – was not to offer employment as cabin attendant to any person whose blood test showed that he or she was HIV positive. SAA justified this on safety, medical and operational grounds. In particular, they argued that persons who are HIV positive may react negatively to yellow fever vaccinations, which cabin crew must have for world-wide duty; that people who are HIV positive are prone to contracting opportunistic diseases, with the consequent risk of infecting passengers; and that the life expectancy of HIV-positive people is too short to warrant the costs of training. Mr. Hoffmann, who was refused employment on these grounds, challenged the constitutionality of SAA's practice.[10] The Constitutional Court accepted medical evidence that asymptomatic HIV-positive persons can perform the work of a cabin attendant competently, and that any hazards to which an immunocompetent cabin attendant may be exposed can be managed by counselling, monitoring and vaccination. The risks to passengers were inconsequential. Even immunosuppressed persons are not prone to opportunistic infections and may be vaccinated against yellow fever as long as their count of "CD4+ lymphocytes" remains above a certain level.

On the basis of this evidence, the Constitutional Court held that Mr. Hoffmann's right to equality, guaranteed by section 9 of the South African Constitution, had been violated and it reinstated him in the job of cabin attendant. Discrimination on grounds of HIV status and the question of testing to determine suitability for employment are now governed by South Africa's Employment Equity Act of 1998, but the facts arose before that Act came into force and the issue was solely a constitutional one. Although section 9 of the Constitution mentions a number of grounds of unfair discrimination, these do not include HIV status. The most significant feature of the judgment in question was therefore its reliance on the human dignity argument: "at the heart of the prohibition of unfair discrimination is the recognition that under our Constitution all human beings, regardless of their position in society, must be accorded equal dignity. That dignity is impaired when a person is unfairly discriminated against".[11]

The judgment, concurred in by the full Bench, went on to stress that South Africa's new democratic era is characterized by respect for human dignity for all human beings: "prejudice and stereotyping have no place" in this era.[12] The fact that *some people* who are HIV positive may, under certain circumstances, be unsuitable for employment as cabin attendants does not justify the exclusion of *all people* who are living with HIV. As a Judge of the Indian Supreme Court recently pointed out: "the State cannot be permitted to condemn the victims of HIV infection, many of whom may be truly unfortunate, to certain economic death" by denying them employment.[13]

It must be obvious from the foregoing analysis that the three approaches to substantive equality – equality of results, equality of opportunity and equality of human dignity – lie at the heart of the notion of decent work. This is not only because the ILO's definition expressly refers to opportunities for women and men, and to conditions of "freedom, equity, security and human dignity", but also because of the universality of the concept. The idea of ending untenable distinctions between different categories of workers has a long history in labour law. It is based on the notion that there must be comparable protection for all those who work. The first European constitution to recognize social rights, that of the Weimar Republic (1919) in its Article 158, required the State to create a "uniform labour law", in particular by linking public and private law. This is reflected in several modern constitutions, such as the Italian Republic's, whose Article 35(1) stipulates that the Republic "protects labour in all its forms and applications".

What is truly innovative in the ILO's concept of decent work, as Amartya Sen (2000) pointed out in his address to the 1999 International Labour Conference, is that it encompasses all kinds of productive work. Unlike classical labour law, it does not presuppose the existence of a contract of employment or an employment relationship. It is not limited to "dependent" or "subordinated" labour, on which labour legislation has traditionally been focused. Indeed, labour law has tended to legitimize inequalities between different categories of workers, between the employed and self-employed, and between those who work and those who are unemployed or cut off from work on grounds of age. The objective of decent work proclaims the basic equality of all those who work or seek work. The concept of substantive equality provides a framework for keeping in mind the needs of the unemployed as well as the employed and self-employed, the aged as well as the young, and those in the informal sector as well as those in the formal sector.

EQUALITY IN THE FRAMEWORK OF FUNDAMENTAL RIGHTS

How does this idea of equality fit into the framework of the rights which are fundamental to a democratic society? The ILO's 1998 Declaration on Fundamental Principles and Rights at Work focuses on freedom of association and the right to collective bargaining, the elimination of forced and compulsory labour, and the worst forms of child labour, as well as discrimination. Action against discrimination aims to achieve equality for disadvantaged groups, such as women, ethnic minorities and people with disabilities. This may be characterized as horizontal equality between workers – a relatively modern concern dating to the Second World War and the ending of colonialism. The more traditional focus of labour law, and of the ILO, has been on what may be called vertical equality between the parties to the employment relationship. Hugo Sinzheimer, one of the founders of labour law in Germany, argued in 1910 that the "special function" of labour law – "the guardian of human beings in an age of unrestrained materialism" – was to ensure some substantive equality between employer and worker (Sinzheimer, 1910, p. 1237). This conception became part of the common law of nations as embodied in ILO Conventions on subjects such as forced or compulsory labour and child labour, and through support for collective organization and collective action in defence of the interests of workers. The principle behind such measures has been described by Paul van der Heijden as "inequality compensation", the aim of which is to compensate by social measures for the economic inequality between employers and workers (van der Heijden, 1994, pp. 135-136). Equality is thus embedded in all elements of the ILO Declaration, making clear the connections between the fundamental rights it protects.

In considering horizontal equality, it is again necessary to distinguish the duty to "eliminate discrimination", in a negative sense, from a broader positive duty to promote equality. Eliminating discrimination, in the sense of avoiding unfavourable actions against individuals, is a negative concept. It usually depends upon *responding* to a complaint or assertion of a right by an individual. That response may be defensive and adversarial, especially when legal proceedings are brought or threatened. Yet this may leave untouched the processes, attitudes and behaviours which, within organizations, lead to prejudice and stereotyping or to practices which unwittingly have the effect of putting women, ethnic minorities, disabled persons and other groups at a disadvantage. Where affirmative action is used, this is seen as a negative exception to the non-discrimination principle. It therefore tends to be sporadic, contested and limited.

By focusing on positive duties to promote equality one can encourage an inclusive, proactive approach. Organizations which have positive duties are compelled to devise coordinated strategies to improve diversity in the workforce or to pursue equality policies in the delivery of services to those who are socially excluded. Instead of passive and defensive responses to complaints of discrimination, organizations are made responsible for reaching stated goals and targets. This will usually involve reasonable adjustments or "special measures". Thus, equality of opportunity increasingly depends not simply on avoiding negative discrimination, but on monitoring, planning, training and improving skills, developing wider social networks and encouraging adaptability. This does not, however, mean reverse discrimination, which can often be counter-productive.

ILO Convention No. 111 anticipated and encouraged the modern emphasis on positive duties. Its Article 2 requires member States "to declare and pursue a national policy designed to promote, by methods appropriate to national conditions and practice, equality of opportunity and treatment in respect of employment and occupation, with a view to eliminating any discrimination in respect thereof". The term "equality" would have been preferable to "equality of opportunity" which, as explained above is both ambiguous and only one of the senses in which substantive equality should be understood. However, there can be no doubt that as long ago as 1958 the ILO envisaged positive promotion and not simply negative prohibition. Article 5 of the Convention provides that "special measures" or "special protection" for certain groups is not discrimination. This leaves ratifying States who wish to do so free to use affirmative action measures. For the reasons already advanced, positive measures will frequently be essential if discrimination is to be eliminated.

There is another reason why positive duties to promote equality and corresponding rights are now necessary: decent work was devised as a model for socially sustainable development. It means productive work which generates an adequate income with adequate social protection. In this respect, there is a growing convergence between the objectives of the ILO and those of the World Bank. Indeed, the *World Development Report 2000/2001* acknowledges the need for a broad social agenda and – of particular relevance here – concludes from the experiences of the 1990s that "inequality is back on the agenda" (World Bank, 2000, p. 33). The *Report* points out the importance of gender, ethnic and racial inequalities as a dimension – and a cause – of poverty. Social, economic and ethnic divisions are "often sources of weak or failed development. In the extreme, vicious cycles of social division and failed development erupt into internal conflict, as in Bosnia and Herzegovina and Sierra Leone, with devastating consequences for people" (World Bank, loc. cit.). The World Bank's "general framework for action" for reducing poverty, like that of the ILO for decent work, obviously requires positive duties on states to grant rights of access to work, health, education, and social security.

An objection to such positive duties which is frequently heard is that social rights cannot be enforced. It is argued that a clear line exists between civil and political rights, on the one hand, and economic, social and cultural rights on the other (see Hepple, 1995). The former are limitations of governmental power – i.e. governments must respect the right not to be discriminated against, etc. – whilst the latter require governments to act, e.g. to provide minimum income, social security, provision of health services and education, etc. Civil rights can be made legally enforceable, while it is said that social and economic rights cannot. However, the creative decisions of the Indian Supreme Court and, more recently, the South African Constitutional Court show that the line between the two classes of rights can become blurred and that it is even possible to give legal effect to certain basic social rights.

An example is the recent South African case of *Mrs. Grootboom*, one of those many thousands of unfortunate people who live in shacks made of cardboard and hessian. The land on which Mrs. Grootboom and many other people lived was subject to flooding, so she and others moved up the hill onto some private land from which they were then rather brutally evicted under a court order. They brought the case to Court relying on section 26 of the new democratic South African Constitution which entitles everyone to the right of access to adequate housing. This right is not absolute because it is subject to the qualification that "the State must take reasonable legislative and other measures, within its available resources, to achieve the progressive realisation of this right". The Constitutional Court decided on 4 October 2000 that the rights in section 26 oblige the State to provide relief for people who have no access to land, no roof over their heads and who are living in intolerable conditions or crisis situations. The South African Government and the local authorities concerned argued that they had a housing programme, and that houses were being built. However, the Court reached the conclusion that Mrs. Grootboom and the others were entitled to this basic protection. They did so on the basis of the rights in the Constitution which guaranteed human dignity, freedom and equality. In the words of Justice Yacoob: "if measures, though statistically successful fail to respond to the needs of those most desperate [like the homeless Mrs. Grootboom] they may not pass the test" of reasonableness.[14] This judgment has great significance for the enforcement of other social rights such as rights to work, to education, to health services and social security. It suggests that the state can be compelled to act "reasonably" in giving effect to fundamental social rights, within the constraints of available resources and the progressive realization of these rights. "Reasonableness", or rationality, requires account to be taken of human dignity, where people are in intolerable or crisis situations.

As this discussion shows, the ILO Declaration and Convention No. 111 must be construed broadly, perhaps even be revised. "Eliminating discrimination" should not be understood simply as a negative duty. The notion should be refocused, so as to emphasize the responsibility of governments, organizations and individuals to generate change by positive actions.

EMPOWERMENT

This leads finally to the question of the implementation of positive duties. This involves designing an optimal system of regulation to reduce inequality by promoting fair representation and eliminating exclusion and institutional barriers to full participation.[15]

There are several designs. One of them concentrates on rights and liabilities allowing individuals to bring legal claims for violation of the right to non-discrimination – this is usually called the American model. Another is that of "command and control" by government or an independent public agency that sets the standards which organizations are required to meet, and enforces them through investigation and legal proceedings. A third model relies exclusively on voluntary self-regulation, with organizations meeting prescribed targets unilaterally without any threat of coercion. A fourth uses enforced self-regulation, applying legal sanctions against those who fail to comply voluntarily. And, finally, there are economic incentives – such as withholding public contracts or subsidies – which may also be used as a means of encouraging compliance.

At one extreme in the debates about the relative advantages and disadvantages of these models are those who want to throw in every kind of policy and legal instrument to tackle inequality – what has been called a "smørgåsbord" approach: "everything is on the table" (Gunningham and Sinclair, 1998, pp. 432-433). In this particular context, however, it rests on the mistaken assumptions that coercion is always necessary and that the resources for enforcement are unlimited. Experience shows that imposing too many bureaucratic requirements on organizations is not only costly, but also likely to engender resistance and adversarialism which make this approach politically unacceptable.

At the other extreme are those who advocate an entirely voluntary approach, encouraging governments and employers to follow best practice without enforceable duties. The trap into which these advocates of "doing good by doing little" fall is to pose one form of regulation (e.g. voluntarism) against another (enforced self-regulation). The point is that a voluntary approach may work in influencing the behaviour of some organizations – e.g. leading edge companies whose markets are among communities receptive to an equal opportunities policy – but fail with others which, for economic or social reasons, are resistant to change.

This has led to the theory of "responsive regulation", now well developed in the environmental field, but not yet so well developed in the field of labour legislation. The idea is that regulation needs to be responsive to the different behaviours of the various organizations subject to regulation. In a recent Independent Review of the Enforcement of UK Anti-Discrimination Legislation which I co-directed, we developed a model of an enforcement pyramid (Hepple, Coussey and Choudhury, 2000, pp. 56-59). As shown in the diagram below, the base of this pyramid consists of what might be called the voluntary means, i.e. persuasion, information and so on. If this fails, the organization is encouraged to have a voluntary plan and when that fails, we move up to investigation by a public body. Eventually the investigation reveals non compliance, and the organization is ordered to comply by compliance notice, traditional enforcement sanctions, ultimately perhaps loss of contracts. In order to work, there must be gradual escalation and, at the top, sufficiently strong sanctions to deter even the most persistent offender. The idea is that the most severe sanctions will rarely be used, but if they are not there the rest of the pyramid is inoperative.

A crucial element in the design of the enforcement pyramid is to identify the potential participants in the regulatory process. In the field of equality, enforcement has traditionally been viewed as a dialogue between the state (or, in some countries, an independent equality commission) and those who are being regulated (employers, service providers, etc.) But this leaves out the disadvantaged groups themselves. Modern regulatory theory offers two critical insights in this respect. The first is that private forms of social control are often more important in changing behaviour than state law enforcement. In other words, more can be achieved by harnessing the enlightened self-interest of employers and service providers than through command and control regulation. There is, of course, a strong "business" case on efficiency grounds for equality and diversity. The second insight – which is the one stressed in this article – is that the quality of regulation depends crucially on empowerment. This, in turn, means bringing into the regulatory process the experience and views of those directly affected, i.e. groups such as employers' organizations and trade unions, community associations and public interest NGOs, etc., which act as watchdogs, educate and inform others, and help individuals to enforce their rights. These groups must be given and effectively enjoy rights to be informed, consulted and engaged in the enforcement process.

The enforcement pyramid involves a tripartite relationship between those who are regulated (business), those whose interests are affected

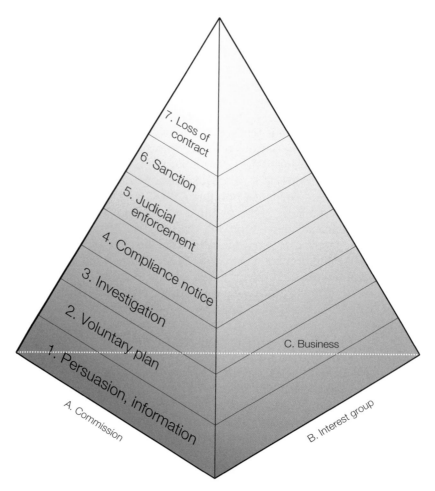

(interest groups) and an independent commission acting as the guardian of the public interest. For example, a strategy of this kind has been introduced in Northern Ireland in respect of a duty on all public authorities to promote equality of opportunity. Section 75 of the Northern Ireland Act 1998 attempts to "mainstream" equality, that is to make equality issues central to the whole range of policy debates and implementation. The reactive and negative approach of anti-discrimination is thereby replaced by proactive, anticipatory and integrative methods. Public authorities must draw up equality schemes. These must set goals and targets, and progress has to be monitored. As a result, public authorities cannot ignore or sideline equality issues.

Central to this new positive duty in Northern Ireland is the empowerment of the local communities themselves. The door has been opened for the people who are affected to get involved in the decision-making process, through rights to information and consultation. A similar positive duty on public authorities has now been enacted in the rest of the United Kingdom in respect of racial equality, and the Government has announced an intention to do the same for gender equality and for disability.

CONCLUDING REMARKS

Does this model of empowerment in the enforcement of a positive duty to promote equality have any relevance to the global Decent Work Agenda? I suggest that it does. The World Bank has proposed as an essential feature of sustainable development the notion that state institutions must be made more accountable and responsive to poor people in political processes and in local decision making. If the barriers that result from distinctions based on gender, ethnicity, race, social status, disability and other disadvantages are to be removed, legal and political processes need to be reformed in this way.

After 42 years, ILO Convention No. 111 still provides a basis for positive policies to promote equality and for the participation of "other appropriate bodies" as well as employers' and workers' organizations in this process (Article 3). This Convention, and the accompanying Recommendation, could now usefully be revised to provide a clearer focus on equality and empowerment. The decent work programme provides an inspiring framework for fulfilling these objectives.

Notes

[1] The full text of the Declaration is published in the special issue of the *International Labour Review* entitled "Labour rights, human rights", Vol. 137 (1998), No. 2, pp. 253-257.

[2] Council Directive 2000/78/EC of 27 November 2000, establishing a general framework for equal treatment in employment and occupation. See *Official Journal of the European Communities* (Luxembourg), L 303, 2 December 2000, pp. 16-22.

[3] See *Official Journal of the European Communities* (Luxembourg), C 364, 18 December 2000, pp. 1-22.

[4] These ideas are elaborated in more detail in Hepple, Coussey and Choudhury (2000, pp. 27-35), Barnard and Hepple (2000), and Fredman (1999).

[5] This provision is worded as follows: "For the purpose of this Convention the term 'discrimination' includes ... any distinction, exclusion or preference made on the basis of race, colour, sex, religion, political opinion, national extraction or social origin, which has the effect of nullifying or impairing equality of opportunity or treatment in employment or occupation".

[6] Case C-408/92, *Smith and Others v. Avdel Systems Ltd.*, ECR 1994, p. I-4435.

[7] Case C-249/96, *Grant v. South West Trains*, ECR 1998, p. I-621.

[8] Art. 1.4 allows "special measures taken for the sole purpose of securing adequate advancement of certain racial or ethnic groups" provided that such measures do not, as a consequence, lead to the maintenance of separate rights for different racial groups, and are not continued after the objectives for which they were taken have been achieved.

[9] Art. 4.1 allows "temporary special measures" aimed at achieving de facto equality between men and women, provided that these measures are discontinued when the objectives of equality of opportunity and treatment have been achieved.

[10] SAA is an organ of the State, not a private employer.

[11] *Hoffmann v. South African Airways,* Case CCT/17/00, Judgment of 28 September 2000, para. 27.

[12] ibid., para. 37.

[13] *MX of Bombay Indian Inhabitant v. M/s ZY and another,* AIR 1997 (Bombay) 406 at 431 (Tipnis J).

[14] *Government of the Republic of South Africa and Others v. Grootboom,* Case CCT 11/00, Judgment of 4 October 2000, para. 44.

[15] This draws extensively on Hepple, Coussey and Choudhury (2000).

References

Barnard, Catherine; Hepple, Bob. 2000. "Substantive equality", in *Cambridge Law Journal* (Cambridge), Vol. 59, pp. 562-585.

Faundez, J. 1994. *Affirmative action: International perspectives.* Geneva, ILO.

Fredman, S. 1999. *A critical review of the concept of equality in UK anti-discrimination law.* Independent Review of the Enforcement of UK Anti-Discrimination Legislation, Working Paper No. 3. Cambridge, Centre for Public Law, University of Cambridge.

Gunningham, Neil; Sinclair, Darren. 1998. "Designing environmental policy", in Neil Gunningham, Peter Grabosky and Darren Sinclair (eds.): *Smart regulation: Designing environmental policy.* Oxford, Clarendon Press, Ch. 6.

Hepple, Bob. 2001. *Work, empowerment and equality.* Geneva, International Institute for Labour Studies.

—. 1995. "Social values and European law", in *Current Legal Problems* (London), Vol. 48-II, pp. 39-61.

—; Coussey, Mary; Choudhury, Tufyal. 2000. *Equality: A new framework – Report of the Independent Review of the Enforcement of UK Anti-Discrimination Legislation.* Oxford, Hart Publishing.

House of Commons (Northern Ireland Affairs Committee). 1999. *The operation of the Fair Employment (Northern Ireland) Act 1989: Ten years on.* Fourth report, Session 1998-99, HC Paper. London, HMSO.

ILO. 1999. *Decent work.* Report of the Director-General of the ILO to the 87th Session of the International Labour Conference. Geneva.

Sen, Amartya. 2000. "Work and rights", in *International Labour Review* (Geneva), Vol. 139 , No. 2, pp. 119-128.

Sinzheimer, Hugo. 1910. "Die Fortenwicklung des Arbeitsrechts und die Aufgabe der Rechtslehre", in *Soziale Praxis,* Vol. 20, p. 1237.

van der Heijden, Paul. 1994. "Post-industrial labour law and industrial relations in the Netherlands", in Lord Wedderburn, Max Rood, Gérard Lyon-Caen, Wolfgang Däubler and Paul van der Heijden (eds.): *Labour law in the post-industrial era: Essays in honour of Hugo Sinzheimer.* Aldershot, Dartmouth, pp. 133-147.

World Bank. 2000. *World Development Report 2000/2001: Attacking poverty.* New York, NY, Oxford University Press.

10

THE VOLUNTARY SECTOR, JOB CREATION AND SOCIAL POLICY: ILLUSIONS AND OPPORTUNITIES

Virginie PÉROTIN *

Voluntary and non-profit organizations have recently attracted a surge of interest in several industrialized countries. The increased visibility of the voluntary sector at a time of stagnating public sector resources and high unemployment, and its apparent ability to tackle certain social problems better than governments, have inspired suggestions that unemployment could be significantly reduced by creating jobs in non-profit organizations, notably in social and community services. However, the voluntary sector's capacity to expand may be limited and dependent on public funding. Increasing public funding to voluntary organizations in social and community services would be justified only if voluntary organizations achieve social policy goals more efficiently than public and for-profit organizations. Though it may not be realistic or desirable to turn the voluntary sector into a large-scale social service provider, the sector may be an important source of innovation for social service provision now, as it has been in the past. This article will outline the terms of this debate, examining the sources and extent of potential job creation in voluntary organizations and the implications for social policy of an expanded role for the non-profit sector.

Several factors have contributed to this renewed attention on the voluntary sector.[1] Much of the debate about privatization over the past two decades has emphasized "government failures" – instances of inefficiency specifically associated with government intervention. In certain cases, the costs arising from government failures have been thought to outweigh the benefits that might be gained from government intervention where markets fail. In certain countries, these considerations, together with concern over

Originally published in *International Labour Review*, Vol. 140 (2001), No. 3.

* This article is based on research undertaken by the author when she was a member of the Cross-departmental Analysis and Report Team, ILO. Access to data and the cooperation of the Comparative Nonprofit Project at Johns Hopkins University are gratefully acknowledged.

government deficits, have induced considerable withdrawal by the State from direct social service provision. At the same time, persistent high unemployment and rapid social and economic change have been accompanied by forms of social exclusion perceived to be inadequately handled by post-war welfare state systems. As a result, the non-profit sector has increasingly appeared as a possible provider of social services, and has been hailed as governments' partner in the fight against social exclusion. Over the same period, in many countries, successful community-level initiatives have been developed by grass-roots organizations in order to deal with social exclusion, unemployment and urban decline. Some of these initiatives have received considerable government support. Tax concessions attached to donations to charities have also increased in several countries. The voluntary sector itself has increased its visibility and professionalism over the past 20 years, and many organizations have developed new skills in tendering for government subsidies and obtaining resources from commercial activities.

The rediscovered potential of the non-profit sector has inspired suggestions that it might be a substantial source of job creation, and even that many current social problems could be solved by promoting non-profit organizations and volunteer work on a large scale. Such hopes have been expressed in a number of contexts and have usually involved one of the following two scenarios. In the first, social services currently provided by government would be massively contracted out to non-profit organizations. Welfare payments to individuals could be used to remunerate community work performed in non-profit organizations by persons presently unemployed. Social and community services could expand and would be cheaper. Savings would come from a reduction in the wasteful bureaucracies that are thought to impose large costs on the welfare state, from the use of voluntary work and donations, and from hiring unemployed people at a low "social wage" rather than additional public employees. Donations and volunteer work would be encouraged by a variety of measures such as additional tax concessions, "shadow wages" for voluntary work, etc. Any extra expenditure not covered by such savings would come from new taxes levied, for example, on polluting activities or luxury goods.

The second scenario involves reorganizing the lifestyle of the working population so that most people are involved in both paid work and volunteer work for non-profit organizations providing community and personal services.[2] Partly financed by public funds, partly by volunteer work and donations and partly by market-generated funds, such services could meet presently unsatisfied needs at a lower cost than if provided by government. The jobs created might involve lower labour costs than public-sector jobs, but would offer better conditions than those offered by personal service jobs in the private sector. The population's involvement in designing and providing the services would ensure needs were adequately covered and would promote community social ties and gift-exchange relationships.

   Though not all supporters of job creation in the voluntary sector make such strong claims for the sector, scenarios such as the ones outlined above have attracted much attention from policy-makers and in the media, and need to be evaluated. After providing a definition of the voluntary sector, this article will first examine the size of the sector and its resources, and the extent to which the sector fits the grass-roots, volunteer-based image evoked in the scenarios described above. The second question to be addressed is whether the sector can expand sufficiently to alleviate unemployment and/or take over social service provision, as proposed. As will be seen, any major expansion of the sector would have to rely on public funding. This implies that public resources would be used to fund the voluntary sector in preference to the public sector or to contracting out social services to for-profit enterprises. The third question to be investigated therefore concerns the optimal circumstances in which the voluntary sector could achieve social policy objectives at the lowest cost, and the cases in which "voluntary sector failures" and inefficiency costs specific to the sector may outweigh the savings achieved by mobilizing non-government resources. It will be argued that governance is a key factor here, and an evaluation will be made of some recent organizational forms which may be associated with more effective and democratic implementation of social policy in both the public and the voluntary sectors.

WHAT IS THE VOLUNTARY SECTOR?

There is no uniform definition of the voluntary sector across countries and disciplines. A clarification of commonly used terms is therefore proposed, together with a fairly standard view of the contours of the sector.

   A variety of terms are used to refer to the voluntary sector or related parts of the economy, including "third sector", "independent sector", "charities", "non-governmental organizations" (NGOs), "non-profits" and "social economy". Usage is sometimes loose, but a fairly standard understanding of what the various terms represent runs as follows. "Third sector" is a helpful notion with which to start. Capitalist market economies can be thought of as comprising a state sector, a conventional private business sector and a third sector that is neither government nor standard private business.[3] The state sector is composed of government and state-owned enterprises, and the private business sector of capitalist enterprises primarily oriented towards the pursuit of profit for their investors. The third sector can be defined as the set of "organizations where a category of agents other than investors ... [are the] explicit, intended beneficiaries of the organization's economic activity" (Gui, 1991, p. 552).[4] This sector includes all private non-capitalist organizations (e.g. cooperatives, mutual insurance funds, credit unions, etc.), and non-profit organizations (i.e. associations, clubs, charities, etc.), which may or may not sell goods and services.[5] Third-sector organizations, and non-profit

---

Box 1. What is the voluntary sector?

According to the JH-CNP definition, the voluntary sector comprises organizations which:

- have some permanent structure, i.e. not just "informal, temporary gatherings of people";
- are private institutions, separate from government, even though they may receive substantial government funding;
- do not distribute profits they generate to their owners or directors: any profit must be ploughed back and used to further the mission of the organization;
- are self-governing;
- involve some degree of voluntary participation.

The International Classification of Nonprofit Organizations (ICNPO) organizes the very wide range of activities carried out by voluntary organizations in the following groups (examples illustrate the wide variety).

Culture and recreation: non-profit media and publishing houses, libraries, photographic societies, theatres, ballet, orchestras, choirs, historical or literary societies, commemoration funds, museums and zoos, sports clubs, playground associations, country clubs, etc.;

Education and research: schools, universities, continuing education institutions and research centres; literacy programmes;

Health: hospitals and residential care facilities for the disabled, the elderly, the mentally ill; outpatient facilities, physiotherapy centres, community health centres, suicide prevention and crisis intervention organizations, health education institutions, emergency medical and ambulance services, etc.;

Social services: child welfare services; delinquency and teen pregnancy prevention, youth centres, YMCAs, Boy Scouts and Girl Scouts; parent education agencies, family violence shelters, sheltered housing, specialized services for the disabled, home helps, recreation and meal programmes for the elderly, self-help support groups and personal counselling; disaster prevention and relief organizations, such as volunteer fire departments, homeless shelters, refugee assistance organizations; and organizations providing cash, food, clothing, etc. to persons in need;

Environment: organizations promoting environmental protection and supplying conservation and environmental services, as well as animal shelters and hospitals, humane societies and wildlife preservation agencies;

Development and housing: community and neighbourhood development associations and organizations working for urban renewal, entrepreneurial programmes, housing associations and assistance, training and counselling, and community employment programmes;

Law, advocacy and politics: organizations protecting the rights of certain disadvantaged groups or the interests of specific ethnic groups, and organizations promoting civil rights and human rights; organizations involved in legal assistance, crime prevention, offenders' rehabilitation or victim support; consumers' associations; and political parties and campaigning organizations;

Philanthropic intermediaries and voluntarism promotion: foundations and organizations providing volunteers and fund-raising to other organizations;

International activities: organizations promoting cultural exchange programmes, international development assistance, disaster relief and human rights;

Religion: religious congregations and their related associations.

Business and professional associations, trade unions.

Source: Information adapted and summarized from Salamon and Anheier (1997), where a more precise definition and the details of the International Classification of Nonprofit Organizations can be found.

---

organizations in particular, may be set up for the mutual benefit of their members, for example, sports clubs or trade associations, or for public benefit, for example, charities (Gui, 1991).

Non-profit or voluntary organizations "do not seek to generate monetary profits for distribution to their owners or officers" (Ben-Ner, 1986, p. 4). This characteristic is often reflected in a legal constraint that they should not distribute profits to their members or owners. In practice, identifying the precise contours of the non-profit sector is not always easy and differences in national usage, tax laws and traditions complicate this task (Salamon and Anheier, 1997). An international definition has been elaborated by the Johns Hopkins Comparative Nonprofit Sector Project (JH-CNP – see Salamon and Anheier, 1996 and 1997), according to which the non-profit sector includes private, self-governing organizations that have some degree of formal existence, do not distribute the profit they may generate to their owners or directors, and involve an element of voluntary participation.

As can be seen from the classification constructed by the JH-CNP (summarized in box 1), the voluntary sector is very heterogenous. Though many of the organizations concerned have a social purpose, others promote business interests or serve groups of individuals who share a hobby. Certain non-profit organizations may even be quite exclusive (e.g. country clubs). Many voluntary organizations exist to further democracy and protect the rights of disadvantaged groups. However, unlike other third-sector organizations such as cooperatives, voluntary organizations are not necessarily run on a democratic basis. If the law of the country allows it, some may even advocate anti-democratic ideals or discriminatory practices (Rock and Klinedinst, 1992). Finally, together with small, volunteer-based associations, the non-profit sector also includes large, highly technical institutions such as hospitals, museums or universities. This diversity is inherent to the voluntary sector, and lies at the heart of its contribution to democracy.

SIZE AND RESOURCES OF THE VOLUNTARY SECTOR

It is of particular interest in the present context to look at personal and community services, as they are often cited as the area where voluntary sector jobs should be created, and also at small, non-bureaucratic organizations using volunteers and pursuing public interest goals (whether organized on a mutual- or public-benefit basis), as they are evoked as sources of jobs at a lower overall cost.[6]

Size

Whether in terms of employment or share of the provision of certain services, the voluntary sector represents a modest but significant part of several major industrialized countries' economies. In 1995, the latest year for which comparable estimates are available, employees in non-profit organizations represented 3 to 12 per cent of total employment in the 13 industrialized countries for which estimates are available (see table 1).[7]

In each country, the place of the sector has been shaped by cultural, social and ideological factors, including the historical role of organized religion and of the State (Salamon and Anheier, 1996, 1998; Kendall and Knapp, 1996; Yamauchi, 1998). The bulk of employment in the non-profit sector is found in health, education and research, social services, and cultural and recreational activities (table 2). Health represents a large portion of voluntary sector employment in countries where it is largely provided privately (e.g. the United States), and a small portion in countries where the State is the major provider (e.g. the United Kingdom and Sweden). Non-profit sector employment in education and research is primarily provided by private (often religious) schools and non-profit universities, which in certain countries receive the bulk of their funding from government (e.g. France and the United Kingdom).

Though the voluntary sector as a whole represents a larger share of employment than might be expected, its grass-roots, public interest portion provides a very small share of all jobs. The bulk of voluntary sector employment is found in industries comprising large, technical institutions that share many characteristics with government and could not rely primarily on volunteer work (health, education and research, and the residential care part of social services), as well as industries primarily composed of mutual interest organizations (the culture and recreation industries). Looking only at the areas

Table 1. Non-profit sector share of total employment, 1995 (%)

Country	Share of full-time-equivalent non-agricultural employment
Australia	7.20
Austria	4.46
Belgium	10.48
Finland	2.96
France	4.90
Germany	4.55
Ireland	11.54
Israel	9.19
Japan	3.54
Netherlands	12.40
Spain	4.52
United Kingdom	6.20
United States	7.83

Source: Salamon et al., 1998, Appendix to table 1.

Table 2.   Distribution of voluntary sector employment by activity, 1995 (%)

Country	Culture	Education	Health	Social ser-vices	Environment	Develop-ment	Advocacy	Foun-dations	Inter-national	Pro-fessional	Other	Total*
Australia	16.8	23.3	18.7	20.2	0.6	10.9	3.2	0.1	0.2	4.3	1.7	100.0
Austria	8.4	8.9	11.6	64.0	0.4	...	4.5	...	0.8	1.4	...	100.0
Belgium	4.9	38.8	30.4	13.8	0.5	9.9	0.4	0.2	0.2	0.9	...	100.0
Finland	14.2	25.0	23.0	17.8	1.0	2.4	8.7	0.0	0.3	7.2	0.3	100.0
France	12.1	20.7	15.5	39.7	1.0	5.5	1.9	0.0	1.8	1.8	...	100.0
Germany	5.8	12.6	33.2	33.8	0.9	6.6	1.8	0.4	0.7	4.2	...	100.0
Ireland	6.0	53.7	27.6	4.5	0.9	4.3	0.4	0.1	0.3	2.2	...	100.0
Israel	5.7	50.3	27.0	10.9	0.8	1.0	0.4	2.0	0.1	1.8	...	100.0
Japan	3.1	22.2	46.6	16.4	0.4	0.3	0.2	0.2	0.4	6.3	4.0	100.0
Nether-lands	3.4	28.3	42.5	19.4	0.9	2.6	0.0	0.4	0.6	2.0	...	100.0
Spain	11.8	25.1	12.2	31.8	0.3	11.2	3.4	0.1	2.0	1.8	0.3	100.0
United Kingdom	24.5	41.5	4.3	13.1	1.3	7.6	0.7	0.7	3.8	2.6	...	100.0
United States	7.3	21.5	46.3	13.5	...	6.3	1.8	0.3	...	2.9	...	100.0

* Totals may not always add up exactly to 100.0 because of rounding errors.   ... Not available.

Source: Salamon et al., 1998, Appendix to table 1.

where grass-roots charities are more common, an upper limit can be estimated for the share of total employment provided by these types of organization. This share is quite small. Together, the voluntary organizations involved in community development and housing, the environment, civic, advocacy and international activities, philanthropic intermediaries and non-profit social services (less residential care in France) provide at most about 2.5 per cent of total employment in Australia, 3.1 per cent in Austria, 2.6 per cent in Belgium, 0.8 per cent in Finland, 1.7 per cent in France, 2.0 per cent in Germany, 1.2 per cent in Ireland, 1.4 per cent in Israel, 0.8 per cent in Italy, 0.6 per cent in Japan, 3.0 per cent in the Netherlands, 2.2 per cent in Spain, 0.8 per cent in Sweden, 1.7 per cent in the United Kingdom and 1.9 per cent in the United States.[8] Actual proportions will be lower, given that for countries other than France these percentages include residential care institutions coming under the "social services" group. In this group, only a subset of organizations provide personal and community services.

Recent changes in employment

Data on the evolution of employment in the voluntary sector confirm the sense prevailing among practitioners that the sector has grown in several countries recently. For the 1980s, estimates available for Germany and the United States indicate that employment in the voluntary sector increased much faster than total employment in these countries, though at a similar rate as employment in services in that period.[9] Fragmentary evidence for France suggests the pattern applies to that country as well.

Table 3 shows the total and annual average growth of non-profit employment in 1990-95 for five countries and the corresponding annual average growth of employment in non-agricultural sectors and in services. In these years, as in the 1980s, employment grew much faster in the voluntary sector than in the economy as a whole in all five countries, several of which went through a severe recession in the early 1990s. However, in the United Kingdom as in the United States, employment growth in the voluntary sector was not much faster than in services.[10] It was substantially faster in Japan and fastest compared to the rest of the economy – including services – in France and, especially, in Germany. In the last two countries, this growth may be explained by the involvement of the non-profit sector in extensive government-subsidized labour market programmes such as employment training schemes (Birkhölzer and Lorenz, 1998a; Demoustier, 1998). For example, in 1995 around 125,000 subsidized *contrats emploi-solidarité* were reported to exist in the voluntary sector in France (Demoustier, 1998), which corresponds to 80 per cent of net job creation in the voluntary sector in that country in 1990-95.[11]

In France, Germany and the United Kingdom, the areas likely to include grass-roots organizations and personal and community services together provided the bulk of voluntary sector job growth in 1990-95 (two-

Table 3. Evolution of voluntary sector employment, 1990-95 (%)

Country	Voluntary sector employment growth[1]		Average annual total non-agricultural employment growth	Average annual employment growth in services
	Overall	Annual (average)		
France	19.6	3.6	0.1	1.1[2]
Germany	46.6	8.6	−0.5[3]	1.1[3]
Japan	18.7	3.5	1.0	1.3
United Kingdom	4.9	1.0	−0.7	0.7
United States	11.2	2.1	0.7[4]	1.5

[1] Full-time equivalent jobs. Technically, the information given here on changes in overall employment and in non-profit employment is not fully comparable, because non-profit employment is expressed in full-time-equivalent terms, whereas overall employment is expressed in numbers of jobs, some of which are part-time. However, the shares of part-time work in the non-profit sector and in the whole economy are unlikely to have changed sufficiently in relation to each other over a five-year period to make a substantial difference in the compared employment growth rates of the voluntary sector and the whole economy in the countries concerned. [2] 1990-96 (source: INSEE). [3] 1991-95 (whole of Germany). [4] Estimate (figure for 1993-94 missing).
Sources: Computed from Salamon et al., 1998; JH-CNP Project,1999; OECD, 1997; INSEE, 1998.

thirds in France and Germany and nine-tenths in the United Kingdom; see table 4). These were precisely the areas targeted for the labour market and development programmes subsidized by several European governments and by the European Union (Salamon et al., 1998). In Japan and the United States, only one-fifth and one-third, respectively, of the new non-profit jobs were created in those areas. It is difficult to assess whether the recent growth

Table 4. Distribution of changes in voluntary sector employment, 1990-95 (%)

	France	Germany	Japan	United Kingdom	United States
Culture	15.8	3.1	−0.1	−4.9	3.1
Education	9.3	8.6	7.7	−3.5	17.7
Health	7.6	18.3	69.1	14.3	44.7
Social services	46.4	54.6	16.9	32.7	29.2
Environment	2.7	2.3	1.3	1.1	...
Development	9.7	6.4	0.4	28.5	3.0
Civic/advocacy	2.1	2.4	0.0	1.0	1.9
Foundations	0.0	0.6	0.5	2.4	...
International	5.6	1.1	0.7	26.2	...
Professional	0.9	2.6	1.8	2.2	0.5
Other	...	...	1.6	...	...
Total	100.0	100.0	100.0	100.0	100.0

... Not available.
Source: JH-CNP Project, 1999.

is a lasting trend, owing to the paucity of available data. The extent to which the jobs created in the voluntary sector are durable is also largely unknown.[12]

Resources

Although a number of voluntary organizations have commercial activities, the market is rarely their primary source of income. Demand for the services of the voluntary sector is mainly expressed in the form of membership fees, donations, government payments and volunteer work supplied to non-profit organizations. The availability of these resources conditions the capacity of the sector to expand.

Financial resources

The distribution of the financial resources of the voluntary sector by source of revenue is shown for 15 countries in table 5. Public sector payments include direct subsidies and government contracts as well as third-party payments, such as state health insurance payments, vouchers, and payments under systems like the United States Medicaid and Medicare programmes. Private donations include direct donations from individuals and businesses as well as foundation grants and funds collected through federated fund-raising campaigns. Private fees and payments primarily include revenue from the sale of services and other market activities, membership dues and investment income.

Table 5.   Distribution of voluntary sector resources, 1995[1] (%)

	Public sector payments	Private donations	Private fees and charges
Australia	31.3	6.4	62.4
Austria	50.4	6.1	43.5
Belgium	77.4	4.5	18.1
Finland	36.2	5.9	57.9
France	57.8	7.5	34.6
Germany	64.3	3.4	32.3
Ireland	77.8	7.0	15.2
Israel	63.9	10.2	25.8
Italy[2]	40.2	4.0	55.7
Japan	34.4	3.3	62.3
Netherlands	60.4	1.5	35.8
Spain	32.1	18.8	49.0
Sweden[3]	26.6	9.4	64.1
United Kingdom	46.7	8.8	44.6
United States	30.5	12.9	56.6

[1] Except for Italy and Sweden.   [2] 1991 – computed from JH-CNP data.   [3] 1992.
Sources: Computed from Salamon, Anheier and Sokolowski, 1995; Salamon et al., 1998.

The most noticeable feature of the distribution of voluntary sector resources in most of the countries of the table is the low share of private donations (table 5). In 1995, this share was less than 10 per cent in all but three of
the countries for which there are data, the exceptions being Israel (10 per
cent), Spain (19 per cent) and the United States (13 per cent). The other salient feature is the often considerable share of the public sector. In 1995, public sector payments represented 30 per cent (United States) to 77-78 per cent
(Belgium and Ireland) of the revenue of the voluntary sector in the countries
for which information is available. Revenue from market activities, often
thought of as a promising source of income, represented between 15 per cent
(Ireland) and 62 per cent (Australia) of voluntary sector revenue in 1995, including membership dues.

In the period 1990-95, the share of private donations dropped in three
of the five countries for which information is available (table 6). Of the other
two, only Japan shows a substantial increase in the share of donations over
the period, but this share remains smaller in that country than elsewhere. In
four of the five countries, the share of market and membership fee income
increased over the period and the share of public sector resources increased
in the United States and in the United Kingdom.[13] Other sources confirm
these trends over a longer period for the United States and suggest a similar
pattern for Ireland.[14]

A larger part of private donations to non-profit organizations come
from individuals or households (excluding membership fees) than from businesses, in the countries for which comparable information is available.[15]
Individual donations revenue depends both on the proportion of people who
give to the voluntary sector and on the amounts involved. In 1991-92, surveys
run as part of the JH-CNP project estimated the proportion of adults making
donations to the voluntary sector in the previous 12 months at 73 per cent in
the United States, 44 per cent in Germany (excluding the church tax) and 43
per cent in France (Salamon, Anheier and Sokolowski, 1995, table 10.13).
Information from later rounds of the same survey in France and from different sources in the United Kingdom and the United States shows that in these
countries the proportion of the population giving to non-profits fluctuated,
with no overall increase, in the 1980s and 1990s.[16]

In 1991-92, the average amount donated to the voluntary sector by
households was estimated at 1.9 per cent of average household income in the
United States and 0.9 per cent in Germany (excluding the church tax – see
Salamon, Anheier and Sokolowski, 1995) which corresponded to amounts
given on average by *all households* of 1.2 per cent and 0.3 per cent of average
household income, respectively. In Japan, this was conservatively estimated
at 0.1 per cent in 1994 (Yamauchi, 1998). Recent estimates put the average
donation of households giving to charity at just under 2 per cent of average household income in the United Kingdom and 0.2 per cent of average
household income in France in 1996.[17] The average level of individual or

Table 6.   Evolution of the distribution of voluntary sector resources, 1990-95 (%)

	France		Germany		Japan		United Kingdom		United States	
	1990	1995	1990	1995	1990	1995	1990	1995	1990	1995
Public sector payments	59.5	57.8	68.2	64.3	38.3	34.4	39.8	46.7	29.6	30.5
Private donations	7.1	7.5	3.9	3.4	1.3	3.3	12.0	8.8	18.6	12.9
Private fees and payments	33.5	34.6	27.9	32.3	60.4	62.3	48.2	44.6	51.8	56.6

Sources: Salamon, Anheier and Sokolowski, 1995, table 10.8; Salamon et al., 1998, Appendix to table 3.

household donations also seems to be stable or declining in relation to income, at least in France, the United Kingdom and the United States (the countries for which information is available).[18]

Only a portion of private donations goes to parts of the sector likely to involve public interest, grass-roots organizations or organizations active in personal, social and community services. Table 7 shows the destination of private donations among the various parts of the voluntary sector in seven countries in or around 1990. Looking again at social services, environment, development and housing, civic and advocacy, philanthropy and international activities, these areas attract 50 per cent or more of private contri-

Table 7.   Distribution of private donations to the voluntary sector (%), 1990

	France	Germany	Italy	Japan	Sweden	United Kingdom	United States
Culture and recreation	10.3	17.8	18.0	2.9	26.4	12.0	5.6
Education and research	34.1	6.1	6.0	68.6	27.1	14.6	22.0
Health	16.3	23.7	5.3	...	0.3	7.5	24.5
Social services	19.4	43.8	31.5	0.1	10.1	36.4	12.2
Environment	1.5	0.2	0.6	1.7	4.8	6.3	0.8
Development and housing	1.6	0.1	0.6	0.0	0.4	3.5	2.6
Civic and advocacy	1.4	1.3	0.9	4.0	9.1	0.4	0.4
Philanthropy	1.7	0.0	14.8	19.2	2.6	6.8	3.4
International activities	10.6	6.5	1.8	3.5	11.4	11.7	2.7
Business associations	3.1	0.4	20.6	...	5.8	0.9	...
Other	...	...	...	...	2.0	...	25.8
Total	100.0	100.0	100.0	100.0	100.0	100.0	100.0
Share in total funding of voluntary sector	7.1	3.9	4.9	1.3	9.4	12.0	18.6
Share of public interest/ grass-roots organizations	36.2	52.0	50.2	28.5	38.4	65.0	22.1

Source: Computed from Salamon et al., 1995, tables 2.2, 3.2, 5.2, 6.2, 7.2, 8.2 and 9.2.

butions in only three of the seven countries considered, about one-third in three other countries and only about one-fifth in the United States. The portion actually allocated to grass-roots, public interest organizations is smaller, because the "social services" group also includes large residential care facilities in most countries. This means that, at the time, households gave on average at most 0.4 per cent of income in the United Kingdom, 0.3 per cent in the United States, 0.2 per cent in Germany and 0.06 per cent in France to non-profit organizations regarded as potential sources of future employment and non-profit revival.

Expanding tax incentives to donors has often been suggested, but limited evidence suggests that the responsiveness of donations may be quite low (Pharoah and Smerdon, 1998; Archambault and Boumendil, 1998; Kendall and Knapp, 1996). If the present trend continues, it therefore seems unlikely that private donations can be expanded to the point of becoming a major source of income for the voluntary sector.[19]

Volunteer work

Volunteer work has been cited as a reason why paid jobs might be cheaper to create in voluntary organizations than in the public sector. It has even been proposed that volunteer work should be generalized, along with reduced hours of paid work, and be commonly used in personal and community services.

Estimates for France, Germany and Italy suggest that volunteer work could represent as much as 40 per cent of all the hours of work performed in non-profit organizations and 25 per cent of all the resources of the voluntary sector in those countries (Salamon, Anheier and Sokolowski, 1995). Table 8 presents the proportion of the adult population (persons aged 18 years or older) doing voluntary work in 14 industrialized countries in 1990. The estimated proportion of volunteers varied considerably according to the country and the definition chosen, but was substantial for most countries.[20] Volunteering is said to be increasing in Japan and has increased in France, both in terms of the proportion of the population involved and for the average number of hours of work done by volunteers (Yamauchi, 1998; Archambault and Boumendil, 1998). The average number of hours has also been increasing in the United Kingdom, but the proportion of volunteers decreased slightly in 1991-97 (to 48 per cent) after increasing (from 44 per cent to 51 per cent) in 1981-91 (Davis Smith, 1998). In the United States, the average number of hours worked by volunteers has remained stable since 1991, but the proportion of volunteers followed a very similar pattern to that of the United Kingdom, going from 45 per cent in 1987 to over 50 per cent in 1989-91 and back to 49 per cent in 1995 (Hodgkinson et al., 1996b).

In what areas of activity do people volunteer? Table 9 shows the allocation of all hours of volunteer work (excluding work undertaken for churches,

Table 8.   Percentages of population volunteering, 1990-91

Country	All volunteering[1]	Religion excluded[1]	Volunteering in past year[2]
United States	46	34	49
Canada	43	39	...
Sweden	39	38	...
Norway	37	34	...
Netherlands	36	33	...
Germany	30	28	13
Belgium	28	27	...
Ireland	26	24	...
Denmark	26	25	...
Italy	24	21	...
France	23	22	19
United Kingdom	22	20	51
Spain	12	10	...
Japan	...	...	28

[1] Percentage of adults aged 18+ currently doing unpaid voluntary work. Source: Dekker and van den Broek, 1998.
[2] Percentage of adults aged 18+ who did volunteer work in the year preceding the survey. Sources: France (1991) and United States (1990): Salamon, Anheier and Sokolowski, 1995; Germany (1990 data in columns 1 and 2 relate to territory of former Fed. Rep. of Germany): Dekker and van den Broek, 1998; (1991 data in column 3 relate to reunified Germany): Salamon, Anheier and Sokolowski, 1995; Japan (1991): Yamauchi, 1998; United Kingdom (1991): Davis Smith, 1998. Estimates from Salamon, Anheier and Sokolowski (1995) do not include church activities.
... Not available.

Table 9.   Distribution of volunteer work, 1990 (% of total hours)

Sector	France	Germany	Italy	Sweden
Culture and recreation	48.8	60.5	33.0	51.6
Education and research	5.3	2.9	9.7	2.4
Health	3.0	6.3	13.2	0.1
Social services	16.3	5.4	36.1	8.1
Environment	10.3	8.8	1.5	2.2
Development and housing	3.4	0.0	3.1	3.8
Civic and advocacy	4.5	9.0	1.7	12.2
Philanthropy	2.2	2.7	0.1	0.0
International activities	3.4	0.9	1.6	2.1
Business associations	2.8	3.3	0.0	15.6
Other	...	...	...	2.0
Total	100.0	100.0	100.0	100.0

... Not available.
Source: Computed from Salamon, Anheier and Sokolowski, 1995, tables 2.1, 3.1, 5.1 and 9.1.

trade unions and political parties) among the various areas of voluntary sector activity in four countries in 1990. A different but related breakdown of volunteer work assignments is available for the United States in 1989 and 1995 (table 10), and for the United Kingdom there is an indication of the percentage of volunteers doing work in each of a series of areas in 1991 and again in 1997 (table 11).[21] Outside the United States, a considerable share of volunteering work occurs in organizations active in culture and recreation. This area receives 49 per cent of volunteer hours in France, 61 per cent in Germany, 33 per cent in Italy and 52 per cent in Sweden (but only 14-15 per cent of volunteer assignments in the United States). In the United Kingdom, a quarter of volunteers are active in sports and one-sixth in "hobbies, recreation and arts". Outside Italy, the United States and possibly the United Kingdom, the share of volunteer work done in social services is considerably smaller than that devoted to cultural and recreational activities. Overall, pooling again all the areas likely to comprise grass-roots, public interest nonprofit organizations and including community and personal services, an estimate can be obtained of the maximum share of volunteering work donated to such organizations: this would be 40 per cent in France, 44 per cent in Italy, 42-43 per cent in the United States, 27 per cent in Germany, and 28 per cent in Sweden.

As with donations, it is difficult to draw any clear conclusion from the limited information available on the evolution of the distribution of volunteering over time in the United Kingdom and the United States, except that the share of personal and community social services has been stable overall in those countries (tables 10 and 11).

If volunteer work is to be relied upon as a way of cutting the cost of employment in personal and community services or of organizing the provision of these services around citizens' involvement, it is important that the burden be shared and that everyone be concerned. There is no overall crossnational pattern in the relative proportions of men and women doing volunteer work. A higher proportion of women than of men volunteered in the United States (1996), Japan (1991) and Australia (1992), a higher proportion of men than women volunteered in France (1996) and equal proportions of women and men volunteered in the United Kingdom (1991).[22] However, men and women do not necessarily volunteer in the same areas. In Australia, the United Kingdom and France, the same pattern was observed: men are more often active in sports and women are more likely to do work involving children's education and social services.[23] Relying on volunteering for personal and community services, in order either to cut the cost of paid jobs or to involve the population in providing the services, is therefore likely to imply relying more on women's voluntary work than on men's.

Finally, it is not known whether individuals would do more volunteer work if they had more free time. In the United Kingdom, as in the United States and in France, the unemployed tend to volunteer less often than the

Table 10.   Distribution of volunteer assignments[1] in public interest charities,
United States, 1989 and 1995 (%)

Type of charity	1989	1995
Arts, culture and humanities	7.1	6.1
Education	15.9	17.3
Environment	6.1	7.0
Health	11.7	13.2
Human services	13.5	12.6
Public and societal benefit	7.6	6.7
Recreation – adults	8.2	7.3
Youth development	15.3	15.2
Work-related	8.5	7.9
Other[2]	6.1	6.6

[1]Formal volunteering only, not including religious or political party activities.   [2]Includes international, private and community foundations and other activities.
Sources: Hodgkinson et al., 1996a, table 1; 1996b, table 2.16.

Table 11.   Voluntary activity[1] by field of interest, United Kingdom, 1991 and 1997,
(% of volunteers [2])

Field of interest	1991	1997
Children's education	23	23
Youth, children	19	14
Adult education	4	4
Sports, exercise	25	26
Health and social welfare	24	19
Elderly people	14	6
Safety, first aid	8	9
Environment	6	5
Justice and human rights	2	3
Local community groups	9	14
Citizens' groups	8	10
Hobbies, recreation, arts	17	18
Work extra to job	3	3
Groups connected with paid work	2	3
Animals	3	3
(Total number of current volunteers in sample)	(747)	(704)

[1]Not including religion or politics.   [2]Total for each year exceeds 100 per cent because some of the volunteers are involved in activities in several different fields of interest.
Source: Davis Smith, 1998, table 3.4.

employed, but this may occur because of factors other than free time, such as income or disability. People who are employed part time volunteer more often than those who are employed full time in the United States, and more detailed information available for the United Kingdom actually reveals a more complex pattern, depending on the number of hours worked.[24]

EXPANDING VOLUNTARY SECTOR SERVICE PROVISION

It will be recalled that the share of employment in non-profit areas of activity likely to include community and personal services and grass-roots, public interest organizations is very small. A comparison of employment in that part of the voluntary sector with the level of unemployment provides an indication of the expansion that would be necessary for those organizations to make a visible dent in unemployment.[25]

In 1995, 13 of the industrialized countries for which information is available had unemployment rates of 5 per cent or more.[26] In these countries, a reduction of unemployment by a quarter would have required employment in the relevant section of the voluntary sector to grow by 60-640 per cent (i.e. a multiplication by 1.6-7.4) depending on the country, the figures for most countries lying between 130 per cent and 420 per cent (i.e. multiplying non-profit employment by 2.3-5.2 in the relevant industries). Even a one-tenth decrease in unemployment would have required this part of the voluntary sector to expand by 25-260 per cent, an increase of 50-170 per cent being necessary in most countries. In contrast, the fast growth of the whole of the voluntary sector observed in Germany and the United States in the 1980s remained of the order of 40 per cent in total over a period of ten years.

The jobs created in the relevant part of the voluntary sector in 1990-95 actually represented only a fraction of the level unemployment might have reached if those jobs had not been created. Compared to that "theoretical" unemployment rate, those five years of job creation represented 0.4 percentage point (or a 4 per cent cut) in France, 0.7 point (a 7 per cent cut) in Germany, 0.4 point (a 4 per cent cut) in the United Kingdom, 0.1 point (a 4 per cent cut) in Japan and 0.4 point (a 6 per cent cut) in the United States. Clearly, personal and community services provided by the voluntary sector would have to grow massively in order to affect unemployment visibly. If in addition the voluntary sector must replace existing government provision in all social services (included in the group of industries above) the expansion required would be colossal.

The need for public funding

As explained, much of the 1990s growth in voluntary sector jobs in Europe was publicly funded. It is unlikely that large-scale growth could be achieved by the voluntary sector on its own. The resources could not come from private donations or volunteer work if the present trend were to continue, even if tax incentives and leisure time were extended. Although revenue from market activities has been increasing faster than the total resources of the voluntary sector in several countries and may continue to do so, that growth remains well below the levels necessary for a massive expansion, considering that it provides only a portion of non-profit organizations' resources and a lower one in social services than in other parts of the voluntary sector. As they grow, market resources may actually crowd out other sources of income, especially private donations (James, 2000). Indeed, if non-profit organizations providing community and personal services were capable of raising enough resources from market activities to finance the expansion required in a short time, there would probably not be an overall job creation problem at all. Excessive reliance on market income may also threaten the independence that enables non-profit organizations to pursue social goals (Weisbrod, 2000b).

If a rapid expansion of those parts of the voluntary sector providing community and personal services were at all possible, it would have to be achieved with a massive influx of public money. The need for government resources is explicitly recognized in both versions of the claims about job creation in the non-profit sector, whether jobs are to be created in public social services contracted out to non-profit providers or in voluntary organizations receiving a combination of public and private funds, in order to offer services that cannot be provided by for-profit enterprises at prices the poor can afford.[27] If substantial public funds are to be redirected from the public to the voluntary sector or to be directed as a priority to the non-profit sector, it must be certain that these funds will be better used there than elsewhere. One issue is whether more jobs could be created in the non-profit sector. The other issue is whether other public interest objectives relating to the services provided would be met most efficiently this way. These two issues are now addressed.

Would public funds create more jobs if they were allocated to the voluntary sector?

The idea that more jobs could be created by existing social services being contracted out to non-profit organizations stems from the belief that voluntary organizations are less bureaucratic than the public sector, and would thus provide service at lower cost. However, it is not known whether a massively expanded non-profit sector would be any less bureaucratic than government. In general, managers of non-profit organizations do not have any more incentive to minimize costs than public sector managers, unlike owners of for-profit enterprises.[28] In social services, non-profit institutions may attract a particular type of manager who is motivated less by self-interest, but this may also be the case in the public sector (see, for example, Posner and Schmidt, 1996). Furthermore, if the non-profit sector expands rapidly because large public subsidies are offered to voluntary organizations, it is likely to attract more opportunistic individuals and organizations (Weisbrod, 1988). Such managers may try to appropriate public funds, for example, through high salaries, large staff, prestige expenditure, etc., which would add to service costs.

Little empirical evidence exists on the comparative performance of public and non-profit service providers. The findings are inconclusive and do not suggest non-profit organizations have a systematic cost advantage (Rose-Ackerman, 1996; Edwards, 1998; Edwards and Hulme, 1996). For example, in one of the most careful studies on the subject, Sloan et al. (1998) found that the only statistically significant difference in performance between public, non-profit and for-profit hospitals in the United States was that public sector hospitals offered a cheaper service, all else being equal, than either non-profit or for-profit hospitals, between which no significant cost difference was observed (there was no significant difference in service quality between the three types of hospital). Compared to the present situation, however, a massive expansion of the voluntary provision of social services would require additional government monitoring of non-profit subcontractors to ensure that public interest objectives were met. This function would be likely to create another form of bureaucracy, especially because massive subsidies might attract unscrupulous individuals into the sector. It is therefore unclear that contracting out social services to the non-profit sector would create extra jobs by saving on service costs or on bureaucracy.

It is often proposed that simply funding extra jobs in grass-roots non-profit organizations supplying personal and community services would create more jobs than funding new public sector services, because the former attract private donations and volunteers and combine market and non-market income. In many countries, the public sector also has access to market resources. However, it can also be argued that the "social entrepreneurs" who create non-profit enterprises are better at putting together resources from different sectors of the economy. This strategy might be impractical on a large scale, given that neither volunteers nor donations are likely to increase considerably. If the current amount of volunteer work, or even a little more than now, had to be redistributed over massively increased service provision this may not have a noticeable impact on costs. Moreover, there may be only a limited number of "social entrepreneurs" in a given society.

It has also been suggested that the flexibility of small, grass-roots organizations and the lower wages paid in non-profit organizations are likely to encourage job creation. Again, it is not clear that small, grass-roots structures can be retained as the sector expands to the extent required and has to meet specified government standards and targets. If they can, this flexibility may constitute a cost advantage. Only limited evidence is available on wage levels in the voluntary sector compared with government and for-profit organizations. Wages do seem lower overall for a given level of skill or qualification in non-profit organizations than elsewhere, but in the United States and Germany voluntary sector wages could be higher than average in a few occupations for women and members of ethnic minorities (Zimmeck, 1998; Kaminski, 1998; Hodgkinson et al., 1994; Anheier, 1991; Preston, 1989). Recent survey evidence suggests that in Italy voluntary sector wages are lower than those in public social services, but are associated with lower skills and higher job satisfaction on average (Borzaga, 2000). There are conflicting hypotheses as to the possible effect of low wages on service quality (Preston, 1989; Handy and Katz, 1998).

SOCIAL POLICY OBJECTIVES AND "VOLUNTARY SECTOR FAILURES"

In social services in general and in personal and community services in particular, efficient provision involves public interest objectives that may motivate government intervention to fund, regulate or directly produce the services. Such social policy objectives typically include redistribution and equity, the promotion of the economic security and dignity of individuals (Barr, 1992), and public health issues. In practice, the pursuit of these objectives may involve the protection of vulnerable groups such as children, the mentally disabled or the frail elderly, the alleviation of poverty, etc. Government intervention may take various forms, depending on the public objectives pursued and how well they can be met by for-profit organizations operating on markets, by non-profit organizations (with or without regulation and government funding), and/or by government itself. Markets (and the for-profit organizations to which they provide incentives) often fail to achieve the public interest objectives of social policy on their own. The market failures involved tend to concern public goods, such as public health or education, and/or services where asymmetric information (information not fully available to all parties) can be used by providers at the expense of users because it is difficult to assess quality before buying, or where service provision is complex, for example, in health care, legal services, elder care or counselling. Governments can fail in other situations, for example, when flexibility is important or service quality is influenced by short-term incentives. A number of voluntary sector failures have been identified. Such failures are not necessarily a problem for organizations set up and funded voluntarily by concerned citizens without public assistance. However, they are a potential problem if government funds voluntary organizations and/or relies on them for meeting public interest goals.

Salamon (1987) listed voluntary sector failures as philanthropic insufficiency, particularism, amateurism and paternalism. Philanthropic insufficiency refers to the inadequacy of charitable funding alone to support sufficient social care provision.[29] This well-known problem need not concern us further here since it has already been established that public funding would be needed to expand the voluntary sector. Funding through private donations could pose other problems, for example, the choices made would reflect the preferences of the unelected, largest donors. Furthermore, funding through private donations is also in a sense regressive compared with tax funding, since the proportion of household income given to charity is inversely related to the level of income, at least in the United Kingdom, Japan and the United States.[30] A more important concern might be that voluntary funding could not ensure security as it is subject to instability because of the ups and downs of fashion and short-term changes in donor preferences. Evidence from the United States and France suggests that the areas of concern in which new non-profit organizations are created depend in part on current events and "new enthusiasms" (Rose-Ackerman, 1996; Forsé, 1984). Though this instability reflects the dynamism of the voluntary sector and its responsiveness to change, it may make it difficult to ensure continuity of provision of certain services. Similar problems may arise with volunteer work: it may be difficult to secure sufficient volunteer work on a lasting and regular basis, so that stable service provision may not be guaranteed on the basis of substantial volunteer input. The experience of centrally planned economies shows that relying on volunteer work on a regular basis for collective services without providing material incentives can mean that citizens are required to do unpaid work "less than voluntarily".

Other voluntary sector failures arise because of characteristics of voluntary sector provision that may require government to regulate the industry or enter into direct service provision, rather than simply funding supply (Steinberg and Young, 1998). Paternalism and particularism may arise because of fundamental conceptual and organizational differences between the voluntary sector and the public sector's approach to social care that has broadly prevailed since the Second World War. Voluntary services depend on the willingness of a part of the population to provide organization, funding and volunteer work for the purposes of offering services. In contrast, social care provided by the public sector is based on the idea that individuals are entitled to the services of the welfare state.[31] Paternalism can be a problem with public interest non-profit organizations, which often direct services at clients who are not themselves members of the organizations. Traditional charities offering social services or income supplementation are typical examples of this group – some analyses have characterized certain charities as instruments of social control of the poor in the United Kingdom (Kendall and Knapp, 1996). Paternalism may take several forms, for example, incorporating into the service goals corresponding to donors' preferences rather than those of clients' (e.g. regarding alcohol consumption, religious practice or living arrangements; Gui, 1991) or conditions not best suited to fostering clients' sense of dignity (e.g. restrictions on freedom, privacy or dress). As Salamon and Anheier (1998) remark, paternalistic organizations are unlikely to be well equipped to foster self-reliance among their clients, a function often claimed to be better performed by the non-profit sector than by government "welfare handouts". Although governments can also be paternalistic, there remains a profound difference, for the dignity of the individuals involved, between receiving charity and claiming a right. As will be seen further on, the risk of paternalism may actually arise because of the governance structure of public interest non-profit organizations.

Particularism occurs in the selection of client groups by non-profit organizations and may be a strength, for example, if it enables the organizations to reach certain populations which do not have access to certain public sector services or do not trust government employees, or to cater to specific needs. However, the choices of groups depend on the preferences of their unelected members. Particularism can be a problem if voluntary organizations selectively administer a service to which everyone is meant to have access (Edwards and Hulme, 1996). Coordination problems may make it difficult to ensure all potential groups of clients are covered.

Amateurism can be a direct consequence of the widespread payment of low wages in the sector, and possibly of volunteer work. The problem can be especially severe if low-skilled, long-term unemployed persons who have become marginalized on the labour market are hired to do personal and community service jobs as a temporary labour market measure – an approach which is often suggested. A substantial proportion of jobs in those areas involve working with vulnerable groups, such as young children or the elderly, and require skilled care and stable, confident staff. Widespread reliance on volunteer work to provide community and personal services can also raise issues of equity, since it implies that poor people who are clients have to rely on someone working for free to provide them with the services they need, while others can afford to pay for such services. In mutual benefit organizations, volunteers are likely to benefit from the service and from someone else's voluntary work at some point. However, in public interest organizations, at least some clients will remain recipients of voluntary work, and never provide the service themselves; the most vulnerable client groups are especially likely to be in this position. In this context, voluntary work has a different meaning, especially in view of the fact that many mutual benefit organizations are involved in leisure-related activities, such as culture or sports, whereas non-profit organizations providing social services are more often public interest organizations. An Australian study of volunteering found that voluntary work was never regarded as cheap labour in sports-related organizations, but was usually so regarded in welfare and social services (ACOSS, 1997). Furthermore, reliance on voluntary work in social and personal services implies counting on voluntary work by women, since most volunteers in those services are women. It is a moot point whether reliance on such voluntary work by women is any more equitable than reliance on women's provision of free care within the family.[32]

When is non-profit best?

Proponents of the idea that more jobs could be created in the non-profit sector generally claim that non-profit provision would meet some of those objectives better than government provision. For example, voluntary organizations may be more flexible and offer services that more closely fit clients' needs; they may be able to reach the poorest clients, who cannot overcome the bureaucratic hurdles to public welfare services, or who trust a voluntary organization more than a government agency; voluntary organizations may be better at helping people regain an active sense of responsibility for their lives, and so on.

The roles of voluntary organizations in society

As has been seen, the voluntary sector encompasses a wide range of activities. Only a proportion of non-profit organizations are service providers, and only some of these supply social, personal and community services that might be funded by government. The heterogeneity of the sector reflects the manifold role played by non-profit organizations in industrialized countries. Non-profit organizations are traditionally seen as playing an advocacy role. Voluntary organizations have often been formed in order to influence state policy and other private organizations. In particular, there have traditionally been non-profit organizations promoting the interests of the "disempowered" (Stromquist, 1998), a function that may be viewed as a factor of democracy in society. In several countries, for example, over the past three decades community development initiatives have emerged from grass-roots organizations originally formed to promote the rights of groups that were formally or informally excluded from the institutions of the State or were "marginalized ... by virtue of race, gender, disability or poverty" (Kendall and Knapp, 1996, p. 59). This role has led certain students of the voluntary sector to propose that its function is to act as an intermediate institution between citizens and the State or the market (e.g. Bauer, 1998).

Two other roles of the voluntary sector are related to this advocacy or representation function: the identification of unmet or changing social needs, and social innovation. Voluntary sector organizations may serve to express social needs when the public interest changes because of evolving economic or social conditions (Willard, 1995). More generally, non-profit organizations may identify needs that are unmet by social policy (Defourny, 1997; Borzaga and Maiello, 1998). Many social needs will not be picked up by for-profit enterprises on the market because they involve redistribution of income, or because certain characteristics, like public goods features, for example, make it unprofitable to supply the corresponding services, so that there may be an argument for government intervention. However, democratic elections, the main channel through which social needs are expressed and the public interest is defined, may not reflect the interests of minority groups or of groups inadequately represented in political institutions. Those groups' interests or preferences may differ from those of the average voter or the average voter may not be well informed of the relevant issues. There may be a consensus that these are social needs, but government may be unable to supply the corresponding services adequately, for example, because it is weak or

261

inefficient (Yamauchi, 1998). In identifying or providing for new, specific or unmet needs, the voluntary sector may be an important source of innovation, either in the type of service supplied or in the way it is organized (Willard, 1995; Defourny, Favreau and Laville, 1998; Kendall and Knapp, 1996; Borzaga and Maiello, 1998). For example, in recent years non-profit organizations have created new personal and community services, such as homework support for children, collective kitchens, work integration enterprises, or shelters for victims of family violence. They have also innovated by replacing the often segmented, bureaucratic approach of government social services with a more holistic approach, taking into account individuals' health needs as well as employment and housing needs, or bringing together public, private and voluntary organizations and resources to handle local problems. The voluntary sector has traditionally offered a space where experimentation can take place, whether with novel ideas or with unpopular or extreme ideologies which can be implemented this way without imposing them on others (Rose-Ackerman, 1996).

The normative aspect of all these roles implies that in some cases non-profit organizations will supply services temporarily, with the understanding that both funding and provision should eventually come from government. Historically, the voluntary organizations that offered social services often actively mobilized political support for direct public provision of the services they supplied (Salamon and Anheier, 1998), and this is still true in many cases today.[33] It is consistent with the historical pattern of government service creation inspired by innovations from the voluntary sector and, more generally, with the cooperation historically observed between governments and non-profit organizations, which has grown largely thanks to government funding in several countries (Salamon and Anheier, 1996; Kendall and Knapp, 1996; Archambault, 1997). Recent economic literature has also identified cases in which non-profit provision is more efficient than either public or for-profit provision. In such cases, even if the service is funded by the State, it would be more efficient for government to contract the service out to non-profit organizations than to supply it directly.

Comparative advantages of non-profit organizations in service provision

Recent studies investigating the reasons why non-profit organizations exist in capitalist economies have identified two main types of goods and services supplied by the voluntary sector: public or quasi-public goods; and private goods and services in which there is an information imbalance between providers and consumers, to the latter's disadvantage. Non-profit organizations may supply public goods that are not provided by the public sector (Weisbrod, 1977b). Perhaps there is excess demand for those goods and services because the government is inefficient or inflexible (Stromquist,

1998). This situation could apply in areas where the voluntary sector could intervene temporarily, as outlined above. Other collective goods may be in high demand in a small section of the population, where people may have specific needs or want services with an unusual set of characteristics that non-profit organizations can be trusted to provide (Ben-Ner, 1986; Ben-Ner and Van Hoomissen, 1991). For example, schools or counselling services with a particular religious or ideological affiliation may be sought by certain consumers, for whom the affiliation acts as a signal of quality (Rose-Ackerman, 1996). In heterogeneous societies with cohesive groups, such as religious or ethnic minorities, consumers are more likely to organize the supply of such local public goods through non-profit organizations (James, 1987).

Education and counselling services have another characteristic that gives an advantage to voluntary organizations – but also, possibly, to government. In these services (as in others, such as health care, residential care, crèches or legal aid), consumers do not have as much information as suppliers about the quality of the service offered before they purchase it, or even until a certain time after the purchase. Moreover, once the initial purchase has been made, it may be difficult to change suppliers, so that competition may not operate to discipline suppliers. In the case of particularly vulnerable groups, such as the very old, young children or certain mentally disabled persons, the consumers of the service may not be the ones who choose the suppliers, and they may not be in a position to voice their dissatisfaction or to complain about abuse. Consumers may feel they can trust non-profit providers, since they do not have an incentive to minimize costs and quality or to cheat consumers (Hansmann, 1980). The non-profit status may also be perceived as a signal of commitment to service quality. As Ben-Ner and Van Hoomissen (1991) point out, if the non-profit provider is controlled by certain consumers or their representatives, the information problem is overcome and this advantage will also benefit other, non-controlling consumers, if the service is available to non-members of the organization.

The same authors view the creation by consumers of a service-providing non-profit organization as an alternative to lobbying for government regulation or public sector supply. In fact, if the quality and provision of the service are well regulated by government, it is not clear that non-profit organizations will retain a substantial efficiency advantage over other types of enterprises (Rose-Ackerman, 1990, 1996). This factor may explain why in several countries government, non-profit and for-profit suppliers coexist in certain industries, such as health care, unless each type specializes in certain types of service or client (ibid.). Historical factors, ideological preference, the extent to which non-profit organizations are constrained to transparency by legislation, and the relative efficiency of certain governments in running public services may imply that consumer trust in the voluntary sector and in government varies across countries,[34] as do the shares of public, non-profit and for-profit providers of certain services.

The role of governance

Much of the argument on trust and information made in the economic literature regarding non-profit service providers relies on the assumption that the supply of those services is consumer-led (see especially Ben-Ner, 1986; James, 1987). Consumer-provided public goods may present characteristics that closely fit consumer preferences and respond to changes in those preferences, while the monitoring provided by controlling consumers can overcome problems of asymmetric information. Furthermore, the operational objectives of those organizations will be defined by consumers rather than by government (OECD, 1996). Thus, mutual interest non-profit organizations may have a definite efficiency advantage in certain areas of community and personal services, where there are information asymmetries, and in local public good provision. However, these arguments hold less well for public interest non-profit organizations, such as charitable associations that provide a service to clients who are not members. In these organizations, members may have objectives which differ from clients' preferences but which have not necessarily been defined as public interest objectives by a democratic process, since voluntary organizations are accountable only to their members. In the absence of contrary regulation, these objectives may be pursued by the organization, and voluntary sector failures may occur (e.g. paternalism). If public interest objectives are also pursued (a requirement if the organization is subsidized by government), it is not clear that the lack of incentives to minimize costs or prevent consumers from being cheated would be greater in voluntary organizations than in public sector ones.

In several countries, a new generation of non-profit organizations have been experimenting with structures borrowed from other parts of the social economy and involving clients as well as providers in the running of public interest non-profit organizations that supply services. This type of governance strengthens the efficiency advantage of non-profit providers of services characterized by an information asymmetry. It also corrects some of the voluntary sector failures that traditionally affect public interest non-profit organizations. In keeping with the traditional role of the voluntary sector, this innovation may even offer a model for running public sector services.

Democratic social enterprises and social cooperatives

The term "social enterprise" has been developed to describe enterprises which operate on a commercial basis to some extent, with or without public funding, but which have a public interest objective and do not aim to pursue profit for their members (even though legally they may not always have a non-profit status).[35] Social enterprises tend to provide social, personal and community services, or to focus on the (re)integration into employment of people who have become marginalized on the labour market as a result of long-term unemployment and/or a disability, or for other reasons such as a criminal record, drug addiction, etc.[36] Many of the social enterprises are consumer-led initiatives, as hypothesized in the economic literature on non-profit organizations, whether they provide collective goods or services characterized by informational asymmetries. In this sense, they are mutual interest organizations, even if their stated objectives include public interest goals. Examples include the 3,300 German "children's shops", which were originally created by parents as grass-roots childcare facilities in empty shop-fronts in the 1970s and have since influenced public nursery school education (Birkhölzer and Lorenz, 1998b); the Swedish day-care cooperatives, also dating back to the 1970s and now employing 5,600 people in 1,800 centres (Stryjan and Wijkström, 1998); some of the new Finnish cooperatives in social and health care, which are organized as users' cooperatives (Pättiniemi, 1998); or certain health cooperatives in Canada, Sweden and the United States, where some Health Management Organizations are set up as consumer- or joint producer-and-consumer cooperatives (Comeau and Girard, 1996).

Other social enterprises are public interest organizations set up by people who were not users of the services, whether to provide collective goods or because the potential user-members of a mutual interest organization needed help in setting it up (Gui, 1991) – for example, it may be difficult for poor people to set up self-help health clinics or mutual credit associations without outside assistance. Among these social enterprises, some have been experimenting with ways of formally involving their clients in the running of the enterprise, by borrowing governance structures and principles from the cooperative movement, such as the principle "one member, one vote" (irrespective of individual capital investment).[37] In some countries, such as Italy (in 1991), Belgium (in 1995) and Portugal (in 1996), these experiments have led to legislative provision enabling the creation of a separate form of company for social enterprises or social cooperatives explicitly allowing for (though not requiring) client or user membership or representation in the management structures running the enterprise.[38]

Perhaps the most interesting form of participatory, public interest social enterprise is the social cooperative of Italy. This movement started in the 1980s and by 1996 had grown to number about 3,000 cooperatives, employing around 75,000 people (Borzaga, 1997). About 30 per cent of these cooperatives were "work integration enterprises". The total number of "disadvantaged" workers employed was at least 5,500, of whom a large majority were cooperative members – therefore shareholders holding rights and participating as client-members in the running of the enterprise (Borzaga, 1997; Zandonai, 1997a, 1997b). The other Italian social cooperatives offer social and personal services to the disabled, the elderly, school- and pre-school children, etc. Most of them are worker cooperatives managed by the majority of their employees who are also members (Zandonai, 1997b) but nearly 100 of them also have clients among their members (Borzaga, 1997). Similar experiments exist in other countries, though on a lesser scale. In Portugal, for example, in the 1970s "social solidarity" cooperatives for the education and rehabilitation of disabled children (CERCIs) began to be formed by teachers, parents and local authorities to provide specialized care for mentally disabled children. CERCIs employed 17,000 people in 1994 (Perista et al., 1998). Similarly, parent-teacher cooperatives, where parents are represented on the governing board of the cooperative, have been created in Spain for the education of disabled children (Vidal, 1998). A number of the Japanese health cooperatives (numbering about 300 in total in 1995), which are primarily producer cooperatives, involve consumers of health care through local client groups (Comeau and Girard, 1996). Some of the Greek "urban cooperatives for special purposes", which provide care and other services to the mentally ill and former prisoners and drug abusers, also involve their clients in the running of the services (Ziomas, Ketsetzopoulou and Bouzas, 1998). As in Italy, enterprises created to help certain groups of the unemployed improve their prospects on the labour market often have clients participating in the management of the enterprise as members in Belgium (Defourny, Favreau and Laville, 1998), and in Finland and Spain, where the unemployed can become members of labour cooperatives that then hire out their labour to enterprises (Pättiniemi, 1998; Vidal, 1998).

Analogous experiments exist in the area of public good provision; examples are the Finnish village societies (Pättiniemi, 1998) and some of the Community Development Corporations in the United States and Canada, which involve trade unions, employers, citizens and associations as well as government in mobilizing local resources for local economic development.[39]

An inspiration for the public sector?

Governance structures that involve users and clients alongside providers in the management of social and collective services give public interest non-profit organizations the type of comparative efficiency advantage identified in the economic literature for the case of consumer-led non-profit service provision. The examples cited above concern primarily the voluntary sector. However, the cases of Community Development Corporations combining public and private participants, and the fact that certain services are offered by both the voluntary sector and government, suggest that participatory governance structures involving clients could in principle be extended to the public sector. Where such governance structures strengthen the comparative efficiency advantages of the voluntary sector, they also – by implication – correct the types of government failure the voluntary sector is thought to remedy, as service characteristics come closer to clients' needs, incentives are provided to increase quality, etc. Thus, social policy could become more efficient and democratic if the public sector were to borrow innovations introduced in the voluntary sector, as so often in the past. In those areas where voluntary sector failures can be a problem, public sector supply could correct those failures, while client involvement of the type promoted in democratic social enterprises might correct common government failures.

It should be noted again that client participation in governance, though it tends to be voluntary, is a type of involvement in service provision that differs significantly from volunteer work performed as part of the service itself – the solution proposed in one of the scenarios described above. Volunteer work has been promoted as a way of countering the passive client reflexes supposedly encouraged by public welfare systems and as a way for social service clients to appropriate the services concerned and to gain a sense of responsibility for their lives. This does not require participation in the actual delivery of the services, which many people may not be able or willing to do. Proposing that clients should perform unpaid "volunteer" work in certain social services implies imposing this option on them because they are poor or vulnerable, since the wealthy may not need the service or may find ways of opting out by paying for private supply. It comes very close to suggesting that the poor should "deserve" or "earn" social services. In contrast, participation in governance is a form of "citizen participation" (ACOSS, 1997). It amounts to a right to participate in decisions, rather than an implicit duty to work for free. Perhaps even more than volunteer work in service delivery, citizen participation in the management of social services implies assuming responsibility for the services, and allows greater input into the design of services.[40]

CONCLUSION

In industrialized countries, the voluntary sector represents a larger portion of the economy than is often thought. Its role is particularly important in social, health and cultural services, and in education. However, suggestions that it could be turned into a major source of employment in community and personal services or could replace government in social service provision are misguided, if well-meaning, attempts to promote the sector.

The scale of the expansion needed to make even a small dent in unemployment implies not only that the proposal is very unrealistic, but also that non-profit organizations could lose some of the distinctive characteristics that make them attractive – such as their non-bureaucratic ways, flexibility, delivery of personalized services – and autonomy. Any substantial expansion could not be supported by the traditional resources of the voluntary sector, and would have to rely in large part on government subsidies. Moreover, it could mean that resources would be drawn away from other parts of the voluntary sector. At the same time, widespread reliance on non-profit organizations and volunteer work to supply social services would raise important issues of equity and efficiency in the pursuit of social policy goals in those areas where "voluntary sector failures" are serious.

Public funding should instead be directed at the organizations that are most efficient at meeting public policy goals, whether in the public, for-profit or voluntary sector. The voluntary sector should thus be supported where it offers distinct efficiency advantages, as for example in the provision of services characterized by information asymmetries, or when voluntary provision meets needs that are not easily expressed on markets or through conventional political processes. The sector's efficiency advantage has been strengthened by recent innovations in governance. Organizations set up as social cooperatives have been promoting client involvement in running personal and community services in a number of countries. These forms of governance solve potential voluntary sector failures, but can also be applied to the public sector in order to counter problems arising in public social services, such as gaps between client needs and service objectives. The voluntary sector could thus become once again a source of inspiration for the public sector and contribute to making social policy more efficient and democratic, as it did in the past. But to think of the voluntary sector as the panacea for problems in employment and social policy would be seriously wrong, both for the voluntary sector itself and for social policy.

Notes

[1] The paper discusses the role of the voluntary sector in industrialized countries. The issues are not the same in transition and less developed countries, because of differences in their political heritage and in the extent of public welfare protection.

[2] Both versions of the argument usually start from the presumption that industrialized economies are reaching the "end of work" and require a general reduction in working time in order to share work around. Both propositions are disputable, but neither is necessary to the argument discussed here, and they will not be examined in this article. For a critique of the "end of work" hypothesis and an assessment of the job creation potential of reductions in working time, see ILO (1996), OECD (1998), and Fitoussi (1998).

[3] This categorization is based on the ownership and governance of organizations (who owns the organizations, what objectives are pursued, who has residual rights) and is more precise than the distinction often proposed between "state", "market" and third sector, because state enterprises as well as non-profit organizations can operate on markets. The term "capitalist" relates to ownership and governance in this way and implies no particular ideological position. Other ways of categorizing economic systems may be based, for example, on forms of coordination – depending on whether resources are allocated by markets or by administrative mechanisms (as with planning).

[4] See also Mertens's elaboration of Gui's classification (Mertens, 1998).

[5] American usage often refers to the "third sector" as comprising only non-profit organizations. The third sector as a whole is also often called "social economy", although the phrase may be used in a slightly more restrictive fashion, for example meaning only democratic, or socially oriented, third-sector organizations (Rock and Klinedinst, 1992). Non-governmental organizations (NGOs) are non-profit organizations operating at the international level (as opposed to governmental organizations, like UN agencies or the IMF).

[6] The only internationally comparable estimates available on voluntary sector employment, funding and economic activity are the JH-CNP data. Apart from information deriving from this project, the figures cited below cover the bulk of the sector but do not always refer to exactly the same definition, so should be regarded as indicating orders of magnitude.

[7] These estimates concern full-time equivalent employment in the voluntary sector as defined in the previous section, excluding the special cases of churches (but not their associated charities) and political parties and trade unions. See Salamon, Anheier and Sokolowski (1995) for methodological notes.

[8] Proportions in 1995 except for Italy and Sweden (1990); see table 2.

[9] In the United States, employment in the voluntary sector increased by an average 3.4 per cent annually in 1980-90 (Salamon, Anheier and Sokolowski, 1995, table 10.7) as against 1.8 per cent for total employment and 3.1 per cent for employment in private sector services (United States Bureau of the Census, 1993). Another source indicates that employment in United States charities increased by an average 3.3 per cent annually in 1977-94 (Hodgkinson et al., 1996a) with a corresponding rate of 1.7 per cent for employment as a whole and 3.0 per cent for private sector services. In Germany, the voluntary sector increased by 3.1 per cent a year on average in 1980-90 (Salamon, Anheier and Sokolowski, 1995, table 10.7) as against 0.5 per cent for total employment and 3.0 per cent in private services (Statistisches Bundesamt, 1993). Anheier (1991) found a similar pattern over the period 1970-87.

[10] In those two countries employment growth in the voluntary sector was about the same as in private services according to my estimates on the basis of United States Bureau of the Census (1993, 1996), Central Statistical Office (1995) and Office for National Statistics (1998).

[11] Under the French *contrats emploi-solidarité* (CES) system, created in 1989, the Government covers 85-100 per cent of the labour costs of the jobs concerned. A similar rate of subsidy applies in the case of the German *Arbeitsbeschaffungsmaßnahmen* (ABM) system (Defourny, Favreau and Laville, 1998).

[12] Attrition rates have been found to be markedly higher among non-profit establishments than among for-profit businesses in the United States (Chang and Tuckman, 1991), though the evidence is less clear for France (see Archambault, 1997). Government-subsidized jobs in the context of labour market policies may also disappear after that funding runs out.

[13] However, the United Kingdom distribution of resources is affected by the shifting of part of higher education from the State to the non-profit sector in the period under study.

[14] In the United States, public interest charities saw the share of government funding increase faster than that of private sector payments in their resources in 1977-92 (31 per cent to 36 per cent as against 44 per cent to 45 per cent), while the share of private contributions dropped from 12 per cent to 9 per cent (see Hodgkinson et al., 1996a, table 4.2). For Ireland, see Powell and Guerin (1998).

[15] In or around 1990, 57 per cent of private giving came from individuals in the United Kingdom, 54 per cent in France, 69 per cent in Germany and 80 per cent in the United States (computed from Salamon, Anheier and Sokolowski, 1995, tables 2.2, 3.2, 8.2 and 9.2). For United States public interest charities, Hodgkinson et al. (1996a) give the share of individual donations and private bequests as 87 per cent of income from private giving in 1996; the share of businesses has not increased overall since the 1960s and declined again recently after a peak in the mid-1980s (ibid.). However, for Japan, Yamauchi (1998) cites estimates suggesting that up to two-thirds of donations revenue could come from corporate giving in that country.

[16] Available estimates concern the percentage of adults making donations in France (Archambault and Boumendil, 1998) and the percentage of households contributing to charity in the United Kingdom (Pharoah and Smerdon, 1998, figure 1.2) and in the United States (Hodgkinson et al., 1996b).

[17] Sources: United Kingdom, Banks and Tanner (1997) cited in Pharoah and Smerdon (1998), and Office for National Statistics (1998); France, Archambault and Boumendil (1998) and INSEE (1998).

[18] Sources: France, Archambault and Boumendil (1998), INSEE (1998) and information on household size provided by Sophie Ponthieux; United Kingdom, Family Expenditure Survey data from Office for National Statistics (1998); United States, Hodgkinson et al. (1995 and 1996b), United States Bureau of the Census (1997 and 1998), and Weisbrod (2000b).

[19] Some of the decline in household contributions to non-profit organizations that was observed in certain countries in the 1990s may be due to recessionary conditions and may be reversed as incomes grow – United States evidence shows donations are related to individuals' economic situation and perceived prospects (Hodgkinson et al., 1996b). However, increases in income seem to be associated with less than proportional increases in donations, at least in the United States, the United Kingdom and Japan (Hodgkinson et al., 1996b, Pharoah and Smerdon, 1998 and Yamauchi, 1998).

[20] It should be noted that in certain countries figures on volunteering may include some volunteer work done in public sector institutions and even in private, for-profit enterprises – though the latter is usually so limited as to be negligible for our purposes. Unless otherwise specified, the figures cited here do not include informal volunteer work done for friends and neighbours. For issues of comparability and measurement of volunteering, see Lyons, Wijkstrom and Clary (1998).

[21] The information available for the United States, and especially for the United Kingdom, is not fully comparable with information for the other countries, because instead of hours or assignments it concerns volunteers, who work longer hours on average in some areas than in others. For example, in France 9 per cent of volunteers were active in health services, but provided only 3 per cent of the total hours of volunteer work in 1990, whereas the 5 per cent who volunteered in environmental protection and conservation provided 10 per cent of all the hours (Archambault, 1997). Furthermore, the same volunteer may be active in more than one type of activity (United Kingdom data).

[22] Sources: for the United States, Hodgkinson et al. (1996b); for Japan, Yamauchi (1998); for Australia, Australian Council of Social Service (1997); for France, Archambault and Boumendil (1998); and for the United Kingdom, Davis Smith (1998). The little information available on recent changes in the proportions of women and men volunteering does not suggest convergence of cross-national gender patterns of volunteering.

[23] See Australian Council of Social Service (1997), Davis Smith (1998) and Archambault and Tchernonog (1994), respectively.

[24] See Davis Smith (1998), Hodgkinson et al. (1996b) and Archambault and Tchernonog (1994), respectively.

[25] The estimates that follow represent orders of magnitude only and ignore the possibility that jobs created in the voluntary sector might correspond to job cuts in other parts of the economy (e.g. because of social services privatization) or, conversely, that job creation in the voluntary sector might have spillover effects in other sectors. The estimates were computed on the basis of Salamon and Anheier (1995), JH-CNP (1999) and ILO (2001).

[26] Those countries (see table 1 for a list) had unemployment rates of 7-12 per cent, with the exception of the United States (5.6 per cent), Finland (15.2 per cent) and Spain (22.9 per cent). The two countries with low unemployment were Austria (3.7 per cent) and Japan (3.2 per cent). See ILO (2001).

[27] Although demand subsidies are often mentioned in this context, the forms proposed, such as coupons redeemable with non-profit organizations, amount to supply subsidies to the non-profit sector.

[28] The lack of incentive to minimize costs in public and non-profit organizations could actually be an advantage in situations where public interest objectives are not well defined or performance is hard to monitor, because it implies that there may also be less incentive to cut quality than in for-profit organizations (Ehrmann and Biedermann, 1990).

[29] Certain voluntary sector failures, such as the insufficiency of funding from charitable sources to meet social needs, have actually been instrumental in leading to government involvement in areas of social care previously served by the voluntary sector; government involvement has often occurred at the request of the non-profit organizations themselves (Kendall and Knapp, 1996; Archambault, 1997; Nyssens, 1998).

[30] See Zimmeck (1998), Yamauchi (1998) and Hodgkinson et al. (1996b).

[31] This right preserves the individual's dignity. The argument goes back at least to Beveridge. See, for example, Barr (1992).

[32] Although gift-exchange relationships may further social ties, not all non-market relationships are non-exploitative, contrary to what is sometimes implied in discussions of community services and solidarity volunteer work. When the power of the parties to the relationship is unequal (e.g. because of differences in class or sex) it may often be the case that a market transaction will actually be less exploitative. Related issues are evoked in Powell and Guerin (1998). See also Maitland (1998) for a provocative discussion of this question from a conservative point of view, and Rodgers (1998) for a review of the issues regarding paid and unpaid work and the sexual division of labour.

[33] See, for example, Nyssens (1998) and Edwards and Hulme (1996). A recent study of a representative sample of non-profit organizations in Ireland found that 54 per cent of the organizations consulted thought there should be more direct state provision of their service (Powell and Guerin, 1998).

[34] On the issue of trust in government and in other institutions, see Knack and Keefer (1997).

[35] See Defourny (1997) for a more precise definition.

[36] For a detailed analysis of those activities and their relation to public labour market policies in several countries, see Defourny, Favreau and Laville (1998).

[37] For the international cooperative principles, see International Co-operative Alliance (2001).

[38] See Borzaga and Santuari (1998).

[39] Favreau (1998); Gunn and Gunn (1991). Several innovative community development experiments are discussed in *Economie et Solidarités*, Vol. 29, No. 2, 1998, and in OECD (1996).

[40] In this respect, it is interesting that in many social enterprises, the extent of volunteer work is highest at the beginning of the life of the enterprise, and tends to be replaced with paid work as the organization grows, while participation in governing boards tends to remain voluntary.

References

Anheier, Helmut K. 1991. "Employment and earnings in the West German nonprofit sector. Structure and trends, 1970-1987", in *Annals of Public and Cooperative Economy* (Louvain-la-Neuve), Vol. 62, No. 4 (Oct.-Dec.), pp. 673-694.

Archambault, Edith. 1997. *The nonprofit sector in France*. Manchester and New York, Manchester University Press.

—; Boumendil, Judith. 1998. "Dons et bénévolat en France", in *Revue des Etudes Coopératives, Mutualistes et Associatives* (Nanterre), No. 267, pp. 17-29.

—; Tchernonog, Viviane. 1994. "Le poids économique du secteur associatif", in *Revue des Etudes Coopératives, Mutualistes et Associatives* (Nanterre), Nos. 253-54, 3rd and 4th quarters, pp. 118-146.

ACOSS (Australian Council of Social Service). 1997. *Volunteering in Australia*. ACOSS Paper No. 74.

Banks, J.; Tanner, S. 1997. *The state of donation: Household gifts to charity 1974-1996*. London, Institute of Fiscal Studies.

Barr, Nicholas. 1992. "Economic theory and the welfare state: A survey and reinterpretation", in *Journal of Economic Literature* (Nashville, TN), No. 30 (June), pp. 741-803.

Bauer, Rudolph. 1998. *Intermediarity: A theoretical paradigm for third sector research*. Paper presented at the Third Conference of the International Society for Third Sector Research (ISTR), Geneva, 8-11 July 1998.

Ben-Ner, Avner. 1986. "Nonprofit organizations: Why do they exist in market economies?", in Rose-Ackerman, pp. 94-113.

—; Van Hoomissen, Theresa. 1991. "Nonprofit organizations in the mixed economy: A demand and supply analysis", in *Annals of Public and Cooperative Economy* (Louvain-la-Neuve), Vol. 62, No. 4 (Oct.-Dec.), pp. 519-550.

Birkhölzer, Karl; Lorenz, Günther. 1998a. "Allemagne. Les sociétés d'emploi et de qualification en appui à la réunification", in Defourny, Favreau and Laville, pp. 127-158.

—. 1998b. "Germany", in Borzaga and Santuari, pp. 255-279.

Borzaga, Carlo (ed.). 2000. *Capitale umano e qualità del lavoro nei servici sociali. Un'analisi comparata tra modelli di gestione*. Rome, Fondazione Italiana per il Volontariato.

—.1997. "L'évolution récente de la coopération sociale en Italie", in *Revue des Etudes Coopératives, Mutualistes et Associatives* (Nanterre), No. 266, pp. 55-63.

—; Maiello, Marco. 1998. "The development of social enterprises", in Borzaga and Santuari, pp. 73-92.

—; Santuari, Alceste (eds.). 1998. *Social enterprises and new employment in Europe*. Trent, Autonomous Region of Trentino-South Tyrol, European Commission and Consorzio Nazionale della Cooperazione Soziale.

Central Statistical Office. 1995. *Annual Abstract of Statistics*. London, Her Majesty's Stationery Office.

Centro Studi CGM (Consorzio Gino Matarelli). 1997. *Imprenditori sociali. Secondo rapporto sulla cooperazione sociale in Italia*. Turin, Edizioni Fondazione Giovanni Agnelli.

Chang, Cyril F.; Tuckman, Howard P. 1991. "Financial vulnerability and attrition as measures of nonprofit performance", in *Annals of Public and Cooperative Economy* (Louvain-la-Neuve), Vol. 62, No. 4 (Oct.-Dec.), pp. 655-672.

Comeau, Yvan; Girard, Jean-Pierre. 1996. "Les coopératives de santé: Une modalité d'offre de services médicaux", in *Revue des Etudes Coopératives, Mutualistes et Associatives* (Nanterre), No. 261(59), pp. 48-57.

Davis Smith, Justin. 1998. *The 1997 National Survey of Volunteering*. London, National Centre for Volunteering.

Defourny, Jacques (ed.). 1997. *EMES: The emergence of social enterprises. New answers to social exclusion in Europe*. Interim Report of the EMES network to the European Commission. Brussels, Jan.

—; Favreau, Louis; Laville, Jean-Louis (eds.). 1998. *Insertion et nouvelle économie sociale: Un bilan international*. Paris, Desclée de Brouwer.

—; Monzon Campos, José L. (eds.). 1992. *The third sector: Cooperative, mutual and nonprofit organizations*. Brussels, De Boeck Wesmael.

Dekker, Paul; van den Broek, Andries. 1998. "Civil society in comparative perspective: Involvement in voluntary associations in North America and Western Europe", in *Voluntas* (New York, NY), Vol. 9, No. 1, pp. 11-38.

Demoustier, Danièle. 1998. "France: Des structures diversifiées à la croisée des chemins", in Defourny, Favreau and Laville, pp. 41-71.

Economie et Solidarités (Sainte-Foy, Quebec). 1998. Special issue on "Le développement social urbain: Revitalisation des quartiers au Nord et au Sud", Vol. 29, No. 2.

Edwards, Michael. 1998. "Are NGOs overrated? Why and how to say 'no'", in *Current Issues in Comparative Education* (http://www.tc.columbia.edu/cice/), Vol. 1, No. 1, 15 Nov.

—; Hulme, David. 1996. "Too close for comfort? The impact of official aid on nongovernmental organizations", in *World Development* (Kidlington), Vol. 24, pp. 961-973 (reproduced in *Current Issues in Comparative Education* (http://www.tc.columbia.edu/cice/), Vol. 1, No.1, 15 Nov.).

Ehrmann, Thomas; Biedermann, Rainer. 1990. "The interest in prima facie inefficient institutions: Housing, supply-subsidies and the role of nonprofit firms", in *Kyklos* (Basel), Vol. 43, Fasc. 2, pp. 277-284.

Favreau, Louis. 1998. "Du local au global: Enjeux et défis des nouvelles initiatives de développement local et d'économie sociale", in *Economie et Solidarités* (Sainte-Foy, Quebec), Vol. 29, No. 2, pp. 1-13.

Fitoussi, Jean-Paul. 1998. "Utopie pour l'emploi (suite)", in *Observations et Diagnostics Economiques* (Paris), No. 64, pp. 9-15.

Forsé, Michel. 1984. "Les créations d'associations: un indicateur de changement social", in *Observations et Diagnostics Economiques* (Paris), No. 6 (Jan.), pp. 125-145.

Gui, Benedetto. 1991. "The economic rationale for the 'Third Sector'. Nonprofit and other noncapitalist organizations", in *Annals of Public and Cooperative Economy* (Louvain-la-Neuve), Vol. 62, No. 4 (Oct.-Dec.), pp. 551-572.

Gunn, Christopher; Gunn, Hazel Dayton. 1991. *Reclaiming capital. Democratic initiatives and community development*. Ithaca, NY, Cornell University Press.

Handy, Femida; Katz, Eliakim. 1998. "The wage differential between nonprofit institutions and corporations: Getting more by paying less?", in *Journal of Comparative Economics* (San Diego, CA), 26, pp. 246-261.

Hansmann, Henry. 1980. "The role of nonprofit enterprise", in *Yale Law Journal* (New Haven, CT), 89 (5), pp. 835-901.

Hodgkinson, Virginia; Weitzman, Murray S. (with Abrahams, John A.; Crutchfield, Eric A.; and Stevenson, David R.). 1996a. *Nonprofit almanac. Dimensions of the independent sector. 1996-1997*. Washington, DC/San Francisco, CA, Independent Sector and Jossey Bass.

—; — (with Crutchfield, Eric A.; Heffron, Aaron J.; and Kirsch, Arthur D.). 1996b. *Giving and volunteering in the United States*. Washington, DC, Independent Sector.

—; —; Noga, Stephen M.; Gorski, Heather A. Undated (1994). *National summary: Not-for-profit employment from the 1990 Census of Population and Housing*. Washington, DC, Independent Sector.

—; Gorski, Heather A.; Noga, Stephen M.; Knauft, E.B. 1995. *Giving and volunteering in the United States, 1994*. Volume II. *Trends and volunteering by type of charity*. Washington, DC, Independent Sector.

INSEE (Institut National de la Statistique et des Etudes Economiques). 1993, 1997 and 1998 editions. *Annuaire statistique de la France*. Paris, La Documentation française.

International Co-operative Alliance. 2001. *Statement on the co-operative identity*. http://www.coop.org/ica/info/enprinciples.html (visited 29.08.01).

ILO. *Laborsta*. 2001. Labour statistics data base. http://laborsta.ilo.org.

—.1996. *World Employment 1996/97. National policies in a global context*. Geneva.

James, Estelle. 2000. "Commercialism among nonprofits: Objectives, opportunities and constraints", in Weisbrod, 2000a, pp. 271-285.

—.1987. "The nonprofit sector in comparative perspective", in Powell, pp. 397-415.

JH-CNP (Comparative Nonprofit Project, Johns Hopkins University). 1999. "Net changes in nonprofit sector employment, by country and field of activity, 1990-1995". Data communicated privately to the author.

Kaminski, Philippe. 1998. "Economie sociale et emploi: le renouveau du dispositif statistique français", in *Revue des Etudes Coopératives, Mutualistes et Associatives* (Nanterre), No. 269, 3rd quarter, pp. 16-31.

Kendall, Jeremy; Knapp, Martin. 1996. *The voluntary sector in the UK*. Manchester/New York, NY, Manchester University Press.

Knack, Stephen; Keefer, Philip. 1997. "Does social capital have an economic payoff? A cross-country investigation", in *Quarterly Journal of Economics* (Cambridge, MA), Vol. 112, No. 4 (Nov.), pp. 1250-1288.

Lyons, Mark; Wijkstrom, Philip; Clary, Gil. 1998. "Comparative studies of volunteering: What is being studied?", in *Voluntary Action* (London), Vol. 1, No. 1, Winter, pp. 45-54.

Maitland, Ian. 1998. "Community lost?", in *Business Ethics Quarterly* (Bowling Green, OH), Vol. 8, No. 4, pp. 655-670.

Mertens, Sybille. 1998. *Nonprofit organizations and social economy: Variations on a same theme.* Paper presented at the Third Conference of the International Society for Third Sector Research (ISTR), Geneva, 8-11 July 1998.

Nyssens, Marthe. 1998. *The development of proximity services: Towards a plural economy? — The case of Belgium.* Mimeo. Louvain, Catholic University of Louvain.

OECD. 1998. "Working hours: Latest trends and policy initiatives", ch. 5 in *Employment Outlook.* Paris, June, pp. 153-188.

—.1997. *Labour Force Statistics.* Paris.

—.1996. *Reconciling economy and society. Towards a plural economy.* Paris.

Office for National Statistics. 1998. *Annual Abstract of Statistics*, No. 134. London, Her Majesty's Stationery Office.

Pättiniemi, Pekka. 1998. "Finland" in Borzaga and Santuari, pp. 195-209.

Perista, Heloísa; Lopez, Margarida Chaga; Espanha, Rita; Rocha, Eugénia. 1998. "Portugal", in Borzaga and Santuari, pp. 397-417.

Pharoah, Cathy; Smerdon, Matthew (eds.). 1998. *Dimensions of the voluntary sector: Key facts, figures, analysis and trends.* West Malling (Kent, UK), Charities Aid Foundation.

Posner, Barry Z.; Schmidt, Warren H. 1996. "The values of business and federal government executives: More different than alike", in *Public Personnel Management* (Alexandria, VA), Vol. 25, No. 3 (Fall), pp. 277-289.

Powell, Fred; Guerin, Donal. 1998. *The Irish third sector and collaboration with the State: A case study on the redefinition of civic virtue.* Paper presented at the Third Conference of the International Society for Third Sector Research (ISTR), Geneva, 8-11 July 1998.

Powell, Walter W. (ed.). 1987. *The nonprofit sector: A research handbook.* New Haven, CT, Yale University Press.

Preston, Anne E. 1989. "The nonprofit worker in a for-profit world", in *Journal of Labor Economics* (Chicago, IL), Vol. 7, No. 4, pp. 438-463.

Rock, Charles; Klinedinst, Mark. 1992. "In search of the 'social economy' in the United States: A proposal", in Defourny and Monzon Campos, pp. 319-379.

Rodgers, Janine. 1998. *The linkage between unpaid and paid work.* Gender in the World of Work Series, Working Paper No. 1. Geneva, ILO.

Rose-Ackerman, Susan. 1996. "Altruism, non-profits and economic theory", in *Journal of Economic Literature* (Nashville, TN), 34 (2), pp. 701-728.

—.1990. "Competition between non-profits and for-profits: Entry and growth", in *Voluntas* (Manchester), Vol. 1, No. 1, pp. 13-25.

— (ed.). 1986. *The economics of nonprofit institutions: Studies in structure and policy.* Oxford/New York, NY, Oxford University Press.

Salamon, Lester M. 1987. "Of market failure, government failure and third-party government: Toward a theory of government-nonprofit relations in the modern welfare state", in *Journal of Voluntary Action Research* (London), Vol. 16, Nos. 1-2, pp. 29-49.

—; Anheier, Helmut K. 1998. "Social origins of civil society: Exploring the nonprofit sector cross-nationally", in *Voluntas* (New York, NY), Vol. 9, No. 3, pp. 213-248.

—; —.1997. *Defining the nonprofit sector. A cross-national analysis.* Manchester/New York, NY, Manchester University Press.

—; —.1996. *The emerging nonprofit sector: An overview.* Manchester/New York, NY, Manchester University Press.

—; —; and Associates. 1998. *The emerging sector revisited: A summary.* Baltimore, MD, Center for Civil Society Studies, Johns Hopkins University.

—; —; Sokolowski, Wojciech. 1995. *The emerging sector: A statistical supplement.* Baltimore, MD, John Hopkins University.

Sloan, Frank A.; Picone, Gabriel A.; Taylor, Donald H., Jr.; Chou, Shih-Yi. 1998. *Hospital ownership and cost and quality of care: Is there a dime's worth of difference?* NBER Working Paper No. 6706. Washington, DC, National Bureau for Economic Research.

Statistisches Bundesamt. 1993 and 1998 editions. *Statistisches Jahrbuch.* Stuttgart, Metzler Poschel.

Steinberg, Richard; Young, Dennis R. 1998. "A comment on Salamon and Anheier's 'Social origins of civic society'", in *Voluntas* (New York, NY), Vol. 9, No. 3, pp. 249-260.

Stromquist, Nelly P. 1998. "NGOs in a new paradigm of civil society", in *Current Issues in Comparative Education* (http://www.tc.colombia.edu/cice/), Vol. 1, No. 1, 15 Nov.

Stryjan, Yohanan; Wijkström, Filip. 1998. "Sweden", in Borzaga and Santuari, pp. 461-489.

United States Bureau of the Census. 1998. *Measuring 50 years of economic change using the March Current Population Survey.* Current Population Reports, P60-203. Washington, DC, United States Government Printing Office.

—.1997. *Money income in the United States: 1996 (with separate data on valuation of noncash benefits).* Current Population Reports, P60-197. Washington, DC, United States Government Printing Office.

—.1993 and 1996 editions. *Statistical Abstract of the United States.* Washington, DC, United States Government Printing Office.

Vidal, Isabel. 1998. "Spain", in Borzaga and Santuari, pp. 421-457.

Weisbrod, Burton A. (ed.). 2000a. *To profit or not to profit. The commercial transformation of the nonprofit sector.* Cambridge, Cambridge University Press.

—.2000b. "The nonprofit mission and its financing: Growing links between nonprofits and the rest of the economy", in Weisbrod, 2000a, pp. 1-22.

—.1988. *The nonprofit economy.* Cambridge, MA, Harvard University Press.

— (ed.). 1977a. *The voluntary nonprofit sector.* Lexington, MA, D.C. Heath.

—.1977b. "Toward a theory of the voluntary nonprofit sector in a three-sector economy", in Weisbrod, 1977a, pp. 51-76.

Willard, Jean-Charles. 1995. "L'économie sociale face à l'Etat et au marché: Interrogations sur quelques mots-clés", in *Revue des Etudes Coopératives, Mutualistes et Associatives* (Nanterre), No. 257, pp. 43-58.

Yamauchi, Naoto. 1998. *Why do nonprofit organizations exist in market economies?* SCOPE Working Paper No. 8. Kanagawa, Graduate University for Advanced Studies. Mar.

Zandonai, Flaviano. 1997a. "Le dimensioni generali del fenomeno", in Centro Studi CGM, pp. 33-49.

—.1997b. "Le risorse umane", in Centro Studi CGM, pp. 115-135.

Zimmeck, Meta. 1998. *To boldly go: The voluntary sector and voluntary action in the new world of work*. London, Royal Society for the Encouragement of Arts, Manufactures and Commerce (RSA).

Ziomas, Dimitris; Ketsetzopoulou, Maria; Bouzas, Nikos. 1998. "Greece", in Borzaga and Santuari, pp. 283-310.

PART II

QUALITY OF WORK, QUALITY OF LIFE

SMALL AND MEDIUM-SIZED ENTERPRISES AND LABOUR LAW

11

Geraldo von POTOBSKY *

INTRODUCTION

For as long as labour law has existed governments have doubted whether it is feasible to apply general labour standards to small and medium-sized enterprises (SMEs). Where these have been accorded special treatment it has generally been for economic and social reasons, to help artisans or independent workers from the middle classes by taking account of such varied considerations as the relationship between the head of an enterprise and his subordinates or co-workers, the overall policy on promoting SMEs or the special case of small family businesses. And the commonest way of adapting labour legislation to suit the needs of such enterprises is simply to exempt them, according to their size or importance, from some or all its provisions.

This divergence from uniform labour law to take account of the specific characteristics of SMEs has long been the subject of debate and conflicting opinion between employers and trade unions. Strong views on the matter have also been expressed by specialists; indeed, differentiation has been challenged in the courts several times as being unconstitutional, on the grounds that it violates the principle of equality. Certainly the trade unions have never – willingly – accepted it. To the employers, on the other hand – and especially to those directly concerned – it seems wholly justified and they have said as much on a number of occasions.

Bearing in mind the remarkable growth of the small enterprise sector, and its importance in terms of flexibility and job creation, this article sets out to make a comparative study of the labour laws applicable to it.[1] First, however, several points bearing on the current situation need clarification. What is meant by small and medium-sized enterprises? Are they homogeneous? How can the current surge in their numbers be explained? How do they fit

Originally published in *International Labour Review*, Vol. 131 (1992), No. 6.

* Former Chief of the Application of Standards Branch and the Freedom of Association Branch of the ILO. Labour consultant.

into the informal sector? Other questions also have to be asked before we turn to specific aspects of labour law. How effective have ILO standards been in this field? What variations can be found within national legislations? Are there any particular trends, whether thematic or temporal, in the differentiation of standards? What is the position regarding family enterprises? And finally, what approach should be adopted in the future?

THE CONCEPT OF SMEs

One of the problems regarding SMEs is to establish objective and uniform criteria by which to define them. A study carried out by the ILO[2] identified more than 50 definitions in 75 different countries, with considerable ambiguity in the terminology used. The enormous variety of criteria applied includes size of workforce or capital, form of management or ownership, production techniques, volume of sales, client numbers, levels of energy consumption, etc. In its report the ILO adopted its own definition, generally taking the expression "small and medium-sized enterprises" in its widest sense, ranging from modern enterprises with up to 50 employees to businesses employing three or four family members, but also including domestic industries, cooperatives, individual enterprises, micro-enterprises, self-employed workers in the informal sector, etc. According to the criterion adopted by the European Community, SMEs may have up to a total of 100 employees. This article takes into account the criteria of both these organizations in outlining the provisions relating to SMEs.

The variety of definitions, and the criteria behind them, also arise from the difference between the sectors concerned – commercial, financial, labour, etc. – each with its own interests and objectives. In an attempt to simplify the process of definition some writers have pointed out that the criteria may be quantitative or qualitative: either they depend on such considerations as the sales figures, the social assets, the equipment (in particular the installed industrial capacity), the number of employees and the value of production or, under the qualitative approach, they draw on vast amounts of data to show how SMEs are run – how decisions are reached, how authority is delegated, etc. – by contrast with larger enterprises. But there are major qualitative differences even between small enterprises. Thus, for example, on the basis of criteria which might be described as economic and technical, micro-enterprises alone can be defined as precarious units geared to survival needs, as small production units, more reliably funded and looking more to the formal market, or as micro-projects with high technical capacity.

Whatever criteria are used, an enterprise can be classified in different ways. Thus, for example, in terms of employee numbers it might be small or medium-sized, but in terms of capital, technology and production value it could be closer to a large enterprise. Such divergences are particularly significant when it comes to measures for the protection or promotion of SMEs, such as exemption from general labour legislation or some other special treatment, which could be justified in some cases and not in others.

The criterion generally applied in labour legislation is quantitative, relating to the number of persons employed. However, sometimes – in some Latin American countries, for example – the capital of an enterprise, its payment capacity or, in maritime labour law, the tonnage of vessels may be taken into account. The family enterprise, too, may be treated as a special case.

Two observations need to be made here. First, we are using the term enterprise in its broadest sense, since legislation may refer to an enterprise, an establishment, a work centre or even a group of enterprises. The specific provisions described below will give some examples of these variations, which gain added significance when staff numbers are calculated, since these form the minimum basis for the application of general legislation.

Equally relevant is the type of employment contract held by the various categories of employee. If apprentices or temporary workers, for example, are excluded from the calculation of staff numbers, or are included on a different basis (e.g. proportionally, in the case of part-time employment), enterprises which have in fact a larger staff than the legal minimum can be exempt from general legislation. In other words, more enterprises receive special treatment – and more workers are deprived of the general protective standards.

THE CURRENT INCREASE IN SMEs

In the 1980s the value of small and medium-sized enterprises once again began to be appreciated in both advanced and developing countries, although the trend had started in the mid-1970s, when the proportion of the population employed in SMEs began to increase in the most developed countries at the expense of employment in large enterprises: a reversal of the earlier trend towards concentration in large enterprises, when small enterprises were looked upon as relics of an outdated economy.[3]

Reflecting the new trend, in 1984 the International Labour Conference adopted the Employment Policy (Supplementary Provisions) Recommendation (No. 169), which contains a section dealing with small enterprises, emphasizing their importance as a source of employment and the need, amongst other things, to improve their conditions of employment. For its part the Commission of the European Communities stressed, in a communication to the European Parliament, that SMEs were an essential component of Europe's industrial and commercial structure, a source of dynamism and vitality in the economy and in job creation and a driving force for economic recovery, restructuring, technological development and improvements in living conditions. As a result, an energetic campaign to promote SMEs was launched both at EC level and within the various countries. Furthermore, the Single European Act of 1986, which amended the Treaty of Rome, included a clause under which any directive adopted under the qualified majority rule on the subject of workers' health and safety should avoid "imposing administrative, financial and legal constraints in a way which would hold back the creation and development of small and medium-sized undertakings" (article 118A). When article 118 was amended in 1991 (under the agreement on social policy annexed to the Maastricht Treaty) extending the list of labour matters to which the majority rule could be applied, this provision for the promotion of SMEs was retained.

Among the factors responsible for the renewed interest in SMEs were: (1) the economic recession, with the resulting unemployment in large production units, especially in industry, and the need for the reconversion of traditional industries, which led workers to seek employment in smaller enterprises or to set up small enterprises of their own; (2) the growth of the service sector, operating in smaller units; (3) the opportunity to avoid labour and taxation laws, as well as less stringent standards, thus bypassing the need for trade unions or other forms of worker representation in the enterprise. Other important factors were SMEs' greater production flexibility and their capacity to adapt to a constantly changing market.

It should be noted, however, that this did not imply any downgrading of large enterprises. Indeed, their importance did not only not decline but actually increased: they merged into even larger companies, in the process restructuring their organization and production, with internal subdivisions into smaller units and extensive subcontracting. In other words, they quickly recognized the need for greater flexibility in adapting to new markets and forms of production through a substantial decentralization of operations.

What SMEs can provide, however, is "flexible specialization", contrasting with the large-scale standardized production of Fordism.[4] The paradigm of small enterprises of this kind is to be found in the so-called industrial districts, especially in central-northern and north-eastern Italy (the "Third Italy"), but also in Germany, Canada, Denmark, Spain and a few other countries, including developing ones. Industrial districts are made up of small production centres or units which, either by specializing or by subcontracting, divide up the work for the manufacture of specific products (textiles, tiles, footwear, foodstuffs, etc.) for a given sector of industry. In other words, production and services are targeted at the manufacture of a specific range of products; they are not regional centres of industrial development with an indiscriminate production policy. The enterprises compete in terms of quality and innovation, but they also cooperate with one another by participating in the collection and dissemination of information on new technology and products, the provision of services, etc.[5]

It is worth mentioning here, by contrast, a characteristic feature of the micro-enterprise in developing countries. This is the so-called informal sector, which is defined in the 1991 Report of the Director-General of the ILO as being very small-scale units producing and distributing goods and services in urban areas of developing countries. According to the Report, these units generally consist of independent, self-employed producers, who sometimes employ family labour or a few hired workers or apprentices. They operate with little or no capital and use a low level of technology and skills; productivity is low, incomes are both low and irregular and employment is unstable.[6] Even though the underground economy of many developed countries may appear to have features in common with the informal sector in the developing countries, the context is substantially different, above all because there is far less unemployment, there is greater access to public services (particularly health and education) and the social security network protects the most vulnerable groups. "Where an underground economy exists, it is generally in order to evade taxes, control and regulation – sometimes perhaps because control and regulation is too bureaucratic and inefficient; but rarely is it a phenomenon associated with survival strategies of the poor as in developing countries."[7] The informal sector can hardly be said to have expanded in the developing countries, except, unfortunately, in the case of survival enterprises. In theory, labour legislation also applies to this sector.

ILO STANDARDS

ILO Conventions and Recommendations generally contain no exceptions or special standards for small and medium-sized enterprises. The situation is different in the case of maritime Conventions, many of which exclude or permit the exclusion of small vessels, those engaged in the coasting trade or in estuary navigation and those of low tonnage (or more commonly of a tonnage below a prescribed amount).[8] A comparatively large number of Conventions also provide for the exclusion of family enterprises. The following paragraphs review the exceptions affecting SMEs (and small enterprises in particular); the special situation of family enterprises will be examined later.

Very few exceptions are to be found in any of the Conventions adopted during the early years of the ILO and up to just after the Second World War. Only subsequently did some Conventions or Recommendations begin to provide for any systematic sort of exclusion for SMEs.

The first Convention which should be mentioned in this regard is the basic social security instrument, the Social Security (Minimum Standards) Convention, 1952 (No. 102). This permits all countries whose economy and medical facilities are insufficiently developed to make temporary reductions in the range of persons entitled to benefits under various parts of the Convention. It also specifically permits a country to exclude small enterprises (employing fewer than 20 workers) when calculating contributions and beneficiaries for some benefits.

In the rural sector several Conventions make provision for exceptions for smallholdings. The Maternity Protection Convention (Revised), 1952

(No. 103), where dealing with agricultural enterprises, refers only to plantations and large enterprises; but the later Plantations Convention, 1958 (No. 110), excludes small enterprises producing for local consumption and not regularly employing hired workers, while the Protocol to the instrument, adopted in 1982, further permits the exclusion of enterprises covering less than five hectares and not employing more than ten workers at any time during the course of a year. The important Minimum Age Convention, 1973 (No. 138), following the formula used in Convention No. 110, authorizes the exclusion of small-scale agricultural holdings. Mention should also be made of the Rural Workers' Organizations Convention, 1975 (No. 141), which specifically includes smallholdings among the organizations it covers.

The Occupational Health Services Recommendation, 1959 (No. 112), and the Occupational Safety and Health Recommendation, 1981 (No. 164), explicitly exclude SMEs from their scope, while others do so implicitly by specifying the size of the enterprise or establishment to which they apply.

Similarly, both the Workers' Representatives Convention, 1971 (No. 135), and the Cooperation at the Level of the Undertaking Recommendation, 1952 (No. 94), refer implicitly to SMEs when they stipulate that account must be taken of the needs, size, capabilities or special circumstances of the different enterprises. The Paid Educational Leave Convention, 1974 (No. 140), allows the adoption of special provisions for small enterprises. The Termination of Employment Convention, 1982 (No. 158), allows some categories of workers to be excluded from its provisions in the event of special problems arising from the "size or nature" of the enterprise. Finally, the Employment Promotion and Protection against Unemployment Convention, 1988 (No. 168), allows ratifying States exemption from a number of obligations (unemployment benefit and other benefits), in line with the formula of Convention No. 102, mentioned above, permitting the exclusion of small enterprises.

A classification of these instruments (except those which refer to specific countries) according to their subject shows that they refer to the following institutions or sectors: termination of employment; workers' representatives; occupational health and safety; paid educational leave; social security and employment; and the rural sector.

Where maritime Conventions are concerned, the provision for exclusion applies to vessels of small tonnage in matters relating to minimum standards under the main labour laws regarding seafarers; articles of agreement; medical examination; officers' competency certificates; wages, hours of work and manning; accommodation; vacations; repatriation; sickness and accidents; and social security. Under two recent Conventions, however – the Holidays with Pay Convention (Revised), 1970 (No. 132), and the Repatriation of Seafarers Convention (Revised), 1987 (No. 166) – exclusion is no longer possible.

OVERVIEW OF LEGISLATION

In order to gain a better overall view of the treatment of SMEs under national labour standards, it may be useful to begin with a comparative summary of current labour law – concerning, in particular, termination of employment, new kinds of contract and workers' representation in the enterprise – which shows a marked change in attitudes to SMEs. There will follow a more detailed examination of the standards in force in various countries, to identify trends towards increased differentiation or, on the contrary, moves towards greater standardization. It will be clear from the examples given that situations vary according to the instruments and countries concerned.

As regards termination of employment, very few countries actually exclude small enterprises from legislation on protection against dismissal without providing workers with some kind of guarantee. What happens most frequently is that laws on dismissal are adapted to the needs of SMEs, offering them special provisions regarding compensation or reinstatement in employment.

If SMEs have to pay compensation, they may be granted financial help from public funds, or the compensation may be set at a lower figure. SMEs are also quite frequently exempt from the obligation to reinstate a worker dismissed without just cause. Other, less common, measures are the introduction of a special termination clause, unavailable to other enterprises, and simplified termination procedures.

Special provisions for collective redundancies on economic grounds are relatively widespread. A variety of formulas is used: exemption from or reduction of prior information and consultation procedures; exemption from the special compensation scheme; reduced compensation; exemption from the obligation to draw up or negotiate a "social plan", which would result in extra expenditure for the enterprise.

New kinds of contract are also subject to special regulations, with a view to facilitating the creation of jobs in SMEs. There are various ways of promoting such "atypical" contracts: for example, SMEs may recruit a higher proportion of workers on atypical contracts; such contracts may be longer and restrictions on granting them may be eliminated; the enterprise may be exempt from social contributions; associations of small enterprises may club together to recruit workers to provide services; and higher age limits may be set for some apprenticeship contracts.

Only in a few countries is provision made for such workers' representation in SMEs at management level, and then only if they have between 25 and 50 employees. As regards elected (non-union) representatives at other levels, some countries stipulate a minimum of five workers, although it is more frequent for the requirement to be at least double this number. Committees or councils are normally required only in the case of larger enterprises or establishments, where the workforce is up to 100 strong. In any case, the powers conferred on these bodies as regards information, consultation and joint decision-making are not always identical and may be reduced according to the size of the enterprise.

In the case of trade union representation, the minimum number of staff required by law or collective agreement is more varied. At one extreme there are inter-union agreements in countries that set no minimum; at the opposite extreme a country may require a labour force consisting of not less than 250 workers. In the latter case, enterprises deemed to be small or medium-sized have no union representation, but only an elected staff delegate or an elected works council. In most Latin American countries, however, where unions usually operate at plant level, the minimum number of members required by legislation precludes unionization in small enterprises.

Apart from a few exceptions, then, workers' representation, whether by trade unions or not, is not obligatory in very small enterprises, although the minimum workforce required may vary considerably according to legislation or collective agreements. Even in larger enterprises, however, the law is frequently not complied with, and a large proportion of SMEs have no staff representatives at all. The number of delegates or members of the works council also depends on the size of the workforce. It may be of limited value to have a single delegate representing more than a certain number of workers, especially if the functions to be carried out involve consultation or, still more, collective bargaining.

As regards staff representation on questions of safety and health, the law generally stipulates the establishment of committees in enterprises with more than 50 workers. In smaller enterprises these functions are carried out by the general representation bodies or by specific representatives.

Other instruments which are sometimes not applied (or applied in a differentiated form) to SMEs are those relating to internal regulations, occupational hazards, profit-sharing under compulsory plans and various social services.

NATIONAL LEGISLATION

Following this overview we will now consider in greater detail the differential treatment accorded to SMEs under various national legislations. In order to limit the scope of this study, we focus on countries in western Europe and Latin America.

Total exemption from labour legislation

At one end of the spectrum some enterprises are totally excluded from the application of labour law. A case in point is rural (agricultural and cattle-raising) enterprises employing at least ten workers on a continuous and permanent basis in the Dominican Republic. On the face of it this exclusion affects only small enterprises, but, since only permanent workers are counted, the influx of large numbers of seasonal workers at certain periods of the year means that the range of enterprises excluded is substantially increased, going well beyond those which are really small or medium-sized. Some larger enterprises thus fall outside the scope of various labour laws.

Termination of employment

This section examines the various measures under which dismissal is made easier and less expensive for the SMEs, taking into account the special character of the relations between employers and workers.

Exclusion of small enterprises from the standards governing dismissals. Protective legislation on dismissals is not applicable to SMEs in Germany, for example, where the Act relating to protection against dismissal (1951) applies only to enterprises which regularly employ more than five workers, who in their turn must have at least six months of service (apprentices are not included). The Employment Protection Act of 1985 also excludes part-time workers who work less than ten hours a week or 45 hours a month, thus increasing the range of enterprises exempted by the law. Moreover, as will be seen below, no provision is made for the establishment in SMEs of works councils, which play an important role in the legal system of protection against dismissal. Workers in such enterprises are protected by other general standards against discriminatory dismissal, arbitrary dismissal without an objective and reasonable basis, dismissal contrary to standard practice and dismissal in reprisal against the exercise of their rights. In Austria the provisions for protection against dismissal also apply only to enterprises with more than five workers, in line with the standards on works councils laid down in the 1974 Act relating to collective labour relations.

In Venezuela the Act relating to protection against unfair dismissal (1974) excluded enterprises normally employing fewer than ten workers, provided that their capital did not exceed a certain amount. The new Basic Labour Law of December 1990 amended the Act, bringing such enterprises within the general scheme governing dismissal. In Italy, too, under Act No. 108 of 1990, workers in small enterprises come under the protection scheme described below. In the United Kingdom the Industrial Relations Act of 1971 excluded enterprises with fewer than four workers from the provisions governing unjustifiable dismissal, although this exclusion was rescinded under the 1975 Employment Protection Act.

Special grounds for dismissal. Among the objective grounds for dismissal (carrying the entitlement only to reduced compensation) contained in the Workers' Statute in Spain, there is one which is applicable only to enterprises with fewer than 50 workers: namely the objectively recognized need to abolish a work post when it is impossible to transfer the worker to other functions in the same enterprise in the same place. The worker concerned is entitled to employment in a vacant post in another establishment of the enterprise in a different place and if the original post is re-established within a year, the worker concerned must be given first refusal.

Causes and procedures. In France, where the law requires certain prior procedures in the case of dismissal for personal reasons (namely, a meeting between the employer and the worker concerned, who may bring an adviser), a recent Act (91-72 of January 1991) extends this requirement in a modified form to enterprises with not more than ten workers; such enterprises were previously excluded. As will be seen below, the special arrangements (including exemption) for enterprises with not more than ten workers also apply to the other provisions on dismissal (it should be noted, however, that this maximum number does not include apprentices or persons without an employment contract; other persons, such as temporary workers, are counted in proportion to their working time).

In Italy, too, the recent Act No. 108 imposed on small enterprises (employing fewer than 16 workers, or six in agriculture) the same obligation as on larger enterprises to notify a dismissal in writing and to state the reasons if requested by the worker, failing which the dismissal is deemed inadmissible. The chances of unreasonable or arbitrary dismissals were thus reduced (except for some categories, such as domestic service workers or workers during their probationary period).

Compensation. Again, in Spain – where there are several legislative antecedents for differential compensation in the event of dismissal – special provisions have been established for enterprises with fewer than 25 workers. If a contract is terminated for technological or economic reasons or owing to *force majeure,* substantial assistance is provided, with the Wage Guarantee Fund covering 40 per cent of the compensation due. Under an earlier law, if an employer opted for the non-reinstatement of the worker the compensation to be paid in cases of unlawful dismissal was as low as 20 per cent (again, partly financed by the Fund). This provision (article 56 (4) of the Workers' Statute) was, however, amended in 1984 under Act No. 32 after being challenged as being discriminatory both against workers and against enterprises employing more than 25 workers, even though this argument was rejected by the court.[9]

In France the law again makes a distinction between enterprises with not more than ten workers and other enterprises. The general rule that any dismissal must have a "true and valid" reason applies to both kinds of enterprise; but whereas in the case of large enterprises the minimum compensation for workers with at least two years' service is six months' wages if such a reason is not established (in addition to a fine on the employer, amounting to up to six months' payment of the worker's unemployment benefit), in small enterprises the compensation payable will depend on the damage suffered, in accordance with the procedure laid down.

In Italy the compensation payable in respect of unfair dismissal, if the worker does not opt for reinstatement, in enterprises which employ more than 15 workers (five in the case of agricultural enterprises) is higher than the compensation to be paid in smaller enterprises in which there is no provision for compulsory reinstatement by the employer (see below).

Colombia is another country where the law has made a distinction between large and small enterprises. For example, in artisanal enterprises where the employer, who also worked in the enterprise, did not employ more than five permanent workers in addition to family labour was formerly not obliged to make redundancy payments.[10] In industrial enterprises, or enterprises in the agricultural, cattle-raising or forestry sectors, with capital below that fixed by the Substantive Labour Code, entitling them to be included in the category of SMEs, the redundancy payment was half that payable by larger enterprises. However, with the adoption of Act No. 50 in December 1990, which made significant amendments to the Code, the whole system of redundancy payments was reformed, making them payable in all enterprises without exception (although the old rules may continue to apply in cases where a contract of employment was concluded before the Act came into force). The new Act also amended the provision that set lower compensation rates for enterprises with less than the prescribed capital. The rate of compensation is now the same for all enterprises, irrespective of their size.

Reinstatement. Italy is one of the countries in which the compulsory reinstatement of unfairly dismissed workers is possible. Legislation has developed considerably in this sphere. The present situation is as follows: reinstatement is obligatory in all enterprises (including small ones) if the dismissal was discriminatory. In the event of unjustifiable or technically incorrect dismissal reinstatement is obligatory only when the work centre employs more than 15 workers, or five in the case of agricultural enterprises; this also applies to employers with more than 60 workers, even if the production unit where the dismissal takes place employs fewer workers in that locality. A worker may request that reinstatement should be replaced by legal compensation. In enterprises or work centres in which the workforce is smaller, reinstatement is not obligatory and may be replaced by compensation set according to the size of the enterprise, the workers' length of service, etc., but is in any case lower than that paid by larger enterprises. Another change is that workers on training contracts and part-time workers now count as staff and the period actually worked is taken into account. The employers' spouse, however, does not count, nor his direct and collateral family members up to the second degree. This is important in the case of small enterprises in Italy, where it is common practice to employ family labour.

In France, reinstatement is not obligatory. The law stipulates, however, that the court may propose reinstatement in the case of enterprises with more than ten workers, although not in smaller enterprises.

In Latin America the legislation of several countries is relevant here. Thus in Mexico, although not specifically mentioned, SMEs come under the provision of the federal labour law exempting employers from reinstating a worker if they pay compensation instead, provided that proof is placed before the Conciliation and Arbitration Board that the worker "by reason of the work he carries out or the nature of his duties is in direct and permanent contact with [the employer] and, in the Board's opinion, taking into account all the circumstances, the normal development of the employment relationship is not possible". More specifically, in Venezuela the new Basic Labour Law stipulates that enterprises with fewer than ten employees are not required to reinstate unfairly dismissed workers if they pay them the legal compensation and benefits. In Panama reinstatement is not obligatory in agro-industrial establishments employing fewer than 20 workers; this number is reduced to 15 if the workplace is a factory, and to ten if it is an agricultural, service or retail trade enterprise. In Colombia, the Substantive Labour Code, prior to its amendment by Act No. 50 of 1990, gave workers with ten years' service the right to reinstatement if unfairly dismissed, although the court could order that reinstatement be replaced by compensation if "reinstatement was not advisable owing to incompatibilities resulting from the dismissal". This provision remains in force for workers who had accumulated the ten years' service before the new Act came into effect, unless they prefer the provisions of the new legislation, which removes the right to reinstatement, thus eliminating any distinction between enterprises.

Length of service. In several countries the law requires a certain period of service before workers become entitled to protection in the event of dismissal, regardless of the size of the enterprise. In the United Kingdom, however, the 1980 Unemployment Act restricted this requirement (two years' service) to workers in enterprises with up to 20 employees. In 1985 this was extended to all enterprises, irrespective of their size.

Collective redundancies on economic grounds. Legislation or collective agreements sometimes exclude SMEs, or else lay down less stringent conditions. This is the case in Belgium, France, Germany, Spain and Colombia.[11] In Belgium the Act of 28 June 1966, which regulates the compensation payable to workers if an enterprise closes down, excludes enterprises with fewer than 20 employees. Various collective agreements also apply here. The agreement of 8 May 1973, which covers a number of industries, stipulates special compensation which again is not payable by SMEs. Under the agreement of 2 October 1975 the employer must inform and consult the works council or the trade union delegate or, if there is none in the enterprise, the workers themselves; but here too enterprises with fewer than 20 workers are excluded. Finally, the agreement of 27 November 1975, applicable to enterprises with more than 50 workers, stipulates that the works council or the trade union delegate must be informed of any delay exceeding three months in the payment by the enterprise of social security contributions or VAT. The employer must also inform the Directorate of Enterprises in Difficulty of the Department of Economic Affairs.

In France there is abundant legislation on the subject, notably Act No. 89-54 of August 1989. The employer is obliged to inform and consult staff delegates or the works council, depending on the number of employees, before taking any measure. If the number of employees is ten or less, however, the law makes no provision for a system of information and consultation. In the case of substantive measures, such as the dismissal of at least ten workers over a period of 30 days, enterprises employing 50 or more workers have to draw up a social plan to avoid such dismissals, reduce their number or facilitate the reclassification of the workers concerned (by providing transfers, part-time work, training and retraining, or reducing working time). If the enterprise has between 11 and 49 employees, however, only a conversion agreement need be proposed by the enterprise (that is, termination of the contract by mutual agreement coupled with payment of compensation). In practice, under the Act, any employee dismissed for economic reasons is entitled to such a conversion agreement, provided that he fulfils the requirements regarding age and length of service; but SMEs are subject to less stringent regulations or are exempted altogether.

In Germany the social plan (generally involving the payment of additional compensation), to be drawn up in consultation with the works council in the event of a reduction of staff, is not obligatory for enterprises which have been in existence for less than four years. And in most cases it is SMEs which benefit from this concession.

In Spain the law stipulates in the case of enterprises whose staff does not exceed 50 (or if the workers affected do not exceed 5 per cent of the labour force in the work centre) that in the event of collective redundancies for technological or economic reasons or owing to *force majeure,* the time limits for the procedures to obtain the necessary official authorization are shorter and the supporting documentation is limited to what is strictly necessary.

Finally, under an amendment to the Substantive Labour Code of Colombia, workers in enterprises with taxable liquid assets totalling less than 1,000 minimum wages – that is, SMEs – are entitled to only 50 per cent of normal compensation.

Trends. The various legislative texts dealing with termination of employment reveal a growing trend towards standardization which is advantageous for workers, in that it extends the protection available to those employed in SMEs. Thus small enterprises are now subject to protective legislation (except as regards reinstatement) and to rules on the payment of compensation for dismissal, the amount of such compensation and the procedures prior to dismissal. But there are also examples showing the opposite tendency: a wider range of small enterprises excluded from legislation; lower compensation payments; special grounds on which termination of employment is permissible; and above all exemption from the obligation (or a reduced obligation) to follow normal procedures on compensation in the case of collective redundancy. In all these examples small enterprises benefit most.

New contractual arrangements

Although SMEs (especially those with fewer than 20 workers) appear to create more job opportunities than large enterprises, it is also true that in the European countries more workers are on atypical contracts, with jobs that tend to be less secure than in larger enterprises. And governments continue to promote such atypical recruitment in small enterprises.

Thus, for example, in Argentina the National Employment Act, which stipulates that workers recruited under new contractual arrangements may not exceed 30 per cent of an establishment's total permanent workforce, raises this limit to 50 per cent in the case of enterprises with between six and 25 workers and to 100 per cent if there are no more than five workers (but no fewer than three). Meanwhile in Italy Act No. 56 of 1987 allows artisanal enterprises to take on apprentices, by collective agreement, aged up to 29, if a high level of occupational content is provided.

In Germany the 1985 Act respecting employment promotion suspended the requirement of an objective reason for the temporary recruitment of new employees and apprentices, with the proviso that the duration of temporary contracts should not exceed 18 months. In new enterprises (those established less than six months) or in those with under 20 workers, however, such contracts may be for up to two years. In the case of enterprises with under five workers, there is no ceiling on temporary contracts, given that workers in such enterprises are not protected against dismissal.

Another way of promoting SMEs is to exempt them from social security contributions. In Spain there is total exemption for enterprises with under 25 employees on training contracts (in this case larger enterprises, too, are given the substantial exemption of 90 per cent). In France a special measure introduced in 1989 exempted small enterprises from social charges for the first salaried employee for the two years following his recruitment. This concession, which resulted in the creation of 60,000 new jobs, was extended in October 1991 to the recruitment of staff in non-profitmaking organizations. Another incentive to employment in small enterprises was introduced in 1985: enterprises with under ten employees were permitted to join forces to recruit workers for an indefinite period who could then be posted to any of the associated enterprises as the need arose.

Such new forms of recruitment show that there is a trend towards promoting small enterprises over larger ones, by facilitating atypical (and precarious) recruitment in the interests of job creation.

Worker representation in enterprises

This section will examine two main types of representation: that organized by trade unions or associations, and bodies elected by all the workers without direct input (even if some influence) from the unions. Representation on occupational safety and health matters will be dealt with separately below.

First, however, a brief word on worker representation in management. Various systems were introduced or extended in the 1970s in several market economy countries (Austria, Belgium, Denmark, the then Federal Republic of Germany, the Netherlands, Sweden). This is relevant here in that some of these systems also apply to SMEs. Thus in Austria a third of the supervisory council in enterprises with more than 40 workers is appointed by the works council; in Denmark a third of the management council of enterprises with more than 50 employees is elected by the staff; in Sweden the workforce may be even smaller to qualify, since in limited companies and cooperatives with more than 25 workers they have the right to appoint two union representatives to the administrative council; in the Netherlands persons proposed by the works council – a worker-elected body – may be coopted on to the supervisory council of enterprises employing over 100 workers.

National legislation commonly debars small enterprises from any kind of representation and restricts representation in medium-sized enterprises (and in large enterprises, too, depending on staff numbers). The minimum number will naturally be different in different countries, for various reasons – the economic factor, of course, but also what has been described as the psychological element, the rejection by the employer of what he considers to be interference in the running of his enterprise. This attitude would be more understandable in the case of small production units, since in-plant staff representation might be an obstacle to the smooth running of the enterprise. But much depends on such factors as the industrial relations climate in a given country. In France the Auroux report (1981) recognized that the cost of staff representation in a small enterprise was excessive and frequently difficult to bear. For example, in the case of an enterprise with 50 workers, the cost of paying for hours off and meetings with the employer would account for 1.45 per cent of the wage bill. The report suggested possible ways to reduce the financial burden for enterprises with between ten and 50 workers, although in an annex dealing with the psychological and economic effects it pointed out that since the estimated cost of hours paid to staff delegates and subsidies granted to the work council came to 2 per cent of the wage bill the psychological effect was greater than the actual financial cost.

In Italy the size of the enterprise is considered relevant here, given the economic hardship involved, the need for a minimum degree of proportionality between representatives and staff and because the right to representation serves a collective interest which outweighs the sum of individual interests. The trade unions have therefore tackled the problem through collective agreements with a view to establishing representation for workers employed in micro-enterprises at the territorial rather than at the enterprise level (area trade union representation for workers in artisanal enterprises; inter-enterprise representation in regions with a high degree of labour and occupational fragmentation). As will be seen below, France has followed a similar path through legislation, although there are also a few collective agreements which have set up local joint committees.

It has already been noted that although the law requires staff representation bodies to be set up in enterprises employing more than a given number of workers, compliance is generally very poor in the case of SMEs. A few examples from developed countries will suffice. In Germany it is estimated that only 6 per cent of establishments with between five and 20 workers have established a committee (and then only with one staff representative, which reduces effectiveness).[12] In France around 65 per cent of establishments with between 11 and 49 employees have no staff delegate; and 45 per cent of establishments with more than 50 workers have no trade union delegate. Works councils exist, however, in around 75 per cent of plants with between 50 and 99 workers.[13]

It should be pointed out that there is little or no unionization in SMEs. Indeed, in Europe a direct relationship has been established between the size of the enterprise and the degree of unionization. Thus, for example, even in Germany, where overall unionization is close to 35 per cent, the rate is only 7 per cent in enterprises with between ten and 100 workers.[14] However, since trade unions generally conduct bargaining negotiations at branch level and the ensuing agreements apply to all enterprises, whether *de facto* or by legislative extension, SMEs too are theoretically covered.

In the countries of Latin America, with the exception of Argentina, Brazil and Uruguay, the typical grass-roots trade union organization is at enterprise level and that is where collective bargaining generally takes place. Since the minimum number of members generally required by legislation is between 20 and 25, however, workers in small and many medium-sized enterprises are deprived of union representation and therefore of collective agreements.

Several countries have passed legislation setting minimum requirements for staff representation. In Argentina Act No. 23551 respecting trade union organizations requires union representation in any enterprise with more than ten employees: one representative for up to 50 employees, with the number rising proportionately to the size of the workforce, if a different proportion has not been fixed by collective agreement. An earlier proposal to fix the minimum at five workers, rising on a sliding scale thereafter, was criticized by the employers (Argentine Industrial Union) as being particularly disadvantageous to SMEs.

In Germany and Austria, as we have seen, works committees may be set up in enterprises with at least five workers; they are directly elected rather than union-based, since trade union bodies do not fall within the scope of legislation. However, the country which has established the widest variety of representative bodies able to coexist and function simultaneously in enterprises is France. First, there are the representatives elected by the whole workforce: these are the staff delegate and the works council. Any establishment with 11 or more workers is entitled to the former, while any with at least 50 workers (for a non-continuous period of 12 months over three years) is entitled to a works council, which is a joint body, with employer representation. A works council may also be set up in enterprises which are legally distinct but belong to the same group of companies. Enterprises with under 50 workers may also set up councils by agreement, with the same powers as the statutory works council.

To encourage worker representation in enterprises with under 11 employees, an Act of 1982 permits the election of an on-site representative in micro-enterprises that are physically and geographically isolated, on condition that there are at least 50 workers at the site; but this option appears to be seldom exercised. Meanwhile, the 1982 Act on collective bargaining (amended in 1985) permits enterprises with fewer than 50 workers to group together at local or departmental level, by collective agreement, in setting up a council of workers – whether from the same occupation or at inter-occupational level, depending on the enterprise – to participate in the negotiation and application of collective agreements, and also in the examination of individual and collective disputes. This is an attempt to compensate for the absence of delegates, who should by law represent the union in collective bargaining at enterprise level.

The presence of a union delegate is, however, required in establishments with at least 50 workers. Where there is a smaller workforce, the union may appoint a staff delegate as its representative. However, any representative trade union is legally entitled to set up a branch within any establishment, however small staff numbers are. The members of the branch have the right to collect contributions, distribute or post up notices and communications, and convene meetings, although for some of these measures agreement must be reached with the employer. The forms of staff representation are so diverse and cause so much difficulty for SMEs, however, that it is proposed to change the law, enabling enterprises with a workforce of between 50 and 100 to amalgamate the functions of the staff delegate, the works council and the committee on occupational safety and health and working conditions.

In Spain, too, the law provides for staff delegates and works councils, but not both in the same enterprise. Where there are more than ten and fewer than 50 workers (or even between six and ten workers, if a majority so decides), one staff delegate represents up to 30 workers and three represent up to 49 workers. If the staff totals 50 or more, the delegates are replaced by works councils, the composition of which varies according to the size of the workforce. For trade union representation there must be at least 250 workers in the enterprise, so this option is closed to SMEs.

In Italy the Workers' Statute regulates only the union presence in the enterprise. This may consist either of branches affiliated to the most representative national confederations or of branches that are not affiliated but have signed collective agreements applicable to the production unit concerned. The branch may be set up within any industrial or commercial production unit (but not enterprise) comprising more than 15 workers, or in agricultural enterprises with more than five workers. In practice the large trade union confederations (the Italian General Confederation of Labour, the Italian Confederation of Workers' Unions and the Italian Labour Union) have established standards amongst themselves governing worker representation at the enterprise level. The most recent agreement, signed on 1 March 1991, makes provision for "single trade union representation", made up of representatives from various unions (including some not belonging to the three main confederations). Additionally there are the collective agreements, mentioned above, enabling workers in micro-enterprises to be represented on a territorial basis; and other agreements, also aimed at micro-enterprises, have reduced the minimum requirement for union representation.

In both Belgium and the Netherlands there is legislation covering works councils (which in Belgium are joint bodies), although along different lines. In Belgium the enterprise must have at least 100 workers. The Government may reduce this figure to 50 but has not yet done so, although the Act has stood since 1948, and moreover the trade unions believe they lack the means to provide the councils with appropriate assistance. Meanwhile in the Netherlands an Act passed in 1981 extended the obligation to set up councils to enterprises with more than 35 workers; in those with between ten and 34 workers, meetings must be held between the employer and the whole workforce at least twice a year. A subsequent Act, passed in 1986, established the right to set up works councils in enterprises with more than ten workers. Trade union representation in Belgium is a matter for inter-union agreement on minimum staff levels: these were set at 25 for white-collar workers under an agreement in 1972. No minimum was set for manual workers under a 1971 agreement.

In some countries the rights of representative bodies depend on the size of the workforce, which disadvantages small enterprises. Thus, for example, in Germany the number of workers with the right to vote must exceed 20 before the works council need be formally consulted on staff reductions, shut-downs, mergers or the introduction of new production methods. This is also the minimum number before the council is allowed the right to joint decision-making on the recruitment, classification, reclassification and transfer of staff or before the enterprise is obliged to present quarterly reports on its financial situation, on its problems, on the social services or on the state of the market. In the Netherlands the works council is entitled to express its opinion on major decisions affecting the organization of the enterprise, but it has fewer powers if the workforce numbers less than 100; and consultation is obligatory only if the proposed changes involve staff reductions of 25 per cent or more.

Overall, this examination of national legislation suggests a distinct trend towards the extension of worker representation to small enterprises. Thus one country has twice in recent years legislated to reduce the minimum requirement and another has seen the requirement reduced in artisanal enterprises through collective bargaining. Elsewhere legal and contractual standards have been introduced to encourage representation in micro-enterprises by grouping them together by area and providing joint representation, thus avoiding the disadvantages of representation within each enterprise.

Occupational safety and health

These very topical and important matters are subject to a wealth of legislation at national and international level. For SMEs, however, they present special difficulties, technically and financially, which have been identified by the ILO, amongst other bodies. One of the preparatory reports for the Occupational Safety and Health Convention, 1981 (No. 155), and Recommendation (No. 164), emphasized that SMEs would need more in the way of assistance and advisory services on prevention. Some countries, such as Australia, the United States and the United Kingdom, have made special efforts in this area. In Japan the Act on occupational safety and health stipulates that the authorities must provide financial and technical incentives for employers (in consultation with workers and their organizations) to improve occupational safety and health conditions, particularly in SMEs. International standards, as we have seen, give few specific indications regarding the size of enterprises and the provision of medical services, etc., merely stating that the recommended measures should be adopted when the size of the enterprise so permits. In several countries legislation prescribes the minimum number of workers for which an enterprise must provide medical services; but this generally applies to larger establishments – in the case of Spain and Brazil, for example, those with more than 100 workers. Colombia appears to be something of an exception, with the Substantive Labour Code requiring facilities to provide assistance in the event of accident or illness to be maintained in enterprises with ten or more workers, while agricultural, cattle-raising and forestry enterprises must have a sick bay and medicines available if the workforce totals 15 or more.

When passing legislation concerning safety and health committees most countries set minimum requirements regarding workforce size generally corresponding to that of medium-sized and sometimes of small enterprises. In Germany safety representatives must be appointed when the workforce numbers 20 or more. In Belgium a committee on occupational safety, health and workplace improvement must be set up if the staff totals 50 or more. As in the case of works councils, the Government may reduce this minimum, although it has not done so to date. In Spain, there has to be a safety and health committee in enterprises with more than 100 workers (fewer in high-risk occupations). In France the minimum is 50 employees. The same applies in Sweden, although the minimum may be lower if the staff of a smaller enterprise specifically requests a safety committee. In Brazil accident prevention committees (CIPAS) are compulsory only in enterprises with at least 50 workers.

However, legislation also frequently provides for representatives with special responsibility for safety and health even in much smaller enterprises. In Germany the representative (just one in enterprises with up to 20 workers) is a member of the works council, which, as mentioned above, is obligatory in enterprises with at least five workers. In Belgium the same function may be carried out by the union delegate representing manual workers, an appointment requiring no minimum workforce. In Spain a safety officer must be appointed in enterprises with more than five workers. In France this task is carried out by the staff delegate, in enterprises with 11 or more workers. In Sweden safety delegates must be elected in enterprises with five workers or more (fewer, in exceptional circumstances). Worker representation on matters of safety and health thus corresponds to the minimum level required for representation generally, sometimes even below the minimum.

FAMILY LABOUR

Work carried out by several members of a family in a small business or micro-enterprise has two characteristics that are relevant to the present study: (1) while definitions of "family" vary from country to country, such enterprises may remain totally or partly outside the scope of labour law; (2) any worker who is not a family member is not – unless formally in possession of an employment contract – counted as part of the workforce for the purposes of determining the minimum base for the application of general labour legislation: yet another category of person who may be excluded from the calculation, thus adding to the number of small enterprises subject to differential labour legislation.

Similarly, many ILO Conventions exclude from their scope family enterprises or workshops, defined as those in which only members of the same family are employed or active or, even more restrictively, only members of the employer's family, or members of the employer's family who are not nor may be considered employees, or enterprises in which a father works alongside his children or wards (children under the care of a father of a family).[15] The exclusion of such enterprises is optional for governments for all Conventions adopted after 1922.

There seem to be two reasons for the exclusion of such enterprises from ILO instruments. First, it is assumed that there will be no abuse within the family environment that might affect the health of the members of the family concerned: a kind of natural protection. It is worth recalling that the Conventions permitting exclusion deal with such basic issues as the workday, the minimum age for work, night work by women and children, medical examination and maternity (but not safety and health).

The second reason appears to be an economic one, given that family enterprises are small, particularly when subject to the restrictive interpretation which suggests that the word "family" refers only to children and wards.[16]

There may be a third reason, relating to working conditions in a family environment, which were believed to fall outside the scope of legislative regulation: weekly rest and paid holidays. The Holidays with Pay (Agriculture) Convention, 1952 (No. 101), for example, permits the exclusion of categories of persons "whose conditions of employment render such provisions inapplicable to them", such as the members of the employer's family who work for that employer. Health considerations do not seem to have been considered relevant. The Holidays with Pay Convention (Revised), 1970 (No. 132), does not expressly exclude family enterprises (as the original Holidays with Pay Convention, 1936 (No. 52), did), but refers only to "all employed persons". On the other hand, the Conventions concerning seafarers' vacations adopted after 1945 no longer exclude vessels whose crews are made up only of members of the shipowner's family.

The Workers' group in the ILO has generally opposed this kind of exclusion: in this context, see the debate at the 1937 Conference when the Minimum Age (Industry) Convention (Revised), 1937 (No. 59), and the Minimum Age (Family Undertakings) Recommendation, 1937 (No. 52), were adopted.

National legislation tends to exclude family labour from its provisions, on the assumption that no employment contract can exist within a family. Thus the Act respecting employment contracts in Argentina refers to "family companies" made up of parents and children (article 27), which may include small enterprises; and the Civil Code excludes any employment relationship between parents and under-age children living at home, and also between spouses.

In Spain the exclusion of family labour from the Workers' Statute (article 3(e)) concerns small enterprises more directly, in that it covers the spouse, parents, children, grandparents, grandchildren and other relatives by blood or by marriage up to and including the second degree, or by adoption. Independent or self-employed groups of workers are frequently considered to be engaged in family labour, on the assumption that no employment relationship exists when such workers live in the same household as the head of the family.

In Germany family members who work with the head of the family are not regarded as employees. They are generally spouses, children or other relatives who provide their services on farms, in workshops or in small businesses without receiving any wage. If a contractual relationship is shown to exist, however, all the provisions of labour law apply, although the practical difficulty of ensuring compliance with labour standards in family enterprises is such that they are permitted to employ cheap labour so that they can compete, if only for a time, with larger, well-established enterprises.

In Italy Act No. 151 of 1975 updates the regulation of employment relationships within the family contained in article 230*bis* (family enterprises) of the Civil Code. This article introduces the concept of family labour cooperation, underlining the fact that the traditional distinction between family labour performed free of charge and that performed in exchange for remuneration is no longer as important as the existence of a subordinate employment relationship and the right to participate in the family enterprise as defined by the article. Thus a family member who works continuously for a family enterprise has the right to subsistence, profit-sharing, a share in the increased value of the family property and a say in basic decisions relating to the business, proportionately to the quantity and quality of the work performed. Under the article the family is taken to mean the spouse, blood relatives up to the third degree and relatives by marriage up to the second degree.

It follows that relationships in enterprises may fall into one of three categories: (a) a subordinate employment relationship; (b) a relationship of cooperation and participation, in the meaning of article 230*bis* of the Civil Code, so that labour law is not applicable; (c) a relationship of work which is performed free of charge, *affectionis causa*, in which no wage is paid but where the other labour laws apply. This covers the whole range of employment relationships, apart from those involving a shared household, and thus enables particular kinds of small enterprises to be set up, exempt from labour legislation.

The Federal Labour Act of Mexico does not apply to small workshops, except as regards occupational safety and health standards. These workshops are defined as ones in which the work is carried out only by spouses, parents, children, grandparents, grandchildren and wards of an owner who is the head of the family. The reason for excluding family enterprises is that it would be impossible to apply criteria based on the formal ownership of family property, since "to oblige the head of a family who works at home and is assisted by his wife and children to comply with the obligations imposed on employers would be tantamount to destroying the family."[17] This would appear to exclude any question of a labour relationship between the head of the family and the members of that family.

Elsewhere family enterprises or workshops are excluded for the same reasons – the financial aspect or to protect the family – as given in the ILO Conventions on which the national legislation is based. This is clearly true of Argentina, where Act No. 11544 and regulatory Decree No. 16115 of 1933 on statutory hours of work exclude establishments employing only family labour (parents, children, grandparents, grandchildren, spouse, brothers and sisters of the head, owner or employer). Similarly, under the Act relating to labour contracts the prohibition on work by children under 14 does not apply to children employed in family enterprises, provided that the work is not harmful, detrimental or dangerous to the child (and is authorized by the guardian).

The same is true of Brazil, where the provisions concerning hours of work do not apply to women employed in workshops in which only members of her family work, under the direction of her husband, father, mother, guardian or child. Nor do the provisions governing minimum age, medical examination of children or apprenticeship apply to workshops in which only members of the child's family work and where the child is under the authority of father, mother or guardian (standards on night work do apply, however, when the premises or services involved are dangerous, unhealthy, or detrimental to the child's morals).

Exclusion may also be for essentially economic reasons. Thus the Substantive Labour Code of Colombia excludes family enterprises in which only the head of the family, the spouse, children and grandchildren work from the provisions relating to occupational accidents and diseases and monetary assistance for non-occupational diseases. (Redundancy payments were also excluded until the adoption of Act No. 50 of December 1990, which amended the Code.)

Finally, social security legislation – and specifically old age protection schemes – in most developing countries, Nicaragua and Panama, for example, are predicated on the existence of an employment relationship, family workers sometimes being expressly excluded.[18]

CONCLUSIONS

The differentiation contained in labour legislation according to the size or importance of an enterprise still applies and indeed is being extended. But it is not a linear process: in some cases respect for the protective principle of labour legislation tends to reduce or eliminate differential standards, while in others they are retained because they are more practical and convenient or because they are in line with a specific social and economic policy.

Attitudes to differentiation vary. Employers, especially in the enterprises concerned, favour less labour regulation for SMEs, or complete deregulation, whereas the unions prefer standardized legislation, even though they sometimes negotiate over regulated standards. International bodies such as the EC and the ILO both accept some flexibility in the treatment of SMEs, but in slightly different ways. For example, the report of the EC Commission, mentioned above, pointed out that differentiation based on staff numbers meant that many SMEs tried either to avoid expanding or to issue atypical contracts (thus, in some countries, excluding staff from the calculation of the minimum workforce) so as to continue enjoying less stringent standards.[19] At the same time, as part of the Maastricht Treaty the EC recently accepted the principle that any directives adopted on social issues should not act as obstacles to the creation and development of SMEs. This amounts to support for some degree of differential treatment for SMEs (although it was made clear that there was no intention to discriminate against workers in SMEs, where safety and health were concerned). For its part, the ILO opposes any kind of deregulation "in the sense of abrogating the most essential protective legislation [which] opens the way for unsatisfactory and even exploitative conditions". But it would accept both the elimination of unnecessary provisions or their replacement by others producing the same results with less bureaucracy and a more flexible application of regulations, if balanced by other acceptable measures under union control.[20] There are also the ILO instruments already referred to which permit partial or total exemption from these provisions for small enterprises (or small vessels).

Among academic writers, Professor de la Villa and Professor Sagardoy Bengoechea of Spain, for example, are in favour of standardized labour law, but on two levels, with the State setting minimum standards and collective agreements establishing sliding scales. The former would be applicable to all workers, whereas collective agreement provisions could make a distinction, based on supplementary protection, between work in large enterprises and in SMEs. For illegal working it would be appropriate to establish a "scale of guarantees, always marginally higher than the state level", with a view to the gradual reincorporation of illegal work into the regular labour market.[21]

This thesis accords with the notion of complementarity between statutory standards and collective agreements and recognizes the dominance of the latter. It acknowledges the differentiation of standards according to the size of an enterprise and its place in the formal or informal sector of the economy, but puts it on a contractual basis. However, the traditional refusal of the unions to accept special treatment for SMEs (although Italy would appear to be an exception[22]) makes it difficult to put this into practice.

It is worth noting that state regulation does not constitute a solid base on which the two sides of industry try to construct improved agreements and higher standards to suit the size of a given enterprise, but on the contrary is very flexible (even to the extent of reducing levels of protection) where SMEs are concerned. In other words, general legislation is subject – with certain exceptions – to some relaxation on minimum requirements for SMEs.

Indeed, state standards generally are growing increasingly flexible under the influence of collective bargaining (which may have an adverse effect on workers in SMEs if disadvantageous agreements are negotiated by weak representatives without proper union backing). The situation is compounded by the fact that even the minimum state standards may be too onerous, both for enterprises in the informal sector which want to reduce labour costs for greater competitiveness and for those in the developing countries which very often find it financially impossible to comply with the regulations.

In Italy, Professor Marco Biagi believes that where protection of basic rights is concerned legislation should not create grey areas exposed to the unilateral power of the employer. However, he also believes, in the interests of pragmatism, that negotiated flexibility is essential, even in the case of SMEs. Taking his cue from a French Bill under which it will be easier to conclude collective agreements with lower standards as an incentive to bargaining in smaller enterprises, where the union presence is weak, he advocates a solution that combines collective bargaining with supervision by the administrative authority.[23]

In practice solutions will inevitably be varied, depending on such factors as the effectiveness and viability of labour legislation on the shop-floor, the real cost involved and the economic and social context in which SMEs develop, not to mention their own size and nature.

Although the various instruments of labour law should be guided by the protective principle, the way they are applied will undoubtedly vary according to which aspect of a given instrument is emphasized. Thus the degree of adaptation necessary to conform to a particular instrument – for example, when adjusting to the difficulties of a shared family enterprise – will largely depend on the social context and the existing tradition of labour relations. Another factor is the mere cost of implementing the relevant instrument, as compared with other production costs.

To take one example: in the case of dismissal on disciplinary grounds or by reason of unsuitability, the protective principle would necessitate the generalized application of the worker's right to defend himself as a prerequisite, even in the case of small enterprises. But in collective redundancies on financial grounds all the preliminary procedures – information, consultation, administrative authorization or a social plan – would be so complex and expensive for SMEs that they would have to be given special treatment. Compensation could also be made flexible in small businesses and micro-enterprises, unless the cost to the employer is already so low under the provisions of the law that the burden on him is comparatively light. On the other hand, any obligation to reinstate workers in SMEs, where employer and workers are in direct contact, would make it difficult to ensure a harmonious atmosphere in the workplace and would thus be unacceptable in practice.

There is a tendency to encourage atypical contracts in SMEs as a means of boosting employment. But a forward-looking social and economic policy must weigh up not only the advantages of greater immediate employment – in any case uncertain in the absence of investment in production – against the disadvantages in the long term of creating a pool of cheap but unstable labour, unmotivated and lacking the necessary training. A competitive market position should rest not on low labour costs, but on quality and adaptability in production. The role of SMEs has special significance here, given their development potential within the context of "flexible specialization" in the modern economy.

Worker representation in the enterprise is important as ensuring not only the protection principle but also the principle of participation in the development of relations within the enterprise. But a country's social context has some effect on this, particularly on participation, and even more so as enterprises get smaller. To achieve recognition for union or electoral representation in a small enterprise may be difficult even in countries with harmonious labour relations. One solution being sought is representation at area level, which may be closer to the social and cultural context in which such enterprises develop.

Mention has been made of the quantitative and qualitative features of SMEs which may be a factor in determining how far a given law should be applied, if at all. Indeed, as we have seen, an enterprise which is small in terms of staff size may be comparable to a large or medium-sized enterprise in terms of capital, technology, etc. Differentiation in labour legislation based only on the criterion of staff numbers may thus be open to question. Various aspects of labour legislation may have to be reconsidered. For example, in the case of dismissal, there is no reason to reduce compensation, but reinstatement may be unacceptable. On the other hand, worker representation for participatory purposes might perhaps be easier in SMEs with larger capital and technological development, in that the staff is more highly qualified, with a higher cultural level and aspirations.

More thought should be given to small enterprises in the informal sector of developing countries, as mentioned at the outset. The problem here is the failure to respect labour standards because of their prohibitive cost. The solution is either to reduce the already low level of standards for SMEs, or to maintain the same level as an objective to be attained over time. In his 1991 Report the Director-General of the ILO opted firmly for the second alternative, believing that "to reduce the standards of protection offered by legislation to workers in the modern sector in order to make them more easily attainable in the informal sector would not only be socially unacceptable, but also of no help to the informal sector".[24] However, he pointed out that there are three types of standards which are so fundamental that their non-observance should not be tolerated: those concerning such basic human rights as freedom of association, protection against forced labour and protection against discrimination; those concerning child labour, where a start should be made by eliminating the most abusive forms of labour exploitation; and those concerning occupational safety and health.

We believe that the progressive application of legislation will require the establishment of time-limits for each of the various categories (holidays, hours of work, dismissal, etc.), as well as for standards on occupational safety and health and on installations and premises used for the production and provision of services (except those for the use of harmful or dangerous substances, the prohibition of which should be immediate). The time-limits should come into effect as soon as the enterprise is registered for production purposes and the enterprise should be given help with their implementation by receiving facilities for credit, taxation, training, etc.

Finally, given the importance of the family in the development of small enterprises, it would be appropriate to examine the possibility of making the family enterprise a special category, to promote such micro-enterprises as a distinct type of SME.

Notes

[1] In addition to national legislation and other works of reference, various specialized studies carried out in Europe have proved very useful. See especially Commission of the European Communities: *Labour law and industrial relations in small and medium-sized enterprises in the EEC countries* (Luxembourg, 1988); national papers presented at the conference organized by the SINNEA Institute, under the direction of Professor Marco Biagi, on the subject of labour law and industrial relations in small enterprises, Bologna, 11 January 1991; national contributions on labour law and small enterprises, published in *Quaderni di diritto del lavoro e relazioni industriali*, 1990, No. 8; Marco Biagi: "Piccole e medie imprese. Rappresentanza sindacale: un'analisi comparata", in *Diritto e pratica del lavoro*, No. 33, 26 Aug. 1991; L. de la Villa and J.A. Sagardoy Bengoechea: *Régimen jurídico laboral de la PYMES en España* (Ministry of Industry and Energy, Madrid, 1985).

[2] ILO: *The promotion of small and medium-sized enterprises*, Report IV, International Labour Conference, 72nd Session (Geneva, 1986), p. 4.

[3] In this connection, see especially Werner Sengenberger, Gary W. Loveman and Michael J. Piore (eds.): *The re-emergence of small enterprises* (Geneva, International Institute for Labour Studies, 1991, 2nd ed).

[4] The best study of the re-emergence of SMEs offering flexible specialization, and the wide range of future possibilities, is the well-known work by Michael J. Piore and Charles Sabel: *The second industrial divide* (New York, 1984).

[5] See in particular F. Pyke and W. Sengenberger (eds.): *Industrial districts and local economic regeneration* (Geneva, International Institute for Labour Studies, 1992).

[6] ILO: *The dilemma of the informal sector*, Report of the Director-General, International Labour Conference, 78th Session (Geneva, 1991), p. 4.

[7] Ibid., p. 13.

[8] The Conventions in question are the Seamen's Articles of Agreement Convention, 1926 (No. 22); the Repatriation of Seamen Convention, 1926 (No. 23); the Officers' Competency Certificates Convention, 1936 (No. 53); the Shipowners' Liability (Sick and Injured Seamen) Convention, 1936 (No. 55); the Social Security (Seafarers) Convention, 1946 (No. 70), and its revision (No. 165); the Medical Examination (Seafarers) Convention, 1946 (No. 73); the Paid Vacations (Seafarers) (Revised) Convention, 1949 (No. 91); the Accommodation of Crews (Revised) Convention, 1949 (No. 92), and the Accommodation of Crews (Supplementary Provisions) Convention, 1970 (No. 133); the Wages, Hours of Work and Manning (Sea) (Revised) Convention, 1958 (No. 109); and the Merchant Shipping (Minimum Standards) Convention, 1976 (No. 147).

[9] On 26 January 1984 the Central Labour Court ruled that the matter concerned compensation under the law equivalent to a penalty clause in the event of non-compliance with a contract,

intended to provide overall compensation for damages but not specifically based on such damages. Thus the difference in the amount was not discriminatory, since it was reasonable and proportionate to the country's economic and social policy objectives, namely the protection of small enterprises and the struggle against unemployment.

[10] The redundancy payment is payable in all cases (except in the event of termination for an unlawful act against the employer, wilful damage to machinery, etc.), on top of the compensation for unfair dismissal.

[11] EC Directive 75/129 on collective redundancies – and its approved draft amendment – excludes from its scope establishments with a labour force of up to 20 workers.

[12] Manfred Weiss: *Industrial relations in medium and small-sized companies in the Federal Republic of Germany,* National paper presented at the Conference of the SINNEA Institute (see note 1).

[13] Report prepared by Gilles Belier, at the request of the Ministry of Labour, on improved worker representation in SMEs. See *European Industrial Relations Review* (London), 1990, No. 198, pp. 23-25.

[14] Commission of the European Communities, op. cit., p. 11.

[15] See especially Hours of Work (Industry) Convention, 1919 (No. 1); Maternity Protection Convention, 1919 (No. 3); Night Work (Women) Convention, 1919 (No. 4), and Revised 1934 (No. 4) and 1948 (No. 89); Minimum Age (Industry) Convention, 1919 (No. 5); Night Work of Young Persons (Industry) Convention, 1919 (No. 6), and Revised 1948 (No. 90); Weekly Rest (Industry) Convention, 1921 (No. 14); Hours of Work (Commerce and Offices) Convention, 1930 (No. 30); Minimum Age (Non-Industrial Employment) Convention, 1932 (No. 33), and Revised 1937 (No. 60); Reduction of Hours of Work (Public Works) Convention, 1936 (No. 51); Holidays with Pay Convention, 1936 (No. 52); Medical Examination of Young Persons (Non-Industrial Occupations) Convention, 1946 (No. 78); Maternity Protection Convention (Revised), 1952 (No. 103); Weekly Rest (Commerce and Offices) Convention, 1957 (No. 106); Plantations Convention, 1958 (No. 110); Minimum Age Convention, 1973 (No. 138), where it refers to agricultural holdings; and several maritime Conventions which exempt vessels manned exclusively by members of the same family.

[16] *International Labour Code*, p. 257, footnote 378.

[17] Mario de la Cueva: *Derecho del trabajo* (Mexico City, 1961), Vol. 1, p. 877.

[18] ILO: *Social security protection in old age,* General Survey of the Committee on the Application of Conventions and Recommendations, International Labour Conference, 76th Session, 1989, pp. 26-27.

[19] Commission of the European Communities, op. cit., p. 13.

[20] ILO: *The promotion of small and medium-sized enterprises,* op. cit., pp. 54, 76 and 77.

[21] De la Villa and Sagardoy Bengoechea, op. cit., preface.

[22] Here special agreements were concluded (in 1983 and 1988) between trade union federations and employers' organizations in the artisanal sector, different from other branch or sector agreements. Furthermore, even regular branch or sector agreements may contain restrictive clauses whereby the negotiated terms may be relaxed in the case of small enterprises.

[23] Biagi, op. cit., pp. 2111 and 2112.

[24] ILO: *The dilemma of the informal sector,* op. cit., pp. 37ff. For background see the analysis of this subject in Victor E. Tokman: "Sector informal en América Latina: De subterráneo a legal", in *Más allá de la regulación – El sector informal en América Latina* (PREALC, ILO, 1990).

THE FUTURE OF WORK, EMPLOYMENT AND SOCIAL PROTECTION (THE ANNECY SYMPOSIUM, JANUARY 2001)

12

Patrick Bollé[*]

Though the labour markets have outlived the recent vogue of apocalyptic predictions about the end of work – or, at least, of wage employment – the fact remains that both work and employment relationships have changed over the past two decades in the industrialized countries. These changes have brought on a heightened sense of insecurity and genuine uncertainty. The explanation may lie in the breakdown of the Fordist model, which combined mass production and consumption with social protection and negotiated sharing of the rewards of productivity gains. For a time, this model appeared to offer boundless prospects for stability and sustainability. Today, however, the organization of work is undergoing rapid changes, as are the content of the employment relationship, the concept of the Welfare State and the scope of social protection. Has the time come to confront a new "social question"? To come up with an answer was one of the aims of a round of symposiums scheduled within the framework of an agreement between the Government of France and the ILO. The first such symposium was held at Annecy (France) on 18 and 19 January 2001.[1]

The purpose of the Annecy Symposium on the Future of Work, Employment and Social Protection was to contribute ideas to the current debate on the new social issues confronting the industrialized countries. This "Perspective" reviews the presentations made at the Symposium as well as the ensuing discussions. The first part presents the general aims of the meeting, together with the underlying issues. This is followed by brief summaries of the presentations made and exchanges held at each of the four panel discussions devoted to the major items on the agenda. A concluding section attempts to bring out some of the alternative options, avenues for reflection and proposals that emerged from the proceedings as a whole.

Originally published in *International Labour Review*, Vol. 140 (2001), No. 4, in the "Perspectives" section.

* French-language editor of the *International Labour Review*.

SOCIAL INSTITUTIONS FOR THE NEW GLOBAL ECONOMY: THE CENTRAL CONCERN

One of the aims of the agreement between France and the ILO is to contribute to the ongoing process of reflection on the new social problems facing the industrialized countries, particularly in regard to issues emerging in the fields of employment and work and the role of work as a factor of economic security and social cohesion. Its other aims are to identify new practices introduced in response to the major changes occurring in this area – examining their scope and whether or not they are innovative, beneficial or risky – and to help develop international strategies which integrate the economic and social dimensions of development.

On this basis, a list of issues was drawn up: [2]

- A first issue centres on the viability – perhaps even the long-term benefit – of strengthening the current strategy underlying the process of globalization, i.e. product differentiation, individualized presentations, and the closest possible matching of "client" needs or, rather, wants. What are the relative micro and macroeconomic costs and benefits of a society structured around the notion of serving the "almighty customer"? Does this not mean sacrificing the producer to the consumer? Taken to an extreme, would it not exacerbate inequalities?

- In the light of these concerns, how would work really need to change in order to ensure that flexibly organized production does not preclude decent work? Could work offering individual and collective social protection be organized in ways that would increase flexibility while reducing worker insecurity? Or do flexibility and security necessarily clash?

- How could social policies come to be seen more in terms of their benefits, instead of being invariably considered in terms of costs? Health, education and training, income stability and a sense of security should not be viewed solely as costs, but also as important factors contributing to efficiency and performance. Can this dimension be incorporated into conventional economic development policies?

- Which specific arrangements need to be made to spare labour the full brunt of what seems to be the inescapable flexibilization of production? Can workers' needs for flexibility over the course of their career be reconciled with the flexibility required for the production of goods and services? What would be the institutional underpinnings of such "flexicurity"?

- Has the time come to set up a system of "special drawing rights" that individuals could make use of at different stages in their career? Since life appears to involve increasingly frequent transitions – between one job and another, between a job and a training course, between jobs and family responsibilities, etc. – can new institutions be designed to manage those transitions?

- How to set up new forms of collective regulation that would accommodate both the social and the economic (through law, collective bargaining or social pacts, and at what level and on which issues)?

- Could there be ways of encouraging employers – in cooperation with existing institutions – to make allowance for the other roles that workers must perform (as citizens, parents, etc.) in order to help them strike a better balance between a career and a family, social and personal life?

The first of the France/ILO symposiums [3] proposed to tackle these questions under four broad headings, each of which was the topic of a panel discussion, namely, the transformation of work and new insecurities; the impact of changes on work and society; the political response to the new challenges; and methods, actors and levels of political action.

TRANSFORMATIONS OF WORK AND NEW INSECURITIES

The first panel discussion opened with a presentation by Eileen Appelbaum [4] which identified four factors of insecurity.

The internationalization of production processes. The growth of international trade causes job loss and wage erosion in industries exposed to international competition, thereby contributing to worker insecurity. This process has been documented and its impact measured. Yet the international integration of production within multinational corporations is just as significant. "These companies exhibit remarkably little concern for the interests of their many stakeholders – the workers, communities, and government of the nations where they are headquartered or their facilities are situated" (see Auer and Daniel, op. cit., p. 18). Such enterprises concentrate on design and marketing while outsourcing and relocating their manufacturing operations as reflected in the spectacular growth of intra-enterprise international trade. The result is a "threat effect" hanging over workers in industrialized countries, compounded by a weakening of their bargaining power and social protection. Also weakened is the regulatory power of States: "Thus, workers confront new insecurities while, at the same time, governments are less able to provide protections" (see Auer and Daniel, op. cit., p. 20). In the face of these developments, Appelbaum proposes that a global social agreement be negotiated with three major objectives: development assistance (infrastructure, social investment, debt relief and technical assistance), compliance with the ILO's basic labour standards, and the introduction of an international tax on global financial transactions, the proceeds of which would serve to finance social investment in the developing countries.

The decline of the standard employment relationship is the second factor of insecurity. In the face of stock market volatility, risk and responsibility are passed on to workers. It is then up to them to maintain their "employability". Precarious employment relationships lessen the employer's social responsibility in respect of both employment security and social benefits. The standard employment relationship is also under threat from the practice of outsourcing. Professionals and managers are no longer sheltered from job loss. This obviously contributes to making employment insecurity more visible. A balance between the needs of business and workers could be struck by providing for wage and benefit parity as between standard and non-standard employment, proper classification of employees (to prevent their misclassification as temporary workers or independent contractors, for example), a broadening of the scope of labour law to include all types of employment, and an increase in the number of "good" part-time jobs.

The marginalization of care work. Comparing the experiences of the United States and of Sweden, Appelbaum shows how an increase in women's labour force participation rates can produce contradictory outcomes. Some countries, like Sweden, use taxpayer money to finance social services that not only offer women jobs but which also enable them to reconcile work and family, because such services are typically based on the caring labour – e.g. childcare – that was traditionally assigned to the "homemaker" in the male breadwinner model. In other countries, like the United States, by contrast, the issue is conceptualized as a matter of personal choice, one that does not call for any social-policy action: "Men and women can work if they conform to the old ideal of the male employee with no domestic work responsibilities; ... Even women who pursue homemaking on a full-time basis are dismissed as 'just a housewife', the important care work they do devalued" (see Auer and Daniel, op. cit., pp. 29-30). Appelbaum advocates a public policy that would promote the sharing of market-based work and recognized care work on the basis of a reduction of working time, equality of opportunity and non-discrimination, a sharing of the cost of care, direct access to benefits bypassing employers, and an update of income security protections.

The ubiquity of digital technology. Information technology has far-reaching consequences for workers. Many of the highly skilled may well enjoy prosperity, but they are nonetheless exposed to the forms of insecurity associated with non-standard employment, i.e. no social protection and on-going training at their own expense. However, many others, who are less qualified, face considerable insecurity on account of their lack of income security and social protection. New technology has boosted productivity and could lead to improvements in people's lives and a reduction of working time. It has improved job quality in high-performance work systems. But there is also a downside: computer technology is contributing to the emergence of trends that undermine workers' security.

Appelbaum concludes that both security and insecurity, whether real or perceived, are strongly determined by labour market institutions, hence the differences observed between industrialized countries in this respect. She also stresses that both segments of the labour market currently face insecurity. This may contribute to broadening awareness of the issues and to reviving trade union activity around issues of common interest.

In the course of the ensuing discussion, Robert Castel[5] pointed out that the process underway is more in the nature of an erosion, than of a collapse, of the regulatory system. In his view, a process of creative destruction is unfolding which could well lead to a new balance between the interests of labour and those of capital. In particular, current demographic trends and a return to full employment can be expected to change the balance of power and thereby lead to the emergence of new regulatory mechanisms.

Jean Gadrey[6] stressed the importance of distinguishing "good flexibility" from bad, and of ensuring that the latter does not crowd out the former. The public authorities can take action to that end, as some French municipalities have done with the launch of "town hours" programmes to reconcile the flexibility of private- and public-sphere activities with certain principles of community life. The authorities can also encourage negotiated management of flexibility over the long term. Gadrey also calls for the international public debate to be enriched with "indicators of labour market quality, job quality and work-related insecurities in order to monitor how they develop over time and to make reliable comparisons between different countries" (see Auer and Daniel, op. cit., pp. 42-43).

Jill Rubery[7] drew attention to what she sees as a tendency to shift or evade responsibilities: as a result of government's weakened job-creation capability and of the shifting of the responsibilities of principal employers to subcontractors, workers are increasingly having to provide for their own "employability" and social protection (care work and income security). The point of her argument is to broaden the scope of social protection to include all care work (without reproducing the old male/female division of labour), to improve social protection for contingent work and to extend social dialogue and intervention by labour market institutions beyond the narrow framework of permanent employment in large organizations.

Summing up the proceedings of this first panel discussion, Bruno Trentin[8] expressed concern over some of the consequences of flexibility for people's private lives and for relations between women and men. Moreover, flexibility can also translate into unilateral enterprise management – by creating an atmosphere of general insecurity – and labour market segmentation. In response to these unfavourable developments he proposes that workers be given more say in the organization of work, together with equal social protection regardless of the form of their contract of employment, neighbourhood services (to be developed through the re-employment of older workers), security of contract with penalties for unjustified dismissals and, lastly, a programme of public and private investments in a system of lifelong learning. For workers, such training would have to be seen as a form of remuneration in kind and, primarily, as an insurance for the future because it offers the best possible protection against insecurity.

THE IMPACT OF CHANGES ON WORK AND SOCIETY

While pondering the causes and consequences of changes in work, it seems only reasonable to attempt to measure their extent. Such was the aim of the presentation given by Raymond-Pierre Bodin.[9] This was based on research that the European Foundation for the Improvement of Living and Working Conditions had been conducting for ten years.[10] As regards numerical flexibility, the period 1990-95 witnessed considerable growth in precarious employment, followed by stabilization at about 20 per cent of total employment today. Significantly, such employment has become widely diversified with a reduction of the proportion of short-term contracts, agency work and internships and a sharp increase in the proportion of "other contracts", which are increasingly difficult to categorize. There are also wide variations across countries (see table 1) and economic sectors not only in respect of the extent of precarious employment but also in terms of its underlying trends and distribution by type. While agriculture and hotels/restaurants remain the sectors with the lowest proportions of permanent jobs (69 and 72 per cent respectively), precarious employment is on the increase in the construction sector and some services. Some variation also occurs according to the personal characteristics of workers, i.e. skill, age and sex.

National and sectoral variations also show up in temporal flexibility. While hours of work display a pattern of increasing diversification, weekly working time has been decreasing slightly. There has been a slight increase in part-time employment: people working less than 30 hours per week accounted for 16 per cent of total employment in 2000, up from 15 per cent in 1995 (see table 2). But this increase is occurring "bottom-up", and it is imposed. In other words, the increase was brought about by growth in the lowest working-time band (less than ten hours per week) and comprises a significant proportion of involuntary part-time work, with 22 per cent of part-timers wanting to work more. In some sectors, part-time work is used as a method of regulation, either in conjunction with numerical flexibility (hotels/restaurants, "other services") or on its own (wholesale and retail trade). Precarious jobs and part-time jobs accounted for 30.5 per cent of wage employment in 2000, while the proportion of full-time permanent contracts appeared to have declined by two percentage points since 1999.

Regarding the organization of work, Bodin observed a slight reduction in the use of flexible hours (evening, night or weekend work), with significant variations between countries, sectors and occupations. Besides, flexible hours and precarious employment often go together. Lastly, whichever form flexibility may take, it adversely affects women: female part-time employment is growing in the lowest working-time bands; the proportion of women in stable jobs is falling; and the number of women working on Sundays is increasing.

Bodin's study leads to the following conclusions:

- Precarious employment is affecting career paths: "rather than being 'passive' in nature, it is being 'actively' used during labour market entry, often as a recruitment filter. It seems that we can speak of 'precarious career paths'. ... This trend is borne out if we look at the breakdown by age. Massive numbers of young people '<25' are experiencing precarious employment, although all the age groups, in particular the '25-34' age group where the use of fixed-term contracts is most marked, are being affected" (see Auer and Daniel, op. cit., p. 56).

- Flexibility falls into three categories: "*individual flexibility* (United Kingdom and Ireland) based on individual relations between employers and workers, *State-driven flexibility* (France, Spain and Finland) where the legislator plays a more important role in constructing regulations, in other words working hours and, to a certain extent, the social entitlements associated with different types of employment, are regulated more by legislation than by collective bargaining and *negotiated flexibility* (Denmark, Netherlands, Germany) where actual working time is set in particular by bargaining and enterprises' quantitative adjustment strategies make only limited use of precarious jobs" (see Auer and Daniel, op. cit., p. 68).

- Though there does not appear to be much growth in the absolute numbers of workers in precarious employment, labour market segmentation seems to have set in: precarious employment now accounts for one-fifth of total wage employment, it is concentrated in specific sectors and affects some categories of workers – particularly women and young workers – more than others.

- Variations across countries highlight the important part played by labour market institutions in containing flexibilization, reducing uncertainty and preventing insecurity. One particular concern is the risk that the new forms of flexibility might be excluded from the scope of collective bargaining. Another is the possible erosion of conditions of employment.

With satisfactory levels of both male and female employment, a significant reduction of unemployment, a low proportion of precarious employment, and a well-preserved Welfare State, Sweden's performance leads Sandro Scocco [11] to raise the following questions: "Are the changes we have seen in the labour market the consequence of changes in production? Or were many changes really due to a different power relationship between employers and employees? The boring truth is that it is both" (see Auer and Daniel,

Table 1.   Precarious employment in Europe: Development levels and recent trends
by country in the year 2000 (precarious employment: fixed-term contracts,
temporary agency work, work experience, other)

Development levels (2000) (% employees)	Recent trends (1995-2000)
Countries with the highest levels of precarious employment:	*Countries where employment has become less stable:*
Spain (35%)	United Kingdom (–6%)
Portugal (24%)	Portugal (–6%)
Finland (21%)	Finland (–4%)
	Austria (–4%)
	Ireland (–3%)
Countries with the lowest levels of precarious employment:	*Countries where employment has become more stable:*
Luxembourg (10%)	France (+7%)
Germany (12%)	Spain (+6%)
Austria (14%)	Belgium (+3%)
Sweden (14%)	
Countries close to the European average:	*Countries where the structure of employment has remained unchanged:*
Ireland (18%)	Denmark
Denmark (18%)	Italy
Netherlands (18%)	Netherlands
United Kingdom (16%)	
France (16%)	

Source: Raymond-Pierre Bodin: "Wide-ranging forms of employment in Europe: Review and challenges for the
players", in Auer and Daniel, op. cit., p. 55.

op. cit., p. 71). In venturing this answer, Scocco concurs with Robert Castel's
conclusion (see above) as to the consequences for that power relationship of
population trends and the return to full employment.

Philippe Lemoine [12] draws attention to the far-reaching implications of
technological changes and the computerization of exchanges – both commercial and non-commercial – which followed that of production and, more
recently, management. Also significant in this respect is the transition from
mass production and consumerism to the belief that service companies need
to organize themselves around their clients: "There are many positive sides
to thinking that the client is king, but I am not convinced that the client has
to be king for all levels of the company, provided that the image of the client
is the same. It is certainly essential that various types of players have their
own ideas about what the client is" (see Auer and Daniel, op. cit., p. 78).

Sabine Erbès-Seguin [13] stresses the key parts played, first, by the institutional framework in maintaining high standards of security and social protection and, second, by the proliferation of different types of flexibility as a

314

Table 2. Part-time work in Europe: Development levels and recent trends by country, in the year 2000 (part time: "less than 30 working hours per week")

Development levels (2000) (% employees and self-employed)	Recent trends (1995-2000)
Countries with the highest levels of part-time work:	*Countries with the highest increase in part-time work:*
Netherlands (30%)	Netherlands (+7%)
United Kingdom (21%)	Ireland (+7%)
Belgium (18%)	Austria (+4%)
Germany (17%)	Belgium (+4%)
	France (+3%)
	Italy (+3%)
Countries with the lowest levels of part-time work:	*Countries where part-time work is declining:*
Portugal (9%)	United Kingdom (–2%)
Finland (9%)	Sweden (–2%)
Sweden (11%)	
Spain (11%)	
Countries close to the European average:	*Countries where there has been little change in part-time work:*
Ireland (15%)	Denmark
France (14%)	Portugal
Italy (14%)	Finland
Austria (14%)	Greece

Source: Raymond-Pierre Bodin: "Wide-ranging forms of employment in Europe: Review and challenges for the players", in Auer and Daniel, op. cit., p. 61.

determinant of workers' heightened sense of insecurity, which is not necessarily related in any direct way to actual insecurity of employment.

THE POLITICAL RESPONSE TO THE NEW CHALLENGES [14]

According to Fritz Scharpf,[15] globalization leads to a decrease in employment in internationally exposed sectors of the economy. As a result, the Welfare State can survive only if it manages to increase employment in sheltered sectors of the economy. In Europe, Scharpf identifies two successful models for coping with this problem. The first is that of the United Kingdom, which is characterized by low taxes and a market approach to social services. In the United Kingdom, low public spending on social services goes hand in hand with a transfer of previously "non-market activities" to the market economy (family work, childcare, public education, public infrastructure). In particular, this is reflected in the high rate of female labour market participation. The second successful model is that of the Scandinavian countries, which is based on high taxes and high social spending, generating equally high employment rates. Continental Europe is in the worst possible position, with an approach that lies somewhere in between the above two models. In Scharpf's view, continental European States need to choose either one of these approaches. Since the Scandinavian model would imply higher taxes, it does not command sufficient political support. The only path these countries can follow in order to increase their employment rates would therefore consist in adopting the United Kingdom's approach of reducing taxes and public spending.

From the ensuing discussion, however, the situation in practice appeared to be less clear-cut than Scharpf suggests. While a comprehensive and all-pervasive Welfare State is not an adequate response to the challenges currently confronting continental Europe, the United Kingdom's model of low taxes and low public spending also has some serious drawbacks, not only for social cohesion but also for the competitiveness of exposed economic sectors. The transfer of public-sector activities to the private sector does not automatically solve the problems of the Welfare State. Besides, overly radical cuts in public spending can have adverse economic effects on the competitiveness of the private sector, which needs an efficient administrative and logistic infrastructure as well as a highly productive workforce.

As regards the effects of the European Union, Scharpf draws attention to the risk of inconsistencies between the common monetary policy and the diversity of national economic situations, with the possibility that the policies of individual Member States may lead to job loss. Maurizio Ferrera[16] also criticizes the fact that the European Union's law on competition hinders regional policy via state aid or differentiated social security contributions. A way has to be found to strike a better balance between the European Union's competition policy and the need to promote economic development in poor regions of the Union.

Bernard Gazier[17] points out that the different levels and modes of labour market regulation are undergoing a process of readjustment and redefinition. This refers to the question of legislation versus collective bargaining, enterprise versus sectoral/regional levels, etc. New modes of regulation are also emerging in some countries, e.g. national pacts for employment and competitiveness, which supplement legislation and help to build up the necessary consensus for reforming social protection systems. Globalization has increased the importance of regional and global regulation, as has become clear from the debates around the liberalization of world trade and the role of the ILO in that context.

Concerning the emergence of new actors for employment regulation, several contributors to the discussion raised the issue of nongovernmental organizations as partners in collective bargaining. However, this poses the problem of the binding nature of collective agreements: under an agreement that regulates working conditions, the actors must be able to deliver what they have agreed upon, and this is only possible for the parties to contracts of employment, i.e. workers and employers. Lastly, with the increasing diversity, discontinuity and dispersal of the professional careers of individuals, labour market regulation needs to facilitate smooth transitions between different activities in the labour market, e.g. from education to employment, from one job to another, from wage employment to self-employment and vice versa, or from unemployment back into employment.

Christian Baudelot's [18] focus is on the educational system. In his view, the educational system – particularly in France – is too concerned with general education and fails to prepare young people adequately for working life by providing them with vocational skills. In meeting the challenges of globalization, the State therefore needs to improve the link between the educational system and the labour market. However, the information society is characterized by the fact that vocational skills become obsolete more and more rapidly and have to be updated through a process of lifelong learning. From this perspective, general education is an important foundation because it should teach young people how to learn and acquire new skills throughout their working lives.

Hornung-Draus concludes her overview of the discussion with the following comment: "we are probably experiencing a change in paradigms. ... [T]he political responses in the 1990s were dominated by deregulation, privatization, tax cuts linked with the reduction of public spending and more specifically of social spending. There is increasing awareness today of the importance of good public infrastructure (education, transport, communication, administration) – which requires public spending – for the international competitiveness of companies. Furthermore, there is an increasing awareness of the importance of social cohesion and hence social spending for the sustainability of the international competitiveness of Europe" (see Auer and Daniel, op. cit., p. 112).

METHODS, ACTORS AND LEVELS OF NEW POLITICAL REGULATIONS

Alain Supiot [19] launched the discussion on "which new forms of regulation might be introduced in response to the current changes in employment and work" (see Auer and Daniel, op. cit., p. 115). The first question, however, is to define what is meant by "regulation".

The meaning of regulation

From the legal point of view, regulation appears to be an attempt to combine two types of rule: legal rules – which draw their strength from a shared belief in the values they are meant to express – and technical rules, which draw their strength from scientific knowledge of the facts they are meant to represent. Yet it would be both dangerous and unrealistic to believe that the knowledge of experts will ever be able to rule out political disputes and con-flicts of interest and would, as it were, rise above the old opposition of State and market. "The sphere of belief is the sphere of what is qualitative and unprovable; it was largely dealt with by laws, public consultation and the State. The sphere of calculation, of what is quantitative, was dealt with by contracts, negotiation and the market. ... It is only when the State takes charge of the incalculable aspects of human life that the market may be viewed as a self-regulation mechanism ... State and market, law and contract thus become inseparably linked" (see Auer and Daniel, op. cit., p. 117). On this basis, regulation can be understood in a more reassuring sense: bargain-ing and contract, on the one hand, and the regulatory authorities, on the other, are both called upon to address issues that extend beyond the limits of the State's cognitive abilities. The regulatory authority thus acts as a new sort of magistrate or judge, taking decisions by referring both to knowledge of the facts and to value judgements. In other words, regulation certainly does not mean the disappearance of the "third party" which characterizes what is known as "the law" in the West.

"Since States are no longer able to define or impose the imperative of 'decent work', it must be expressed through other institutional channels, par-ticularly at international level. Redefined in this way, the concept of regula-tion provides a suitable framework for tackling the problems currently facing labour law. This law incorporates 'regulatory' mechanisms for transforming relationships based on strength into legal relationships. By allowing workers representation and collective action it acknowledges that they are genuinely entitled to challenge the law; on the other hand, it channels these collective forces to promote the ongoing development of the law. These mechanisms are what we now call 'social dialogue', which actually refers to a wide range of instruments for confronting employers' and workers' interests: rights to information, to consultation, to strike, to be represented, to negotiate ..." (see Auer and Daniel, op. cit., p. 118).

No regulation without a regulator

The State is growing weaker. This is especially true of the Welfare State that serves people's well-being through public services and protections attaching to wage employment. And it applies both to the international level, where the law of competition (neo-liberalism) rules, and to the national level, where solidarity and security needs are addressed through negotiation with the representatives of different interest groups (neo-corporatism). "How-ever, it is unlikely that the space vacated by the retreat of the State will stay empty for long. The myth expounded in the west that society is being ground down to a dust made up of rational individuals maximizing their interests ignores the basics of anthropology" (see Auer and Daniel, op. cit., p. 121) – as reflected in the surge of demands articulated around religious, ethnic or regional identities. "This is why we need to ask what the new foundations for regulation might be in an economy and a world which are open to trade" (ibid., p. 122).

The social and the economic. With the opening up of frontiers, national solidarities operating within States are becoming subordinate to the principles of free competition upon which the international markets are founded. The old distinction between public and private is thus overtaken by the distinction between economic rights ("rights of ...") and social rights ("rights to ..."). But this distinction is purely ideological: any legal relationship necessarily embodies both an economic dimension and a social dimension. One must therefore be careful to distinguish between the scientific value of the distinction – which is zero – and its value as a dogma, which is considerable. "This distinction underlies the legal structures which have come about as a result of globalized markets. ... EU law shows that the consideration of social rights can counterbalance the rules of free competition, not only nationally but at a supranational level too. This is an extremely interesting way of building an international social order which will act as a counterweight to the economic order" (see Auer and Daniel, op. cit., p. 124).

Principles and procedure. Another distinction – that between law and contract – is also becoming blurred. Here, principles need to be distinguished from procedure. There are two levels of legislation corresponding to two main types of rule: on the one hand, the law, which is deliberate and unilateral, reflecting the public interest, and on the other, the contract, which is negotiated, bilateral and reflects individual interests. The globalization of the market economy is believed to lead inescapably to enlargement of the province of contract to the detriment of imperative law. But the situation is not that straightforward. Indeed, what is happening is more in the nature of a change affecting both contract and law. While the law is admittedly relinquishing the job of ruling on substance, it is concentrating instead on upholding principles and laying down procedures. And these procedures pass on to contracts the burden of the qualitative issues being offloaded by the law. Thus the State is both withdrawing, disengaging from the management of social matters, and reaffirming, restoring its role as the guardian of common assets. Within the European Union, an example of this type of regulation is Council Directive 94/45/EC of 22 September 1994 on the establishment of a European Works Council or a procedure in Community-scale undertakings and Community-scale groups of undertakings for the purposes of informing and consulting employees. "At international level the ILO did something similar, adopting in 1998 a Declaration on Fundamental Principles and Rights at Work which requires all member States to respect, to promote and to realize these principles in good faith" (see Auer and Daniel, op. cit., p. 126).

Power and authority. Whereas the State used to combine power and authority in the face of market forces, these two attributes now need to be dissociated. The opening up of markets has been accompanied by a proliferation of national, regional and international regulatory authorities. These lie beyond the reach of state control. Their powers are as diverse as the areas they cover, but they have two features in common: they draw their legitimacy from the scientific or technical expertise of their members and they are held to be independent of both government and private operators. Being responsible for markets, however, these authorities do not see it as their job to address the social dimension of the problems they deal with. This means that there is no one to authorize States to invoke social considerations as a way of limiting the effects of competition law. It thus leads to decisions which can, at a single stroke, destroy the livelihood of entire societies, most notably the poorest. There are two ways of escaping such follies. The first would be to "de-specialize" regulatory authorities and enable them to take equal account of the economic and social aspects of such issues as they are required to rule upon. The other would be to set up authorities with special responsibility for regulating the social dimension of markets. "These authorities could rule on disputes where a State or a trade union believed that the application of competition law infringed fundamental social principles or, conversely, cases in which a State or a company thought that specific social legislation constituted an unfair barrier to free trade. There might also be a role for them in regulating the forces operating within the labour market and ensuring that a proper balance was maintained between those forces" (see Auer and Daniel, op. cit., p. 129).

No regulation without a balance of forces

As a result of new corporate structures, changes in the organization of work, opening up to international competition, and the new rules of corporate governance, Supiot argues that: "The balance of forces between the economic action of companies and the collective action of workers, which is necessary for 'social regulation', is thus disrupted, and it is social regulation which loses out. One of the great tasks facing labour lawyers in years to come will be to invent ways of restoring that balance, many possibilities for which are already available in practice" (see Auer and Daniel, op. cit., p. 133).

The whole complex of law governing collective labour relations needs to be reconsidered with a view to adapting it to the new forms of corporate organization and their new dimensions (international centres, company networks, groups, trades, etc.) and to the diversification of types of employment (contract work and other types of atypical work). The same goes for systems of trade union representation: "we would have to extend the scope for action and collective representation to areas currently out-of-bounds to them ... Two types of method can be employed here. The first involves using the new freedoms inherent in globalization: the freedom of choice enjoyed by consumers and investors and freedom of information offer ways to influence the social policy of business-owners. The second involves the reverse: restraining global competition law by emphasizing the distinction between the economic and social fields and by strengthening the authority of institutions concerned with social issues" (see Auer and Daniel, op. cit., p. 134). Here, Supiot suggests a number of leads that could be followed: workers' representatives should be given access to the information technology networks of enterprises; relations should be established between the workers of subcontractors and those of the contracting company; trade union organizations should be given the right to provide social and environmental information to the public; the right to boycott should be recognized and incorporated into international legislation. Some corporations have issued "codes of conduct and social labels, the effectiveness and sincerity of which are open to question in the absence of reliable certification procedures covering their content and application" (see Auer and Daniel, op. cit., p. 136). In order to avoid the wide range of possible manipulations, two conditions must be met: the first is the establishment at international level of proper social regulation authorities which would guarantee the validity of the information disseminated; the second is to give trade unions and consumers' associations the financial resources to provide social information for the public. Lastly, the ability of States to take measures restricting freedom of competition on social grounds presupposes "the involvement of social regulation authorities able to ensure that such measures are likely to promote the equalization of working conditions throughout the world and do not serve to protect the richest countries which would prefer to close their borders to both workers and products from the poorest countries. ... Such an authority could be called on to intervene, either directly or by way of a complaint to the market economic authorities (for example the WTO's Dispute Settlement Body)" (see Auer and Daniel, op. cit., p. 136).

In the course of the ensuing debate, Hans Borstlap[20] considered that the problems confronting Europe stem not from flexibility and globalization, but from the inability to adapt European social policies to these new challenges. Strong public regulations at the international level are definitely needed, but the commitment to social policy must also be renewed through an investment programme and public regulation. In addition to the equalization of rights as between full-time and part-time workers, another of Borstlap's recommendations – proceeding from the assumption that workers' security depends on training and skills – is to make lifelong learning a legal obligation along the lines of what was done with education about a century ago.

Danielle Kaisergruber[21] took the view that the demand for flexibility is not being pressed by employers alone, for each and every individual is all at once a worker, a user, a consumer, an Internet user. The type of regulation that is needed therefore has to display the following five characteristics: regulations and social negotiations should be at grass-roots level; they should be made consistent with changes in the size and structure of enterprises through decentralization and the adjustment of trade union organization; they should be grounded in negotiation rather than in the law; they should involve new players (such as subcontractors and local-level government); and they should spell out the procedures to be followed by workers in transit between one status and another in order to secure their working life trajectories rather than their particular situation at a given point in time.

Taking the example of Silicon Valley, Amy B. Dean[22] spelled out the features that make the new economy different from the old, namely:

- internationalization and regional concentrations;

- corporate restructuring through networking and externalization of non-core activities;

- changing notions of justice in society;

- changes in the pace of work and of the renewal of skills;

- primacy of intellectual capital;

- an "hour glass" profile of job distribution, with many high-skilled and low-skilled jobs, but few intermediate jobs.

This requires trade union organizations to refocus their role as labour market institutions in order to take an active part in coordination between small and medium-sized enterprises, between the various players involved in training, during workers' transitions between jobs, and between labour supply and demand. At the political and social levels, Dean argues, the challenge to labour in the United States is to press for an overhaul of labour law to remove legal impediments to labour's capacity to organize. She also argues the case for regional-level regulations suited to the needs of the new economy, adding: "I am not of the belief that there will be some international regulatory order, nor some international regulatory body of law any time soon. However, the idea of the hybrid approach [of marrying contractual obligations so that you create a parity of power between interests and make this a condition of our trade agreements ...] is not only politically viable but also consistent" (see Auer and Daniel, op. cit., p. 148).

Summing up the proceedings of the fourth panel discussion, Allan Larsson[23] concludes that everything has changed in the world of work and that both institutions and working life need to follow suit. The debate as to whether trade unions should adjust to change, resist it or seize the initiative is under way; yet a number of points need to be stressed. In particular, this applies to the necessity of solidarity between the more successful workers and those at risk of becoming marginalized. New rights need to be recognized in order to reconcile flexibility and security, such as the right to lifelong learning. The ILO, for its part, should, at the substantive level, focus on the quality of work and, from the point of view of method, develop guidelines and benchmarks in addition to setting minimum standards.

ADDITIONAL PERSPECTIVES

Aside from the exchanges held during the panel discussions, two keynote speakers were invited to share their visions of the future of work.

Working to live or living to work?

These are the two visions of society contrasted by Richard B. Freeman.[24] The live-to-work vision has four distinctive characteristics: everyone works; there is limited social protection; there is great inequality; and trade unions are weak. At best, this is the world of shared capitalism. At its worst, it is "an insecure rat race". Conversely, the characteristics of the work-to-live vision are: limited hours of work; extensive social protection; long periods of joblessness; and powerful trade unions. "At its best, this is a world where security generates risk-taking and where leisure generates stronger families, limited hours produce deep insights and labour-saving innovation. At its worst, this is a world where the employed guard their positions against newcomers, which makes entrepreneurship costly, and where the young remain in their parents' homes for years while they wait for the good job" (see Auer and Daniel, op. cit., p. 156).

The two visions reflect the positions of the United States and of continental Europe, respectively. The paradox, according to Freeman, is that the live-to-work model offers the best prospects for attaining full employment, whereas the work-to-live model is the one that works best in conditions of full employment and at times of economic difficulty. Moreover, the two models generate equivalent hourly productivity. And the fact that the United States and Scandinavia are in the forefront of the Internet economy suggests that either model can lead the modern technological revolution.

The role of consumers and producers in the promotion of fair labour standards

Eddy Laurijssen[25] challenges the logic of the distinction typically drawn between consumers and producers, because better wages lead to higher consumption and, consequently, increased need for production. In a global economy, however, this virtuous circle cannot be achieved when governments gear all their efforts towards export maximization by depressing wages and curbing workers' rights. Laurijssen is confident nonetheless: "It is said that markets know the price of everything, but the value of nothing. The same cannot be said of the modern consumer. … The growing awareness by consumers of the effect of their purchases on conditions of workers as well as the dangers of products and their consequences for the environment does not just exercise itself in the market. Consumers are also workers and the public. They are helping to restrain the excesses of free market dogma" (see Auer and Daniel, op. cit., p. 160). Discarding the assumption of short-term maximization of profits as a primary objective of companies and their shareholders, one can increasingly observe that there exists a common cause, a convergence of the interests of consumers with those of producers. Unfortunately, what is actually happening is a trend towards shifting risk onto individual workers, away from enterprises and society as a whole. At worst, Laurijssen deplores, flexible employment "may mean that people are thrown on the social scrap heap" when they are no longer needed (see Auer and Daniel, op. cit., p. 161). It is therefore important to remember that labour law recognizes the unequal power of the parties to an employment relationship: social protection in the context of atypical work requires more, not less, solidarity, in the same way as the global economy and demographic pressures mean more, not less, international solidarity. In particular, the global economy requires global social dialogue: "The challenge for the ILO itself as well as for the social partners is: How can social dialogue rooted in respect for freedom of association and collective bargaining be expanded in ILO member countries?" (see Auer and Daniel, op. cit., p. 162).

CONCLUDING REMARKS

In spite of the variety of topics addressed, views expressed and approaches taken by participants, there are a number of major issues and proposals that cut across the discussions. These are presented in this concluding section, together with excerpts from the closing remarks of Juan Somavia, the Director-General of the ILO.[26]

Perceived insecurity versus real insecurity. "Whatever conclusion you draw from the discussion we had, whether jobs are truly becoming more or less precarious, the fact is that uncertainty is growing. On that we are broadly in agreement. There is for some reason a sense of unease – I may have a sure job today but will I have it tomorrow? We have to deepen the understanding of that. I think that people are not afraid of change, they are afraid of uncertainty" (see Auer and Daniel, op. cit., p. 165).

Labour market segmentation. Conditions of employment do not appear to be deteriorating in a general sense. Nor is the share of wage employment shrinking. Yet the status of such employment and the protection it affords are substandard for a significant, albeit stable, proportion of workers. "We were told yesterday that there has not been much change in the proportion of precarious jobs, but 20-30 per cent of precarious jobs in a developed society is not something to be proud about" (see Auer and Daniel, op. cit., p. 167). Accordingly, almost all of the participants call for equal rights and social protection to be extended to all types of employment. It must indeed be remembered that the current segmentation affects some categories of workers more than others, such as young workers, women and the least skilled. Moreover, atypical employment is associated – and this may be the explanation – with a transfer of certain costs or certain risks to the worker. Some contingent workers, for example, have to pay for their own unemployment, sickness or old-age insurance.

Transferring responsibilities and risks to the worker. As has just been pointed out, there is a tendency now to shift certain risks and certain responsibilities away from the enterprise or society to the worker. One example relates to the concept of employability: "[T]here is a tendency to say, look, if you do not have a decent job it is your fault, you are inadequate, you are not adapted, you are unfit, you are incompetent, it is your problem. ... We came back to the notion of personal responsibility which somehow had been lost. We came back to the idea that in the end we do have a responsibility for our own reality and for our own life and it is up to us to be able to cope with many of the issues that we face. I think that up to a point this has been a positive evolution. But it can go too far, and some people end up arguing that institutions and policies are not that important, only individual responsibility counts. We have to re-establish the balance between the spaces of personal responsibilities and the spaces of institutional needs. I think we discussed this issue here very well" (see Auer and Daniel, op. cit., p. 168). One of the issues this raises is whether this transfer is the hallmark of a more individualistic society or the result of a shift in the balance of power that governs bargaining over conditions of employment.

Changes driven by production or by power relations. As pointed out above, changes in conditions of employment are probably both dictated by the needs of globalized production and driven by a change in power relations. It would be interesting – particularly for the purposes of social policy – to distinguish the respective effects of these two factors. Population trends together with a return to full employment – where applicable – will no doubt make a difference. A further determinant will be the ability of trade unions to adjust their systems of representation to new corporate structures and to the wide variety of workers' employment situations. Even so, as Supiot points out, some of the "rules of the game" will need to be adapted, whether at the national, European or global level. This is a matter of political will: "We tend to say that economic changes are irreversible and the only possibility that we have is to adapt to them. I would say to that, yes and no. Yes, open economies are better than closed economies, yes, open societies are better than closed societies, yes, the information and communication technology revolution is irreversible. But policies can be changed, whether they are macroeconomic policies, trade policies, development policies, financial policies. Policies are not biological phenomena. They are made by people and institutions and they can be changed. You need a double adaptation. An adaptation of people and institutions to the reality of the changes but also an adaptation of the process of change to the needs of people" (see Auer and Daniel, op. cit., p. 166). Regarding the issues of political will, the transfer of responsibility (employability), and of reconciling flexibility and security, particular consideration deserves to be given to Hans Borstalp's proposal to make lifelong learning a legal obligation modelled on the legislation of compulsory education last century.

The ILO: The global authority on social issues. Here again, with only one exception, all participants concurred on the idea that the world needs a body – an authority – that regulates social matters. As the economy goes global, existing social-policy instruments – as embodied in international labour standards – appear to lack supporting authority, if not legitimacy. As Somavia points out: "I think that we fit into the legitimacy sphere rather than the power sphere" (see Auer and Daniel, op. cit., p. 169). Yet every single participant recognized that the ILO should be that international social authority, also suggesting that its standard-setting and supervisory work should be supplemented by such mechanisms as may be needed to redress the balance of power, to gain knowledge of the conditions prevailing in the world of work, and to evaluate "decent work". The two proposals made along these lines warrant special attention, namely, the development of qualitative indicators of work and the establishment of a certification system covering conditions of work and employment in enterprises upholding a code of conduct. On this point, it is worth mentioning that a number of agreements have already been signed under the auspices of the ILO between multinational corporations and international trade secretariats on the protection of fundamental rights at work.

Notes

[1] For an account of the proceedings of the second symposium, held at Lyons on 17-18 January 2002, see *International Labour Review* (Geneva), Vol. 141 (2002), No. 3, pp. 275-290.

[2] See the preparatory *Background document* for the round of discussions at: http://mirror/public/english/bureau/inst/papers/confrnce/annecy2001/back.htm.

[3] For a full record of proceedings, see Peter Auer and Christine Daniel (eds.): *The future of work, employment and social protection: The search for new securities in a world of growing uncertainties.* Geneva, ILO, 2002. All of the quotations in this "Perspective" are taken from this source (hereinafter referenced "Auer and Daniel, op. cit.").

[4] Director of Research, Economic Policy Institute, Washington, DC (see "Transformation of work and employment and new insecurities", in Auer and Daniel, op. cit., pp. 17-44).

[5] Centre d'études des mouvements sociaux, Paris (see "Erosion rather than collapse of the regulatory system", in Auer and Daniel, op. cit., pp. 39-40).

[6] Faculté des Sciences économiques et sociales, Université de Lille I, France (see "The rights and wrongs of labour flexibility", in Auer and Daniel, op. cit., pp. 41-43).

[7] Manchester School of Management, UMIST, Manchester (see "Shifting of risks and responsibilities in labour markets", in Auer and Daniel, op. cit., pp. 45-46).

[8] Member of the European Parliament, Rome (see "Rebalancing the employment relationship", in Auer and Daniel, op. cit., pp. 47-49).

[9] Director, European Foundation for the Improvement of Living and Working Conditions, Dublin (see "Wide-ranging forms of work and employment in Europe: Review and challenges for the players", in Auer and Daniel, op. cit., pp. 61-78).

[10] The findings presented by Bodin were primarily those of the third European survey of working conditions carried out in the spring of 2000 on the basis of a representative sample of the working population consisting of 1,500 people per country (500 for Luxembourg) for each of the Member States of the European Union (face-to-face questionnaires).

[11] Economist, Swedish Confederation of Trade Unions (LO), Stockholm (see "The Swedish paradox", in Auer and Daniel, op. cit., pp. 71-73).

[12] Co-chairperson of the board of the "Galeries Lafayette" group, Paris ("The links between technical progress, employment and work", in Auer and Daniel, op. cit., pp. 75-78).

[13] Director of Research, Centre national de la recherche scientifique, Paris (see "Impact of transformations on work and society", in Auer and Daniel, op. cit., pp. 79-80).

[14] The summary of the proceedings of this third panel discussion is largely based on the overview presented by Renate Hornung-Draus, Director for European and International Affairs, Confederation of Employers' Associations of Germany (BDA), Berlin (see "The political response to the new challenges: Raising the issues", in Auer and Daniel, op. cit., pp. 109-112).

[15] Director, Max Planck Institute for the Study of Societies, Cologne (see "New challenges and political responses", in Auer and Daniel, op. cit., pp. 83-98).

[16] Professor, Poleis, Luigi Bocconi University, Milan (see "The south of the South", in Auer and Daniel, op. cit., pp. 99-100).

[17] Professor, Maison des sciences économiques, University of Paris I (see "New approaches to negotiation", in Auer and Daniel, op. cit., pp. 101-103).

[18] Department of Social Sciences, École normale supérieure, Paris (see "Using education to tackle unemployment, and its limits", in Auer and Daniel, op. cit., pp. 105-107).

[19] Professor, University of Nantes, Maison des Sciences de l'Homme Ange-Guépin, Nantes (see "Towards an international social order? Preliminary observations on the 'new regulations' in work, employment and social protection", in Auer and Daniel, op. cit., pp. 115-138).

[20] Director General for Strategy and the Labour Market, Ministry of Education, Culture and Science, the Netherlands (see "The threats to job security", in Auer and Daniel, op. cit., pp. 139-141).

[21] President, Bernard Brunhes Consultants, Paris (see "New regulation", in Auer and Daniel, op. cit., pp. 143-144).

[22] President, South Bay AFL-CIO, San Jose, CA (see "The view from Silicon Valley", in Auer and Daniel, op. cit., pp. 145-148).

[23] President, Swedish Television Corporation, Soltsjö-boo (see "Social institutions for change and security", in Auer and Daniel, op. cit., pp. 149-152).

[24] University of Harvard/National Bureau of Economic Research, Cambridge, MA (see "Working to live or living to work?", in Auer and Daniel, op. cit., pp. 155-157).

[25] International Confederation of Free Trade Unions (ICFTU), Brussels (see "Consumers and producers – Their role in the promotion of fair labour standards", in Auer and Daniel, op. cit., pp. 159-162).

[26] See "closing remarks", in Auer and Daniel, op. cit., pp. 163-171, the source of all the quotations given in this concluding section.

GOOD JOBS, BAD JOBS: WORKERS' EVALUATIONS IN FIVE COUNTRIES

13

Joseph A. RITTER* and Richard ANKER**

How good or bad is a particular job? How good or bad is my own job? These are questions that everyone has asked or been asked. They are important questions, because they go to the heart of the issues of job quality and personal welfare.

One direct way to evaluate the extent to which jobs are good or bad is to rely on the opinions of workers by asking them about their own job satisfaction. Understanding job quality is indeed important for several reasons. First, careful evaluation of labour market policies requires that account be taken of their effects on all aspects of employment, not merely wages and employment levels. In this respect, the value of job satisfaction data stems from the existence of subjective, but important, aspects of the employment relationship, coupled with the near impossibility of measuring all the objective characteristics of a job. And even if measurement difficulties could be overcome, measurements of each characteristic would then need to be combined in order to create what economists call a utility index. In constructing such an index, job satisfaction data allow the job incumbent's personal values to be used instead of those of the policy-maker or researcher. In short, no simple, externally imposed taxonomy of "good jobs" and "bad jobs" is likely to capture what is obvious to labour market participants about their own jobs.

Second, although a number of large-scale surveys have included questions about job satisfaction,[1] there has been relatively little systematic exploration of cross-sectional variation in job satisfaction within large socio-economic groups (as distinct from employees of a specific organization or group of organizations).[2] As a result, the meaning of high, low, or changing levels of job satisfaction in larger socio-economic groups is not yet well understood. Not only has existing research in this field focused predominantly on

Originally published in *International Labour Review*, Vol. 141 (2002), No. 4.

* International Labour Organization and University of Minnesota. ** International Labour Organization. The authors are grateful to María Mercedes Jeria Cáceres and Deborah Levison for helpful comments and discussions.

industrialized economies, but none of it has tried to determine how relationships between job satisfaction and its covariates compare across dissimilar national labour markets.

Third, job satisfaction has been shown to be an important predictor of quits and other objective outcomes (Freeman, 1978; Akerlof and Dickens, 1982; Akerlof, Rose and Yellen, 1988; Clark, 2001). In this respect, job satisfaction can be viewed as an important organizational indicator. Seashore (1974) and Clark (1998) argue that job satisfaction can be viewed as an important output or outcome of organization and labour markets – a direct measure of well-being. Keon and McDonald (1982) found a two-way relationship between job satisfaction and life satisfaction. In other words, job satisfaction is both an organizational indicator and a social indicator.

This article examines job satisfaction data collected by the People's Security Surveys (PSSs) of the ILO in five countries. Its objectives are to evaluate (1) the determinants of job satisfaction in each country, (2) the extent to which similar patterns appear within each country, and (3) whether those patterns support the use of job satisfaction data as an indicator of job quality. Following a background section presenting the study data and analytical framework, the second section of the article relates measured job satisfaction to other information from the surveys to determine whether observed patterns integrate sensibly with economics and psychology in a specific national context. The findings are confirmed by regression analysis in the third section, and a final section offers some concluding remarks.

DATA AND FRAMEWORK

Before beginning our analysis, it is important to note some limitations to the use of job satisfaction information. Job satisfaction data complement objective information on wages, hours, and so forth, but may sometimes produce evaluations of job quality which – from the researcher's point of view – appear to be at variance with the objective facts. The main reason is that respondents answer job satisfaction questions from their own frames of reference. The respondents' use of frames of reference is part of the purpose of examining job satisfaction data and part of what we set out to analyse. Nevertheless, it is important to keep in mind that these frames vary in ways which we do not pretend to understand or measure.

Job satisfaction data

The data for this study are drawn from the PSSs conducted in Argentina, Brazil, Chile, Hungary and Ukraine during 2000 and 2001. The surveys differ somewhat in coverage, as shown in table 1.[3]

All five surveys used a sequence of questions that invited the respondent's evaluation of her or his job satisfaction on six dimensions: pay, non-

Table 1. Scope of selected People's Security Surveys

	Overall sample size	Target population	Geographic coverage
Argentina	2 920	Ages 15-64	Metropolitan Buenos Aires, Cordoba, Rosario
Brazil	4 000	Ages 15-64	Metropolitan Rio de Janeiro, São Paulo, Recife
Chile	1 188	Ages 15-64	Metropolitan Santiago, Concepción, Valparaíso
Hungary	1 000	Ages 18-60	National
Ukraine	8 099	Individuals on official registers*	National

*Individuals on official registers of employees in the industrial sector, service sector, public budgetary sphere, agricultural sector; unemployed workers; students; and pensioners. Self-employed were excluded from the sampling frame.

wage benefits, nature of work, autonomy or independence, opportunities for promotion, and opportunities for skill upgrading. In each case, responses were gathered on a five-point scale ranging from "very dissatisfied" to "very satisfied".[4] The distributions of responses are shown in figure 1.[5] Means are shown in table 2. Job satisfaction tends to be higher in the three Latin American countries than in the two transition economy countries. This is partly related to the fact that the Latin American samples were entirely urban; the means for urban respondents in Hungary and Ukraine were 0.24 and 0.31 higher than the overall means. Chile displays the highest level of job satisfaction and Ukraine the lowest. Among the six aspects of job satisfaction, respondents in all five countries tended to be the most satisfied with the nature of their work and least satisfied with their pay and benefits.

This article analyses the *total job satisfaction score* obtained by summing the six job-satisfaction scores in order to produce a total score between 6 and 30 (see figure 2). This procedure is commonly followed where multiple job-satisfaction indicators are available, though the total score is subject to more than one interpretation. The simplest interpretation is that the total job-satisfaction score offers a measure of overall job satisfaction.[6]

However, the analysis offered in this article is based on a somewhat more complex interpretation. The six job-satisfaction scores tend to move up and down together, and this tendency can be quantified using factor analysis. A factor analysis performed on the six specific job-satisfaction scores produces the same result for all five countries: an individual who reports being highly satisfied with pay also tends to report high satisfaction with the degree of autonomy, and so on. In statistical terms, we found a single dominant factor, and this estimated factor has roughly the same positive relationship to the six specific job-satisfaction scores in all five countries.[7] The correlation of this factor with the total job-satisfaction score exceeds 0.99 for every analysis reported in this article.

Figure 1. Job satisfaction scores (employees)

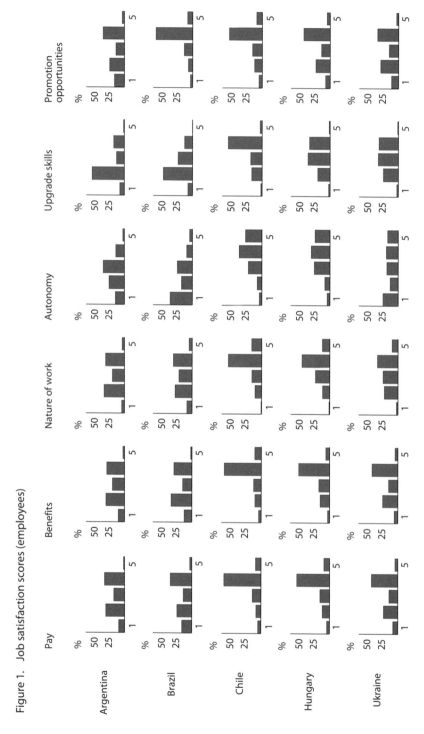

Table 2. Job satisfaction scores (employees)

	Argentina	Brazil	Chile	Hungary	Ukraine
Wages					
Mean	2.9	2.8	3.0	2.6	2.5
Satisfied, very satisfied (%)	37.9	34.6	39.0	19.3	19.6
Unsatisfied, very unsatisfied (%)	41.7	43.6	35.8	42.7	66.9
Benefits					
Mean	2.9	2.8	3.0	2.3	2.5
Satisfied, very satisfied (%)	41.8	35.0	40.0	16.3	15.1
Unsatisfied, very unsatisfied (%)	42.9	48.9	34.2	57.9	60.0
Nature of work					
Mean	3.6	3.7	3.7	3.8	3.4
Satisfied, very satisfied (%)	71.7	73.4	70.6	66.2	62.1
Unsatisfied, very unsatisfied (%)	13.2	13.8	11.9	10.8	18.8
Autonomy					
Mean	3.5	3.4	3.6	3.7	3.1
Satisfied, very satisfied (%)	64.9	60.7	60.8	58.7	38.3
Unsatisfied, very unsatisfied (%)	18.0	20.3	14.7	14.0	24.2
Opportunities to upgrade skills					
Mean	3.1	3.2	3.3	2.9	3.1
Satisfied, very satisfied (%)	50.6	50.6	48.5	39.6	37.0
Unsatisfied, very unsatisfied (%)	33.9	32.8	26.5	40.1	28.4
Promotion opportunities					
Mean	2.9	2.8	3.2	2.7	2.8
Satisfied, very satisfied (%)	39.9	35.1	43.2	30.4	22.6
Unsatisfied, very unsatisfied (%)	43.5	46.9	32.0	41.0	35.7
Total job satisfaction score[a]					
Mean	18.8	18.6	19.8	18.0	17.4
Standard deviation	5.0	4.5	5.8	5.0	4.1
24 or higher (%)	15.2	14.4	25.2	11.3	6.9
12 or lower (%)	8.7	9.8	6.2	11.7	10.9
25th percentile	16	16	17	14	15
Median	19	19	20	18	18
75th percentile	22	22	24	22	20
Observations	781	1 458	433	437	5 731

[a]Sum of six scores above.

Figure 2. Distribution of total job satisfaction scores

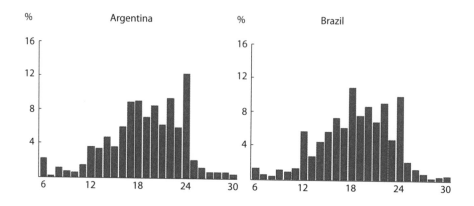

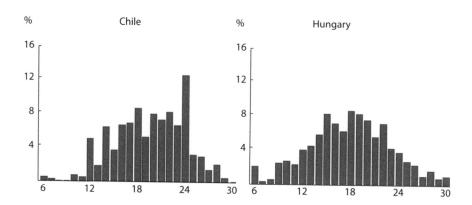

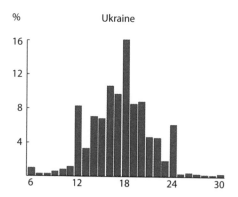

An economic interpretation of the existence of this factor would suggest that labour markets function in ways that package jobs so that they *tend* to be good, bad or mediocre on all six dimensions. A psychologist, by contrast, would be likely to argue that the six job satisfaction questions tap into a latent psychological construct that might naturally be termed "job satisfaction". In practical terms, this would cause the responses for each dimension to move up or down with the underlying level of overall satisfaction. Psychologists' preferred interpretation of the factor analysis result is that it reveals this latent "job satisfaction" construct statistically. These economic and psychological explanations of the finding of statistical regularity are not just different words for the same phenomenon, nor are they mutually exclusive. Although we know of no methodology for measuring their relative validity, it is unlikely that either is completely correct or incorrect: both are incomplete to the extent that the six satisfaction scores do not move in lockstep.

Table 2 indicates that, on average, respondents were fairly neutral about their jobs, with average total scores ranging from 17.4 for Ukraine to 19.8 for Chile. The distributions of total job-satisfaction scores for the five samples are shown in figure 2.

Analytical framework

Job satisfaction outcomes are determined by the characteristics of both the individual incumbent and the job/employer. Certain kinds of individuals have an advantage in getting matched to a "good" job. Certain kinds of jobs or employers will deliver higher levels of job satisfaction. More specifically, job satisfaction outcomes are determined by the interplay of:

(1) The technical characteristics of the job. Is it, for example, inherently dangerous?

(2) The employer's decisions about how to position the job and the firm in the labour market. Has the employer chosen, for example, to provide generous compensation relative to other employers competing for similar workers?

(3) The characteristics of the individual. Is he or she highly educated, for example?

(4) The individual's choices about how to position herself in the labour market. For example, has the worker chosen a demanding but highly paid job?

(5) The individual's frame of reference. Is he or she highly educated, for example?

The same example is deliberately chosen for items 3 and 5 in order to highlight an inherent difficulty in interpreting subjective measures such as job satisfaction: the individual's frame of reference, when asked about job satisfaction, is inevitably correlated with her/his own characteristics. A highly educated individual is very likely to have high pay relative to the labour market as a whole, but this generates a frame of reference which includes the expectation of high absolute pay (Clark and Oswald, 1996). If, then, s/he perceives that s/he is underpaid relative to other highly educated people, s/he is likely to report lower job satisfaction.[8]

Relative position effects of this sort are not static. Suppose, for example, that discrimination against women becomes a highly visible issue. This could induce a shift in women's frame of reference away from women in similar circumstances and toward men doing comparable work. This shift would, in turn, tend to reduce women's reported job satisfaction. Similarly, a significant drop in the returns to education in a particular labour market might induce highly educated workers to believe that they are underpaid, reducing their reported job satisfaction.

Thus, it is important to keep in mind that job satisfaction data measure the quality of jobs *as filtered through the perceptions of the individual holding the job.*

BIVARIATE ANALYSIS

This section explores the relationships between total job satisfaction scores and variables in the following categories:

- characteristics of the respondent;
- employer size and self-employment status;
- the respondent's evaluation of workplace safety;
- perceived job security;
- earnings on the job;
- transferability of skills used on the job;
- union membership;
- the respondent's perception of employer attitudes.

These relationships are examined one at a time, with four subsections devoted to employees, and a fifth to the self-employed. The following section then goes on to use regression analysis to assess the extent to which the bivariate relationships overlap as part of a more integrated picture.

Individual characteristics of respondents

Table 3 shows the overall means of total job satisfaction, as well as means by sex, age and educational attainment. In this and subsequent tables, the rows labelled "*t*-statistic" display the test statistic for a test of the null hypothesis that the means of the first and last categories are equal (a two-tailed test). The rows labelled "significance level" use asterisks to indicate whether the null hypothesis is rejected at standard significance levels of 10, 5, and 1 per

Table 3. Job satisfaction by employee characteristics (average total job satisfaction score, employees)

	Argentina	Brazil	Chile	Hungary	Ukraine
All employees	18.8	18.6	19.8	18.0	17.4
Women	18.8	18.3	20.1	18.6	17.5
Men	18.8	18.9	19.7	17.4	17.2
Tested difference[a]	0.0	0.6	−0.4	−1.2	−0.4
t-statistic [a]	0.1	2.4	0.8	2.6	3.4
Significance level[b]		**		***	***
Age in years[c]					
< 30	19.2	19.0	19.5	18.4	17.6
30 to 39	18.0	18.3	19.9	18.2	17.3
40 to 49	18.9	18.4	19.6	17.2	17.5
≥ 50	19.0	18.8	20.4	18.1	17.3
Highest education completed[d]					
Primary or less	17.9	18.3	18.3	14.9	15.7
Vocational				17.1[e]	
Secondary	19.1	19.0	19.6	18.8	16.6
Special secondary					17.5[f]
University[g]	20.7	19.2	21.4	19.8	17.8
Tested difference[a]	2.8	1.0	3.1	4.9	2.1
t-statistic [a]	6.4	2.2	4.2	6.3	4.1
Significance level[b]	***	**	***	***	***
Employees in samples	771-781	1 456-1 458	433	437	5 731

[a] For t-test of equality of means of first and last categories. [b] *** = 0.01; ** = 0.05; * = 0.10. [c] Test of difference between extreme categories not performed. [d] Respondents were asked about their highest level of education and offered a pre-coded list of possible responses (i.e. they were not asked for years of education). [e] Somewhat less educational attainment than *secondary*. [f] Three to four years' technical education substituting for the last two years of secondary education and securing admission to the third or fourth year of university, i.e. considerably more than ordinary *secondary*. [g] Includes all post-secondary education (e.g. university and "college" for Hungary; undergraduate and post-graduate studies in the Latin American countries).

cent. In some cases, as noted in later tables, where the number of observations in the first category is small, the test compares the second category or merged first and second categories to the final category.

The first panel of table 3 shows that women are generally less satisfied than men in Brazil, but more satisfied in Hungary. In Argentina, Chile and Ukraine, the difference between women and men is less than half a total job-satisfaction point. However, because the Ukraine sample is more than three times larger than the next largest sample, the small 0.3 point difference between men and women in Ukraine is statistically significant.

There does not seem to be a simple relationship between age and job satisfaction in any of the five countries (second panel of table 3), though the data do hint at a U-shaped relationship. The *t*-test comparing the youngest and oldest workers is therefore omitted. That no clear pattern emerges is not really surprising; there is no *a priori* reason to expect a direct relationship, and age differences mirror a number of indirect and, possibly, conflicting influences. First, research in many countries has found that age typically has an inverted-U relationship with earnings. Second, there are large inter-generational differences in the countries surveyed here: older people in Hungary and Ukraine lived most of their working lives under communism; and in Latin America, average levels of education have been rising. Third, younger workers are more likely to be found in less satisfactory jobs, which they subsequently leave for positions that suit them better.

The relationship between education and job satisfaction is shown in the last panel of table 3. In every country, higher education is consistently associated with higher average job satisfaction. The differences between *university* and *primary or less* range from one to 4.9 total job satisfaction points in Brazil and Hungary, respectively; and the difference is statistically significant in every case. At least part of the association between education and job satisfaction probably reflects the composite effect of the well-documented positive relationship between education and earnings and a strong positive association between earnings and job satisfaction. As Freeman (1978) points out, however, "by altering the way in which persons respond to questions, variables like education (which raises aspirations) ... could have very different effects on job satisfaction than on objective economic conditions".

Employer and workplace characteristics

Employer size is similar to age in the sense that it is a catch-all variable that blends a number of separate effects. Table 4 reinforces this view; the relationship with job satisfaction is neither consistent among countries nor unidirectional in any of the five countries. One interesting pattern is that the smallest employers generate the lowest job satisfaction in Latin America (though the number of observations in the under 10 category is very small for Argentina), but the highest job satisfaction in Hungary and Ukraine. This may stem from historical differences in the nature of small-scale establishments in these countries. Small enterprises in Latin America are often unregulated, informal-sector establishments with relatively poor prospects. In the transition economies, small establishments are typically more dynamic, comprising workers who have left rigid, previously state-run enterprises.

The second panel of table 4 looks at the respondent's evaluation of workplace safety. This is the first of several variables that are the employee's subjective evaluation of an objective situation.[9] In all five countries, respondents were asked to describe the safety of their workplace on a five-point scale ranging from "very unsafe" to "very safe".[10] These questions are subjective in a different way than the job satisfaction questions. The latter ask for a rat-

Table 4. Job satisfaction by employer and workplace characteristics
(average total job satisfaction score, employees)

	Argentina	Brazil	Chile	Hungary	Ukraine
Employer size					
Under 10 employees	17.7	18.4	19.9	18.1	18.1
10 to 50[a]	20.2	18.9	19.9	17.9	17.7
50 to 100[b]	20.9	19.5	19.7	17.1	17.2
Over 100	20.1	19.2	20.1	18.0	17.3
Tested difference[c]	2.3	0.8	0.2	–0.2	–0.8
t-statistic[c]	4.3	2.6	0.3	0.2	4.2
Significance level[d]	***	***			***
Workplace safety evaluation					
Very unsafe	14.2	15.9	17.8	15.0[e]	16.7
Unsafe	16.8	16.6	17.4		16.6
Neutral	17.3	17.5	17.7	16.4	16.5
Safe	19.4	19.2	20.3	18.4	17.8
Very safe	21.7	20.5	22.8	19.4	19.3
Tested difference[c]	4.8[f]	3.9[f]	5.5[f]	4.3[g]	2.6
t-statistic[c]	7.6[f]	8.5[f]	5.0[f]	4.2[g]	7.5
Significance level[d]	***	***	***	***	***
Employees in sample	635	1 234	369	388	5 521

[a]Actually 11 to 50 for the Latin American countries and 10 to 49 for Ukraine and Hungary. [b]Actually 51 to 100 for the Latin American countries and 50 to 99 for Ukraine and Hungary. [c]For *t*-test of equality of means of first and last categories, except as otherwise noted. [d]*** = 0.01; ** = 0.05; * = 0.10. [e]First and second categories combined because of small cell sizes in both. [f]For equality of means of second and last categories. [g]For equality of mean of last category with mean of combined first and second categories.

ing of the worker's emotional (affective) response to different aspects of the job, whereas the workplace safety and job security questions elicit an evaluation of an objective condition.

The results point to a strong link between job satisfaction and perceived workplace safety, both statistically and quantitatively: the difference between the best and worst categories ranges from 2.6 job satisfaction points in the Ukraine sample to 7.5 points in the Argentina sample. The Ukraine results are somewhat puzzling because there is no strong relationship between perceived safety and job satisfaction for those in the worst three categories; the relationship only emerges when comparing "neutral" to "safe" or "very safe".[11]

Job characteristics

Table 5 starts with another subjective evaluation: prospective job security over the coming 12 months. Without exception, higher confidence that the job can be retained is related to higher job satisfaction, with the gap between "very unconfident" and "very confident" ranging from 3.3 (Ukraine)

Table 5.   Job satisfaction by job characteristics (average total job satisfaction score, employees)

	Argentina	Brazil	Chile	Hungary	Ukraine
Keep job one year?					
Very unconfident	16.5	15.5	17.3	13.2	15.6
Unconfident	16.5	17.0	15.5	14.6	16.1
Neutral	18.7	18.2	19.1	16.5	16.7
Confident	19.6	19.5	20.5	19.2	18.0
Very confident	21.2	19.9	22.6	19.8	18.9
Tested difference[a]	4.7	4.4	7.1[b]	5.2[b]	3.3
t-statistic [a]	6.8	6.3	7.3[b]	6.7[b]	7.8
Significance level[c]	***	***	***	***	***
Skills transferable?					
No	17.4	18.1	19.2		
Yes, partly	18.8	18.5	19.8		
Yes, mostly	19.7	19.2	20.6		
Tested difference[a]	2.3	1.0	1.4		
t-statistic [a]	4.7	3.2	1.7		
p-value	0.00	0.00	0.10		
Significance level[c]	***	***	*		
Computer user?					
No				16.7	17.2
Yes				19.9	18.3
Tested difference[a]				3.2	1.1
t-statistic [a]				6.9	8.7
Significance level[c]				***	***
Employees in samples	764-771	1 451-1 452	385-426	432-433	4 691-5 731

[a] For t-test of equality of means of first and last categories, except as otherwise noted.   [b] For equality of means of second and last categories.   [c] *** = 0.01; ** = 0.05; * = 0.10.

to 6.6 points (Hungary).[12] The difference is statistically significant at the 0.01 level in every case. Given the strength of this result (and of the results for safety reported above), it is worth emphasizing that none of the six job satisfaction questions asked directly about job security or job safety. Nor were the safety and security questions posed as questions about satisfaction regarding the levels of job safety and security.

The reasons why job safety and security influence job satisfaction are obvious. A bit less transparent is the use of transferable skills on the job. The underlying reasoning involves two steps. The starting point is the economic theory of labour markets, which argues that workers are compensated for transferable skills they use on the job. The argument rests on the observation that transferable skills can be sold to another employer. This, in turn, has two consequences for job satisfaction. First, transferability of skills may partly be a proxy for earnings; and second, the transferability of skills partially insures the worker against job loss because the worker is more likely to be able to find a new job generating comparable income.

In Argentina, Brazil and Chile, use of transferable skills was measured with a direct (subjective) question: respondents were asked whether they thought the skills and knowledge associated with their main job were transferable to other jobs. But because of the general nature of this question, the reported skills may include some of those acquired through formal education. In Hungary and Ukraine, by contrast, the survey asked whether the respondent knew how to use a computer – a specific transferable skill – and whether the respondent had access to a computer at work.[13] If the computer is used at work, the above reasoning about the link between transferable skills and job satisfaction applies. And, of course, a positive association may also indicate that people like using computers or having the kinds of jobs in which computers are used (white-collar jobs).

The association between job satisfaction and different levels of transferable skills is fairly strong – between 1.1 and 3.2 points using the available measurements – though transferable skills are clearly not as important a consideration as job security.

Table 6 shows a modest positive relationship between *time on current job* and job satisfaction in Argentina, Brazil and Chile, but no statistically

Table 6.   Job satisfaction by job characteristics (average total job satisfaction score, employees)

	Argentina	Brazil	Chile	Hungary
Time on current job				
< 2 years	18.2	18.4	19.1	17.6
2 to 5 years	18.6	18.7	19.2	17.3
> 5 years	19.6	18.9	20.7	18.3
Tested difference[a]	1.4	0.5	1.6	0.7
t-statistic [a]	3.5	2.0	2.4	1.0
Significance level[b]	***	**	**	
Earnings on job				
1st quartile (lowest)	16.4	16.7	18.4	
2nd quartile	18.1	18.6	17.4	
3rd quartile	19.5	18.9	19.8	
4th quartile (highest)	20.5	20.1	23.1	
Tested difference[a]	4.1	3.4	4.7	
t-statistic [a]	7.0	9.3	7.1	
Significance level[b]	***	***	***	
Employees in samples	671–778	1 386–1 455	380–430	434

[a]For *t*-test of equality of means of first and last categories.   [b]*** = 0.01; ** = 0.05; * = 0.10.

significant relationship is evident for Hungary (no data are available from the Ukrainian survey). For two reasons it is somewhat surprising that a stronger positive relationship does not appear. First, earnings are typically positively related to seniority in the job. Second, unsatisfied employees would be more likely to filter out of their jobs over time, leaving senior employees who are, on average, more satisfied.

It is unfortunate that the PSS questionnaires did not gather information about earnings on the job in Hungary and Ukraine, since earnings can be expected to be one of the most important determinants of job satisfaction. Indeed, for the three Latin American countries, table 6 documents a very strong relationship: those in the highest earnings quartiles have total job satisfaction scores that are 3.4 to 4.7 points higher than those in the lowest quartile.[14] It is striking, however, that these differences are roughly comparable to those identified in respect of job safety and job security; pay is not obviously the most important determinant of job satisfaction.[15]

Employer-employee relationships

Table 7 turns to measurements of the quality of employer-employee relationships. All five data sets make it possible to identify union members. For the Latin American countries, however, the respondent was not asked about union membership unless there was a union at the workplace. In Hungary and Ukraine, two questions addressed employer attitudes directly. The first asked whether the worker felt able to *express concerns* and grievances. The second asked whether the employer could be trusted to look after the worker's interests (*trust employer*). Employer attitudes were not directly addressed in the Latin American surveys, but all five surveys contain a question about whether there is a *safety department* or committee at the workplace. For reasons connected to the regression analysis below, this variable is considered to be a good proxy for the existence of processes to safeguard the employees' interests rather than being simply an indicator of a safer workplace.

Union membership is associated with significantly higher job satisfaction in every country but Chile. The association is fairly weak in Argentina, Brazil and Ukraine, but rather strong – 2.1 points – for Hungary. On their own, these results seem to be of only modest interest, but they are strikingly different from the standard finding from industrialized countries, where a robust negative relationship between job satisfaction and unionization has been found.[16]

The data from Hungary and Ukraine offer evidence of the importance of intangible aspects of employer-employee relationships. Whether workers can discuss concerns with their employer or trust their employer is part of a larger picture that encompasses notions of fairness, reciprocity and dignity. The glimpse these two questions provide of that larger picture is compelling.

Table 7. Job satisfaction and employeer-employee relations (average total job
satisfaction score, employees)

	Argentina	Brazil	Chile	Hungary	Ukraine
Union status					
Non-member	18.9	18.7	20.0	17.5	17.2
Member	19.9	19.4	19.8	19.6	17.7
Tested difference[a]	1.1	0.7	–0.2	2.1	0.5
t-statistic [a]	2.4	2.6	0.4	4.1	4.5
Significance level[b]	**	***		***	***
Safety department					
No	18.1	18.0	18.3	17.2	17.2
Yes	20.6	19.7	21.0	18.4	17.7
Tested difference[a]	2.5	1.6	2.7	1.3	0.5
t-statistic [a]	7.0	6.9	4.6	2.5	4.2
p-value *	0.00	0.00	0.00	0.01	0.00
Significance level[b]	***	***	***	**	***
Can discuss concerns with employer					
No				15.5	16.4
Don't know					17.1
Yes				18.4	18.4
Tested difference[a]				2.9	2.0
t-statistic [a]				3.9	15.1
Significance level[b]				***	***
Trust employer					
No				15.2	16.5
Yes				19.0	18.6
Tested difference[a]				3.7	2.1
t-statistic [a]				7.0	19.8
Significance level[b]				***	***
Employees in samples	631-642	1 264-1 297	373-402	408-437	5 731

[a]For t-test of equality of means of first and last categories. [b]*** = 0.01; ** = 0.05; * = 0.10.

Interestingly, the Ukrainian data show that certainty that the employer is not open to discussion is worse than uncertainty, and that nearly a third of the sample answered "don't know" to this question. The perception that the employer is open to discussions about concerns and problems is associated with higher job satisfaction (2.0 to 2.9 points on average in Ukraine and Hungary, respectively). The broader question about trusting the employer to look after the worker's interests produces a similar spread for Ukraine (2.1 points) and an even larger gap for Hungary (3.7 points). The correlation between answers to the openness and trust questions were 0.54 and 0.43 in Hungary and Ukraine, respectively – high, but far from 1.0.

As mentioned earlier, the presence of a safety department seems more likely to reflect the existence of internal processes that safeguard workers' interests than an increment in workplace safety (for further elaboration, see the discussion about this variable in the regression analysis below). In table 7, the association of this variable with job satisfaction is positive and statistically significant in every country, but the magnitude of the difference is noticeably smaller in Hungary and Ukraine. In Brazil, Chile and Ukraine, large employers are required by law to set up safety departments (subject to different thresholds), so some of the observed difference may be echoing other employer-size effects. The regression analysis conducted in the next section controls for employer size, however, and the relationship remains statistically important.[17]

Self-employed workers

The number of self-employed individuals is large enough for detailed analysis only in the Argentina and Brazil samples, though some limited conclusions can be drawn from the Chile sample as well (the self-employed were not included in the sampling frame for the Ukrainian PSS). Unlike earlier tables, table 8 reports cell sizes because so many are small enough to be of note, particularly for Chile, where we found it necessary to merge cells in several cases.

The top of table 8 compares job satisfaction between the usual three employment status categories, including employers, which are excluded elsewhere in this article. In the Argentine data, employees' job satisfaction is 1.4 points higher than that of the self-employed. The gap is neither large nor statistically significant in the Brazilian and Chilean data. The small number of employers in each sample have substantially higher job satisfaction than employees and self-employed workers.

Table 8 demonstrates that many of the relationships between job satisfaction and individual or job characteristics are qualitatively similar for the self-employed and employees. Here attention will therefore be drawn only to substantial differences from the patterns observed for employees. There are relatively few such differences, and those few are matters of magnitude; the directions of differences is completely consistent.

In the Brazilian sample, the climb in job satisfaction as we move into higher educational categories is much steeper in table 8 than in table 3 – a 3.7 point gap between *university* and *primary or less* for the self-employed versus 1.0 point for employees. Also in the Brazilian sample, the difference between more than five years on the job and less than two years is associated with a difference of only 0.5 point for employees, but 1.4 points for the self-employed.

The difference in average job satisfaction between the highest and lowest earnings quartiles is smaller for the self-employed in Argentina, but

Table 8. Average total job satisfaction score, self-employed

	Argentina		Brazil		Chile	
	Mean	Observed	Mean	Observed	Mean	Observed
Employer	19.3	42	22.1	41	22.3	18
Self-employed	17.4	373	18.7	520	19.2	121
Employee	18.8	781	18.6	1 458	19.8	433
Tested difference [a]	1.4[b]		−0.1[b]		0.6[b]	
t-statistic [a]	4.7[b]		0.3[b]		1.0[b]	
Significance level[c]	***					
Female	17.6	148	18.4	205	19.4	36
Male	17.2	225	18.9	315	19.2	85
Tested difference [a]	−0.4		0.5		−0.2	
t-statistic [a]	0.8		1.1		0.2	
Significance level[c]						
Age in years [d]						
< 30	17.9	73	18.8	114	21.4	15
30 to 39	18.2	88	18.4	131	19.9	29
40 to 49	17.3	103	19.0	168	18.3	42
> 50	16.4	109	18.5	107	19.2	34
Highest education, completed						
Primary or less	16.5	182	18.0	354	19.1	43
Secondary	17.7	131	19.7	129	18.6	57
University	19.1	54	21.8	37	20.9	21
Tested difference [a]	2.5		3.7		1.8	
t-statistic [a]	4.1		5.8		1.1	
Significance level[c]	***		***			
Workplace safety evaluation						
Very unsafe	15.5	15	15.0	27	16.7[e]	43
Unsafe	15.5	86	17.5	95		
Neutral	17.5	60	18.5	82	20.4	19
Safe	18.1	184	19.2	253	20.9[e]	57
Very safe	19.5	26	19.9	63		
Tested difference [a]	2.6[f]		2.4[b]		4.1[g]	
t-statistic [a]	3.9[f]		2.8[b]		2.5[g]	
Significance level[c]	***		***		**	
Keep job one year?						
Very unconfident	14.0	44	16.3	18	15.9[e]	24
Unconfident	17.0	87	16.7	124		
Neutral	16.9	79	18.0	91	18.5	32
Confident	18.7	113	19.8	183	20.7[e]	62
Very confident	19.4	42	20.2	102		
Tested difference [a]	5.3		3.5[b]		4.8[g]	
t-statistic [a]	5.2		5.3[b]		2.8[g]	
Significance level[c]	***		***		***	

(continued overleaf)

Table 8. Average total job satisfaction score, self-employed *(concl.)*

	Argentina		Brazil		Chile	
	Mean	Observed	Mean	Observed	Mean	Observed
Skills transferable?						
No	16.0	92	18.5	160	19.4	19
Yes, partly	17.6	157	18.2	228	18.5	51
Yes, mostly	18.2	118	19.8	126	20.4	38
Tested difference [a]	2.2		1.3		1.0	
t-statistic [a]	3.2		2.3		0.6	
Significance level[c]	***		**			
Time on current job						
< 2 years	16.7	96	17.8	143	17.7	34
2 to 5 years	17.1	63	18.8	132	19.6	20
> 5 years	17.7	214	19.2	245	20.0	67
Tested difference [a]	1.0		1.4		2.3	
t-statistic [a]	1.6		2.9		1.6	
Significance level[c]			***			
Earnings on job						
1st quartile (lowest)	16.6	82	16.5	144	16.3	35
2nd quartile	17.5	54	18.5	94	18.9	12
3rd quartile	17.5	46	19.3	100	21.0	30
4th quartile (highest)	19.0	74	20.8	113	20.5	23
Tested difference [a]	2.4		4.3		4.3	
t-statistic [a]	3.4		7.9		3.4	
Significance level[c]	***		***		***	

[a]For *t*-test of equality of means of first and last categories. [b]For equality of means of second and last categories. [c]*** = 0.01; ** = 0.05; * = 0.10. [d]Test of difference between extreme categories not performed. [e]Categories combined because of small cell sizes in both. [f]For equality of "safe" and "unsafe" categories. [g]For equality of mean of last two categories combined with mean of first two categories combined.

larger in Brazil. (As mentioned earlier, the earnings quartiles are calculated using data for both employees and the self-employed.)

There were only 121 self-employed individuals in the Chilean sample. The resulting observations, however, are sufficient to confirm tentatively that higher job satisfaction for the self-employed is associated with higher education, safer workplaces, higher job security, more time on the job, and higher earnings.

REGRESSION ANALYSIS

The comparisons of sub-sample means discussed in the preceding section suggest explanations for the observed cross-sectional distribution of job satisfaction. It is clear, however, that these explanations overlap because of correlations among the categories (conditioning variables). This can be illustrated by an example such as university-educated workers, who are more likely to work in office environments that are, on average, safer than other workplaces. In Argentina there is a 7.5 point job satisfaction difference between the two extreme safety categories and a 2.8 point gap between the highest and lowest education categories. But because of correlation between education and safe workplaces, the effects of education and safety – as well as other factors correlated with education – are commingled in both numbers. In this section, regression analysis is used in an attempt to separate these effects.

Employees

Table 9 reports the results of regressing total job satisfaction scores on regressors comparable to the categories used in tables 3-6. All of these regressors are indicator variables.[18] The reference (omitted) categories are: age less than 30 years, primary education or less, fewer than ten employees, the middle (neutral) categories for the job safety and job security evaluations,[19] skills not transferable, not a computer user at work, not a union member, no safety department, cannot express concerns and grievances, and does not trust employer. The coefficients reported in table 9 are the difference in total job satisfaction points associated with each explanatory variable after statistically controlling for (holding fixed) the other explanatory variables.

Earnings were not used in the regressions because theoretical considerations and empirical evidence suggest that earnings would be an endogenous regressor, biasing the regression results (see Ritter and Anker, 2002). The theoretical argument is simply that more satisfied employees are more likely to be successful, achieving higher earnings.

Except for the job safety and job security sections of table 9, a test of the null hypothesis that the coefficient on the highest category (university, for example) is zero gives results comparable to those of the *t*-tests reported in tables 3-6. For the safety and security variables the comparable test uses the null hypothesis that the difference of two coefficients is zero (e.g. the difference between the coefficients on the very safe and very unsafe indicators). The results of these tests are reported in the discussion below.

In general, the regression results are consistent with the comparisons of means discussed in the previous section in terms of the direction of the associations. As expected, the magnitudes of the effects are generally smaller, however, because of the correlations among explanatory variables.

The largest effects are still those of perceived job safety, job security, and the employer-employee relations variables. The differences between "very safe" and either "unsafe" or "very unsafe" categories – depending, as in table 4, on cell size – range from 1.4 to 3.5 job satisfaction points. The differences are statistically significant at the 0.01 level, except in the Hungary

Table 9. Regression of total job satisfaction score, employees

	Argentina	Brazil	Chile	Hungary	Ukraine
Female	−0.49	−0.53**	0.89	0.13	−0.22*
	(0.37)	(0.24)	(0.55)	(0.48)	(0.13)
Age					
30 to 39	−1.21**	−0.48	−0.49	−0.05	−0.17
	(0.48)	(0.30)	(0.80)	(0.57)	(0.17)
40 to 49	0.20	−0.39	−1.12	−1.07*	0.16
	(0.48)	(0.31)	(0.89)	(0.60)	(0.16)
50 and over	−0.25	−0.15	−0.10	0.16	−0.02
	(0.58)	(0.46)	(0.93)	(0.86)	(0.19)
Completed education					
Vocational				1.41*	
				(0.81)	
Secondary	0.06	−0.20	0.02	1.76**	0.39
	(0.44)	(0.25)	(0.66)	(0.81)	(0.60)
Special secondary					1.04*
					(0.60)
University	0.48	−0.07	2.19***	2.26**	0.98
	(0.54)	(0.46)	(0.67)	(0.94)	(0.60)
Employer size					
10 to 50	1.36***	0.23	−0.55	−0.57	−0.51**
	(0.47)	(0.33)	(0.68)	(0.72)	(0.21)
50 to 100	1.92***	0.75*	−0.69	−1.58*	−0.98***
	(0.57)	(0.45)	(0.97)	(0.84)	(0.23)
>100	1.17**	0.08	−1.04	−0.64	−0.72***
	(0.59)	(0.35)	(0.72)	(0.78)	(0.20)
Workplace safety evaluation					
Very unsafe	−2.96*	−1.00	2.18	0.59	0.14
	(1.64)	(0.93)	(1.85)	(1.43)	(0.19)
Unsafe	−1.34*	−0.47	0.14	0.00	−0.14
	(0.74)	(0.47)	(0.99)	(0.94)	(0.37)
Safe	0.92	1.45***	2.03***	1.47***	0.61***
	(0.60)	(0.32)	(0.72)	(0.54)	(0.15)
Very safe	1.86**	2.58***	3.67***	1.42**	1.57***
	(0.83)	(0.42)	(0.92)	(0.58)	(0.36)
Keep job one year?					
Very unconfident	−0.93	−1.68	−0.83	−2.27	−0.57
	(0.81)	(0.77)	(1.35)	(1.17)	(0.39)

Table 9. Regression of total job satisfaction score, employees *(concl.)*

	Argentina	Brazil	Chile	Hungary	Ukraine
Keep job one year? *(concl.)*					
Unconfident	–1.28**	–0.79	–2.43	–1.13	–0.25
	(0.62)	(0.37)	(0.93)	(0.88)	(0.30)
Confident	0.00	0.80	1.01	1.79	0.93
	(0.48)	(0.31)	(0.69)	(0.60)	(0.13)
Very confident	0.96*	0.95	2.25	2.19	1.51
	(0.58)	(0.39)	(0.78)	(0.61)	(0.18)
Skills transferable?					
Yes, mostly	1.25**	0.67**	0.88		
	(0.55)	(0.32)	(0.78)		
Yes, partly	0.92*	0.44	0.14		
	(0.56)	(0.31)	(0.69)		
Computer user				1.45***	0.67***
				(0.54)	(0.14)
Time on current job					
2 to 5 years	0.13	–0.36	–1.53**	–1.32*	
	(0.51)	(0.34)	(0.76)	(0.77)	
More than 5 years	0.73	0.00	0.35	–1.16*	
	(0.47)	(0.29)	(0.75)	(0.67)	
Union member	0.10	0.29	–0.72	1.81***	0.24**
	(0.43)	(0.28)	(0.65)	(0.52)	(0.12)
Safety department	1.75***	1.20***	2.56***	0.88*	0.27**
	(0.41)	(0.27)	(0.58)	(0.46)	(0.13)
Express concerns?					
Yes				1.21	0.92***
				(0.82)	(0.15)
Don't know					0.52***
					(0.14)
Trust employer				2.38***	1.43***
				(0.51)	(0.12)
Constant	16.45***	16.84***	16.26***	14.29***	16.24***
	(0.90)	(0.49)	(0.96)	(1.26)	(0.66)
R^2	0.27	0.16	0.40	0.38	0.17
Observations	526	1 158	282	341	4 559

Significance levels: *** = 0.01; ** = 0.05; * = 0.10.   Standard errors in parentheses.

sample.[20] The peculiar finding for Ukraine – that the difference between "very unsafe" and "neutral" does not matter – persists in the regression results.

The coefficients for perceived job security show a similar pattern of decreasing magnitudes. The differences between coefficients on "very confident" and "very unconfident" (or "confident", depending on cell size) range from 1.9 to 4.7 points across the five countries studied, and all are statistically significant at the 0.05 or 0.01 level.[21]

As mentioned earlier, the natural interpretation of the apparent effect of the *safety department* variable on job satisfaction in table 7 is that it serves as a proxy for workplace safety. But the regression results strongly suggest that this interpretation is misleading. Since the regressions control for workers' direct evaluation of safety, the effects of *safety department* seem far too large to represent a further increment in workplace safety. Furthermore, when the *very unsafe* to *very safe* variables are excluded from the regression, the coefficient on *safety department* changes little, increasing by about 0.2 for Argentina, Brazil and Hungary and remaining virtually unchanged for Chile and Ukraine. Therefore we interpret the *safety department* variable as a proxy for the existence of processes that safeguard, or reflect concern for, workers' interest (especially, perhaps, safety). This interpretation is strengthened by the results for Hungary and Ukraine: when the *express concerns* and *trust employer* variables are excluded, the *safety department* coefficients are much larger and statistically significant in both samples. In short, the evidence suggests that the existence of a safety department is closely related to these more direct measures of employer attitudes.

It is clear overall that employer attitudes are very important determinants of job satisfaction. In Hungary, the combined impact of *safety department*, *express concerns*, and *trust employer* is 4.5 job satisfaction points; and in Ukraine, it is 2.6 points. Thus the importance of these variables in determining job quality is estimated to be comparable to, or greater than, that of perceived job security.

Self-employed workers

Table 10 reports analogous regressions for self-employed individuals in the Latin American samples. The results for Chile are reported for completeness, but the small sample size leads to large standard errors, thereby severely limiting the usefulness of the regression.[22] The regressions leave out several variables used in the employee regressions that have little meaning for self-employed workers.

As was the case for employees, the regressions for self-employed workers find that the magnitude of effects is generally smaller than it was in the comparisons of conditional means given in table 8. However, there are some notable contrasts with the regression results for employees shown in table 9.

Table 10. Regression of total job satisfaction score, self-employed workers

	Argentina	Brazil	Chile
Female	0.23	−0.83**	1.26
	(0.50)	(0.39)	(1.09)
Age			
30 to 39	0.10	−0.34	−0.70
	(0.72)	(0.55)	(2.09)
40 to 49	−0.88	0.22	−1.22
	(0.77)	(0.55)	(2.11)
50 and over	−1.83***	−0.45	−0.41
	(0.69)	(0.66)	(1.97)
Completed education			
Secondary	0.07	1.13**	−0.13
	(0.56)	(0.46)	(0.95)
University	1.69***	3.09***	2.18*
	(0.58)	(0.64)	(1.26)
Workplace safety evaluation			
Very unsafe	−1.51	−3.46***	−2.19
	(1.17)	(1.11)	(1.98)
Unsafe	−1.66**	−0.37	−3.36**
	(0.72)	(0.55)	(1.67)
Safe	0.11	0.25	0.86
	(0.60)	(0.49)	(1.36)
Very safe	1.37	0.45	0.97
	(0.97)	(0.80)	(1.98)
Keep job one year?			
Very unconfident	−2.33**	−1.77	−0.07
	(0.92)	(1.20)	(2.22)
Unconfident	0.52	−1.13**	−1.63
	(0.71)	(0.54)	(1.15)
Confident	1.59***	1.61***	1.87
	(0.60)	(0.46)	(1.19)
Very confident	1.83**	1.86***	1.70
	(0.90)	(0.61)	(1.22)
Skills transferable?			
Yes, mostly	1.31**	1.01*	0.87
	(0.65)	(0.54)	(1.45)
Yes, partly	1.00*	−0.50	−0.93
	(0.58)	(0.43)	(1.27)
Time on current job			
2 to 5 years	−0.34	0.68	2.49*
	(0.83)	(0.54)	(1.51)
More than 5 years	0.96	0.83*	3.33***
	(0.65)	(0.48)	(1.04)
Constant	16.25***	17.45***	17.12***
	(1.03)	(0.72)	(2.79)
R^2	0.22	0.21	0.47
Observations	351	512	103

Significance level: *** = 0.01; ** = 0.05; * = 0.10. Standard errors in parentheses.

First, the effect of a university education is much larger for self-employed individuals than for employees; and the same goes for the effect of secondary education in Brazil. Second, for self-employed Brazilians, the effects of different levels of perceived workplace safety are negligible except for a large coefficient of –3.46 on the "very unsafe" indicator.[23] The magnitude is roughly the same as the difference between the "very safe" and "very unsafe" coefficients in the employees regression, but there the effect is not concentrated in the jump from "unsafe" to "very unsafe".

CONCLUDING REMARKS

Individual workers' expressions of job satisfaction relate in predictable ways to worker, employer and job characteristics. First, job satisfaction is strongly associated with perceived job security in all five countries. Though it may be tempting to regard this finding as tautological, it is important to remember that the dependent variable does not directly measure job security. Second, the worker's evaluation of workplace safety is strongly related to job satisfaction in all five countries, though the specific pattern of results is somewhat puzzling for Chile, Hungary and Ukraine. Here again, it is important to keep in mind that the dependent variable does not directly measure workplace safety. Third, highly educated workers are more likely to report high job satisfaction levels. Fourth, employer attitudes, as perceived by workers, have large and highly significant effects. And fifth, in sharp contrast to previous research findings on the United Kingdom, the United States, Canada and Australia, union membership is not negatively related to job satisfaction.

The PSS questionnaires were structured largely around the conceptual framework for understanding socio-economic security proposed by Standing (1999). That framework describes seven dimensions of economic security and offers a different perspective on our findings. Specifically, the results reported in this article indicate that job satisfaction is closely related to what Standing terms work security (the safety measures), employment security (the job stability measures), security of occupational skills (the transferable skills variables) and voice representation security (unionization and employer attitude variables).

Given the large differences among the five labour markets studied, especially between the Eastern European and Latin American countries, the results reported here are satisfyingly consistent. Job satisfaction data thus prove to be credible indicators of job quality, generally responding sensibly and consistently to various characteristics of the employment relationship.

Notes

[1] For example, the General Social Survey in the United States has inquired about job satisfaction every year since 1972. The British Household Panel Survey has followed job satisfaction since 1991.

[2] A recent exception is Clark (1996), who analyses job satisfaction data from the British Household Panel Survey in detail. Clark (1998) provides the only multi-country study we are aware of, using data from the International Social Surveys Programme Work Orientations I module.

[3] For more details on methodology, see Jeria Cáceres, 2001.

[4] In Argentina, Brazil and Chile, a seventh question asked about the work environment. The responses to this question are not used in this article in order to allow closer comparability with the Hungarian and Ukrainian data.

[5] Figures 1 and 2 use unweighted counts. All tables use weighted data.

[6] The PSS questionnaires did not include a question about overall job satisfaction.

[7] The single factor is dominant in the sense that its associated eigenvalue exceeds 2.0 in all five countries, while the eigenvalue associated with the second factor is always less than 0.5. The estimated factor loadings are approximately the same size in all five countries. For details, see Ritter and Anker (2002).

[8] Unfortunately, the data do not include the respondent's perception of the fairness of any aspect of employment.

[9] We assume that there is a connection between actual job safety and workers' evaluations, though it is the perceptions themselves, whether realistic or not, that are relevant to job satisfaction. The approach of measuring objective circumstances using subjective responses has also been used in the health field where subjective evaluations of health have been demonstrated to be good predictors of objective outcomes, specifically mortality (Golini and Calvani, 2001).

[10] The surveys also gathered information about work-related injuries and illness, as well as exposure to specific workplace hazards. The incidence of injuries was low and, not surprisingly (given the very small cell sizes), no statistically significant relationships with job satisfaction emerged. It is very difficult to collect detailed workplace hazard data in general surveys, so there were three problems with the approach to measuring workplace safety for this study: (1) the list of categories was not exhaustive; (2) like injuries, some hazards showed a very low incidence; and (3) some exposures were too broadly specified (e.g. "exposure to hazardous chemicals" rather than, say, "*frequent* exposure to hazardous chemicals *without protective equipment*"). Consequently, the relationship between job satisfaction and exposure to hazards did not display consistent patterns.

[11] In the Ukraine PSS the subjective job-safety query is immediately preceded by two questions about whether the respondent or any fellow worker has been off work due to injury, illness or stress. In the Latin American surveys, the preceding question is about the respondent's own injury, illness or stress and there is no question about a larger group. In Hungary, the safety evaluation question is preceded by unrelated questions. Since the respondent is much more likely to recall a specific problem when asked about fellow workers, the placement of questions on the Ukraine PSS tended to emphasize unsafe aspects of the work environment just prior to the subjective question. This may partly account for the relatively high level of "very unsafe" responses and could have changed the relationship with the job satisfaction question.

[12] It is likely that the range is smaller for Ukraine partly because the question was framed in a more pessimistic fashion. For Argentina, Brazil, Chile and Hungary, the endpoints of the scale were: "very (or fully) confident" and "very unconfident". For Ukraine, the endpoints were: "Confident I will keep present job" and "Expect to lose present job". For the sake of brevity, however, this article uses the "very confident" to "very unconfident" labels. A large "don't know" group on this question in Ukraine – almost 18 per cent of the sample – reported mean job satisfaction slightly better than those in the neutral category, but they have not been included in the analysis.

[13] For *computer user* to be coded yes, the requirement was that the respondent both knew how to use a computer and had access to one at work. This was the closest we could get to the desired concept using PSS data, though it does not preclude the possibility that the respondent knew how to use a computer and had access to one at work, but did not *use* one at work.

[14] The earnings quartiles were calculated from the PSS data, including individuals who were self-employed or employers.

[15] This finding also emerges from parallel tabulations replacing the total job satisfaction score with the pay component only.

[16] The relationship has been found in the United States (Freeman, 1978; Borjas, 1979), Canada (Meng, 1990), Australia (Miller, 1990) and the United Kingdom (Clark, 1996).

[17] Respondents who say they work for large employers where safety departments are mandated do not uniformly report that there was a safety department at their workplace. Since job satisfaction is a subjective variable, it is respondents' knowledge of such a department, not its actual existence, that is relevant. Adalberto Cardoso has pointed out to us (in personal communication) that Brazil presents a special case, however. In Brazil, the safety department requirement is actively enforced, and the required safety departments, which are widely known by their acronym (CIPA), are elected by the workers. Since these facts seem to rule out widespread disregard of the regulation and unawareness by the workers, the reference to a "safety department" rather than a CIPA in the PSS question was almost certainly misunderstood by some of those who worked for large employers and answered in the negative. This error in the data biases downward the difference in job satisfaction between those with and without a CIPA because some of those with a CIPA and high job satisfaction are misclassified as not having a CIPA, thus raising the non-CIPA mean.

[18] Therefore, the regression is equivalent to an ANOVA without interactions. Regressions using a quadratic specification for age and tenure produce similar results.

[19] The middle category is used because the extreme categories contained small numbers of cases in some samples.

[20] In a regression not reported here, the "very unsafe" and "unsafe" categories were combined in the Hungary data to increase the cell size. The difference with the "very safe" coefficient was still insignificant.

[21] Kelley, Evans and Dawkins (1998) found a similarly large effect of job security on job satisfaction using Australian data.

[22] The sample is smaller than in table 8 because the regression requires complete information on all variables.

[23] There are 65 observations in this category.

References

Akerlof, George A.; Dickens, William T. 1982. "The economic consequences of cognitive dissonance", in *American Economic Review* (Nashville, TN), Vol. 72, No. 3 (June), pp. 307-319.

Akerlof, George A.; Rose, Andrew K.; Yellen, Janet L. 1988. "Job switching and job satisfaction in the U.S. labor market", in *Brookings Papers on Economic Activity* (Washington, DC), No. 2, pp. 495-582.

Borjas, George J. 1979. "Job satisfaction, wages, and unions.", in *Journal of Human Resources* (Madison, WI), Vol. 14, No. 1 (Winter), pp. 21-40.

Clark, Andrew E. 2001. "What really matters in a job? Hedonic measurement using quit data", in *Labour Economics* (Amsterdam), Vol. 8, No. 2 (May), pp. 223-242.

—. 1998. *Measures of job satisfaction: What makes a good job? Evidence from OECD countries.* Labour Market and Social Policy Occasional Papers, No. 34 (DEELSA/ELSA/WD(98)5). Paris, OECD.

—. 1996. "Job satisfaction in Britain", in *British Journal of Industrial Relations* (Oxford), Vol. 34, No. 2 (June), pp. 189-217.

—; Oswald, Andrew J. 1996. "Satisfaction and comparison income", in *Journal of Public Economics* (Amsterdam), Vol. 61, No. 3 (Sep.), pp. 359-381.

Freeman, Richard B. 1978. "Job satisfaction as an economic variable", in *American Economic Review* (Nashville, TN), Vol. 68, No. 2 (May), pp. 135-141.

Golini, Antonio; Calvani, Plautilla. 2001. *Relationships between perceptions of health, chronic diseases and disabilities*. Nihon University Population Research Institute, Research Paper Series, No. 73. Tokyo, Nihon University.

Jeria Cáceres, María. 2001. *People's Socio-economic Security Survey methodology: Note on sampling designs*. Paper presented at the ILO Technical Conference on People's Socio-economic Security Surveys, 28-30 Nov., Geneva, ILO.

Kelley, Jonathan; Evans, M.D.R.; Dawkins, Peter. 1998. "Job security in the 1990s: How much is job security worth to employees?", in *Australian Social Monitor* (Melbourne), Vol. 1, No. 1 (Sep.), pp. 1-7.

Keon, Thomas L.; McDonald, Bill. 1982. "Job satisfaction and life satisfaction: An empirical evaluation of their interrelationship", in *Human Relations* (New York, NY), Vol. 35, No. 3, pp. 167-180.

Meng, Ronald. 1990. "The relationship between unions and job satisfaction", in *Applied Economics* (London), Vol. 22, No. 12 (Dec.), pp. 1635-1648.

Miller, Paul W. 1990. "Trade unions and job satisfaction", in *Australian Economic Papers* (Adelaide), Vol. 29, No. 55 (Dec.), pp. 226-248.

Ritter, Joseph A.; Anker, Richard. 2002. *Empirical modeling of job satisfaction: Results from five nonindustrialized countries*. Unpublished manuscript. Geneva, ILO.

Seashore, Stanley E. 1974. "Job satisfaction as an indicator of the quality of employment", in *Social Indicators Research* (Dordrecht), Vol. 1, No. 2 (Sep.), pp. 135-168.

Standing, Guy. 1999. Global labour flexibility: Seeking distributive justice. London, Macmillan Press.

LABOUR LAW AND NEW FORMS OF CORPORATE ORGANIZATION

14

Marie-Laure MORIN *

In today's global economy, the drive for corporate competitiveness and flexibility has led to sweeping changes in the ways enterprises are organized, economically, financially and in terms of their workforce (Boyer and Durand, 1998; Castels, 1998). Developments such as the emergence of global financial networks, outsourcing, relocation and the establishment of networks of enterprises have had far-reaching consequences for labour relations and labour law enforcement. This article examines a few of the issues raised by these transformations together with the ways in which they could be managed – tentatively at this stage – in law, particularly with reference to the experience of France and Europe.[1]

Born of the second industrial revolution, contemporary labour law is, historically, the outcome of a gradual process of construction, concomitant with that of productive organization itself, within national boundaries. Such law, be it statutory or contractual, was strongly influenced by the integrated large-scale enterprise model. It conceptualizes wage employment relationships in terms of binary relations between employers and workers. It is therefore hardly surprising that the reorganization of firms, under the combined effects of financial concentration and productive decentralization, should give rise to a new set of needs for protection.

The necessary evolution of labour law has already been the subject of important contributions (Supiot, 1999; Simitis, 1997; Verge and Vallée, 1997). Since the early 1980s, a process of important legal reform has been under way at the national level. At the international level too, the adjustment process is beginning to bear fruit. Examples include the European Commission's Green

Originally published in *International Labour Review*, Vol. 144 (2005), No. 1.

* Director of research, National Centre for Scientific Research (CNRS), Adviser to the Court of Cassation, France. Email: marie-laure.morin@justice.fr.

Paper on corporate social responsibility (European Commission, 2001), the Declaration on Fundamental Principles and Rights at Work adopted by the International Labour Conference in 1998 (ILO, 1998; Duplessis, 2004), and the work of the World Commission on the Social Dimension of Globalization (ILO, 2004).

As a contribution to this ongoing process, this article begins by analysing the ways in which enterprises have effectively changed in order to bring the real issues into sharper focus. Then, by reference to a few of the central concerns of labour law, it attempts to identify the legal techniques or concepts which are already being used, or which could be used, to further the construction of that body of law in such a way as to take account of those changes in productive organizations.[2]

NEW FORMS OF CORPORATE ORGANIZATION: THE SEARCH FOR AN ANALYTICAL FRAMEWORK

In the absence of a legal definition, the notion of "an enterprise" has provoked much debate among labour law specialists, as it has in other branches of law for that matter (Despax, 1957; Lyon-Caen and Lyon-Caen, 1978; Farjat et al., 1987). There have also been a great many economic and sociological studies of the enterprise and the changes it has been through (Storper and Salais, 1993). These will not be rehearsed here. Rather, this study proposes to take a multidisciplinary approach based on an analysis of labour relations and of how they relate to productive organization. From the economic and legal perspectives alike, when a person supplies labour to another the resulting relationship can be considered from either of two angles. The first is that of the productive organization within which the employment relationship occurs and of the determination of the organization's centre of power. The second is that of the sharing of the economic and social risks relating to production and to the work of the people involved (Morin, Dupuy and Larré, 1999). The first angle calls for a descriptive approach to the organization of firms. It also offers an opportunity to comprehend those issues that labour law is concerned with in relation to the enterprise, i.e. the objectives it pursues. The second angle involves a more theoretical analysis: how to interpret the changes under way? What is the nature of the legal issues that they raise in labour law?

Levels of corporate organization

Taking the descriptive approach, one can indeed identify different levels of organization of "the firm" in which employment relationships occur. The term "firm" is used deliberately here in preference to "enterprise" because it is broader and, legally speaking, neutral.[3] These levels of organization are structured hierarchically, though the whereabouts of the dominant level – the main focus of labour law – has shifted over time.

In today's labour law, it is common practice to distinguish the establishment, the undertaking and the group of undertakings (Gaudu, 1999; A. Lyon-Caen, 2003). In actual fact, these distinctions refer to the different levels of corporate organization with which labour law has, historically, been successively concerned in order to focus on the centre of effective power and thus ensure the protection of employees. Yet, while seeking to ensure workers' protection, labour law also contributes to organizing the production of goods or services. While spelling out the rules that govern the individual contract of employment – i.e. the master–servant relationship – between a legally identified employer, be it a legal or natural person, and the employee, labour law is also concerned with the organization – endowed with a centre of power and governed by labour relations – of which the employee is a part by virtue of the contract of employment (Jeammaud, 1989). Employment relationships are thus legally structured around two essential focal points to which particular attention will be devoted below (Jeammaud, Lyon-Caen and Le Friant, 1998).[4]

The firm as "producer"

Historically, labour law began by conceptualizing "the firm" as "a producer", i.e. the meeting place of capital and tangible labour where goods are manufactured for the market. Hence its focus on the factory, the establishment, the place where tangible labour was performed and where it was necessary to protect wage-earners or, rather, bodies at work. Early industrial legislation, particularly in the field of occupational health and safety, was establishment-level legislation, targeting the locus of tangible labour – the subject matter of the contract of employment. It was also from these tangible workplaces that collective solidarity networks first emerged, leading to the first collective actions.

As the first level of corporate organization, the establishment remains a major framework for the application of labour law. For example, this is reflected in the concept of the establishment used in German law, which forms the basis of the establishment's "social constitution" (Rémy, 2001). Another example is the notion of a "transferred economic entity" which carries on its activity while retaining its identity, as provided for in the European Directive on transfers of undertakings.[5] Such an entity is indeed characterized by a set of organized interactions between capital and labour, aimed at the pursuit of some form of activity.[6] The producer is above all the owner, the manager of the asset who is, at the same time, the employer, being a party to the contract of employment. This conceptualization of the productive firm remains very close to the concepts of farm assets and stock-in-trade which were hallmarks of the as yet very rural societies of the first industrial revolution (Gaudu, 2001).

The firm as an economic and social organization

Labour law subsequently went on to concern itself with the second level of organization of "the firm" which governs the latter's economic activity in relation to the market. In other words, the firm's economic organization was for a long time left to the complete discretion of the employer, without any interference from labour law beyond its focus on the performance of the contract of employment itself. From a consideration of the firm's economic organization – as opposed to a narrow focus on the labour-related aspects of the organization of production – it turns out that the firm can carry on multiple economic activities; it can comprise several branches of activity and have any number of establishments (Desbarats, 1996). Yet it is characterized by a single economic management which also governs the organization of its workforce. The firm's organizing principle is thus no longer production but economic decision-making power in relation to the market. The enterprise can then be conceptualized as an organization, both economic and social, under a single management. This classic notion of the firm, typified by the large Fordian enterprise, still lies at the heart of the conceptualization of the enterprise in labour law. In Germany and, later, in France, it gave rise to institutional theories of the enterprise as the locus of the exercise of private power, which the law has endeavoured to frame as such, although persistent debate has carried on in the realm of theory, both legal and economic, between the proponents of the contract and those of the organization.

Consideration of the enterprise as an economic and social organization was labour law's starting point for developing the modern concept of employment, both in the passive sense – i.e. to be employed – and, more importantly, in the active sense, i.e. to have a job and thus to play a part in an organization (Gaudu, 1996). This, in turn, laid the foundations for the legal construction of protection of the long-term employment relationship based on attachment to the enterprise, as reflected in the law of dismissal and more particularly in that of redundancy, an institution particular to the contract of employment. Social protection mechanisms based on the holding of a job were developed accordingly (Supiot, 1997). In the field of collective labour law, the reconceptualization of the firm around this level of organization led to the development of enterprise-level worker representation in continental Europe and, gradually in the post-war period, to the development of workers' rights to information and consultation on management's economic decision-making, particularly when such decisions were likely to affect employment. Hence the emergence of a body of law governing the exercise of executive power within the enterprise. Enterprise law and employment law are thus the corollaries of an understanding of the enterprise as an organization with both social and economic dimensions under a single economic management. From the standpoint of industrial relations, and again in the context of Europe, the development of industry-level bargaining paved the way for the organization of the social and labour aspects of competition between enterprises on the national markets for goods (affiliation to a particular industry being determined by the enterprise's main line of business).

The firm as a financial group

The third, financial level of organization of the firm is that concerned with resource allocation. It is also at this level that shareholder value is monitored and distributed. When a single company or person exercises majority control over the entire range of companies – whether through direct or indirect ownership of majority shares in the companies of the group or through the power to appoint company executives – there is "unity of governance" at the group level, which then becomes the locus of real decision-making power. This unity can then serve as a basis for tracing the boundaries of the firm.

European labour law and the law of some countries take account of this level of decision-making and recognize groups of companies as entities. The classic paradigm of the enterprise is indeed still effective when unity of governance can be identified as such (Supiot, 1985; Teyssié, 1999), though innovative approaches are needed to accommodate the separation between the legal employer, be it a corporation or a natural person, and the actual locus of decision-making power, as well as such discretionary scope as may be enjoyed by the individual enterprises within the group. Indeed, a group can encompass a variety of economic activities such that the locus of economic decision-making and that of financial decision-making may not always coincide. In practice, a supervisory relationship takes over – one of "controlled autonomy", to use a concept more sociological than legal (Appay, 1993) – which may give some scope for economic decision-making to individual enterprises within the group. The group and the enterprise may happen to coincide when, say, "economic and social unity" can be readily identified in terms of the concept developed under French law on this point (Boubli, 2004). But this is not always the case since a group can comprise several enterprises in the economic sense. Under French law, the institution of the group-wide works council and its recognized terms of reference represent an attempt to provide for such relationships; they also serve as the legal basis for the obligation to re-employ workers within the group in the event of redundancies and, more recently, recognition of group-wide collective bargaining.[7] Under European law, the directives on group-wide works councils and the status of workers in European companies also extend the scope of labour law to this level of decision-making.[8]

At present, this level of organization of the firm is the one that determines the hierarchy among the other levels in the sense that economic decision-making is dominated not so much by the market for goods as by the necessity of increasing value for shareholders. Indeed, with the development of the financial market economy, the 1990s witnessed a crucial turning point. The need to create value for shareholders,[9] together with the notion of shareholder value, led to an evaluation of the financial performance of an enterprise which was no longer based on its fundamental value but on the typical remuneration that its shareholders had come to expect. Applying this concept to the strategic management of the enterprise produces "a radical change of perspective that subordinates the firm's economic performance to an ex ante requirement for financial reward" (Baudru and Morin, 1999).[10] This radical shift obviously had far-reaching consequences for employment relationships since workers had no power whatsoever to influence shareholders' decisions on the financial market. The financial level of decision-making can indeed be very far removed from the establishments that have to face the consequences of decisions taken in response to financial logic. In such cases, the legal means of getting the decision-making centre involved are not always straightforward, especially in regard to international groups. This can be illustrated by the European Union's painful soul-searching over corporate restructuring projects.[11]

To sum up, labour law began by focusing on employment relationships at the establishment level in order to regulate the conditions of tangible labour and extend protection to workers' physical bodies. It then sought to protect employment and to organize collective relations within the economic boundaries of the enterprise – the economic entity then being the main locus of decision-making. Nowadays, it is painstakingly endeavouring to extend its reach to the group, as the embodiment of the dominant level, so as to ensure that workers' interests can be taken into account at that level too.

Questioning the unity of the firm

In its quest for the unifying feature of the firm, or at least for the level at which decisions are taken, labour law has come up against new obstacles. Aside from globalization which is weakening the overall effectiveness of national-level regulation, this unity-seeking approach to the firm is being challenged both downstream and upstream. This process is leading to a form of partitioning that labour law – initially constructed within the binary framework derived from the contract of employment – is ill-equipped to cope with.

Upstream, investors – many of them pension funds – are not interested in taking control of firms or in exercising economic decision-making power and taking responsibility accordingly. By acquiring shares, often on a relatively small scale, their objective is typically to reap financial rewards by wielding such influence as will sway the financial markets. Moreover, alongside groups characterized by unity of governance, which can thus be influenced by the decisions of minority shareholders, there are also various forms of inter-firm alliances without majority shareholdings (e.g. equity swaps, bank-industry alliances) which also have implications for firms' strategic decision-making. Within such networks (or financial arrangements), labour law has become something of an irrelevance, particularly when the underlying relationships are tenuous. In this model of financial market capitalism (Aglietta, 1998; Aglietta and Rebérioux, 2004), whose workings are increasingly disconnected from the real economy, capital mobility is generally accelerating. Faced with the influential power of minority shareholders within these financial networks, the means of action open to workers necessarily differ from those available within groups of companies whose unity of governance can be identified as such. Employee shareholding or the development of employee savings funds could be used to add another dimension to shareholders' decision-making which otherwise remains purely financial. But the quest for appropriate responses is clearly still on – and it is not confined to labour law alone.

Also on the upstream side, commercial alliances are being developed by networking enterprises on the basis of varying degrees of economic interdependence.[12] Such networks also pose new challenges to labour law. Examples include teamwork by the employees of several enterprises working on a common project, common systems of labour relations based on new information and communication technology between enterprises within a given network, the nature of employment within distribution networks (i.e. wage employment versus self-employment), etc. Such configurations also give rise to relations of "controlled autonomy" between enterprises, based not only on institutional financial interdependency but also on contractual economic interdependency. In all such cases, new forms of "allegiance" are emerging (Del Cont, 1998; Virassamy, 1986; Supiot, 2001).

Downstream, at the producer level of the firm, i.e. the establishment level, the sweeping drive towards "productive decentralization" – outsourcing of service functions, subcontracting arrangements – is also undermining the traditional unity of the enterprise as a social and economic organization (Morin, 1994 and 1996). At the production level itself and at the workplace, workforces are fragmented, working under different sets of collective rules, and parts of the production process may be relocated elsewhere. Internationally, these practices have revived the issue of competition, not only among enterprises but also, and perhaps more importantly, in the labour market. This, in turn, has undermined the regulatory function of industry-level collective agreements as envisaged within the framework of the dominant national markets of the twentieth century, which were consistent with the enterprise being organized as an economic and social entity. Arguably of even greater concern is the difficulty of identifying the employer responsible for working conditions and conditions of employment. In this respect too, inter-enterprise relationships tend to be relations of "controlled autonomy" in which hierarchy is determined less by the exclusive economic dependence of a subcontractor on a prime contractor than by specific requirements pertaining to quality, delivery deadlines, training, etc., which can directly impact on working conditions without entailing any responsibility whatsoever on the part of the prime contractor.

As Supiot (2002) points out, such networked enterprises combine autonomy in the subordination of employees (who are evaluated on performance) with allegiance in the independence of the enterprises within the network which can thus sidestep the constructs of labour law based on master-servant relationships and hierarchic organization.

From the legal perspective, these sweeping changes raise two major issues. The first is the identification of the employer, since it has typically become impossible to piece together an enterprise with a single management. And the second, just as crucial, concerns the ways and means of providing for these forms of productive organization not only for the purposes of employment security, but also in terms of workers' ability to influence the decisions taken in particular workplaces, and the protection of working conditions.

The sharing of risks and responsibility

New organizational configurations and the transfer of risks

The developments outlined above and the underlying rationale have been the subject of many different interpretations. The one considered here, hypothetically, is that these changes may be driven by a shift in the terms on which responsibility is taken for the risk inherent in any economic enterprise.

The sharing of economic risk in a market economy, together with the corollary issue of responsibility for social risks in a wage-employment society like western Europe's, have indeed been at the very heart of the construction of labour law and, more generally, social law (Deakin, 2002; Ewald, 1986; Morin, 2000). A worker who makes her labour available to an employer takes no responsibility for entrepreneurial risk. She accepts a position of subordination in return for a measure of security based on the operation of collective solidarity, be it in the form of social insurance or regulations protecting labour and employment. The recent developments at issue here are contributing to the disruption of the terms of the trade-off between security and subordination, as already discussed by Supiot (1999 and 2002, inter alia).

The way firms are structured financially most certainly follows a financial rationale as to the sharing of financial risk. The networking of firms – into groups or contractual networks of enterprises – allows for the sharing of economic risk (and of the burden of investment). But the resulting distribution of economic and financial risks also entails a sharing of the employment risk, which is both a component of the risk of entrepreneurship borne by the employer and a social risk borne by the employee in the event of job loss and, consequently, loss of livelihood. The incorporation of subsidiaries and out-sourcing are assuredly means of transferring to other enterprises – if not to the employee or state authorities – the risks attaching to employment and work. The employment risk is not confined to labour costs: it also includes the risk of having to adjust the labour force to changes in employment, which may mean dismissals. As for the work-related risk, it comprises the risks that arise from the work itself,[13] from the very conditions in which it is performed collectively, taking account of the ever-present possibility of conflict, and from the safety of workers.

In today's financial market economy, such a transfer of risks poses a daunting question about responsibility, not so much in the legal sense of the term – responsibility being borne by whoever causes damage – as in an etymological sense: who is to be held accountable for events that are likely to affect working and employment relationships? And who is to contribute not only to compensation but also to preventing them? From this perspec-tive, the emergence and significance of debates over corporate social respon-sibility are – however this concept is understood – probably indicative of the new light in which the question is being posed as to the work and employ-ment responsibilities of enterprises and, more generally, of each of their stakeholders (Igalens, 2004).

Labour law options for accommodating the changes under way

The conventional responses that labour law has come up with fall into two categories. On the one hand, it spells out the responsibilities of the entre-preneur or, rather, of the legal employer, which derive from her/his entrepre-neurial capacity, both within the collective framework of the enterprise and within the individual framework of the contract of employment, while endeavouring to strike a balance between the right to employment and free-dom of enterprise. On the other hand, it organizes collective protection for jobless workers in the labour market.

In a situation where the reorganization of firms is accompanied by the development of various "controlled autonomy" relations and transfer of risks as described above, the problem is not only a matter of how the enter-prise can be reconceptualized so as to come up with binary relationships again, with a responsible employer or entrepreneur. From the legal stand-point, it is indeed just as much a question of how to accommodate trilateral relationships, be they contractual or institutional, in order to establish the respective responsibilities of the parties and organize collective guarantees more appropriately.

In a landmark article written over a decade ago, Teubner (1993) ex-plored the relationships between new forms of corporate organization and the law, proposing three types of approach that may achieve such accommodation. All three of them are indeed helpful in this respect.

The first approach, being the most conventional, consists in seeking out fraud. In the case of subcontracting operations, for example, the aim is to distinguish between those that are bona fide and those that are not, in order to identify who the real employer is. In particular, it is always essential to establish whether labour has been leased unlawfully. However, subcontracting or the incorporation of subsidiaries to carry out some of a firm's work may be entirely legitimate even when it involves a change of employer.

The second approach consists in piecing together the constituent parts of the enterprise in order to get a picture of the firm's economic and social unity in practice, following the classic paradigm of the enterprise.[14] This is the approach underlying France's legal doctrine and case law on economic and social unity (Boubli, 2004).

The third approach, on which Teubner lays particular emphasis, consists in examining the contractual or financial relationships between firms in order to retrace the chain of responsibility. Under French law, the obligation to re-employ redundant workers within a group of companies reflects an attempt at this approach. The same goes for other recent developments in Europe's positive law. European regulations on occupational safety and health in the event of joint work, for example, actually organize the sharing of responsibility for occupational safety between the prime enterprise and the other enterprises involved. Here, the aim is neither to crack down on fraud in order to identify the real employer nor to piece together a full picture of the enterprise, but to take account of inter-firm relationships so as to determine each firm's respective share of responsibility for such events as may occur over the course of the employment relationship.

This last approach will now be examined in the light of three classic concerns of labour law which corporate reorganization is once again bringing to the fore, namely, the powers of the enterprise's chief executive, the identification of the employer for the purposes of contractual relationships, and accountability for the conditions in which the work itself is performed.

NEW FORMS OF CORPORATE ORGANIZATION AND RESPONSIBILITY

The various approaches outlined above are already being used in positive law to establish the responsibilities of various parties, say, in identifying the locus of power for the purposes of collective labour relations, or in identifying the employer for the purposes of the individual contract of employment, or yet in seeking to establish responsibility for working conditions. A more detailed overview of the means used to these ends may help to give some idea of what the future holds.

The exercise of power and industrial relations

On this point, trends in the development of industrial relations law suggest, albeit tenuously, a few leads.

The broadening of workers' rights to information and consultation

Under European law, the right to information and consultation of workers' representatives now seems to be established as a matter of general principle, though not yet as a general right (Rodière, 2002). At any rate, this principle is reflected in a fair number of European directives – including those on European works councils,[15] on information and consultation of employees,[16] and on the European company statute[17] – and in the provisions on mandatory information to be provided to workers' representatives in the event of a transfer of enterprise ownership or redundancy.

This broadening of rights to information brings to mind a parallel that other authors have drawn already (Supiot, 2001). In the same way as corporate governance in the context of financial market capitalism rests on the principle of information transparency vis-à-vis shareholders, should such transparency not be provided on the same terms to the workers of the enterprises within the group? New information and communications technologies can play a crucial part in this respect. At present, European law lays down a principle of useful information, i.e. the provision of such data as will furnish a basis for adequate consideration (which is in fact the precondition for useful consultation – a substantively meaningful exchange of views aimed at eliciting a considered response and, if possible, reaching agreement). The relevant directives also establish the principle of equal access to information concerning the undertakings within a group. The principle of information transparency could, however, be extended a little further: as stakeholders in the firm, should employees not have access to the same information as shareholders, as opposed to information that is merely "appropriate"?

The European Court of Justice, for its part, considers that the right to information presupposes worker representation.[18] In other words, the representation of workers' interests must be organized at an appropriate level. Although the directives on European works councils and the European company statute do organize representation at the level of the centre of power, the fact remains that in less structured enterprise networks and in contractual networks the representation of workers' interests has yet to be organized at the level where problems actually arise (Gaudu, 2001). Affirmation of the principle of information transparency could thus serve as a catalyst for improving the structure of representation itself.

Appropriate levels of collective bargaining

Over the past 20 years there has been much talk about the decentralization of enterprise bargaining. Elaborating on this idea, France's legislation of 4 May 2004 enshrines the principle of subsidiarity in industry-level bargaining.[19] The effectiveness of this principle is questionable, however, at a time when the boundaries of the firm are becoming blurred both upstream and downstream.

Upstream, some legal systems like France's now recognize group-level bargaining.[20] Under European law, the establishment of a group-wide works council must proceed from bargaining at that level. In actual fact, group-level collective agreements had been concluded even before these legislative initiatives (Vachet, 1999). These were mostly framework agreements or procedural agreements designed to lay down principles whose practical application was then left to each individual enterprise within the group. This was indeed one way of accommodating the "controlled autonomy" that governs relations within the firm. From a legal perspective, the key issue concerns the extent to which a group-level agreement may or may not limit the scope of enterprise-level bargaining in areas where enterprise bargaining is recognized as a right in itself. France's recent legislation, for example, does not settle this issue.[21]

Downstream, in response to the decentralization of production, another avenue being explored ever so tentatively is that of location-based inter-enterprise bargaining or territorial bargaining covering enterprise networks. In the United States, for example, a notable decision of the National Labor Relations Board has established that the employees of the prime enterprise together with the agency employees working for it make up a multi-employer bargaining unit.[22] This approach has been taken in a number of countries (though not in France), and many authors have stressed the need for this bargaining format (Texier, 2003; Supiot, 1999; Trentin, 2002; Morin, 1999).[23]

The main issue raised by this form of bargaining is its purpose. Indeed, it may be tempting to think of this in terms of securing equal pay for the workers of separate enterprises participating in the same production venture at the same location, particularly in scenarios involving subcontracting. In positive law, the European directive on services lays down the principle of equal treatment – to some minimum standard at least – when the workers of an enterprise based in the European Union are sent to perform services in an enterprise located in another country of the Union. However, the application of this principle presupposes that the employees of the first enterprise hold jobs similar to those of the employees of the host enterprise. Yet, except in the event of subcontracting to make up for under-capacity, the outsourcing of certain tasks such as security surveillance or highly specialized subcontracting tends by definition to be concerned precisely with those jobs that have no equivalent in the host enterprise or which are outside its line of business. Indeed, such jobs would most probably not even be covered by the same collective agreement.

For these reasons, production-site bargaining would seem to be better suited to issues such as the standardization of fringe benefits (e.g. catering, transport, etc.), provisions for training or labour mobility within the network or across a given location, or the establishment of production-site commissions. Such bargaining could also focus on some sort of social clause that would spell out required minimum standards applicable to the employees of subcontractors wishing to prequalify for work with a prime contractor. This idea has already been taken up in the codes of conduct adopted by several major multinationals, sometimes at the outcome of collective bargaining. Such codes or agreements, however, are now more typically concerned with respect for certain fundamental rights than with the specification of minimum standards, as are collective agreements.[24]

The obstacles to the wider development of this form of bargaining are in effect more sociological than legal. They stem primarily from the composition of workers' collective representation and their willingness to accommodate enterprises' new organizational configurations. But they also stem from employers' reluctance to enter into legally binding commitments.

Upholding corporate social responsibility

The third lead is given by the concept of corporate social responsibility as defined in the Green Paper of the European Union, "whereby companies integrate social and environmental concerns in their business operations and in their interaction with their stakeholders on a voluntary basis" (European Commission, 2001, para. 20; Desbarrats, 2003; Sobczak, 2002 and 2004). It follows directly from the developments in collective bargaining outlined above, albeit with greater openness to the entire range of concerns surrounding corporate activity.

The actual scope of this concept remains the subject of intense debate (Sobczak, 2004; Gendron, Lapointe and Turcotte, 2004). Some see it as a means of promoting corporate self-regulation independently from government regulation, while others take the view that the practices deriving from corporate social responsibility foreshadow the way government standards and market standards will eventually come to interact on the basis of new standard-setting instruments.

Initially, the concept of corporate social responsibility was indeed used in reference to the codes of conduct that multinationals required their subcontractors to abide by. Typically, this meant that subcontractors (or enterprises within a given group) had to respect workers' fundamental rights or applicable collective agreements, sometimes subject to supervisory mechanisms. The literature on the subject highlights the significance of this growing practice, initiated by the multinationals themselves, but also the difficulty of securing compliance with these arrangements at the most basic level in spite of the emergence of supervisory mechanisms and social labelling schemes that function with the support of consumer groups.

In legal terms, the underlying trend raises two issues. The first is the scope of the very notion of fundamental rights. How does it differ from recognition of a wage employment status enshrined in a collective agreement? A tentative answer may be that it aims primarily to secure the rights of the wage-earner as an individual, rather than as a worker (Waquet, 2003; Valdés Dal Ré, 2003; Lyon-Caen and Vacarie, 2001). The rights in question appear to be characterized by their source (constitutional or international conventions) – such that their international application can indeed be envisaged – and by their objective, i.e. protecting the life or dignity of human beings. This last proposition obviously includes collective freedoms, but it also extends to commitments to occupational safety, protection of privacy and decent remuneration.

The second issue relates to the nature of penalties for non-compliance with codes of conduct. More specifically, what would be the liability of an enterprise that has adopted such a code if its subcontractors failed to abide by its provisions? On this particular point, Sobczak (2004) cites a ruling of the Supreme Court of California, in *Kasky vs. Nike Inc.* to the effect that non-compliance with a commitment made in a code of conduct, together with false information given in a social audit report, entail liability to prosecution for misrepresentation through advertising.[25]

Within the conceptual framework of a corporate social responsibility extending to inter-firm relations, the practice of adopting codes of conduct is thus underpinned by three important ideas. First, the aim is to secure the fundamental rights of workers as individuals. Second, the legal actionability of such codes is grounded in a mix of company law, consumer law and labour law. And third, the effectiveness of the codes is conditional upon a certain amount of publicity and, therefore, on a degree of transparency in their application. In other words, the system does not directly promote corporate responsibility in the sphere of labour relations; rather, it does so through the economic power that firms wield.

Social responsibility and restructuring

The issue of social responsibility obviously comes up in the context of corporate restructuring as well (redundancies, plant closures, etc.). In this context, however, the point is not to understand relations between firms per se, but to make a direct determination of the share of responsibility falling to an enterprise that closes down a given plant in relation to that plant's environment. In European law, efforts to give effect to the notion of corporate social responsibility in respect of restructuring have run into serious difficulty.[26] However, within the domestic systems of member States, including French law in particular, the framing of legal rules on this subject features a number of interesting developments. One of these, in France, is the obligation to re-employ redundant workers within the group. This obligation is particularly significant: although it places a burden on companies implementing redundancy plans, the very fact that the obligation is provided for shows that corporate responsibility can go beyond the strict confines of the contract of employment. Such reasoning could be extended to contractual networks of enterprises so that such networks also might be recognized as "spheres of mobility". French case law offers a few examples of contractual networks being considered in this way.[27] But it may be necessary to go further still and recognize a prime contractor's specific responsibility for employment relationships among subcontractors. The practices of certain large enterprises actually point in that direction (Raveyre, 2001). The extension of corporate responsibility beyond corporate boundaries and the need for joint action with other parties (local authorities, for example) are also reflected in the obligations recently prescribed in section 118 of France's Social Modernization Act of 17 January 2002. This requires very large enterprises to contribute to the development of alternative employment opportunities in areas affected by the complete or partial closure of one of their establishments. In such circumstances, the underlying idea is that whoever is responsible for economic decision-making has to take account of its consequences for third parties in accordance with new rules that apply regardless whether a fault was committed or an accident has occurred.

Another set of emerging issues centres on transfers of enterprise or establishment ownership, typically a key instrument of corporate restructuring. In actual fact, the law has long embodied solutions for maintaining production units in operation in such cases. This is especially true of European law and those domestic systems that provide for continuity of the contract of employment and, to some extent, the maintenance of collective regulatory frameworks. However, the reconfiguration of firms is now raising two kinds of issues. The first relates to the transferred entity being defined in such a way as to allow the contract of employment to be maintained, particularly in the service industry. The question here is whether the maintenance of economic activity is sufficient to identify the economic entity – and the outsourcing of business services makes this question ever more pressing. In other words: what is it that makes the firm a firm? Is it a set of contracts covering particular aspects of economic activity or is it a particular form of organization? Debates on enterprise ownership transfers thus raise a question about the very concept of the firm, calling for fresh thinking about its most basic level of organization. The "haziness" (Bailly, 2004) of the concept of a transferred economic entity may well be a reflection of the ease with which today's work organizations can be reconfigured. Another question that also relates to this first level of organization is about each worker's individual right to choose, which is recognized in some European legal systems and in the European directive on transfers. Specifically, the question here is whether a change of employer can be imposed on the worker; and, should the worker refuse to accept such a change, what are his/her rights (Ionescu, 2002)? There is no standard answer to these questions, though case law reflects some attempts to restrict outsourcing operations. In France, the so-called Perrier judgements follow a highly conventional approach to the enterprise, requiring verification that the transferred economic entity genuinely constitutes a unit with which the jobs of transferred workers are connected (Waquet, 2000).[28] Elsewhere, as in Australia for example, the approach taken is arguably more innovative: it is up to the court to verify that the transfer process is not a ploy designed to evade compliance with collective rights by challenging the applicable collective agreement.[29] But both approaches – i.e. maintaining the unity of the enterprise and preventing fraud – appear to be little more than partial responses to the development of outsourcing operations as an instrument of corporate strategy.

The contract of employment and determination of the employer

Driven by new forms of corporate organization, the growing incidence of triangular relations between a worker and one or more enterprises highlights the need for new forms of protection precisely because the employer is now not necessarily the party with the real decision-making power (Morin, 2001). On this point, the ILO's (2003) report on the scope of the employment relationship makes an important contribution to the literature on account of the wealth of insights it provides.

From the standpoint of workers' employment, several configurations are indeed possible. For example, one might involve putting an employee at the disposal of several enterprises within a group or requiring the employee to work for each of them in succession. Another, more conventional, involves subcontracting or service provision whereby the employees of one enterprise engage in work on the premises of another or are placed at its disposal to perform a particular job (they could also be self-employed workers). Yet another, also common, involves contract work through an agency, whereby an enterprise uses labour hired by a third-party employer responsible for the employment relationship (Morin, Dupuy and Larré, 1999).

In the face of such practices, the ILO report offers a comparative evaluation of at least two ways of taking account of inter-firm relations and, thereby, of establishing the responsibility of those firms that have taken decisions likely to affect the contract of employment.

Joint employers

Two enterprises can be considered jointly as a worker's employer, with joint responsibility for the employment relationship. In French law, this device is used in dealing with the companies within a group. It has also been used in cases where the employee of one enterprise is seconded to another for a protracted period (e.g. brand-specific salespersons working in department stores) and where the host enterprise exercises a measure of management authority.[30] The general idea is that whenever the host enterprise exercises a degree of control over an employee placed at its disposal, it can be considered as that employee's joint employer. This offers a starting point from which to construct a legal framework for the practice of assigning employees to work for another enterprise – a framework which would also help to address other issues that arise (see below). But where the employees of several enterprises work together, it may not be feasible to ascertain whether the supervisory control requirement is fulfilled.

However, some countries have enacted provisions that allow for all of the enterprises participating in the arrangement to be held jointly responsible for the employment relationship.[31] Of course, effective supervision of work rests with the enterprise at whose disposal the employee has been placed (and he/she may be assigned to several enterprises either simultaneously or in succession), but responsibility for the employment relationship rests jointly with all the enterprises in the network. While this approach thus distinguishes the use of labour from the overall employment connection, it relies on the notion of "networked employers" to establish the joint responsibility of all of the participants in the arrangement for the continuation of the employment relationship (unlike what happens, say, in the case of temporary or agency work where the user of the labour bears no responsibility for employment).

The joint liability of employers

The legal construct just described is indeed that of joint liability in respect of all or part of the employer's obligations to the worker. Finland, for example, has legislation that makes a prime contractor accountable for respect for workers' fundamental rights by its subcontractors.[32] This is in fact a means of giving legal effect to codes of conduct through the controlling enterprise itself. In the same spirit, a New York district court annulled a contract for the supply of garments because its terms offered inadequate safeguards for the payment of applicable minimum wages. Here too, the court's decision is grounded in the idea that the principal cannot ignore the consequences of its operations in terms of respect for the fundamental rights of a subcontractor's workforce.

In the same spirit, the inclusion in sub-contracts of "social clauses" specifying the workers' rights that the subcontractor must respect would offer a means of establishing the prime contractor's liability. The latter would then be let off only if the terms of the sub-contract make adequate provision for respect for those rights. Here again, a focus on the need to uphold workers' fundamental rights is helpful in the search for innovative solutions.

Under the laws of some countries, the prime contractor may be held accountable for, say, the social security registration of subcontractors' workers. French legislation on undisclosed employment is based on this approach.[33] It is then up to the party entering into a contract with an enterprise to ensure that it complies with its social obligations.

The notion that the principal or prime contractor may be held jointly liable thus offers considerable potential. In fact, it comes up in a variety of provisions, sometimes in very old statutes, whereby the prime contractor is under an obligation to guarantee compliance by subcontractors, notably in respect of wages (as is the case with the provisions of the French Civil Code governing subcontracting in construction and public works). As regards temporary agency workers, joint obligations in regard to wages also extend to the enterprise using their labour.[34]

Liability and performance of work

This question is another textbook classic. It takes us back to the issues that arise at the establishment level, involving tangible labour performed at a workplace. It is worth mentioning, however, that it has been at the heart of significant advances in the legal framing of new forms of corporate organization.

The basic idea is that the user of the labour – i.e. the party to which the labour is supplied – is responsible for enforcing the rules applicable to the performance of work although that party's liability for employment may be limited. This notion is reflected in numerous provisions of French law, though it has not been systematically codified as yet. The rules in question will not be detailed here; suffice it to say that the notion is an important one.[35] Indeed, it could serve as a basis for developing a law of secondment/labour supply, if only to establish a clear legal framework for the many working arrangements that can occur in a host enterprise whose legal status remains largely unsettled, e.g. project-specific team work, secondment of an employee to another enterprise, joint provision of services, etc. (Morin, Dupuy and Larré, 1999).

Another idea, which follows from the first, is recognition of the concept of joint work or "co-working" in French law. This is more specifically concerned with occupational safety as provided for in the European Directive on workers' safety and health. The term joint work should be understood to refer to situations where workers from several enterprises take part in a common undertaking.[36] The Directive is based on three principles, namely: responsibility rests with the employer who is a party to the contract of employment; preventive action must be taken in respect of risks arising from joint work; and enterprises sharing a workplace must cooperate, exchange information and coordinate protection. In French law, recognition of joint work has produced two sets of rules that are interesting in terms of provision for the respective responsibilities of each of the enterprises involved.[37] These rules were recently expanded in the legislation of 15 July 2003 on major technological hazards.

First, there are rules that effectively organize information-sharing on risks and preventive action between the host enterprise and the labour-supplying enterprise or, as the case may be, among the various enterprises sharing a given workplace. Such coordination of information and preventive action is linked to a sharing of responsibility between the prime contractor and the subcontractor(s) in respect of their workers. Responsibility for coordination, however, rests with the prime contractor. The extent of the latter's responsibility is further increased under the recent legislation on major technological hazards: it is up to the prime contractor to ensure that the subcontractors comply with prevention requirements (an illustration of the second mechanism described above).[38]

Second, these statutory provisions (including the legislation on major technological hazards) prescribe a variety of rules that organize relations between the workers' representatives of the various enterprises sharing responsibility for occupational safety. Under the legislation on major technological hazards, provision is also made for joint, inter-enterprise representation on major worksites – through a "committee on occupational health and safety and working conditions" (CHSCT) – and for the workers' representatives of sub-contracting enterprises to attend the prime contractor's CHSCT.

In short, the coordination of enterprises' responsibilities needs to be matched by coordination of workers' representation. Although it is outlined here in very general terms, this idea is important because it highlights the need to ensure that representation genuinely takes account of the conditions experienced by workers. Unity of representation or bargaining must be organized or reorganized in the light of how tangible work is performed: it is not something that can be pre-determined. In France, this is the position taken in judicial decisions. Indeed, recent case law requires that all of the workers of independent enterprises contributing to the operations of a client enterprise must be counted as part of the latter's own workforce for the purposes of electing workers' representatives.[39] The establishment – now more broadly understood as a worksite – has thus regained its position as a major focus of the law.

CONCLUDING REMARKS

However patchy, the foregoing overview of incipient developments in the way positive law is coming to grips with new forms of corporate organization and the sharing of associated risks suggests three main themes. A focus on these themes could, in turn, help to chart the course of future developments in labour law, taking account of the various aims of workers' protection at different levels of corporate organization.

The first of these themes is in line with the general objective of respect for workers' fundamental rights. At the international level, this ties in with – not to say substitutes for – the objective of employment security that was central to the construction of national labour law systems in the second half of the twentieth century. The pursuit of this objective is evidenced both by the current debates over corporate social responsibility and by the adoption of the ILO's Declaration on Fundamental Rights and Principles at Work (ILO, 1998).

The other two themes are more specifically concerned with intra-firm or inter-firm relations. First, as regards industrial relations, the key issue seems to be transparency of information across enterprise networks. Such transparency opens up the possibility of establishing relations between workers' representatives and separate workforces either within a given firm or within a network of firms. It can help to set up new bargaining units or new units for collective action on the basis of the common interests of workers at different organizational levels. And second, as regards the responsibilities associated with the very exercise of freedom of enterprise in today's new corporate configurations, further consideration deserves to be given to recognition of the joint liability of distinct enterprises for all or part of the employer's obligations, according to the purpose of their collaboration and the nature of their relationships, so as to address the implications of new forms of corporate organization and the way work and employment risks are being shared as a result.

Notes

[1] This article is based on a presentation given at a round-table discussion during the seventeenth Congress of the International Association for Labour Law, held at Montevideo on 25 September 2003. It draws on the findings of empirical research conducted in France and Europe-wide by the Interdisciplinary Laboratory for Research on Human Resources and Employment (LIRHE), CNRS Social Sciences University of Toulouse, and on ILO (2003).

[2] The following discussion owes much to earlier seminar work on this topic, particularly in France: "The Boundaries of the Enterprise and Labour Law", a seminar organized by the French Association for Labour Law (AFDT), Paris, December 2000 (see *Droit Social*, No. 5, May 2001), and the contributions of G. Vallée on codes of conduct; and the international symposium of May 2003 on "Equity, Efficiency and Ethics: The Social Regulation of Global Business", organized by the Inter-University Centre for Research on Globalization and Work (University of Montreal, Laval University, HEC Montreal), Montreal, 2003 (see Murray and Trudeau, 2004).

[3] This reasoning draws on multidisciplinary research on the concept of "the enterprise" conducted by economists and legal experts (see, in particular, Jeammaud, Kirat and Villeval, 1996; Morin and Morin, 2002).

[4] These authors consider additional focal points to be procedures for defending interests, collective bargaining and the role of the State.

[5] Council Directive 98/50/EC of 29 June 1998 amending Directive 77/187/EEC on the approximation of the laws of Member States relating to the safeguarding of employees' rights in the event of transfers of undertakings, businesses or parts of businesses (*Official Journal of the European Communities*, No. L201, 17 July 1998, pp. 88-92).

[6] See Case 24/85, *Jozeph Maria Antonius Spijkers vs. Gebroeders Benedick Abattoir CV and Alfred Benedik en Zonen BV*, ECJ 1986, p. 1119, on the maintenance of workers' rights in the event

of enterprise transfers, as subsequently confirmed by case C-13/95, *Ayse Sûzen vs. Zehnackar Gebâudereinigung Gmbh Krankenhausservice*, ECJ 1997, p. I-1259.

[7] Act No. 2004-391 of 4 May 2004 concerning lifelong vocational training and social dialogue, in *Journal Officiel* (Paris), 5 May 2004; new article L.132-19-1 of the French Labour Code.

[8] Council Directive 2001/86/EC of 8 October 2001 supplementing the Statute for a European company with regard to the involvement of employees, in *Official Journal of the European Communities* (Luxembourg), No. L294, 10 November 2001, pp. 22-32.

[9] A concept proposed by Stewart III (1991), cited by Gendron, Lapointe and Turcotte (2004).

[10] Cited by Gendron, Lapointe and Turcotte (2004).

[11] See *Liaisons Sociales Europe* of 6 February and 17 April 2003.

[12] For example, the Sky alliance between eight airline companies from different continents operates common services to the various companies with the result that the employees of different enterprises occasionally work together or in shared premises. Another example is given by distribution networks based on agreements between retailers and suppliers.

[13] Which also tends to be increasingly transferred to the employee, particularly through today's new forms of remuneration (A. Lyon-Caen, 1996).

[14] This paradigm actually characterizes this approach, which may also be combined with the fraud-seeking approach (Urban, 2000).

[15] Council Directive 94/45/CE of 22 September 1994 on the establishment of a European Works Council or a procedure in Community-scale undertakings and Community-scale groups of undertakings for the purpose of informing and consulting employees, in *Official Journal of the European Communities* (Luxembourg), No. L254, 30 September 1994, pp. 64-72.

[16] European Parliament and Council Directive 2002/14/CE of 11 March 2002 establishing a general framework for informing and consulting employees in the European Community, in *Official Journal of the European Communities* (Luxembourg), No. L080, 23 March 2002, pp. 29-34.

[17] See note 8 above.

[18] See case C382/92, *Commission of the European Communities vs. United Kingdom of Great Britain and Northern Ireland*, ECJ 1994, p. I-2435, on the maintenance of workers' rights in the event of enterprise transfers.

[19] In relation to individual enterprises, though not in relation to the group (new article L.132-19-1 of the Labour Code).

[20] In a new article of the Labour Code introduced by the legislation of 4 May 2004.

[21] The issue was raised by the so-called AXA judgement that preceded statutory recognition of group-level bargaining in France. See Court of Cassation, Social Chamber, 30 April 2003, Case No. 1283, in *Revue de jurisprudence sociale* (Levallois-Perret), No. 916, July.

[22] M. B. Sturgis, Inc. and Textile Processors, Service Trades, Health Care, Professional and Technical Employees International Union local 108, 331 NLRB, No. 173, 25 August 2000 (cited by Gaudu, 2001).

[23] A somewhat dated example is the Agreement on the Ariane Espace Base at Kourou between Ariane Espace and the subcontractors working on the base. For a more recent example of location-wide social dialogue (though not actual bargaining) at the CGE Alsthom site at Nantes, see Texier (2003).

[24] See, for example, the agreement on social responsibility concluded between General Motors and its European works council, in *Liaisons Sociales Europe* (Paris), No. 67, 27 November 2002; or the agreement of 11 May 2001 between the IUF, the Coordinating Committee of Banana Workers' Unions (COLSIBA) and Chiquita Brands International (cited in ILO, 2003).

[25] *Kasky vs. Nike Inc.*, Supreme Court of California, 27 CAL 4th 939, No. SO87859, 2 May 2002.

[26] Following initial consultations, work on restructuring is now at a standstill. For empirical work taking a comparative European perspective, see Segal, Sobczak and Triomphe (2002).

[27] Court of Cassation, Social Chamber, 9 June 2004, appeal No. 01-46584 (available at www. legisfrance.gov.fr).

[28] Court of Cassation, Social Chamber, 18 July 2000, Appeal No. 98-18037, in *Bulletin Civil de la Cour de Cassation* (Paris), part V, No. 285, July, p. 225.

[29] *Australian Municipal, Administrative, Clerical Service Union vs. Greater Dandenong City Council* (2000), 48 Australian Industrial Law Reports, 4-236.

[30] Court of Cassation, Social Chamber, 19 January 1999, in *Bulletin Civil de la Cour de Cassation* (Paris), Part V, No. 35, January. See also Lemière (1997).

[31] See, for example, article L.127-1 of the French Labour Code.

[32] Cited in ILO (2003, p. 69).

[33] Article L.324-13-1 of the Labour Code.

[34] See articles L.143-6 and L.143-8 of the Labour Code on construction workers and articles R.124-22 and L.125-2 on temporary employment and labour-supplying agencies.

[35] On temporary work and labour contracting agencies, see Articles L.124-4-6 and L.125-2 of the French Labour Code.

[36] This definition is taken from the circular issued in France in March 1993 pursuant to the Decree of 20 February 1992 to give effect to Council Directive 89/391/EEC of 12 June 1989 on the introduction of measures to encourage improvements in the safety and health of workers at work, in *Official Journal of the European Communities* (Luxembourg), No. L 183, 29 June 1989, pp. 1-8.

[37] For the purposes of occupational safety and health, French law considers joint work to be a particular form of work. See Articles R.237-1 et seq. of the Labour Code, on involvement of an enterprise in the workplace of another, and Articles L.235.1 et seq. on construction and civil engineering works.

[38] A number of codes of social responsibility make provision for the safety of the workers of sub-contracting enterprises or for the establishment of worksite commissions. Examples include the above-mentioned General Motors agreement and the CGE Alsthom experiment reported by Texier (2003).

[39] See *Syndicat CGT Renault v. Société Renault* (Court of Cassation, Social Chamber, 26 May 2004, Judgement No. 1073), in *Bulletin civil de la Cour de cassation* (Paris), Part V, No. 141, May.

References

Aglietta, Michel. 1998. "Le capitalisme de demain", in *Note de la Fondation Saint Simon* (Paris), No. 101, Nov.

—; Rebérioux, Antoine. 2004. *Dérives du capitalisme financier*. Paris, Albin Michel.

Appay, Béatrice. 1993. "Individu et collectif: questions à la sociologie du travail et des professions. L'autonomie contrôlée", in *Cahier du Gedisst* (Paris), No. 6.

Bailly, Pierre. 2004. "Le flou de l'article L 122-12, alinéa 2 du Code du travail", in *Droit Social* (Paris), No. 4 (Apr.), pp. 366-374.

Baudru, Daniel; Morin, François. 1999. "Gestion institutionnelle et crise financière, une gestion spéculative du risque", in Conseil d'analyse économique (ed.): *Architecture financière internationale*. Supplement to Report No. 18. Paris, La Documentation française, pp. 151-169.

Boubli, Bernard. 2004. "L'unité économique et sociale à l'époque des vœux. Etat des lieux et souhaits de réforme", in *Semaine Sociale Lamy* (Paris), No. 1156 and No. 1157 (Feb.).

Boyer, Robert; Durand, Jean-Pierre. 1998. *L'après-fordisme*. Paris, Syros.

Castells, Manuel. 1998. *The rise of the network society*. Paris, Librairie Arthème Fayard.

Deakin, Simon. 2002. "The evolution of the employment relationship". Paper presented at the Second France/ILO Symposium on the Future of Work, Employment and Social Protection, Lyons, 17-18 Jan. 2002. Available online at: www.ilo.org/public/english/bureau/inst/download/deakin.pdf

Del Cont, Catherine. 1998. *Propriété économique, dépendance et responsabilité*. Paris, l'Harmattan.

Desbarats, Isabelle. 2003. "Codes de conduites et chartes éthiques des entreprises privées, regard sur une pratique en expansion", in *JCP G Semaine Juridique (Edition générale)* (Paris), No. 9, pp. 337-343.

—.1996. *L'entreprise à établissements multiples en droit du travail*. Paris, LGDJ.

Despax, Michel. 1957. *L'entreprise et le droit*. Paris, LGDJ.

Duplessis, Isabelle. 2004. "La déclaration de l'OIT relative aux droits fondamentaux au travail. Une nouvelle forme de régulation efficace?", in *Industrial Relations* (Quebec), Vol. 59, No. 1, pp. 52-72.

European Commission. 2001. *Green Paper: Promoting a European framework for corporate social responsibility*. COM/2001/0366. Available online at: http://europa.eu.int/comm/employment_social/soc-dial/csr/greenpaper_en.pdf

Ewald, François. 1986. *L'Etat Providence*. Paris, Grasset.

Farjat, Gérard et al. 1987. "Une reconnaissance de l'entreprise en droit privé", in *Revue Internationale de Droit économique* (Brussels), p. 521.

Gaudu, François. 2001. "Entre concentration économique et externalisation: les nouvelles frontières de l'entreprise", Colloque "Les frontières de l'entreprise", in *Droit Social* (Paris), No. 5 (May), pp. 471-477.

—.1999. "Entreprise et établissement", in Editions Dalloz (ed.): *Prospectives du droit économique. Livre d'amitié à Michel Jeantin*. Paris, Dalloz, p. 47.

—.1996: "Les notions d'emploi en droit", in *Droit Social* (Paris), No. 6 (June), pp. 569-576.

Gendron, Corinne; Lapointe, Alain; Turcotte, Marie-France. 2004. "Responsabilité sociale et régulation de l'entreprise mondialisée", in *Industrial Relations* (Quebec), Vol. 59, No. 1, pp. 73-100.

Igalens, Jacques (ed.). 2004. *Tous responsables*. Paris, Editions d'Organisation.

ILO. 2004. *A fair globalization: Creating opportunities for all*. Report of the World Commission on the Social Dimension of Globalization. Geneva.

—.2003. *The scope of the employment relationship*. Report V, International Labour Conference, 91st Session. Geneva.

—.1998. *ILO Declaration on Fundamental Principles and Rights at Work*. International Labour Conference, 86th Session. Geneva. Available online at: www.ilo.org/public/english/standards/relm/ilc/ilc86/com-dtxt.htm.

Ionescu, Valentin. 2002. "Le droit d'opposition des salariés au transfert de leur contrat de travail: mythe ou réalité", in *Droit Social* (Paris), No. 5 (May), pp. 507-515.

Jeammaud, Antoine.1989. "Les polyvalences du contrat de travail", in Editions Dalloz (ed.): *Les transformations du droit du travail. Etudes offertes à Gérard Lyon-Caen*. Paris, Dalloz, pp. 299-316.

—; Lyon-Caen, Antoine; Le Friant, Martine. 1998. "L'ordonnancement des relations du travail", Chronique, in *Recueil Dalloz* (Paris), pp. 359-368.

—; Kirat, Thierry; Villeval, Marie-Claire. 1996. "Les règles juridiques, l'entreprise et son institutionnalisation: au croisement de l'économie et du droit", in *Revue Internationale de Droit Economique* (Brussels), pp. 99-141.

Lemière, Séverine. 1997. "La relation salariale des démonstrateurs(trices) dans les grands magasins", in *Droit Ouvrier* (Paris), July, pp. 274-277.

Lyon-Caen, Antoine. 2003. "Géographie du droit du travail", in *Semaine Sociale Lamy* (Paris), special supplement edited by P. Waquet ("Les lieux du droit du travail"), Oct., pp. 16-18.

—.1996. "Les clauses de transferts de risques sur le salarié", in *Revue juridique de l'Ile de France* (Paris), No. 39/40, p. 151.

—; Vacarie, Isabelle. 2001. "Droit fondamentaux et droit du travail", in Editions Dalloz (ed.): *Droit syndical et droits de l'homme à l'aube du XXIe siècle. Mélanges en l'honneur de Jean-Maurice Verdier.* Paris, Dalloz, pp. 421-453.

—; Lyon-Caen, Gérard. 1978. "La doctrine de l'entreprise", in LITEC (ed.): *Dix ans de droit de l'entreprise.* Paris, LITEC, pp. 599-621.

Morin, François; Morin, Marie-Laure. 2002. "La firme et la négociation collective. La question des frontières en économie et en droit", in USST (ed.): *Mélanges dédiés au Président Michel Despax.* Toulouse, Presses de l'Université des sciences sociales de Toulouse, p. 97.

Morin, Marie-Laure. 2001. "Les frontières de l'entreprise et la responsabilité de l'emploi", in *Droit Social* (Paris), No. 5 (May), pp. 478-486.

—.2000. "Partage des risques et responsabilité de l'emploi – contribution au débat sur la réforme du droit du travail", in *Droit Social* (Paris), No. 7/8 (July-Aug.), pp. 730-738.

—.1999. "Espaces et enjeux de la négociation collective territoriale", in *Droit Social* (Paris), No. 7/8 (July-Aug.), pp. 681-691.

—.(ed.). 1996. *Sous-traitance et relations salariales. Aspects du droit du travail.* Cahier du LIRHE. No. 2. Toulouse, Université des sciences sociales de Toulouse.

—.1994. "Sous-traitance et relations salariales. Aspects de droit du travail", in *Travail et Emploi* (Paris), No. 60, pp. 23-43.

—; Dupuy, Yves; Larré, Françoise. 1999: *Prestation de travail et activité de service.* Cahier Travail Emploi Series. Paris, La Documentation française.

Murray, Gregor; Trudeau, Gilles. 2004. "Une régulation sociale de l'entreprise mondialisée? Introduction", in *Industrial Relations* (Quebec), Vol. 59, No. 1, pp. 3-14.

Raveyre, Marie. 2001. "Implication territoriale des groupes et gestion du travail et de l'emploi, vers des intermédiations en réseaux", in *Revue de l' IRES* (Paris), No. 35, pp. 35-59.

Rémy, Patrick. 2001. "Le groupe, l'entreprise et l'établissement: une approche en droit comparé", in *Droit social* (Paris), No. 5 (May), pp. 505-513.

Rodière, Pierre. 2002. *Droit social de l'Union européenne.* Second edition. Paris, LGDJ.

Segal, Jean-Pierre; Sobczak, André; Triomphe, Claude-Emmanuel. 2002. "Douze entreprises européennes socialement responsables?", in *Liaisons Sociales Europe* (Paris), No. 65, Oct.

Simitis, Spiros. 1997. "Le droit du travail a-t-il encore un avenir?", in *Droit Social* (Paris), No. 7/8 (July-Aug.), pp. 655-668.

Sobczak, André. 2004. "La responsabilité sociale de l'entreprise: menace ou opportunité pour le droit du travail", in *Industrial Relations* (Quebec), Vol. 59, No. 1, pp. 26-51.

—.2002. "Le cadre juridique de la responsabilité sociale des entreprises en Europe et aux Etats-Unis", in *Droit Social* (Paris), No. 9/10 (Sep.-Oct.), pp. 806-811.

Stewart III, Bennett. 1991. *The quest for value*. New York, Harper Collins.

Storper, Michael; Salais, Robert. 1993. *Les mondes de production. Enquête sur l'identité économique de la France*. Paris, Les Editions de l'EHESS.

Supiot, Alain. 2002. *Entre marché et régulation: les nouvelles régulations sociales assurent-elles une sécurité tout au long de la vie?* Introductory paper presented at the Second France/ILO Symposium on the Future of Work, Employment and Social Protection, Lyons, 17-18 Jan. 2002. Available online at: www.ilo.org/public/french/bureau/inst/download/supiot.pdf.

—.2001. "Revisiter les droits d'action collective", in *Droit Social* (Paris), No. 7/8 (July-Aug.), pp. 687-704.

—.2000. "La contractualisation de la société", in Y. Michaux (ed.): *Qu'est-ce que l'humain?, Université de tous les savoirs*. Paris, Editions Odile Jacob, Vol. 2, pp. 157-167.

—.(ed.). 1999. *Au-delà de l'emploi, transformation du travail et devenir du droit du travail en Europe*. Paris, Flammarion.

—.1997. "Du bon usage des lois en matière d'emploi", in *Droit Social* (Paris), No. 3 (Mar.), pp. 229-242.

—.1985. "Groupes de sociétés et paradigme de l'entreprise", in *Revue trimestrielle de Droit Commercial* (Paris), pp. 621-644.

Teubner, Gunther. 1993. Nouvelles formes d'organisation et droit", in *Revue française de gestion* (Paris), No. 96 (Nov.), pp. 50-68.

Texier, Jean-Yves. 2003. "L'entreprise plurielle. L'émergence des logiques de site", in *Les nouvelles formes de travail, Cadres-CFDT* (Paris), No. 403 (Feb.), pp. 62-66.

Teyssié, Bernard (ed.). 1999. *Les groupes de sociétés et le droit du travail*. Paris, Editions Panthéon-Assas.

Trentin, Bruno. 2002. *Potential changes in systems of industrial relations*. Paper presented at the Second France/ILO Symposium on the Future of Work, Employment and Social Protection, Lyons, 17-18 Jan. 2002. Available online at: www.ilo.org/public/english/bureau/inst/download/trentin.pdf

Urban, Quentin. 2000. "Piercing the veil, Cour d'appel de Caen 21 septembre 1999", in *Droit Social* (Paris), No. 4, pp. 385- 391.

Vachet, Gérard. 1999. "La négociation collective dans les groupes de sociétés", in Teyssié, pp. 105-123.

Valdés dal Ré, Fernando. 2003. *Droit du travail et droits fondamentaux des personnes*. General Report on Fundamental Rights, XVIIth World Congress on Labour and Social Security Law, Montevideo, 2-5 Sep.

Verge, Pierre; Vallée, Guylaine. 1997. *Un droit du travail? Essai sur la spécificité du droit du travail*. Québec, Les Editions Yvons Blais Inc.

Virassamy, G.-J. 1986. *Les contrats de dépendance, essai sur les activités professionnelles exercées dans une dépendance économique*. Paris, LGDJ.

Waquet. Philippe. 2003. *Droit du travail et droits fondamentaux des travailleurs*. Report of France to the XVIIth World Congress on Labour and Social Security Law, Montevideo, 2-5 Sep.

—.2000. "Libres propos sur l'externalisation", in *Semaine Sociale Lamy* (Paris), No. 999, p. 7.

NIGHT WORK OF WOMEN IN INDUSTRY: STANDARDS AND SENSIBILITY

15

George P. POLITAKIS *

In the course of the twentieth century, the ILO's Conventions concerning the prohibition of night work for women in industry were gradually relegated from the status of memorable achievements for the protection of female workers to being an embarrassment to the Organization's commitment to promote gender equality and non-discrimination at work. The instruments in question are the Night Work (Women) Convention, 1919 (No. 4), the Night Work (Women) Convention (Revised), 1934 (No. 41), the Night Work (Women) Convention (Revised), 1948 (No. 89), and the Protocol of 1990 to the Night Work (Women) Convention (Revised), 1948. Since their adoption, these four instruments have received a total of 165 ratifications, but also 72 denunciations – a clear sign that for numerous member States these instruments have fallen into obsolescence.

Against this background, the Governing Body of the ILO requested the Committee of Experts on the Application of Conventions and Recommendations to undertake the first General Survey on the application of the Conventions concerning women's night work in industry (ILO, 2001).[1] Specifically, the Committee was requested to take stock of ILO's standard-setting activities in this field over a span of 80 years and, also, to offer guidance on the unresolved question of whether the ILO instruments dealing with this matter are still relevant and suited to present needs, principles and values.

The purpose of this article is to present a synthesis of the Committee's findings. The article opens with a presentation of the general background to the current controversy over the legal prohibition of women's night work,

Originally published in *International Labour Review*, Vol. 140 (2001), No. 4.

* Legal/Labour Law Specialist, Social Protection and Labour Conditions Branch, International Labour Office.

including relevant aspects of women's labour force participation and selected findings on the effects of night work. This is followed by a short history of ILO standards on the night work of women in industry and, in a third section, a review of national law and practice in this field. The discussion then turns to the conflict between legal "protection" of female workers and the principles of non-discrimination and equal treatment. The article ends with the Committee of Experts' main findings on this issue, followed by a recapitulatory concluding section and a "postscript" outlining the positions expressed by the ILO's constituents during the discussion of the General Survey at the International Labour Conference in June 2001.

FEMALE LABOUR, NIGHT WORK AND SEX EQUALITY

The rationale behind the first national measures on night-time work in factories, adopted during the last quarter of the nineteenth century, was that women together with children belonged to a specific category of factory workers needing special protection because they were physically weaker than men and more susceptible to exploitation.[2] The idea of protecting adult women and children against arduous working conditions also found expression in the Preamble to the ILO Constitution and later led to the adoption of several Conventions such as the Maternity Protection Convention, 1919 (No. 3), the Night Work of Young Persons (Industry) Convention, 1919 (No. 6) and the Night Work (Bakeries) Convention, 1925 (No. 20). The first ILO Convention on the night work of women thus embodied the convergence of two preoccupations – i.e. humanizing working conditions by limiting night work in general, while setting up women-specific protective rules principally on account of their reproductive role and traditional family responsibilities.

Nowadays, however, the basic premise underlying all three Conventions on women's night work in industry appears critically flawed. Indeed, there seems to be little justification for legal rules that seek to restrict access to night-time employment on the basis of sex rather than the worker's physical aptitude.[3] Particularly problematic is the compatibility of such rules with the Discrimination (Employment and Occupation) Convention, 1958 (No. 111), or with the Workers with Family Responsibilities Convention, 1981 (No. 156), both of which seek to promote a completely different approach. The uneasy relationship between the current ILO standards on the night work of women in industry and such fundamental principles of non-discrimination and equality of opportunity and treatment between men and women is further confirmed by the 1979 United Nations Convention on the Elimination of All Forms of Discrimination Against Women, European Community laws and the jurisprudence of the European Court of Justice (see, for example, Heide, 1999; Ellis, 1998, pp. 190-260; ILO, 2000, pp. 6 and 78).

The ILO's delicate balancing act

Over the past 15 years, the Organization has made considerable efforts to evaluate the effectiveness and relevance of standards on women's night work in industry and, on that basis, to assess the willingness of its constituents to abandon protective legislation applying to women in favour of night-work regulations applicable to all workers. Most of these efforts, however, have remained inconclusive, at best confirming the persistence of profoundly differing opinions about the benefits or negative effects of special protective legislation prohibiting women's work at night. In 1984, the Office gave a legal opinion advising member States that they were bound to review their protective legislation in accordance with the United Nations Convention on the Elimination of All Forms of Discrimination Against Women and that, following this review, member States might need to denounce the relevant ILO Conventions at the appropriate time. The text concluded, however, that "there need not be any contradiction between the obligations arising under the UN Convention and those assumed by a State having ratified ILO Conventions providing for special protection for women for reasons unconnected with maternity, namely Convention No. 45 and Conventions Nos. 4, 41 and 89" (ILO, 1984, p. 6, para. 17).

In 1985, a resolution of the International Labour Conference on equal opportunities and equal treatment for men and women in employment called upon member States to "review all protective legislation applying to women in the light of up-to-date scientific knowledge and technological changes and to revise, supplement, extend, retain or repeal such legislation according to national circumstances" (ILO, 1985, p. 80). In 1989, the Meeting of Experts on Special Protective Measures for Women and Equality of Opportunity and Treatment came to the conclusion that "special protective measures for women alone in the case of dangerous, arduous and unhealthy work are incompatible with the principle of equality of opportunity and treatment unless they arise from women's biological condition"; the experts recommended that "there should be a periodic review of protective instruments in order to determine whether their provisions are still adequate in the light of experience acquired since their adoption and to keep them up to date in the light of scientific and technical knowledge and social progress" (ILO, 1990a, pp. 79-80). In its conclusions, however, the Meeting of Experts made it clear that special protective measures for women concerning night work were expressly excluded from the scope of their recommendations, probably because of the well-known sensitivity of this issue and the upcoming Conference discussion of a draft instrument revising Convention No. 89.

In the framework of the ILO Governing Body's Working Party on Policy regarding the Revision of Standards, the Office put forward on two occasions the idea of shelving Conventions Nos. 4 and 41 but the proposal met with the strong opposition of the worker members who called for a detailed examination of all three night-work Conventions and emphasized the need to promote the ratification of Convention No. 89 (ILO, 1996b, paras. 47-49). It was finally agreed to promote the ratification of Convention No. 89 and its Protocol of 1990 or, where appropriate, of Convention No. 171, and to denounce, as appropriate, Conventions Nos. 4 and 41. In approving the proposals of the Working Party, the Governing Body considered that Conventions Nos. 4 and 41 "retain their value on an interim basis for States party" and that therefore the shelving of these instruments is not called for under present conditions (ILO, 1997, Appendix I, para. 21).

Apart from the evolving yet somewhat irresolute ILO position, the practice of member States in recent years is also of importance. Whereas the 1990 Protocol to Convention No. 89 has received only three ratifications since its adoption some eleven years ago, Convention No. 89 has been denounced in the same period by as many as 14 countries, thus confirming earlier evidence that the international labour Conventions on women's night work in industry have been among the most widely denounced ILO instruments (Widdows, 1984, p. 1062).

The hidden face of the "feminization" of labour

Although women's participation in the labour market has been increasing steadily, the male-female gap in relation to conditions of work persists (United Nations, 2000, pp. 109-137). Employment opportunities may be expanding – due to factors such as the growth of the services sector and, more recently, information and communications technologies and globalization – but women often have to cope with a "double burden" in striving to reconcile family responsibilities with market work. Women remain concentrated in atypical employment and spend much of their working time doing unpaid work. They continue to receive less pay than men, and they are disproportionately affected by unemployment, financial crises and migration. Seen from the perspective of growing flexibilization and casualization of employment, the term "feminization" of labour thus really means that "female labour is still available when needed and dispensable when it is not"(United Nations, 1999, p. xvii).

Women's employment in export-oriented industries in developing countries offers a good example of poor working conditions, including extensive use of irregular hours, overtime and night work. In addition, female labour in such industries is often synonymous with low wages, long commuting times, minimal job security and denial of basic maternity protection (ILO, 1998; ILO/UNCTC, 1988; United States Department of Labor, 1989; ICFTU, 1998). Under the circumstances, some countries find it difficult to abide by ILO standards, including those prohibiting night work for women, and decide either to denounce the relevant Conventions or to exclude export processing zones (EPZs) from the scope of restrictive labour legislation. In

1983, for instance, Sri Lanka denounced Convention No. 89 on the grounds that the prohibition against women's night work would discourage the establishment of foreign enterprises in its EPZ. In Mauritius, where night work is generally prohibited, EPZ workers are specifically exempted from the prohibition by virtue of the 1993 Industrial Expansion Act.

Night work and its effects

The number of permanent night workers has quadrupled in the past 15 years with shift workers now accounting for 20-25 per cent of the working population in most industrialized countries. Spurred by globalization and the new economy, businesses and individuals are forging new working patterns, making increasing use of night hours and capitalizing on the economic potential of round-the-clock production and services. Today's information technology allows some workers to choose their hours and place of work. The growth of night work is thus the result of the 24-hour society and its unrelenting search for flexibility in working time. And as lifestyles change, there is growing acceptance of "night-time" as part of the working "day". Available figures for North America and Europe show that one in five people now works a non-traditional schedule, in which most of the working hours are outside the traditional "nine to five".

Although statistics are scarce, women appear to be particularly affected by the rising incidence of night work, especially in so far as it concerns lower skilled jobs such as data processing and jobs in credit card billing centres or call centres. Moreover, the "flexibilization" of working time leads to the development of atypical and precarious forms of employment which are frequently characterized by inferior conditions. As pointed out in an earlier ILO study, "destandardizing" the duration and arrangement of working time could have detrimental effects on the safety, health and well-being of workers while flexibility in working time should not be equated with the dismantling of social protection (ILO, 1995, p. 24). The health implications of rotating shift systems or extensive night-work arrangements are known to include over-fatigue, sleep disturbances, increased gastro-intestinal and cardiovascular problems and a weakened immune response because of the disruption of the body's circadian rhythms. Apart from such physical symptoms, studies have demonstrated that night work may also cause psychological disorders, such as stress and depression, and have adverse effects on family and social life.[4]

The antinomy between the ban on women's night work and gender equality advocacy

The promotion of women's rights, equality and non-discrimination between the sexes has gained significant momentum in the past twenty years and is now central to international discourse on policy-making relating to human rights and social development. The 1979 United Nations Convention on the Elimination of All Forms of Discrimination Against Women, the European Social Charter, as last revised in 1996 (see Council of Europe, 1995 and 1999), or the European Council's Equal Treatment Directive of 1976,[5] all endorsed the principle that restrictions on the employment of women for night work are justifiable only in the case of maternity. This principle echoes long-established scientific evidence that there are no physiological differences between women and men as regards tolerance of shift work or adaptation to night work: "from the medical point of view there is no justification for protecting only women workers except insofar as their function of reproduction is concerned because of the risks to the children" (Carpentier and Cazamian, 1977, p. 41; see also Hakola, Härmä and Laitinen, 1996; Nachreiner, 1998; Ogínska, Pokorski and Ogínski, 1993).

In the light of these developments and findings, the ILO has had a difficult time defending the continued relevance of standards which effectively perpetuate stereotypical assumptions about women's role in society and at the workplace. In the words of an ILO report, "the subject is complex. Its analysis involves conflicting values as well as competing legal doctrines and international labour standards on preventing discrimination in employment and ensuring the safety and health of workers. The ILO seeks to rationalize the various interests and doctrines into a coherent policy that ensures equal opportunity and at the same time prevents the deterioration of working conditions" (ILO, 1990a, p. 1). The crux of the matter comes down to an uncomfortable dilemma: is it preferable, in certain cases, to maintain special protective laws for women workers at the risk of preserving gender stereotypes about the place of women in society and the labour market, or should one rather push for the repeal of all laws and regulations inconsistent with the principle of equality of opportunity and treatment between men and women even when such action would accentuate the *de facto* inequalities and gender discrimination suffered by women at home and at the workplace?

For example, women employed in the construction industry in India are reported to carry out work of the same physical difficulty as men, meaning 32 tonnes of concrete mixture a day, or up to 21 tonnes of mud from an excavation site (Ramakrishnan, 1996, p. 169). Can this be viewed solely from an "equal treatment" perspective or does it call for public intervention, protective measures and stricter enforcement? The same goes for those Chinese women reportedly working up to 16 hours a day, often without a single day of rest in a month, or those female workers in Viet Nam's export processing zones who, according to some accounts, total 6,000 hours per year as compared to 2,000 stated by the law (Asia Monitor Resource Center, 1998, pp. 179 and 232). Here again, can one reason in terms of women's "empowerment" rather than shocking exploitation?[6]

NIGHT WORK OF WOMEN IN INDUSTRY: ILO STANDARDS
IN HISTORICAL PERSPECTIVE

The origins of the first ILO Convention dealing with the night work of women in industrial undertakings can be traced to the pioneering work of the International Association for Labour Legislation (IALL) and to the 1906 Bern Convention on the prohibition of night work for women. The latter, together with the Convention on the prohibition of the use of white phosphorus in the manufacture of matches, were the first international legal instruments to focus on working conditions and human welfare.[7] The Bern Convention laid down a blanket prohibition of industrial night work for all women without exception. The prohibition applied to all industrial enterprises employing more than ten workers, while the notion of compulsory night rest for women referred to an 11-hour period, including the interval between 10 p.m. and 5 a.m. At the time of the Bern Conference the prohibition of night work for women was justified as a measure of public health designed to reduce the mortality of women and children, and to improve women's physical and moral well-being through longer periods of night rest and more relaxed devotion to housekeeping tasks (IALL, 1904, p. 9; Collis and Greenwood, 1921, pp. 211-242).[8]

The provisions of the 1906 Bern Convention were left practically untouched at the first session of the International Labour Conference, which was held in Washington in 1919. The only substantial changes were to give a more detailed definition of the term "industrial undertaking" and to delete the provision limiting the application of the Convention to industrial undertakings of more than ten employees. In adopting Convention No. 4, member States generally shared the view that the new Convention "would constitute a valuable advance in the protection of the health of women workers, and, through them, of their children, and that of the general population in each country, by making the prohibition of night work for women engaged in industry more complete and more effective than it has ever yet been" (ILO, 1919, p. 246).[9]

The first appeals for flexibility in the application of ILO Convention No. 4 were made in 1928 and concerned female engineers who were excluded from certain supervisory positions in electrical power undertakings. Beginning in 1931, the Office sought to amend Convention No. 4 by means of a clause to the effect that it "does not apply to persons holding positions of supervision or management". But the revision failed because of conflicting interpretations of the scope of Article 3 of the Convention, which finally gave rise to a formal request to the Permanent Court of International Justice for an advisory opinion.[10]

In the event, Convention No. 41, which was adopted in 1934, partially revised Convention No. 4 to allow, first, the substitution in exceptional circumstances of the period 11 p.m. to 6 a.m. for the period 10 p.m. to 5 a.m. in the definition of the term "night" and, second, the exemption from the prohibition of night work of "women holding responsible positions of management who are not ordinarily engaged in manual work" (see ILO, 1934, pp. 650-654).

Further appeals for revision were voiced after the Second World War. What was most urgently needed, in the opinion of certain governments, was a more flexible definition of the term "night" in order to facilitate the operation of the double day-shift system (an important feature of the post-war economy). Attention was also drawn to the possibility of broadening the exception applying to women in managerial positions and adding a clause to provide for the suspension of the prohibition in cases of serious national emergency. As finally adopted, Convention No. 89 provided for a night rest period of at least 11 consecutive hours, including an interval of at least seven consecutive hours falling between 10 p.m. and 7 a.m. The "competent authority" could prescribe different intervals for different areas, industries, undertakings or branches of industries but had to consult the employers' and workers' organizations concerned before prescribing an interval beginning after 11 p.m. The scope of the Convention was also revised to exclude from the prohibition of night work not only women holding responsible positions of management but also of a technical character, as well as "women employed in health and welfare services who are not ordinarily engaged in manual work". Furthermore, a new article was inserted in the Convention to provide for the possibility of suspending the prohibition of night work for women "when in case of serious emergency the national interest demands it" (see ILO, 1948, pp. 494-499).

The idea of a critical appraisal of Convention No. 89 started to take shape in the early 1970s, the Swiss Government being the first to argue that the Convention was outdated and that the prohibition of night work in its current form could lead to discrimination against women. In subsequent years, the Organization sought without success to design a consensual policy on the revision of the 1948 Convention. Most of its initiatives ended in a helpless acknowledgment of the irreconcilable positions of its constituents as to the advisability of adopting new standards on night work. In his reports on the night-work Conventions, submitted to the Governing Body in 1973 and 1975, the Director-General of the ILO confined himself to describing the different schools of thought and to confirming the persistence of diametrically opposed opinions as to the purpose and scope of a revision exercise or the scope of any new standards (ILO, 1973, p. 30, and 1975, p. 7). The Tripartite Advisory Meeting on Night Work, held in 1978, failed to formulate any recommendations on future ILO action because of the considerable diversity of views among participants and their apparent unwillingness to seek agreement on a middle-ground solution (ILO, 1978). In its 1986 General Report, the Committee of Experts on the Application of Conventions and Recommendations expressed concern over the application of the Convention in certain countries and drew the Governing Body's attention to the importance of seeking a rapid solution.

By 1989, when the International Labour Conference held its first discussion on a draft Protocol revising Convention No. 89, the prohibition of night work for women had become such a divisive and polemical issue that no single instrument could possibly satisfy the conflicting expectations of governments, employers and workers. For the representatives of workers' organizations, Convention No. 89 still had an important role to play because the problem which had prompted its adoption persisted. To the employers' organizations, the Convention was inherently discriminatory and an impediment to economic and social progress. As for the government representatives, many of them expressed strong views to the effect that there was no reason for differential treatment between men and women, except in respect of maternity protection.

The compromise solution favoured at the time was a two-pronged approach that consisted in adopting, on the one hand, a Protocol to Convention No. 89 allowing for exemptions from the prohibition of night work and variations in the duration of the night period by agreement between employers and workers, and, on the other, a new Convention setting out protective standards for all night workers, irrespective of their sex, in all industries and occupations (ILO, 1989a, p. 69; Kogi and Thurman, 1993).[11] It was thus hoped that a generous dose of substantive flexibility (which under certain circumstances could practically mean a waiver of the prohibition) would accommodate the concerns of those countries seeking greater sensitivity to women's rights and consensual solutions to the problems of shift work organization, while allowing Convention No. 89 to remain open to further ratifications. The futility of the Office's efforts to "square the circle" is illustrated by yet another inconsistency: the draft Protocol and the new night work Convention were not designed as mutually exclusive instruments so that member States could, in theory at least, apply sex-specific prohibitions on night work and, at the same time, enforce regulations regarding the safety and health of *all* night workers, both men and women.[12]

Today, the approach taken in 1990 calls for some critical assessment. The fact that two of the three States (Czech Republic, Cyprus) which had accepted the Protocol have already proceeded to denounce it betrays an uncomfortable sense of failure.[13] Moreover, only two of the States parties to Convention No. 89 (Bangladesh, Slovenia) have indicated that they are favourably considering ratification of the Protocol. This would seem to contradict the Committee of Experts' finding that "Convention No. 89, as amended by the 1990 Protocol, remains the most pertinent legal instrument for those member States which would not yet be prepared to dismantle all protective regimes for women in the name of gender equality, while at the same time seeking flexibility in the application of such protective legislation and of course giving full consideration to the ratification of the Night Work

Convention, 1990 (No. 171)" (ILO, 2001, p. 134, para. 179). Yet, there are still no signs of Convention No. 171 being widely accepted either. More than ten years after its adoption, the number of ratifications it has received remains surprisingly low. Some governments openly question its very ratifiability because of what they see as the excessively regulatory character of some of its provisions. So far, only Brazil has reported that the Bill ratifying Convention No. 171 is being processed by its parliamentary machinery. A further two countries have reaffirmed their intention to ratify the Convention, and four others have simply indicated that consultations with the social partners have been initiated without giving further details as to ratification.

In concluding the chapter of the General Survey tracing the history of ILO standards on women's night work in industry, the Committee of Experts states that "rarely have standards given rise to such prolonged controversy", adding that the issue "epitomizes a century-long debate over sensitive questions which have divided policy-makers, trade unionists and even women's organizations themselves" (ILO, 2001, p. 51, para. 85).

REVIEW OF NATIONAL LAW AND PRACTICE

National laws and practice make up an extremely diversified picture, even though in most countries there would seem to exist some form of legislative or regulatory provision restricting the employment of women workers during the night. On the one hand, 50 countries effectively apply a general prohibition against the night work of women, without distinction of age, in all industrial undertakings. In contrast, two countries are in the process of introducing legislative amendments lifting all restrictions on women's night work; five countries have introduced such broad exceptions that they practically nullify the comprehensive prohibition which continues to apply only in theory; and in three countries the provisions proscribing women's night work are not legally enforced (see ILO, 2001, pp. 53-56). There are also some 18 countries which have ceased to apply the provisions of the relevant ILO Conventions even though they are still parties to one or more of those instruments. The Committee of Experts has expressed concern about the extent of this practice:

the significance and implications of the growing tendency among States parties to Conventions Nos. 4, 41 and 89 to no longer give them effect cannot be underestimated; yet, the Committee considers it of critical importance to recall that it is not sufficient to invoke the principle of non-discrimination in employment and occupation or the principle of equality of treatment to nullify the obligations incumbent upon a member State by virtue of its formal acceptance of an international Convention (ILO, 2001, p. 61, para. 93).

This wording may be seen as a tactful way of suggesting that national law should be brought into conformity with national practice and that, where the reintroduction of a prohibition on women's night work was not envisaged, the ILO Convention(s) on night work should be denounced in accordance with established procedures.

On the other hand, there are 36 countries whose legislation does not provide for any sex-specific regulations on night work in order to ensure respect for the principle of non-discrimination between men and women at work and in employment. Among these countries, five have enacted legislation providing for a general ban on night work for all workers, while the remaining 31 countries do not prohibit the employment of women at night either because their legislation does not distinguish between night work and day work or because it does not apply different standards to male and female workers.

Irrespective of where they stand on women's access to night employment in general, almost all of the countries whose legislation was reviewed in the General Survey apply specific regulatory regimes to night work for two categories of workers with special needs, namely expectant or breast-feeding mothers and minors. With respect to pregnant workers and nursing mothers, many countries apply a blanket prohibition on night work covering the entire period of pregnancy as well as a specified period after childbirth which may vary from three months to three years. In some countries the period during which night rest is compulsory does not exceed the duration of maternity leave, while in other cases the prohibition is not absolute and applies only at the worker's request. Finally, a few industrialized countries have adopted a new occupational safety and health approach to the protection of pregnant workers whereby new or expectant mothers are not, in principle, prohibited from working on night shifts, though the employer is under obligation to assess the possible hazards of night work in each individual case and take mandatory action as appropriate. Generally speaking, the special protection afforded to pregnant women and nursing mothers is not limited to those employed in industrial undertakings, but applies to all sectors of economic activity.

The review of national law and practice reveals that the term "night", used in connection with the employment of female workers, is construed to cover a period which may vary from six to 12-and-a-half hours, though most States opt for a compulsory night rest period between seven and nine hours. However, the legislation of most of the States parties to the Conventions under review provides for an 11-hour ban period including either the interval between 10 p.m. and 5 a.m. in accordance with the provisions of Conventions Nos. 4 and 41, or a seven-hour interval between 10 p.m. and 7 a.m. pursuant to the terms of Convention No. 89.

There is also remarkable diversity in the legal prescriptions setting the grounds for exemptions from the prohibition of night work. In numerous countries the prohibition does not apply to family undertakings, undertakings processing perishable materials, or in case of *force majeure*; and women in managerial positions or employed in health services are also excluded from the scope of any prohibition or restriction on night work. In many cases, however, national laws and regulations provide for far-reaching exceptions bearing little relevance to the provisions of the Conventions. For example, the general ban on women's night work does not apply to economic sectors with "special needs" or to such work or occupations as may be designated by Ministerial decision, or yet to undertakings that meet certain requirements (typically in relation to health, security and transport). Further grounds for exemption include the attainment of production targets, compensation for an interruption of work due to a strike, the nature of certain work requiring dexterity, speed and attention, or the location of a factory within an export processing zone. Moreover, the notion of "national interest in case of serious emergency" – as a permissible ground for the suspension of the prohibition of night work for women under Convention No. 89 – is often construed broadly to cover situations of serious economic crisis, threats to national security, grave danger, or urgent interests of society, all of which have little in common with the relevant provision of the Convention.

THE STIGMA OF DISCRIMINATION: NIGHT WORK AND THE PRINCIPLE OF EQUAL TREATMENT

An omnipresent concern of ILO member States is the uneasy relationship between the ILO Conventions concerning the night work of women in industry and the fundamental principle of non-discrimination and equality of opportunity and treatment between men and women. For the great majority of governments which provided replies for the purposes of the General Survey, all Conventions on night work of women are synonymous with sex discrimination (ILO, 2001, p. 123, para. 156). Several States invoked principles enshrined in national constitutional law, while some referred to recent supreme court or constitutional court judgments explicitly declaring the unconstitutionality of any legislative provision prohibiting the access of women workers to night employment. Many governments also expressed the view that the mere intention to regulate women's employment during night hours differently from men's was evidently discriminatory and unjustifiable. Others, while qualifying the prohibition as an obstacle to equal employment opportunities, linked the problem to that of promoting full employment. Significantly, all of the 19 member States that have so far denounced Convention No. 89 have invariably invoked the principle of gender equality and non-discrimination as being the principal motive for their decision.

The analysis of the Committee of Experts offers a balanced mix of progressive interpretation and pragmatism. First, the Committee appears to be restating established rules while adapting them to contemporary conditions, in that it considers special protective measures to be justifiable only when they aim at restoring a balance, as part of a broader effort to eliminate inequalities. To quote from the General Survey:

differences in treatment between men and women can only be permitted on an exceptional basis, that is when they promote effective equality in society between the sexes, thereby correcting previous discriminatory practices, or where they are justified by the existence, and therefore the persistence, of overriding biological or physiological reasons, as in the case in particular of pregnancy and maternity. This requires a critical re-examination of provisions which are assumed to be "protective" towards women, but which in fact have the effect of hindering the achievement of effective equality by perpetuating or consolidating their disadvantaged employment situation (ILO, 2001, pp. 125-126, para. 161).

In this connection, the Committee of Experts recalls the conclusions of its 1996 *Special Survey on equality in employment and occupation in respect of Convention No. 111* (ILO, 1996a), which expressed the same idea, i.e. that practices which create advantages or disadvantages on the basis of sex are permissible only if they are designed to compensate for existing discrimination with the aim of ensuring equality of opportunity and treatment in practice. On this criterion, any rule restricting or prohibiting night work for women would clearly fail to qualify as a justifiable special protective measure.[14]

But the Committee also recognizes the need for pragmatism and that, depending on the needs and priorities of each country, a phased approach may be called for:

the Committee is aware that, as a long-term goal, the full application of this principle will only be attained progressively through appropriate legal reforms and varying periods of adaptation, depending on the stage of economic and social development or the influence of cultural traditions in a given society. The Committee believes that, for some parts of the world, progress towards full implementation of the principle of non-discrimination will proceed at a more gradual pace. The Committee cannot be expected to identify at which stage a country or a particular part of a country will be able to determine the actual impact of any existing special protective measures prohibiting or restricting night work for women and to take appropriate action. Nor should it substitute its own view for the view of those best placed to decide this issue, not least the women themselves. The protections afforded by Convention No. 89 and its Protocol should therefore be available to those women who need them, but they should not be used as a basis for denying all women equal opportunity in the labour market (ILO, 2001, p. 128, paras. 168-169).

Indeed, the Committee cautions against the risk of swift or premature action in conditions which might adversely affect women workers:

it would be unwise to believe that eliminating at a stroke all protective measures for women would accelerate the effective attainment of equality of opportunity and treatment in employment and occupation in countries at different stages of development. Before repealing existing protective legislation, therefore, member States should ensure that women workers will not be exposed to additional risks and dangers as a result of such repeal (ILO, 2001, p. 126, para. 163).

The Committee of Experts concludes its discussion of the relationship between the prohibition of night work for women and the principle of equality of opportunity and treatment on an unequivocal note: "a blanket prohibition on women's night work, such as that reflected in Conventions Nos. 4 and 41, now appears objectionable and cannot be defended from the viewpoint of the principle of non-discrimination" (ILO, 2001, p. 126, para. 162). As regards Convention No. 89, the Committee's conclusion is somewhat more qualified:

in those countries where technological progress has removed or reduced the hazards involved in industrial occupations and where the evolution of ideas about women's role in society has led to effective measures being put in place to eradicate discrimination and removed the need for special protective measures, Convention No. 89 may appear to be an anachronism (ILO, 2001, p. 128, para. 169).

Ratification prospects and problems

Based on the replies of member States, the Committee considers the ratification prospects[15] of Convention No. 89 and its Protocol to be thin (ILO, 2001, p. 131, para. 173). In fact, only one State (Papua New Guinea) indicated that there are good prospects of its ratifying Convention No. 89 and its Protocol in the context of a major review of labour laws, while two States parties to Convention No. 89 (Bangladesh, Slovenia) have reported that they are favourably considering the possibility of ratifying the 1990 Protocol. In contrast, eight countries[16] have announced their decision to denounce Convention No. 41 or Convention No. 89 and its Protocol, as the case may be, while another three Members (Brazil, Ghana, Malawi) have stated that Convention No. 89 had ceased to apply following the recent enactment of new legislation. In addition, more than 20 governments have indicated that they did not envisage ratifying any of the instruments under review. Most of these countries firmly objected to the idea of denying women access to night employment as a form of direct discrimination, while others expressed concern about the implications that prohibitions or restrictions on women's night work would have on unemployment.

The Committee concludes that the outlook for acceptance of the Protocol in the coming years appears uncertain: the fact that the 1990 Protocol cannot be ratified separately from Convention No. 89 seems to constitute a disincentive to ratification for those countries which, although interested in the flexibility afforded by the Protocol, still have serious objections to the basic premise of banning night work for women in general as set forth in Convention No. 89 (ILO, 2001, p. 134, para. 179).

With Convention No. 89 currently open to denunciation (27 February 2001-27 February 2002), it may be reasonably expected that it will be the subject of a large number of denunciations, probably as numerous as those registered in 1991-92 following the ruling of the Court of Justice of the European Communities in the *Stoeckel* case, according to which Convention No. 89 was found to contradict Community law.[17]

The Committee's findings: Where do we stand?

In drawing its conclusions as to the continued relevance of the instruments on women's night work, the Committee of Experts was guided by two clear, yet conflicting indicators. On the one hand, there is ample evidence that the impact of Conventions Nos. 4, 41 and 89 on national law and practice is weakening. In fact, according to the replies of member States, no less than 19 countries formally bound by the Conventions have ceased to apply them. Many of these countries have legislation in conflict with their provisions, while others are in the process of introducing legislative amendments lifting all restrictions on women's night work; others still have announced their intention to proceed with their denunciation. On the other hand, 66 States are formally bound by the provisions of Convention No. 89 or Convention No. 41; a further 12 States enforce prohibitions or restrictions on women's night work without being parties to any of the relevant instruments, thus obliging the Committee to admit that the number of member States whose national legislation continues to conform to the provisions of Conventions Nos. 4, 41 or 89 is still significant.

The Committee concludes that Convention No. 4 is "manifestly of historical importance only" and that it "no longer makes a useful current contribution to attaining the objectives of the Organization" (ILO, 2001, pp. 139-140, para. 193). The Committee therefore recommends that this instrument should be "shelved" and join those Conventions which will be eventually considered for abrogation. As regards Convention No. 41, the Committee notes that it is "poorly ratified and its relevance is diminishing" (ILO, 2001, p. 140, para. 194) and suggests that it would be in the interest of the States parties to this Convention to ratify Convention No. 89 and its Protocol instead. Finally, with respect to Convention No. 89, as revised by the 1990 Protocol, the Committee considers that it "retains its relevance for some countries as a means of protecting those women who need protection from the harmful effects and risks of night work in certain industries, while acknowledging the need for flexible and consensual solutions to specific problems and for consistency with modern thinking and principles on maternity protection" (ILO, 2001, p. 143, para. 201).

In sum, the Committee sees little reason for retaining protective standards for female workers only. At most, such standards should serve to respond to specific situations or sources of exploitation and abuse, they should be limited in time and scope, kept under regular review, and above all they should be maintained only for as long as the women workers themselves recognize their usefulness:

the Committee considers that international labour legislation should not be divested of all regulatory provisions on night work of women, on condition and to the extent that such regulation still serves a meaningful purpose in protecting women workers from abuse. In particular situations where women night workers are subject to severe exploitation and discrimination, the need for protective legislation may still prevail, especially where the women themselves are anxious to retain such protective measures. The Committee will therefore have to consider whether prohibitions on night work for women in certain situations serve to protect those women from abuses of their rights, in relation in particular to security and transport issues, quite apart from and in addition to health risks for pregnant women or nursing mothers caused by their working at night. In such situations the protective function of the night work standards may, for the time being and on a limited basis, subject to regular review, be legitimately considered by some constituents to be justified (ILO, 2001, pp. 47-48, para. 75).

The General Survey ends by offering some guidance with respect to ILO's future action in matters of night work as well as a subtle word of caution addressed to member States. As regards the Organization's standards policy in the field of night work, the Committee advises that its aims should be to promote ratification of the Night Work Convention, 1990 (No. 171) and to assist those constituents still bound by Convention No. 89, but not yet ready to ratify Convention No. 171, in realizing the advantages of modernizing their legislation in line with the provisions of the Protocol. As a result of the low number of ratifications of Convention No. 171 thus far – coupled with the growing tendency among member States to denounce or no longer to give effect to Conventions Nos. 4, 41 or 89 – "there is risk of a complete deregulation of night work through the removal of all protective measures for women and the failure to replace them with a legislation offering appropriate protection to all night workers" (ILO, 2001, p. 143, para. 202).

CONCLUDING REMARKS

The first General Survey on the night work of women in industry, conducted by the ILO Committee of Experts on the Application of Conventions and Recommendations, has been an opportunity for fresh inquiry and some expert advice on persistent questions concerning both the advisability of regulating night work in general and the acceptability of special protective measures for women having regard to the principles of non-discrimination and gender equality. The essence of the Committee's analysis may be captured in the following propositions.

The detrimental effects of night work on the health and on the social and family life of *all* workers are largely acknowledged. More generally, the introduction of new working-time patterns, flexible work schedules and complex rotating shift arrangements, which typically imply irregular hours of work, calls for increased occupational health awareness and protective measures adapted to new needs. The factors affecting tolerance of night work are unrelated to sex. Yet, biological conditions such as pregnancy or deep-rooted social traditions such as the uneven sharing of family and household responsibilities between men and women may leave female workers more exposed to the adverse effects of night work.

The impact of the Conventions in question is weakening rapidly. Their current relevance is extremely limited, being largely confined to the possible ratification of the 1990 Protocol by those countries which are still bound by the provisions of Convention No. 89 but which are not yet prepared to ratify Convention No. 171. There is overwhelming evidence that, in most national legal systems, prohibitions on women's night work have either been struck out or ceased to be enforced. Even among those countries which continue to give effect to the provisions of the relevant ILO Conventions there seems to be general recognition of their transitional nature and the need ultimately to create such conditions as would permit them to move away from sex-specific legislation, with the sole exception of laws aimed at protecting maternity.

Whatever their residual value, the ILO standards on women's night work in industry are in a state of flux due to the advancement of the overriding principles of non-discrimination and equality of opportunity and treatment between men and women. The two sets of ideas interact: the more the action in furtherance of equality bears its fruits, the more sex-specific protection retreats. The international obligation to conduct periodic reviews of all protective legislation applying to women only – as set out in the 1979 Convention on the Elimination of Discrimination Against Women or the 1985 ILO resolution on equal opportunities – is a clear manifestation of the continuous action required for the promotion of equality of opportunity and treatment. Ever-changing social conditions call for well-adjusted policies: night-work protection for women is therefore set to vanish as rapidly, or as sluggishly, as the goals of non-discrimination and gender equality in employment and occupation are attained.

Each of the four instruments on women's night work was drawn up in response to specific needs at a given point in time and thus necessarily reflects the ideas prevailing at the time of its adoption. These instruments are therefore to be evaluated on their merit of giving expression to constantly evolving priorities and expectations in the world of work, not as embodying timeless standards. Faced with a hard choice between protection *or* equality, the ILO has always endeavoured to achieve protection *and* equality. The following passage, quoted from a 1921 report prepared for the third Session of the International Labour Conference, testifies to the remarkable consistency of ILO's action and objectives:

the principal importance of the Conference which is about to be held lies not in the special measures that it may adopt for the protection of women workers, so much as in the proposal to put men and women on a footing of almost complete equality in all protective measures contemplated. It is in this direction that women desire to see the development of protection for women workers. They no longer ask for privileges – they demand absolute equality. Most of the draft Conventions submitted to the Conference ought, in the view of the Governing Body of the International Labour Organisation, to apply equally to women and men. They are a step towards the complete unification of social legislation which is the real object of the whole movement of working women (ILO, 1921, p. 11).

Postscript

In accordance with usual practice, the Conference Committee on the Application of Standards at the 89th Session (June 2001) of the International Labour Conference devoted part of its general discussion to the examination of the Committee of Experts' General Survey.[18] Practically all the 30 members of the Committee who took part in the discussion addressed the central question of whether or not special protective measures for women, with the exception of standards and benefits related to maternity protection, were contrary to the principle of equal opportunity and treatment between men and women. Most speakers acknowledged the challenging nature of the subject pointing out the specificity of the General Survey which, instead of limiting itself to a technical evaluation of the practical application of standards relating to women's night work, addressed first and foremost the very relevance of those standards. The discussion confirmed the existence of two well-entrenched lines of argument and – after 25 years of intense debate – the persistent sensitivity of the issue.

The Employer members saw the maintenance of sex-biased restrictions on night work as a test for the Organization's credibility and authority, stressing that the protection seen as social progress 100 years ago could now represent a social impediment and a disadvantage. The time had finally come, they argued, to consign to history all ILO instruments on women's night work. In their opinion, the Organization now needs courage to move forward in a spirit of realism lest it should be overtaken by modern developments. The perpetuation of outdated instruments which are not applied in practice, even by countries which have ratified them, could not be beneficial either to the ILO or to workers. Several government representatives (Canada, Denmark, Japan, Portugal, South Africa, Sweden, Zimbabwe) also supported the view that singling out women for special protection under the night work Conventions was anachronistic, blatantly discriminatory and scientifically unfounded.

The Worker members, for their part, deplored the use of equality arguments to lower standards on working conditions, particularly with regard to night work, and pointed out that the dilemma was not what to choose between equality and protection but how to best guarantee both. They emphasized that there was a real risk of complete deregulation, given the current tendency to erode protection in the name of equality and render employment precarious for all night workers. Other Worker members (France, India, Pakistan, Senegal) noted that, although the situation might be different in the industrialized world, there was still great need to protect female workers in developing countries. It was surprising, they felt, that despite the rampant discrimination against women workers throughout the world, especially in relation to wages and career prospects, so many people championed the cause of equality only where it related to lifting the ban on women's night work.

Several specific references were made to export processing zones (EPZs), with the argument that poor working conditions and a total lack of social protection tended to be endemic in EPZ workplaces: in certain EPZs where labour law was not generally observed, it was already difficult to ensure adequate protection of women by day, and the situation would clearly be much more critical at night. It was therefore suggested that the supervisory bodies of the ILO should specifically address the question of the application of ILO standards in EPZs, while the Office should consider ways of improving the conditions of millions of EPZ workers.

As regards the prospects for ratification of the instruments concerning women's night work, the government representatives of Egypt and Lebanon indicated that ratification of the 1990 Protocol was under consideration, while the government representatives of Slovakia and South Africa confirmed that their countries intended to proceed with the denunciation of Convention No. 89 by the end of 2001.

With reference to the Night Work Convention, 1990 (No. 171), most speakers regretted that this instrument had been left outside the purview of the General Survey and expressed interest in shifting emphasis away from a specific category of workers and sector of economic activity to the safety and health protection of all night workers, irrespective of sex, in all sectors and occupations. Several Worker members (Argentina, France, Italy) and government representatives (Denmark, Italy, Portugal) considered that Convention No. 171 reflected current thinking with regard to the problems of night work and shift work and endorsed the conclusion of the Committee of Experts that the ratification of that instrument should be encouraged. In contrast, other Government members (Canada, Sweden, Switzerland), while recognizing that Convention No. 171 generally represented a step forward, indicated that ratification was not envisaged at this stage.

In sum, the key points of the Conference Committee discussion included wide acknowledgement of the adverse effects of night work on workers' health and social and family life; diminishing support for instruments endorsing a general prohibition of night work for women; growing awareness of the need for regulations covering all night workers, both male and female, coupled with widespread approval of the standards set out in Convention No. 171; broad acceptance of the prohibition/restriction of night work for young workers and pregnant or nursing mothers; the persistent inequality and vulnerability of female workers which, in some circumstances, called for carefully designed protective measures along with the pursuit of genuine conditions of equality and non-discrimination.

With respect to the issue of compatibility between the prohibition of night work for women and the principle of equality of opportunity and treatment at the workplace, both the General Survey and the Conference discussion have helped to clarify the dialectics of a balanced approach combining a sustained effort for the eradication of all forms of discrimination against women with circumscribed provision of protection, especially where women themselves demand it. Even though some of the views expressed appear to be unbridgeable, some common ground could be found, say, the fundamental nature of the principle of equality of opportunity and treatment as codified in the United Nations Convention on the Elimination of All Forms of Discrimination Against Women, or ILO Convention No. 111; the existence of situations – distinct from the health risks to pregnant women or nursing mothers – which might justify concrete protective measures of limited scope and/or of temporary duration; and recognition that, in certain parts of the world, the implementation of the principle of non-discrimination might need to be phased in according to local conditions, given the widely varying socio-economic circumstances of different countries.

The thorough analysis undertaken by the Committee of Experts in its General Survey, coupled with the rich debate at the ILO Conference Committee on the Application of Standards, is expected to allow the Governing Body's Working Party on Policy regarding the Revision of Standards to draw definitive conclusions on the standard-setting policy to be followed in matters of night work regulation.[19]

Notes

[1] The General Survey draws principally on information provided by 109 member States in accordance with article 19 of the Constitution as well as on information contained in the regular reports submitted under articles 22 and 35 of the Constitution by those member States parties to one or more of the instruments in question. It also takes account of the observations and comments submitted by 18 employers' and workers' organizations.

[2] Early legislation addressed the questions of women's freedom to work underground in mines, working hours and conditions of work, especially women's safety around moving machinery. Later came measures on maternity protection such as maternity leave and prohibitions on work with toxic substances. The United Kingdom was the first country to prohibit women from working underground in 1842 and, two years later, to restrict their work at night.

[3] Convention No. 4, adopted in 1919, provided for an outright prohibition of night work for women of any age in any public or private industrial undertaking other than an undertaking in which only members of the same family were employed, it being understood that "night" should cover a period of at least 11 consecutive hours including the interval from 10 p.m. to 5 a.m. Convention No. 41, adopted in 1934, excluded from the scope of the night-work prohibition women holding responsible positions of management and also provided for a possible variation in the seven-hour interval specified in the definition of the term "night". Convention No. 89, adopted in 1948, laid down new exception and suspension possibilities and also made the definition of "night" more flexible. As for the Protocol to Convention No. 89, adopted in 1990, it allows for variations in the duration of the night period and exemptions from the prohibition of night work which may be introduced by governments after consulting the employers' and workers' organizations. It also provides for the protection of pregnant women and nursing mothers by prohibiting the application of such variations and exemptions during a period before and after childbirth of at least 16 weeks.

[4] See, for example, Harrington (1978), Maurice (1975), Taylor (1969, pp. 15-30), Härmä et al. (1998), *Ergonomics* (1993), Rosa and Tepas (1990), Helbig and Rohmert (1998), Kogi (1998), Knauth (1998) and Bunnage (1979). See also the following web sites:

www.matrices.com/Workplace/Research/shiftworkresearch.html;

www.members.tripod.com/~shiftworker/swlinks.html;

www.sleepfoundation.org/publications.html;

www.stmarys.ca/partners/iatur/index.htm;

www.workingnights.com/library.htm

[5] In July 1991, the Court of Justice of the European Communities delivered its ruling in the *Stoeckel* case by which it affirmed that the Council Directive 76/207/EEC on the implementation of the principle of equal treatment for men and women as regards access to employment, vocational training and promotion, and working conditions was "sufficiently precise to impose on the Member States the obligation not to lay down by legislation the principle that night work by women is prohibited, even if that obligation is subject to exceptions, where night work by men is not prohibited" (see case C-345/1989, *Ministère public v. Stoeckel*, ECR 1991, p. I-4047, judgment of 25 July 1991; see also cases C-197/1996, *Commission of the European Communities v. French Republic*, ECR 1997, p. I-1489, judgment of 13 March 1997, and C-207/1996, *Commission of the European Communities v. Italian Republic*, ECR 1997, p. I-6869, judgment of 4 December 1997). The same finding was confirmed and further elaborated in the infringement proceedings initiated by the European Commission against France and Italy in 1999. However, in its judgment in the *Levy* case, the Court found that a national jurisdiction could set aside its obligation to ensure full compliance with article 5 of the Equal Treatment Directive if the national provisions incompatible with Community legislation were intended to implement an international agreement to which the Member concerned had become a party prior to the entry into force of the EEC Treaty – in this case ILO Convention No. 89. Reference should also be made to the European Parliament's resolution on night working and the denunciation of ILO Convention No. 89, dated 9 April 1992, which "deplores the carelessness of the Commission in permitting a situation to arise in which no night working legislation exists at Community level, since Member States are no longer required to respect minimum international standards" (Kilpatrick, 1996, p. 188).

[6] See also the following sources:

www.un.org/womenwatch;

www.unifem.undp.org;

www1.umn.edu/humarts/links/women.html;

www.library.yale.edu/wss/

[7] On the work of the Bern Conference, see Caté (1911), Hopkins (1928, pp. 16-26), Lowe (1935, pp. 112-131) and Troclet (1952, pp. 218-244). For an interesting account of the first efforts to cope with the "social question" in the late nineteenth century – i.e. the deterioration of workers' living standards and the lack of protective legislation for the working masses – as perceived by the women's movement, see Wikander (1995, pp. 29-62) and Bauer (1903).

[8] The Bern Convention entered into force in 1912, and by 1919 had received 11 ratifications. But some countries objected to the discriminatory nature of the agreement: the Convention was rejected the first time it was presented to the Swedish Parliament, while Denmark, which had only signed with reservations, never ratified it (see Ravn, 1995, pp. 210-234; Karlsson, 1995, pp. 235-266; Hagemann, 1995, pp. 267-289).

[9] Nordic countries expressed their opposition to special protective measures for women except for pregnant women and nursing mothers and favoured the prohibition of absolutely unnecessary night work for all workers. Within ten years of its adoption, Convention No. 4 had been ratified by 36 countries and had met with almost universal application.

[10] The Court found that the wording of Article 3 of Convention No. 4 was unambiguous so that the prohibition applied to all women workers without exception and that if the intention was to exclude women holding positions of supervision or management from the operation of the Convention, a specific clause to that effect would have been inserted into the text (see PCIJ, 1932, p. 373).

[11] For the Conference discussions, see also ILO (1989b, pp. 30/30-30/35; 1990b, pp. 26/21-26/26).

[12] In this respect, an analogy could be drawn between the evolution of ILO standards concerning night work and those concerning underground work in mines; much like the new Night Work Convention, 1990 (No. 171) reflects a new approach to the problems of night and shift work in that it is designed to protect the health and rights of all night workers without distinction, the Safety and Health in Mines Convention, 1995 (No. 176) shifts emphasis from the protection of

women, as provided for in the Underground Work (Women) Convention, 1935 (No. 45), to the protection of mine workers irrespective of their sex.

[13] Even though these denunciations appear to be dictated by reasons of political expediency rather than by problems connected with the practical application of the Protocol.

[14] In contrast, the Committee of Experts makes no reference to the 1988 General Survey on Convention No. 111 (ILO, 1988), or to the comments made then about special protective measures, especially with regard to Article 5(1) of Convention No. 111. It will be recalled that the Committee in its 1988 General Survey (para. 140) expressly included Conventions Nos. 4, 41 and 89 among the ILO instruments which provide for special measures of protection or assistance and whose application might result in distinction or preferences not deemed to be discriminatory in terms of Article 5 of the Convention. Moreover, the Committee clearly stated that "rules adopted in application of the principles established in international Conventions concerning the night work of women in industry come under the provisions contained in Article 5, paragraph 1, of the Convention" (ILO, 1988, para. 142).

[15] By ratification prospects, reference is made only to Convention No. 89 because Convention No. 41 has been closed to ratification since the adoption of Convention No. 89, and the 1990 Protocol cannot be ratified on its own, while Convention No. 4, adopted some 82 years ago, is highly unlikely to attract any new ratifications.

[16] Austria, Cyprus, Czech Republic, Dominican Republic, Estonia, South Africa, Suriname and Zambia.

[17] As at 8 October 2001, four instruments of denunciation had been registered (Austria, Cyprus, Czech Republic, Zambia). Moreover, Convention No. 4 was denounced by Austria and Italy on 26 July and 6 August 2001 respectively.

[18] See International Labour Conference, 89th Session, 2001, *Provisional Record No. 19*, paras. 159-207 and *Provisional Record No. 22*, pp. 22/2-22/10.

[19] The question of the deferred examination of Conventions concerning night work of women was placed on the agenda of the Working Party for the November 2001 Session of the Governing Body (see GB.282/LILS/WP/PRS/2 at www.ilo.org/public/english/standards/relm/gb/index.htm).

References

Asia Monitor Resource Center. 1998. *We in the zone – Women workers in Asia's export processing zones*. Hong Kong.

Bauer, Etienne. 1903. "Préface", in Association internationale pour la protection légale des travailleurs (ed.): *Le travail de nuit des femmes dans l'industrie – Rapports sur son importance et sa réglementation légale*. Iéna, Gustave Fischer.

Bunnage, David. 1979. "Study on the consequences of shiftwork on social and family life", in European Foundation for the Improvement of Living and Working Conditions (ed.): *The effects of shiftwork on health, social and family life*. Dublin.

Carpentier James; Cazamian, Pierre. 1977. *Night work: Its effects on the health and welfare of the worker*. Geneva, ILO.

Caté, Marcel. 1911. *La Convention de Berne de 1906 sur l'interdiction du travail de nuit des femmes employées dans l'industrie*. Paris, E. Larose.

Collis, Edgar L.; Greenwood, Major. 1921. *The health of the industrial worker*. London, J. & A. Churchill.

Council of Europe. 1999. *Equality between women and men in the European Social Charter*. Human rights/Social Charter monographs, No. 2. Strasbourg.

—.1995. *Women in the working world: Equality and protection within the European Social Charter*. Human rights/Social Charter monographs, No. 2. Strasbourg.

Ellis, Evelyn. 1998. *EC sex equality law*. Second edition. Oxford, Clarendon Press.

Ergonomics (London). 1993. "Special issue: Night and shiftwork", Vol. 36, Nos. 1-3 (Jan.-Mar.), pp. 1-321.

Hagemann, G. 1995. "Protection or equality? Debates on protective legislation in Norway", in Ulla Wikander, Alice Kessler-Harris and Jane Lewis (eds.): *Protecting women – Labor legislation in Europe, the United States, and Australia, 1880-1920*. Chicago, IL, University of Illinois Press.

Hakola, Tarja; Härmä, Mikko; Laitinen, Jarmo T. 1996. "Circadian adjustment of men and women to night work", in *Scandinavian Journal of Work, Environment & Health* (Helsinki), Vol. 22, No. 2 (Apr.), pp. 133-138.

Härmä, Mikko; Barton, Jane; Costa, Giovanni; Greenwood, Ken; Knauth, Peter; Nachreiner, Friedhelm; Rosa, Roger; Åkerstedt, Torbjörn. 1998. "New challenges for the organization of night and shiftwork: Proceedings of the XIII International Symposium on Night and Shift Work, 23-27 June 1997, Finland", in *Scandinavian Journal of Work, Environment & Health* (Helsinki), Vol. 24, Supplement 3, pp. 1-155.

Harrington, J. M. 1978. *Shift work and health: A critical review of the literature*. London, Employment Medical Advisory Service/Health and Safety Executive.

Heide, Ingeborg. 1999. "Supranational action against sex discrimination: Equal pay and equal treatment in the European Union", in *International Labour Review* (Geneva), Vol. 138, No. 4, pp. 381-410.

Helbig, Rolf; Rohmert, Walter. 1998. "Fatigue and recovery", in Jeanne Mager Stellman (ed.): *Encyclopaedia of Occupational Health and Safety*. Fourth edition. Geneva, ILO, Vol. 1, pp. 29.38-29.41.

Hopkins, Mary D. 1928. "The employment of women at night", in *Bulletin of the Women's Bureau* (Washington, DC), No. 64.

IALL (International Association for Labour Legislation). 1904. *Memorial explanatory of the reasons for an international prohibition of night work for women*. Basel.

ICFTU (International Confederation of Free Trade Unions). 1998. *Behind the wire – Anti-union repression in the export processing zones*. Brussels.

ILO. 2001. *Night work of women in industry: General Survey of the reports concerning the Night Work (Women) Convention, 1919 (No. 4), the Night Work (Women) Convention (Revised), 1934 (No. 41), the Night Work (Women) Convention (Revised), 1948 (No. 89), and the Protocol of 1990 to the Night Work (Women) Convention (Revised), 1948*. International Labour Conference, 89th Session, 2001, Report III (Part 1B). Geneva.

—. 2000. *ABC of women workers' rights and gender equality*. Geneva.

—. 1998. *Labour and social issues relating to export processing zones*. Report for discussion at the Tripartite Meeting of Export Processing Zones-Operating Countries, Geneva, 1998. TMEPZ/1998. Geneva.

—. 1997. *Follow-up on the recommendations of the Working Party: General Paper*. Document GB.270/LILS/WP/PRS/1/1. Geneva.

—. 1996a. *Equality in employment and occupation: Special Survey on equality in employment and occupation in respect of Convention No. 111*. International Labour Conference, 83rd Session, 1996, Report III (Part 4B). Geneva.

—. 1996b. *Report of the working Party on Policy regarding the Revision of Standards – Part II: Conventions in need of revision (Phase 2)*. Document GB.267/LILS/4/2 (Rev.). Geneva.

—.1995. *Conditions of Work Digest – Vol. 14: Working time around the world.* Geneva.

—.1990a. *Special protective measures for women and equality of opportunity and treatment.* Documents considered at the Meeting of Experts on Special Protective Measures for Women and Equality of Opportunity and Treatment, Geneva, 1989. MEPMW/1989/7. Geneva.

—.1990b. International Labour Conference, 77th Session, 1990: *Record of Proceedings.* Geneva.

—.1989a. *Night Work.* International Labour Conference, 76th Session, 1989, Report V (1). Geneva.

—.1989b. International Labour Conference, 76th Session, 1989: *Record of Proceedings.* Geneva.

—.1988. *Equality in employment and occupation: General Survey of the reports on the Discrimination (Employment and Occupation) Convention (No. 111) and Recommendation (No. 111), 1958.* International Labour Conference, 75th Session, 1988, Report III (Part 4B). Geneva.

—.1985. International Labour Conference, 71st Session, 1985: *Record of Proceedings.* Geneva.

—.1984. *Note on the question of compatibility between the UN Convention on the Elimination of all Forms of Discrimination Against Women and certain ILO Conventions on the protection of women.* Document GB.228/24/1. Geneva.

—.1978. *Report of the Tripartite Advisory Meeting on Night Work.* Document GB.208/8/4. Geneva.

—.1975. *Revision of the Night Work (Women) Convention (Revised), 1948 (No. 89).* Document GB.198/SC/1/1. Geneva.

—.1973. *Draft report of the Governing Body of the International Labour Office on the working of the Convention concerning Night Work of Women Employed in Industry (Revised 1948) (No. 89) and of the corresponding Conventions of 1934 and 1919 (Nos. 41 and 4).* D.5. Geneva.

—.1948. International Labour Conference, 31st Session, 1948: *Record of Proceedings.* Geneva.

—.1934. International Labour Conference, 18th Session, 1934: *Record of Proceedings.* Geneva.

—.1921. *The international protection of women workers.* Studies and reports, Series 1, No. 1. Geneva. Oct.

—.1919. International Labour Conference, First Session, 1919: *Record of Proceedings.* Geneva.

ILO/UNCTC (United Nations Centre on Transnational Corporations). 1988. *Economic and social effects of multinational enterprises in export processing zones.* Geneva.

Karlsson, L. 1995. "The beginning of a 'Masculine Renaissance': The debate on the 1909 prohibition against women's night work in Sweden", in Ulla Wikander, Alice Kessler-Harris and Jane Lewis (eds.): *Protecting women – Labor legislation in Europe, the United States, and Australia, 1880-1920.* Chicago, IL, University of Illinois Press.

Kilpatrick, Claire. 1996. "Production and circulation of EC night work jurisprudence", in *Industrial Law Journal* (Oxford), Vol. 25, No. 3 (Sep.), pp 169-190.

Knauth, Peter. 1998. "Hours of work", in Jeanne Mager Stellman (ed.): *Encyclopaedia of Occupational Health and Safety.* Fourth edition. Geneva, ILO, Vol. 2, pp. 43.2-43.15.

Kogi, Kazutaka. 1998. "Sleep deprivation", in Jeanne Mager Stellman (ed.): *Encyclo-paedia of Occupational Health and Safety*. Fourth edition. Geneva, ILO, Vol. 1, pp. 29.52-29.55.

—; Thurman, J.E. 1993. "Trends in approaches to night and shift work and new inter-national standards", in *Ergonomics* (London), Vol. 36, Nos. 1-3, pp. 3-13.

Lowe, Boutelle Elsworth. 1935. *The international protection of labor: International Labor Organization, history and law*. New York, NY, Macmillan.

Maurice, Marc. 1975. *Shift work: Economic advantages and social costs*. Geneva, ILO.

Nachreiner, Friedhelm. 1998. "Individual and social determinants of shiftwork toler-ance", in *Scandinavian Journal of Work, Environment & Health* (Helsinki), Vol. 24, Supplement 3, pp. 35-42.

Ogínska, H.; Pokorski, J.; Ogínski, A. 1993. "Gender, ageing, and shiftwork intolerance", in *Ergonomics* (London), Vol. 36, Nos. 1-3 (Jan.-Mar.), pp. 161-168.

PCIJ (Permanent Court of International Justice). 1932. *Interpretation of the Convention of 1919 concerning employment of women during the night*. Advisory Opinion, PCIJ. Series A/B, Fasc. No. 50, 15 Nov.

Ramakrishnan, G. 1996. "A struggle within a struggle: The unionization of women in the informal sector in Tamil Nadu", in Marilyn Carr, Martha Chen and Renana Jhab-vala (eds.): *Speaking out – Women's economic empowerment in South Asia*. London, IT Publications.

Ravn, A.-B. 1995. "Lagging far behind all civilized nations: The debate over protective labor legislation for women in Denmark, 1899-1913", in Ulla Wikander, Alice Kessler-Harris and Jane Lewis (eds.): *Protecting women – Labor legislation in Europe, the United States, and Australia, 1880-1920*. Chicago, IL, University of Illinois Press.

Rosa, Roger; Tepas, D. 1990. "Factors for promoting adjustments to night and shift work: Special issue", in *Work and Stress* (London), Vol. 4, No. 3 (Jul.-Sep.), pp. 201-283.

Taylor, Peter J. 1969. "The problems of shift work", in Å. Swensson (ed.): *Night and shift work: Proceedings of an international symposium, Oslo, Jan. 31st-Feb. 1st, 1969*. Stockholm, National Institute of Occupational Health, pp. 15-30.

Troclet. Léon-Eli. 1952. *Législation sociale internationale*. Brussels, Editions de la Librai-rie Encyclopédique.

United Nations. 2000. *The World's Women 2000: Trends and statistics*. Social Statistics and Indicators, Series K, No. 16 (ST/ESA/STAT/SER. K/16). New York, NY.

—. 1999. *1999 World Survey on the Role of Women in Development: Globalization, gender and work*. New York, NY.

United States Department of Labor. 1989. *Working conditions in export processing zones in selected developing countries*. Washington, DC. Oct.

Widdows, Kelvin. 1984. "The denunciation of international labour Conventions", in *Inter-national and Comparative Law Quarterly* (London), Vol. 33, No. 4 (Oct.), pp. 1052-1063.

Wikander, Ulla. 1995. "Some kept the flag of feminist demands waving" – Debates at International Congresses on Protecting Women Workers", in Ulla Wikander, Alice Kessler-Harris and Jane Lewis (eds.): *Protecting women – Labor legislation in Europe, the United States, and Australia, 1880-1920*. Chicago, IL, University of Illinois Press.

EMPLOYMENT, SOCIAL JUSTICE AND SOCIETAL WELL-BEING

Joseph E. STIGLITZ *

16

The purpose of economic activity is to increase the well-being of individuals, and economic structures that are able to do so are more desirable than those that do not. This proposition might seem anodyne, but on closer inspection it is far more complex. To be sure, all politicians – left, right and centre – pay homage to it. Yet, the policies that are pursued often turn out to be antithetical to it. Much of traditional economics has indeed provided considerable comfort to those politicians who have a different agenda, and created considerable confusion for those who are sympathetic.

A second proposition, also deceptively anodyne, is that for a large fraction of the world's population, work – employment – is important. For individuals who lose their jobs, it is not *just* the loss of income that matters, it is also the individual's sense of self. Unemployment is associated with a variety of problems and pathologies, from higher divorce rates, higher suicide rates to higher incidences of alcoholism. And the relationship is not just a correlation: there is a causal connection. Some individuals can keep themselves happy and gainfully "employed" without a job. But for many, employment – the fact that someone else recognizes their "contribution" by paying them – is important.[1]

This article aims to explain how standard economic theory – reflected in much of the popular policy folklore – has served to undermine the above propositions or runs counter to them. The first section shows how policies based on a neoclassical view of the labour market ultimately weaken workers' bargaining position because of pervasive market failures. The next

Originally published in *International Labour Review*, Vol. 141 (2002), No. 1-2.

* Columbia University. This article is based on a lecture given at the International Labour Office on the occasion of the Global Employment Forum, held in Geneva from 1 to 3 November 2001. The author wishes to acknowledge helpful discussions with David Ellerman and Jerry Levinson, and financial support from the Ford and Rockefeller Foundations. The views expressed are solely those of the author, and not of any organization with which he is or has been affiliated.

two sections critically discuss the welfare and employment implications of a wider set of policies – from capital market liberalization to pro-cyclical fiscal and monetary management – which are pursued on the theoretical assumption that efficiency and equity/distribution can be dealt with separately. The fourth section is a plea for labour to be seen as an end in itself, not a means of production, and development as a transformation of society; while the fifth section looks at the role of the international community in setting the objectives of socio-economic development. A concluding section sums up the discussion and offers some policy proposals aimed at providing full employment and better working conditions.

LABOUR AND NEOCLASSICAL ECONOMICS

One of the great "tricks" (some might say "insights") of neoclassical economics is to treat labour like any other factor of production. Output is written as a function of inputs – steel, machines, and labour. The *mathematics* treats labour like a commodity, lulling one into thinking of labour like an ordinary commodity, such as steel or plastic. But labour is unlike any other commodity. The work environment is of no concern for steel; we do not care about steel's well-being (though to be sure, we may take care that the environment does not lead to its rusting or otherwise adversely affect its performance characteristics). Steel does not have to be *motivated* to work as an input. Steel does whatever it is "told" to do. But management is generally highly concerned with *motivating* labour.

The distinction arises from labour's *human aspect*. Individuals *decide* how hard they work, and with what care. The environment affects their behaviour, including the incentives with which they are confronted. In standard theory, individuals contract to perform a certain job, and are paid if and only if they complete that job. It is assumed that contract enforcement is costless – partly because of the assumption that information exists about whether the task (which is specified in infinite minutia) has been completed. Yet, information imperfections abound in the economy, and these information imperfections have profound impacts on the way an economy behaves, a fact recognized by the 2001 Nobel Prize (which focused in particular on information *asymmetries*). While this is not the occasion to review all of the implications of information imperfections, I want to highlight three that are particularly germane to the theses of this article.

First, imperfect information leads to imperfect competition; but the striking result of our research was that even a little bit of information imperfection – even a small cost of searching for a new job, for instance – can have a large effect. Economists always knew that information was imperfect, but they hoped that a little bit of imperfection would only change the equilibrium in a small way, and that the imperfections were indeed small. These hopes were not based on analytical work, but rather on the realization that if these assumptions were *not* true, the models that economists have used for decades, and the conclusions derived from these models, would be of little relevance. To put it perhaps over-grandly, it would have made much of economic analysis obsolete overnight. The new information economics showed, however, that even a small search cost could enable the equilibrium real wage to fall from the competitive level to the monopsony level (see Diamond, 1971; Stiglitz, 1985b and 1987a).

Observers of labour markets had long been concerned with bargaining power asymmetries. Workers' mobility is limited; employees who are fired – e.g. because they demand higher wages or better working conditions – may have a stigma, making it difficult for them to obtain another job, even if employers do not act collusively (and there may be tacit collusion); credit market imperfections (credit rationing, which itself can be explained by information imperfections) can make it difficult for a worker who is unemployed to live well for long, putting the worker in a far more precarious position than the employer who has lost whatever rents were gained from the worker's labour. What our analysis showed is that, despite other market imperfections that may exist, these alone put workers in a decidedly disadvantageous position.

Second, imperfect information leads to unemployment: even when wages are so high that the demand for labour is less than the supply, wages will not fall; for if a firm lowers its wages, workers' effort or the quality of workers hired may decrease (or their turnover costs increase). To most of the world, this is hardly news. But to standard economic theory it is: neoclassical theory said that markets always clear; what seemed to be unemployment was nothing more than a sudden change in the demand for leisure. Information economics also emphasized that the decentralized *adjustment* process often worked imperfectly, leading to temporary unemployment rates which even exceeded the *equilibrium* unemployment rates associated with efficiency wages. Yet traditional theory paid no attention to this – after all, with perfect information it is easy to move to the new equilibrium whenever the economy is disturbed.

Third, information economics has challenged the traditional economic theory which argues that markets are *self-adjusting* and *efficient*, and that the nature of the equilibrium (and its efficiency) depends neither on distribution nor on institutions. To traditional economists, the law of demand and supply determines the allocation of resources (including incomes), not institutions like sharecropping. Issues of efficiency could thus conveniently be separated from issues of distribution. Information economics has challenged each of these propositions: Bruce Greenwald and I showed that when information is imperfect or markets incomplete – that is, always – markets are not even constrained Pareto efficient, i.e. that in principle, there existed interventions in the market which took account of the costs of information and of creating a market, and which made everyone better off (see Greenwald and Stiglitz,

1986). Our analysis found that there were pervasive market failures that might, in principle, be addressed by government intervention. The retort that we ignored information imperfections in the public sector was simply wrong. We took them into account. We had, in fact, gone further, and identified reasons which made government's information set, powers and constraints different from those of a decentralized private sector, and which provided an explanation for why, at least in principle, government might undertake welfare-improving actions (see, for example, Stiglitz, 1989).

We also showed that the nature of the equilibrium, including its efficiency, could well depend on the distribution of wealth. This can be seen most clearly in the case of simple agricultural economies, but in fact it holds true more generally. The agency problems associated with sharecropping arise because of the disparity between the ownership of land and capital. Problems of information asymmetry do not arise when workers work their own land.[2]

Whether there was a political agenda in the back of the minds of those who formulated and developed the neoclassical theories, I will not venture to guess. But it is clear that the theories proved convenient for those with a particular set of interests. If, as neoclassical theory claimed, one could separate out efficiency issues from equity, one could pursue a political programme that focused only on the former – saying that *if* society wanted to change the distribution of income through its political process, *that* was an issue which it could turn to at any time; regardless of one's views on equity, it then made sense to remove distortions in the economy which impeded efficiency.

In standard competitive models, any interference with the free workings of the economy had an adverse effect on efficiency, whether it was minimum wage laws or trade unions – which introduced imperfect competition in labour markets – or requirements on working conditions. After all, an employer who offered workers worse conditions would only be able to recruit by paying commensurately higher wages. Firms would therefore carefully balance the extra cost of improving the conditions against the extra wage costs of not doing so, and these extra wage costs represented the marginal benefit of improved working conditions. Interventions to enhance job security were criticized, not only when they were made by government, but even when they resulted from collective bargaining because they were perceived as evidence of trade unions' monopoly power. Public pension schemes were also criticized, with payroll taxes seen as leading to higher labour costs and thus explaining the rise in unemployment.

It was, of course, inconvenient that many of the central propositions had little empirical support. Card and Krueger's (1995) work strongly demonstrated that minimum wage legislation does not have the serious adverse effect on employment predicted by the standard theory – and that it may even have a positive effect. But economic theory did not lend credence to many of the propositions either, even without recourse to modern information theories. Even if benefits did not depend on contributions, payroll taxes should largely be shifted backwards (except for minimum wage workers), and hence have no effect on employment; and to the extent that benefits depend on contributions, there may be little or no effect on labour supply (not even a positive one). But information economics explained clearly why market equilibrium was generally inefficient, e.g. why firms "undersupplied" contract provisions enhancing job security (see, in particular, Shapiro and Stiglitz, 1984).

In short, the mantra of increased labour market flexibility was only a thinly disguised attempt to roll back – under the guise of "economic efficiency" – gains that workers had achieved over years and years of bargaining and political activity. To be sure, sometimes unions may have more than corrected the imbalance of bargaining power that previously existed, and used their power to push for *excessive* protection for their members, at the expense of other workers in the economy. If that happens, however, the answer is not to pretend that in the absence of such protections, the competitive market place would lead to efficient *or equitable* outcomes; but rather to try to redress the imbalances.

While freedom of association and trade union rights are important in correcting the power imbalances that exist in labour markets, even workers enjoying such rights are typically in a disadvantageous position. It is far easier for an employer to replace recalcitrant workers than for employees to "replace" a recalcitrant employer, especially when the unemployment rate is high. Thus, there is an important role for government, e.g. in ensuring occupational health and safety.

"MARKET-FRIENDLY POLICIES": AT WHOSE RISK?

There is a range of other policies – sometimes seemingly quite remote from the labour market – which affect the outcome of the bargaining process. Capital market liberalization enhances the bargaining power of capital: effectively, it gives "capital" the right to announce that if it is taxed unduly, or if other measures that it dislikes are adopted, it will leave the country. It enhances the threat point of capital, and therefore tilts the outcome more in its favour. In the extreme, it means that capital cannot be taxed at all. Had similar measures been adopted to enhance labour mobility, they would have restricted the ability to tax labour as well (see, for example, Stiglitz, 1983a and 1983b). A well-known standard result in tax theory says that the optimal taxes should be inversely related to the elasticity of supply; capital market liberalization thus leads to a lower optimal tax.

"Labour market flexibility" and "capital market liberalization" may thus appear as symmetric policies, freeing up the labour and capital markets, respectively; but they have very asymmetric consequences – and both serve to enhance the welfare of capital at the expense of workers. So ingrained have these prescriptions become in the mantra of good policy that their distributional consequences have been almost totally ignored; and of course, if efficiency and distribution could be separated, as traditional theory argued they could be, the lapse might not have been so important.

It is not, of course, just that the advocates of these policies overlook the imperfections of competition and information. There are other market imperfections (some derived from imperfections of information) to which they turn a blind eye too. With imperfect insurance markets, individuals worry about the volatility of their income. They can smooth only imperfectly and often at great cost. Risk matters more than it would if markets were perfect. Indeed, surveys of poor workers suggest that insecurity is among their main concerns, and that instability is among the most important causes and manifestations of poverty (see World Bank, 2000). Yet, the so-called Washington Consensus has not only pushed policies which enhanced instability, but it has also pushed for the elimination of job security protections (which markets by themselves will often not provide).

Another important set of market imperfections concerns corporate governance. Managers of firms may not act in the interests of shareholders, majority shareholders may not act in the interests of minority shareholders and, more broadly, the concerns of other stakeholders may not be adequately reflected in the firm's decision-making process (see Stiglitz, 1985a).

The advocates of these "market friendly policies" (which might more aptly be called "capital market friendly" policies) have not consistently followed the neoclassical model's symmetries. For instance, they talk about the discipline provided by capital market liberalization – the discipline of a capricious market place, exhibiting not only irrational exuberance but, from time to time, irrational pessimism. Those who subject themselves to this discipline know too that it has particular perspectives and ideologies. Imagine how different the discipline might be if skilled labour, or unskilled labour, were perfectly mobile. It might, for instance, threaten to leave a country that did not provide adequate air quality, or which otherwise had a degraded environment.

Another manifestation of "capital market friendly policies" is the recent push for privatization of social security, with the replacement of defined-benefit programmes by defined-contribution programmes. While this is not the occasion for a full debate on the issues,[3] it should be clear that privatization would be of immense benefit to those firms that managed the pension funds and provided the annuities, but it would at the same time impose greater risks on workers, since the market in most countries does not provide securities that are fully indexed for inflation. Moreover, there is evidence suggesting that even in highly efficient capital markets, like the United Kingdom's, transaction costs are so high that benefits under privatization are reduced by 40 per cent (Murthi, Orszag and Orszag, 1999).

Advocates of the (capital) market friendly doctrines have not argued that all institutions do not matter. They argue that monetary institutions matter. Not content to change the broader economic environment in ways which tilt the balance of power, they have pushed for monetary institutions which tilt the balance of power further still, pressing for independent, non-representative central banks with a mandate solely for price stability. They try to use economic "reasoning" to support their conclusion, with regressions showing that countries with independent central banks have lower inflation.[4] But they confuse ends with means – just as the entire enterprise which sees labour merely as input into production confuses ends with means. Inflation is of concern only to the extent that it leads to worse *real* outcomes, e.g. lower growth, more poverty, and greater inequality. And the link between independent central banks and these *real* outcomes is tenuous at best.[5]

Even if one believed that *institutionally* it is preferable to have an independent central bank,[6] independence is not the same as non-representativeness. One can have an independent central bank, in which the differing interests of different stakeholders are represented. It is not the case that there is a single Pareto dominant policy,[7] one to which all "reasonable" people can agree. And so long as that is the case, one cannot – or, at least, should not – delegate decision-making to technocrats. Still less should one delegate decision-making to one group whose interests are markedly different from those of other groups. I shall return to this point at the end of the next section.

LEVEL OF EMPLOYMENT

The previous section argued that there is a role for government in the labour market: at the minimum, ensuring the right to collective action and enforcing minimum standards. The notion that markets fail to ensure socially efficient (and desirable) outcomes has long been recognized. Keynes pointed out that there might be persistent unemployment. But by a sleight of hand, what came to be called the neoclassical synthesis (Samuelson, 1997) argued that, once we correct for the market failure of massive unemployment, markets work efficiently. Thus, the standard neoclassical model – with its implications of efficiency – prevailed. The neoclassical synthesis was simply an assertion, a hope, an attempt by those committed to the market model to limit the scope for potential government intervention. Bruce Greenwald and I argued that it was far more plausible to assume that there were pervasive market failures, of which massive unemployment was the most obvious manifestation, the tip of the iceberg that could not be ignored (Greenwald and Stiglitz, 1987). Research on the economics of information helped to explain what was wrong with the standard neoclassical model: why there could be equilibrium unemployment,[8] why shocks to the economy could be amplified and result in the economy operating well below its "potential" for extended periods of time, and in the persistence of levels of unemployment far higher than the "equilibrium" level (see, for instance, Greenwald and Stiglitz, 1993).

Since Keynes and the Great Depression, few have believed in Say's law, that an increase in the supply of labour would automatically bring about an increase in demand. The theories referred to above explained how government intervention could help stabilize the economy with less volatility and higher *equilibrium* levels of employment. The precepts of counter-cyclical fiscal and monetary policy have come to be taught as part of standard macroeconomics in universities around the world. Remarkably, however, if we look at the data, we see that governments in less developed countries regularly engage in pro-cyclical fiscal policies. Worse still, we have seen how the IMF has advocated fiscal and monetary tightening in the face of an impending recession. We have seen how these policies exacerbated the recessions in East Asia, helping to turn one into a depression, from which some have yet to fully recover. The IMF has also put in place strategies for financial market restructuring which have adversely affected macroeconomic performance. In its structural adjustment programmes, it has often combined trade liberalization with interest rates so high that job and enterprise creation would have been impossible even in the best of economic circumstances, let alone in the more adverse circumstances prevailing in most developing countries. As the affected countries could not compete with the highly subsidized agricultural goods from the United States and elsewhere, the principles of comparative advantage did not play out in the way predicted by standard textbooks. Rather than moving from low productivity sectors to higher productivity, resources simply moved from low productivity to unemployment.

In transition economies as well, the policy framework all too often failed to lead to job creation. Even if the absence of a safety net implied that some employers did not fire their workers – resulting in less open unemployment than there might otherwise have been – it meant that they were underemployed, and often not paid. We now know the devastating effects – a GDP in Russia that is 40 per cent lower than ten years ago, and a poverty rate that has soared from 2 to 40 per cent or higher. Privatization, which was supposed to be the basis of wealth (and job) creation, laid the foundation for asset stripping and job destruction.

Repeatedly, we have seen a vicious cycle come into play: with excessively high unemployment rates, deteriorating social cohesion, accompanied by a multitude of societal manifestations from urban violence to riots and civil strife, creating an unattractive environment for investment and job creation. We saw that in Indonesia, where I predicted in December 1997 that if the highly contractionary monetary and fiscal policies that had been imposed on that country were maintained, there would be civil and political turmoil within six months. My prediction, unfortunately, proved all too correct.

While high interest rates prevent job creation, in the case of heavily leveraged firms large increases in interest rates contribute to job destruction – again as we saw in East Asia. They force firms into bankruptcy, and even if the resources *eventually* get reallocated (though in the process there may be considerable losses in assets and asset values), in the interim there can be high unemployment. And unfortunately, lowering interest rates at that point does not undo the damage: the bankrupt firms do not become unbankrupt. This is one of a number of important hysteresis effects within the labour market.

In development, transition and crises – or even in ordinary economic downturns – markets do not automatically quickly lead to full employment, and it is now almost universally recognized that government has an important role in facilitating employment creation and the maintenance of the economy at full employment. We now know a great deal about how to design effective stimulus programmes. We know that monetary policy is more effective in constraining an economy in a boom than in stimulating an economy in recession, and that we therefore need to rely on fiscal measures. We also know a great deal about how to design effective fiscal measures, i.e. measures which operate quickly, which have high multiplier effects, and which do not exacerbate social divisions in countries where such divisions are strong.[9] An example might be policies which change intertemporal prices to encourage consumption and investment during a period of expected unemployment (in which the shadow prices of resources are low) and which reduce liquidity constraints that limit expenditures either on investment or on consumption.[10] Such policies are indeed more effective than, say, tax cuts for the rich or permanent investment tax credits.

No matter how well we manage the economy, there will be downturns and, with downturns, unemployment. Yet while we know more about macroeconomic management,[11] economic crises have become more frequent and deeper around the world: close to a hundred countries experienced crises in the last quarter of the twentieth century. I believe there are some reasons for this: changes in the global economic architecture, including capital market liberalization, have heightened risks beyond the coping ability of many developing countries. Thus, while countries need to be urged to construct adequate safety nets,[12] anyone who is concerned with employment and decent work must be concerned about those features of the global economic architecture which contribute to volatility. Conversely, it seems perverse to argue simultaneously for measures that enhance global volatility *and* against measures that enhance worker security. Remarkably, however, this is precisely the position that advocates of the neo-liberal doctrines have taken.

The fact that there is a great deal of uncertainty in the dynamics of any economy implies that there is a great deal of uncertainty about the consequences of any policy. Today, for instance, we do not know how deep the recession will be, or would have been were it not for government intervention.

All decision-making must take these risks into account; this entails a process of sequential decision-making, with policies revised as new information becomes available. But the policy structures must also take account of irreversibilities and non-linearities, such as the fact, noted earlier, that while small increases in interest rates may not force a company into bankruptcy, large increases may, with huge implications for the dissolution of organizational capital; and subsequent lowering of interest rates may not undo the damage. Different policies entail different risks, with the risks being borne by different groups within societies. Not surprisingly, the policies advocated by those with financial interests result in a disproportionate share of the risks being borne by workers.

In framing macroeconomic policies, we need to keep our eyes on the ultimate objectives, not on intermediate variables – i.e. on employment, growth and living standards, not interest rates, inflation rates or exchange rates. Such variables are important only to the extent that they affect the variables of fundamental importance. Typically, however, macroeconomic analysis is framed around a trade-off between a variable that is of *direct* concern – employment and output today – and an intermediate variable: inflation. It is *asserted* that higher inflation will lead to lower growth, though it is hard to find evidence of such a relationship being statistically and economically significant for countries which, like the United States, face low inflation. It is *asserted* that once inflation starts to grow, it will be difficult to turn it back – that the economy is on the edge of a precipice of price stability, from which it is easy to fall. Again, there is no evidence for this "precipice theory". Finally, it is asserted that once inflation begins, it is very costly to reverse. The evidence however, is to the contrary – that the "augmented Philips curve" is linear or convex, not concave, at least for the United States (Stiglitz, 1997).

No wonder then that there has been so little analysis of trade-offs between variables of *fundamental* concern: it is remarkably hard to establish such trade-offs. But even if one could, the analysis needs to focus on risks: what are the risks associated with excessively aggressive policies? With insufficiently aggressive policies? And who bears those risks? It should be clear that alternative policies force different groups within society to bear these risks.[13] It follows then that macroeconomic policy is not a purely technical matter, and should therefore not be delegated to technocrats. It follows even more strongly that it is, to say the least, problematic to delegate decision-making to an independent central bank which is unrepresentative of the various groups affected by macro-policy, which is dominated by financial interests, and which pays little if any attention to employment.

A concern for employment and workers thus leads us to advocate not only for strong macroeconomic policies committed to the maintenance of full employment, policies which lead to greater economic stability, and strong safety nets to protect workers against the inevitable fluctuations that remain even with the best of economic policies, but also for institutional arrangements which ensure that the interests and concerns of workers are adequately reflected. Throughout the world, even social democratic governments have failed, by their acquiescence in unrepresentative and independent central banks. There is indeed little evidence to support the view that countries with independent central banks enjoy faster growth, high employment, higher living standards, or higher real wages (holding everything else constant). It is, of course, hardly surprising that an independent central bank focusing exclusively on inflation leads to lower inflation; but as I said before, inflation is only an intermediate variable. Besides, even if one agrees on independence, it does not follow that the mandate of the central bank should focus exclusively on inflation. I would argue that the Federal Reserve's broader mandate, which embraces employment and growth, has served the United States well. And if one argues that monetary policy should take account of employment and other objectives, it implies that if the central bank is independent, it should not be dominated by financial interests; workers should have a voice, and an important one at that.

LABOUR AS A MEANS VERSUS AN END, AND DEVELOPMENT AS A TRANSFORMATION OF SOCIETY

While much of this article focuses on *economic analysis* – e.g. institutions and policies which contribute to increasing employment, and the inadequacies of the neo-liberal model – I would be remiss if I failed to note that what is at stake is not just models of how the economy works but also *objectives*. As noted earlier, much of the neo-liberal doctrine has seen labour solely as an input into production, an input just like any other input. But if improving living standards is the objective of economics, then improving the welfare of workers becomes an end in itself; and only if one believes that the market leads to efficient outcomes can one feel confident in not paying explicit attention to workers' welfare, trusting that the market will make all the correct trade-offs.[14]

Elsewhere (Stiglitz, 1998), I have argued that development is more than just the accumulation of capital and the reduction of distortions (inefficiencies) in the economy. It is a transformation of society, a departure from traditional ways of doing things and traditional modes of thinking. If development were mainly a matter of capital accumulation, then successful development would entail primarily making a country more attractive for capital, enhancing the "security" of capital.[15]

If, however, development is to be broader based, then we must pay at least as much attention to workers and *their* security. We must persuade them that change can benefit them. But if they are exposed to increased insecurity and higher unemployment it will not; and many of the "reform" policies have done exactly that. On a more positive note, successful democratic development entails questioning authority and participation in decision-making:

democratic workplaces [16] as well as democratic political processes. These entail more democratic governance structures at all levels. [17]

THE ROLE OF THE INTERNATIONAL COMMUNITY

The principles set forth in this article so far are hardly radical, though in the terms of market-fundamentalist doctrines, which prevail in certain circles, they might seem so. This last section on the role of the international community begins with a simple premise, which should not be controversial either, though I am afraid it may appear to be so. That is, the international community should not push policies that *contravene* the above principles. Yet, that is precisely what the international community has been doing, through the Washington Consensus policies that have prevailed within the international economic institutions. They have pushed macroeconomic policies that have resulted in unnecessarily high unemployment, with *pro-cyclical* monetary and fiscal policies, the worst and most dramatic manifestations of which were witnessed in East Asia. To those who have worked in developing countries, however, their effects have been clear for years. The international economic institutions have pushed financial policies that have replaced automatic stabilizers with automatic destabilizers: as economies go into recession, non-performing loans increase, and strict enforcement of capital adequacy standards forces banks to cut back credit, automatically accelerating the decline. They have pushed privatization of old-age pensions: this exposes the elderly to risks from which they might otherwise have been protected and imposes transaction costs which, while enriching the providers of financial services, markedly diminish the benefits received by the elderly. They have not only pushed policies like capital market liberalization which expose countries to enormous risks they cannot manage well, but they have also pushed "labour market flexibility", making workers bear more fully the brunt of the adverse consequences of those policies. They have opposed, or at least not supported, demands for rights to collective action on the argument that this would intrude into politics – though in a myriad of other contexts, they feel perfectly comfortable doing so. This is not the occasion to try to explain why the institutions in question have taken such stances, though given their governance structure they can hardly come as a surprise: they are run by finance ministers and central bank governors, whose interests, perspectives and ideology are often not fully sympathetic with the concerns of workers.

But I think the international community should go further. The IMF was established more than a half century ago out of fear that, as the Second World War came to an end, the world would once again sink into a global recession. The IMF was supposed to put pressure on countries to pursue *expansionary* policies – recognizing that a downturn in one country has spillover effects on others (a negative externality) – and to provide the resources with which that could be done. It has not only abandoned its original mandate; it has, perversely, taken up the opposite cause, all too often providing funds to countries only on the condition that they engage in *contractionary* policies. As noted earlier, many developing countries have pro-cyclical fiscal policies. All too often this perversity arises not from a lack of knowledge of modern economics, but from a lack of resources. As the expression goes, banks love to lend to those who do not need their money; so when developing countries go into recessions, they pull their loans, exacerbating the downturn. Thus, developing countries may not only face exorbitant interest rates – with risk premiums that reflect an irrational pessimism which is the counterpoint to the excessive exuberance of the boom – they may also find themselves unable to access credit. There is now considerable support for the hypothesis that there may be credit rationing (Eaton and Gersovitz, 1981), the presence of which can be explained by theories of imperfect and asymmetric information (see, for example, Stiglitz and Weiss, 1981). The presence of such credit rationing (sometimes referred to as liquidity constraints) provides the *rationale* for the IMF: why an international *public* institution is required. But unfortunately, rather than providing needed liquidity to developing countries to enable them to pursue full employment policies, the IMF typically provides liquidity to countries only on the condition that they pursue contractionary policies.

But there is a more fundamental criticism of IMF strategies, one which focuses on countries' trade deficits. Countries with large trade deficits are told to cut them back, but never is a word of criticism levelled at the countries maintaining sustained trade surpluses. If deficits are vice, then surpluses must be virtue. How different from Keynes' conception: it was then surplus countries that were seen as the source of the problem, as their insistence on high levels of savings contributed to "underconsumption" and an insufficiency of aggregate demand, which threatened global prosperity. There was even discussion of imposing penalties on surplus countries.

The more modern IMF seems to have missed a central point: the sum of all trade surpluses and deficits must add up to zero, so if some countries – like Japan and China – insist on having large surpluses, other countries *must* have correspondingly large deficits. The deficits are like hot potatoes. As one country is forced to eliminate its deficit, it *must* show up somewhere else in the system. With a focus on trade deficits, no wonder there is always an impending crisis somewhere in the world.

These issues have taken on a greater urgency today as the world is slipping into a major slowdown. The issue is not whether growth will be negative: the point is that the global economy is performing markedly below its potential, and the gap will inevitably result in increases in unemployment.

There is a simple remedy. As has just been observed, problems of insufficiency of global aggregate demand were very much on the minds of Keynes and others at the time the IMF was established. There is a framework for enhancing aggregate purchasing power, namely through the creation of Special

Drawing Rights (SDRs). One way of thinking about this is the following: assume that the nations of the world wish to maintain reserves equal to a fixed percentage of their GDP; with global GDP of around US$40 trillion and growth of around 2 per cent, if reserves were equal to 5 per cent of GDP, aggregate reserves would grow by US$40 billion a year. Given the surpluses of China and Japan, a number twice that size might be more realistic. An annual issue of SDRs in that amount would just offset the purchasing power set aside in reserves and thus not be inflationary. The SDRs could be used to pursue global interests – from helping the poorest countries to improving the global environment.

For the past several decades, the IMF has focused on bailing out creditors and pushing the neo-liberal agenda. The time is ripe for the IMF to return to its original mission – i.e. ensuring global liquidity, to enable sustained global growth and, with that growth, full employment. But I think the international community should go still further: it is not enough just to do "no harm", or to have the IMF return to its role in promoting global economic prosperity. The international community should push for *decent work*, for full employment and better working conditions. Today there is international *surveillance* of countries in terms of their conformity to international norms for macroeconomic policies and financial institutions. The IMF's Article IV Consultations have grown beyond a review of whether countries are complying with the articles of agreement, to an intrusive review of a variety of policies. But while some macroeconomic indicators get enormous attention, others, such as the level of employment, the level of wages and disparities in pay, are virtually ignored. I believe very strongly that information helps shape behaviour: if we focus on unemployment, we will almost inevitably seek to ensure that it remains within reasonable limits, and if it does not, we will inquire into why not. If we demand that there be a "labour impact statement" before programmes (such as structural adjustment programmes) are adopted, then it is more likely that policies which minimize the adverse impacts on workers will be adopted.

Labour market experts must conduct the reviews. It is high time that we recognize that there are trade-offs in economic policies, that there is not a single Pareto-dominant policy. We should also recognize that there is a great deal of uncertainty about the consequences of economic policies and that there is, perhaps unsurprisingly, a correlation between those with particular perspectives/interests and the dominant views of the economy. It was those from the financial community who were the most ardent advocates of capital market liberalization, sliding over both the absence of compelling empirical and theoretical evidence that it increased growth and the presence of compelling evidence that it increased instability. Within the economics profession, labour economists are the most sceptical about claims that even moderate minimum wages result in significant unemployment. But even if one does not accept the Card and Krueger (1995) findings that there is no adverse effect, their results make a compelling case that if there is an adverse effect, it is not large.

We need a new framework for Article IV Consultations, one that is conducted with greater openness and transparency, with broader participation. These consultations would serve not to impose conditions on countries, but rather to enhance the kinds of dialogue on economic policy that should be central to democracy.

This may be a modest reform, but it is a small step that we can take towards the creation of economic policies that promote social justice and societal well-being.

CONCLUDING REMARKS

Labour policy has in many countries been subsumed under broader economic policies which, all too often, have come to be dominated by commercial and financial interests. Those defending such interests have been successful in propagating the idea that policies which advance their interests benefit all – a new version of trickle-down economics which suggests that workers do not even have to wait long, or at all, to receive the benefits of these wise policies. They claim there is a single Pareto-dominant set of policies, and therefore economic policy can simply be entrusted to technocrats, whose job is to craft that Pareto-dominant policy. For too long labour has acquiesced, sometimes becoming a more effective advocate of that Pareto-dominant policy than those whose interests it serves.

What I am calling for is not a return to class warfare, but a simple recognition of long-standing principles: there are trade-offs; there is uncertainty; different policies affect different groups differently; the role of the economic adviser is to inform policy-makers of the consequences of different decisions; and it is the role of the political process to make those decisions.

The fact that these principles have often been subverted has some important implications. While we all speak passionately about the importance of democratic principles, we also recognize that our democracies are imperfect, and that some groups' voices are heard more loudly than others. In the arena of international economic policy, the voices of commercial and financial interests are heard far more loudly than those of labour and consumer interests. As just noted, they have tried to convince others, with remarkable success, that there is no conflict of interests – which means that there are no trade-offs. The consequences speak for themselves: the growing dissatisfaction with the reform policies[18] is partly a consequence of the fact that so many have actually been made worse off. In Mexico, for instance, the incomes of the poorest 30 per cent of the population have actually declined over the past 16 years. All of the income gains (reflected in increases in *average* GDP per capita) have occurred among the richest 30 per cent, and especially among the richest 10 per cent. According to the Inter-American

Development Bank, no country in Latin America for which data on income distribution are available can boast a decline in income inequality during the 1990s (IDB, 2000).

Government – and the international economic institutions, which are *intergovernmental* public institutions[19] – play a role in determining the economic framework (including on those issues that affect labour relations). Therefore, one cannot separate politics from economics, as they are intimately intertwined. This was recognized by Teddy Roosevelt at the turn of the last century: his attack on trusts was not so much motivated by the loss of efficiency from the Harberger triangles resulting from monopoly power, as by the loss of democracy from the concentration of political power that follows from the concentration of economic power. The more stringent laws concerning the concentration of media power reflect similar concerns. Yet the economic policies that the international institutions have often pushed have resulted in the devastation of the middle classes and the aggrandizement of economic power. When national monopolies are sold prior to the establishment of effective regulatory and anti-trust institutions, those who hold these monopoly powers will use their wealth to perpetuate it. The Bill Gateses and the John D. Rockefellers of the world have clearly not been the strongest advocates of competition policy! The interplay between politics and economics has been seen most dramatically in Russia, where the privatization process resulted in the devastation of the middle class, and the creation of huge inequalities and an oligarchy which, if it seeks to establish a rule of law, will use its wealth and power to try to ensure that that rule of law favours itself.[20]

I have tried in this article to broaden the discussion beyond the confines of economics: there are market failures, and there is a role for government in correcting those market failures. Markets by themselves may fail not only to create full employment, but also to provide the right kind of working conditions. There are imperfections of competition and imperfections of corporate governance, and laws granting workers the rights to association and collective bargaining may serve to redress the balance, to give more effective voice to the concerns of workers, to enhance overall economic efficiency.

Advanced industrialized countries have developed a variety of institutions – including a strong independent academia, think tanks and NGOs – which give voice to broader national concerns, to the interests of consumers and workers, and which limit the scope, even if imperfectly, of special interests. This is not so in many developing countries. Yet what is at stake for these countries is not just a matter of economic efficiency, but the kind of society into which they will evolve, and the creation or survival of meaningful political democracy. In other words, income distribution and the creation of institutions which give effective voice to the concerns of workers matter, not just for economic efficiency, but for the dynamics of political and economic change. To take but one example: land reform. In many countries of the world, land is highly inequitably distributed, and much of the land is held in the form of sharecropping. The 50 per cent share which farmers must pay attenuates incentives. Were a government to impose a 50 per cent tax, however, the international economic institutions would speak out loudly about the attenuation of incentives. The seeming lack of concern on the part of the IMF[21] is hardly a surprise: land reform would disturb established economic interests and might even question existing property rights, regardless of how those property claims had come to be established. An even stronger case for land reform can be made: several of the most successful developing countries carried out major land reforms prior to – or at early stages of – their development transformation. With interests of trade unions coinciding with those of the landless,[22] the two can be a potent force for land reform.

Development is more than just the accumulation of capital and the enhanced efficiency of resource allocation; it is transformation of society. Equitable, sustainable and democratic development requires basic labour rights, including freedom of association and collective bargaining.

If we, as an international community, are to promote equitable, sustainable and democratic development – development that promotes societal well-being and conforms to basic principles of social justice – we must reform the international economic architecture. We must speak out more loudly against policies which work against the interests of workers. At the very least, we must point out the trade-offs, we must insist on democratic processes for determining how economic decisions are made. We have remained silent on these issues for too long – and the consequences have been grave.

Notes

[1] These attitudes are, of course, socially determined; in Western societies, for instance, there is increasing demand by women to participate in the labour force, a demand which is not just a reflection of economic factors.

[2] Though information asymmetries may still be important in credit markets.

[3] For a discussion of some of the fallacies underlying the standard arguments for privatization, see Orszag and Stiglitz (2001).

[4] New classical doctrines reinforced these perspectives: they argued that there was no trade-off in the long run. But even if there is no trade-off in the long run, there may be one in the short run. So long as the NAIRU is uncertain, different policy frameworks impose different risks (see Stiglitz, 1997).

[5] One of the reasons is, of course, that it is hard to establish a significant adverse relationship between inflation and growth for low inflation economies (see Bruno and Easterly, 1996).

[6] The case for which I find more compelling in countries with a long history of high inflation than in those with no such history.

[7] Though one strand of research in modern macroeconomics – that which contends that there is a vertical Phillips curve – has tried to argue something close to this.

[8] See the large literature on efficiency wages (e.g. Stiglitz, 1974 and 1987b; Shapiro and Stiglitz, 1984), much of which derives from problems of information imperfections.

[9] These are, of course, not the only desiderata that stimulus packages should meet: they should also strengthen the economy's long-run position, or at least not do undue harm.

[10] The constraints themselves are explained by asymmetries of information (see, for example, Stiglitz and Weiss, 1981).

[11] Indeed, in the United States, while there are still economic fluctuations, there is little evidence of a regular business cycle; expansions have become longer, and contractions shorter.

[12] Though, at the same time, one should recognize the inadequacy of such safety nets – even in advanced industrialized countries – in the agricultural and self-employment sectors, sectors which predominate in less developed countries.

[13] The nature of these risks depends, of course, on underlying structural relationships. For instance, if it is easy to reverse a slight increase in inflation (as the evidence seems to suggest) then one should be more willing to be more aggressive (see Stiglitz, 1997; Council of Economic Advisers, 1996 and 1997).

[14] While I have focused on several of the market failures, there are others, especially relating to education and training, with imperfect contracting (see, for example, Arnott and Stiglitz, 1985).

[15] We put aside here the question of whether the actual policies which the IMF has pushed have actually succeeded in doing so; arguably, capital market liberalization, while it has opened up access to capital, has also led to increased volatility, a higher incidence of crises, and in that sense, at a global level, may have actually not increased capital's "security". There are some who argue that the intent was not so much to increase the security of capital as the returns to capital. Increased capital mobility, as already noted, limits the scope for the taxation of capital, and, given the higher ability of higher income individuals and large corporations to bear risks, the increased riskiness of the global economic environment redistributes income in their favour.

[16] There is some evidence that more democratic workplaces enhance economic efficiency (see Blinder, 1990; Levine, 1995).

[17] By contrast, IMF conditionality often serves to undermine democratic processes, especially when (as in Korea) the conditionality extends beyond issues directly related to the crisis, and into core political issues (see Feldstein, 1998).

[18] For Latin America, a study by the Inter-American Development Bank (IDB) suggested that 60 per cent of the population think the economy is in trouble and 70 per cent see no possibility of improvement in the near term (IDB, 2000).

[19] They have been instrumental in perpetuating the myth that there is a single Pareto-dominant strategy – and the notion that economic policy is apolitical. Not only are they not supposed to enter into political matters (though they do so regularly and inevitably), they refer to the member governments as their shareholders, suggesting that they are more akin to corporations than to political institutions.

[20] See Hoff and Stiglitz (2001) for a discussion of how macroeconomic and other policies induced policies of asset stripping rather than wealth creation, and enhanced the likelihood of success of policies that were more congenial to the former than the latter.

[21] The World Bank has actually begun to push for market-based land reforms.

[22] Land reform reduces migration pressure, which induces downward pressure on urban wages.

References

Arnott, Richard J.; Stiglitz, Joseph E. 1985. "Labor turnover, wage structure and moral hazard: The inefficiency of competitive markets", in *Journal of Labor Economics* (Chicago, IL), Vol. 3, No. 4 (Oct.), pp. 434-462.

Blinder, Alan S. (ed.). 1990. *Paying for productivity: A look at the evidence*. Washington, DC, The Brookings Institution.

Bruno, Michael; Easterly, William. 1996. "Inflation and growth: In search of a stable relationship", in *Federal Reserve Bank of St. Louis Review* (St. Louis, MO), Vol. 78, No. 3 (May-June), pp. 139-146.

Card, David; Krueger, Alan B. 1995. *Myth and measurement: The new economics of the minimum wage*. Princeton, NJ, Princeton University Press.

Council of Economic Advisers. 1997. *Economic Report of the President*. Washington, DC.

—.1996. *Economic Report of the President*. Washington, DC.

Diamond, Peter. 1971. "A model of price adjustment", in *Journal of Economic Theory* (San Diego, CA), Vol. 3, pp. 156-168.

Eaton, Jonathan; Gersovitz, Mark. 1981. "Debt with potential repudiation: Theoretical and empirical analysis", in *The Review of Economic Studies* (Edinburgh), Vol. 48, No. 2 (Apr.), pp. 289-309.

Feldstein, Martin. 1998. "Refocusing the IMF", in *Foreign Affairs* (Palm Coast, FL), Vol. 77, No. 2 (Mar.-Apr.), pp. 20-33.

Greenwald, Bruce C.; Stiglitz, Joseph E. 1993. "Financial market imperfections and business cycles", in *Quarterly Journal of Economics* (Cambridge, MA), Vol. 108, No. 1 (Feb.), pp. 77-114.

—; —.1987. "Keynesian, new Keynesian and new classical economics", in *Oxford Economic Papers* (Oxford), Vol. 39, No. 1 (Mar.), pp. 119-133.

—; —.1986. "Externalities in economies with imperfect information and incomplete markets", in *Quarterly Journal of Economics* (Cambridge, MA), Vol. 101, No. 2 (May), pp. 229-264.

Hoff, Karla; Stiglitz, Joseph E. 2001. "Modern economic theory and development", in Gerald Meier and Joseph E. Stiglitz (eds.): *Frontiers of development economics: The future in perspective*. Oxford, Oxford University Press, pp. 389-459.

IDB (Inter-American Development Bank). 2000. *Economic and social progress in Latin America: Development beyond economics*. IPES 2000. Washington, DC.

Levine, David I. 1995. *Reinventing the workplace: How business and employees can both win*. Washington, DC, The Brookings Institution.

Murthi, Mamta; Orszag, Michael J.; Orszag, Peter R. 1999. *The charge ratio on individual accounts: Lessons from the U.K. experience*. Birbeck College Working Paper 99-2. London, University of London, Mar. [Available at http://www.econ.bbk.ac.uk/ukcosts].

Orszag, Peter R.; Stiglitz, Joseph E. 2001. "Rethinking pension reform: Ten myths about social security systems", in Robert Holzmann and Joseph E. Stiglitz (eds.): *New ideas about old age security: Toward sustainable pension systems in the 21st century*. Washington, DC, World Bank, pp. 17-56.

Samuelson, Paul. 1997. *Economics: The Original 1948 Edition*. New York, NY, McGraw-Hill Professional.

Shapiro, Carl; Stiglitz, Joseph E. 1984. "Equilibrium unemployment as a worker discipline device", in *American Economic Review* (Nashville, TN), Vol. 74, No. 3 (June), pp. 433-444.

Stiglitz, Joseph E. 1998. *Towards a new paradigm for development: Strategies, policies and processes*. Ninth Raul Prebisch Lecture, delivered at the Palais des Nations, Geneva, 19 Oct. Geneva, UNCTAD.

—.1997. "Reflections on the natural rate hypothesis", in *Journal of Economic Perspectives* (Nashville, TN), Vol. 11, No. 1 (Winter), pp. 3-10.

—.1989. "The economic role of the State: Efficiency and effectiveness", in Arnold Heertje (ed.): *The economic role of the State*. Oxford, Basil Blackwell, pp. 9-85.

—.1987a. "The causes and consequences of the dependence of quality on prices", in *Journal of Economic Literature* (Nashville, TN), Vol. 25, No. 1 (Mar.), pp. 1-48.

—.1987b. "Design of labor contracts: Economics of incentives and risk-sharing", in Haig Nalbantian (ed.): *Incentives, cooperation and risk sharing*. Totowa, NJ, Rowman & Allanheld, pp. 47-68.

—.1985a. "Credit markets and the control of capital", in *Journal of Money, Credit and Banking* (Columbus, OH), Vol. 17, No. 2 (May), pp. 133-152.

—.1985b. "Equilibrium wage distributions", in *Economic Journal* (Cambridge), Vol. 95, No. 379 (Sep.), pp. 595-618.

—.1983a. "Some aspects of the taxation of capital gains", in *Journal of Public Economics* (Lausanne), Vol. 21, pp. 257-294.

—.1983b. "Public goods in open economies with heterogeneous individuals", in Jacques-François Thisse and Henry G. Zoller (eds.): *Locational analysis of public facilities*. Amsterdam, North-Holland Publishing Company, pp. 55-78.

—.1974. "Alternative theories of wage determination and unemployment in LDCs: The Labor Turnover Model", in *Quarterly Journal of Economics* (Cambridge, MA), Vol. 88, No. 2 (May), pp. 194-227.

—; Weiss, Andrew. 1981. "Credit rationing in markets with imperfect information", in *American Economic Review* (Nashville, TN), Vol. 71, No. 3 (June), pp. 393-410.

World Bank. 2000. *World Development Report, 2000/2001: Attacking poverty*. Washington, DC.

PART III

FRESH PERSPECTIVES, NEW IDEAS

THE LABOUR MARKET: A LAWYER'S VIEW OF ECONOMIC ARGUMENTS

17

Pietro ICHINO *

The broadest possible protection of workers through peremptory standards or standards of public policy – considered by orthodox labour lawyers to be a positive value – is a negative value in the eyes of orthodox economists, given that such protection prevents the market from operating freely and therefore efficiently. Conversely, formal freedom and autonomy of individuals are considered positive by the orthodox economist but negative by the labour lawyer, who sees in them an inherent risk of dominance of the weak by the strong. How, given these contradictions, can a common language be found and dialogue established between orthodox economists and orthodox labour lawyers?

Over the past century, the legislators and trade unions of continental Europe found an effective means of countering workers' weak labour market position by building up a system of protection with two main objectives. The first was to prevent employers from negotiating workers' conditions of employment on a one-to-one basis, by imposing on both parties, through legislation and collective agreement, a standardized (model) arrangement of their mutual interests in the form of a binding contract. The second objective was to ensure that a worker who has been hired by an enterprise remains as far removed as possible from the labour market, hence the prevailing model of the stable employment relationship of unspecified duration. Although this system functioned well for decades, it is less effective today in the more developed countries, particularly in those of continental Europe. The notion of a permanent job guaranteed for life increasingly appears to be incompatible with the very rapid obsolescence of technologies and changes in production systems and, although standard models of work organization are

Originally published in *International Labour Review*, Vol. 137 (1998), No. 3.

* Director of the Institute of Labour Studies, Milan. These thoughts were prompted by exchanges during seminars and debates between the author and the economists of the Faculty of Political Sciences in Milan, where he has lectured in labour law since 1991.

regularly updated and adjusted, they cannot keep pace with those changes. As a result, the scope of legislation supporting trade union involvement in enterprises and statutory protection of workers is constantly shrinking. The working population is thus becoming divided between a group of insiders enjoying protected regular employment and a group of outsiders comprising temporary and casual workers and the unemployed – some of them in a state of permanent exclusion.

Through conversations with economists, the possibility has occurred to lawyers that the market could be transformed in such a way that, instead of constituting a threat for workers, it may offer them – including the more or less permanently excluded – a means of strengthening their bargaining position. This calls for experimentation with new forms of protection which, without being incompatible with, or aiming to replace the traditional forms, would make the requisite information and services generally available, minimize transaction costs (search, information, negotiation, etc.) and make transactions transparent.

However, even in a mature labour market that is well-provided with services for workers, labour law remains indispensable, even in the thinking of orthodox economists. On grounds of public interest, sound reasons still exist as evidenced in theory by particular economic models – for maintaining the contract of employment as a form of insurance for workers. And the contract can perform this function effectively only through the enforcement of peremptory rules. A general "safety net" is thus still necessary and should be extended to all those who work for their living, including those working outside the sphere of employer-employee relationships.

The same goes for trade unions. It is indeed in the interest of all workers that a coalition should defend their rights, both in the labour market and at the workplace, and represent them effectively in negotiations on their conditions of employment. Once the fundamental rights of all workers on the labour market and their protection within the contractual relationship are guaranteed ("safety net"), collective autonomy and individual autonomy must be brought to coexist and complement each other. Similarly, trade unions will have to learn to represent and promote the interests of outsiders as well as those of insiders. This may indeed prove to be an area in which labour lawyers and orthodox economists can find common ground. This article very briefly summarizes personal thoughts on the subject.

THE JUSTIFICATION OF LABOUR LAW

The first question that arises is: What is the justification, in terms of economic rationality, for state intervention in imposing conditions on employment relationships, i.e. the establishment of a standard of treatment (and, specifically, the distribution of risk between employer and worker) through rules from which private autonomy can make no exception?

The first answer to this question offered by economic science is based on the concept of structural monopsony – a market consisting of a single buyer and a large number of suppliers. This was precisely the situation of the original labour market at the outset of industrial development, when the factory was a "cathedral in the desert" – the desert of an almost exclusively agricultural economy in which workers were for the most part underemployed. Orthodox economists agree with labour lawyers and trade unionists that a monopsonic labour market does not produce optimal outcomes. Indeed, the employer buys less labour – engages fewer workers than he/she could – and pays them less than if other employers were competing for the available labour. In a monopsonic market, therefore, the purpose of legislation or collective agreement is to impose a peremptory standard of treatment – such as obligatory maximum working hours and a minimum wage – which will improve the general well-being.

This is the justification for labour law that is given, more or less explicitly, in the introductory chapters of most texts on labour law. However, the structure of the European labour market has certainly changed since the beginning of the industrial revolution. A large number of enterprises are now competing for labour. The former justification, based on the model of the monopsonic market, no longer suffices.

Labour law as protection for insiders

An alternative view, although by no means a justification of labour law, is that based on the model suggested by Lindbeck and Snower (1988), better known under the name of the "insider-outsider theory". This theory explains the basic workings of the labour market by viewing trade unions and labour law as instruments that enable workers in a stable situation (insiders) to protect themselves against competition from unemployed, casual or temporary workers (outsiders). This theory considers legislated or collectively agreed minimum conditions of employment as means of reducing the potential advantages of replacing an insider by an outsider. Restrictions on dismissal are regarded as a further means of increasing the cost of such substitution.

To someone who has worked for trade unions for several years, who has devoted a lifetime to labour law, and who considers it to be a prime expression of civil progress and solidarity between citizens, it is unpleasant to be told that trade unions and labour law may serve to protect the privileges of the most fortunate workers to the detriment of the excluded. In this view, trade unions and labour law would be primarily an expression of the selfishness of the richest workers towards the poorest.

The common interest model

Rejecting the model based on the conflict of interests between insiders and outsiders, economists who are closer to the trade unions offer models based on the idea that the two groups have a common interest in state intervention and collective bargaining, whether for establishing minimum conditions of employment, for reducing disparities in earnings between workers, or for apportioning to wages the largest possible share of the value-added produced. According to them, the fact that outsiders currently benefit neither from state-enforced protection nor from trade union protection does not in itself imply that they have no interest in maintaining or even in strengthening such protection. Indeed, they may expect to benefit from it in the future. If outsiders can realistically expect to find a stable job within a reasonable period, they too will perceive that anything that contributes to maintaining at a high level or even enhancing the peremptory standards of treatment for those in regular employment will ultimately be to their advantage.

THE DUAL NATURE OF THE LABOUR MARKET IN ITALY AND OTHER EUROPEAN COUNTRIES

The problem for outsiders lies in the fact that the labour market in continental Europe, and in Italy in particular, is characterized by very limited interchange between insiders and outsiders.

In this respect, the situation of the Italian labour market is hardly enviable, as demonstrated by the figures in table 1. In 1997, Italy, with a high overall unemployment rate, had almost seven unemployed workers out of ten (66 per cent) unemployed for over a year (classified under ILO and OECD criteria as long-term unemployed); six out of ten were seeking their first job; and five out of ten were under 25 years of age. In Italy, particularly in the southern regions, the unemployed are mostly young people who encounter serious difficulties in entering the job market, or adults who have been unemployed for a considerable period and whose difficulty in finding another job increases year by year. The situation is slightly better in other European countries, with long-term unemployment rates of 55.5 per cent in Spain, 49 per cent in the Netherlands, 48 per cent in Germany (1996), 41 per cent in France, and 39 per cent in the United Kingdom. Yet these figures still highlight a major divergence between Europe and the United States where, in 1996, only 9 per cent of the jobless were in the long-term unemployed category.

Empirical studies have revealed a striking positive correlation between the average duration of unemployment among outsiders and the duration of stable employment among insiders (Grubb and Wells, 1993; Blanchard and Portugal, 1998). Of course, this does not necessarily imply a positive correlation between the stability of employment of insiders and overall unemployment.

From this marked duality of the labour market, and the remote possibility that outsiders will find stable employment, it would be reasonable to conclude that, at least in Italy, a large majority of such workers are unaffected

Table 1. Long-term unemployment rates and standardized unemployment rates
in selected European countries and in the United States (1997)

Country	Long-term unemployment rate[1]	Standardized unemployment rate
Italy	66.3	12.1
Belgium	60.5	9.2
Portugal	55.6	6.8
Spain	55.5	20.8
Netherlands	49.1	5.2
Germany (1996)	47.8	8.9
France	41.2	12.4
United Kingdom	38.6	7.1
European Union	50.2	10.6
United States	8.7	4.9

[1] 12 months or longer, as a percentage of total unemployment.
Source: OECD, 1998, Statistical annex, tables A and G; OECD: *Standardized unemployment rates,* Press release, Paris, 15 Sep. 1998.

by the maintenance of protective legislation or public policy or by legislation which encourages unionization in large or medium-sized enterprises (except as an ideological choice which has nothing to do with their economic interests).

In the current economic system, raising conditions of employment above a given level entails not only a narrowing of the labour market segment to which they apply, but also a restriction on access to that segment. The most significant example is clearly that of restrictions on dismissals, the aim of which is to improve conditions of employment and to protect the dignity and moral freedom of the worker by preventing the employer from acting arbitrarily. However, such restrictions not only reduce the likelihood that an employer will hire further workers (given uncertainty regarding future demand), but they also increase the cost of replacing insiders, with the result that the competitive position of outsiders is further eroded. It might therefore be assumed, at least for the short and medium terms, that negative correlations exist both between the level of protection and the number of people who have access to that protection, and between the level of protection and the ease with which those who benefit from it may change places with those who do not. This is another reason, in Italy at least, why millions of outsiders have no interest in the general system of employment protection.

These considerations must be borne in mind when discussing worker protection. Stability of employment, for instance, may be very important for insiders, but it hampers outsiders' access to regular employment. Consequently, job stability should be protected not as an absolute value, but as a relative value, in the sense that outsiders may be paying the price for the stability of insiders.

Similarly, under a system of collective bargaining that covers all workers (i.e. negotiation with *erga omnes* effect, as in France) it is necessary always to consider who benefits from collective agreements. Lest such agreements reflect insiders' concern to protect themselves from the competition of outsiders, instead of the common interest of the two groups, it is essential that both somehow be represented at the negotiating table. For an agreement to have *erga omnes* effect, it must be concluded by a trade union confederation whose representativeness is demonstrably not confined to insiders. This was the approach put forward by Solow (1990) and of which the present author has suggested a practical application in the context of industrial relations in Italy (Ichino, 1996). A prior condition for the *erga omnes* effect of collective agreements is that the signatory unions must represent the majority, their representativeness being measured not only in enterprises in terms of numbers of workers, but also on the basis of regular consultations with the unemployed, organized by the public employment agencies where they are registered.

To date, labour lawyers have said little about the price paid by outsiders for the protection of insiders. But a price certainly is paid, and this may well explain the recent waning of Italy's popular consensus in support of labour law and trade union organizations. In a referendum in 1995, 66 per cent of Italians voted for the repeal of a legislative provision intended to strengthen trade union presence and activities at the workplace level.

INFORMATION ASYMMETRY

In Italy – though the same arguably applies to much of continental Europe – the model based on the conflict of interest between insiders and outsiders appears to provide a more accurate reflection of labour market reality than does the model of common insider-outsider interests. This does not, however, give sufficient cause for denying the economic rationale for the mandatory limitation of competition between workers.

Economics teaches that perfect competition can only exist if information for both sides of the market is perfectly symmetrical. But such symmetry of information is precisely what the labour market lacks most.

The employer's lack of information

The first asymmetry to emerge relates to the information available to the employer and to the worker regarding the latter's personal qualities: the worker is fully aware – certainly much more aware than the employer – of his or her own ability to adapt to new situations, chances of falling sick, or reproductive plans. The model developed by Aghion and Hermalin (1990) around this asymmetry is extremely interesting for labour lawyers because it explains the positive function of labour law as a means of distributing the risks of negative eventualities between the worker and the employer in the best possible way.

In the absence of a law or contract that restricts the employer's right to dismiss workers, the risk of failure to carry out a task or to produce a result – for example, the risk of interruption of service by reason of illness or child-birth (i.e. absence), or the risk of skill obsolescence – is borne solely by the worker, since failure to provide the service would entail dismissal. A contract restricting the employer's freedom to dismiss workers transfers at least part of the risk from the worker to the employer, even if it also provides for lower earnings (which can be seen as an insurance premium paid by the worker). Such a contract thus strikes a balance of interests in this respect. A law (or collective agreement) which imposes such a transfer of risks by restricting the employer's freedom to dismiss workers is justified in that workers nego-tiating their employment conditions might otherwise refrain from demand-ing a clause restricting the possibility of dismissal for fear of identifying themselves as "risky" individuals. Given the imperfect information available to enterprise managers regarding the qualities and characteristics of workers offering their services, the latter would be tempted to make a show of great confidence when negotiating their conditions of employment, with the result that the risk of failure to provide a service or produce a result, or of other negative eventualities, would then subsequently be borne by the worker.

In other words, in the absence of a state-imposed requirement that the employer should assume a share of the risk – thereby automatically attribut-ing an insurance function to the employment contract – the market would not of its own volition optimize transactions in terms of the respective parties' ex-posure to risk. Employment contracts would imply greater security for enter-prise managers, who are typically more inclined to take risks, and greater in-security for workers who are generally more inclined to seek security.

It should be emphasized that while this model justifies the requirement that risk should be shared between the employer and the worker (i.e. a re-striction on the freedom to dismiss), it does not justify peremptory standards regarding minimum wages. Thus, the same reasoning cannot be applied to all provisions of labour law.

In regard to the insurance function of the employment contract, it is also interesting to note that this reasoning implicitly denies the rationale for any distinction between the peremptory standards governing employer-employee relationships and those governing self-employment in cases where there is a continuous relationship with a single contractor.

But this line of reasoning also highlights the fact that any restriction of the employer's freedom to dismiss turns the employment contract into an insurance contract, with a trade-off taking place between stability of employ-ment and level of earnings (because of "the insurance premium" that the worker pays the employer). The imposition of stability of regular employ-ment therefore implies a cost not only for outsiders (in that it becomes more difficult for them to gain access to the protected sphere), but also for those it protects, since it reduces their earnings. This may go some way towards explaining the deliberate "flight" of workers out of employer-employee relationships and into self-employment in countries where stability is most rigidly imposed (on this correlation, see Grubb and Wells, 1993; on the characteristics of this phenomenon in Europe see Loutfi, 1991; OECD, 1992, chapter 4, pp. 155-194).

The worker's lack of information

A second information asymmetry which can serve to explain the positive role of labour law (and which is also acceptable to orthodox economists) is a counterpart asymmetry to that discussed above. Here, the information concerns not the quality or characteristics of the worker but supply and demand on the labour market, a matter on which the employer has more information than the worker.

The employer is familiar with the labour market, since he or she is regularly in touch with it and can thus select workers from a broad pool of labour. The worker, by contrast, is generally not familiar with the labour market since he or she may only have to enter it a few times in the course of his or her lifetime. Just as a foreigner alone in an unknown country must accept the deal offered by the first hotelier encountered if he/she does not want to spend the night in the open, so the worker, on a market on which he/she does not know how to behave, must accept the first job on offer for want of any other solution. This accounts for workers' fear of the market and their weak bargaining position, which are a direct consequence of their limited range of choice, even when the market features a large number of employers competing for labour. So, although the market may have the potential for perfect competition on the demand side – which would enhance workers' bargaining position – scant information on possible choices and the inadequacy of services to disseminate information make the labour market a *de facto* monopsony. In other words, the employer benefits from the fact the worker is not in a position to choose. And this applies both to the initial phase of negotiation on conditions of employment and to the phase consisting of the employment relationship itself.

The *dynamic monopsony* model is based on these considerations. It explains the dysfunctions of a labour market that is left to itself in a developed economy and shows that peremptory rules are needed to correct the ensuing distortions. For example, Card and Krueger (1995) used this model to explain why the imposition of a minimum wage did not have a depressive effect on employment levels in the United States.

THE DISEQUILIBRIUM OF THE LABOUR PROTECTION SYSTEM

The very purpose of labour legislation is to correct distortions of the free market. However, since it is primarily enacted in response to demands by insiders and organizations defending their interests, labour legislation – like trade unions – tends to protect workers who are already in employment, not workers on the labour market. Workers enjoy adequate assistance within enterprises once they have succeeded in obtaining employment, but the assistance available to them outside, on the market, is totally inadequate. In this sense, the labour law of continental Europe – with the possible exception of Sweden – can be said to lack one of the two pillars on which a modern labour protection system should rest; and over-emphasis on one of the two components of the system – i.e. protection of workers in employment relationships – does not make up for the inadequacy of the second, i.e. worker protection on the market.

This structural imbalance, in turn, seriously undermines the effectiveness of the standards that protect workers in employment. Indeed, a worker in a weak and isolated position on the labour market is likely to end up in a weak position in any contractual relationship with an employer. A person who fears the labour market will also fear his/her employer to some extent; he/she will be disinclined to stand up for his/her rights and, in the absence of an alternative solution, will submit to the employer's terms. Of course, there are other solutions; but workers are not in a position to resort to them, for lack of information and for lack of the services needed to obtain information (particularly information and retraining services that could direct workers towards opportunities on the job market).

According to another, now classic theory, workers' lack of information can constitute an excessively high transaction cost, which prevents the market from functioning at maximum efficiency (Coase, 1960). In economic terms, this explains and justifies peremptory intervention by the State, although the same theory holds this to be merely a lesser evil since the imposition of a mandatory balance of interests between two individuals will necessarily produce results which are less efficient than those that would have been achieved by a competitive market if transaction costs could be eliminated.

If transaction costs could be removed, the labour market might cease to be a source of weakness and danger for workers and instead become a source of greater freedom and enhanced bargaining capacity. If the market were equipped with a dense network of efficient services, rid of its innumerable pitfalls, and turned into a more accessible and safer place that was easier to understand, it could offer workers the best possible means of utilizing their skills and fulfilling their aspirations.

What the long-term unemployed lack most is indeed information and access to the opportunities available on the market, vocational training which could equip them to apply for jobs, and services to facilitate geographical mobility and thereby enhance their chances of finding a suitable job. If new forms of protection were to be tested – consisting not in imposing obligations, but rather in making information and the necessary services widely available and in making transactions transparent – the market might be able to provide everyone with access to regular employment, including for those who are now more or less permanently excluded. If the latter were granted priority access to such services, they would indeed be placed on a more even footing with workers in a stronger position.

SUGGESTIONS FOR ACHIEVING A BETTER BALANCE

To strike a better balance between the interests of insiders and those of outsiders, the labour market must be strengthened by a wide range of public and private services which, though in competition, should all be permanently networked so as to constitute an overall observatory of supply and demand and to serve as a structure through which the two can meet. Indeed, Italian legislators drew inspiration from this idea when they passed Act No. 469, of 23 December 1997, which requires all public and private employment services to hook up to a national computer network and to use it daily to communicate all available information on the nature and volume of demand for and supply of labour. Within such a framework, the duty of the public employment service and of the services administered by trade unions, nonprofit organizations and local authorities should be first and foremost to reintegrate the weakest workers and provide them with genuine leverage in bargaining and competition by compensating for their occupational, cultural or social weakness through the provision of a surplus of what they most need, namely, information, training and mobility. A market rendered efficient by a system that reduces transaction costs to a minimum for all workers – and particularly for the weakest and most disadvantaged – would offer them the most reliable means of emerging from exclusion. And here the distinction is not between public services and private services, but between services that are provided openly and services that are provided to the grey market and which cannot sustain such transparency (ILO, 1994, pp. 52-53 and 56-58).

Obviously, an economic development policy that seeks to create jobs remains essential in combating unemployment. But job creation alone cannot, and never could, eliminate the disadvantages suffered by those who are the worst off. Therefore, it is essential that they should be offered real equality in terms of information, training and mobility – in short, what is understood today in European Union parlance by "employability". It is not simply a matter of appealing to workers' individual responsibility, but of ensuring that all workers – and particularly the weakest – have the means of exercising that responsibility (Sen, 1997).

It should be emphasized, moreover, that such a policy may achieve notable results in terms of social equity, even in a situation of permanent imbalance between the supply of and demand for labour. Take a hypothetical rate of unemployment of 10 per cent.[1] It can mean either of two quite different things. It could mean that each labour force participant can expect an average of six months' unemployment for every five-year period of work; or it could mean that 10 per cent of labour force participants are excluded from employment for protracted periods, with the other 90 per cent occupying all the jobs offered on the market. While economic development policy should seek to reduce the level of unemployment, the aim of "employability" policy is, for any given level of unemployment, to distribute the risk of unemployment fairly. In other words, it must create a situation in which all workers – and not only 90 per cent of them – stand a chance of obtaining the jobs offered day by day by the economy.

Besides, the underprivileged will not be the only ones to benefit from the effectiveness of the labour market services provided through such a policy. Since lack of information and occupational and geographical mobility have always been among the principal reasons for the general imbalance between the bargaining positions of workers and employers, these deficiencies must be corrected if that imbalance is to be eliminated or significantly reduced. Indeed, a labour market offering a network of efficient services and underpinned by widely available education could go a long way towards redressing the balance between the bargaining positions of workers and employers. The fairness of the transaction may be assured, on a mature market, by guaranteeing symmetry of information between employers and workers, transparency of negotiations between them and qualified assistance in such negotiations. And the outcomes could be more efficient than those achieved merely by imposing a standard model of employment relationship through state-enforced public regulations.

It is already apparent today that competently advised workers who are fully informed of their rights, of standard employment conditions on the national and local job markets, and of the occupational options available on the market are effectively in a position to choose the time, mode and place of work best suited to their interests. Such workers are emancipated, mature and equipped to negotiate with their prospective employers; they are not afraid of the market. The bargaining strength of workers will be further enhanced if all are offered assistance and equal access to information, just as the range of their options will be extended if they have access to appropriate services to facilitate their mobility and to provide them with training that helps them to find real jobs. The new forms of protection concentrate on boosting the bargaining power of workers in general, so that all of them – and not just those who were the best off to begin with – are put in a position optimally to administer their own interests as mature individuals.

Once the "safety net" is ensured for all – i.e. the three fundamental labour market rights (information, training and mobility) and essential protection in the employment relationship – it will be possible to give everyone freedom of choice between the many possible models for combining interests. These range from situations where the employer accepts inflexibility and an obligation to provide greater security to the worker in exchange for a lower wage, to situations where the worker offers greater flexibility in exchange for higher pay. With inalienable rights thus guaranteed, the labour market could fully become a market for working time, for flexibility and sta-bility of that working time; a market in which different models of organ-ization and of worker participation in the enterprise can be compared and placed in competition; a market on which all individuals – both workers and employers – can opt for what best suits them.

Trade unions would also have an important role to play in such a job market. Trade unions are much needed by workers – even before represent-ing them in their relations with an employer – to assist them in the labour market by guaranteeing compliance with their rights to information, training and mobility. In this sphere, it will be possible for trade unions to serve not only the relatively restricted circle of workers in large enterprises or in the public sector – as occurs today in most cases – but also others who are excluded from this circle and are today in the majority.

Collective bargaining on conditions of employment will continue to be the typical and essential function of trade unions, since individual workers can never have as great a knowledge as trade unions do of the state of the economy, the position of the enterprise on the market and the countless cir-cumstances affecting employment relationships. However, on a mature labour market that is well provided with services, it will be possible to do away with the traditional concept of collective autonomy as a negation of individual autonomy or a "colonization of the individual by the collective" (Simitis, 1990). The role of collective bargaining should come to concentrate less on imposing peremptory rules on the organization of employment rela-tionships, leaving more scope for individual contract, because a wider formal freedom for the worker implies real bargaining strength and effective free-dom of choice.

CONCLUSIONS

The following conclusions are offered tentatively, without any pretension of certainty.

The model of a dual labour market teaches that, in a mature economic system, an inverse correlation generally exists between the level of protec-tion of stable employment and the ease of access to protection by those who are excluded from such employment; legislation and collective bargaining should therefore always take into account all the interests at stake, not exclu-sively those of insiders.

Nonetheless, insiders and outsiders may have a shared interest in main-taining high wage levels and job stability, imposed by law and collective contract, under the common interests model; however, this applies only if outsiders have a real prospect of obtaining stable employment within a reasonable period.

The model formulated by Aghion and Hermalin (1990) demonstrates that the asymmetry of information on the personal qualities of the worker causes a distortion in the functioning of the free market which should be corrected by state-imposed or collectively agreed regulations which transfer to employers a share of the risk borne by workers (who are on average less inclined to take risks than are employers); here, some restriction of the employer's freedom to dismiss is certainly necessary and justified.

However, job stability is also a relative value, not an absolute one. Any restriction on the employer's freedom to dismiss turns the employment contract also into an insurance contract, whereby a trade-off takes place between stability of employment and the corresponding wage level. Indeed, job stability carries a cost not only to outsiders – by making it more difficult for them to enter the protected sphere – but also to insiders in that their earnings are reduced (the "insurance premium" that the worker pays the employer).

The dynamic monopsony model, which fits the situation in most developed countries more closely than does the structural monopsony model, shows that the asymmetry of information on labour supply and demand also produces a distortion in the functioning of the free market in these countries. This may be corrected by offering all workers on the market a plethora of information, training and mobility services, rather than through rigid regulation of the employment contract.

The costs and benefits of every public policy standard, of every article of labour law and trade union law, of every trade union action should always be carefully assessed not only in so far as they affect those in stable employment, but also as to their implications for those who are excluded. This is a difficult exercise both for lawyers and for economists, since it simultaneously requires economic expertise and legal expertise, one of which they lack. But this exercise is essential to meet the urgent need to shift the centre of gravity of labour law away from protecting workers in their contractual relationship with the employer and towards protecting all of them on the labour market. This does not imply any weakening of the workers' position vis-à-vis the employer, since a worker who is strong and self-confident on the market will also be strong and self-confident in the workplace.

Note

[1] A figure which is, moreover, that of the average level of unemployment in the European Union as at August 1998.

References

Aghion, Philippe; Hermalin, Benjamin. 1990. "Legal restrictions on private contracts can enhance efficiency", in *Journal of Law, Economics and Organization* (Oxford), No. 2, pp. 381-409.

Blanchard, Olivier; Portugal, Pedro. 1998. *What hides behind an unemployment rate: Comparing Portuguese and US unemployment.* NBER Working Paper No. 6636, Cambridge, MA, National Bureau for Economic Research.

Card, David; Krueger, Alan B. 1995. *Myth and measurement: The new economics of the minimum wage.* Princeton, NJ, Princeton University Press.

Coase, Ronald Harry. 1960. "The problem of social cost", in *Journal of Law and Economics* (Chicago, IL) No. 3, pp. 1-44.

Grubb, David; Wells, William. 1993. "Employment regulation and patterns of work in EC countries", in *OECD Economic Studies* (Paris), No. 21, Winter, pp. 7-58.

Ichino, Pietro. 1996. Il *lavoro e il mercato.* Milan, Mondadori.

ILO. 1994. The *role of private employment agencies in the functioning of labour markets.* International Labour Conference, 81st Session, Geneva, 1994, Report VI. Geneva.

Lindbeck, Assar; Snower, Dennis J. 1988. *The insider-outsider theory of employment and unemployment.* Cambridge, MA, MIT Press.

Loutfi, Martha F. 1991. "Self-employment patterns and policy issues in Europe", in *International Labour Review* (Geneva), Vol. 130, No. 1, pp. 1-19.

OECD. 1998. *Employment outlook.* Paris. June.

—.1992. *Employment outlook.* Paris. July.

Sen, Amartya. 1997. "Inequality, unemployment and contemporary Europe", in *International Labour Review* (Geneva), Vol. 136, No. 2, pp. 155-172.

Simitis, Spiros. 1990. "Ii diritto del lavoro e la riscoperta dell'individuo", in *Giornale di diritto del lavoro e di relazioni industriali* (Milan), No. 45, 1990/1, pp. 87-113.

Solow, Robert M. 1990. *The labor market as a social institution.* Cambridge, MA, Blackwell.

WORK AND RIGHTS

Amartya SEN

18

This is a crucial moment in the history of working people across the world. The first flush of globalization is nearing its completion, and we can begin to take a scrutinized and integrated view of the challenges it poses as well as the opportunities it offers. The process of economic globalization is seen as a terrorizing prospect by many precariously placed individuals and communities, and yet it can be made efficacious and rewarding if we take an adequately broad approach to the conditions that govern our lives and work. There is need for well-deliberated action in support of social and political as well as economic changes that can transform a dreaded anticipation into a constructive reality.

This is also a historic moment for the ILO as custodian of workers' rights within the United Nations system. Its new Director-General – the first from outside the industrialized world – has chosen to lead the organization in a concerted effort to achieve decent work for all women and men who seek it across the globe (see ILO, 1999). My own close association with the ILO goes back much more than a quarter of a century. In the seventies, I had the privilege of advising the ILO, and doing some work for it (see, e.g., Sen, 1975, 1981). But my first working association with the ILO was in 1963, when I was despatched to Cairo. Already in the 1970s I was trying to persuade the ILO to take a broad approach to the idea of working rights – though admittedly what I did then was rather crude and rough. I was trying to invoke ideas not only of rights but also of metarights. So I do particularly welcome this new initiative of the ILO to achieve decent work.

What, then, is the nature of this start, and where does all this fit into the contemporary intellectual discourse on economic arrangements, social values

Originally published in *International Labour Review*, Vol. 139 (2000), No. 2.

* Master, Trinity College, Cambridge, and Lamont University Professor Emeritus, Harvard University. This article is based on his address to the 87th Session of the International Labour Conference, Geneva, 15 June 1999.

and political realities? I should like to identify four specific features of the approach which may be especially important to examine. I shall have the opportunity of scrutinizing only two of these issues in any detail, but I shall briefly comment on the other two distinctive features.

OBJECTIVES AND GOALS

The first important feature in the new ILO vision is the articulation of its goal: the promotion of "opportunities for women and men to obtain decent and productive work, in conditions of freedom, equity, security and human dignity" (ILO, 1999, p. 3). The reach of this objective is indeed momentously large: it includes *all* workers, wherever and in whatever sector they work; not just workers in the organized sector, nor only wage workers, but also unregulated wage workers, the self-employed, and the homeworkers. The ILO aims to respond to the terrible fact that "the world is full of overworked and unemployed people" (ILO, 1999, pp. 3, 4).

This universality of coverage, pervasiveness of concern and comprehensive conception of goals is a well-chosen alternative to acting only in the interest of *some* groups of workers, such as those in the organized sector, or those already in employment, or those already covered by explicit rules and regulations. Of course universality implies facing many difficult questions which need not arise if the domain of concern is restricted to narrower groups, such as workers in the organized sector (leaving out the unorganized sector), or even all wage workers (leaving out homeworkers), or even all people actively in work (leaving out the unemployed).

The case for choosing such a broad focus rests on the importance of a comprehensive approach. There are different parts of the working population whose fortunes do not always move together, and in furthering the interests and demands of one group, it is easy to neglect the interests and demands of others. Indeed, it has often been alleged that labour organizations sometimes confine their advocacy to very narrow groups, such as unionized workers, and that narrowness of the outlook can feed the neglect of legitimate concerns of other groups and also of the costs imposed on them (unorganized labourers, or family-based workers, or the long-term unemployed, for example). Similarly (on the other side), by focusing specifically on the interests of workers in the informal sector, it is also possible to neglect the hard-earned gains of people in organized industry, through an attempt – often recommended (if only implicitly) – to level them down to the predicament of unorganized and unprotected workers.

Working people fall into distinct groups with their own specific concerns and plights, and it behoves the ILO to pay attention simultaneously to the diverse concerns that are involved. Given the massive levels of unemployment that exist in many countries of the world today – indeed even in the rich economies of western Europe – it is right that policy attention be focused on expanding jobs and work opportunities. And yet the conditions of work are important too. It is a question of placing the diverse concerns within a comprehensive assessment, so that the curing of unemployment is not treated as a reason for doing away with reasonable conditions of work of those already employed, nor is the protection of the already-employed workers used as an excuse to keep the jobless in a state of social exclusion from the labour market and employment. The need for trade-offs is often exaggerated and is typically based on very rudimentary reasoning. Further, even when trade-offs have to be faced, they can be more reasonably – and more justly – addressed by taking an inclusive approach, which balances competing concerns, than by simply giving full priority to just one group over another.

The aged and the unemployed

The need for a broad and inclusive approach can be well illustrated by referring to another issue – that of ageing and the dependency ratio – which is often juxtaposed, in an unexamined way, to the problem of unemployment and availability of work. There are two principles in some tension with each other that are frequently invoked simultaneously in dealing with these different issues in an intellectually autarchic way.

Addressing the growing proportion of the aged population, it is often lamented that since old people cannot work, they have to be supported by those who are young enough to work. This leads inescapably to a sharp increase in the so-called dependency ratio. As it happens, this fact itself demands more scrutiny. There is, in fact, considerable evidence that the increase in longevity that has resulted from medical achievements has also elongated the disability-free length of working lives over which a person can work (see, for example, Manton, Corder and Stallard, 1997). The possibility of elongating working lives is further reinforced by the nature of technical progress that makes less demand on physical strength.

This being the case, it is natural to suggest that one way of reducing the burden of dependency related to ageing is to raise the retirement age – or at least give people in good health the option to go on working. In resisting this proposal, it is frequently argued that if this were done, then the aged will replace the younger workers and there will be more unemployment among the young. But this argument is in real tension with the previous claim that the root of the problem lies in the fact that old people cannot work, and the young who can work have to support the old.

If health and working ability ultimately determine how much work can potentially be done (and certainly social and economic arrangements can be geared to make sure that to a great extent the potential is realized), then surely the trade-off with youthful unemployment is a real *non sequitur*. The absolute size of the working population does not, in itself, cause more unemployment; for example, it is not the case that countries with a larger working population typically have a larger proportion of unemployment (consider the United States compared to France or Italy or Spain or Belgium). There are many big issues to be faced in scrutinizing proposals for revising the retirement age, but linking unemployment to the absolute size of the working population does not enrich this discussion. Indeed, we see here a messy argument based on combining two mutually contrary gut reactions: (i) the gut reaction that the source of the problem related to an ageing population is that the old cannot work and the young must support them; and (ii) the gut reaction that the young must lose jobs if the older people do work. The combination of these unscrutinized feelings is to produce a hopeless impasse which rides just on unexamined possibilities, based on a simple presumption of conflict that may or may not actually exist.

The practice of being driven by imagined conflicts and being led by partisan solutions is as counterproductive in dealing with issues of ageing and employment as it is in addressing the problem of working conditions on one hand and the need for employment on the other. Conflicts cannot be made to go away by simply ignoring them on behalf of one group or another. Nor need conflicts invariably arise merely because some elementary textbook reasoning suggests that they might conceivably exist, under certain hypothesized conditions. There is a need for facing empirical possibilities with open-mindedness. There is also a need for openly addressing ethical issues involving conflict, when it does arise, through balancing the interests of groups with contrary interests, rather than giving total priority to the interests of one group against another.

Child labour and its prevention

Similar questions arise in dealing with the difficult problem of child labour. It is often claimed that the abolition of child labour will harm the interests of the children themselves since they may end up starving because of a lack of family income and also because of increased neglect. It is certainly right that the fact of family poverty must be considered in dealing with this issue. But it is not at all clear why it must be presumed that the abolition of child labour will lead only to a reduction of family income and further neglect of children, without any other economic or social or educational adjustment. In fact, that would be a particularly unlikely scenario for "the worst forms of child labour" (slavery, bondage, prostitution, trafficking) which are the focus of the recently adopted Convention concerning the prohibition and immediate action for the elimination of the worst forms of child labour (Convention No. 182 (1999)).

The case for a broader and more inclusive economic analysis and ethical examination is very strong in all these cases. One must not fall prey to unexamined prejudices or premature pessimism.

RIGHTS OF THE WORKING PEOPLE

The second conceptual feature that needs to be stressed is the idea of rights. Along with the formulation of overall objectives, the domain of practical reasoning extends beyond the aggregative objectives to the recognition of rights of workers.

What makes this rights-based formulation particularly significant is that the rights covered are not confined only to established labour legislation, nor only to the task – important as it is – of establishing new legal rights through fresh legislation. Rather, the evaluative framework begins with acknowledging certain basic rights, whether or not they are legislated, as being a part of a decent society.[1] The practical implications that emanate from this acknowledgement can go beyond new legislation to other types of social, political and economic actions.

The framework of rights-based thinking extends to ethical claims that transcend legal recognition. This is strongly in line with what is becoming increasingly the United Nations' general approach to practical policy through rights-based reasoning. The framework of rights-based thinking is thus extended from the pure domain of legality to the broader arena of social ethics. These rights can thus be seen as being prior (rather than posterior) to legal recognition. Indeed, social acknowledgement of these rights can be taken to be an invitation to the State to catch up with social ethics. But the invitation is not merely to produce fresh legislation – important as it is – since the realization of rights can also be helped by other developments, such as creation of new institutions, better working of existing ones and, last but not the least, by a general societal commitment to work for appropriate functioning of social, political and economic arrangements to facilitate widely recognized rights.[2]

There are really two contrasts here: one between legal rights and socially accepted principles of justice, and another between rights-based reasoning and goal-based formulations of social ethics. In scrutinizing the approach, we have to ask how well rights-based reasoning integrates with goal-based programming. These two basic precepts have sometimes been seen, especially by legal theorists, as providing alternative ethical outlooks that are in some tension with each other (see, for example, Dworkin, 1977). Are we to be guided, in case of a conflict, by the primacy of our social goals, or by the priority of individual rights? Can the two perspectives be simultaneously invoked without running into an internal contradiction? I believe that the two approaches are not really in tension with each other, provided they are appropriately formulated. However, the underlying methodological question has to be addressed, and I shall briefly examine the reasons for thinking that there is no deep conflict here.[3]

Rights and goals

The question that has to be faced is this: why cannot the fulfilment of rights be among the goals to be pursued? The presumption that there must be a conflict here has indeed been asserted, but the question is why we should accept this claim. There will quite possibly be a real impasse here if we want to make the fulfilment of each right a matter of absolute adherence (with no room for give and take and no possibility of acceptable trade-offs), as some libertarians do. But most rights-based reasoning in political debates, for example on human rights, need not – and indeed does not – take that form.

If the formulation is carefully done to allow trade-offs that have to be faced, then it is indeed possible to value the realization of rights as well as the fulfilment of other objectives and goals. The rights at work can be broadly integrated within the same overall framework which also demands opportunities for women and men to obtain decent and productive work, in conditions of freedom, equity, security and human dignity. To pay attention to any of these demands does not require us to ignore – or override – all other concerns. For example, the rights of those at work can be considered along with – and not instead of – the interests of the unemployed.

Rights and obligations

There is a different type of question that is sometimes raised, focusing on the relation between rights and duties. Some have taken the view that rights can be sensibly formulated only in combination with correlated duties. Those who insist on that binary linkage tend to be very critical, in general, of any discussion of rights (for example, invoking the rhetoric of "human rights") without specification of responsible agents and their duties to bring about the fulfilment of these rights. Demands for human rights are then seen just as loose talk. And similar scepticism is aimed at such statements as "all those who work have rights at work".

A basic concern that motivates some of this scepticism is: how can we be sure that rights are, in fact, realizable unless they are matched by corresponding duties? Indeed, some do not see any sense in a right unless it is balanced by what Immanuel Kant called a "perfect obligation" – a specific duty of a particular agent for the actual realization of that right (Kant, 1788).

This presumption can be the basis of rejection of rights-based thinking in many areas of practical reason. Indeed, aside from general scepticism that tends to come from many lawyers, there are also distinguished philosophers who have argued in favour of the binary linkage between rights and exact duties of specified individuals or agencies (see, for example, O'Neill, 1996).

We can, however, ask: why this insistence? Why demand the absolute necessity of a co-specified perfect obligation for a potential right to qualify as a real right? Certainly, a perfect obligation would help a great deal towards the realization of rights, but why cannot there be *unrealized* rights? We do not, in any obvious sense, contradict ourselves by saying: "These people had all these rights, but alas they were not realized, because they were not institutionally grounded." Something else has to be invoked to jump from pessimism about the *fulfilment of* rights, all the way to the *denial* of the rights themselves.

This distinction may appear to be partly a matter of language, and it might be thought that the rejection can be based on how the term "rights" functions in common discourse. But in public debates and discussion the term "rights" is used much more widely than would be permitted by the insistence on strict binary relations. Perhaps the perceived problem arises from an implicit attempt to see the use of rights in political or moral discourse through a close analogy with rights in a legal system, with its demand for specification of correlated duties. In contrast, in normative discussions rights are often championed as entitlements or powers or immunities which it would be good for people to have. Human rights are seen as rights shared by all – irrespective of citizenship – advantages that everyone *should* have. The claims are addressed generally (and as Kant might say, "imperfectly") to anyone who can help, even though no particular person or agency may be charged to bring about singlehandedly the fulfilment of the rights involved. Even if it is not feasible that everyone can have the fulfilment of their rights in this sense (if, for example, it is not yet possible to eliminate undernourishment altogether), credit can still be taken for the *extent* to which these alleged rights are fulfilled. The recognition of such claims as rights may not only be an ethically important statement, it can also help to focus attention on these matters, making their fulfilment that much more likely – or quicker.

This is indeed the form in which many major champions of rights-based thinking have tried to use the idea of rights, going back all the way to Tom Paine and Mary Wollstonecraft.[4] The invoking of the idea of rights is neither in tension with a broadly goal-based ethical framework, nor ruled out by some presumed necessity of perfect obligations allegedly needed to make sense of the idea of rights. The broad approach can be defended not just in terms of good commonsense appeal, but also in terms of capturing the variety of values and concerns that tend to arise in public discussions and demands.

SOCIAL AND POLITICAL BROADENING

Another distinguishing feature of the approach is that it situates conditions of work and employment within a broad economic, political and social framework. It addresses, for example, not merely the requirements of labour legislation and practice, but also the need for an open society and the promotion of social dialogue. The lives of working people are, of course, directly affected by the rules and conventions that govern their employment and work, but they are also influenced, ultimately, by their freedoms as citizens with a voice who can influence policies and even institutional choices.

In fact, it can be shown that "protection against vulnerability and contingency" is, to a great extent, conditional on the working of democratic participation and the operation of political incentives. I have argued elsewhere that it is a remarkable fact in the history of famines that famines do not occur in democracies. Indeed, no substantial famine has ever occurred in a democratic country – no matter how poor.[5] This is because famines are, in fact, extremely easy to prevent if the government tries to prevent them, and a government in a multi-party democracy with elections and a free media has strong political incentives to undertake famine prevention. This would indicate that political freedom in the form of democratic arrangements helps to safeguard economic freedom (especially from extreme starvation) and the freedom to survive (against famine mortality).

The security provided by democracy may not be sorely missed when a country is lucky enough to be facing no serious calamity, when everything is running along smoothly. But the danger of insecurity arising from changes in economic or other circumstances (or from uncorrected mistakes of policy) can lurk solidly behind what looks like a healthy state. This is an important connection to bear in mind in examining the political aspects of the recent "Asian economic crisis".

The problems of some of the east and south-east Asian economies bring out, among other things, the penalty of undemocratic governance. This is so in two striking respects, involving the neglect of two crucial instrumental freedoms, viz. "protective security" (what we have been just discussing) and "transparency guarantee" (an issue that is closely linked with the provision of adequate incentives to economic and political agents). Both relate directly or indirectly to safeguarding decent work and to promoting decent lives.[6]

Taking the latter issue first, the development of the financial crisis in some of these economies was closely linked with the lack of transparency in business, in particular the lack of public participation in reviewing financial and business arrangements. The absence of an effective democratic forum has been consequential in this failing. The opportunity that would have been provided by democratic processes to challenge the hold of selected families or groups – in several of these countries – could have made a big difference.

The discipline of financial reform that the International Monetary Fund tried to impose on the economies in default was, to a great extent, necessitated by the lack of openness and disclosure, and the involvement of unscrupulous business linkages, that were characteristic in parts of these economies. The point here is not to comment on whether the IMF's management of the crises was exactly right, or whether the insistence on immediate reforms could have been sensibly postponed until financial confidence had returned in these economies. No matter how these adjustments would have been best done, the contribution of the lack of transparency and freedom in predisposing these economies to economic crises cannot be easily doubted.

The pattern of risk and improper investments, especially by politically influential families, could have been placed under much greater scrutiny if democratic critics had demanded this in, say, Indonesia or South Korea. But of course neither of these countries then had the democratic system that would have encouraged such demands to come from outside the government. The unchallenged power of the rulers was easily translated into an unquestioned acceptance of the lack of accountability and openness, often reinforced by strong family links between the government and the financial bosses. In the emergence of the economic crises, the undemocratic nature of the governments played an important part.

Second, once the financial crisis led to a general economic recession, the protective power of democracy – not unlike that which prevents famines in democratic countries – was badly missed. The newly dispossessed did not have the hearing they needed. A fall of total gross national product of, say, even 10 per cent may not look like much, if it follows the experience of past economic growth of 5 or 10 per cent every year for some decades. And yet that decline can ruin lives and create misery for millions if the burden of contraction is not shared together but allowed to be heaped on those – the unemployed or those newly made economically redundant – who can least bear it. The vulnerable in Indonesia may not have missed democracy acutely when things went up and up, but that very lacuna kept their voice muffled and ineffective as the unequally shared crisis developed. The protective role of democracy is strongly missed when it is most needed.

The comprehensive view of society that informs the approach adopted in the ILO vision of decent work (ILO, 1999) provides a more promising understanding of the needs of institutions and policies in pursuit of the rights and interests of working people. It is not adequate to concentrate only on labour legislation since people do not live and work in a compartmentalized environment. The linkages between economic, political and social actions can be critical to the realization of rights and to the pursuit of the broad objectives of decent work and adequate living for working people.

INTERNATIONAL VERSUS GLOBAL

I turn now to the fourth and final distinctive feature of the approach under discussion. While an organization such as the ILO has to go beyond national policies (without overlooking the instrumental importance of actions by governments and societies within nations), there is a critical distinction between an "international" approach and a "global" one. An *international* approach is inescapably parasitic on the relation between nations, since it works through the intermediary of distinct countries and nations. In contrast, a truly *global* approach need not see human beings only as (or even primarily as) citizens of particular countries, nor accept that the interactions between citizens of different countries must be inevitably intermediated through the relations between distinct nations. Many global institutions, including those central to our working lives, have to go well beyond the limits of "international" relations.[7]

The beginnings of a truly global approach can be readily detected in the analysis underlying the new directions of the ILO. The increasingly globalized world economy calls for a similarly globalized approach to basic ethics and political and social procedures. The market economy itself is not merely an international system; its global connections extend well beyond the relation between nations. Capitalist ethics, with its strong as well as weak points, is a quintessentially global culture, not just an international construct. In dealing with conditions of working lives as well as the interests and rights of workers in general, there is a similar necessity to go beyond the narrow limits of international relations.

A global approach is, of course, a part of the heritage of labour movements in world history. This rich heritage – often neglected in official discussions – can indeed be fruitfully invoked in rising to the challenges of decent work in the contemporary world. A universalist understanding of work and working relations can be linked to a tradition of solidarity and commitment. The need for invoking such a global approach has never been stronger than it is now. The economically globalizing world, with all its opportunities as well as problems, calls for a similarly globalized understanding of the priority of decent work and of its manifold demands on economic, political and social arrangements. To recognize this pervasive need is itself a hopeful beginning.

Notes

[1] A key instrument that reflects this is the ILO Declaration on Fundamental Principles and Rights at Work. For the full text of that 1998 Declaration and for helpful discussion, see the special issue of the *International Labour Review* on "Labour Rights, Human Rights" (Vol. 137 (1998), No. 2, pp. 253-257 and pp. 223-227 respectively).

[2] This and related issues are discussed in Sen, 1999a.

[3] I have discussed these issues in Sen, 1982, 1985 and 2000.

[4] Tom Paine's *Rights of man* and Mary Wollstonecraft's *A vindication of the rights of woman* were both published in 1792.

[5] I have discussed this in Sen, 1983 and 1984; and jointly with Jean Drèze in Drèze and Sen, 1989.

[6] I have investigated these connections in Sen, 1999a.

[7] I have discussed the distinctions involved in Sen, 1999b.

References

Drèze, Jean; Sen, Amartya. 1989. *Hunger and public action.* Oxford, Clarendon Press.

Dworkin, Ronald. 1977. *Taking rights seriously.* London, Duckworth.

ILO. 1999. *Decent work.* Report of the Director-General of the ILO to the 87th Session of International Labour Conference. Geneva.

Kant, Immanuel. 1788. *Critique of practical reason.* Translated by L.W. Beck. New York, NY, Bobbs-Merrill, 1956.

Manton, Kenneth G.; Corder, Larry; Stallard, Eric. 1997. "Chronic Disability Trends in Elderly United States Populations: 1982-1994", in *Proceedings of the National Academy of Sciences*, 94 (March 1997).

O'Neill, Onora. 1996. *Towards justice and virtue.* Cambridge, Cambridge University Press.

Paine, Thomas. 1792. *Rights of man: Being an answer to Mr Burke's attack on the French Revolution.* Boston, Faust.

Sen, Amartya. 2000. "Consequential evaluation and practical reason", in *Journal of Philosophy* (New York), Vol. 97, No. 9, pp. 477-502.

—.1999a. *Development as freedom.* New York, NY, Alfred A. Knopf, and Oxford, Oxford University Press.

—.1999b. "Global justice: Beyond international equity", in Inge Kaul, Isabelle Grunberg and Marc A. Stern (eds): *Global public goods: International cooperation in the 21st Century.* New York, Oxford University Press.

—.1985. "Well-being, agency and freedom: Dewey Lectures 1984", in *Journal of Philosophy* (New York), Vol. 82, No. 4, pp. 169-221.

—.1984. *Resources, values and development.* Cambridge, MA, Harvard University Press.

—.1983. "Development: Which way now?", in *Economic Journal* (Oxford), Vol. 93, No. 372 (Dec.), pp. 742-762.

—.1982. "Rights and agency", in *Philosophy and Public Affairs* (Princeton), Vol. 11, No. 1, pp. 3-39.

—.1981. *Poverty and famines: An essay on entitlement and deprivation.* A study prepared for the ILO within the framework of the World Employment Programme. Oxford, Clarendon Press.

—.1975. *Employment, technology and development.* A study prepared for the ILO within the framework of the World Employment Programme. Oxford, Clarendon Press.

Wollstonecraft, Mary. 1792. *A vindication of the rights of woman: With strictures on political and moral subjects.* Boston, Thomas and Andrews. [Text available online at: http://www.constitution.org/woll/row.txt. Visited on 11 May 2000.]

WOMEN AND EQUALITY: THE CAPABILITIES APPROACH

19

Martha NUSSBAUM *

I found myself beautiful as a free human mind.

> Mrinal, in Rabindranath Tagore's "Letter from a wife" (1990, p. 102)

It is obvious that the *human* eye gratifies itself in a way different from the crude, non-human eye; the human *ear* different from the crude ear, etc. ... The *sense* caught up in crude practical need has only a *restricted* sense. For the starving man, it is not the human form of food that exists, but only its abstract being as food; it could just as well be there in its crudest form, and it would be impossible to say wherein this feeding activity differs from that of *animals*.

> Marx, *Economic and Philosophical Manuscripts* (1844)

SEX AND SOCIAL JUSTICE

Human beings have a dignity that deserves respect from laws and social institutions. This idea has many origins in many traditions; by now it is at the core of modern democratic thought and practice all over the world. The idea of human dignity is usually taken to involve an idea of *equal* worth: rich and poor, rural and urban, female and male, all are equally deserving of respect, just in virtue of being human, and this respect should not be abridged on account of a characteristic that is distributed by the whims of fortune. Often, too, this idea of equal worth is connected to ideas of freedom and opportunity: to respect the equal worth of persons is, among other things, to promote their ability to fashion a life in accordance with their own view of what is deepest and most important.

But human dignity is frequently violated on grounds of sex. Many women all over the world find themselves treated unequally with respect to employment, bodily safety and integrity, basic nutrition and health care,

Originally published in *International Labour Review*, Vol. 138 (1999), No. 3.

* Ernst Freund Professor of Law and Ethics, The Law School, The Divinity School, and the Departments of Philosophy and of Classics, The University of Chicago.

education and political voice. In many cases these hardships are caused by their being women, and in many cases laws and institutions construct or perpetuate these inequalities. All over the world, women are resisting inequality and claiming the right to be treated with respect.

But how should we think about this struggle? What account shall we use of the goals to be sought and the evils to be avoided? We cannot avoid using some normative framework that crosses cultural boundaries when we think of concepts such as women's "quality of life" their "living standard" their "development" and their "basic entitlements". All of these are normative concepts, and require us to defend a particular normative position if we would use them in any fruitful way. In default of an alternative, development economics will supply some less than perfect accounts of norms and goals, such as increased GNP per capita, or preference satisfaction. (These approaches are criticized below.) This article first addresses the worries that arise when we attempt to use any cross-cultural framework in talking about improvements in women's lives. Next, the dominant economic approaches are examined. Finally, there is a defence of the "capabilities approach", an approach to the priorities of development that focuses not on preference satisfaction but on what people are actually able to do and to be. It is argued that this approach is the most fruitful for such purposes, that it has good answers to the problems that plague the other approaches.[1]

THE NEED FOR CROSS-CULTURAL OBJECTIVES

Before we can advance further defending a particular account of the objectives of development, we must face a challenge that has recently arisen, both in feminist circles and in discussions of international development policy. The question that must be confronted is whether we should be looking for a set of cross-cultural objectives in the first place, where women's opportunities are concerned. Obviously enough, women are already doing that in many areas. Women in the informal sector, for example, are increasingly organizing on an international level to set goals and priorities.[2] But this process is controversial, both intellectually and politically. Where do these normative categories come from? – it will be asked. And how can they be justified as appropriate for cultures that have traditionally used different normative categories? The challenge asks us to defend our entire procedure, showing that it is not merely an exercise of colonial power.

Now of course no critical social theory confines itself to the categories of each culture's daily life. If it did, it probably could not perform its special task as theory, which involves the systematization and critical scrutiny of intuitions that in daily life are often unexamined. Theory gives people a set of terms with which to criticize abuses that otherwise might lurk nameless in the background. Terms such as "sexual harassment" and "hostile work environment" are some obvious examples of this point. But even if one defends theory as in general valuable for practice, it may still be problematic to use concepts that originate in one culture to describe and assess realities in another – and all the more problematic if the culture described has been colonized and oppressed by the describer's culture. For such reasons, attempts by international feminists today to use a universal language of justice, human rights, or human functioning to assess the lives of women in developing countries is bound to encounter charges of Westernizing and colonizing – even when the universal categories are introduced by activists who live and work within the very countries in question. For, it is standardly said, such women are alienated from their culture, and are faddishly aping a Western political agenda.

Sometimes this objection is simply a political strategem to discredit opponents who are pressing for change. The right reply to such strategies is to insist on the indigenous origins of the demand for change, and to unmask the interested motives of the objector. But sometimes, too, a similar objection is made in good faith by thinkers about culture. Three standard arguments are heard, all of which must be honestly confronted.

First, one hears what is called here the *argument from culture.* Traditional cultures, the argument goes, contain their own norms of what women's lives should be: frequently norms of female modesty, deference, obedience and self-sacrifice. Feminists should not assume without argument that those are bad norms, incapable of constructing good and flourishing lives for women. By contrast, the norms proposed by feminists seem to this opponent suspiciously "Western", because they involve an emphasis on choice and opportunity.

An answer to this argument will emerge from the proposal to be made here. It certainly does not preclude any woman's choice to lead a traditional life, so long as she does so with certain economic and political opportunities firmly in place. But we should begin by emphasizing that the notion of tradition used in the argument is far too simple. Cultures are scenes of debate and contestation. They contain dominant voices, and they also contain the voices of women, which have not always been heard. It would be implausible to suggest that the many groups working to improve the employment conditions of women in the informal sector, for example, are brainwashing women into striving for economic opportunities: clearly, they provide means to ends women already want, and a context of female solidarity within which to pursue those ends. Where they do alter existing preferences, they typically do so by giving women a richer sense of both their own possibilities and their equal worth, in a way that looks more like a self-realization (as Tagore's heroine vividly states) than like brainwashing. Indeed, what may possibly be "Western" is the arrogant supposition that choice and economic agency are solely Western values! In short, because cultures are scenes of debate, appealing to culture gives us questions rather than answers. It certainly does not show that cross-cultural norms are a bad answer to those questions.

Let us now consider the argument called here the *argument from the good of diversity*. This argument reminds us that our world is rich in part because we do not all agree on a single set of practices and norms. We think the world's different languages have worth and beauty, and that it would be a bad thing, diminishing the expressive resources of human life generally, if any language should cease to exist. So, too, cultural norms have their own distinctive beauty; the world risks becoming impoverished as it becomes more homogeneous.

Here we should distinguish two claims the objector might be making. She might be claiming that diversity is good as such; or she might simply be saying that there are problems with the values of economic efficiency and consumerism that are increasingly dominating our interlocking world. This second claim, of course, does not yet say anything against cross-cultural norms; it just suggests that their content should be critical of some dominant economic norms. So the real challenge to our enterprise lies in the first claim. To meet it we must ask how far cultural diversity really is like linguistic diversity. The trouble with the analogy is that languages do not harm people, whereas cultural practices frequently do. We could think that threatened languages such as Cornish and Breton should be preserved, without thinking the same about domestic violence: it is not worth preserving simply because it is there and very old. In the end, then, the objection doesn't undermine the search for cross-cultural norms, it requires it: for what it invites us to ask is whether the cultural values in question are among the ones worth preserving, and this entails at least a very general cross-cultural framework of assessment – one that will tell us when we are better off letting a practice die out.

Finally, we have the *argument from paternalism*. This argument says that when we use a set of cross-cultural norms as benchmarks for the world's varied societies, we show too little respect for people's freedom as agents (and, in a related way, their role as democratic citizens). People are the best judges of what is good for them, and if we say that their own choices are not good for them we treat them like children. This is an important point, and one that any viable cross-cultural proposal should bear firmly in mind. But it hardly seems incompatible with the endorsement of cross-cultural norms. Indeed, it appears to endorse explicitly at least some cross-cultural norms, such as the political liberties and other opportunities for choice. Thinking about paternalism gives us a strong reason to respect the variety of ways citizens actually choose to lead their lives in a pluralistic society, and therefore to seek a set of cross-cultural norms that protect freedom and choice of the most significant sorts. But this means that we will naturally value religious toleration, associative freedom, and the other major liberties. These liberties are themselves cross-cultural norms, and they are not compatible with the views that many real people and societies hold.

We can make a further claim: many existing value systems are themselves highly paternalistic, particularly toward women. They treat them as unequal under the law, as lacking full civil capacity, as not having the property rights, associative liberties and employment rights of males. If we encounter a system like this, it is in one sense paternalistic to say, sorry, that is unacceptable under the universal norms of equality and liberty that we would like to defend. In that way, any bill of rights is "paternalistic" vis-à-vis families, or groups, or practices, or even pieces of legislation, that treat people with insufficient or unequal respect. The Indian Constitution, for example, is in that sense paternalistic when it tells people that it is from now on illegal to use caste or sex as grounds of discrimination. But that is hardly a good argument against fundamental constitutional rights or, more generally, against opposing the attempts of some people to tyrannize others. We dislike paternalism because there is something else that we like, namely liberty of choice in fundamental matters. It is fully consistent to reject some forms of paternalism while supporting those that underwrite these basic values.

Nor does the protection of choice require only a formal defence of basic liberties. The various liberties of choice have material preconditions, in whose absence there is merely a simulacrum of choice. Many women who have in a sense the "choice" to go to school simply cannot do so: the economic circumstances of their lives make this impossible. Women who "can" have economic independence, in the sense that no law prevents them, may be prevented simply by lacking assets, or access to credit. In short, liberty is not just a matter of having rights on paper, it requires being in a material position to exercise those rights. And this requires resources. The State that is going to guarantee people rights effectively is going to have to recognize norms beyond the small menu of basic rights: it will have to take a stand about the redistribution of wealth and income, about employment, land rights, health, education. If we think that these norms are important cross-culturally, we will need to take an international position on pushing toward these goals. That requires yet more universalism and in a sense paternalism; but we could hardly say that the many women who live in abusive or repressive marriages and have no assets and no opportunity to seek employment outside the home are especially free to do as they wish.

The argument from paternalism indicates, then, that we should prefer a cross-cultural normative account that focuses on empowerment and opportunity, leaving people plenty of space to determine their course in life once those opportunities are secured to them. It does not give us any good reason to reject the whole idea of cross-cultural norms, and gives some strong reasons why we should seek such norms, including in our account not only the basic liberties, but also forms of economic empowerment that are crucial in making the liberties truly available to people. And the argument suggests one thing more: that the account we search for should seek empowerment and opportunity for each and every person, respecting each as an end, rather than simply as the agent or supporter of ends of others. Women are too often treated as members of an organic unit,

461

such as the family or the community is supposed to be, and their interests subordinated to the larger goals of that unit, which means, typically, those of its male members. However, the impressive economic growth of a region means nothing to women whose husbands deprive them of control over household income. We need to consider not just the aggregate, whether in a region or in a family; we need to consider the distribution of resources and opportunities *to each person,* thinking of each as worthy of regard in her own right.

THE DEFECTS OF TRADITIONAL ECONOMIC APPROACHES

Another way of seeing why cross-cultural norms are badly needed in the international policy arena is to consider what the alternative has typically been. The most prevalent approach to measuring quality of life in a nation used to be simply to ask about GNP per capita. This approach tries to weasel out of making any cross-cultural claims about what has value – although, notice, it does assume the universal value of opulence. What it omits, however, is much more significant. We are not even told about the distribution of wealth and income, and countries with similar aggregate figures can exhibit great distributional variations. Circus girl Sissy Jupe, in Dickens's *Hard Times* (1854), already saw the problem with this absence of normative concern for distribution: she says that the economic approach doesn't tell her "who has got the money and whether any of it is mine". So, too, with women around the world: the fact that one nation or region is in general more prosperous than another is only a part of the story – it doesn't tell us what government has done for women in various social classes, or how they are doing. To know that, we would need to look at their lives; but then we need to specify, beyond distribution of wealth and income itself, what parts of lives we ought to look at – such as life expectancy, infant mortality, educational opportunities, health care, employment opportunities, land rights, political liberties. Seeing what is absent from the GNP account nudges us sharply in the direction of mapping out these and other basic goods in a universal way, so that we can use the list of basic goods to compare quality of life across societies.

A further problem with all resource-based approaches, even those that are sensitive to distribution, is that individuals vary in their ability to convert resources into functionings. Some of these differences are straightforwardly physical. Nutritional needs vary with age, occupation and sex. A pregnant or lactating woman needs more nutrients than a non-pregnant woman. A child needs more protein than an adult. A person whose limbs work well needs few resources to be mobile, whereas a person with paralysed limbs needs many more resources to achieve the same level of mobility. Many such variations can escape our notice if we live in a prosperous nation that can afford to bring all individuals to a high level of physical attainment; in the developing world we must be highly alert to these variations in need. Again, some of the pertinent variations are social, connected with traditional hierarchies. If we wish to bring all citizens of a nation to the same level of educational attainment, we will need to devote more resources to those who encounter obstacles from traditional hierarchy or prejudice: thus women's literacy will prove more expensive than men's literacy in many parts of the world. If we operate only with an index of resources, we will frequently reinforce inequalities that are highly relevant to well-being.

If we turn from resource-based approaches to preference-based approaches, we encounter another set of difficulties.[3] Preferences are not exogenous, given independently of economic and social conditions. They are at least in part constructed by those conditions. Women often have no preference for economic independence before they learn about avenues through which women like them might pursue this goal; nor do they think of themselves as citizens with rights that were being ignored, before they learn of their rights and are encouraged to believe in their equal worth. All of these ideas, and the preferences based on them, frequently take shape for women in programmes of education sponsored by women's organizations of various types. Men's preferences, too, are socially shaped and often misshaped. Men frequently have a strong preference that their wives should do all the child care and all the housework – often in addition to working an eight-hour day. Such preferences, too, are not fixed in the nature of things: they are constructed by social traditions of privilege and subordination. Thus a preference-based approach typically will reinforce inequalities: especially those inequalities that are entrenched enough to have crept into people's very desires.

THE CAPABILITIES APPROACH

A reasonable answer to all these concerns – capable of giving good guidance to government establishing basic constitutional principles and to international agencies assessing the quality of life – is given by a version of the *capabilities approach* – an approach to quality of life assessment pioneered within economics by Amartya Sen[4] and by now highly influential through the *Human Development Reports* of the UNDP (see UNDP, 1993, 1994, 1995, 1996, 1997, 1998, 1999).[5] The version of this approach argued here is in several ways different from Sen's; it is laid out as currently defended.

The central question asked by the capabilities approach is not, "How satisfied is this woman?" or even "How much in the way of resources is she able to command?" It is, instead, "What is she actually able to do and to be?" Taking a stand for political purposes on a working list of functions that would appear to be of central importance in human life, users of this approach ask: "Is the person capable of this, or not?" They ask not only about the person's satisfaction with what she does, but about what she does, and what she is in a position to do (what her opportunities and liberties are). They ask not just about the resources that are present, but about how those resources do or do not go to work, enabling the woman to function.

The intuitive idea behind the approach is twofold: first, that there are certain functions that are particularly central in human life, in the sense that their presence or absence is typically understood to be a mark of the presence or absence of human life. Second – and this is what Marx found in Aristotle – that there is something about doing these functions in a truly human way, not a merely animal way. We judge, frequently enough, that a life has been so impoverished that it is not worthy of the dignity of the human being, that it is a life in which one goes on living, but more or less like an animal, not being able to develop and exercise one's human powers. In Marx's example, a starving person cannot use food in a fully human way – by which he seems to mean a way infused by practical reasoning and sociability. He or she just grabs at the food in order to survive, and the many social and rational ingredients of human feeding cannot make their appearance. Similarly, the senses of a human being can operate at a merely animal level – if they are not cultivated by appropriate education, by leisure for play and self-expression, by valuable associations with others; and we should add to the list some items that Marx probably would not endorse, such as expressive and associational liberty, and the freedom of worship. The core idea is that of the human being as a dignified free being who shapes his or her own life, rather than being passively shaped or pushed around by the world in the manner of a flock or herd animal.

At one extreme, we may judge that the absence of capability for a central function is so acute that the person is not really a human being at all, or any longer – as in the case of certain very severe forms of mental disability, or senile dementia. But that boundary is of lesser interest (important though it is for medical ethics) than is a higher one, the level at which a person's capability is "truly human", that is, worthy of a human being. The idea thus contains a notion of human worth or dignity.

Notice that the approach makes each person a bearer of value, and an end. Marx, like his bourgeois forebears, holds that it is profoundly wrong to subordinate the ends of some individuals to those of others. That is at the core of what exploitation is, to treat a person as a mere object for the use of others. What this approach is after is a society in which individuals are treated as each worthy of regard, and in which each has been put in a position to live really humanly.

It is possible to produce an account of these necessary elements of truly human functioning that commands a broad cross-cultural consensus, a list that can be endorsed for political purposes by people who otherwise have very different views of what a complete good life for a human being would be. The list is supposed to provide a focus for quality of life assessment and for political planning, and it aims to select capabilities that are of central importance, whatever else the person pursues. They therefore have a special claim to be supported for political purposes in a pluralistic society.[6]

The list represents the result of years of cross-cultural discussion,[7] and comparisons between earlier and later versions will show that the input of other voices has shaped its content in many ways. It remains open-ended and humble; it can always be contested and remade. Nor does it deny that the items on the list are to some extent differently constructed by different societies. Indeed part of the idea of the list is that those items can be more concretely specified in accordance with local beliefs and circumstances. The box on page 466 sets out the current version of functional capabilities.

The list of capabilities is, emphatically, a list of separate components. We cannot satisfy the need for one of them by giving people a larger amount of another one. All are of central importance and all are distinct in quality. The irreducible plurality of the list limits the trade-offs that it will be reasonable to make, and thus limits the applicability of quantitative cost-benefit analysis. At the same time, the items on the list are related to one another in many complex ways. One of the most effective ways of promoting women's control over their environment, and their effective right of political participation, is to promote women's literacy. Women who can seek employment outside the home have more resources in protecting their bodily integrity from assaults within it. Such facts give us still more reason not to promote one capability at the expense of the others.

Among the capabilities, two, practical reason and affiliation, stand out as being of special importance, since they both organize and suffuse all the others, making their pursuit truly human. To use one's senses in a way not infused by the characteristically human use of thought and planning is to use them in an incompletely human manner. Tagore's heroine describes herself as "a free human mind" – and this idea of herself infuses all her other functions. At the same time, to reason for oneself without at all considering the circumstances and needs of others is, again, to behave in an incompletely human way.

The basic intuition from which the capabilities approach begins, in the political arena, is that human abilities exert a moral claim that they be developed. Human beings are creatures such that, provided with the right educational and material support, they can become fully capable of these human functions. That is, they are creatures with certain lower-level capabilities (called here "basic capabilities"[8]) to perform the functions in question. When these capabilities are deprived of the nourishment that would transform them into the high-level capabilities that figure on the list, they are fruitless, cut off, in some way but a shadow of themselves. If a turtle were given a life that afforded a merely animal level of functioning, we would have no indignation, no sense of waste and tragedy. When a human being is given a life that blights powers of human action and expression, that does give us a sense of waste and tragedy – the tragedy expressed, for example, in Tagore's

---

Central human functional capabilities

1. Life. Being able to live to the end of a human life of normal length; not dying prematurely, or before one's life is so diminished as to be not worth living.

2. Bodily health. Being able to have good health, including reproductive health;* to be adequately nourished; to have adequate shelter.

3. Bodily integrity. Being able to move freely from place to place; to be secure against violent assault, including sexual assault and domestic violence; having opportunities for sexual satisfaction and for choice in matters of reproduction.

4. Senses, imagination and thought. Being able to use the senses, to imagine, think and reason – and to do these things in a "truly human" way, a way informed and cultivated by an adequate education, including, but by no means limited to, literacy and basic mathematical and scientific training. Being able to use imagination and thought in connection with experiencing and producing works and events of one's own choice, religious, literary, musical, and so forth. Being able to use one's mind in ways protected by guarantees of freedom of expression with respect to both political and artistic speech, and freedom of religious exercise. Being able to have pleasurable experiences, and to avoid non-necessary pain.

5. Emotions. Being able to have attachments to things and people outside ourselves; to love those who love and care for us, to grieve at their absence; in general, to love, to grieve, to experience longing, gratitude, and justified anger. Not having one's emotional development blighted by fear and anxiety. (Supporting this capability means supporting forms of human association that can be shown to be crucial in people's development.)

6. Practical reason. Being able to form a conception of the good and to engage in critical reflection about the planning of one's life (which entails protection for the liberty of conscience).

7. Affiliation.
A. Being able to live with and toward others, to recognize and show concern for other human beings, to engage in various forms of social interaction; to be able to imagine the situation of another and to have compassion for that situation; to have the capability for both justice and friendship. (Protecting this capability means protecting institutions that constitute and nourish such forms of affiliation, and also protecting the freedom of assembly and political speech.)
B. Having the social bases of self-respect and non-humiliation; being able to be treated as a dignified being whose worth is equal to that of others. This entails protections against discrimination on the basis of race, sex, sexual orientation, religion, caste, ethnicity, or national origin.

8. Other species. Being able to live with concern for and in relation to animals, plants and the world of nature.

9. Play. Being able to laugh, to play, to enjoy recreational activities.

10. Control over one's environment.
A. Political. Being able to participate effectively in political choices that govern one's life; having the right of political participation, protections of free speech and association.
B. Material. Being able to hold property (both land and movable goods); having the right to seek employment on an equal basis with others; having freedom from unwarranted search and seizure. In work, being able to work as a human being, exercising practical reason and entering into meaningful relationships of mutual recognition with other workers.

* The 1994 International Conference on Population and Development (ICPD) adopted a definition of reproductive health that fits well with the intuitive idea of truly human functioning that guides this list: "Reproductive health is a state of complete physical, mental and social well-being and not merely the absence of disease or infirmity, in all matters relating to the reproductive system and to its functions and processes. Reproductive health therefore implies that people are able to have a satisfying and safe sex life and that they have the capability to reproduce and the freedom to decide if, when and how often to do so" (United Nations, 1995, p. 40, para. 7.2). The definition goes on to say that it also implies information and access to family planning methods of their choice. A brief summary of the ICPD's recommendations, adopted by the Panel on Reproductive Health of the Committee on Population established by the National Research Council specifies three requirements of reproductive health: "1. Every sex act should be free of coercion and infection. 2. Every pregnancy should be intended. 3. Every birth should be healthy" (see Tsui, Wasserheit and Haaga, 1997, p. 14).

heroine's statement to her husband, when she says, "I am not one to die easily." In her view, a life without dignity and choice, a life in which she can be no more than an appendage, was a type of death of her humanity.

We begin, then, with a sense of the worth and dignity of basic human powers, thinking of them as claims to a chance for functioning, claims that give rise to correlated social and political duties. And in fact there are three different types of capabilities that play a role in the analysis. First, there are *basic capabilities*: the innate equipment of individuals that is the necessary basis for developing the more advanced capability, and a ground of moral concern. Second, there are *internal capabilities*: that is, states of the person herself that are, so far as the person herself is concerned, sufficient conditions for the exercise of the requisite functions. A woman who has not suffered genital mutilation has the *internal capability* for sexual pleasure; most adult human beings everywhere have the *internal capability* for religious freedom and the freedom of speech. Finally, there are *combined capabilities*, which may be defined as internal capabilities *combined with* suitable external conditions for the exercise of the function. A woman who is not mutilated but who has been widowed as a child and is forbidden to remarry has the internal but not the combined capability for sexual expression – and, in most such cases, for employment, and political participation (see Chen, 2000 and 1995). Citizens of repressive non-democratic regimes have the internal but not the combined capability to exercise thought and speech in accordance with their conscience. The above list, then, is a list of *combined capabilities*. To realize one of the items on the list entails not only promoting appropriate development of people's internal powers, but also preparing the environment so that it is favourable for the exercise of practical reason and the other major functions.

OBJECTIVES OF DEVELOPMENT: FUNCTIONING AND CAPABILITY

We have considered both functioning and capability. How are they related? Getting clear about this is crucial in defining the relation of the "capabilities approach" to our concerns about paternalism and pluralism. For if we were to take functioning itself as the goal of public policy, a liberal pluralist would rightly judge that we were precluding many choices that citizens may make in accordance with their own conceptions of the good. A deeply religious person may prefer not to be well-nourished, but to engage in strenuous fasting. Whether for religious or for other reasons, a person may prefer a celibate life to one containing sexual expression. A person may prefer to work with an intense dedication that precludes recreation and play. Does the declaration of the list mean that these are not fully human or flourishing lives? Does it mean to instruct government to nudge or push people into functioning of the requisite sort, no matter what they prefer?

It is important that the answer to these questions is no. Capability, not functioning, is the appropriate political goal. This is so because of the very great importance the approach attaches to practical reason, as a good that both suffuses all the other functions, making them fully human, and also figures, itself, as a central function on the list. The person with plenty of food may always choose to fast, but there is a great difference between fasting and starving, and it is this difference that we wish to capture. Again, the person who has normal opportunities for sexual satisfaction can always choose a life of celibacy, and the approach says nothing against this. What it does speak against (for example) is the practice of female genital mutilation, which deprives individuals of the opportunity to choose sexual functioning and, indeed, the opportunity to choose celibacy as well (see Nussbaum, 1999, chaps. 3-4). A person who has opportunities for play can always choose a workaholic life; again, there is a great difference between that chosen life and a life constrained by insufficient maximum-hour protections and/or the "double day" that makes women unable to play in many parts of the world.

Once again, we must stress in this context that the objective is to be understood in terms of *combined capabilities.* To secure a capability to a person it is not sufficient to produce good internal states of readiness to act. It is necessary, as well, to prepare the material and institutional environment so that people are actually able to function. Women burdened by the "double day" may be *internally* incapable of play – if, for example, they have been kept indoors and zealously guarded since infancy, married at age six, and forbidden to engage in the kind of imaginative exploration that male children standardly enjoy. Young girls in rural Rajasthan, for example, have great difficulty *learning* to play in an educational programme run by local activists – because their capacity for play has not been nourished early in childhood. On the other hand, there are also many women in the world who are perfectly capable of play in the internal sense, but unable to play because of the crushing demands of the "double day". Such a woman does not have the *combined capability* for play in the sense intended by the list. Capability is thus a demanding notion. In its focus on the environment of choice, it is highly attentive to the goal of functioning, and instructs governments to keep it always in view. On the other hand, it does not push people into functioning: once the stage is fully set, the choice is theirs.

CAPABILITIES AND THE HUMAN RIGHTS MOVEMENT

One might construct a view based on the idea of capabilities without giving a large place to the traditional political rights and liberties, which have historically been so central to the international human rights movement. Thus one might imagine a capabilities approach that diverged sharply from the international human rights approach. The version of the capabilities approach presented here, however, by making the idea of human choice and freedom central, entails a strong protection for these traditional rights and liberties. The political liberties have a central importance in making well-being human. A society that aims at well-being while overriding these has delivered to its members an incompletely human level of satisfaction. As Amartya Sen has recently written, "Political rights are important not only for the fulfilment of needs, they are crucial also for the formulation of needs. And this idea relates, in the end, to the respect that we owe each other as fellow human beings" (Sen, 1994, p. 38).[9] There are many reasons to think that political liberties have an instrumental role in preventing material disaster (in particular famine [10]), and in promoting economic well-being. But their role is not merely instrumental: they are valuable in their own right.

Thus capabilities have a very close relationship to human rights, as understood in contemporary international discussions. In effect they encompass the terrain covered by both the so-called first-generation rights (political and civil liberties) and the so-called second-generation rights (economic and social rights). Further, the list incorporates some sex-specific rights (in the area of bodily integrity, for example) that have been strongly defended by feminists in the human rights movement, and added, with some struggle, to international human rights instruments. The role played by capabilities is also very similar to that played by human rights: they provide the philosophical underpinning for basic constitutional principles. Because the language of rights is well-established, the defender of capabilities needs to show what is added by this new language.[11]

The idea of human rights is by no means crystal clear. Rights have been understood in many different ways, and difficult theoretical questions are frequently obscured by the use of rights language, which can give the illusion of agreement where there is deep philosophical disagreement. People differ about what the *basis* of a rights claim is: rationality, sentience, and mere life have all had their defenders. They differ, too, about whether rights are prepolitical or artifacts of laws and institutions. (Kant held the latter view, although the dominant human rights tradition has held the former.) They differ about whether rights belong only to individual persons, or also to groups. They differ about whether rights are to be regarded as side-constraints on goal-promoting action (meaning that one may pursue one's other goals only within the constraints imposed by people's rights), or rather as one part of the social goal that is being promoted. (The latter approach permits trade-offs between rights and other goals, whereas the former makes rights sacrosanct.) They differ, again, about the relationship between rights and duties: if A has a right to S, then does this mean that there is always someone who has a duty to provide S, and how shall we decide who that someone is? They differ, finally, about what rights are to be understood as rights *to*. Are human rights primarily rights to be treated in certain ways? Rights to a certain level of achieved well-being? Rights to resources with which one may pursue one's life plan? Rights to certain opportunities and capacities with which one may make choices about one's life plan?

The account of central capabilities has the advantage of taking clear positions on these disputed issues, while stating clearly what the motivating concerns are and what the goal is. Bernard Williams put this point eloquently, commenting on Sen's 1987 Tanner Lectures:

I am not very happy myself with taking rights as the starting point. The notion of a basic human right seems to me obscure enough, and I would rather come at it from the perspective of basic human capabilities. I would prefer capabilities to do the work, and if we are going to have a language or rhetoric of rights, to have it delivered from them, rather than the other way round (Williams, 1987, p. 100).

As Williams says, however, the relationship between the two concepts needs further scrutiny, given the dominance of rights language in the international development world.

In some areas, the best way of thinking about what rights are is to see them as capabilities. The right to political participation, the right to religious free exercise, the right of free speech – these and others are all best thought of as capacities to function. In other words, to secure a right to a citizen in these areas is to put them (both in terms of their internal powers and in terms of their material and institutional environment) in a position of capability to function in that area. (Of course there is another sense of "right" that is more like "basic capabilities": people have a right to religious freedom just in virtue of being human, even if the state they live in has not guaranteed them this freedom.) By defining rights in terms of capabilities, we make it clear that a people in country C don't really have the right to political participation just because this language exists on paper: they really have this right only if there are effective measures to make people truly capable of political exercise. Women in many nations have a nominal right of political participation without having this right in the sense of capability: for example, they may be threatened with violence should they leave the home. In short, thinking in terms of capability gives us a benchmark as we think about what it is really to secure a right to someone.

There is another set of rights, largely those in the area of property and economic advantage, which seem analytically different in their relationship to capabilities. Take, for example, the right to shelter and housing. These are rights that can be analysed in a number of distinct ways: in terms of resources, or utility (satisfaction), or capabilities. (Once again, we must distinguish the claim that "A has a right to shelter" – which frequently refers to A's moral claim in virtue of being human – from the statement that "country C gives its citizens the right to shelter". It is the second sentence whose analysis is being discussed here.) Here again, however, it seems valuable to understand these rights in terms of capabilities. If we think of the right to shelter as a right to a certain amount of resources, then we get into the very problem discussed above: giving resources to people does not always bring differently situated people up to the same level of capability to function. The utility-based analysis also encounters a problem: traditionally deprived people may be satisfied with a very low living standard, believing that this is all they have any hope of getting. A capabilities analysis, by contrast, looks at how people are actually enabled to live. Analysing economic and material rights in terms of capabilities thus enables us to set forth clearly a rationale we have for spending unequal amounts of money on the disadvantaged, or creating special programmes to assist their transition to full capability.

The language of capabilities has one further advantage over the language of rights: it is not strongly linked to one particular cultural and historical tradition, as the language of rights is believed to be. This belief is not very accurate: although the term "rights" is associated with the European Enlightenment, its component ideas have deep roots in many traditions. [12] Where India is concerned, for example, even apart from the recent validation of rights language in Indian legal and constitutional traditions, the salient component ideas have deep roots in far earlier areas of Indian thought – in ideas of religious toleration developed since the edicts of Ashoka in the third century BC, in the thought about Hindu/Muslim relations in the Mogul Empire, and, of course, in many progressive and humanist thinkers of the nineteenth and twentieth centuries, who certainly cannot be described simply as Westernizers, with no respect for their own traditions (see Sen, 1997a). [13] Tagore portrays the conception of freedom used by the young wife in his story as having ancient origins in Indian traditions, in the quest of Rajput queen Meerabai for joyful self-expression. (Meerabai left her privileged palace life to become an itinerant singer, joyfully pursuing both independence and art.) The idea of herself as "a free human mind" is represented as one that she derives, not from any external infusion, but from a combination of experience and history.

So "rights" are not exclusively Western, in the sense that matters most; they can be endorsed from a variety of perspectives. None the less, the language of capabilities enables us to bypass this troublesome debate. When we speak simply of what people are actually able to do and to be, we do not even give the appearance of privileging a Western idea. Ideas of activity and ability are everywhere, and there is no culture in which people do not ask themselves what they are able to do, what opportunities they have for functioning. Certainly in international discussions of women's work, ideas of control over the conditions of one's activity are absolutely central, and nobody would suggest that these ideas are exclusively Western. They arise when women get together to discuss what they want, and what their lives lack.

If we have the language of capabilities, do we also need the language of rights? The language of rights still plays four important roles in public discourse, despite its unsatisfactory features. First, when used in the first way, as in the sentence "A has a right to have the basic political liberties secured to her by her government", this language reminds us that people have justified and urgent claims to certain types of urgent treatment, no matter what the world around them has done about that. As suggested earlier, this role of rights language lies very close to "basic capabilities", in the sense that the *justification* for saying that people have such natural rights usually proceeds by pointing to some capability-like feature of persons (rationality, language) that they actually have at least on a rudimentary level. And without such a justification the appeal to rights is quite mysterious. However, there is no doubt that one might recognize the basic capabilities of people and yet still deny that this entails that they have rights in the sense of justified claims to certain types of treatment. We know that this inference has not been made through a great deal of the world's history. So appealing to rights communicates more than does the bare appeal to basic capabilities, without any further ethical argument of the sort supplied here. Rights language indicates that we do have such an argument and that we draw strong normative conclusions from the fact of the basic capabilities.

Second, even at the next level, when we are talking about rights guaranteed by the State, the language of rights places great emphasis on the importance and the basic role of the corresponding spheres of ability. To say, "Here's a list of things that people ought to be able to do and to be" has only a vague normative resonance. To say, "Here is a list of fundamental rights", is more rhetorically direct. It tells people right away that we are dealing with an especially urgent set of functions, backed up by a sense of the justified claim that all humans have to such things, in virtue of being human.

Third, rights language has value because of the emphasis it places on people's choice and autonomy. The language of capabilities was designed to leave room for choice, and to communicate the idea that there is a big difference between pushing people into functioning in ways you consider valuable and leaving the choice up to them. But there are approaches using an Aristotelian language of functioning and capability that do not emphasize liberty in the way that the approach presented in this article does: Marxist Aristotelianism and some forms of Catholic Thomist Aristotelianism are illiberal in this sense. If we have the language of rights in play as well, it helps us to lay extra emphasis on the important fact that the appropriate political goal is the ability of people to choose to function in certain ways, not simply their actual functionings.

Finally, in the areas where we disagree about the proper analysis of rights talk – where the claims of utility, resources, and capabilities are still being worked out – the language of rights preserves a sense of the terrain of agreement, while we continue to deliberate about the proper type of analysis at the more specific level.

CAPABILITIES AS OBJECTIVES FOR WOMEN'S DEVELOPMENT

Legitimate concerns for diversity, pluralism and personal freedom are not incompatible with the recognition of cross-cultural norms. Indeed, cross-cultural norms are actually required if we are to protect diversity, pluralism, and freedom, treating each human being as an agent and an end. The best way to hold all these concerns together is to formulate the objectives as a set of capabilities for fully human functioning, emphasizing the fact that capabilities protect, and do not close off, spheres of human freedom.

Used to evaluate the lives of women who are struggling for equality in many different countries, developing and developed, the capabilities framework does not look like an alien importation: it squares pretty well with demands women are already making in many global and national political contexts. It might therefore seem superfluous to put these items on a list: why not just let women decide what they will demand in each case? To answer that question, we should point out that the international development debate is already using a normative language. Where the capabilities approach has not caught on – as it has in the *Human Development Reports* of the UNDP – a much less adequate theoretical language still prevails, whether it is the language of preference-satisfaction or the language of economic growth. We need the capabilities approach as a humanly rich alternative to these inadequate theories of human development.

Women all over the world have lacked support for central human functions, and that lack of support is to some extent caused by their being women. But women, unlike rocks and trees, have the potential to become capable of these human functions, given sufficient nutrition, education and other support. That is why their unequal failure in capability is a problem of justice. It is up to all human beings to solve this problem. A cross-cultural conception of human capabilities gives us good guidance as we pursue this difficult task.

Notes

[1] More extensive versions of the arguments made here (and more case studies from development work in India) can be found in Nussbaum (2000, chap. 1). For earlier articulations of the author's views on capabilities see Nussbaum (1988, 1990, 1992, 1993, 1995a, 1995b, l997a, 1997b and 1999, chap. 1, pp. 29-54).

[2] See WIEGO (1999); the steering committee of WIEGO (Women in Informal Employment: Globalizing and Organizing) includes Ela Bhatt of SEWA, and Martha Chen, who has been a leading participant in discussions of the "capabilities approach" at the World Institute for Development Economics Research, in the "quality of life" project directed by Martha Nussbaum and Amartya Sen (see Chen, 1995).

[3] Nussbaum (2000, chap. 2) gives an extensive account of economic preference based approaches, arguing that they are defective without reliance on a substantive list of goals such as that provided by the capabilities approach.

[4] The initial statement is in Sen, 1980 (reprinted in Sen, 1982); see also various essays in Sen (1984, 1985a, 1985b, 1992, 1993 and 1995) and Drèze and Sen (1989 and 1995).

[5] For related approaches in economics, see Dasgupta (1993), Agarwal (1994), Alkire (1999), Anand and Harris (1994), Stewart (1996), Pattanaik (1998), Desai (1990), Chakraborty (1996). For discussion of the approach, see Aman (1991) and Basu, Pattanaik and Suzumura (1995).

[6] Obviously, this is a broader view of the political than is that of many theorists in the Western liberal tradition, for whom the nation state remains the basic unit. It envisages not only domestic

deliberations but also cross-cultural quality of life assessments and other forms of international deliberation and planning.

[7] For some examples of the academic part of these discussions, see Verma (1995), Chen (1995), Nzegwu (1995), Valdes (1995), and Li (1995).

[8] See the fuller discussion in Nussbaum (2000, chap. 1).

[9] Compare Rawis (1996, pp. 187-188), who connects freedom and need in a related way.

[10] Sen (1981) argues that free press and open political debate are crucial in preventing food shortage from becoming full-blown famine.

[11] The material of this section is further developed in Nussbaum (1997b).

[12] On India and China, see Sen (1997a); see also Taylor (1999).

[13] On Tagore, see Sen (1997b) and Bardhan (1990). For the language of rights in the Indian independence struggles, see Nehru, 1936, p. 612.

References

Agarwal, Bina. 1994. *A field of one's own: Gender and land rights in South Asia.* Cambridge, Cambridge University Press.

Alkire, Sabina. 1999. *Operationalizing Amariya Sen 's capability approach to human development: A framework for identifying valuable capabilities.* Unpublished D. Phil. Dissertation. Oxford, Oxford University.

Aman, K. (ed.). 1991. *Ethical principles for development: Needs, capabilities or rights.* Montclair, NJ, Montclair State University Press.

Anand, Sudhir; Harris, Christopher J. 1994. "Choosing a welfare indicator", in *American Economic Review* (Nashville, TN), Vol. 84, No. 2 (May), pp. 226-231.

Bardhan, Kalpana. 1990. "Introduction", in Kalpana Bardhan (ed.): *Of women, outcastes, peasants, and rebels: A selection of Bengali short stories.* Berkeley, CA, University of California Press, pp. 1-49.

Basu, Kaushik; Pattanaik, Prasanta; Suzumura, Kataro (eds.). 1995. *Choice, welfare, and development: A festschrift in honour of Amartya K. Sen.* Oxford, Clarendon Press.

Chakraborty, Achin. 1996. *The concept and measurement of the standard of living.* Unpublished Ph.D. Thesis. Riverside, CA, University of California at Riverside.

Chen, Martha A. 2000. *Perpetual mourning: Widowhood in rural India.* Delhi, Oxford University Press/Philadelphia, PA, University of Pennsylvania Press.

—. 1995. "A matter of survival: Women's right to employment in India and Bangladesh", in Nussbaum and Glover, pp. 37-57.

Dasgupta, Partha. 1993. *An inquiry into well-being and destitution.* Oxford, Clarendon Press.

Desai, Meghnad. 1990. "Poverty and capability: Towards an empirically implementable measure". Suntory-Toyota International Centre Discussion Paper No. *27.* London, London School of Economics, Development Economics Research Programme.

Dickens, Charles. 1854. *Hard times.* London, Bantam Classic, 1991.

Drèze, Jean; Sen, Amartya. 1995. *India: Economic development and social opportunity.* Delhi, Oxford University Press.

—; —. 1989. *Hunger and public action.* Oxford, Clarendon Press.

Li, Xiaorong. 1995. "Gender inequality in China and cultural relativism", in Nussbaum and Glover, pp. 407-425.

Marx, Karl. 1844. "Economic and philosophical manuscripts", in Penguin Classics (ed.): *Karl Marx: Early writings*. London, Penguin, 1992.

Nehru, Jawaharlal. 1936. *Autobiography*. The centenary edition. Delhi, Oxford University Press, 1986.

Nussbaum, Martha. 2000. *Women and human development: The capabilities approach*. Cambridge, Cambridge University Press.

—.1999. *Sex and social Justice*. New York, NY, Oxford University Press.

—.1997a. "The good as discipline, the good as freedom", in David A. Crocker and Toby Linden (eds.): *Ethics of consumption: The good life, justice, and global stewardship*. Lanham, MD, Rowman and Littlefield, pp. 312-411.

—.1997b. "Capabilities and human rights", in *Fordham Law Review* (New York, NY), Vol. 66, No. 2 (Nov.), pp. 273-300.

—.1995a. "Aristotle on human nature and the foundations of ethics", in J.E.J. Altham and Ross Harrison (eds.): *World, mind and ethics: Essays on the ethical philosophy of Bernard Williams*. Cambridge, Cambridge University Press, pp. 86-131.

—.1995b. "Human capabilities, female human beings", in Nussbaum and Glover, pp. 61-104.

—.1993. "Non-relative virtues: An Aristotelian approach", in Martha Nussbaum and Amartya Sen (eds.): *The quality of life*. Oxford, Clarendon Press, pp. 242-276.

—.1992. "Human functioning and social justice: In defence of Aristotelian essentialism" in *Political Theory* (Thousand Oaks, CA), Vol. 20, No. 2, pp. 202-246.

—.1990. "Aristotelian social democracy", in R. Bruce Douglass, Gerald Mara and Henry Richardson (eds.): *Liberalism and the good*. New York, NY, Routledge, pp. 203-252.

—.1988. "Nature, function, and capability: Aristotle on political distribution", in *Oxford Studies in Ancient Philosophy* (Oxford), Supplementary Vol. 1, pp. 145-184.

—; Glover, Jonathan (eds.). 1995. *Women, culture, and development: A study of human capabilities*. A study prepared for the World Institute for Development Economics Research (WIDER) of the United Nations University. Oxford, Clarendon Press.

Nzegwu, Nkiru. 1995. "Recovering Igbo traditions: A case for indigenous women's organizations in development", in Nussbaum and Glover, pp. 444-465.

Pattanaik, Prasanta. 1998. "Cultural indicators of well-being: Some conceptual issues", in UNESCO (ed.): *World Culture Report: Culture, creativity, and markets*. Paris, UNESCO, pp. 333-339.

Rawls, John. 1996. *Political liberalism*. New York, NY, Columbia University Press.

Sen, Amartya. 1997a. "Human rights and Asian values", in *The New Republic* (Washington, DC), 14-21 July, pp. 33-41.

—.1997b. "Tagore and his India", in *New York Review of Books* (New York, NY), 26 June, pp. 55-63.

—.1995. "Gender inequality and theories of justice", in Nussbaum and Glover, pp. 153-198.

—.1994. "Freedoms and needs", in *The New Republic* (Washington, DC), 10-17 Jan., pp. 31-38.

—.1993. "Capability and well-being", in Martha Nussbaum and Amartya Sen (eds.): *The quality of life*. Oxford, Clarendon Press, pp. 30-53.

475

—.1992. *Inequality reexamined.* Oxford, Clarendon Press/Cambridge, MA, Harvard University Press.

—.1985a. *Commodities and capabilities.* Amsterdam, North-Holland.

—.1985b. "Well-being, agency, and freedom: The Dewey Lectures", in *Journal of Philosophy* (New York, NY), Vol. 82, No. 4 (Apr.), pp. 169-220.

—.1984. *Resources, values, and development.* Oxford, Basil Blackwell/Cambridge, MA, MIT Press.

—.1982. *Choice, welfare, and measurement.* Oxford, Basil Blackwell/Cambridge, MA, MIT Press.

—.1981. *Poverty and famines: An essay on entitlement and deprivation.* Oxford, Clarendon Press.

—.1980. "Equality of what?", in S. McMurrin (ed.): *The Tanner Lectures on Human Values – Volume 1.* Cambridge, Cambridge University Press.

Stewart, Frances. 1996. "Basic needs, capabilities, and human development", in Avner Offer (ed.): *In pursuit of the quality of Life.* Oxford, Oxford University Press.

Tagore, Rabindranath. 1990. "Letter from a wife", in Bardhan, pp. 96-109.

Taylor, Charles. 1999. "Conditions of an unforced consensus on human rights", in Joanne R. Bauer and Daniel A. Bell (eds.): *The East Asian challenge for human rights.* Cambridge, Cambridge University Press, pp. 124-146.

Tsui, Amy O.; Wasserheit, Judith N.; Haaga, John G. (eds.). 1997. *Reproductive health in developing countries.* Washington, DC, National Academy Press.

UNDP. Various years. *Human Development Report 1993-1999.* New York, NY, United Nations Development Programme.

United Nations. 1995. *Report of the International Conference on Population and Development – Cairo, 5-13 September 1994.* Document A/CONF.171/13/Rev.1. New York, NY.

Valdds, Margarita M. 1995. "Inequality in capabilities between men and women in Mexico", in Nussbaum and Glover, pp. 426-432.

Verma, Roop Rekha. 1995. "Femininity, equality, and personhood", in Nussbaum and Glover, pp. 433-443.

WIEGO. 1999. *Report on the proceedings of the Annual Meeting and Public Seminar*, 12-14 April. Ottawa.

Williams, Bernard. 1987. "The standard of living: Interests and capabilities", in Amartya Sen and Geoffrey Hawthorn (eds.): *The standard of living.* Cambridge, Cambridge University Press, pp. 94-102.

PRAGMATISM AND DARING IN INTERNATIONAL LABOUR LAW

REFLECTIONS OF A LABOUR LAWYER

20

Jean-Claude JAVILLIER *

The ILO is celebrating its seventy-fifth anniversary shortly before the year 2000. The end of a century, especially if it is also the end of a millenium, entails considerable apprehension and a sense of foreboding. Some will look back on the century with profound disillusionment, so promising it seemed to be for humanity, at least in terms of technological progress. Once again we have recession and unemployment, violence and war. Economic development and social progress have not been definitively achieved. Hunger and poverty manifestly still exist in the very heart of great cities, where wealth, not to say opulence, appeared to have been established and could have benefited many. Thus are sown the seeds of doubt. Doubt intensified by the decline, if not the disappearance of political and economic alternatives, of cohesive ideological and cultural certainties. Have we lost our bearings? Where are we to find that social state to which economic advancement was expected to lead? Must we now dismantle everything or reconstruct again? Few can claim to be untroubled. Lawyers are aware of this, as they witness the hesitation of the economist, the doubts of the legislator, the judge's fears and the confusion of the expert. It is not evident that current economic and legal theories will lead us out of this dense social and economic fog.

These misgivings can, however, be turned to good account. Doubt and criticism, especially in respect of industrial relations and international and national labour legislation, are indispensable to anyone wishing to advance further. Account can be taken of the range of interests of employers and workers, governments, regions and continents. Above all, one must not lose sight of the need for doubt and criticism and for an assessment of the changes which have occurred, especially as the end of the millenium approaches. However, scientific scepticism must not lead to a state of apathy.

Originally published in *International Labour Review*, Vol. 133 (1994), No. 4.

* Holder (1993) of the Chair in Honour of the ILO's Nobel Peace Prize (the David Morse Chair); Professor at Panthdon-Assas (Paris II) University; President of the French Association of Labour Relations Studies.

On the contrary: now more than ever, energy should be directed to furthering the development of more open and dynamic industrial relations systems and more effective labour law appropriate to particular social and economic contexts. It is not enough merely to take note of the changes which have occurred. It is necessary to construct a new legal dynamic for working conditions and industrial relations, drawing on the most profound of those changes. For this reason, we should welcome and encourage pragmatism, especially in the legal field, as demonstrated from its earliest days by the International Labour Organization (part one of this article refers). Such prudence should be accompanied by a certain daring, which is essential to meeting the challenges of the coming millenium. For labour lawyers this means creativity and innovation in addressing all legal issues (part two refers).

PRAGMATISM IN STANDARD SETTING: READINESS TO ACCEPT CHANGE

One is now called upon to confront challenges in virtually all fields. Moreover, such testing may be harder, or more acutely felt, in countries or regions where it has been customary to consider geopolitical maps as changeless, with frontiers drawn for all eternity or at least a few centuries. But the political sphere is not the only one assailed by doubt of institutions and of strategies. In the economic field, hitherto stable and secure situations have been profoundly, and perhaps permanently, affected. The words crisis (depression and unemployment), competition (liberalization of markets), social dumping (relocation of jobs and precariousness of social welfare) are commonly heard. Labour relations and the laws that govern them are also affected by significant, almost constant change. Much has been said of the scale and complexity of these phenomena, though all too often there has been a wide gap between analysis and action, between law and practice. The social partners and governments are clearly alert to the changes, but it appears to be very difficult to adapt rapidly, to reorient strategies designed for another time, in many cases for the last century. We shall, in the following pages, confine ourselves to mentioning certain aspects relating only to law, aspects which are of immediate concern to labour lawyers, or some among them, it being understood that there is no cleavage between domestic and international labour law, as they both deal with the same issues, though the legal bases or the machinery for handling standards may differ between them. One must argue for a close association of all disciplines, especially legal disciplines, that concern labour.

Development of law

Everyone is affected by the changes taking place as this century draws to a close, but no one can have more than a very partial conception or imperfect understanding of these changes. Therefore, one must take some distance from one's customary universe and professional reflexes. Then a certain continuity appears to emerge. Specialists in domestic and international labour law may observe, with some justification, that many debates considered to be new are, in fact, no more than a return to those held at the very inception of contemporary labour law and labour relations systems. At the end of the nineteenth century, when it was a question of developing standards to protect workers (or some categories among them), the arguments advanced against state intervention were couched in terms strangely resembling those put forward today, in certain circles, in favour of deregulation or, more modestly, of flexibility in labour standards. It is not uncommon for debates on this topic to sound like religious wars. Some are vehemently accused of seeking to demolish the hard-won measures of social protection gained since the nineteenth century by workers (through, for some, a ruthless and unrelenting class struggle); others maintain that social welfare measures have turned against the very people whom they were designed to benefit, by causing loss of competitiveness and a consequent loss of jobs. We are, however, permitted to reject the rigidity and simplicity of these extreme points of view. From its earliest days, the ILO has painstakingly avoided such rigidity in its standard setting – a rigidity which may sometimes be satisfying to a lawyer but which is likely to result in widespread and persistent inadequacy and ineffectiveness in international labour law. It is a pity that in many academic circles, among lawyers and economists alike, no serious and reasoned reference is made to ILO competence in the matter of flexibility in standard setting – though this has been brought out by certain authors.[1]

Fundamentally, it is to a large extent a question of continual renewal in standard setting. Quarrels between champions of flexibility and advocates of legal constraint, between supporters of state intervention or abstention in economic and social matters, are unlikely to end. Nonetheless, it is important not to succumb too readily to the temptation of seeing the current debates merely as a reappearance of the logic of the past, a repetition of earlier alternatives, or the eternal division of the social and economic worlds into two ideological and political camps. To illustrate this point, a few comments are offered on the role accorded to labour law and on labour relations in contemporary societies.

An expansion of the law?

Every lawyer should ponder on the increasing number of legal standards, laws and codes, rulings and judgements of all kinds. One seems to see a hypertrophy of law, accompanied by a growing complexity; individuals and even enterprises seem to be no more than helpless spectators. The third millenium might be characterized by ubiquitous, not to say socially oppressive and economically paralysing, laws, a labyrinth of standards, from which it is not possible to emerge. National law (in some cases, regional law) and international law could lead almost automatically to an endless accumulation of standards. Some can come to terms with this; others complain vigorously. On the workers' side, the idea persists that some social benefit can always be reaped from the accumulation of protective standards; on the employers' side, where flexibility in standard setting can become an article of faith, it is considered that most can be gained from free competition and unconstrained business management, even in the interest of the workers.

It is not evident how such a profusion of standard setting can be managed. Contradictions and conflicts abound. To some extent the law appears not to have been designed to be truly effective. One sees so many regulations – with so much detail and so little law on essentials. This could even herald the end of law as such. If this is correct, international labour law will not escape the fatal outcome in which people, even specialists, will cast doubt on its efficiency or, worse, its effectiveness. Furthermore, there will be no consolation to be gained from the fact that all legal disciplines suffer the same illness. But, in fact, such doubt may not be an evil. It might be a good, even a great benefit to contemporary societies to become technocratic and legalistic. Advance the rule of law, long live the reign of regulation!

To be sure, the hypothesis that the law suffers from hypertrophy – which some would not hesitate to turn into a thesis, to be promoted or refuted, as the case may be – may appear excessive as well as simplistic. Yet it should not be dismissed. It is, in fact, not inconceivable that the result of this growth may prove to be a creeping and insidious legal deregulation. In such a context, the reaction of enterprises, especially small and medium-sized enterprises,[2] the increasing economic importance of which is now universally recognized, is highly relevant. Thought should also be given to the increasing difficulties experienced by certain state institutions, labour inspection in particular, which are responsible for implementing regulations.

There may be an inexorable shift towards the codification of labour relations and of industrial relations in general. It is not enough to realize (with or without pleasure) that the law penetrates all spheres. One must draw all the inferences in respect of the adoption, interpretation and application of new standards, especially international standards.

Complexity versus universality

The complexity of societies seems to doom the simplest, shortest, most transparent and, doubtless also, the most stylishly written legal instruments to failure. There is no longer any social or economic question that can be legally formulated in simple, unequivocal and, what is more serious for lawyers, abstract and permanent terms. The diversity of situations, contexts and analyses seems to dissolve the unity of issues, the global nature of solutions – in law as in many other matters affecting working life. This could even be the end of common law and the failure of universal law. Obviously, we cannot subscribe to such a view; indeed we take the opposite stance. More than ever before, recourse to general principles and to basic standards is required in order to deal with any question relating to labour relations and industrial relations in a relevant and durable manner. The development of the rule of law is quite naturally accompanied by a possible measure of opposition and free discussion concerning any legal standard. One should, no doubt, be glad of this since the basic rights of the individual can thus be guaranteed. However, in a more profound and complex manner, it is the sacrosanct aspect (or, at least, a certain conception of it) of legal and social norms which is gradually being called into question. This risk is apparent within even the most stable and homogeneous continents, legal systems and social groups. Such a development is not unconnected with the fact that legal standards are increasingly contingent on particular situations and with the undeniable increase in the number of lawsuits.

Some speak of the users or consumers of law, which suggests legal "distributors" from which one could select ready-made standards. In reality, everyone knows that it is never like that. Every standard needs to be interpreted and adapted. A great danger for contemporary societies lies in separating law from the human sphere, rendering the law arid.

The increase in the number of lawsuits is disturbing as, if one is not wary, a growing ineffectiveness of labour law could result. Users sometimes experience profound dissatisfaction in the face of expectations fostered by reforms presented as fundamental by the media, only to be disappointed as soon as they seek to obtain practical, concrete benefits from those new laws. One would like to see less ardour in the reform of a code or law or in a reversal of jurisprudence and more attention given to the situation of the person who would seek its application, or more simply, waits for justice to be done.

Thought should therefore be given to the effects of such developments on international labour law[3] and on the work of the ILO. One hypothesis that might be advanced is that those standards not advertised by some media campaign could be consigned to a sort of "law museum", which would no doubt be much appreciated by a handful of enthusiasts but would scarcely draw in the general public. To advance such a hypothesis is to invite everyone concerned to seek the means of maintaining the legal, social and media link between international labour law and varying national laws, which are constantly evolving and contingent on economic trends.

A person is often bewildered by the profusion of standards and litigation. Worse, it is becoming increasingly difficult, even for specialists, to distinguish the essential from the incidental, the principle from the exception, the reasonable from the unreasonable. But it is precisely this situation that gives international labour law its increasing relevance and decisive importance. Its value lies not in regulating detail or passing economic trends, but in its universality concerning the essentials of the worker's condition and the development of labour relations. It is in being a body of law concerned more with structures and principles than with details and contingencies.

International labour law must not fall victim to the trends, hesitations and upheavals that affect many national legal systems. For this reason, and probably more than ever before, the questions placed on the agenda of the International Labour Conference take on a symbolic value, reflecting options fraught with consequences for the future of the International Labour Organization and the laws and institutions of the member States. It is undoubtedly also the reason why the procedure for formulating international standards should be given consideration.[4] Critical comment and suggestions for future reform of those procedures should be sought. The choice, indeed the number, of questions before the International Labour Conference cannot be dictated merely by the legitimacy achieved through consensus among participants or by some institutional custom. It is not so much a question of adding standards year after year, but of analysing issues question by question.

The influence of economic questions

Economic factors constitute a force of attraction which is revealed in many ways, of which two will be mentioned here. Economic concerns lie at the root of legal texts, which tend increasingly to be drafted by economists. At the macroeconomic level, they govern a number of issues and technical procedures in labour or industrial relations. This is particularly important in employment policy. It goes without saying that great sensitivity to economic questions does not necessarily imply ignorance or rejection of the social and human objectives of labour law. Indeed, the opposite is sometimes the case.[5]

Certain lawyers have a perception of the law which is far removed from economic or social realities. Economic considerations allow the cost of reforms and also their viability to be measured. Likewise, consideration must be given right from the conception as to how economic factors can be integrated into the labour relations system, in society as a whole as well as in the socio-cultural microcosm of the enterprise. Too many generous legal texts are stillborn for the obvious reason that they ignore realities, especially economic realities, which give standards their true significance and prominence.

However, we must never lose our critical sense. It may very well be a good thing that the law is not exclusively in the hands of legal experts, but is entrusted (sometimes entirely) to economists or administrators. Nevertheless, legal rigour, the consistency of laws, the precision of concepts and the assignment to legal categories are indispensable, and the lawyer must always bear them in mind. If it were otherwise, legal considerations would be swamped by economic and conjunctural factors. This would also lead, sooner or later, to the death of standard setting and to the end of security before the law for citizens as well as for the social and economic actors.

In labour and industrial relations, it is undoubtedly a time for relativism in the light of economic trends; but it is also a time for norms and absolute values. True to its origins, the ILO can allow no room for doubt or equivocation. A hierarchy of standards was established following a process of rigorous deliberation on the priorities of all standard setting activity,[6] as well as on the complementarity between standard setting and technical cooperation.[7] This distinction between what is essential and what is incidental for the individual, between the absolute and the relative in the law, should give rise to a new dynamic in international labour law, in national law and in industrial relations systems.

Regionalization of the law

The proliferation of standards is the result not only of a sort of "instrumentalization" of the law, especially in labour relations. It is also an effect of the development of regional legal systems. This phenomenon is of vital importance to the ILO. The spirit of universality, present in the ILO since its inception, has never ceased to inspire every international labour standard. But the situation in the regions has been undergoing profound changes, especially in recent years.

In Europe, Community labour law is being developed; hesitantly, to be sure, but progressively. However, one cannot but regret the fact that new regional standards are often established ignoring ILO standards. Comparing the labour standards of European Community (Union) origin with those that are not (Council of Europe), the contrast is quite striking; the latter are largely inspired by international labour law. Clearly, the institutional contexts are very different. In Strasbourg, there is a sort of institutional proximity to the ILO (though without the important element of tripartism). In Brussels, the institutional structure is still being developed: whether to be a federation or confederation has not yet been resolved. And, undoubtedly, there is some enthusiasm for developing a system of laws which some, at least, would like to see as entirely new, or even clear proof that Europe is actually being built.

The development of detailed regulations on working conditions in the European Union should not be taken as a model in all aspects and all spheres. There may even be a danger of wishing to adopt or reproduce some of these regulations worldwide. Comparative labour law teaches us that no standard can be simply transposed from one country to another. And if a cogent reason were necessary, it would obviously be the essential link with the industrial relations system. Any legal standard, if it is to be truly assimilated, needs to be integrated into this system. The force of an international labour standard lies in this adaptation and acceptance into the different systems of industrial relations, it having been observed that several such systems may even exist in a single country. Over the past few years, some may have had the impression that European-style labour law carried too much weight in the development of international labour law, and was incompatible with the universality of the ILO's principle of standard setting. To which may be added that these laws produced by the European Union suffer from excessive detail and technocracy. This is another sign of the unfortunate tendency to confuse law with regulation. And this is exactly what the ILO must avoid at all costs if international Conventions and Recommendations are to retain their importance and influence. Certain recently adopted Conventions may, moreover, have given the impression that the "temptation" to give in to technocracy was becoming even greater. This, according to some, would lead to another form of "temptation": the non-ratification of standards. True or false, pretexts or not, these criticisms should be taken very seriously, especially on the European side, as they represent the views of others on a "European" law that would have no universal value.

New regional developments are to be expected within the next few years, though it may be premature to consider them geopolitically stable and institutionally definitive. Europe will certainly not be the Europe envisaged by those who designed its institutions, in the context of a world divided between East and West, between communism and capitalism.

The political changes and economic upheavals that have occurred in South America are likely to give rise to new institutions, new forms of intergovernmental cooperation, new perspectives, especially in respect of policies on employment and working conditions,[8] and, surprisingly for some, to an unexpected synergy in transnational labour relations. Many standard setting and social developments may well occur in the Americas, in the context of Mercosur or NAFTA.[9] Nor is Asia likely to escape this movement that is turning whole regions of the world, no longer just States, into new economic, and eventually political and social, actors. Here, too, the consequences of such developments for the ILO and for international labour law may well be crucial. Economic links and cooperation, proximity and political agreements between States in the different regions of the world will call into question – perhaps even without its being noticed – a number of classic analyses and conceptions concerning international law. No serious development in international (labour) law can ignore these constellations of factors. Above all, it is important to ensure that international achievements in social matters, the legal know-how of the ILO, should save time for everyone. All are in a hurry to succeed in their integration. As far as labour relations and industrial relations are concerned, each must be able to reap the greatest political, social and also economic benefit from this standard setting heritage of international labour Conventions and Recommendations. It is also important to ensure that the same regional developments do not debase this heritage or conflict with the ideals that give it its force and sustain its transcendence.

INNOVATION AND AUDACITY IN LEGAL THINKING

Audacity is the reverse of timidity and the opposite of fear. It also means creativity, refusal of repetition and, more fundamentally, the rejection of conformism. It would be wrong to insinuate that daring plays no part in ILO standard setting activity or in the functioning of the International Labour Office. One need only refer to the invitation formulated by the Director-General of the ILO in one of his reports to the International Labour Conference devoted to the dilemma of the informal sector.[10] This sector "presents as much of a challenge to the ILO as it does to the member States. While remaining firm on the principles that should continue to guide the ILO's activities, we must be imaginative and innovative in devising new methods of action and new approaches to the problems that it presents."[11]

Such an objective is not easily attained. To innovate in law, through the law, is not as easy as it appears, especially to non-lawyers, and even more so in institutions where diplomacy calls rather for caution which, in its turn, can result in resistance to change. Thus, in order to avoid shocking people, it would perhaps be more fitting, in many fields, to avoid using an original vocabulary, and to avoid developing a distinct point of view. A frank critical approach should also lead us to ponder the bottlenecks which a tripartite, or even bipartite, structure can create in labour relations at national or international level. In certain economic and political situations, the tripartite system can inhibit change, hold up the development of new approaches and modes of action. This immobility is as true of institutions as it is of individuals; sometimes unwittingly, they tacitly agree to avoid re-opening certain questions or upsetting established custom. Consensus in human groups is peculiar in that it can encourage the most radical developments, as well as hold back the most inevitable revolutions, especially in institutions. But it can also prevent the worst kinds of disorder and destruction. Economic reforms have been aborted, ending in social and political violence.

Daring and innovation should go hand in hand in all spheres. However, the author would like to draw attention to two questions of crucial importance to labour lawyers and industrial relations specialists in a context of profound and permanent change. In the first place, the connection between workers' protection and economic development should be considered in the broadest and most open manner possible. No one can be in any doubt today that employment is at the core of the whole issue of labour and industrial relations. But a certain audacity is required to draw the necessary conclusions as regards standard setting. In the second place, relations between the individual and the group cannot be envisaged in the same terms as in the recent past. Developments have occurred which imply, especially at the workplace, a challenge to the classic structure of relations between the worker and the group of which he/she is part and also, in a more complex and subtle way, to relations between the worker and the various groups to which he/she may belong at any given moment or in the course of time.

Labour, the economy, the law

It is risky – especially for a lawyer – to try in a few words to stress the urgent need to re-examine existing relations between social questions and economic questions.

The dilemma of the informal sector [12] is probably one of the most striking illustrations of the lucidity needed to adapt new procedures, especially in the legal field. The ILO has done vital work in this area.

New forms of work

There are some lawyers for whom the law must be hard and fast, the application of standards must be simple and mechanical, and the only legitimate quest is for total and mechanical effectiveness of national or international standards. Labour law should be applied and extended to all domains, since the entire population will eventually be wage-earning. In other words, the natural tendency would be towards an (expansionist) labour law. In actual fact, such a situation would only be a translation into the standard setting context of the inevitable ascendancy of "typical" employment, which constitutes a sort of ideal: full-time, permanent employment in a factory, for one and the same employer. In an industrialized, organized and regulated world, many have no doubt foolishly thought that "atypical" employment would gradually disappear, or be confined to archaic or uncompetitive productive sectors. That is clearly not the case. We must have the courage to accept the many complex factors that together imply that typicality and atypicality may well attract each other, if not merge with (or complement) each other, from both the legal and the social points of view. But at this point, we cannot evade the basic questions raised by any form of atypical employment. To what extent does the employee really have freedom of choice? What are the organizational constraints on the enterprise? Is atypicality chosen or intended? At the very least, the complex nature of the situations and the limitations of freedom should be clearly identified, so that they can be effectively dealt with by law. [13]

Labour law in the final decade of the twentieth century seems to have been caught unawares by technological change and economic crisis, and we are witnessing the reappearance or the development of forms of employment and conditions of work that existed in the last century. Urbanization, computerization, robotization: magic inventions which were supposed to banish the demons of solitude, drudgery, subordination. Such confidence could not fail to end in disappointment and this has undoubtedly contributed to the present social resentment. The city has demolished all social solidarity and put an end to economic self-sufficiency. Computerization has introduced hitherto unknown methods of controlling human activity. As for robotization, it has reduced human labour quantitatively, to a point where it has rendered the physical presence of the worker at the production place virtually unnecessary and caused increased unemployment among the unskilled. All these developments have been only partially taken into account by (international) labour law.

So we are condemned, at national and international level, always to concern ourselves with all possible forms of human labour. No formula can be considered as belonging definitively to the past. The most appalling and reprehensible employment practices are continually being revived – a humiliating rebuttal of prophecies rashly announcing a new era of human labour.

Any standard setting action must therefore be based on clearly stated premises. Contrary to earlier beliefs, the informal sector is not going to disappear spontaneously with economic growth. It is, on the contrary, likely to grow in the years to come, and with it the problems of urban poverty and congestion. This stark fact presents a dilemma to policy-makers, to organized employers and workers and to the ILO itself: should the informal sector be allowed to continue to expand outside the framework of laws and institutions governing social and economic life, and thus provide a convenient low-cost way of absorbing labour that cannot be employed elsewhere; or should attempts be made to bring it into the legal and institutional framework of the rest of society, with the risk of impairing its capacity to absorb labour? Is it possible to reconcile the two objectives of labour absorption and regulation? [14]

Appropriate responses

The answer to the last two questions should be a firm yes. The mere fact of directly and rationally addressing the question of the non-observance of (international) labour law represents a huge step forward. Not seeing it as an accidental phenomenon, considered by many to be pathological, but as a widespread and lasting situation in a number of sectors and in practically all regions of the world. The surfeit of laws and regulations referred to earlier exists alongside a vacuum in respect of standard setting. This may well serve economic needs and ensure the survival of a sizeable proportion of the population, especially in cities.

Daring does not merely consist in not "resigning ourselves to the non-observance of ILO standards in the informal sector". [15] We must also resolve to devise a strategy to meet the major standard setting challenge, the existence and importance of which, for governments and social partners alike, are no longer in question. A correlation must be clearly established between the application of legal standards and the implementation of employment policies and of economic policies in general.

Of course, the lawyer must assess the risk incurred when problem situations develop to the point at which the entire standard setting structure is called into question. Thus, as pointed out by some authors, [16] a new balance must be struck between the market economy, which has become planetary or nearly so, and a restored but still fragile democracy. "We need standards guaranteeing a minimum of protection in order that the economy may become increasingly free, without giving rise to excesses or abuses, which could trigger reactions dangerous both for the economy itself and for democracy."[17] A clear and firm demarcation line must therefore be established between essential, fundamental regulations and others. As regards the informal sector referred to earlier, one cannot afford delay; it is necessary to "concentrate in the first instance on the promotion of certain fundamental, core standards that are essential for a decent human existence and that it should be possible to apply in the informal sector without imposing an impossible burden on informal sector enterprises".[18] There can be no question of letting (international) standards concerning fundamental human rights – abolition of forced labour, equal opportunity and treatment, freedom of association – or those aimed at eliminating intolerable forms of worker exploitation – child labour, health and safety – fall by the economic wayside.

Audacity and innovation will be required for all the essential issues. There is still a great deal to be done to reinforce the action and influence of the International Labour Organization and Office.

I shall mention just one question of serious concern, that of cooperation with international financial or economic organizations. The linkage to be established between labour, the economy and the law cannot be envisaged within a single international organization, however multidisciplinary its orientation. It has been repeatedly observed in all quarters that organizations tend to ignore each other. It is perhaps an exaggeration to suggest that contacts do not exist, that meetings do not take place or that no communication occurs. But much remains to be done before all are convinced of the need for complementarity in action, expertise and solutions – unless one suddenly succumbs to pessimism, induced by unbridled impatience, and advocates radical institutional change. Can international negotiations be conducted on economic issues without direct and full discussion of labour questions? Is it not, in fact, derisory to deal with the development of free competition between countries without raising the question of social disparities and their complex and often horrendous effect on entire regions? Perhaps one should resort to a sort of social GATT. In any case, it is unthinkable that in the next few years the International Labour Organization and Office should not have made a basic contribution to the solution of such problems as "social dumping", in terms of analysis and strategy, for the benefit of governments and the social partners. Obviously, many legal structures could be developed. The social clauses in economic and financial agreements have an essential role to play.[19]

The individual, the group, the independence of standard setting

It would be foolish to think that cultural changes, technological innovations and political revolutions are of no consequence or of little importance to the development of international law and to the various activities of the ILO. The implications are wide: "The dismantling of the Berlin Wall in November 1989 is no doubt the most striking symbol of the change, but the movement had started in Southern Europe around 1975 and spread to Latin America before returning to Central and Eastern Europe. More recently, the process has been having some interesting developments in Africa and Asia as well. In short, this historic sequence of events conveys the impression of an almost universal movement towards democracy."[20]

This situation requires an increased effort on the part of lawyers to participate usefully in devising and establishing procedures which take into account the economic context and constraints as well as the broad patterns of social equilibrium in the medium and long terms. In the present period, which may well be termed historic from a geopolitical point of view, the Director-General of the ILO has rightly emphasized the decisive nature of the ILO's role "in helping member States that are applying a policy of democratization [which] will consist in supporting their effort to establish a framework of laws and regulations guaranteeing respect for fundamental rights and adequate protection of the rights of workers".[21] It is, therefore, essential that the ILO "expand appreciably the help it can offer to member States wishing to revise their labour legislation, wholly or in part, and to those intending to establish tripartite institutions, which are essential to the maintenance of constructive industrial relations".[22]

Thus the opportunity is offered, not only to those wishing to revise their legislation, wholly or in part, within the framework of a policy of democratization, but to all, governments and social partners alike, to promote constructive industrial relations. For, in many ways, concepts and techniques, especially in the legal field, should be reviewed, if not radically changed. As has already been emphasized, it is not so much a question of formulating new standards, but of giving a new dynamic to an existing set of standards. Such a dynamic would seem to imply, among other things, a prospective study of relations between the individual and the group, or between state intervention and the social partners' independence in standard setting. In these two areas, it is not enough to rely on present analyses, which are too strongly marked by the past and are the cause of major social and economic stumbling blocks.

Bearing in mind that various forms of atypical employment[23] are likely to develop and, perhaps, even predominate in the organizational structure of enterprises, it goes without saying that relations between the worker (wage-earning or not) and the groups around him/her will undergo profound changes in their nature and meaning. This development is not unconnected with the cultural and technological environment in which all are evolving.

Thus one should consider the linkage between individual aspirations and collective expression and options which is essential to the survival of any group whether economically oriented or not. There are signs of an inevitable rise in individualism and a concomitant decline in the "collective". It would appear that, in certain countries which have recently experienced decades of totalitarian regimes, under which pre-eminence was given to the collectivity with the systematic limitation of all individual initiative especially in the economic and political field, this very concept is intolerable to many.

It is possible to advance the hypothesis that new and more appropriate forms of participation must urgently be defined for individuals in the groups that represent them or of which they are a part. In some countries, traditional methods of representing individuals, of declaring interests, of participation pure and simple, are being called into question, or, at least put into competition with other systems. A fumbling quest for alternative institutional (or other) solutions to ensure participation, especially in the workplace, will undoubtedly be a significant aspect of the development of industrial relations systems. This phenomenon is also to be observed in the civil and the political contexts.

The issue is even more important when one considers that there can be no genuine tripartite system unless each individual who belongs to a particular group feels actually involved with the social actor representing him/her, in situations both ordinary and extraordinary, of conflict or concertation. It is not unusual these days for employment relations to be multilateral, competitive, heterogeneous and subject to outside influence. It is no longer a matter of a duel between easily identified employers and employees, between workers and their natural antagonists, the capitalists. Relations now tend to be multilateral, to involve business partners and financiers. Complexity, ambivalence and a multiplicity of legal alternatives seem to prevail. Hence the confusion in the minds of certain labour lawyers, accustomed as they are to a clear and conclusive, but also binary and radical division of territories and roles, techniques and institutions. We all need the courage to recognize this situation, subject it to criticism if need be, draw all the necessary conclusions and abandon certain legal preconceptions, or even invent new concepts and suggest relevant techniques and institutions.

This may produce a fracture in the classic legal approach. The present-day worker often belongs simultaneously to a number of groups. Consumer law and environmental law as well as labour law concern the entire population. They cannot afford to ignore each other as they have done for too long. Neither should the clash of interests that may arise between these fields be ignored or concealed, for they are increasingly at the centre of all major conflicts in society. Unemployment also can lead to a sort of deprivation or loss of social and legal identity. In industrial relations systems that have developed on the basis of (full?) industrial employment, the problems created by unemployment are such that, sooner or later, they may seriously challenge representative institutions and settlement methods, especially dispute settlement. Some would almost say that unemployment, like poverty, constitutes the greatest challenge to international labour law and governments' social and economic policies. As for the employers' and workers' organizations, their very future may be at stake.

In other words, the relation between the individual and the group is undergoing profound change; analysis of labour issues and of industrial relations in general can no longer be limited, reduced and focused solely on the relation between employers and employees, between bosses and unions. This limitation has become inadequate, as it neglects the fact that it is becoming frequently impossible to seek and propose an appropriate solution without taking societal (as well as social) dimensions fully and genuinely into consideration. As observed earlier, the very concepts of employment or work can no longer be regarded as a straightforward stable job in one enterprise, with an economic (in the narrow sense of productive and industrial) objective. The terms used must be taken seriously into consideration, in as much as they reflect equivalences and alternatives, parallels and differences. Work, activity, production, re-entry, subordination, partnership, informal sector, integration, all these terms have been fragmented or broadened, renewed or discarded. Let us open our legalistic minds and transform into a new dynamic, especially in international labour law, what is often a source of discouragement, if not anguish, for governments, employers and workers.

Attaching the greatest importance to economic and social contexts, it seems possible to use labour standards to bring about a new synergy between the law and the economy, between social welfare and economic growth, between production and participation, between heteronomy and autonomy. Let us as lawyers continue to be uncompromising on absolute values, on matters concerning the worker's dignity and the development of democracy; but let us be flexible, in contributing to the prosperity of enterprises, to free competition in the economic field, without which there can be no abiding protection for the worker and no true freedom for the individual. A quarter of a century ago David Morse wrote:

If the ILO is to continue to meet its original challenge and the challenge as we now see it for the years which lie ahead, it will be essential that the Organization continue to be alert to change and to continue to adapt, modify and alter its structure, functions and programmes to the needs of a dramatically changing world. I believe that ... this will certainly be done.[24]

By sharing his conviction and confidence, the ILO will be able to adapt to a changing world; it will take up the great standard setting challenges confronted by all – employers, workers and Governments.

Notes

[1] See N. Valticos: *Droit international du travail, Traité de droit du travail*, second edition (Paris, Dalloz, 1983), especially para. No. 277ff., pp. 226ff., and para. No. 829, p. 652; G.W. von Potobsky and H. G. Bartolomei de la Cruz: *La Organización Internacional del Trabajo* (Buenos Aires, Editorial Astrea, 1990); M. Montt Balmaceda: *Principios de derecho internacional del trabajo* (Santiago de Chile, Editorial Jurídica de Chile, 1984); A. Süsskind: *Direito internacional do trabalho* (São Paulo, Editora Ltr, 1983).

[2] See G.W. von Potobsky: "Small and medium-sized enterprises and labour law", in *International Labour Review*, Vol. 131, 1992, No. 6, pp. 601-628.

[3] See N. Valticos: "Fifty years of standard-setting activities by the International Labour Organization", in *International Labour Review*, Vol. 100, No. 3, Sep. 1969, pp. 201-237; and E.A. Landy: "The influence of international labour standards: Possibilities and performance", in *International Labour Review*, Vol. 101, No. 6, June 1970, pp. 555-604.

[4] See J.M. Servais: "Le droit international du travail en mouvement: déploiement et approches nouvelles", in *Droit social* (Paris), 1991, No. 5, May, pp. 447-452.

[5] See the book published by R. Cortazar, until recently Minister of Labour in Chile: *Política laboral en el Chile democratico y desafíos en los noventa* (Santiago de Chile, Ediciones Dolmen, 1993).

[6] ILO: *International labour standards*, Report of the Director-General, International Labour Conference, 70th Session, Geneva, 1984.

[7] ILO: *The role of the ILO in technical cooperation*, Report VI, International Labour Conference, 80th Session, Geneva, 1993.

[8] An in-depth study of the evolution (extension) of the concept of working conditions is of crucial importance to the development of international labour law; see M. G. Spyropoulos: "Conditions de travail: élargissement du concept et problématique juridique", in *Droit social* 1990, No. 12, Dec., pp. 851-861.

[9] We shall follow with interest the analyses published in the new review *Relasur* (Montevideo, ILO and the Spanish Ministry of Labour and Social Security), of which issue No. 2, 1994, contained the text of the North American Agreement on Labor Cooperation, p. 15ff.

[10] ILO: *The dilemma of the informal sector*, Report of the Director-General (Part 1), International Labour Conference, 78th Session, Geneva, 1991.

[11] ibid., p. 61.

[12] Ibid.

[13] See the remarkable analyses presented on the occasion of the adoption of new standards on part-time work. ILO: *Part-time work*, International Labour Conference, 80th Session, Geneva, 1993, Report V (1 and 2), and International Labour Conference, 81st Session, Geneva, 1994, Report IV (1, 2A and 2B).

[14] ILO: *The dilemma of the informal sector*, op. cit., p. 63.

[15] ibid., p. 57.

[16] See H. G. Bartolomei de la Cruz: "Strength through renovation", in *World of Work* (Geneva), No. 1, Dec. 1992, pp. 4-5.

[17] ibid., p. 5.

[18] ILO: *The dilemma of the informal sector*, op. cit., p. 57.

[19] See M. Hansenne: "Libéralisation des échanges et progrès social. Comment appliquer la clause sociale?", in *Le Monde* (Paris), 21 June 1994.

[20] ILO: *Democratization and the ILO*. Report of the Director-General (Part 1), International Labour Conference, 79th Session, Geneva, 1992, p. 8.

[21] ibid., p. 65.

[22] ibid., p. 65.

[23] See Gerry and Janine Rodgers (eds.): *Precarious jobs in labour market regulation. The growth of atypical employment in Western Europe* (Geneva, International Institute for Labour Studies and Free University of Brussels, 1990).

[24] David A. Morse: *The origin and evolution of the ILO and its role in the world community* (Ithaca, New York, Cornell University, 1969), p. 114.

THE DYNAMICS OF CHANGE AND THE PROTECTION OF WORKERS

21

Patrick Bollé*

The first France/ILO Symposium on the Future of Work, Employment and Social Protection, held at Annecy (France) in 2001,[1] provided a broad overview of the changes under way in those areas and policy options for coping with them. Despite the wide variety of views and approaches expressed by participants, the consensus was that social integration and cohesion must be secured both by providing decent work for all and by striking a new balance between flexibility and security. The discussions centred on the content of responsible political action, avoiding the extremes of some single-minded market dogma, on the one hand, and blind faith in all-out regulation, on the other. In concluding, the first Symposium had stressed the importance of holding further exchanges between researchers, experts, the social partners and policy-makers from different disciplines and countries.

The *International Labour Review*'s "Perspective" on that Symposium had highlighted a number of trends, areas and issues which called for further consideration and research: perceived insecurity versus real insecurity, labour market segmentation, the transfer of responsibilities and risks to the worker, whether changes are driven by production or by power relations, and the role of the ILO as the global authority on social issues.

Following up on the work of the Annecy Symposium, the organizers decided that the theme of the second Symposium would be *The dynamics of change and the protection of workers*. Accordingly, the second France/ILO Symposium, held on 17-18 January 2002 in Lyons (France), comprised three sessions on the following topics:

- Preventing exclusion and promoting inclusion: Transitions on the labour market;

- Reconciling work and family: An approach based on life cycles/ transitions;

Originally published in *International Labour Review*, Vol. 141 (2002), No. 3, in the "Perspectives" section.
* French-language editor of the *International Labour Review*.

- Between the market and regulation: Do the new social regulations provide lifelong security?

This "Perspective" reports the substance of the Symposium's proceedings, beginning with the implications of the increasing frequency and diversity of labour market transitions for statistics, public policy, the role of the social partners, and labour law. The second part of this "Perspective" is devoted to the challenge of reconciling career and family responsibilities.[2]

TRANSITIONS, RISKS AND SECURITY

Typology of transitions

The "transitions" under discussion here fall into three broad categories (Gazier, 2002, pp. 28-29).

Individual transitions. These are changes that affect the position, tasks and status of a worker throughout his or her working and non-working life. Such transitions may be imposed or voluntary, protected and socially monitored to various degrees. Specifically, they refer to transitions between the following situations: wage employment, vocational training, self-employment, unpaid work in a family enterprise, initial education and training, unemployment, retirement, inactivity, etc. Some of them may be negative, dangerous and "excluding". A related issue concerns the extent to which individual career paths are irreversible: "your fate can change diametrically, from inclusion to exclusion, depending on how you are 'channelled' on the labour market" (Gazier, 2002, p. 28).

Collective transitions. These are the transitions from the education system to working life, and from working life to retirement. Today, these transitions are less clear-cut than they used to be because of the proliferation of alternating training and other such schemes at the start of a working life and of gradual retirement schemes before full retirement.

Global or systemic transitions. These are the transitions that affect the labour markets and employment policies of a country as a whole. They come about as a result of the pressures of competition and globalization, but they can also be triggered by poverty, unemployment, inequality and population ageing.

The complexity and diversity of individual transitions is illustrated by a study on changes in employment status over one year in 11 Member States of the European Union (Schmid, 2002, pp. 65-70). The main findings of this survey can be summed up as follows:

- Women go through more transitions than men. About 60 per cent of all individuals having experienced a transition within one year are women; around 40 per cent are men.

- About a quarter of the individuals undertaking transitions within one year change their status more than once. There are thus many more transitions than there are individuals making transitions.

- Only about half of all new transitions are related to employment or unemployment flows. In other words, half the transitions involve statuses that are unrelated to the labour market in the narrow sense.

- Some 60 per cent of all inflows into unemployment come from employment.

- About 60 per cent of all the outflows from unemployment go into employment, with the remainder going into self-employment, education or training, retirement or other "inactivity" statuses, special labour market policy schemes, community or military service.

New risks

The foregoing observations "on the dynamics and patterns of transitions – even if they are admittedly still very preliminary and sketchy – demonstrate that a narrowly defined unemployment insurance system which focuses only on flows between unemployment and employment is likely to overlook important risks related to these flows" (Schmid, 2002, p. 68).

In order to evaluate transition-related risks, the authors of the study looked at the kind of labour contract that formerly unemployed workers were engaged on. They find that in most countries – the exceptions being Italy, Greece and Denmark – non-standard employment relationships have increased to an average Europe-wide level of about 30 per cent. They conclude that, even in the absence of any trend towards the structural demise of stable employment relationships (see Auer and Cazes, 2000), transitions around the core of stable jobs are increasing and even "stable jobs" are affected by new income risks on account of result-oriented wages or concession bargaining.

To sum up, one can say that, first, the risks related to gainful employment are increasing. Second, and more important, these risks are not necessarily related to unemployment but to income or status insecurity. Third, and much neglected, these risks are more and more related with a wide range of disabilities, be they health or psychological problems. Fourth, even in the case of a so-called standard employment relationship – which means permanent full-time contracts in dependent employment – we find more and more elements of commercial contracts built into these contracts, for instance, success-related wages, wages in the form of equity shares and so on. On the one hand, we find more and more people not covered by the conventional social insurance systems, and on the other, more and more 'hard working wage earners' and small employers under high competitive pressure reluctant to contribute into the collective social security funds (Schmid, 2002, p. 70).

Statistical issues

A number of speakers at the Symposium drew attention to the great difficulty and high cost of accurately monitoring transitions in the life cycle. Not

Box.   Possible typology for "pattern of activities during year t"

1.   Stable employment
   (a)   Employed whole period: Same job.

2.   Mobile employment
   (a)   Employed whole period: Changed industry at least once, same occupation.
   (b)   Employed whole period: Changed occupation at least once, same industry.
   (c)   Employed whole period: Changed both industry and occupation at least once.

3.   Unstable employment
   (a)   Employment followed/interrupted by at least one unemployment spell lasting not more than t weeks in total, no spells, not in the labour force.
   (b)   Employment followed/interrupted by at least one spell not in the labour force lasting not more than t weeks in total, no unemployment spells.
   (c)   Employment followed by a spell of unemployment lasting more than t weeks.
   (d)   Employment followed by a spell not in the labour force of at least t weeks.
   (e)   Unemployment followed by a spell of employment lasting more than t weeks.
   (f)   Not in the labour force and in training followed by one spell of employment lasting more than t weeks.

4.   Stable unemployment
   (a)   Unemployed whole period.

5.   Long-term unemployment
   (a)   Unemployment followed/interrupted by one or more employment spells lasting not more than t weeks in total.
   (b)   Unemployment followed/interrupted by one or more spells not in the labour force of not more than t weeks in total.
   (c)   Unemployment followed by a spell not in the labour force lasting more than t weeks.

6.   Turbulent labour force status
   (a)   Not in the labour force and in training followed/interrupted by at least one spell of employment and/or unemployment.
   (b)   Not in the labour force and not in training followed/interrupted by at least one spell of employment and/or unemployment.
   (c)   Combinations of periods of employment, unemployment and not in the labour force not classified elsewhere.

7.   Stable not in the labour force: in training
   (a)   Not in the labour force and in training the whole period
   (b)   Not in the labour force and in training part of the period.

8.   Stable not in the labour force: Not in training
   (a)   Not in the labour force whole period: Not in training during any part of the period.

Source: ILO, 1998, p. 43.

only does this call for collecting a huge amount of data, but the consequences of transitions over time need to be traced as well. For example, participation in some employment policy programme, such as a training course, can turn out to be a positive experience for one person but a negative one for another. Similarly, temporary or agency-brokered employment can be a stepping stone to stable employment for some people, but a dead end for others. The promotion of part-time employment may well give people more freedom of choice, but it can just as well increase the level of underemployment (see Bollé, 1997). Such mixed outcomes can be experienced by individuals, by specific categories of people (e.g. women, young workers, etc.) or by a country as a whole. The complexity of statistical observation of labour market dynamics was highlighted in a report submitted to the Sixteenth International Conference of Labour Statisticians, which provides a number of working hypotheses together with an outline of variables that could be used to monitor changes of status over the course of a year (see box).

Government policies

Can flexibility be reconciled with security? The term "flexicurity" was coined "to characterize this successful combination of adaptability to a changing international environment and a solidarity-type welfare system, which protects the citizens from the more brutal consequences of structural change" (Madsen, 2002, p. 49). Denmark seems to have succeeded in creating a unique combination of stable economic growth and social welfare since the mid-1990s, at a time when liberals were arguing that the Scandinavian model was no longer able to cope with the demands of flexibility and structural change arising out of technological progress and international competition. Danish unemployment was halved between 1993 and 1999, dropping from 10.2 to 5.2 per cent, while the employment rate increased to 76.5 per cent – the highest of the entire European Union. Significantly, these improvements were achieved without balance-of-payments deficits or any significant wage inflation, and with growing budget surpluses. This outstanding performance is no doubt partly attributable to the country's sound macroeconomic policy – of demand-driven growth – and to the reduction of labour supply through early retirement and long-term paid leave schemes. But another major contributing factor was the so-called "golden triangle" of flexicurity. This concept combines flexibility (measured by high labour mobility and low employment protection), generous social security systems, and active labour market policies. Contrary to what one might expect, the high level of job mobility and low level of employment protection have not generated any widespread feelings of insecurity among Danish workers, whatever their occupational category. The explanation probably lies in the relative ease with which they can find a new job if they lose theirs, as a result of both lower unemployment and Denmark's industrial structure, which is dominated by small and medium-sized enterprises, thereby making strong internal labour markets less important than in other countries. A further explanation lies in the duration and generosity of unemployment benefits. Such benefits, however, are conditional upon mandatory full-time "activation" after 12 months of unemployment for adults and six months of unemployment for persons under the age of 25. This activation policy aims both to motivate and to train the unemployed so as to help them find new jobs. Despite the potential perverse effects inherent in such policies (e.g. creaming or slackening job-search efforts during participation in activation programmes), various studies have pointed to a significant reduction of unemployment among training programme beneficiaries.

One of the components of the "golden triangle" plays a particularly important part, namely, the generosity of social protection. But whereas the cost of generous paid leave schemes, early retirement and unemployment benefits appears to have been long since accepted in the Scandinavian countries, it comes up against very strong political and economic pressures for lower taxes and social contributions in the other countries.

Social protection

The increasing frequency of transitions and related risks calls for reconsideration of risk management, i.e. social protection. A distinction can be drawn between "internal" or "manufactured" risks related to individual choices – e.g. a change of job and location dictated by divorce or a partner's career requirements – and "external" risks related to economic downturns or technological change. Since internal risks are becoming increasingly frequent, Günther Schmid (2002, pp. 63-64) proposes that unemployment insurance be redesigned to incorporate elements of mobility insurance and to operate in conjunction with active labour market policy measures, so as to build up a system of "employment insurance". Such a system would foster the development of "transitional labour markets", understood as institutional arrangements that empower individuals to transit between various employment statuses during their life cycle. This system would secure the participation of the middle class and of the rich in a comprehensive social security system. In practice, the proposed system of employment insurance would rest upon three pillars. The first would consist of conventional unemployment insurance, covering the risk of involuntary unemployment due to external shocks. Its financing would include a redistributive element by abolishing wage-income ceilings, by making non-wage income subject to contributions, and by granting reductions in contributions or even exemptions in respect of the lowest paid jobs so as to encourage employment and work. The second pillar would consist of various individualized social security or employability accounts. The third pillar would consist of active labour market policy programmes funded through general taxation. Mobility accounts could be used to establish drawing rights or vouchers to "ensure" the income risks related to various kinds of transitions during the life cycle. These schemes would enable workers to finance and to manage their own transitions adequately. "A voucher system might also halt the ongoing legalization of the labour market, enhance labour market flexibility and allow for a 'reflexive deregulation' that does not neglect the fundamental need for social security during risky transitions" (Schmid, 2002, p. 80).

However, the idea of decoupling social protection from labour legislation seems somewhat radical at a time when the increasing frequency of transitions and the proliferation of different types of employment relationships have been fuelling intense debate over the legal status of workers and their terms and conditions of employment, social protection included.

The employment relationship and labour law

Yet the law does provide for transitional situations, which act as 'antechambers', as staging posts between one legal situation and another; ... A new field of research appears to be opening up here, namely those legal acts which, because they mark the moments of a passage from one status to another, may be termed transitional acts: starting up a business; recruitment; 'hiving off'; moving from public- to private-sector employment; the replacement of a statutory by a contractual relationship; involuntary early retirement; involuntary lay-off; departure on or return from sabbatical leave or leave for family reasons; assistance to the unemployed to start up a business; legal acts giving effect to a transformation of an employment relationship, sometimes even the creation of a new form of employment relationship. Information on this last type of case is scarce – especially as regards the proper giving of consent by the parties concerned, and this suggests that provision will need to be made for a new area of dispute settlement (Lyon-Caen, 1996, pp. 700-701).

Historically, the contract of employment evolved out of the employment relationship itself, as a governance mechanism which linked together work organization with labour supply in such a way as to make it possible to manage long-term economic risks. The State became the implicit third party to the contract, channelling risks of insecurity among the workforce as a whole through the social insurance system or, in a wider sense, social protection (Deakin, 2002, p. 191). Yet some of the very foundations of the contract of employment are now being called into question. The first of these is the notion of subordination, which is out of step not only with the new forms of semi-self-employment or para-self-employment but also with the new forms of work in which workers are given greater autonomy in return for meeting the targets they are assigned (Supiot, 2002, p. 153). The employment relationship is evolving into something of an exchange between, on the one hand, a willingness on the part of the worker to perform a task or to achieve a given objective on the basis of her or his skills – and to be accountable for the results of the work, but with no consideration of the insecurity of the employment relationship in terms of its duration – and, on the other hand, pay and working time determined on the basis of demonstrated skills and the results of the service provided in terms of quantity and quality (Trentin, 2002, pp. 207-208). In Supiot's view, "autonomy in subordination and allegiance in independence are simply two complementary sides of the same approach to network organization" (Supiot, 2002, p. 154). A second foundation of the traditional employment model which is now under threat is the division of labour between the commercial and domestic spheres, whereby the male was made the sole breadwinner – a notion that is becoming increasingly anachronistic with the feminization of the labour market (see below). A third is that the contract of employment was based on the model of the nation State whose powers of regulation and taxation are being undermined by the liberalization of capital flows. Lastly, the employment model is based on the linear and homogeneous concept of working life between the end of schooling and retirement. This concept too has become unrealistic given the increasing frequency of the intervening transitions discussed above.

In practice, subcontracting and outsourcing of production have resurfaced, largely as a consequence of government measures aimed at cutting public expenditure and undermining the floor to wages and conditions of employment. From the perspective of labour law, the problem lies not so much in the growth of self-employment at the expense of protected forms of labour as in the blurring of the divide between the two and in the emergence of a "grey zone" of workers who are neither clearly employees nor self-employed. Furthermore, employment policy measures aimed at supporting the indeterminate or open-ended employment relationship and at actively suppressing casual hirings have being discontinued and reversed, with access to short-term and insecure employment now seen as factors likely to promote the employability of those seeking work (Deakin, 2002, pp. 196-197). The fact remains, as Supiot argues, that the market economy cannot get by without labour law. Indeed, the market economy calls for nature, money and labour to be treated as products or merchandise with a trade value, rather than just the value they have when they are used. Yet this idea is without substance, since nature, labour and money are not products: only law – the law of property, labour law and commercial law – can give it substance (Supiot, 2002, p. 150).

The point is that the above developments and trends could lead to exacerbated and persistent labour market dualization. Addressing this risk, Deakin supports the proposals put forward in Supiot's 1999 report *Beyond employment*, which aim to reconceptualize security on the basis of three principles:

Employment status should be redefined to guarantee the continuity of a career rather than the stability of specific conditions. The prime aim is to protect workers during transitions between jobs. ...

Labour force membership status should no longer be determined on the basis of the restrictive criterion of employment, but be based on the broader notion of work. Social law may no longer disregard non-marketable forms of work. ...

This broadened labour force membership accordingly covers three of the four circles of social law: the rights inherent in wage-earning work (employment), common rights connected with occupational activity (health and safety), and rights ensuing from unwaged work (care for others, voluntary work, training on one's own initiative, etc.) together constitute the three circles of rights associated with the notion of labour force membership. Universal social rights, guaranteed irrespective of work (health care, minimum social assistance), fall outside this notion and should therefore be protected under specific legislation. The principle of equal treatment for men and women, however, applies to all four circles.

Broadened labour force membership goes hand-in-hand with various kinds of social drawing rights. ... [T]hey are exercised on a discretionary basis rather than in the unexpected occurrence of risks (Supiot, 1999, pp. 221-222).

As mentioned earlier, collective approaches seem to be losing ground to individualization driven by the diversification of personal situations and the increasing frequency of transitions. This pattern – which is reflected in statistical observation, public policy, including active labour market policies, and labour law and the status of workers – leaves trade unions little choice but to reconsider their own organization and means of action.

The social partners

Michael Piore argues that the collapse of the United States' old system of work and employment – built around four key institutions: the family, the productive enterprise, the trade union, and the nation State – is attributable to a shift in political power towards management, deregulation and globalization, which increased competitive pressure on wages, particularly at the bottom of the labour market. However, the main cause of the system's demise was probably the decline of trade union membership, which virtually collapsed during the 1990s. As a result, inequality increased, as did income and employment insecurity – trends that met with little resistance. With the considerable weakening of collective bargaining, social regulation was left to legislation and the courts, including in the field of occupational health and safety. Another factor contributing to this process was the way in which women and other socially stigmatized groups came to see their problems in the workplace as related to their social identities and not to their identities as workers. Following the approach taken by the civil rights movement, they sought to solve their problems through legislative and judicial remedies rather than through trade unionism and collective bargaining (Piore, 2002, p. 178).

It is difficult to determine with any certainty the direction of causality as between the decline of trade unionism and the emergence of new forms of employment. Besides, there are good reasons to believe that in Europe the problem can be seen from a different angle, although European countries have also witnessed a relative increase in the activity of identity groups. Bruno Trentin, a former trade union official and current member of the

European Parliament, considers the problem in terms of the content of the employment relationship, whereby workers are obliged to produce a result while employers preserve unilateral decision-making powers, including in respect of the duration of the employment relationship and its termination. Such inequality might well explain the weakening of workers' bargaining power and erosion of the right to strike. Clearly, the imbalance cannot be overcome simply by patching up the old rules governing industrial relations (Trentin, 2002, p. 208). In the circumstances, Trentin proposes four strategic objectives for trade unions:

- Training throughout working life would be the primary objective of collective bargaining. From the workers' perspective, such continuing training would have to be seen as some sort of payment in kind and, more importantly, as an insurance for the future because it offers the best possible protection against insecurity.

- The second objective would be to gain control over processes linked to the restructuring of the enterprise, the geographical mobility of the labour force and occupational mobility within the enterprise.

- The third objective would have to do with participation in decisions involving the organization of work and working time within the enterprise, together with bargaining at the local level with a view to an organization of time that makes it possible – particularly in towns and cities – to reconcile the operation of public services with work and private life.

- The fourth objective, relating to social protection and population ageing, would be to secure a higher rate of labour force participation by encouraging people to continue voluntarily to work despite their advancing years.

Such a wide-ranging reform of collective bargaining would entail new forms of representation and the appearance of new actors: "contract based" and "semi-self-employed" workers, workers who do not have a fixed workplace, people looking for their first job, and unemployed workers looking for a new job – all of the groups that are typically not represented by trade unions in active labour policy negotiations. This would require trade unions to support charitable organizations which would enable atypical or unemployed workers to participate, alongside the trade unions, in some forms of collective bargaining aimed at the conclusion of "framework" agreements spelling out the roles, rights and duties that would be an integral part of any employment relationship and any form of welfare (Trentin, 2002, p. 210).

By way of conclusion on this discussion, it might be argued that the appropriate response to the increasing frequency of transitions, increasing sources of uncertainty, and the diversification of employment situations would be to broaden the concepts of work and worker. This applies not only to trade union representation but also to social protection and the exercise of rights and legal protection. The question of the definition of work – in the broadest possible sense – also lies at the heart of the debate on reconciling career and family life.

WORK AND FAMILY [3]

The papers presented in the panel on the relationship between work and family focused on countries in which participation in paid employment was quite high for mothers of young children, namely, the United States, France, Sweden and Denmark (Appelbaum, 2002a; Anxo, 2002; Esping-Andersen, 2002; Fagnani, 2002).

The facts

The Scandinavian countries have succeeded in enabling women both to work and to have children, though the Scandinavian model would be difficult to establish in other countries. Indeed, the welfare state and public sector employment are unlikely to be expanded in countries that have not already done this. Besides, the Scandinavian countries' high rates of female labour force participation and work/family balance come at the cost of relatively severe occupational segregation, the confinement of women to certain jobs and public sector employment (see Melkas and Anker, 1997).

Women in the United States face the opposite problem – or perhaps only the other side of the same coin. They come closer than women in other industrialized economies to achieving gender equality in the workplace, provided they are willing to sacrifice their families in the interest of keeping their jobs. Women who pursue full-time jobs or careers find themselves facing contradictions that arise from the incompatibility between motherhood and employment in the United States. Most American women pay a high price for motherhood in terms of lost opportunities for steady employment, rising wages, or a career.

The French example suggests that progress may be possible through a commitment to create childcare facilities and subsidize the cost of quality childcare, and through a reduction in weekly working time. But this approach is not without its drawbacks. Some employers may make up for perceived increases in costs by demanding more irregular or atypical hours, which are difficult to reconcile with the operating hours of childcare services. The question is whether public policy should accommodate the demands on working parents – and especially mothers – to work asocial or irregular hours in order to keep their jobs or have a career, even if this contradicts the biological rhythms of children and families, or whether public policy should resist the development of atypical and flexible working arrangements, which may restrict the employment opportunities of mothers in certain occupational categories.

Individual working families in many industrialized countries have taken up the only option available to them – they have reduced fertility. In many countries, women are now having one child, since the problems of compatibility of work and motherhood are most extreme when there are two or more children whose schedules have to be juggled. This results in a loss of well-being, since most young women express a desire for two or three children. But the problem goes beyond a decline in the well-being of some individuals. Many countries where it is difficult for mothers to work – e.g. Germany, Italy and Japan – face an extreme and sustained decline in fertility that is expected to lead to an actual decline in the native-born population over the next several decades. Clearly, this situation is not sustainable. The minimum requirement for sustainable economic development is that economic activity must assure the succession of generations. The long-term sustainability of the economy – of rising levels of output and the ability to support an ageing population – depends on resolving the incompatibility that exists in many countries between work and children.

Going backwards to an older situation is not an option. Globalization and downward pressure on wages make it unlikely that companies will again pay a family wage to men; rising education levels and women's aspirations make it unlikely that they will again accept a high degree of dependence on a man for access to earnings and social insurance.

Solutions

Several approaches to resolving this dilemma were suggested during the discussion that followed the panel presentations. They can be summed up as follows:

- To focus on children and reconceptualize the discussion in terms of the rights of children. The case for this approach can be strengthened by the requirement in modern societies for strong cognitive development during the early years – beyond what most parents can provide privately for their children up to the age of six years.
- To rethink the current linear career path. The greatest time demands within the family occur when there are younger children. Currently, this coincides with the period of greatest time demands on the job as people establish themselves at work. Can the career path for men and women be changed, rather than the current effort to shoehorn women into the traditional career path?
- To make the integration of paid and unpaid work and time off for family care responsibilities politically legitimate – as men's annual military service is in Switzerland.
- To address the difficulties associated with a career interruption: while on parental leave, parents could engage in training activities until they rejoin the labour force.

- To broaden the concept of work so as to include training, paid employment, and unpaid work in the household.

- To focus on older women as well because they are often needed to care for elderly persons when they are in their forties and fifties and working themselves. Also, as women increase their employment, there are challenges ahead in terms of the social rights and protections that women now enjoy – e.g. claim on a man's pension to compensate for women's careers and jobs that were not well paid.

The discussion also gave rise to a number of questions. Should governments develop services for the care of young children and the elderly? Should they provide child allowances and allowances for child care to families? Should crèches be kept open 24 hours a day to reconcile the different demands on the time of parents?

The solution may lie in considering motherhood as one of the many transitions that workers make over their life cycle and in developing a range of social protections that every member of the labour force could expect to call on at one time or another in the course of a working life. Temporary reduced working time options, with social insurance benefits to maintain income levels need not be limited to maternity or parental leave – which provides firms with incentives for statistical discrimination against women. Such options could also be exercised in the event of an involuntary reduction in hours during periods of slack demand (partial unemployment insurance), jury duty or community volunteer activities, military service, part-time training to upgrade skills, pursuit of higher education on a part-time basis, or phased retirement (partial pensions).

Workers could be exempt from fluctuating or atypical hours for fixed periods of time at various points in their life cycle and for a variety of reasons – e.g. care of young children or elderly relatives, enrolment in a training or education programme, age or health of the worker. Volkswagen currently exempts employees from rotating shifts for these and other reasons. In principle, every worker would have access, as needed over the life cycle, to reductions in hours and income supports or to regular hours at key periods. The very universality of this approach would make discrimination by firms difficult; it would overcome the resistance of workers without young children to "special" treatment of parents; and it might make possible a political coalition to push for such a policy.

Here again, participants in the discussion repeatedly suggested that the concept of work be broadened to encompass a wider variety of situations (employment, maternity leave, parental leave, training) and to provide workers with security during their transitions, notably through a system of credits and drawing rights.

BY WAY OF CONCLUSION

It is now an established fact that workers' careers involve increasingly frequent transitions, both within the labour market and between employment/ unemployment and various statuses of inactivity. There also appears to be growing diversity in forms of employment and in the content of employment relationships, though it is as yet unclear how much of this trend is dictated by the technical requirements of production and demand for goods and services, as opposed to the imbalance of bargaining power between labour supply and demand.

For a number of reasons, workers are having to take on an increasing burden of risk. First, the cost of insurance against certain risks, which used to be shared by employers, is now often borne by workers alone, e.g. where wage employment is replaced by a contractual relationship between a client company and a worker in "semi-, para-, pseudo- or spurious" self-employment. Second, there is the risk of persistent labour market segmentation, whereby some categories of workers – typically female, elderly, young and unskilled workers – risk being confined to the "bad" segment, e.g. in "permanent" temporary employment or involuntary part-time work. And third, the most vulnerable workers run the risk of social exclusion, lacking the means of effecting the necessary transitions or of adapting to new forms of employment.

How, in the face of these risks, can the inherent flexibility of new labour markets be reconciled with workers' security? For a start, the trend towards diversification calls for replacing the concept of employment – and the implied status of "employee" – by that of work – and worker – whatever the nature of the employment relationship, also taking account of the fact that work performed in the domestic sphere is also work even though it takes place outside the market.

Thus, with the growing individualization of situations that range from inactivity to full-time, permanent employment, but which also include unemployment, training, parental or sabbatical leave, etc., the concepts of work and legal and social protection need to be broadened. Accordingly, new practices like time credits and social drawing rights are emerging. This broadening of the traditional framework poses a challenge to the social partners. For the trade unions, the challenge is to represent all workers, whatever their status. For employers, it is to widen the scope of bargaining to include new forms of "remuneration" in time off or training, for example. In this connection, attention must again be called to the necessity of lifelong learning – a necessity for workers concerned with their own security, for employers concerned with productivity, and for States concerned with the future of their citizens.

The main difficulty is that reconciling flexibility and security carries a cost – the cost of social protection. In Europe, taxation and social contributions have come under intense economic and political pressure. The situation is often exacerbated by the pursuit of restrictive macroeconomic policies, although priority should be given to growth and job creation – not only for the sake of state budgets, but also for the sake of social justice. To quote Juan Somavia, the Director-General of the ILO, speaking at the final round table of the Symposium: "Unemployment is probably one of the main enemies of labour rights, because the more people out of work there are who are prepared to accept anything just to have a job – as is the situation in the Third World – the more difficult the situation becomes for those trying to defend labour rights. So creating employment is indeed one way of promoting labour rights" (see Auer and Gazier, 2002, p. 234).

Notes

[1] See Bollé, 2001; see also Auer and Daniel, 2001, for the full record of proceedings.

[2] Contributions to the Symposium were too numerous to be recorded individually in this "Perspective", hence the selective focus on the question of transitions and on career/family responsibilities. The full proceedings of the Symposium are available in Auer and Gazier (2002).

[3] This section draws on a synthesis of panel presentations prepared by Eileen Appelbaum (2002b).

References

Anxo, Dominique. 2002. "Time allocation and the gender division of labour in France and Sweden", in Auer and Gazier, pp. 99-108.

Appelbaum, Eileen. 2002a. "Shared work/valued care: New norms for organizing market work and unpaid care work", in Auer and Gazier, pp. 93-98.

—.2002b. "Synthesis", in Auer and Gazier, pp. 141-146.

Auer, Peter; Cazes, Sandrine. 2000. "The resilience of the long-term employment relationship: Evidence from industrialized countries", in *International Labour Review* (Geneva), Vol. 139, No. 4, pp. 379-408.

—; Gazier, Bernard (eds.). 2002. *The future of work, employment and social protection: The dynamics of change and the protection of workers.* Record of proceedings of the France/ILO Symposium, Lyons, 17-18 Jan. 2002. Paris, Ministry of Social Affairs, Labour and Solidarity/Geneva, ILO, International Institute for Labour Studies.

—; Daniel, Christine (eds.). 2001. *The future of work, employment and social protection: The search for new securities in a world of growing uncertainties.* Record of proceedings of the France/ILO Symposium, Annecy, 18-19 Jan. 2001. Paris, Ministry of Employment and Solidarity/Geneva, ILO, International Institute for Labour Studies.

Bollé, Patrick. 2001. "The future of work, employment and social protection (the Annecy Symposium, January 2001)", in *International Labour Review* (Geneva), Vol. 140, No. 4, pp. 453-474.

—.1997. "Part-time work: Solution or trap?", in *International Labour Review* (Geneva), Vol. 136, No. 4, pp. 557-579.

Deakin, Simon. 2002. "The evolution of the employment relationship", in Auer and Gazier, pp. 191-205.

Esping-Andersen, Gosta. 2002. "Towards a post-industrial gender contract", in Auer and Gazier, pp. 109-128.

Fagnani, Jeanne. 2002. "Family policy, life cycle and linking working life and family life in France: New factors, new choices to be made", in Auer and Gazier, pp. 129-140.

Gazier, Bernard. 2002. "Labour markets and transitions", in Auer and Gazier, pp. 27-32.

ILO. 1998. *General report*. Report IV, Sixteenth International Conference of Labour Statisticians. Geneva, 6-15 Oct. 1998. ICLS/16/1998/IV. Geneva, ILO.

Lyon-Caen, Gérard. 1996. "By way of conclusion: Labour law and employment transitions", in *International Labour Review* (Geneva), Special Issue: "Perspectives on the nature and future of work", Vol. 135, No. 6, pp. 697-702.

Madsen, Per Kongshøj. 2002. "Security and flexibility: Friends or foes? Some observations from the case of Denmark", in Auer and Gazier, pp. 49-62.

Melkas, Helinä; Anker, Richard. 1997. "Occupational segregation by sex in Nordic countries: An empirical investigation", in *International Labour Review* (Geneva), Vol. 136, No. 3, pp. 341-363.

Piore, Michael J. 2002. "The reconfiguration of work and employment relations in the United States at the turn of the 21st century", in Auer and Gazier, pp. 171-189.

Schmid, Günther. 2002. "Employment insurance for managing critical transitions during the life cycle", in Auer and Gazier, pp. 63-82.

Supiot, Alain. 2002. "Between market and regulation: New social regulations for life-long security?", in Auer and Gazier, pp. 149-155.

— (ed.). 1999. *Au-delà de l'emploi. Transformations du travail et devenir du droit du travail en Europe*. Report for the European Commission. Paris, Flammarion. [Published in English as *Beyond employment: Changes in work and the future of labour law in Europe*, Oxford, Oxford University Press, 2001].

Trentin, Bruno. 2002. "Potential changes in systems of industrial relations", in Auer and Gazier, pp. 207-215.

PERSPECTIVES ON WORK: INTRODUCTION

Alain SUPIOT *

22

The "Great Transformation" (Polanyi, 1944) that gave birth to industrial society initially centred on free trade. The transformation of work came only later. The unforeseen consequences of the liberalization of trade and industry made it necessary to rethink the issue of work and to turn nation states into Welfare States. But the Welfare State is now falling apart. Under the combined effects of technological and political change, international trade is growing while national institutions are undermined. Foremost among these is national labour law, which is suspected of impairing economic efficiency, as were trade guilds in the past. It may be a sign of the times that the new World Trade Organization has moved into the former building of the International Labour Organization on the verdant shores of Lake Geneva.

Like the industrial revolution, today's great transformation is bound to raise the issue of work in the context of international trade. In fact, the issue is already being raised: debates on the inclusion of a social clause in international trade agreements offer a foretaste of what lies ahead (Servais, 1989; Moreau, Staelens and Trudeau, 1993; Emmerij, 1994; van Liemt, 1989; Hansenne, 1994; Besse, 1994; Maindrault, 1994). Indeed, goods cannot be traded indefinitely in disregard of the fate of the people who make them. To some, the breakdown or disruption of the legal status and values attaching to work means joblessness and uselessness to the world. To others, it means too much work and no time for the world. In either case, the outcome is something like a social death that threatens the very foundations of human existence and reproduction (particularly for lack of money or time to bring up children). This is bound to lead to violence because people cannot be reconciled to social death indefinitely. Whether it is religious, criminal or nationalist, violence will in turn pose a threat to business and to the very survival of the market economy. The age of simplistic arguments for labour deregulation (e.g. dismantle labour law and all will be for the best in the best of

Originally published in *International Labour Review*, Vol. 135 (1996), No. 6.

* Professor at the Faculty of Law and Political Science, University of Nantes.

all possible worlds) is drawing to a close and will have been short-lived. Far from being sidelined by the globalization of the market economy, the issue of labour is assuming unprecedented proportions. This no doubt explains why the past two years have witnessed a proliferation of studies on the question of work, analysing how it has changed, proclaiming its decline or projecting its future. The contributions presented in issue No. 6, Vol. 135, of the *International Labour Review* should be seen within that context.[1]

A MULTIDISCIPLINARY APPROACH TO THE SOCIAL SCIENCES

Colloquia, seminars and other such gatherings have become so common and specialized that one might be forgiven for forgetting what they were originally intended for. Etymologically, the term colloquium implies intent to "speak with" someone, as opposed to a succession of soliloquies. The issue then is with whom to speak. In a world where knowledge has become so specialized, it is tempting to converse only with experts in one's own field of specialization. Ever since knowledge about human behaviour and society became organized into "sciences", on the model of the natural sciences, the whole approach to the study of social affairs appears to have become irremediably bent to the rules of specialization. This would mean that the quest for the ultimate truth underlying social phenomena bears fruit only by narrowing the scope of investigations. The division of labour, as theorized by Durkheim, finds particularly vivid expression in the field of scientific research. Just as there are no longer any specialists on Byzantium – but specialists in Byzantine art, institutions or customs – no one can go on claiming to be a labour specialist. Now there are only labour lawyers, labour sociologists, labour economists or labour historians. Moreover, each of these categories tends to split into a myriad of subdivisions, with the result that no specialist in trade union law would confidently venture into the province of specialists on the law of dismissal; nor would a historian specialized in eighteenth-century labour attempt a foray into the preserve of colleagues specialized in medieval labour. In many respects, this process of specialization is both inevitable and beneficial, but it none the less presents serious drawbacks.

It is conducive to autistic behaviour among experts themselves. Economists tend to read (and cite) only other economists (preferably those from their own school), as do sociologists other sociologists, jurists other jurists, and so forth. Taken to extremes, this tendency makes self-citation the preferred form of reference. Between the increasingly narrow fields of knowledge, there is little or no communication. And within each field, self-reference has become the standard approach.[2] While there is nothing new about autism among experts, this condition is now underpinned by scientific authority. Hence the rather special relationship experts have with the outside world. People can have difficulty making sense of what experts say about the society in which they live, either because they present a jigsaw of which the pieces do not fit together, or because the pieces have been forced together to suit the experts' own way of thinking, then presented as some universal and definitive Truth.[3] For the sake of that Truth, entire areas of human experience may be consigned to the scrap heap. Yesterday, it was the end of religion, the end of philosophy, the end of law, even the end of history. Today, it is the end of work (Rifkin, 1995).[4]

The common aim underlying the articles in this issue of the *Review is* the endeavour to avoid these pitfalls. As experts specialized in particular fields, the authors could only avoid the trap of self-reference by comparing their points of view on the question of work. This means comparing ways of conceptualizing work at different historical moments, in different disciplines and in different countries. Just as there is no single way of looking at a landscape – but as many ways as there are angles from which it can be viewed (with each angle itself offering a variety of prospects depending on the daylight) – there is no single way of seeing work and the changes it is currently undergoing. The concept of work itself must not be allowed to mask the great diversity of situations it actually encompasses (see Salais and Storper, 1993). Comparing points of view invariably amounts to making them relative, less absolute, especially as regards the point of view of the person drawing the comparison.

This is the reason for bringing together different perspectives on work. First, the notion of perspectives implies that the question be addressed by contrasting points of view that normally take no account of one another, namely, those of specialists from different disciplines (economics, law, anthropology, philosophy, sociology) and those of different countries (France, Germany, Greece, Italy, Japan, Spain, United Kingdom). Second, perspectives imply an aim – in this case, to extract from the narrow confines of academe a pool of knowledge on the transformation of work with a view to making a practical reappraisal of the legal and institutional categorization of work today.

HOW LAW RELATES TO THE SOCIAL SCIENCES

The special importance given to law in these articles calls for an explanation. The point is not to analyse the transformation of work according to existing legal categories, but rather to conduct a legal analysis of the transformations of work. Law is not a social science and has nothing to offer on the ultimate truth of social relationships. Law can only mirror what societies believe those relationships ought to be. This peculiarity is misunderstood by all those who so diligently endeavour to incorporate law into some theory of regulation, confusing the rule of law with scientifically observed or practised regularity. However, provided that legal categories are taken for what they really are, they can be useful not only to understand but also to manage social change in general and the transformation of work in particular.

The understanding that law can provide derives from the fact that the legal approach can help to identify the standards inherent in each of the conceptual categories (especially the statistical) that pervade the social sciences (see Legendre, 1983). What the term "worker" has come to mean in the course of this century, the way in which it is understood throughout the social sciences, is the outcome of classification processes, of inclusions and exclusions, which set standards both in principle and in effect. The same goes for the term "unemployed" (Salais, Baverez, Reynault, 1986; Mansfield, Salais, Whiteside, 1994). Legal analysis is thus akin to what Bachelard called the "psychoanalysis of objective knowledge", which he considered necessary to clear the obstacles inherent in any quantitative knowledge (Bachelard, 1938, pp. 211 et seq.).

Law is also needed to manage the transformation of work. Considerable information is available on the transformation itself from historical, economic, philosophical, sociological and other perspectives. But this sum of knowledge will be of no practical value unless it can at some point be used to facilitate adaptations in the legal status of work. Hence the point of communication between legal specialists and social scientists. Obviously, such communication can have only a modest influence on historical developments, which are essentially shaped by power play. The metamorphosis of the world of work, now under way, looks set to be a painful process. But without the appropriate intellectual means to guide its course, the pain will be all the greater.

TRANSFORMATIONS OF WORK

Current thinking on employment conveys a notion of work which crystallized over a century ago and represents only one of the avatars assumed by human activity in the course of its long history. That notion is the product of a standard definition of work that combined inputs from both law (with the emergence of labour law) and the then incipient social sciences (particularly political economy and sociology).

Any attempt to reconsider the notion of work must therefore begin by stripping it of the qualities of eternity and universality that the western mind so readily assumes its products to possess.[5] Accordingly, issue No. 6, Vol. 135, of the *Review* opens with historical, anthropological and philosophical perspectives on work. Robert Castel, whose work has had such a profoundly refreshing influence on perceptions of the emergence of wage employment in western societies (Castel, 1995), retraces the historical steps that led Europe to make work the primary source of people's utility. Gerard Heuzé-Brigant's anthropological contribution on work and identity in India illustrates the lesser importance attached to the wage employment model in cultures where the notions of employment and employee were imported by the colonial powers and where work *per se* never became central to the system of values. The value attached to work is the subject of Dominique Méda's philosophical investigation. Drawing on the arguments set out in her book predicting the end of the value attaching to work (Méda, 1995), she introduces some nuances here: work is now understood to embody a product of the recent historical developments that made economic transaction central to social life. Méda's retrospective shows how work came to be identified with the very essence of humankind, either as a victory of the spirit over matter, or as a means of fulfilment in relation to the self, to others and to nature.

This first set of perspectives leads to the conclusion that law has a central role to play in recasting the concept of work. As shown by Castel, it is indeed through its legal underpinnings that work acquired the value and dignity it now has in Europe. Heuzé-Brigant explains that it is a particular legal perspective – rather than some value attaching to work itself – which makes public sector employment the model and unemployment a failing of the State in India. Méda, in turn, calls for a new "normative ideal", an institutional recasting of individual identity and of the public sphere, thus giving work a less central position than it occupies today.

THE SHIFTING BOUNDARIES OF WAGE EMPLOYMENT

The above approaches converge upon one issue, namely, the meaning that law gives, or fails to give, to work. What is work in the legal sense? And how is its meaning changing today? Addressing these questions calls for a fresh look at the boundaries of wage employment. The hypothesis adopted for this purpose assumes that work, as understood in labour law, can be defined by reference to a set of four contrasts:[6]

(a)   wage employment vs. self-employment;

(b)   remunerated vs. unremunerated work;

(c)   private-sector wage employment vs. public service employment;

(d)   work vs. training.

A common feature of these four distinctions is that they dissociate work from the person of the worker (i.e. the subject of law), which makes it possible to treat work as the object of a specialized market, namely the labour market. This institutional definition of work excludes any human activity involving values other than market values (e.g. self-fulfilment, the interest of the family or children, the public interest, personal freedom).

The validity of all four distinctions is currently challenged by two tendencies. First, the private-sector wage employment model is finding its way into areas of activity outside its traditional scope through the development of work-based training, the introduction of wage employment relationships into the domestic sphere, public-sector privatization, and the statutory incorporation of self-employed workers into structures upon which they become economically dependent. Second, there is a reverse tendency whereby private-sector labour law is incorporating values that were previously characteristics of public-sector and non-wage employment: the right to vocational training and certification; the right to suspend employment for personal reasons (e.g. parental or sabbatical leave); enterprise claims to social and environmental responsibilities (expressed clumsily by the notion of corporate citizenship); development of non-subordinate wage employment (executive wage employment, statutory wage employment status,[7] wage employment of traditionally self-employed workers; and, more generally, a blurring of the notion of subordination in employment relationships. All these developments are generally changing the way workers relate to their work, either by "marketing" occupations that previously fell outside the scope of private-sector wage employment (self-employment, public service) and thereby weakening the legal foundations of their distinctiveness, or by transposing into the sphere of private-sector wage employment values that were hitherto exclusively associated with public service and non-wage employment.

These changes are undermining the basic assumptions of both labour-related institutions (those providing for social protection, in particular) and the social sciences – especially sociology and economics – whose statistical and other analytical categories are based on a standard representation of labour and employment.

The criterion of subordination no longer applies to the whole range of employment relationships. This, in turn, calls for consideration of a legal status for working people which would extend beyond the current boundaries of private-sector wage employment. Remuneration, which used to characterize only employment relationships, is irresistibly gaining ground among previously unremunerated forms of work concerned with what are probably the most vital aspects of human life. Conversely, new forms of unremunerated work are finding their way into the sphere of wage employment itself. The previously clear-cut distinction between private-sector and public-sector employment is giving way to a much more complex situation, in which regulatory methods from the private sector (primarily collective bargaining) are being extended to the public sector, while the State is increasingly active as a supervisor and guarantor of work in the private sphere whenever it affects the public interest. As a result, features that used to distinguish work in the public interest are becoming common to both the private and the public sectors. Lastly, the boundary between training and work is also becoming blurred. This affects the very terms of employment contracts and puts in a different light the question of legal recognition of vocational skills.

THE FUTURE OF LABOUR LAW

This examination of current transformations logically leads to conjecture regarding the future of labour law. Such is the purpose of the last three articles in this issue, which discuss prospects from three different angles.

Jean-Baptiste de Foucauld was formerly head of France's General Planning Commission, which oversaw the preparation of the recent report on "Work in 20 years" (Commissariat Général du Plan, 1995).[8] Here he offers a reappraisal of the aims of labour law. Recognizing that two requirements must be met – first, continuous adjustment and mobility of both people and organizations, and, second, personal security, without which economic development would no longer be synonymous with progress – he argues for "the construction of a system that can provide security, continuity and stability to people who are now faced with a multiplicity of possible situations and who are continuously required to adapt". This is not far removed from Méda's view that everyone should be guaranteed "access to the whole range of activities which the individual is capable of undertaking alone or as a part of a group".

Basing his contribution on the conclusions of an important work published in Germany (Matthies et al., 1994), Ulrich Mückenberger projects a new social citizenship that would reconcile economic efficiency with respect for human diversity. To that end, he constructs a discursive model that takes account of all the basic needs at stake in the issue of work: those of enterprises, those of workers and those of society as a whole, including the societal needs which are left out of the dominant models of collective bargaining.

The comparison of the French and German points of view on the future of labour law is enlightening. The French approach, both past and present, looks at the issue in terms of personal rights guaranteed by the State, whereas the German approach does so in terms of collective organization.[9] But the outlook is ultimately the same in both cases: a redefined legal status of work allowing for the diversity of human activities.

By way of conclusion, Gérard Lyon-Caen looks at how labour law would cope with transition from one position to another, highlighting the double meaning of transition in this context. First, there is the transition from the old to the new labour law, which would at last become fully fledged after breaking free of the narrow confines of legally defined subordination, and, second, the transition from one job to another, since the primary objective of that new labour law would be to reduce the risks involved in making such professional moves, which are now increasingly frequent.

AMBIGUITY OF WORK

According to Roland Barthes, "history never procures a clear-cut victory of one opposite over its opposite: as it unfolds, it reveals unimaginable outcomes, unforeseeable syntheses" (Barthes, 1957, p. 246). The history of work alone would suffice to corroborate the veracity of that statement, as would better still the history of labour law, which has variously managed in different countries to reconcile work as a tradeable (i.e. the object of a contract) and work as an expression of the person of the worker (i.e. a living subject).

Indeed, work has withstood all attempts at defining it narrowly in terms of opposites, beginning with polarization between the economic and the social – that decoy of contemporary thinking whose ideological and contingent nature has been exposed so convincingly by Emile Durkheim,[10] Louis Dumont (Dumont, 1976) and Karl Polanyi (Polanyi, 1944). Concomitantly subjecting people to the material world and the material world to people, work is part of both material and social life. This fundamental ambiguity of work must be fully recognized if there is to be any chance of glimpsing the unimaginable outcomes its future holds in store.

It then follows that markets – and labour markets in particular – should be conceived not as metaphysical entities to which law and institutions are applicable, but as spheres of trade created by law. The creative role of law in this respect is twofold. First, law sets out the rules of trade without which the market would not function, i.e. the law of contracts, defining the principles of freedom and equality between market operators. Second, it regulates relations between the market and those spheres of social life which lie outside the scope of the rules of commercial trade, e.g. the political sphere (in the broad sense of the Greek *polis*) and the sphere of private life (particularly the family sphere, that of human reproduction). Yet only the first of the two is effectively provided for in today's labour law. Work is identified with that particular form of labour which is supplied by a subordinate in return for pay, through a market. Besides, market institutions were set up nationally,[11] and are therefore ill-prepared for the liberalization of capital movements and trade.

It is the most vulnerable who are now having to bear the brunt of those two shortcomings, in the form of unemployment, precarious living conditions or poverty-line wages. The prerequisites of a balanced life are thus being sapped by lack of work, time or money. The security attaching to work is under threat from the merciless law that capital enforces on labour in the global economy, and from the consequent realignment of legal protection worldwide. The need to adapt work-related human rights to present conditions is thus more pressing than ever.

WORK-RELATED HUMAN RIGHTS

Work-related human rights must extend to each and every form of activity that a person may carry on in the service of another, it being understood that different forms of activity can be carried on concomitantly or successively over a lifetime.

A first distinction must be drawn between unremunerated and remunerated activities. Unremunerated work is probably the more vital for the survival of society. This obviously includes all work performed in the family sphere for the maintenance and reproduction of the labour force (domestic tasks, children's education). But it also includes all the work performed in the public or non-profit sphere within the context of so-called volunteer activities. Generally speaking, this unremunerated work is not performed under contract, but by virtue of a set of rules governing a person's position in society. It remains largely ignored in economic analysis and many still refuse to recognize it as work, preferring to describe it loosely as "activity". Others, however, claim it has huge job creation potential, arguing that all such work should be brought within the scope of paid employment (e.g. through demands for a maternity wage or incentives for hiring domestic help). Either way the result would be to eliminate such work, to deny its intrinsic distinctiveness. Yet any socially useful work should, on the contrary, be underpinned by a coherent set of labour rights and a legal status that would recognize it as being part of a normal working life without detriment to its distinctiveness. Such rules would have to provide for rights already enshrined in labour law, the foremost among them being the principle of equality between men and women.

Remunerated work, by contrast, remains largely polarized between wage employment and self-employment. Indeed, despite its growing imprecision and the proliferation of grey areas, that distinction itself is still meaningful. But this is less true of its implications.

The reason why it remains meaningful is that no market economy could conceivably do without labour markets where capital can procure the human resources it needs for its own development. The futuristic vision of a population of stand-alone teleworkers all connected to the internet has slim chances of ever materializing, whereas subordinated workers producing tangible things – not just symbols – still have a future. Subordination relationships are changing but continue to exist none the less. And subordination calls for a range of specific rights and safeguards, which have been worked out in the course of the historical development of labour law. By contrast to civil law, which is geared to equality and the individual, labour law offers an avenue for legal reasoning on hierarchy and collective issues. From the legal point of view, the distinctiveness of wage employment lies in the fact that it necessarily implies some impairment of personal freedom. It is indeed the very object of wage employment law to limit the extent of that impairment. This is done first by restricting the employer's powers to the strict requirements of the contract of employment and, second, by making up for the workers' loss of personal freedoms with collective rights (trade union rights, right to collective bargaining, right to strike). Along with social security, labour law has been the major legal innovation of this century, and its main lines of reasoning have lost nothing of their relevance (employment contract conferring wage employment status, collective agreement, freedom of association and right to strike). They only need to be continuously adjusted to socioeconomic changes, all the while maintaining their underlying values.

It is thus the implications of the distinction between wage employment and self-employment which need to be seen in less polarized terms. Indeed,

517

while reconciling subordination with personal freedom is an issue that arises only in the context of wage employment, the need for workers' security is common to both wage employment and self-employment. In either case the difficulty lies in reconciling the short time it takes to complete an economic transaction under contract with the length of the human life span. Protection of the worker's physical and economic security is a value common to all forms of contractual work. Yet, it tends to be adequately provided for only in the context of wage employment. Hence the need to develop a common labour law that would apply equally to self-employment and to wage employment. Signs of a move in that direction are already apparent in the fields of occupational safety and health, vocational training and old-age pension rights.

NEW RIGHTS AND ORGANIZATION OF WORK AT THE INTERNATIONAL LEVEL

There are definitely prospects for a comprehensive overhaul of the rights attaching to work. Unless the need for such new rights is taken seriously at the international level, it is bound to exacerbate the nationalist sentiments that are already on the rise everywhere. For this reason, a genuine organization of work at the international level has become more necessary than ever before. Labour is not some "human material" (see Klemperer, 1975) to be moulded to the requirements of industry or trade. For the past 20 years, however, it has been considered a secondary issue throughout the world, as the object of some sort of engineering of human resources. On the one hand, every effort has been made to turn labour into a flexible material, adaptable in real time to the needs of the economy. On the other, social or humanitarian schemes have been devised for the swelling flood of people whom this has deprived of an opportunity to work for a living, in order to provide them with a minimum subsistence or to keep them busy. This approach, combining efficiency and goodwill, makes the issue of labour subordinate to all others and is therefore doomed to failure. Indeed, it is hardly conceivable that millions of people will indefinitely agree to being relegated to the ghetto of the useless. The status given to work is not merely a matter of human resource engineering; it is in effect pivotal to the establishment of a just order.

Notes

[1] All of them are based on presentations to a colloquium "Perspectives on work" held at the Maison des sciences de l'Homme Ange-Guépin, at Nantes (France) on 12-13 April 1996. The proceedings of the colloquium, comprising some 50 presentations, will be published by LGDJ (see Supiot, 1998). The articles published here have been recast by their authors for the benefit of the readers of the *International Labour Review*.

[2] On the theory of self-referencing applied to law, see Teubner, 1994.

[3] This tendency fits the description of what Lucien Sfez (Sfez, 1988) calls "tautism" which occurs when there is no longer any distinction between a given system of representation and what it is supposed to represent.

[4] Under its millennialist title, this rich book offers a thought-provoking vision of the future of work. To Rifkin, the "end of work" is both the decline of jobs that can be done by machines and a question mark hanging over the purpose and meaning of human work in a mechanized world. Far from predicting the end of work, the author concludes that millions of jobs are just waiting to be created in the third sector, "a third force that flourishes independent of the marketplace and the public sector" (p. 239).

[5] This exercise is not without precedent. For a useful investigation of the question of work dating back to the time of France's "social state" in the immediate aftermath of the Second World War, see for example the contributions of Lucien Febvre, André Aymard, Paul Vignaux, Marcel Mauss, Marc Bloch and Georges Friedmann in *Journal de psychologie normale et pathologique* (Paris), Vol. 41 (1948), No. 1 (Jan.-Mar.), a special issue on work and technology

[6] Three of these boundaries of wage employment are examined in other articles in this issue, namely, those by Raymond Le Guidec, Alain Supiot and Françoise Favennec-Hdry. On the distinction between employment and self-employment, see Patrick Chaumette (forthcoming) and the numerous publications of the International Labour Organization on this subject (especially ILO, 1990).

[7] This covers occupations which the law of some countries presumes to fall within the category of wage employment regardless of the degree of subordination that the employment relationship involves (journalists, travelling sales staff, performing artists, etc.).

[8] See also Jean Boissonnat: "Combating unemployment, restructuring work: Reflections on a French study", in *International Labour Review* (Geneva), Vol. 135 (1996), No. 1, pp. 5-15; and in the same issue: "Perspectives: What is the future of work? Ideas from a French report", pp. 93-110.

[9] On the existence of a dominant influence in national legal systems – already observed by Georges Scelle (*Le droit ouvrier: Tableau de la legislation française actuelle*, Second Edition, Paris, A. Cohn, 1929, pp. 212-216) – see Brian Bercusson, Ulrich Mückenberger and Alain Supiot: "Diversité culturelle et droit du travail en Europe", in *Convergence des modèles sociaux européens*, Actes du 4e séminaire sur l'Europe sociale, Paris, Ministry of Labour, Department of Research and Statistics, 1992, pp. 319-328.

[10] According to Durkheim, "since all economic facts – those needed to explain prices, wages, markets, market-driven phenomena – ultimately amount to beliefs or ideas, there is no reason to erect a barrier between economic facts and other facts" (cited by Maurice Halbwachs: *Classe sociale et morphologie,* Paris, Edition de minuit, 1972, p. 393).

[11] Except for the social measures taken in conjunction with the creation of regional markets; on the European case, which makes up in experience what it lacks in substance, see Brian Bercusson: *European labour law*, London, Butterworth, 1996, and "The concept and structure of European labour law", in Alain Supiot (ed.): Actes *du colloque "Le travail en perspectives"*, Paris, LGDJ, 1998.

References

Bachelard, Gaston. 1938. *La formation de l'esprit scientifique: Contribution à une psychanalyse de la connaissance objective.* Fourteenth edition (1989). Paris, J. Vrin.

Barthes, Roland. 1957. *Mythologies.* Paris, Seuil.

Besse, Genevieve. 1994. "Mondialisation des échanges et droits fondamentaux de l'homme au travail", in *Droit social* (Paris), No. 11 (Nov.), pp. 841-849.

Castel, Robert. 1995. *Les métamorphoses de la question sociale: Chronique du salariat.* Paris, Fayard.

Chaumette, Patrick. Forthcoming. "Travail dépendant et travail indépendant", in Alain Supiot (ed.): *Actes du colloque «Le travail en perspectives».* Paris, LGDJ.

Commissariat général du Plan. 1995. *Le travail dans vingt ans* (report of the commission chaired by Jean Boissonnat). Paris, Odile Jacob/La Documentation française.

Dumont, Louis. 1976. *Homo æqualis I. Genèse et épanouissement de l'idéologie économique*. Paris, Gallimard (published in English under the title: *From Mandeville to Marx. The genesis and triumph of economic ideology*. Chicago, University of Chicago Press, 1977).

Emmerij, Louis. 1994. "The employment problem and the international economy", in *International Labour Review* (Geneva), Vol. 144, No. 4, pp. 449-466.

Hansenne, Michel. 1994. "La dimension sociale du commerce international", in *Droit social* (Paris), No. 11 (Nov.), pp. 839-840.

ILO, 1990. *The promotion of self-employment*. International Labour Conference, 77th Session, Report VII. Geneva, ILO.

Klemperer, Victor. 1975. *LTI Notizbuch eines Philologen*. Leipzig, Reclam Verlag.

Legendre, Pierre. 1983. *L'empire de la vérité: Introduction aux espaces dogmatiques industriels*. Paris, Fayard.

van Liemt, Gijsbert. 1989. "Minimum labour standards and international trade: Would a social clause work?", in *International Labour Review* (Geneva), Vol. 128, No. 4, pp. 433-448.

Maindrault, Marc. 1994. "Les aspects commerciaux des droits sociaux et des droits de l'homme au travail", in *Droit social* (Paris), No. 11 (Nov.), pp. 850-855.

Mansfield, Malcolm; Salais, Robert; Whiteside, Noel. 1994. *Au sources du chômage 1880-1914: Une comparaison interdisciplinaire entre la France et la Grande-Bretagne*. Paris, Belin.

Matthies, H.; Mückenberger, U.; Offe, C.; Peter, E.; Raasch, S. 1994. *Arbeit 2000, Anforderungen an eine Neugestaltung der Arbeitswelt*. Reinbek bei Hamburg, Rowohlt Taschenbuch Verlag.

Méda, Dominique. 1995. *Le travail: Une valeur en voie de disparition*. Paris, Aubier.

Moreau, Marie-Ange; Staelens, Patrick; Trudeau, Gilles. 1993. "Nouveaux espaces économiques et distorsions sociales", in *Droit Social* (Paris), No. 7/8 (Jul.-Aug.), pp 686-694.

Polanyi, Karl. 1944. *The Great Transformation: The political and economic origins of our time*. New York, Rinehart.

Rifkin, Jeremy. 1995. *The end of work.. The decline of the global labour force and the dawn of the post-market era*. New York, Putnam.

Salais, Robert; Storper, Michael. 1993. *Les mondes de production: Enquète sur l'identité économique de la France*. Paris, Editions de l'Ecole des hautes études en sciences sociales.

—; Baverez, Nicolas; Reynaud, Bénédicte. 1986. *L'invention du chômage: Histoire et transformations d'une catégorie en France des années 1890 aux années 1980*. Paris, PUF.

Servais, Jean-Michel. 1989. "The social clause in trade agreements: Wishful thinking or an instrument of social progress?", in *International Labour Review*, Vol. 128, No. 4, pp. 423-448.

Sfez, Lucien. 1988. *Critique de la communication*. Paris, Seuil.

Supiot, Alain (ed.). 1998. *Actes du Colloque «Le travail en perspectives»*. Paris, LGDJ.

Teubner, Gunther. 1994. *Droit et réflexivité: L'auto-référence en droit et dans l'organisation*. Paris, LGDJ.

NEW PERSPECTIVES ON WORK AS VALUE

23

Dominique MÉDA *

Developing "perspectives on work" calls for an understanding of how work came to play the all-important role it has in society today: what was the underlying historical process? what forces brought this situation about? In other words, what needs to be done is to lay bare the rationale whereby work – a historically determined construct if ever there was one has come to be regarded as an inherent feature of the human condition, as the only means of fulfilling all individual and social aspirations.

It is high time to put an end to the fruitless debates about whether work is or is not at the centre of modern life and to reveal the historical process whereby work has come to dominate the entirety of individual and social time and space. This is an urgent task – for unless it is undertaken there can be no understanding both why work is today the main vehicle for the formation of social relationships and for self-fulfilment, and that this has not always been the case or will be in the future. The place taken by work in contemporary social organization is an outcome, a fact, not a structural feature of all human societies.

In other words, it is by accident and not on account of the immutable nature of things that work has become the essential mechanism for the achievement of social integration and self-fulfilment, and the origins of this fact lie not buried in the mists of time but in the response to a certain historically situated state of affairs from which the world may now be emerging, and from which it is certainly desirable to emerge. It is necessary to distinguish the question of the amount of work which will be available in the future from the question of the place that work rightfully occupies in personal and societal life.

Originally published in *International Labour Review*, Vol. 135 (1996), No. 6.

* Philosopher. This article is a revised and updated version of an earlier one on the future of work ("La fin de la valeur travail?" in *Esprit* (Paris), No. 214 (Aug.-Sep.), 1995).

The interesting question – and which should be of major concern to every politician and citizen – is this: what are the necessary conditions for the construction and preservation of the good society, that is, a society forming a well-integrated whole, providing a mooring and a source of identity for its citizens, able to deal with all manner of strains, both internal (xenophobia, violence, inequality...) and external, a society unlikely to dissolve into atoms, i.e. into individuals, at the first threat? It is the question of the good constitution, of good government, which all previous societies have had to ask themselves, which has for centuries lain at the heart of political philosophy and practice, and which, alone, our own civilization has neglected to ask.

Work alone – in the sense of paid participation by individuals in the productive process – cannot weave together and sustain the system of social relationships which is central to a society's cohesion and its insertion in a particular historical period. This is especially evident when one sees how the notion of work prevailing today is a misshapen creature resulting from the numerous meanings conferred on the word over the past two hundred years.

THE INVENTION OF WORK

"Work" as a category passed through three broad stages before acquiring the meaning it has today. In the eighteenth century it appears both as a means of increasing wealth and as a mechanism for the emancipation of the individual – another category then emerging. That these two dimensions coincided was significant: if work is an individual service which can be the subject of exchange and of contractual arrangements, it is also the sum of all individual effort – of the efforts and industry of an entire nation – whereby the individual is integrated into society as a whole and social relationships are organized. But at the time work was neither positively valued nor glorified. In the nineteenth century a further crucial dimension was added. The nineteenth century's distinctive contribution was to transform, civilize and humanize the world, whilst also enabling individuals to develop their potential; this process was termed *Bildung* by contemporary German culture and eventually came to be known simply as work. Whether termed a movement of the Spirit, of God or of humanity, it was the leading factor in the humanization of the world.

A true ideology of work emerges during this period, contemporaneously with the proliferation of inhuman working conditions and with the debate on pauperism. Work is presented on the one hand as a truly creative freedom, a symbol of human endeavour whose full realization is fettered by the way in which production is organized and which will provide the basis for the eventual creation of a more just social order based on capacities, on the individual's contribution to production; and, on the other hand, as the facilitating factor of common endeavour.

Work thus becomes a synonym for creation (in the sense that something of the producer's self goes into the object produced, it is a means of self-expression) and at the same time a collective creation (in the sense that by expressing self an image of self is produced for others). As Marx says, once work is no longer alienated and people can produce freely there will be no more need for money since the goods and services produced will reveal people to each other as they are revealed to themselves: "Suppose we had produced things as human beings... Our productions would be so many mirrors reflecting our nature."[1]

This illustrates very well the type of future society imagined by the nineteenth century in general and by Marx in particular: in this vision, production and therefore work are the site of the alchemy of social relationships in a philosophy of mutual expressiveness and recognition. Marx succeeds in synthesizing English political economy and the German philosophy of expressiveness, placing himself in the tradition of a philosophy of humanization: humanity is seen as pursuing not only material affluence, but also the humanization and civilization of the world. From that moment on all utopian hopes and efforts concentrated on the productive sphere: production would not only improve material living conditions but would also create the conditions for the full realization of potential at both personal and social levels. In the same period, in Marx, Proudhon, Louis Blanc and in socialist (and also liberal) philosophy as a whole, work became synonymous with fully human endeavour: the activity proper to humankind is work, and the most fundamentally human activity is work itself.

However, Marx remains consistent, he is aware that work has yet to become a liberating creative activity – or at least that it is still only potentially so, not yet a reality. That basic need will be satisfied only when humanity comes to produce in conditions of absolute freedom, when wage labour is abolished and a world of abundance created. Then work will no longer be equated with drudgery, suffering or sacrifice, it will be pure self-fulfilment, pure expressive power; then and only then will the difference between work and leisure disappear.

Also relevant to our subject, the third stage (which was theorized in German social democracy) consists of a recovery of the socialist heritage the belief in the inherently fulfilling nature of work and in the necessity of the pursuit of abundance – combined with a fundamental change in its doctrinal content. Instead of abolishing wage labour, in both its discourse and practice German social democracy made wages into the vehicle whereby wealth was to be distributed and a new social order – more just because based on labour and on capacities, and truly collective through the organization of the producers – gradually come into being. From then on the State was entrusted with the related tasks of guaranteeing continued economic growth and full employment, in other words of offering to all access to the riches which were pouring forth. But this stands in total contradiction with the thought of Marx, because in the original discourse of social democracy fulfilment was to come from work itself, whereas in this new version it is only thanks to increasing wages and consumption that this can be achieved. In the words of Habermas:

> For the burdens that continue to be connected with the cushioned status of dependent wage labour, the citizen is compensated in his role as client of the welfare state bureaucracies with legal claims, and in his role as consumer of mass-produced goods with buying power. The lever for the pacification of class antagonisms thus continues to be the neutralization of the conflict potential inherent in the status of the wage labourer.[2]

In other words social democracy, which in this sense remains the dominant view today, is based on a profound contradiction (from which contemporary left-wing parties have been unable to extricate themselves) in that it approaches work as the principal path to human fulfilment, both personal and collective, but without providing the means of producing a work of creation (since work is undertaken for a purpose extraneous to itself) let alone a collective work of creation achieved through authentic cooperation. Thus social democracy has confused two conceptions of work which socialist thought had traditionally taken care to distinguish: actually existing, alienated work which is the object of political action aimed at reducing the time it takes up, and freed work, which one day should become life's most basic need albeit fundamentally changing its meaning.

What do we learn from this historical summary? That work is a construct, that it has definitely not always been associated with the creation of value, with the transformation of the natural world, or with self-fulfilment; that it is multi-faceted because of its multiple meanings (as a factor of production, as creative freedom, as a mechanism for the distribution of income, status and security), but also because it is a mixture of elements, some objective and some made up largely of utopia, fantasy and dream. From this two consequences follow: on the one hand we are the victims of a retrospective illusion, believing as we do that work has always existed – are we not told that it is already there in the Bible, that men have worked since time immemorial, even though it is centuries of reinterpretation which forced into one category activities which in their time were experienced in highly diverse ways?[3] On the other hand, contemporary discourse on work does not distinguish between its different dimensions. Does it mean work as a factor of production whose efficiency must constantly increase thus creating ever more wealth, whatever the consequences for the way in which work is undertaken? Does it mean work as the vision of an activity inherent to the human condition, enabling humanity to express itself, for humans to gain mutual recognition and to engage together in creative effort? Or does it simply refer, more prosaically, to employment and the system whereby income, status and security are distributed?

WORK AND THE SOCIAL BOND

This backward glance shows how for the last two centuries work has been the central social bond, the basis for the construction of the "social contract", the foundation of the hierarchy of positions and pay. It then follows – indeed to say so becomes a tautology – that to have work is today the primary condition for belonging to society, the central factor in the construction of a person's identity; that people who are without work lack everything; and that work is the only available collective endeavour, since the rest belongs to the private sphere. This must be the case, since work has become the central axis around which social relations as a whole have come to be organized, in societies which for the last two centuries have made the pursuit of affluence their sole concern. So we simply cannot imagine any other collective endeavour, any way of expressing ourselves or any basis for relating socially to one another save through work. Are we forever condemned to reinvent work, forever driven to place everything under "man's yoke", in accordance with the theories of Bacon, Saint-Simon and Marx, and to do so exclusively in the form of work? As advanced societies succeed in satisfying their needs with an ever-decreasing expenditure of time, will they still feel impelled to seek out ever more opportunities for the creation of value, ever newer horizons to strive towards? When will we finally decide that we have attained this famous state of abundance, the dream after which we have hankered for so long? The answer, of course, is never. Abundance is a limitless concept, the path to it an asymptotic curve leading nowhere.

But perhaps today a point in history has been reached when this line of reasoning ceases to be tenable, when it can finally be realized, on the one hand, that work cannot fulfil all the functions heaped upon it over such a short period, and on the other, that it is precisely on account of our inability to extricate ourselves from traditional modes of thought that we cannot solve our problems. If work is not the only means whereby an individual can achieve self-fulfilment, if it is not necessarily the main vehicle for the tying of social bonds, if the use made of the world can be measured in non-monetary terms, maybe then the attempt to save the social bond by making all activities into work will be seen for the absurdity which it surely is. For, once again, the central problem in contemporary societies is not the growing scarcity of production but rather, first, the criteria of distribution of what is produced, and therefore the question of universal access to what remains the main vector of income distribution and of status allocation; and, second, the extreme fragility of the social bond. Has the time not come to employ some mechanism other than work as the basis for distributing the wealth of a nation and for cementing the social bond?

Returning to the utopian and contradictory expectations which humanity has of work, two points should be emphasized.

First, the idea that work, in the sense of paid participation in the production of goods and services, would be the most appropriate vehicle for personal fulfilment – as some would have it, a "positive passion".[4] This idea should be approached with extreme caution, because it contradicts the fact that work is primarily the means to an end, production, and is therefore subordinate to a force external to itself, namely the logic of ever-increasing efficiency. Also because access to fulfilling types of work is nowadays a realistic prospect for only a small part of the economically active population. And finally, because the small number of surveys of people's perceptions and aspirations show that once the issue of income is removed from the picture, individual aspirations shift to other, freely chosen activities, undertaken under different conditions, at different levels of intensity, and fulfilment ceases to depend exclusively on work. This idea needs developing: work is not the only way for individuals to find fulfilment, and if one could but recall that the reduction operated by Marx in relation to Hegel's thought consisted precisely in combining the many means of civilizing the world into the single category of work, it would become clear that what in German is called "culture" cannot and should not be reduced to work.

The time has come to restore to words their proper meaning and to stop confusing culture – the development of human capacities with all the suffering, creation, and joy that entails – with work alone, as if reading, learning, education, art, friendship, cuisine, and no doubt much else besides should all be subsumed under the heading of work. To believe that these are all merely work, to confound these highly varied activities and ways of living out one's humanity with a paid activity whose sole recompense is as a contribution to national product, is to confound action with production – yet, as Aristotle already explained, life is action not production. Stated in even clearer terms, the last two centuries have seen not the reduction of a timeless pseudo-concept of work to paid work, but rather the reduction of the entire range and variety of activities to work alone – and thus the invention of the concept of work itself.

And second, it is also time to undertake a thorough reappraisal of the idea that work is the only way to create and maintain the social bond indeed, to question the very nature of a social bond which is shaped by work. To be sure, there will be some who say that over time work has been intimately related to economics and that economics itself creates a particular social bond in which all are needed for each individual's subsistence and in which participation in the functioning of society is linked to each person's ability to contribute to production and therefore to exchange. But is this type of social bond an adequate basis for society? As Louis Dumont and, more recently, Alain Supiot[5] and Robert Castel[6] have said, it is on account of the institution of contract and of the labour market that it became possible for a more "egalitarian" social order to emerge, for the dominance of ties of personal dependence to be overcome, and for individuals to be emancipated from traditional forms of authority. At the same time the chance to transform part of one's abilities into money, into unconstrained purchasing power, has contributed greatly to strengthening the basis of individual independence. This no one could deny, least of all women for whom this emancipation has recently progressed at an accelerated pace. But the problem is whether this is history's last word or whether, after the successive stages of communities founded on personal dependence *(Gemeinschaft)* and later on contract and personal autonomy, it is now possible, indeed indispensable, to move on to a third stage in which the advantages of the first two would be preserved and, above all, the disadvantages of contract-based societies overcome.

In other words, does the economic bond alone suffice to create a true sense of belonging, of belonging together, a true solidarity among the members of society? For that is the central issue in the debate on the social "fracture" and on social "cohesion" (two concepts which should also one day be subjected to a more critical gaze). That is undeniably the issue at stake, when the question is asked whether society can achieve a measure of cohesion and whether we have the means to implement policies to reduce the social polarization currently attracting so much attention. But before such policies can be evolved, society needs first to be represented as having a reality, a good of its own, its existence and cohesion must themselves be regarded as a good. And in that case, is there any use for the model of society and its underlying philosophy offered by the discipline of economics?

CRITIQUE OF ECONOMICS

It is reasonable to hold that contemporary economics, whose theoretical foundations are those developed by eighteenth-century economists despite the vast changes in the subject since then, continues to be based on a profoundly dated conception of humanity and society, in which society only ever appears as the external framework for autonomous individuals who conduct exchanges according to rules which, though social in nature, are still, like society, ultimately the creation of those individuals alone. Economics has kept to the individualist and contractualist assumptions of a period which never succeeded in imagining society as something more than the result of a contract between individuals who perforce lost something of themselves on their entry into that society. For the same reason, the eighteenth century was never able to imagine social riches as something more than the sum of individuals' enrichment through exchange, and had no concept of wealth as a heritage held in trust. In other words, economics sees no value in an individual's development towards a goal other than exchange, or in any form of "enrichment" of society which has a truly collective (as opposed to an aggregative) dimension or is measurable in terms other than those of "production".

527

For economics, then, no value can be placed either on the existence of healthy, peace-loving, happy, civically aware, tolerant, non-violent individuals, or on the establishment of a "good society", that is a just, peace-seeking, closely knit and cultivated society. Economics conceives of social wealth only in the form of increasing GNP because it continues to hold to a representation of society as a mere "collection of individuals". And it cannot develop a broader conception thereof because it continues to believe in the eighteenth-century assumptions that the expansion of wealth will suffice for individuals to become sufficiently employed and civilized so as to live together. Economists also continue to believe that increasing production is good in itself, since in that way all those vast unsatisfied needs can be met, even though for the most part this expansion does not meet the needs of the most deprived, because such issues are regarded as falling outside the subject's competence – as belonging rather to ethics. I would only recall the following from the critique of economics which I have developed at greater length elsewhere:[7] just as the invention of the contract signified an enormous step forward in the formalization of human relations in the eighteenth century and provided the basis for individual autonomy, so economics provided the extremely valuable tools which opened the way to the formalization and conceptualization of the increase in production which our countries needed, and thus underpinned a particular way of developing the world. In the process, however, economics concentrated all attention on one particular means of creating value, and concealed from view other dimensions, other means of translating human capabilities into value and developing them, in short, other ways of living in society.

Even if economists respond to this criticism by maintaining that they do not confuse growth indicators with welfare indicators, that confusion does exist, and all the more so because of the absence of the time, the space and the structures necessary to translate the world into value by means other than those measured in monetary terms. When Hegel said that civil society – the locus of political economy, needs and individual interest – should be circumscribed and integrated in a political community, he meant precisely that there are several ways of approaching the civilization of the world and of participating in the life of society: to be sure, contribution to the production of goods and services has its place, but so do political activities, religion, art, philosophy, science, and the elaboration of ever more sophisticated ways of living and cooperating, whether in the form of political institutions, rules of justice or whatever.

From the beginning of the nineteenth century a particular current of thought drew attention to the dangers arising from a purely economic approach to the development of the world, and also to the dual character of the economic bond: its emancipatory potential, but also its potential for bringing about the dissolution of established societies. Hegel and Tocqueville developed their theories at the same time and on the same theme: civil (or bourgeois) society represented the destruction of the old feudal order and the rise of a new one based on individual freedom and equality, but also contained the seeds of a new danger: the "atomization" of society, on account of its inability to preserve a minimum of solidarity and effective bonds. Hence these writers' obsessive concern to confine purely economic logic within certain limits and their desire to integrate it into a political community of rights and duties based on institutions and giving substance to the social bond. Thus it can be seen – as an entire German tradition from Hegel to Habermas, passing through Hannah Arendt, has insisted – that to make a society, and especially a good society, production alone is not enough, political institutions must also be built, loci where social bonds are forged in some other way than by mere juxtaposition in mechanical productive cooperation. It is also necessary to talk, discuss, debate, and participate, to provide not only for the sphere devoted to production, but also for the continuous existence of a public sphere set aside for debate, for specifically political activity.

Smith and Marx both believed that the social order could be founded on production, and also that these conflicts, agreements and disagreements, taken together, could be solved in the sphere of production alone. They denied the need for a specifically political sphere which could impose rules and limits on the productive sphere but also counterbalance it, raise issues and develop types of relationship having nothing to do with production of any kind. This belief seems to be shared by those who, today, disagree with the need to reduce the space occupied by work, production and economics so as to create a truly public, and therefore political, space. Such is the place taken by production that this is now thought to be virtually impossible: very little room is left between those who believe that individuals would use time freed up in this way not to take part in politics but rather to extend their leisure activities, and those who think that politics is far too serious a business to be left to the ignorant masses.

And yet, with a populist note entering the highly justified criticism of elites which has been going on, though barely audibly and quite ineffectively, perhaps the time has come to reflect on the relationship between economic and productive development on the one hand, and the "depoliticization of the masses", as Habermas calls it, on the other. The issue is not one of repoliticizing the masses, but rather of developing public spaces where choice and democracy can be effectively exercised, which means at the most local level, and in this way to redistribute not only work (and its fruits) but also political activity in the simplest, noblest and most straightforward sense of the word – namely the discussion of ends to pursue, of the means to be marshalled to attain them, and of the sharing-out of wealth and functions. In other words, the task ahead is to reduce the space occupied by work so as to make way for the activity which is essential to the long-term cohesion of societies and which has the best prospect of cementing the social bond, namely the activity of politics.

THE AMBIGUOUS NOTION OF A FULLY ACTIVE SOCIETY

This idea presupposes two simultaneous shifts: a reduction of the place taken by work in individual and social life (with the work to be done spread across the whole working population), and the development, in the time and space thus vacated by work, of new private and public activities – related on the one hand to friendship, family and emotional and cultural life, on the other to the public sphere and politics in particular – which are at least as essential to individual fulfilment and to democracy. This idea deserves the status of a normative ideal to guide action, and thus to ward off the worst of the fates now haunting society, namely polarization, fragmentation and atomization.

Other "solutions" have recently been proposed to these problems. The ideas of a universal social benefit (in recognition of the weakening link between work and income) or of the emergence of a third sector (of voluntary, "convivial" or solidarity-based activities to provide for those excluded from the formal productive sector)[8] both seem to contain the seeds of a process of polarization. Both are founded on the incapacity of an ever-increasing number of individuals to remain within the traditional productive system for whom a "softer" alternative is arranged, leading in all likelihood in the medium-to-long term to a second-rate existence compared with that led by the managers of the established productive system. A life with less security, fewer rights and lower status.

Other possible solutions remain stuck in the narrow and misguided framework of traditional indicators of wealth and continue to focus exclusively on the growth of commercial exchanges of goods and services, without any concern for the content of this growth or for its redistribution. These solutions do nothing to help solve the central issue of the quality of the individual elements constituting the social bond and offer no response to the "democratic deficit" which is as much a problem for society today as the employment deficit and the uneven distribution of work.

The normative ideal proposed here points towards what might well be called a fully active society, but only on condition that such full activity characterizes not only society as a whole but also each individual. A society in which it is acceptable that some can have good, secure and well-paid jobs, while others undertake socially useful jobs with less security and less pay, cannot avoid the risk of division.

A fully active society is one which ensures each individual access to the entire range of human activities or, more precisely, to the whole range of activities which the individual is capable of undertaking alone or as part of a group. This means that everyone should simultaneously have access to political, productive and cultural activities, as well as to the private activities involving friendship, family and emotional ties. Thus the idea of full activity goes far beyond the merely productive to encompass the entirety of human activities necessary for personal and social fulfilment in all its diversity and richness.

This does not mean replacing work with political or private activity. It means preventing productive activity from invading all the available individual and social time and space, thus permitting a new organization of the various uses individuals make of their time, and their coordination with the allocation of time by society as a whole.

With this ideal of multi-activity it will be possible to intervene legitimately in the time-space left to work: only once the value of speech, debate, education, and leisure time to our immediate surroundings and to the functioning of society itself has been demonstrated, will the formulation of consistent work and employment policies be possible.

For the time being, if these ideas appear utopian, that is because there is no scale by which to measure the benefits for society of healthy individuals, inclined to peaceful coexistence and mature discussion, untainted by racism and living in a less polluted atmosphere. And this is because of the limitations of eighteenth-century conceptions of wealth – which would be called medieval did they not date back merely two hundred years – and of the contractualist vision of society which was the cornerstone of the "science", especially the economics, of that time.

So long as the "wealth" of a society continues to be defined exclusively as the result of the commercial exchange of material goods and services – a definition roughly embodied in national accounts – one remains caught in this vicious circle. For this reason, if society aspires to the possibility one day of a careful redistribution of work among individuals, to a genuine practice of political activity in an appropriate public sphere (above all, the city) and to the articulation of different social time frames, then one must reconsider what is meant by the wealth of a society (in terms of flows but especially stock, comprising human as well as material qualities) and by the vision which underlies it.

It is possible to describe this solution as "full employment" (avoiding misleading debates on the disappearance or replacement of work, or the alarmist talk about people renouncing the goal of full employment). In this perspective, full employment would simply mean that everyone has access to employment on a fair and equitable basis, but that this employment occupies fewer hours, leaving everyone the space and time to devote to other private and collective activities.

If this is the desired form of full employment and if the real question is the best way to base the political community on solidarity and to breathe life into the social bond, then it must also be the case that the solution to the employment problem necessitates a vast public debate on the purpose of life in society, on the nature of society's riches, and on the distribution of basic goods (including work itself) which will do most to promote social cohesion.

With this approach as given, one can but agree with the provocative view recently expressed by Renaud Camus that there is no employment problem.[9]

Notes

[1] Karl Marx: "Excerpt-notes of 1844", in G. Hillman (ed.): *Texte zu Methode und Praxis*, Hamburg, 1966, pp. 180ff; translated in David McLellan: *Marx before Marxism*, London, Macmillan, 1970, p. 179. For an interpretation of Marx's concept of work, see Dominique Méda: *Le travail: une valeur en disparition*, Paris, Aubier, 1995, Ch. IV.

[2] Jürgen Habermas: "The new obscurity: The crisis of the Welfare State and the exhaustion of utopian energies", in *The new conservatism: Cultural criticism and the historian's debate*, Cambridge, Polity Press, 1989, p. 55.

[3] For further details on the way in which history is retrospectively represented, and on societies without work, see Dominique Méda, op. cit., Ch. II, "Des sociétés sans travail?".

[4] Daniel Mothé: "Le mythe du temps libéré", in *Esprit* (Paris), No. 204 (Aug.-Sep.), 1994.

[5] Alain Supiot: "Le travail, liberté partagée", in *Droit social* (Paris), No. 9/10 (Sep.), 1993, p. 715.

[6] Robert Castel: *Les métamorphoses de la question sociale: chronique du salariat*, Paris, Fayard, 1994.

[7] Dominique Méda, op. cit., Ch. VIII, "Critique de l'économie", and Ch. IX, "Réinventer la politique".

[8] As in, for example, Jeremy Rifkin: *The end of work*, New York, G. B. Putnam's Sons, 1995; or Jean-Marc Ferry: *L'allocation universelle*, Paris, Cerf, 1995.

[9] Renaud Camus: *Qu'il n'y a pas de problème de l'emploi*, Paris, P.O.L., 1994.

WORK AND THE PUBLIC/PRIVATE DICHOTOMY

Alain SUPIOT *

24

An opposition between the public and the private, between the State and civil society permeates conceptions of society. Thus it is hardly surprising that this opposition should also have influenced conceptions of work. Both through privileges and through the specific responsibilities attaching to them, the service of the public has become distinct from that of the private individual.

The Welfare State led to steady growth in the number of persons working for or in the public sphere, whilst state control over employment relationships in the private sphere increased. But the 1980s were marked by a reaction to this growing ascendancy of the public sphere. Privatization replaced nationalization as a political motto, and deregulation policies reduced state-imposed requirements under labour law (that is to say, the ascendancy of the public authorities over employment relationships).

As a result, the question of work could not be put in perspective today without reflecting on the opposition between public and private: what impact does it still have on the organization of employment relationships? Is there an irreducible distinctiveness to work in the public service? Or is the model of work in the private sphere being generalized? These questions are not merely academic. The strikes held in France in December 1995 showed how public service interests can be invoked in opposition to economic globalization and its impact on the situation of working people.

The main contribution of academic work is not so much to find answers to such questions (practice takes care of that, with more or less success); rather it is to help formulate the questions aptly. Indeed, where work is concerned, the opposition between public and private is deceptive in many respects.[1] Its real nature is only revealed upon closer observation.

Originally published in *International Labour Review*, Vol. 135 (1996), No. 6.

* Professor at the Faculty of Law and Political Science, University of Nantes.

The pertinent question is no longer that of the respective importance of the public and private spheres in the establishment of employment relationships, but that of the relationship between work and the public interest.

PUBLIC V. PRIVATE – A DECEPTIVE DICHOTOMY

A successful illusion effectively deceives the eye and, viewed from a distance, presents a sight whose deceptiveness is revealed only on closer inspection.

The view from afar: The public sphere losing ground to the private

The first impression which emerges from the examination of employment relations in Europe is that the public sphere is generally in retreat relative to the private sphere.

This is epitomized by the situation in the United Kingdom, where the various forms of privatization undertaken have been analysed in depth:[2]

(a)   the most radical form is the direct substitution of the private for the public: public enterprises or services are incorporated as limited companies and their shares sold to investors;

(b)   an intermediate form is where the private and public spheres are made to compete: the law may require that certain services be opened to subcontracting; the service concerned can itself invite tenders on the opened market, and so-called "non-commercial" considerations (which include the working conditions of the subcontractor) do not have to be taken into account in awarding a contract;

(c)   the last form of asserting the private model consists in requiring the public service to reorganize as if it were private. This is the "quasi-market" approach whereby a public service is broken up into autonomous entities, which are linked by customer-supplier-type "contracts".

Although public servants in the United Kingdom do not have a separate status in relation to other workers, the trend towards privatization has considerably affected the working conditions of the employees concerned: collective bargaining has become fragmented or has quite simply disappeared; priority is given to returns to shareholders; and, finally, the pressure of competition forces down labour costs.

The situation in Italy shows privatization in a different light:[3] the privatization of employment rather than of employers. Unlike the United Kingdom, Italy had legislated a special employment status for public servants. But it has now undertaken to subject employment in the public sector to standard labour law, which has thus become the common body of law governing employees in both the public and the private sectors. Pursuant to Decree No. 29/1993, which was the outcome of legislative developments begun in 1982, public administration employees are governed by the provisions of the Civil Code pertaining to salaried employees. The situation of those workers no longer depends on unilateral decisions by public authorities, but on collective agreements to be negotiated sector by sector. This constitutes a veritable legal revolution, which has made private law the sole reference for all types of employment relationships.

In between the British and Italian models one finds those countries which, although retaining a distinct body of public service law, have reduced its scope or distinctiveness.

The reduction in the scope of public service law is a corollary of the privatization of services of common economic interest (postal services, telecommunications, railways, etc.), which is variously under way in all European countries. In Germany, for example, standard labour law will be applied gradually to all such services, and civil service recruitment has ceased.

That public sector employment has become less distinctive is a result of the transposition of certain labour law principles: the general tendency is to bring modes of public service management into line with the managerial model of private undertakings,[4] to contractualize employment relationships and to reduce the number of rules laid down unilaterally by the public authorities. These trends are highlighted by the experience of the Dutch[5] and French[6] public services, especially that of France's *entreprises à statut du personnel*, public enterprises whose staff is subject to public service employment rules.[7]

The principles of private sector labour law are also making inroads into the public sphere at the international level. The ILO's Labour Relations (Public Service) Convention, 1978 (No. 151), makes no distinction between the private or the public nature of the post held. The same applies under the European Union law with the principle of equality between men and women, the European Council's Framework Directive No. 89/391/EEC of 12 June 1989 on safety at work (*Official Journal of the European Communities (OJEC)* (Brussels) No. L 83, 29 June 1989), Directive 93/104/EEC of 23 November 1993 on working time (*OJEC*, No. L 307, 13 Dec. 1993), or with certain essential provisions of the Community Charter of Fundamental Social Rights. And although the Treaty of Rome does recognize the specificity of public service employment (Art. 48), the Luxembourg Court of Justice has interpreted this concept restrictively.[8]

The fact that the public sector is being challenged by the values and procedures of the private sector is felt very strongly by the workers themselves. This was shown by a survey of Paris public transport employees involved in the large-scale strike in December 1995 to defend their special retirement schemes.[9] These public employees saw the plans for bringing their pensions into line with the general pension scheme for salaried employees as a threat to their public law employment status, that embodying the fundamental quid pro quo which gives meaning to their work and substantiates their obligations. To them, defending their distinctive status meant defending public service values, while at the same time defending themselves against a drift towards the most precarious forms of private employment.

The vision of a public sphere losing ground to the values and methods of the private is thus socially meaningful. It determines the behaviour of public sector employees, just as it prompted privatization policies. But closer scrutiny of current developments shows that vision to be distorted: what is really happening is less a decline of the public sphere than a restructuring of relations between the private and public spheres.

A closer look: The intermeshing of public and private

In the transformations under way, the private and the public remain indissociable elements of institutional structures within which the public has lost nothing of its strength or importance. The continuance of those structures is manifest in the new forms of public service organization. It is also reflected in the changing pattern of employment relationships in the private sector, where the State continues to play a decisive role.

The decline in the role of the State as employer has gone hand in hand with a rapid expansion of its regulatory function. This shift is particularly obvious in the case of the United Kingdom where, far from being in decline, the role of the State has never been so pronounced (Deakin, see note 2). It was the State which, for the sake of promoting competition, imposed the restructuring of entire branches of the economy. It is the State which issues operating licences and controls the pricing system and the quality of services through regulatory agencies in industries which it considers essential. It is again the State which requires that certain services be subcontracted on such terms as it dictates (hence the British Courts' extension of certain rules specific to civil servants to the employees of subcontractors). And, lastly, it is also the State which organizes the "quasi-markets" within the non-privatized public services.

This persistent role of the State can be seen in other countries as well. In Italy, for example (Ballestero, see note 3), although the public sector is open to collective bargaining, it is the State which dictates the very inflexible framework for that bargaining, defines bargaining sectors, and conducts the bargaining through a central agency which is directly responsible to the Government *(ARAN: Agenzia per la rappresentanza negoziale)*. The law makes provision for a public interest reservation clause entitling the State to intervene unilaterally in labour relations at any time it deems necessary. It also excludes several crucial issues from the scope of collective bargaining – payroll development, the rules governing access to employment and the rules governing "incompatibilities" (i.e. conflicts of interest) – which still fall exclusively within the purview of the public authorities.

In the Netherlands, where collective bargaining has been made compulsory in the civil service, the resulting collective agreements are not self-executing. Their implementation requires regulations whose effect *erga omnes* is without parallel in the general law of collective bargaining in that country. The State as an employer thus remains indissociable from the State as a public authority with the capacity to impose provisions unilaterally at any time (Rood, see note 5). The same applies in France, where the introduction of collective agreements in public enterprises has not led to the elimination of the public service employment status, the conditions of which are determined unilaterally by the State (Moreau, see note 4; Maggi Germain, see note 7).

However, the continuing role of the State is not confined to employment relationships in the public service; it can also be seen in the changes brought about in the private sector. In this sense, deregulation would seem to be a particularly deceptive concept. This was one of the lessons of a comparative analysis of the role of the State and of the social partners in the economic transformations which came about in Western Europe during the 1980s.[10] That analysis debunks generally accepted ideas by demonstrating the decisive role played by the State in those transformations in most European countries. This is hardly surprising in the case of France, where the weakness of both employers' and workers' organizations allowed the State full scope to take the economic lead. But the State's role was just as important in the United Kingdom, where an alliance between the Conservative Government and employers made it possible to break a system of industrial relations previously characterized by the absence of intervention by the public authorities. In Germany, however, the State was until recently unable to sway the social partners, who were sufficiently strong and responsible to determine the course of change themselves. To the extent that "less State" is a value, this value has been respected most in those countries which have "deregulated" employment relations the least.

Developments in labour law in Europe during this period also run counter to the idea of a decline of the public sphere. In its own way, every country's labour law makes private-law relationships subject to a number of public policy rules. And while such rules have admittedly been relaxed on some points (e.g. on employment security, with the development of precarious contracts or abolition of the administrative clearance requirement for dismissal), they have been tightened on others (including in the United Kingdom, e.g. in respect of gender equality or workers' representation, particularly under the influence of European Union law). What has happened is not a decline of state supervision, but a shift in its focus. While state protection is diminishing for the most vulnerable workers, it is continuing to increase for regular employees and even more so for managerial staff, as reflected in the recent developments in French labour law. This trend reflects a "dualization" of the world of work, not the deregulation of work in the legal sense of the term.

Thus the issue is not so much a decline of the public sphere in relation to the private as a profound transformation of the way the two interact. In every country, contractual arrangements are increasingly being used to stimulate competition both amongst undertakings and amongst workers themselves. Yet in no instance has this trend meant that services in the public interest have been simply abandoned to the "laws" of the market. The question is not one of opposition between public and private, but the relation between work and the public interest.

REDEFINING THE LINK BETWEEN WORK
AND THE PUBLIC INTEREST

Rather than the relative importance of public versus private sector employment or the rules by which each is governed, it is the root of the relation between work and the public interest that must be examined. First of all, by its very nature, work can be in the public interest. The question is then whether work in the service of the community must obey particular rules. Yet work is not only the *means* of serving certain interests; it is also the *end* of a number of public policies. In other words, work is itself a matter of public interest. Each of these two aspects of the question calls for investigation, devoting attention not only to legal or macroeconomic factors but also to actual work situations.[11]

The concept of work in the public interest

The time has come to recast the concept of public service. In Western Europe, public service is still clearly constrained by requirements of continuity and general access, to which no private undertaking would subject itself voluntarily. There is serious cause to doubt that competition invariably promotes economic efficiency, and one can query the implications of public incentives which reduce costs in the short term but encourage neither the quality of labour nor that of the products and services supplied (Deakin, see note 2). In Europe, however, the situation in this respect resembles that of a country whose government has been reduced to a competition council (Moreau, see note 4). The view that the current organization of work has lost sight of public interest is widely shared by workers who strike in defence of the public service.[12] As a Paris bus driver put it, "The private sector isn't interested in providing transport for three people ... it isn't profitable ... So they do the morning and evening rush hour, and the rest of the time it's your problem. That's the way it is. Public service is on its way out!"

Even where the State or undertakings dependent on it provide such services, public service requirements are not necessarily satisfied. Indeed, the public has come to expect more than just continuity and generality of service. According to a recent European survey, the foremost requirement is now quality.[13] Except for minimum services designed for those who cannot afford to procure higher quality services on the market, public services cannot ignore the demand for quality, which stems from the diversification of supply and needs.

The quality requirement implies that the nature of the service provided takes precedence over the legal status of the undertaking which provides it. Anyone trying to view the situation through the old public! private prism is therefore bound to end up squinting. A case of this "institutional squint" can be observed in what happened to the concept of services of general economic interest provided for in the Treaty of Rome (Art. 90). This concept could have provided an opportunity to arrive at a Community definition of welfare. But the institutional criterion exerted such a strange influence over the definition of those services that, instead of providing a basis for dynamic reflection on the concept of European public interest, Article 90 has become a conservatory – ill-tended, at that – of national representations of public interest.[14] The same applies to European transport policy. As regards roads, the policy is one of total *laissez-faire, laissez-passer*[15] entailing a spectacular deterioration of the environment, working conditions and safety: 50,000 people are killed and 1.6 million injured on Europe's roads every year (referring to the Community of 12 countries).[16] As regards railways, by contrast, Europe is a juxtaposition of national, State-controlled networks.[17] The overall picture looks as though the reference to "service of general economic interest" only makes sense at the national level.[18]

For things to change, the question of public interest in transport would have to be seen as a whole,[19] taking road transport and railway transport together. For both modes of transport, this might result in agonizing soul-searching. On the one hand, it would have to be acknowledged that public interest considerations call for much greater constraints on road transport, particularly for social and environmental reasons. On the other hand, the public benefit of the monopolies and rules governing the rail sector would have to be thoroughly reconsidered. In both cases, reflection on the public interest in transport would inevitably affect the rules governing employment in that sector.

To take the pragmatic approach, based on the nature of the service provided, would imply acknowledging not only that work performed in the private sphere can serve the public interest but also, conversely, that serving the public interest can, in some cases, be incompatible with serving the State. This is particularly true of activities which contribute to the exercise of a number of public rights or freedoms. For example, journalism, trade unionism, teaching, research, and defence at law are activities which presuppose independence both from the public authorities and from the influence of private interests. Whether such activities are carried out in the private or in the public sphere is less important than whether or not there are rules guaranteeing their independence.

It is from that perspective that the need for separate rules on work in the public interest must now be examined. This can only be done case by case, having regard to the particular nature of each service. By managing the inter-dependencies it creates, a service in the public interest actually replicates the whole range of economic and social situations which the market tends to manage in a unidimensional way (Moreau, see note 4). The professional rules needed to meet the requirements of generality, continuity and quality of service should therefore be set for each individual type of service. The rules are bound to vary depending on whether the service involves providing transport or information, supplying energy, providing care or teaching, though they can be common both to the private and public sectors and to a set of countries, such as those of the European Union.

Some have used the term "professional codes of ethics" to refer to the sets of rules which could be negotiated at the union level and subsequently applied to all providers of a particular service (Moreau; Supiot; Villeneuve, see notes 4, 14 and 13, respectively). But the idea of a code of ethics may present a drawback in that it stresses only those duties incumbent upon workers, whereas serving the public interest implies special duties for both workers and employers. Besides, the constraints inherent in this type of service must be compensated through special rights for the undertakings and workers providing the service.

The public interest in work

All work involves both private and public considerations and, contrary to what is naively argued by deregulation advocates, private contract law cannot suffice to govern employment relationships. As is the case with public services, the question of labour law cannot be resolved by recourse only to the private sphere. Labour law embodies a combination of public and private concerns, and it is their combination which needs to be recast.

Firstly, a combination of public and private concerns is inevitable when it comes to the rights of the person at work. In this respect, any distinction between a labour law governed by private law rules and a public service law governed by public law is bound to be approximate at the least. For the last century there has been a two-way process whereby public policy rules have been penetrating labour law and rules protecting the individual have been penetrating public service law. The State cannot ignore work in the private sphere, for the conditions, volume and quality of that work directly affect the physical, psychological and economic state of the nation. Conversely, under a democratic constitution, the State can no longer deny its employees rights or freedoms which it guarantees in the private sphere (freedom of association, gender equality, etc.).

Here again, there can be no question of returning to the mythical purity of a labour law purged of all public regulation or a public service law purged of trade unionism, public servants' strikes and all forms of collective bargaining. Rather, the point would be to ensure that the balance of public and private concerns achieved in both cases continues to meet public interest requirements satisfactorily. But it is doubtful whether this is actually happening, for labour law and public service law both present symptoms of increasing dualism: protection and guarantees for the weakest workers are being eroded, while protection and guarantees for those at the top of the scale are being extended. France, for example, would only stand to gain from subjecting its senior civil servants and the top management of its major corporations (whether private or public) to the values of insecurity and responsibility which they are so eager to preach to the country's workers, and, conversely, from extending to workers in precarious employment the economic security through job diversity which is currently the prerogative of those high-ranking officials.

Secondly, the combination of public and private concerns derives from the close connections between work and the life of the community. Industrial work in particular has imposed its pace and requirements on every aspect of social life. Time is organized accordingly, as are the forms of solidarity to which people still adhere in large part. In this respect, the interests of a nation could be identified with those of its enterprises: whatever was good for Ford was good for the United States. Today, however, international capital mobility, technological change and the individualization of life-styles in Western countries are divesting the enterprise of its role as a focal point of social life. Hence the idea that the private, market sphere and the public, citizenship sphere are ineluctably drifting apart, divesting work of its formerly central role in social life. In line with that view, the various forms of social solidarity (such as social security) should devolve to the public sphere alone and enterprises would no longer have any responsibility in that respect.

Opposing the public and the private spheres in this way leads to an underestimation of the bonds which unite them and to the belief that those bonds are being lost, whereas they are in fact just changing. The concept of economic globalization, while pertinent in many respects, must not be equated with the fantasy of "an economy without a territory". On the contrary, it is the comparative advantages of a given territory or society which attract capital to one country rather than another. This locational concern [20] means that where the enterprise ceases to be a focal point for the community, it is the community which becomes a focal point for the enterprise. No enterprise can thrive sustainably in an impoverished and dangerous public environment. The fact that major enterprises have opened up to concerns of public interest and to the quality of their social and natural environment derives not from any particular virtue of citizenship but from the pursuit of their own interests (Villeneuve; Moreau, see notes 13 and 14, respectively).

* * *

The analysis of the opposition of public and private which served as the point of departure has thus proved fruitful. Once stripped of their political and ideological trappings, moves to privatize or deregulate employment relationships suggest a redefinition of the relation between public and private rather than a decline of the public in relation to the private. The underlying challenge is to redefine the public interest which work is to serve or embody. The real issue is thus to agree on what that interest is and on what its implications are for the status of work in society.

Notes

[1] Alain Supiot (ed.): *Actes du Colloque "Le travail en perspectives"*, Paris, Presses Universitaires de France, forthcoming. This publication will bring together the papers presented to the Colloquium "Perspectives on Work" held at the Maison des sciences de l'Homme Ange-Guépin, Nantes, France, 1213 April 1996.

[2] Simon Deakin: "Privatisation des entreprises et droit du travail en Grande-Bretagne", in Supiot (ed.), op. cit. (see note 1).

[3] Maria-Vittoria Ballestero: "Emploi privé, emploi public: de la différence au droit commun", in Supiot (ed.), op. cit. (see note 1).

[4] Yannick Moreau: "Transformation de la relation de travail dans les entreprises publiques", in Supiot (ed.), op. cit. (see note 1).

[5] Max Rood: "Some aspects of Dutch civil servants law", in Supiot (ed.), op. cit. (see note 1).

[6] Jacques Caillosse: "Le statut de la fonction publique et la division de l'ordre juridique français", in Supiot (ed.), op. cit. (see note 1).

[7] Nicole Maggi-Germain: "La contractualisation des relations de travail dans les entreprises publiques à statut", in Supiot (ed.), op. cit. (see note 1).

[8] Court of Justice of the European Communities (CJEC): *Commission of the European Communities v. the Kingdom of Belgium*, judgment of 17 Dec. 1980, case 149/79, in *European Court Reports* (Luxembourg), 1980-8, pp. 3881-3919; *Commission of the European Communities v. the French Republic*, judgment of 3 June 1986, case 307/84, in *European Court Reports* (Luxembourg), 1986-6, pp. 1725-1740; *Commission of the European Communities v. the Italian Republic*, judgment of 16 June 1987, case 225/85, in *European Court Reports* (Luxembourg), 1987-6, pp. 2625-2754; *Pilar Allué and Carmel Mary Coonan v. Università degli studi di Venezia*, judgment of 30 May 1989, case 33/88, in *European Court Reports (Luxembourg)*, 1989-5, pp. 1591-1613. See also V. L. Dubouis: "La notion d'emploi dans l'administration publique et l'accès des ressortissants communautaires aux emplois publics", in *Revue française de droit administratif* (Paris), 1987, pp. 949-962.

[9] Olivier Schwartz: "Enquête sur la question corporative dans le mouvement social de décembre 1995", in Supiot (ed.), op. cit. (see note 1).

[10] Bob Hanké: "Labour relations, business coordination and economic adjustment in Western Europe 1980-1990", in Supiot (ed.), op. cit. (see note 1).

[11] Yves Schwartz: "Le juridique et l'industrieux", in Supiot (ed.), op. cit (see note 1).

[12] Olivier Schwartz: "Figures et tensions du collectif dans le monde salarié d'aujourd'hui: le cas des machinistes de la RATP", in Supiot (ed.), op. cit. (see note 1).

[13] Robert Villeneuve: "Dialogue social élargi et excellence territoriale", in Supiot (ed.), op. cit. (see note 1).

[14] Alain Supiot: "Le travail au service de l'intérêt général", in Supiot (ed.), op. cit. (see note 1).

[15] The quotas designed to avoid excess supply were scrapped (see Council Regulation (EEC) No. 1841/88 of 21 June 1988, in *OJEC*, No. L 163, 30 June 1988; and Council Regulation (EEC) No. 881/92 of 26 Mar. 1992, in *OJEC*, No. L 95, 9 Apr. 1992). Charging the carriers of one State for using the infrastructure of another was ruled contrary to the Treaty (see CJEC: *Commis-*

sion v. Germany, judgment of 12 July 1990, case C-195/90R, in *OJEC,* No. C 199, 8 Aug. 1990). Road transport prices were deregulated (see Council Regulation (EEC) 4058/89 of 21 Dec. 1989, in *OJEC,* No. L 390 of 30 Dec. 1989), resulting in lower pay for those working in the sector and prompting demands for a "mileage/safety rate" (see *Transport Bulletin* 1990.593).

[16] European transport policy in 1992, Commission of the European Communities, European File, August 1992.

[17] The first instances of significant intervention by the Community are of recent date, with the introduction of the obligation to separate infrastructure accounts from operating accounts (a rule known as unbundling) and the granting of transit rights to international carriers. See Council Directive 91/440/EC of 29 July 1991 on the development of the Community's railways, in *OJEC,* No. L 237, 24 Aug. 1991, p. 25 (and implementation directives No. 95/18/EC of 19 June 1995 on the licensing of railway undertakings, in *OJEC,* No. L 143, 27 June 1995, pp. 70-74; and No. 95/19/EC of 19 June 1995 on the allocation of railway infrastructure capacity and the charging of infrastructure fees, in *OJEC,* No. L 143, 27 June 1995, pp. 75-78).

[18] Obviously, being relegated to the fringe of European Union policy in this fashion, the idea of service in the public interest is liable to stay rigid. In the eyes of the public, Europe is a destroyer of national public services, not the inventor of transnational public services. The Swiss were quite right in identifying the European Union with the unbridled liberalization of heavy goods vehicle traffic.

[19] This seems to have been done only on an experimental basis with the harmonization of the accounting rules applicable to the infrastructure of rail, road and inland waterway transport; see Council Regulation (EEC) No. 1108/70 of 4 June 1970 (in *OJEC,* No. L 130, 15 June 1970), as amended by Council Regulation (EEC) No. 1384/79 of 25 June 1979 (in *OJEC,* No. L 167, 5 July 1989, p. 1).

[20] Bob Hanké: "Travail, capital et Etat: relations de travail et ajustement économique dans l'Europe des années 1980", in Supiot (ed.), op. cit. (see note 1).

WORK AND TRAINING: A BLURRING OF THE EDGES   **25**

Françoise FAVENNEC-HÉRY *

Getting a perspective on work is like trying to focus on a moving target, for the obvious reasons that no one can tell where the notion of work begins and ends, and that the nature of work itself is constantly evolving. Training is a crucial factor contributing to this evolutionary process, and it is easy to see how closely the two are linked, sometimes even to the point of merger: training for work, training through work, training as a form of employment and so on.

The question of the links between work and training is not new, it lies at the heart of the changes wrought in "post-industrial" society. In the great debates on work and integration, the notion of training is perceived as laden with promise. But is this a passing fashion, a reliable solution or just an unavoidable outcome? The scope and complexity of the subject are such that it is wise to narrow one's focus and draw on a wide variety of sources.

Clearly, a multi-disciplinary approach is required: vocational training needs to be analysed from historical, socioeconomic and legal angles to establish, for example, its role in education, suitable methods of certification, how it is viewed in recruitment practice, and the skill evaluation criteria used by companies. Such an analysis should include a comparative approach, but avoid hasty generalizations based on lessons drawn from national experience.

An exploration of the relationship between work and training, however, should not venture further than the links between them, to avoid getting lost in the variety of meanings ascribed to these terms. The meaning of training is very broad and does not admit of precise definition: it is not just the acquisition of knowledge or techniques, it is more generally a training of the self. Training may be perceived as an intrinsically valuable structural element in an individual's overall activity. It can also be approached from the standpoint of the functions it performs. In that sense, it is not simply an

Originally published in *International Labour Review*, Vol. 135 (1996), No. 6.

* Professor at the Faculty of Law and Political Science, University of Nantes.

instrument for entry into an occupation and thus for integration into society: it can also serve to exclude or marginalize certain categories of people, for example, when a given level of knowledge is required to sit an examination or to obtain certain jobs or enter certain occupations. The notions of work and employment are equally unclear, which adds to the difficulty of establishing the respective roles of training, work and employment.

Because of these definitional difficulties, "work and training" are best approached not as static objects of study, but rather as an ongoing process. For the seemingly simple, linear path leading from training to work is currently undergoing major changes with regard to the purpose of training, the training process itself and forms of certification.

THE PURPOSE OF TRAINING

Work and training often concern related goals, and they are then seen as linked in a linear and sequential manner: first you train, then you work. This teleological view of training is giving way to other approaches which affect the order in which training and work occur in time, the separate stages of training and work (which are sometimes the same or very similar) and the actual purpose of training which may basically be to enable the individual to become integrated in society. The links between training and work may thus be perceived as teleological, as pathological and as therapeutic.[1]

The teleological link

The link is a normal, linear one between training first followed by work. This form of training aims to equip the recipient for work. Unlike a job, training is merely a means of obtaining one. The training provided in school is regarded in this way, never as productive work. The status of pupil is not the same as that of worker, even if the same vocabulary applies, and the status of student is evolving. For the time being, pupils and students are recognized as having only the duties and none of the rights of workers.[2]

Nevertheless, this sequential distinction, which assigns roles between different players, is not absolute. Both in practice and in the law, the two stages often overlap.

Take the manner in which the concept of apprenticeship is treated under French and Spanish law. Is work or training the purpose of an apprenticeship contract? A good argument can be made both that apprenticeship is the last link in the training chain and that it is the first in the work chain. The same can be said of all forms of alternating training contract. In some ways work and training are perceived to be alike, even to be one and the same. The apprentice or holder of an alternating training contract also enjoys some of the rights of a wage-earner. However, although there is a similarity in legal terms, the need for a period of training separate from productive employment still applies. Thus, in French law, a Court of Appeal ruling considered that "theoretical training being an essential part of the skills training contract,[3] an employer who impedes such training commits a serious offence which justifies the employee in breaking the contract".[4] According to this ruling, therefore, employment remains subordinate to the training objective and must not displace it.

The pathological link

In other circumstances, employment and training may be linked through the need to address dysfunctions or "pathologies" in society. The goal of training through work is not simply to train people but also to integrate them into society. This secondary aim is becoming increasingly important. It affects both people who have come out of the education system without any qualifications and manage to obtain "job-starter" contracts (i.e. contracts combining training and work) and people who have lost their jobs and are seeking to retrain. Such contracts then become, in some instances, a way of providing low-cost employment rather than a means of training the young for work and of retraining the not-so-young. This can be said of the Spanish law on training contracts, as is clear from the explanatory preface to the first reform of that law in 1984: "The level of youth unemployment makes it advisable to refine the types of contract which help young people to be gradually integrated into the labour force. All these types of contract are widely used in Western countries with disturbing levels of youth unemployment, in order to give young people the opportunity of a period of adjustment to work on leaving school, and to create jobs which allow them to gain some experience of working life".[5]

This trend towards integration through work is also found in French law in alternating training contracts (such as the contracts providing first exposure to a variety of work experiences,[6] training for recognized qualifications, training programmes based on company needs,[7] and programmes to help hard-to-place workers re-enter the labour market). But legal precedent ensures that the theoretical side of training is maintained when so required by the law;[8] the lack of provision for such training in the labour market entry contract was one of the grounds for its withdrawal.[9] However, the employment and solidarity contract,[10] which provides opportunities for young people who cannot get a normal job, fully satisfies the goals of social and occupational integration. Nevertheless, in such cases, training is only intended to play an ancillary part in improving the beneficiary's chances of regaining a place in society, i.e. the training goal becomes secondary.[11]

The therapeutic link

Here the work-training link has a therapeutic aim, namely the integration through work of groups excluded from society because of a handicap or extreme social deprivation and marginalization. Legislative measures combining training and work enable people suffering such handicaps to live as normal citizens and workers. Integration through work can take place either in ordinary enterprises, in special recruitment centres or in companies providing protected employment. Spanish law provides for programmes targeting young people from seriously deprived backgrounds. The programmes consist of a special education phase, a vocational training phase to help the social integration of the participants and a final phase offering work-oriented vocational training.

Clearly, the notion of training is multifaced and fulfils a variety of functions. Its links with work and the world of work have changed, as has the process of training.

THE TRAINING PROCESS

Changes in the training process, in both the French and other European systems have occurred over time in a gradual, well-established way; some have been more recent.

Firstly, it is clear that training has become a continuing, lifelong process and is no longer a fixed stage in working life. Though not a new idea, it is increasingly prevalent in the relevant legal instruments and principles governing training policy.

Secondly, there has been a redistribution of roles between school, enterprises and other training organizations.

Thirdly, companies are increasingly turning to personalized, individualized forms of training, and this has brought about a real change in vocational training law.

Training as an ongoing process

Training and work no longer occur sequentially, they form an ongoing process,[12] have been absorbed into productive work and contribute to the continuing self-development process.

In the first place, the distinction between initial and continual training no longer applies – an observation made against the background of high levels of unemployment, which call for a total reappraisal of the issue. As already noted, the transition between school and work is getting longer and longer. To mitigate the failures of the school system, the focus of attention has moved to employers and to types of contract which seek to facilitate the acquisition of qualifications or preparation for a specific job. In French law, there has been a boom in alternating training contracts mainly targeting the young: contracts providing exposure to a variety of work experiences, training for recognized qualifications, programmes based on company needs, etc. Somewhat similar measures, such as the employment and solidarity contract and the contract to help hard-to-place workers re-enter the labour market,[13] are aimed at unemployed wage-earners. Despite rather unconvincing results, this has become a firm trend and has modified the chronological order of training and work, often reversing it.

Reasonably stable employment contracts sometimes allow for training to occur throughout their duration. The right to training has even been granted to employees on fixed-term contracts and to temporary employees. In this context, in French law, the focus of both general collective agreements and the legislation has been training rather than agreements on working time. Responsibility for organizing training (including the financial aspects) has been shared between public bodies, the social partners and enterprises. Training may be a matter of implementing company policy, notably under a training plan, or the expression of the employee's individual right to acquire a skill. In France this usually takes the form of individual study leave. The rulings of the Court of Appeal have also helped establish the notion of "lifelong training" by placing a duty on companies to retrain employees.[14] The law, collective agreements and court rulings all make training an integral part of the employment contract. At European Union level, the Treaty of Maastricht itself (art. 127) requires the Union to "facilitate adaptation to industrial changes" and to "improve continuing training". The employment contract thus provides for a measure of convergence between training and employment. This slow process has gradually come to apply in some of the professions. Training is thus one of the areas on which there is a convergence of views and where common rules could be drawn up applying both to salaried employees and self-employed professionals.

Distribution of training roles

The second force for change, closely linked to the first, concerns the distribution of responsibility for training. Should this lie with educationalists, with employers or with training professionals? Historically, training was a vocational instrument to integrate the individual in the working community. Subsequently, and to varying degrees depending on the country, this function of producing and reproducing the labour force was transferred from the enterprise to the school, thus incidentally contributing to the breakdown of the social and community network which had grown up around industrial sites. There was a gradual shift from a society where manual and other workers were integrated in the enterprise to one which offers them merely a passing involvement through "work interactions". A work-based community with shared values has evolved into a temporary association of individuals bound merely by legal ties and circumstance. Where the workplace no longer has the overall common integrating role, then the school takes over – the world of school on one side, the world of work on the other. Training then serves to help individuals find a place in society rather than to integrate them into a community. In fact, at the initial training stage, the role of the school is not to introduce the pupil immediately into the production process. Its first social function is to provide an apprenticeship in the meaning of work itself and, secondly, it equips the pupil with the necessary vocational skills. As a result of this separation of the two worlds, families now exert strong pressure on schools and there has been an upgrading of training, with as concomitant risks the devaluation of academic qualifications and problems of integration.

Without going as far as to speak of a reversal of roles, there are now signs that the worlds of education and work are attempting to draw closer, and even compete, in the training sphere. Hence the introduction of so-called "work-related" training within the overall education system. However, this vocational training has not had the expected results and its social effect has been very limited.[15] On the other hand, some companies are evolving forms of parallel training directly reflecting company needs and no longer linked to branches of the general education system. Thus some "work-related" programmes now provide a form of skills training which is determined by company objectives.[16] As a result of such requirements, vocational training professionals have developed a number of methods which determine the nature of the teaching content. There is a kind of redistribution of roles: a general training without any very precise goal, provided by the state education system, and initial or continuous vocational training based on the company, which has a defined knowledge base and ensures the preparation needed for specific jobs.

The dominant role played by training institutions in the French system should also be mentioned. In France continuing vocational training has relied for the last 20 years on several different actors – companies, the social partners, the State and training-providers – coordinating their activities. The involvement of the training-providers raises the issue of training content and there has been legislation on a number of occasions to exercise greater control over bodies jointly managed by the social partners and agencies operating in the training market.[17]

Vocational skills and the personalization of training

The third change that has occurred in France is due to the impact of skills theory on companies, resulting in procedures to make training a needs-based, personalized process. Though far from a general trend, it is taking hold. Under this approach, the purpose is no longer to try to furnish the individual with a general qualification but to require the employee to have a number of specific, attested skills. The company then makes demands of the employee which relate to a set of predetermined standards. This approach, which was introduced by well-known collective agreements, including "A Cap 2000",[18] relies on the integration of training in the production process. It requires assessment of the skills already acquired by the employee and a procedure for progressing by stages through a form of specific vocational training. This trend is no longer confined to the internal organization of companies. It has had a direct influence on the relevant legal provisions and has been recognized in law. Through concepts such as the skills audit, collective agreements and the law now focus on the individualization of career paths.[19]

This trend, which is a new departure in training law and originates in companies' quality-enhancing policies, raises the issues of the assessment of training and of who is competent to undertake that assessment. But how convincing, how objective are companies' internal assessment procedures? Is there not a risk of deregulation? These questions lead in turn to that of the certification of training.

CERTIFICATION OF TRAINING

The key question here is the role of paper qualifications in the training–work relationship. Because of the ever-present gap between trainers and job providers, some form of recognition of training is needed. As these two worlds start to merge, the certification process is changing.

This development invites three observations:

(a) Firstly the relative importance of paper qualifications in the recruitment process. A significant sociological study on "private sector recruitment methods",[20] has shown that in the hiring process, the importance of such qualifications varies according to the level of skills required by the job. As a criterion in recruitment it was cited in a survey six times more often for managers than for salaried employees or manual workers, where experience was at a premium, or for marketing staff where the main criterion was personality. A paper qualification requirement often allows a preliminary sort in the selection process. In practice, the qualification is proof more of a certain level of training than of knowledge. It serves as evidence of the candidate's individual performance and as an indicator of conformity. Its importance varies according to the person recruited (female, male, young, not so young) or the type of employer.

This change in the value of qualifications (which has paradoxically been accompanied by a scramble to obtain them) can be explained by the fact that within a very few years they have ceased to be the guarantors of value and content that they once were. The mad rush to ever more specialized qualifications has led to growing insecurity among the holders of the qualifications and among employers, with neither side really knowing the value of what the other was offering, except in the comprehensive systems of the French *grandes écoles* or the training courses under the control of the various occupational branches.

(b) With the relegation of academic qualifications to a lesser status, new forms of assessment have emerged. The loss of reference points together with the development of skills theory mentioned above have led to the emergence of other forms of non-academic certification. Vocational training now involves reference or benchmark systems, and contracts between trainees, trainers and employers. These assessment methods are based on objective criteria. The human resource management policies discussed earlier have introduced evaluation of the skills required for specific jobs and an assessment of those acquired by the employee; training is thus becoming an integral part of human resource management. Methods of certification of acquired skills are diversifying. In these different scenarios, the problem is deciding who conducts the evaluation, using what standards and with what measure of transparency. The establishment of such certification alongside state diplomas may be a matter for collective bargaining[21] and there have been moves in this direction in some occupational sectors in France. In some collective agreements, therefore, may be found "certificates of qualification in the sector" or "skills portfolios" or other forms of training identification. Paper qualifications, or more generally the form of certification, are becoming occupation-based. The acquisition of skills through training is then recognized either by the salary level or by the opportunity of promotion to higher-grade work.[22]

(c) This issue is important at national level and crucial at European level. Developing a highly skilled work force is a major area of common European interest. It assumes the mobility of workers and transparency in the way their training is recognized within the European Union (EU). Measures in relation to training can be grouped under four headings: improving vocational training facilities in the member States, improving vocational training provision, developing language skills and innovation, and establishing a network for cooperation between States, particularly as regards monitoring and assessment procedures.[23] As a general system for the recognition of diplomas and vocational training under EU law, it is currently governed by two kinds of regulations. A vertical regulatory system consists of sectoral directives on the regulated professions (doctors, nurses, midwives, veterinary surgeons, dentists, chemists, architects) containing arrangements for automatic recognition of qualifications. More generally, there is a horizontal regulatory system comprising a common body of law governing the recognition of higher-education diplomas and professional education and training which allow nationals of one country to obtain recognition of qualifications acquired in their country of origin in order to carry on an equivalent profession in another member State. By contrast with sectoral arrangements, there is no automatic recognition of qualifications, and the migrant worker may have to meet additional requirements in the event of substantial differences between the training already acquired and that required in the host country. There are two directives in force. One is Council Directive 89/48 of 21 December 1988 on a general system for the recognition of higher education diplomas awarded on completion of professional education and training of at least three years' duration. The second, Council Directive 92/51 of 18 June 1992, supplements the first and covers short post-secondary education and training. A draft directive on a general system is under discussion. The general system involves a recognition for training and not academic recognition of diplomas. Its goal is to take account not of titles as such but of qualifications acquired in the country of origin in order to carry on a regulated profession in the host country.[24] This method applies only to those professions not covered by a sectoral directive. Conversely, however, automatic recognition of qualifications is confined to the professions covered by sectoral directives. For the moment, the dominant trend in EU law is to take account of qualifications rather than recognition of any academic certification involved.

The changing goals of training, the shift to lifelong training and the changes in methods of certification bear witness to the enduring nature of the link between employment and training. They also highlight the broad scope of the employment-training bond, which extends far beyond the sphere of paid employment.

If work is viewed through the prism of its links with training, then a true unity will be restored to the meaning of work: unity of time through lifelong work; and unity of place through work whatever the legal jurisdiction governing it.

Notes

[1] This distinction is taken from A. Marzal: "La dialectique formation-travail dans le droit espagnol", in Alain Supiot (ed.): *Actes du colloque «Le travail en perspectives»*, Paris, LGDJ, 1998.

[2] See C. Durand-Primborgne: *Le droit de l'éducation*, Paris, Hachette éducation, 1992; and "Le statut du travail scolaire", in Supiot (ed.), op. cit.

[3] This was a case of a labour market integration contract intended to provide the young person with vocational training alternating between the workplace and a training institution (see in this connection, art. L980-2 et seq. and art. L980-1 of the Labour Code).

[4] Cour de cassation, 12 Apr. 1995, in *Droit social* (Paris), 1995, p. 597.

[5] Quoted by Marzal, op. cit.

[6] "Contrat d'orientation": A measure intended to place unskilled young people in an environment where they can work out a personal career plan (see decree of 20 October 1992, in *Journal Officiel* (Paris), 3 Oct. 1992; decree of 11 January 1994, in *Journal Officiel* (Paris), 13 Jan. 1994).

[7] "Contrat d'adaptation": A contract enabling young people to enter the labour force by means of additional training (see art. L980-6 of the Labour Code).

[8] Chambre sociale de la Cour de cassation (hereinafter Soc.), 18 Nov. 1992, in *Droit social* (Paris), 1993, p. 54; Soc., 31 Mar. 1993, in *Droit social* (Paris), 1994, p. 511; Soc., 12 Apr. 1995, in *Droit social* (Paris), 1995, p. 597.

[9] See G. Couturier: "Le contrat d'insertion professionnelle", in *Droit social* (Paris), 1994, p. 204: "Within the framework of the labour market entry contract, there was no specified period of compulsory training". The purpose of the agreement was "to promote the first exposure to work and subsequent integration of certain categories of young people".

[10] "Contrat emploi-solidarité": A contract intended to encourage occupational integration of unemployed young people by developing activities based on community needs.

[11] On these various contracts, see: *Droit de l'Emploi*, Paris, Dalloz action, 1996, p. 78.

[12] See, in France, the vocational training reform in progress to establish a law on developing lifelong training and alternating education, "Bref social No. 12268, rapport Virville", in *Liaisons sociales* (Paris), Vol. 111/96.

[13] See J. Savatier: "Les contrats initiative-emploi", in *Droit social* (Paris), 1995, p. 965.

[14] On this point, see: Soc., 25 Feb. 1992, in *Droit social* (Paris), 1992, p. 379; A. Lyon-Caen and J.-M. Luttringer: "L'émergence d'un droit à la formation professionnelle", in *Liaisons sociales* (Paris), C3 No. 6606, 12 Dec. 1991; and A. Lyon-Caen: "Adapter et reclassifier: quelques arrêts stimulants de la Court de Cassation", in *Semaine sociale Lamy* (Paris), 21 Apr. 1992.

[15] P. Cam: "Insertion et cheminement professionnel des jeunes", in Supiot (ed.), op. cit.

[16] Ropé, F.; L. Tanguy: *Savoir et compétences. De l'usage de ces notions dans l'école et l'entreprise,* Paris, L'Harmattan, 1994; see also A. Lyon-Caen: "Le droit et la gestion des compétences", in *Droit Social* (Paris), 1992, p. 573.

[17] J.-M. Luttringer: "La formation professionnelle: nouveaux chantiers", in *Droit social* (Paris), 1993, p. 192.

[18] Agreements of 17 Dec. 1990 and 25 Jan. 1991, in *Liaisons sociales* (Paris), C2 No. 6506.

[19] Law No. 91/1405 of 31 Dec. 1991, art. L-931 *et seq.* of the Labour Code; see J.-M. Luttringer: "L'accord national interprofessionnel du 3 juillet relatif à la formation et au perfectionnement professionnels", in *Droit social* (Paris), 1991, p. 803.

[20] A.-C. Dubernet: "L'embauche, approche sociologique des modes de recrutement dans le secteur privé", doctoral thesis in sociology, University of Nantes, 1995.

[21] See J.-M. Luttringer: "Réflexions sur les rapports entre formation continue et négociation collective", in *Le droit collectif du travail,* Paris, Mélanges Sinay, Peter Lang, 1994, p. 43 et seq.

[22] ibid

[23] See R. Blanpain and J.C. Javillier: *Droit du travail communautaire,* second edition, Paris, LGDJ, 1995, p. 108.

[24] In this respect, see J.-M. Favret: "Le système général de reconnaissance des diplômes et des formations professionnelles en droit communautaire: l'esprit et la méthode", in *Revue trimestrielle de Droit européen* (Paris), Apr.-June 1996.

COMBATING UNEMPLOYMENT, RESTRUCTURING WORK: REFLECTIONS ON A FRENCH STUDY

26

Jean BOISSONNAT *

Consider this enigma: over the past 20 years or so Europe has been flooded with unemployment, while growth in production has continued unabated (with moderate falls only in 1975 and in 1993). In the 1930s when production collapsed, people understood why unemployment increased. However, over the past 20 years when the annual economic growth rate has averaged about 2.5 per cent, the unemployment rate in the countries of the European Union has almost tripled (4.2 per cent in 1975, 11.6 per cent in 1994). It can be demonstrated that, at this growth rate, production in absolute (not relative) terms is now rising faster than in the immediate post-war era when, under the effects of the reconstruction and catching-up necessitated by the years of crisis and war, the same countries' annual growth rate was around 5 per cent. Economic growth creates more jobs today than it did then. For the countries of the European Union as a whole, with an immediate postwar growth rate of 5 per cent, the annual increase in jobs was only 0.2 per cent. By contrast, during the 1980s, with an annual growth rate of 2.5 per cent, the annual average growth in employment was 0.5 per cent.[1] In other words, the job content of growth has quadrupled. To summarize, there has never been a collapse in growth and yet there has never been so much unemployment. What lies behind this contradiction?

The answer lies in the nature of the work being done. The question therefore arises whether, unless society takes into consideration the changing nature of work, the efforts it makes to push back the tide of unemployment are not futile. The supply and demand of work are changing at a speed beyond our comprehension – and one for which no allowance is made in people's calculations.

Originally published in *International Labour Review*, Vol. 135 (1996), No. 1.

* Member of the Bank of France's Committee on Monetary Policy, and also Chair of the Working Group on "Employment and Work to the Year 2015", General Planning Commission, France.

As far the jobs on offer are concerned, workers have already experienced considerable change. After the Second World War, in France, two-thirds of wage-earners were blue-collar workers employed mostly on factory production lines. In effect, they were little more than cogs in the wheel, just another form of machine. Currently, blue-collar workers account for under a third of the active population (90 per cent of which consists of wage-earners); 20 years hence, they will account for no more than 10 to 15 per cent. In France, in 1967 middle managers outnumbered farm workers for the first time; in 1994, their number rose above that of blue-collar workers. The skills required in the workplace are no longer the same. Yesterday, workers were slaves to the machine and to materials; today, the important skills are those of communication, of adaptability, and the ability constantly to renew one's work motivation.

As far as the job seekers are concerned, the change has been equally pronounced. Today people will no longer accept just any work for the sake of a wage. In France, indeed, over a third of household income does not derive directly from work (social security benefits, various allowances). Family income has trebled since the war and families can – at least for a certain time – meet the needs of their out-of-work members. And everyone has come to expect a greater say in their choice of work and working conditions.

In other words, it is not so much that jobs are in short supply as that work itself is changing. Unless our institutions and our mode of behaviour adjust to those changes, there is no chance of absorbing unemployment. Some time back, Alfred Sauvy the French demographer pointed out that, as regards jobs, "we are not solving the supply and demand problem". And now we are faced with the same situation again.

This was the fact guiding the Working Group which the French Government entrusted with the task of examining the likely evolution of employment and work over the next 20 years, and whose report came out in 1995.[2] This article will make no attempt to summarize the Working Group's actual deliberations, but will try to draw out its underlying philosophy.

Briefly put, the Working Group sketched out four different scenarios, intended to result in new frameworks to help redefine work and employment over the next 20 years.

TRENDS AND VARIABLES

These scenarios were conceived by juxtaposing certain major trends not expected to change over the coming 20 years with various, less stable strategic variables. Naturally, the trends included the revolution in information and telecommunication technology – a veritable third industrial revolution where the microprocessor has the role played in the two earlier industrial revolutions by the steam engine and then by the electric motor and the internal-combustion engine. The other major trends taken into consideration were the globalization of economic, commercial and financial activities and the emergence of Asia's enormous economic power; the individualization of all aspects of social behaviour; and the general ageing of the population. Viewed in the specifically French context, a particularly important factor is the demographic upheaval that country is undergoing, which a few figures will illustrate. Looking at the population of working age (18-64 years) and breaking down the trend into 20-year periods, the following pattern emerges: from 1955 to 1975, the population grew by 3.7 million persons; between 1975 and 1995, by 5.2 million persons; and between 1995 and 2015, by an estimated 2.3 million persons. For the period between 2015 and 2035, assuming the most probable hypothesis (the French birth rate comes into line with the European average of 1.5 children per woman of child-bearing age), the astounding projection is a fall of 4 million persons in the population of working age. Yet, over same period, because of an increase in life expectancy, the total population of France will be virtually static. This means that, unless there is a significant inflow of foreign labour, the French economy could be doomed to stagnation and the French people could experience a fall in their standard of living. Unemployment may not necessarily disappear since (not for the first time in history) a labour shortage would be accompanied by unemployment. This trend is unlikely to vary over the coming two decades – though with an appropriate family policy, Sweden has been able to achieve a turn-around in its birth rate from 1.6 up to 2 children per woman of child-bearing age.

Four strategic variables were placed in juxtaposition to the major trends: the (rising or falling) degree of worldwide economic cooperation; the public's preferences for income or for leisure time (which may also change significantly); the restructuring of the production apparatus (which may occur more or less rapidly); and society's varying ability to reform the institutional framework of work and employment.

FOUR SCENARIOS

In combining the trends and the variables, various scenarios emerged. Four which contained sufficient contrast to facilitate the Working Group's deliberations were then selected (see table). Two scenarios were relatively grim (the most likely) and two relatively rosy (the most desirable).

In the first (the "sinking") scenario the variables move in the wrong direction: the overall environment is not favourable (for example, there is no progress towards European union); enterprises adjust too slowly to new situations; income/free time options remain unchanged; and the reform of the institutional framework does not take place (the State retains too much standard-setting power, which condemns it to playing the roles of both policeman and welfare provider, bankrupting itself in the attempt to repair the effects of its own regulatory activities). According to this scenario, at the

Four scenarios

Key spheres	1. "Sinking" scenario	2. Hyper-competition or "devil-take-the-hindmost" scenario	3. Adjustment scenario	4. Cooperation scenario
International environment (Europe, the world)	Uncooperative	Cooperative (integrated Europe)	Not very cooperative	Cooperative (Europe, the world)
French production system	Competition Inadequate adjustment Segmentation Rigid labour market	Search for competitiveness Technological innovation Individualized wages Segmentation of production network Externalization	Organizational and technological innovation Return inwards "Chain" cooperation	Activity networks "Global" performance Local development New management tools Negotiated change
Values, expectations, social behaviour	Wage demands Rigid working time Little regulation Introversion	Individual differentiation and arbitration Acceptance of growing wage gaps Everyone for him/herself	New approach to time and leisure Classic (narrow) collective bargaining	Personal choice on work vs. leisure time Diversity of work patterns Cooperation Collective regulation of employment, wages, time, social protection
Legal and institutional framework	Defensive adjustment State regulatory power Attention to unemployment State's role as welfare provider or policeman	Offensive adjustment Enterprise regulatory power Weak trade unions Attention to poverty Refocusing of the State	Gradual construction of institutional framework Reduction in legal working hours State as guarantor	Radical change of institutional framework Redistribution of social responsibility State as partner

Source: Le travail dans vingt ans, op. cit., p. 171

end of an economic cycle unemployment never falls to a level lower than that experienced in the preceding cycle; and finally a social explosion occurs, opening the door to all manner of political adventurers.

The second ("devil-take-the-hindmost") scenario involves importing into Europe the main features of the United States social model. Labour relations move towards a system in which the employment contract is gradually absorbed into commercial law and all bargaining becomes individualized. However, the production apparatus undergoes rapid modernization; flexibility is significantly enhanced; unemployment falls; and poverty increases. In the United States, between 1964 and 1988 real wages increased by 40 per cent in the top 5 per cent earnings bracket and fell by 5 per cent in the lowest decile.[3] In the United States, the ratio of wages in top and bottom deciles is 6:1; in Germany, it is 2:1. However, in the United States the significant reduction in the labour cost of the least-skilled segment of the workforce has, in fact, made it possible to create more jobs than in Europe: between 1970 and 1992, employment increased by 49 per cent in the United States but by only 9 per cent in the (then) European Community of 12 Member States.[4] In Europe goods are going cheap; in the United States it is wages.

The third ("adjustment") scenario is more voluntarist. Despite an unfavourable environment and much internal resistance, political will and a high degree of social commitment make it possible to overcome some of these obstacles, and the spirit of reform wins out over sclerosis. But such a climate is seldom encountered except during periods of major social upheaval, or in times of war or civil strife – and such a climate, by definition, cannot be planned for.

In the fourth ("cooperation") scenario, there is a positive interaction between a number of favourable circumstances. In a socially cooperative environment, growth accelerates, enabling a change in the relation between time spent on income generation and on leisure, which in turn promotes restructuring of the production apparatus then reform of the regulatory framework, and a renewal of dialogue between the social partners. Unemployment falls, without a concomitant widespread increase in precarious employment.

In order to establish a reference scenario situated between the adjustment scenario and the cooperation scenario (reflecting a minimal ability to change in a not entirely favourable environment), the Working Group employed a "philosophical" approach which, while it was not fully explicit, may be expressed as follows.

PHILOSOPHICAL CHOICES

The first item in this philosophy is based on the belief that, over the next 20 years, a paid occupation will continue to be the basic means of social integration. The family and school will still have a role to play in this context – indeed, having reverted to being the base camp in the assault on growing unemployment, the family may even assume a significant role once again. Nevertheless, social integration through work will remain important – which means that (in France) it would be better to have a growing proportion of part-time work than the current division between fewer (but full-time) jobs and more unemployment.

The second assumption underlying the work of the Working Group relates to the growing individualization of demand for products, services and work. In every sphere, society is trading up from the "ready-to-wear" to the "tailor-made" – a phenomenon which has led the American consultant Stanley Davis to comment that, soon, "every client will be a market and every wage-earner, an entrepreneur".[5] This is a deep and irreversible trend, the new "invisible hand" in industrial civilization. It will be a very powerful lever for social change, and will have no need for a supporting ideology or for organized forces to make progress. It will bring about changes of status within a single working life, and will bring "workers" and "consumers" closer together, blurring the distinction currently made between the two.

In this new society, contrary to the predictions of the proponents of the minimalist State, the State will still have a major role to play. Certainly, the State will be less pervasive; it will regulate less and levy less. But it will remain a determining factor since the law defines the structure of the market. The phenomenon will be even more significant in Europe where the social protection model that has gradually evolved stands in marked contrast to its American and Japanese equivalents. This model appears in various guises, depending on the country: in Northern Europe, it is called social democracy, in Germany the social market economy, and in France the mixed economy. These are all variants of the basic model, which is the result of a compromise between the degree of flexibility needed for the market economy to operate, and a basic level of social protection for individuals. Admittedly, this model has been through difficult times (for example, the crisis currently affecting social security schemes, and excessive public levies), but it will change, not disappear, since it is central to European social perceptions. Economic liberalism in its post-social democracy form cannot merely be a replica of its earlier form.

Under these conditions, is it right to present the struggle against unemployment as the absolute aim of collective action, when it may lead into a dead-end? The retreat of unemployment will most probably be brought about through action to promote growth and to reorganize work – but such action would have become necessary in any case, even if there had been no unemployment.

SIX FRAMEWORKS

On this implicit philosophical basis, therefore, six frameworks were evolved by the Working Group to help thought and action;[6] six frameworks which should enable a balance to be struck between flexibility and social protection, between the operation of the market and the safety of the individual – a balance that ensures the least possible wastage of human, natural and material resources.

"Economy" implies "economical". The best system is the one most economical of social costs (the aim of the social contract), of natural resources (the "ecological" contract with nature) and of financial resources (the profitability of invested capital). The international cooperation framework will be crucial to the pace of economic growth. In this framework, the Working Group emphasized the need to implement the plan to introduce a single European currency, this being the best way to bring real interest rates in Europe down to a reasonable level and give the "Old World" the means of consolidating the international monetary system and to provide the new World Trade Organization with the opportunity to play its role as regulator of international trade. It is foolish to believe that the advanced industrial countries will long maintain their employment levels by seeking to protect themselves from competition from the emerging economies – their own future clients. Yet the necessary transition will have to be handled intelligently in order to avoid isolated incidents causing public opinion to call for protective measures. Michel Hansenne, Director-General of the International Labour Office, put the problem clearly when he wrote, "the link to be made between the development of trade and social progress should not be one that excludes the developing countries from access to the developed countries' markets, since the former are not in a position to meet the labour standards achieved by the latter ... Such a link ought to promote in parallel, and bearing in mind each country's particular circumstances and chosen policies, both the economic development that results from trade liberalization and social progress".[7]

Studies conducted by the various international organizations estimate that the potential growth of the developed countries lies between 2.5 and just over 3 per cent per annum, so it is clear that growth alone can reduce unemployment only gradually. For unemployment to be reduced to around 5 per cent of the active population by the year 2000 (a figure below which it is difficult to go in the rich countries where both technology and social behaviour are in a state of flux), growth rates of between 4 and 6 per cent will be needed, depending on the country.[8]

However, the aim of this article is to demonstrate that an active policy on the restructuring of work would efficiently complement the effects of growth on employment. Thus in the five other frameworks the aim is a better adjustment of the structures of work to conditions in the new industrial society. Much could be said in this respect about improving the structures of production and training, and the latter – especially in France – will be the object of a new contract between the education system and production. Sandwich training courses alternating study and work experience will have to start earlier and recur throughout people's working lives – which is why this form of training should be regarded as genuine, organized, supervised, paid work.

However, this article will dwell on the three frameworks which attracted the greatest attention when the Working Group's report was published: reducing hours of work, establishing a new legal framework (the activity contract), and breathing new life into organized dialogue between the social partners.

HOURS OF WORK

History shows that technological change has never failed to bring about a reduction in hours of work. In France, hours of work are estimated to have been cut by half over the past 100 years. Broadly speaking, if this reduction had not occurred, today's production levels would be attained with the efforts of only 12 million workers. Assuming that the remaining persons of working age had nevertheless looked for work (though obviously the situation would have evolved very differently), the number of unemployed people in France today would be 15 – not three – million! Without dwelling longer on such hypotheses, it should be remembered that in industrial society generally, productivity-induced advances always entail a choice between distributing the results in the form of increased incomes or of reduced hours of work. Though only partly a conscious choice, it is nevertheless a real one.

However, although the fall in hours of work is certain, the way in which it occurs varies. When there is talk today of granting more people a four-day week or a sixth week of paid holiday, the reasoning employed is that of the industrial era when time could be sliced into standard blocks without any untoward effects (in France, the 40-hour week was adopted in 1936 but did not actually become a reality for 40 more years; in the intervening period it was merely a way of increasing wages, since overtime was paid 25 per cent more).

In years to come, reductions in hours of work will occur in a far more diverse way. Bringing the working week down to 35 hours may be achieved by working one hour less per day or one day less per fortnight, by allowing time credits to build up and be used during certain periods of the year (for example, when order books are low) or for certain tasks (linked to family responsibilities, for example). There will be an increase in the number of part-time jobs and shared-time jobs (with the same person working for several enterprises at a time), etc. In due course, even the concept of hours of work may gradually lose significance. Payment will be made for carrying out a specific task or mission rather than for the number of hours worked.

At this stage, it may be useful to establish a general framework to guide collective bargaining in this area. This is why the Working Group proposed that over the next 20 years average annual hours of work should be reduced from 1,650 to 1,500, provided that 10 per cent of that time is devoted to training or retraining. Today, these 1,650 hours of work per year are no more than an average calculated between hours worked full time (employees working an annual average of 1,785 hours) and hours worked part time (an annual average of 1,000 hours).[9]

Part-time work (whether or not the result of personal choice) is expected to become more widespread in France, where the situation lags far behind the majority of northern European countries: around 15 per cent of wage-earners work part time in France, compared with nearly 30 per cent in the Nordic countries. In other words, if twice as many people in France worked part time, there would be some 1.5 million extra jobs. Demand for part-time work will necessarily grow in line with the individualization of hours and forms of work. At present the demand side acts as a brake on such developments, since firms are cautious about getting organized along these lines and the regulations now in force – despite some real progress – do not sufficiently support part-time work.

THE ACTIVITY CONTRACT

The issue of working hours leads on to a problem at the heart of another framework, one which has already attracted much attention: the establishment of a new form of employment contract, the "activity contract". The basic idea derives from the observation that the existing form of employment contract no longer provides an adequate framework for the organization of different types of paid activity. In the circumstances, it is very tempting to do away with the employment contract completely, ultimately letting labour law be absorbed into commercial law. The worker would then be bound to an employer only by an ordinary supplier-to-client contract. In social policy terms, this would certainly be a major step backwards, since the contractual relationship between, for example, a vendor and a purchaser of galvanized steel sheet is more equal than the contractual relationship between a job seeker and an employer. The trade unions are rightly concerned about the risks involved in such a trend.

This is why an activity contract should include, but not replace, an employment contract. It would enable workers to change jobs or work status without being consigned to the dustbin of history. Today, a firm that has to get rid of some of its employees has no choice but to entrust their fate to the public authorities to which it pays contributions or taxes. This has led the French industrialists François and Edouard Michelin to comment that, "in human resource management terms, the way in which these workers have to be treated is contrary to human dignity. Abruptly throwing people on to the labour market is tantamount to preventing them from finding work again. By contrast, if it were possible to say three or four years in advance, 'in five years' time we will no longer have satisfactory work for you, so let us examine together the terms on which you might leave', wage-earners could in future take the necessary steps to find other work, and we could help them do so." [10]

The existence of an activity contract would make it possible to lower significantly, if not do away with, the divisions between the various types of "activity" in which people can engage: full- or part-time wage-earning work for a fixed or unlimited period, in-service training, setting up one's own company, leave for family reasons, etc. Despite changes of job or work status, workers would have a steady level of social protection. The activity contract could be drawn up with some sort of "network", consisting of firms, training bodies, local and regional authorities, chambers of commerce or industry. The contract could be signed for a fixed number of years and could obviously involve undertakings on both sides. How would payment be made? and by whom? Conceivably through some form of mutual arrangement, with the contracting firms in the network paying into a common fund some of the sums that they currently pay to government to distribute unemployment benefits, finance training or provide job placement services. However, this would not be a system of universal allowance, payable to everyone regardless of their status. For, in effect, such an allowance would make it possible, with a clear conscience, to exclude people from the production system – and we have already seen the impact on social integration of such exclusion. On this point, François Gaudu comments pertinently, "Today, economic ultraliberalism favours the generalized payment of a basic survival income, since this is the only way to maintain the purity of market forces. In order to allow the market to exclude people, no obligations must be placed on those who receive a minimum income". [11] But the same author recalls that there can be no authentic recognition of rights without a statement of obligations. Traditional rural society excluded no one – but laid down strict rules of behaviour for those who remained in the village. To a certain extent, the left-wing parties have kept the suburbs stable for several years now by very rigorously applying a system of support for the population. Bringing people back into the community also means imposing constraints on them.

Viewed objectively, the activity contract can be seen as another way of enabling a compromise to develop between the flexibility needed by the market and the legitimate social protection of people according to the "European model", which weighs so heavily in European history and culture. In common with any breakthrough, this one raises many questions; but the critical evaluation process it calls for can usefully be carried out only by all the social actors involved, not just by the State.

RENEWED DIALOGUE BETWEEN THE SOCIAL PARTNERS

This is why renewed dialogue between the social partners is the first step towards the reorganization of work. But for this dialogue to be fruitful, participants must regularly demonstrate their representativeness. This applies both to the employers' organizations and to the trade unions – and in France, over the past 25 years, the latter have lost between a half and two-thirds of their members (notably in the private sector). To build a new system for work and employment, collective bargaining must cast its net wider and involve a broader range of agents. Such involvement is probably the best way of revitalizing the institutions that mediate between the citizen and the State in French society – for a sense of responsibility goes hand in hand with representativeness.

What are the chances today that French society will shift its efforts from the abortive fight against unemployment towards an ambitious policy aimed at reorganizing work? They cannot be assessed in political terms only, by asking whether the Left is doing better than the Right or *vice versa*. People are spurred to action by the realities of their own experience. But such realities are constantly changing, leading into dead ends and out again. There are changes in social behaviour – and not necessarily along ideological lines. Competition comes from unexpected quarters, such as the Asian economies or the telecommunications revolution. In service economies, needs are renewed without the space limitations imposed by the renewal of material goods in industrial societies. Today, these needs cluster around the family, the home, health, and leisure, giving rise to new commercial services and, consequently, to new forms of enterprise. In the United States, between 1987 and 1991, large companies lost 2.4 million jobs; over the same period, enterprises with fewer than 20 employees gained 4.4 million jobs.[12] The future is wide open.

Notes

[1] See *EC Economic data,* Luxembourg, Office for Official Publications of the European Community, Oct. 1995.

[2] *Le travail dans vingt ans,* Paris, Editions Odile Jacob, La Documentation française, 1995.

[3] Chinhui Juhn; Kevin M. Murphy; Brooks Pierce: "Wage inequality and the rise in returns to skills", in *Journal of Political Economy* (Chicago), 1993, Vol. 101, No. 3 (June), pp. 410-442.

[4] Commission of the European Communities: *Growth, competitiveness, employment. The challenges and ways forward into the 21st century. White Paper,* in *Bulletin of the European Communities,* Supplement 6/93 (Brussels, 1993).

[5] Stanley M. Davis: *2020 vision: Transform your business today to succeed in tomorrow's economy*, London, Business Books, 1991.

[6] International cooperation; reducing hours of work; establishing a new legal framework (the activity contract); renewal of dialogue between the social partners; the production system; and training. See the Perspective "What is the future of work?", in *International Labour Review* (Geneva), Vol. 135 (1996), No. 1, pp. 93-110.

[7] Michel Hansenne: "La dimension sociale du commerce international", in *Droit Social* (Paris), 1994, No. 11 (Nov.), pp. 839-840.

[8] ILO: *World Employment 1995*, Geneva, 1995.

[9] Estimated by the Commissariat Général du Plan, Paris.

[10] Interview in *Le Figaro* (Paris), 11 July 1995.

[11] François Gaudu: "Du statut de l'emploi au statut de l'actif", in *Droit Social* (Paris), 1995, No. 6 (June), pp. 535-544.

[12] Estimates by David Birch for the research consultancy Cognetics, cited by Charles Handy in *Le temps des paradoxes,* Paris, Editions Village mondial, 1995.

WHAT IS THE FUTURE OF WORK? IDEAS FROM A FRENCH REPORT[1]

Patrick BOLLÉ*

27

Certain recent events illustrate people's fears about the value of their work amidst the acute employment crisis and widespread talk about globalization. In December 1995 France experienced its longest and toughest period of strike action since May 1968. At the time there was talk of "the first strike against globalization"[2] and of "resistance to social insecurity".[3] In January 1996, AT&T shares rose sharply when the company announced 40,000 redundancies (though fewer were carried out in the event). Conversely, on the announcement that the United States had created 750,000 new jobs in February 1996 and 140,000 in March – both record figures exceeding all expectations – the Dow Jones Industrial Index fell by over 3 per cent and 1.5 per cent, respectively.

Decision-makers and informed observers did not fail to remark that there are limits to the degree of social insecurity a society can tolerate. For example, on the strikes in France, the labour law specialist Alain Supiot wrote: "Directed mainly against the new iron law that capital imposes on labour in the globalized economy, this call for more social justice can be interpreted as a call for the establishment of a new international (and especially European) social order as much as a call for a return to national values".[4] It appears that redundancies, once the symptom of a company's failure, are now a sign of its success. This is what prompted Robert Reich, the United States Secretary of Labor, to point to the gap between financial results and people's economic security, raising the issue of an enterprise's responsibility towards its employees and towards the community.[5] In a similar vein, Rosabeth Moss Kanter, former Editor of the *Harvard Business Review,* in her address to the February 1996 World Economic Forum at

Originally published in *International Labour Review*, Vol. 135 (1996), No. 1, in the "Perspectives" section.

* French-language editor of the *International Labour Review*.

Davos (Switzerland), stressed the need to give workers confidence and to organize cooperation between firms, so that local communities, cities and regions benefit from globalization. Otherwise, she warned, there would be a resurgence of social unrest such as has not been seen since the Second World War.[6] And Michel Hansenne, Director-General of the International Labour Office, speaking at the G-7 Employment Conference at Lille (France) in April 1996, emphasized that: "these changes and this feeling of insecurity should not be underestimated. This feeling is by no means irrational. Solutions must be found that appeal to the enlightened self-interests of workers and employers. This task will be made easier if it is clearly recognized that they have a common stake in bringing about lower unemployment, higher growth and greater social cohesion."[7]

No one denies that there is a sense of insecurity – real or imagined. The debate is over the relative importance of its various causes. Is it fear of the unknown in the face of the transformation of work itself, of the social value of work? Is it a shortage of jobs due to weak economic growth? Is it a deterioration in conditions of employment brought about by an unfair division between labour and capital? This perspective examines the first of these hypotheses – one which has caused much debate and a lot of ink to flow.[8]

The starting point here is the findings of the Working Group on "Work and employment to the year 2015", established by France's General Planning Commission and chaired by Jean Boissonnat, a member of the Bank of France's Monetary Policy Committee (for an article by Mr. Boissonnat commenting on the report of the Working Group, see chapter 26 in this volume). This perspective begins by outlining the Working Group's report. Then, on the basis of other sources, it reviews different aspects of the transformation of work (work content, place and hours of work, worker status) and examines the extent and implications of the changes involved. Finally, it considers the most radical of the hypotheses evoked – i.e. the end of work – and concludes that, of the three hypotheses mentioned above, the one that causes the most heated discussion is not necessarily the one weighing most heavily on people's sense of insecurity.

THE WORKING GROUP'S APPROACH

The Working Group comprised specialists in diverse fields (lawyers, philosophers, economists, demographers, sociologists, statisticians, industrialists, consultants, etc.). So as to avoid a reductionist (economic, sociological or legal, for example) representation of the determinants of work and employment and of their interrelationships, they chose a "system" approach, that is, they considered them as "a combination of factors together defining an aggregate, of which the whole is more than the sum of its parts": the work-employment system (GPC, p. 320). The report is structured as follows: the first part looks at the emergence of the modern conception of work and analyses the current situation. The second part examines major trends and determining factors, going on to describe the scenarios resulting from their combination. In the third part, a number of proposals are put forward for discussion, the aim being to help bring about the most "rosy" scenarios.

The facts

Over the past two hundred years the evolution of work, labour law and work-related institutions has not only made wage-earning employment (that creation of industrial society) the most widespread form of employment, but also turned it into a standard: "The very notion of work has thus become increasingly identified with the standard represented by wage-earning employment. The relative shortage of jobs experienced in recent years has strengthened the hold this standard has on us, even if more diverse forms of work have been emerging" (GPC, p. 59). Work and employment in France today are having to adjust to several phenomena: the changing pace and nature of the integration of the world economy, which is no longer relational (based on the exchange of goods and services) but structural (the activities themselves have become internationalized); the reorganization of economic activity with the growth of services; the slow-down of productivity growth; the new forms of enterprise and work organization; the difficulty of regulating the labour market; a less operational system of labour law; and changing expectations from work, especially as regards the trade-off between income and free time. In the light of this diagnosis of the present situation, the major – inescapable – trends for the years to come are already clear: the age pyramid is being inverted, with population ageing; there will be increased geographical and occupational mobility; patterns of work are changing and globalization is becoming more pronounced; expectations and values are being transformed, and new demands are emerging in relation to social identity, protection, time use and training.

Variables

What are the variables that can be brought into play? **The international environment:** "With the gradual structuring of an increasingly globalized economy, there are two possible ways forward: either through intensified international cooperation, which would help develop instruments of political action to regulate the consequences of globalization and encourage the development of a growth strategy, or through a system of international cooperation which, though inadequate, lastingly commits the world economy to a 'disharmonizing', exclusionist and mercantilist logic of market shares". The **productive system** could take one of three courses: segmentation, which encourages external flexibility and successive subcontracting at the expense of research and development and long-term investment, especially in human resources; cooperation based on a system of networks, exchange of information and intangible investment; and finally, "global performance" which shares the same principles as those of cooperation, but where "cooperative organization extends beyond the industrial sector, for it is the foundation of relations between the productive system and society" (GPC, p. 155). Changes in work-related **expectations and attitudes** will depend on five determinants: the values people place on work, money and time; the capacity to produce as much or more wealth with less and less labour; the ability to invent activities which fulfil the same functions (for the individual) as employment but without the characteristics of paid employment; readiness to accept redistribution of income; and the type of regulatory mechanism adopted. These factors will determine whether present social attitudes are maintained, whether individual decisions come to predominate, whether regulation is based on collective bargaining in the conventional sense – i.e. wage bargaining – or whether regulation through collective bargaining covers the whole package of "employment, wages, time and social protection". The **legal and institutional system** will either adjust or change: adjust defensively (deregulation and social assistance) or offensively (redistribution of the State's prescriptive power to the social partners); or change gradually (new areas for negotiation, new rules governing worker and employer representation) or radically (redefinition of the legal concept of work).

Four scenarios

The future will depend upon how these variables evolve. The Working Group conceived of four scenarios – obviously possible visions of the future, not forecasts, still less predictions. (The scenarios are summarized in the table in GPC, p. 8.) Cooperation and adjustment are the two distinctive attitudes shaping these scenarios. The first scenario (which the French authors call *enlisement*, or the process of sinking) is characterized by a lack of cooperation – on an international scale, between enterprises, between the productive sector and society – and by a lack of adjustment – in production, law, labour relations. As a result a country turns in on itself, its working population shrinks (in proportionate terms), there is persistent mass unemployment and a preference for income rather than free time, society becomes segmented and the State is bankrupted by social welfare spending on the unemployed. The second scenario (hyper-competition) is that of unrestrained adjustment: competition rules supreme, the State's role is reduced to the minimum, the trade unions are further weakened, deregulation leads to lower unemployment accompanied by increased poverty, precarious working conditions and inequality. Social divisiveness grows. The third scenario (adjustment) involves a low level of international cooperation but rapid changes in the productive system, in social behaviour, expectations and institutions. Consumption gains from individuals opting for free time and reduced working hours; the productive system is characterized by flexibility and renewed productivity gains; active working life is prolonged; working time and training time merge. Unemployment is reduced and there is less strain on social cohesiveness. In the fourth scenario, there is cooperation at all levels. International regulation in the monetary sphere (as elsewhere) allows interest rates to fall and stimulates world growth. In combination with institutional reforms (in training, labour law), the reorganization of activities throughout the life cycle (work, training, civic activities, leisure) and the creation of enterprise networks, this growth makes it possible to loosen the stranglehold of short-termism and break with unemployment and economic insecurity.

PROPOSALS OF THE WORKING GROUP

Seeking to ensure that one of the rosier scenarios materializes in France, the Working Group made a series of proposals – presented as six frameworks for discussion and action. They concern: international cooperation, the production system, training, working time, labour law and dialogue between the social partners.

Openness to the world

In the international sphere, the Working Group advocated intensified co-operation: accepting globalization but rejecting the logic of "economic warfare in which any gain is necessarily achieved at someone's expense" (GPC, p. 223). They considered the single European currency necessary in order to "restore a certain margin for manoeuvre to an economic policy which favours growth, and makes the regions of Europe attractive to investors, thus encouraging employment" (GPC, p. 223). The Working Group stressed the need to build a social Europe, notably by promoting rules established through European-level collective bargaining (the first example of which may prove to be the agreement on the right to parental leave, recently signed by European employers and workers). International cooperation should also be applied in monetary and financial matters in order to lower interest rates and make the monetary and financial systems serve the real economy rather than constrain it. As regards international trade and labour standards, "better information on the links between economic development and social progress will be needed to establish the institutional framework and consensus-based practical procedures for the harmonization of labour standards between countries involved in international trade. Hopefully, the standards laid down by the International Labour Organization – given its experience in supervisory activity – will provide the basis for a policy of multilateral supervision of labour practices as they relate to economic development" (GPC, p. 230).

The networking enterprise

In the second framework, the key word is *network*: "Field observation shows, above all, that the efficient enterprise has access to information networks, which allow it to pick up changes in its environment and to adjust quickly". Networking would make it possible to limit the economic uncertainty associated with subcontracting (which then becomes a form of partnership or co-contracting) and with the survival of small and medium-sized enterprises by sharing risks or pooling certain functions, including the management of personnel. These area-based networks could include other partners, such as training institutions or local authorities, which have a role to play in the development of employment in the personal services sector or neighbourhood services, though effective demand in this area is unknown.

Lifelong learning

Training will be a lifelong process, which implies a redistribution of roles between the school system and the productive sector. Moreover, skills and qualifications are being redefined, with "problem-solving ability" becoming just as important as "know-how".[9] The school must therefore "refocus on its general education and socialization functions. Relieved of the impossible task of providing adequate training for employment, the school will be able to develop all aspects of knowledge, ... to improve pupils' understanding of reality, develop comparative approaches, and increase pupils' independence and sense of responsibility" (GPC, p. 254). A similar idea is put forward by Robert Reich in *The work of nations*, where he expresses regret that: "learning to collaborate, communicate abstract concepts and to achieve a consensus are not usually emphasized within formal education".[10] As for what comes after school – which requires the ability to adjust to employment or, preferably, to a variety of jobs – this should be of greater concern to the social partners, who "would be persuaded to negotiate ... in a manner that takes individual skills into account in pay scales and career plans. ... While the employment contract in the employer/employee relationship involves the management and exchange of individual skills, the function of collective bargaining is to regulate this management and exchange in accordance with the principle of equality. Legislation might be enacted granting workers a collective right of co-determination as regards the conditions on which they may dispose of time previously allocated to training and retraining" (GPC, p. 264).

The reduction of working time

On the question of working time, three lessons may be learnt from the past:
– reduction of working hours is an adjustment method that is complicated to implement, but effective in increasing the employment-

intensity of growth, provided it is accompanied by genuine and socially desirable organizational change;

–   compulsory, uniformly applicable state measures to shorten the working week with immediate effect must be ruled out;

–   multiform, "spontaneous", decentralized processes to reduce working time cannot, alone, provide a satisfactory response to the full scale of the problem [of unemployment] and are not a reliable source of more employment-intensive growth (GPC, p. 272).

The Working Group therefore proposed to combine substantial, generalized reduction in statutory working time with a very wide range of specific measures arising out of negotiation and agreements. Statutory working hours would be calculated on an annual, not a weekly, basis, the object being to arrive at 1,500 hours in France by 2015 (down from 1,670 hours in 1992), 10 per cent of which would be devoted to training. Working time, in the strict sense of the term, would thus be shortened by between 20 and 25 per cent over the next 20 years. Both the number and the pattern of hours worked would be decided jointly by the employer and the worker.

Activity contracts

This is undoubtedly the core proposal of the report. Firstly, because it serves as a focal point for the various questions raised in the rest of the document. Secondly, because this idea will certainly meet with opposition both in people's minds and in practice. At any event, the proposal's main strength is to raise the questions of how to tackle legal and economic insecurity and whether there is a will to do so.

Labour law, which is largely modelled on the standard of wage-earning employment in a Taylorist organization, now faces a multiplicity of new forms of employment and work organization. Thus, today:

–   the relationship of subordination, which characterizes the employment contract, is becoming more tenuous in the new systems of job assignments, new working time arrangements and changing work hierarchies, while at the same time certain self-employed workers are gradually losing their independence since, in practice, they now often depend on enterprises;

–   there is a blurring of the legal boundaries that used typically to define the object of the employment contract as being directly performed and temporally quantifiable production work, distinct from the person of the worker and directly related to the activity of the profit-making enterprise (GPC, p. 89).

The long labour market series published by the INSEE (French National Institute of Statistics and Economic Studies) shows that "the traditional model of full-time paid employment, for a specified duration in a given trade or occupation, which has prevailed since the beginning of this century, is losing its standard-setting value. New forms of temporary employment are developing, periods of employment and unemployment alternate with increasing frequency, and job mobility is increasing" (GPC, p. 95). There are also ever more new forms of employment designed to fight unemployment in certain population groups. These are inevitably accompanied by a dense mass of regulations, packed with exceptions and otherwise confusing provisions. As a result, many labour laws no longer have any real impact.

Economic insecurity. From the worker's point of view, mobility will therefore be of the essence: changes of employer, sector, work status and geographical area; periods of unemployment, training or voluntary inactivity; modified work patterns. Such mobility is bound to result in some economic insecurity, as regards income level maintenance and social security coverage, which is linked to employment.

An activity contract would be concluded between an individual and a number of employers (enterprises, associations, local authorities, training institutions) organized in a network, for a period of several years (five, for example), during which periods of employment under a conventional contract would alternate with periods of self-employment, training or leave devoted to community or social service activities. It is designed as a legal instrument that would regulate employment with a view to preventing social exclusion (though making no claim to "repair" it); placing work and vocational training on an equal basis; equating self-employment with wage-earning employment; maintaining social protection and organizing the social responsibilities of the various actors, including enterprises.

Dialogue between the social partners

In calling for the promotion of collective bargaining as a means of regulation, the report alludes to certain features characterizing the situation in France: the supremacy of state law, low union density, a fragmented trade union movement, and the lack of cooperative spirit. The Working Group suggested measures "that would enable the trade unions to achieve genuine representativeness again and enhance their capacity to assume greater responsibility in the social/human resource management of enterprises and sectors of activity" (GPC, p. 306):

- at enterprise level, the representativeness of a trade union should no longer be presumed, but should be shown to be genuine and justified;

- in collective bargaining, the complexity of French procedural law seems pointless and often harmful; a simple general obligation to bargain in good faith should suffice;

- the French legal system should move towards genuine co-determination, in particular as regards the organization of working time.

To avoid a situation where only large enterprises would be subject to rules introduced through collective bargaining, it was suggested that in small and medium-sized enterprises where there is no representative union, enterprise agreements (currently negotiable only by the unions) might be negotiated by the works council provided that they tie in with existing agreements at the industry level or above. It should be noted that a few days after the report was published, the French employers' organization (CNPF) and three unions signed a national inter-occupational agreement introducing an experimental scheme which will, under certain conditions, allow collective agreements to be negotiated and concluded in enterprises where there are no union representatives. In such cases, those entitled to negotiate will be either a group of workers mandated by a representative trade union or staff representatives (delegated or elected to the works council); and the provisions of any agreement they conclude will be submitted to a joint committee at industry level.[11]

This set of proposals applies to France. Their aim is to make up for certain weaknesses or delays which hinder that country's institutions from adjusting or from intervening in the new economic and social situation of global integration, mass unemployment and strained social fabric. Bernard Perret, the rapporteur of France's *Conseil scientifique de l'évaluation* (Scientific Evaluation Council) has pointed out that: "for the first time, an official report dealing with this issue is not just a collection of prescriptions for reducing unemployment, but a genuine prospective study which takes account of all aspects of work, including the most 'qualitative'".[12] Though some of the proposals may seem utopian, others are quite realistic, as evidenced by the agreement referred to in the preceding paragraph. This ambivalence brings us back to the question of the scale of the changes affecting work. Is there a deep, structural transformation going on, manifestations of which are being felt throughout the world? Or are there differentiated, sectoral and cyclical developments, perception of which is clouded by the employment crisis? Does this transformation spell the end of paid employment, indeed the end of work, as some predict?

TRANSFORMATION OF WORK

Taylorist work organization may be said to have obeyed the rule of unity of time, place and action applied by seventeenth-century dramatists when structuring their plays. Workers gathered together in one establishment, for a fixed number of hours, performing given tasks. To this one may add that they enjoyed the benefits of a contract of indefinite duration, a fixed wage based on time worked and skills, and complete independence from their employer outside working hours. "Nevertheless, in the past few years we have seen the start of a new era in which each of these components has been whittled away by the spread of new forms of employment. Is the model about to collapse? No, but it will gradually lose ground to an expanding 'grey area'".[13] Let us examine these components.

Work content

According to the Report,

Technological innovation and organizational changes have made their presence felt at the workplace by dissociating the worker from his/her machine. ... Blue-collar work is moving in four different directions: supervision (actively overseeing the process), optimization (improving the performance of the technical system), maintenance, and flow management (close matching of production with orders). Workers at all levels are having to become versatile, but their autonomy is limited by a new interdependence with other workers and teams. The concept of qualification or skill is gradually shifting towards that of competence. We no longer talk of the "worker performing a task" but of the "operative who can handle uncertainty and solve problems" (GPC, pp. 126-127).

These comments certainly apply to high-technology industries and to many tertiary sector activities. But do they apply generally? A note of caution is called for. Robert Reich has drawn up a typology of occupations in the global economy: routine production services, in-person services, and symbolic-analytic services. It is often assumed that the expansion of services and the modernization of industry will inevitably reduce the share of routine production services in favour of symbolic-analytical services. And yet: "many information-processing jobs fit easily into [the category of routine production services]. The foot soldiers of the information economy are hordes of data processors stationed in 'back offices' at computer terminals linked to worldwide information banks. They routinely enter data into computers or take it out again. ... [the] raw data ... must be processed in much the same monotonous way that assembly-line workers and, before them, textile workers processed piles of other raw materials".[14]

The workplace

According to the Report,

In parallel with the trend towards extensive decentralization in decision-making ..., there is an increasing tendency for large firms now to refocus on their "core business". At the same time, there is a tremendous shift towards subcontracting, involving a network of service firms that operate on the periphery of large enterprises (GPC, p. 128).

Telework and home work both seem to be on the increase in many countries, though there are important distinctions to be made when it comes to employment and working conditions: subcontracting in the strict sense must be distinguished from labour-only contracting. In the first case, the object of the contractual relationship between enterprises is the supply of goods or services; in the second case, it is the supply of labour.[15] Subcontracting in the strict sense includes the provision of a skill or service by a third party, as well as contracting out or contracting in.[16] Telework and home work have one feature in common, namely that the activity is carried on in the worker's own home.[17] They differ in that telework implies the use of electronic means of communication, which may also, as we have seen, involve repetitive tasks.

The effects of these changes in the place where work is performed stem primarily from the fact that they also entail changes in worker status, form of remuneration, working time, etc. For example, the home worker is paid piece rates rather than by the hour. Empirical observation of subcontracting in the aerospace and the textile/garment industries led Marie-Laure Morin to note that:

In both industries, subcontracting appears to have resulted from the decision to contract out the less profitable operations and those entailing the highest labour costs. ... Subcontracting – as a form of employment flexibility and personnel management reorganization – is one of the various ways of creating concentric circles of peripheral jobs around the core staff of large (and not-so-large) enterprises, either by strictly legal means (through temporary employment agencies, contract labour) or by both legal and organizational means (subcontracting).[18]

In the cases of home work and telework, there is a blurring of the boundary between private and working life that is found in wage-earning employment.

Worker status

The contracting out of certain functions entails a reorganization of the enterprise and of employment. Within the enterprise, there remains a core of stable employees with contracts of indefinite duration; on the periphery, there are two other categories of workers. The first comprises employees with fixed-term contracts, trainees and temporary workers; and the second, workers external to the enterprise, generally service suppliers, subcontractors or self-employed workers (GPC, p. 79).

The diversification of forms of work is most evident in this respect: self-employment, fixed-term contracts and temporary work increase at the expense of wage-earning employment under contract of indefinite duration. Although this shift has so far affected only a limited proportion of the workforce, there is little doubt as to its nefarious consequences for workers' economic security.

A survey of self-employed workers in the United Kingdom[19] shows a very wide range of incomes with a highly polarized distribution. These workers are three times more likely than wage-earners to be in the poorest decile of the population (the greatest threat being to women, young people and the long-term unemployed). Inequality is perpetuated into retirement, as poorer self-employed workers have fewer acquired rights and so have smaller pensions. Another aspect of the question is the so-called "pseudo-self-employed" – persons whose work does not differ from that of wage-earners (notably as regards the relationship of subordination), but who are bound by a commercial contract rather than an employment contract, which means that all social security contributions are paid by the worker.[20]

What goes for self-employed workers also applies to wage-earners in insecure or precarious work: lower wages and less social security coverage, difficulty in obtaining housing or credit, less satisfactory working conditions, labour inspection problems as regards occupational health and safety, etc. In France, such workers are the victims of twice as many employment injuries and of industrial accidents twice as serious as are permanent employees.[21] In social policy terms, their vulnerability is fraught with consequences. The sociologist Robert Castel places the individual on two axes: the axis of relational integration, which ranges from "insertion" in stable sociability networks to total "isolation"; and the axis of relation to work, ranging from stable employment – through participation in various forms of precarious, intermittent, seasonal occupations – to complete loss of work (exclusion).

The correlation of these two axes delimits different zones of [the] social space according to the degree of *social cohesion* they provide. Put schematically: at one extreme, being in the *integration zone* means that one has guaranteed permanent employment and solid relational support mechanisms; in the middle, the *vulnerability zone*, employment is precarious and relations are fragile; and at the other extreme, the *disaffiliation zone*, there is both lack of work and social isolation.[22]

Thus, the development of "peripheral" jobs – or a secondary labour market – at the expense of the "core" – or primary labour market – could involve the risk of social exclusion, particularly since on the other, relational axis, there are strains on such bonds as family ties.

Working time

Changes in this area have been threefold: an arguable weakening of the trend reduction in working time; an increase in part-time work; and the reorganization of working time, with the decline of the concept of the working week. Three factors have been at work here: workers' demands for shorter working hours in return for productivity gains; employers' emphasis on flexibility to extend plant operating time or adapt work schedules to cyclical or seasonal fluctuations in demand; and the relative values placed by the individual on free time and income.

The trend decline in annual working time in the industrialized countries has levelled off since the late 1970s (with a few exceptions, as in Japan). The fluctuations observed during the 1980s and into the 1990s have been cyclical. While this development may be attributed to stagnant productivity, it is not clear whether it marks only a pause in a declining trend, or a floor. The answer depends partly on whether the emerging tendency to conclude agreements reducing and reorganizing working time will have any significant impact on actual average working time.[23] The same applies to the trade-off between reduced hours of work and wages, whether in the form of work-sharing or of part-time work.

In the OECD countries, the incidence of part-time employment is increasing nearly everywhere, with women accounting for between 60 and 85 per cent of part-time workers.[24] In this connection two points deserve careful consideration: first, whether part-time work is freely chosen or not, and second, whether or not it translates into precarious employment. A recent study by the Canadian Council on Social Development shows considerable overlap between temporary work and part-time work, neither of which is freely chosen in most cases.[25] Other studies suggest an increase in part-time work undertaken out of necessity and in combination with various forms of precarious employment, resulting in lower income.[26]

Working time is organized through collective bargaining and the flexibility demanded by employers is typically traded off either for the maintenance of jobs or for shorter working hours. Several European countries have introduced incentives to encourage this trade-off.[27] Flexibility in the organization of working time covers a wide variety of work patterns: annual calculation of working hours, night or weekend shifts, job sharing, flexitime and core time, part-time work, overtime, etc. The introduction of these new patterns raises two issues.

Firstly, flexibility should not be confused with deregulation. One of the lessons Gerhard Bosch draws from surveys conducted in eight OECD countries is that:

Both firms and employees are interested in more flexible working hours. Often, however, their interests do not coincide. This divergence of interests is dealt with in very different ways in different countries and sectors. In the capital-intensive sectors of manufacturing industry, firms seek to reduce their capital costs by extending operating hours and are able to offer attractive compromises to their highly unionized work forces. In the labour-intensive service sector, however, flexible working time arrangements are intended to reduce staff costs which, in a sector dominated by small firms and price competition and with a high proportion of women workers, may lead to unattractive time arrangements for employees. Unregulated flexibility means that the interests of firms predominate, with trade unions forced to react defensively because of their lack of opportunity to participate in the determination of working time. Regulated flexibility, by contrast, can create a balance between the interests of employees and those of firms. It increases the acceptance of flexible time arrangements and avoids negative consequences for individual sectors, such as persistent recruitment problems in sectors with unfavourable working-time regulations.[28]

Here, too, the question arises as to the extent to which workers can actually dispose of their free time, if "flexibility" is pushed so far that working hours become unpredictable.

Secondly, changes in working time cannot be considered separately from remuneration, whether in part-time employment or in short-time employment for economic reasons. This is evidenced by the fact that part-time work is generally performed by women and is most widespread in high-income countries. Similarly, agreements on the reorganization of work,

Income/free time preferences

1993-95	Preference (%)	
	Income	Free time
End 1993	54	43
End 1994 ·	47	49
End 1995 ·	45	53
By income level (FF)		
< = 8 000	59	37
8 000 to 12 000	45	52
12 000 to 24 000	35	61
> = 24 000	39	61

Source: *Liaisons sociales – Le mensuel* (Paris), Mar. 1996.

shorter hours, lower wages and new work patterns seem to be more readily accepted and more effective in enterprises, sectors or countries enjoying high levels of remuneration and social protection. The same can be said of the trade-off that individuals make between income and free time.

Individual preferences for extra income or more free time are difficult to assess otherwise than by opinion poll. Surveys conducted in France by the CREDOC (Research Centre for the Study and Observation of Living Conditions) show an increasing preference for free time, and that this is linked to income (see table). Studies conducted in Germany also show a change over time, and from one generation to another, in the priority given to work and leisure.[29]

And what is the trend?

The wide variety of changes and their scale are clear, as shown in a report prepared by the ILO for the International Labour Conference in 1996:

It is true that new forms of work have emerged such as teleworking and outsourcing of work previously done by a core, in-house workforce. Some of this outsourcing is even being done across national frontiers. But the overall magnitudes involved have to be put into perspective. Whether or not it is the wave of the future remains to be seen. In the meantime it would be prudent to examine whether aggregate statistics on changes in the structure of employment in the past two decades or more do reveal any clear trends in this direction.

The last two decades have indeed seen the emergence of non-standard forms of work. Among these the most important numerically have been self-employment, part-time employment and temporary work. Each of these forms deviates from the standard full-time regular employment by one or more characteristics. They usually offer lower levels of social security coverage and employment rights than regular jobs. Part-time and temporary work are usually associated with lower wages.[30]

In order to assess the extent of this trend, the ILO monitored the following indicators: the shares in total employment of self-employment in non-agricultural sectors (a measure of self-employment) and of part-time employment (including women's share in this type of employment); the share of temporary employment in total wage employment; the rate of turnover and job tenure (measures of employment stability); and the occupational distribution of employment (indicating job "quality"). This study demonstrates that the share of non-standard employment has been increasing in OECD countries since the early 1970s, but that the increase is neither as spectacular as one might think nor uniform – some countries have even recorded a decrease in self-employment and temporary work. Only part-time employment has gained ground practically everywhere, though in varying proportions. Moreover, there has been rapid employment growth at the top of the occupational scale (professional, technical, administrative and management personnel); the economy is actually generating more "good" jobs. Turnover and job tenure rates have, on the whole, remained remarkably stable. The ILO report concludes "... the slight changes recorded so far do not support the view that the 'job for life' has ceased to exist or that jobs in general have become dramatically more unstable. On the contrary, a large core of the workforce is still in stable and secure jobs, even though instability and insecurity have increased in other segments of the labour market." [31]

THE END OF WORK?

And yet, some not only proclaim the transformation of work, they even predict its end:

In the past, when a technological revolution threatened the wholesale loss of jobs in an economic sector, a new sector emerged to absorb the surplus labor. ... Today, however, as all these sectors fall victim to rapid restructuring and automation, no "significant" new sector has developed to absorb the millions upon millions of workers who are being displaced. The only new sector on the horizon is the knowledge sector ... The new professionals – the so-called symbolic analysts or knowledge workers – come from the fields of science, engineering, management, consultancy, teaching, marketing, media, and entertainment. While their numbers will continue to grow, they will remain small compared to the number of workers who will be displaced by the new generation of "thinking machines". [32]

This is the old theory of technology-induced unemployment decked out in new attire, the one that – implicitly or explicitly – underlies the theories of jobless growth, delinking income from work, or "full activity" as a substitute for full employment. Basically, the idea is that since jobs cannot be created in sufficient numbers, the labour market could be cleared and social exclusion prevented if everyone were given an opportunity to engage in a subsidized occupation or if all citizens were paid a minimum income, allowing them to choose freely between full- or part-time work, casual work, non-commercial or leisure activities. [33]

These ideas are countered both in *Le travail dans vingt ans* – in principle – and in the ILO Report on *Employment policies in a global context* – in fact. According to the first:

The activity contract is intended to encourage a form of mobility that implies neither precariousness, nor insecurity nor yet exclusion (GPC, p. 284) ... However, the aim of the activity contract is not to disguise the reality of unemployment or to promote a concept of "full activity" which would blur the differences between employment, work and activity and thereby justify public funding for a universal allowance or subsistence income for a part of the population which would, in effect, be permanently excluded from work (GPC, p. 286).

According to the second:

Thus aggregate data do not provide any support for the imminent "end of work", or even the beginnings of jobless growth. ... The reality is that high current unemployment is largely the result of the slower growth of output and productivity rather than of the labour-displacement effects of hyperproductive new technologies.[34]

MUCH ADO ABOUT NOTHING?

Work is undoubtedly changing. Indeed, has it ever stopped changing? It is, however, highly likely that the process is in an accelerating phase, owing to the revolution in communications and information technology. What is debatable is the relation between these changes and the employment crisis, and, even more so, the relation between these changes and the instability, insecurity and deterioration of wage employment – which, according to some, is about to become extinct. Despite their differences, the two reports *Le travail dans vingt ans* and *Employment policies in a global context* have one virtue in common: they both reject the oversimplification and fatalism implied in equating change with workers' insecurity. A study on flexibility of work in the United Kingdom revealed that precarious jobs are on the increase, but to a limited extent and as a result of the lower social cost of precarious jobs rather than technical causes. The *Financial Times* has argued that: "Job-getting is a multi-billion dollar industry in its own right. But much of the industry has a vested interest in the movement of employees in and out of work. It needs turnover."[35] On a more serious note, however, consider the conclusions reached by Richard B. Freeman, Professor of Economics at Harvard University and at the London School of Economics: "The growth of flexibility, notably of the unfettered right to hire and fire, has a largely redistributive effect ... I am convinced that flexibility has no impact on output and employment levels, but that it strongly influences the redistribution of incomes in favour of the employers. ... The real problem is that of restoring strong economic growth conducive to massive job creation – not seeking to move people around more easily from one job to another."[36]

Notes

[1] Commissariat général du Plan: *Le travail dans vingt ans* (Report of the Working Group on "Work and employment to the year 2015", chaired by Jean Boissonnat), Paris, Editions Odile Jacob/

La Documentation française, 1995. All further references to this report are given as GPC (General Planning Commission), followed by the relevant page number(s).

[2] *Le Monde* (Paris), 7 Dec. 1995.

[3] *Le Monde diplomatique* (Paris), Jan. 1996, pp. 8-9.

[4] Alain Supiot: "Malaise dans le social", in *Droit social* (Paris), 1996, No. 2 (Feb.), p. 115.

[5] *Le Nouveau quotidien* (Lausanne), 15 Jan. 1996, p. 16.

[6] *Le Nouvel économiste* (Paris), No. 1034, 9 Feb. 1996, p. 25.

[7] Address to the G-7 Employment Conference, held in Lille, 1 Apr. 1996.

[8] Some contributions to the debate are cited in this perspective. Others to which reference could be made are Dominique Méda: *Le travail. Une valeur en voie de disparition*, Paris, Aubier, 1995; Alain Supiot: *Critique du droit de travail*, Paris, PUF, 1995; Gérard Blanc (ed.): *Le travail au XXIe siècle*, Paris, Dunod, 1995; and two special issues of the periodical *Esprit* (Paris), 1995, No. 214 (Aug.-Sep.) and No. 217 (Dec.), respectively entitled "The future of work" and "Towards a multiactivity society?".

[9] The evolution of the idea of skill as problem-solving ability is discussed in "A job classification to facilitate occupational mobility", in *International Labour Review* (Geneva), Vol. 133 (1994), No. 2, pp. 259-264.

[10] Robert Reich: *The work of nations*, New York, Vintage Books, 1992, p. 233.

[11] *Liaisons sociales – Le quotidien* (Paris), 9 Nov. 1995. On this subject, see also Gabriel Coin: "Politique contractuelle: l'accord interprofessionnel du 31 octobre 1995", in *Droit social* (Paris), 1996, No. 1 (Jan.), p. 3.

[12] *Espace social européen* (Paris), 10 Oct. 1995, p. 28. Bernard Perret is the author of *L'avenir du travail. Les démocraties face au chômage*, Paris, Le Seuil, 1995. The Scientific Evaluation Council is a body appointed to evaluate the effectiveness of government policies.

[13] Jacques Lesourne: "Allons-nous vers la mort du salariat?", in *Liaisons sociales – Le mensuel* (Paris), Oct. 1995, p. 98.

[14] Reich, op. cit., p. 175.

[15] See International Labour Conference (ILC), 85th Session, Report VI (1): *Contract labour*, Geneva, ILO, 1996; see also the article by Lee and Sivananthiran in this issue.

[16] See Marie-Laure Morin: "Sous-traitance et relations salariales, Aspects de droit du travail", in *Travail et emploi* (Paris), 1994, No. 60 (May), pp. 23-43.

[17] See ILC, 82nd Session, Report V (1): *Home work*, Geneva, ILO, 1994.

[18] Morin, op. cit., pp. 28 and 31.

[19] N. Meager, G. Court and J. Moralee: *Self-employment and the distribution of income* (IMS Report No. 270), Brighton Institute of Manpower Studies, 1994.

[20] See *Revue du travail* (Brussels), Apr.-May-June 1995, an issue largely devoted to the question of the "pseudo-self-employed". See also ILC, 77th Session, 1990, Report VII: *The promotion of self-employment*, Geneva, ILO, 1990.

[21] According to a survey conducted by the *Institut national de recherche et de sécurité*; see *Santé et Travail* (Paris), 1994, No. 8 (Apr.), and *Libération* (Paris), 27 July 1995.

[22] Robert Castel: "De l'indigence à l'exclusion: la désaffiliation. Précarité du travail et vulnérabilité relationnelle", in Jacques Donzelot (ed.): *Face à l'exclusion. Le modèle français*, Paris, Editions Esprit, 1991. By the same author, see also *Les métamorphoses de la question sociale. Une chronique du salariat*, Paris, Fayard, 1995.

[23] See Vittorio Di Martino: "Megatrends in working time", in *Journal of European Social Policy* (Harlow, Essex), 1995, Vol. 5, No. 3, pp. 235-249.

[24] For a comprehensive international study of part-time work and related issues, see ILC, 80th Session, 1993, Report V (1): *Part-time work*, Geneva, ILO, 1992.

[25] Grant Schellenberg and Christopher Clark: *Temporary employment in Canada: Profiles, patterns and policy considerations*, Ottawa, Canadian Council on Social Development, Mar. 1996.

[26] Vittorio Di Martino: "La nuova disciplina del lavoro a tempo parziale nelle fonti dell'Organizzazione Internazionale del Lavoro", in *Diritto delle relazioni industriali* (Milan), 1995, No. 1/5, pp. 123-134.

[27] See "Working time and employment: New arrangements", in *International Labour Review* (Geneva), Vol. 134 (1995), No. 2, pp. 259-272.

[28] Gerhard Bosch: "Synthesis report", in OECD (ed.): *Flexible working time: Collective bargaining and government intervention*, Paris, OECD, 1995, pp. 38-39.

[29] Hans Lenk: "Value changes and the achieving society: A social-philosophical perspective", in OECD (ed.): *OECD societies in transition: The future of work and leisure*, Paris, OECD, 1994, pp. 81-96.

[30] ILC, 83rd Session, 1996, Report V: *Employment policies in a global context*, Geneva, ILO, 1996, p. 22.

[31] ibid., p. 25.

[32] Jeremy Rifkin: *The end of work: The decline of the global labor force and the dawn of the post-market era*, New York, G.P. Putman's Sons, 1995, p. 35.

[33] For a review of the various versions of this idea, see Denis Clerc: "La pleine activité, fille indigne du plein emploi", in *Alternatives Economiques* (Paris), 1996, No. 134 (Feb.), pp. 64-67.

[34] ILC, 83rd Session, 1996, Report V: *Employment policies in a global context*, Geneva, ILO, 1996, pp. 19 and 21.

[35] Richard Donkin: "Realistic picture of work remains elusive", in *Financial Times* (London), 15 Mar. 1996.

[36] Interview in *Alternatives économiques* (Paris), 1996, No. 135 (Mar.), pp. 60-61.

DECLINE AND RESURGENCE OF UNREMUNERATED WORK

Raymond LE GUIDEC*

28

Before addressing the opposition between remunerated and unremunerated work, a few definitions need to be specified. Firstly, the notion of work itself. This certainly encompasses the activity involved in producing goods and services in a mercantile society, where work is a means of increasing the community's wealth and is central to the development of economic relations. But work can also be understood as a broader social activity where relationships do not always lend themselves easily to economic measurement even though they require skill and expenditure of time. In this sense, the notion of work covers all sorts of activities, including those which contribute to maintaining and strengthening social bonds. In place of work in the strict economic and legal sense, one can define social activity, which both includes it and transcends it.

The distinction between remunerated and unremunerated work is essentially legal. Remunerated work implies a consideration – i.e. some payment or obligation – to be given by the party for whom the work is done. In contrast, unremunerated work is characterized by the absence of such an exchange: a person receives and benefits without owing anything in return. In this case there is nothing to counterbalance the parties' losses and gains. In civil law, the pure form of an unremunerated act is a gift. This occurs where a material loss is consented to voluntarily, for no remuneration or other consideration whatsoever. This implies the intention of benefiting another.[1]

In a mercantile society remunerated work is the norm, especially when it concerns the production of goods and services. Today at least, the fact that there is generalized wage employment renders it obvious that work should be remunerated. Indeed, remuneration is a powerful, if not the only, sign of social and legal recognition of work as distinct from voluntary or charitable

---

Originally published in *International Labour Review*, Vol. 135 (1996), No. 6.

* Professor at the Faculty of Law and Political Science, University of Nantes.

activity. In this sense also, work is synonymous with employment; it requires and confers professional qualifications, gives entitlement to social benefits, and is measured by its cost within the overall economic system. This is why voluntary, unremunerated work raises an issue of recognition and identification. At first glance, such work would appear to be the exception. Indeed, its very existence may seem questionable.

THE DISAPPEARANCE OF TRADITIONAL FORMS OF UNREMUNERATED WORK

Traditional forms of unremunerated work are in constant retreat as they come to be recognized as actual work and are given social recognition through remuneration and legal status. In the long run, unremunerated work thus seems destined to disappear. But counter to this historical trend, today's organization of work is bringing out new forms of unremunerated work that are characteristic of the current crisis of work and employment. Because it is costly by nature, work – and therefore employment – tends to become scarce in an economy under stress. Hence the idea – now widely applied – of integrating work into a socially productive process in which direct remuneration is either managed differently or even eluded.

Taken together, attempts to define the current role and state of what are conveniently described here as traditional forms of unremunerated work convey the impression of a heterogeneous range of activities. The overall picture, however, shows a decline of unremunerated work, which in turn reflects the historical tendency towards the social recognition of work.

One example of unremunerated work, which has probably disappeared entirely, is that of productive labour in private charitable establishments during the second half of the nineteenth century.[2] These institutions received orphans and people – mostly women – who had fallen on hard times. Their work consisted essentially of tailoring and housework, combining education and apprenticeship. The family-like structure of the establishment placed them in a situation of extreme dependence. They were provided with board and lodging, but their work was unpaid as such, except for a very small amount which remained under the exclusive control of the establishment until they left. Though such institutions scarcely exist any longer, unremunerated work in the context of training continues to be common practice.

An ancient form of unremunerated work which has survived is that performed by people serving a sentence.[3] Such work may be either the object of the sentence itself, or an aspect of prison life. In France, for example, work was first introduced as a penalty in the form of community service in 1983. In this case, since work is an alternative to some other penalty, it is obviously not remunerated and has scarcely any skill-enhancing value (e.g. cleaning up public spaces, maintenance of the national heritage, environmental improvement). Prison work, by contrast, reflects a sort of right to work granted to detainees. It consists of traditional manufacturing work – sometimes involving dangerous tasks – governed by a wide range of complex administrative rules. Although such work is not entirely unremunerated, the rate of pay is extremely low and what little prisoners do earn is set aside for them until their release. Clearly, such work does not constitute employment: they have no labour contract and enjoy none of the rights associated with wage employment, such as freedom of association or the right to strike. Nevertheless, they are granted some social protection – which is expanding such as protection against industrial accidents and family allowances. This quasi-unremunerated work has been criticized as a source of unfair competition against private sector work. Conceived as a means of rehabilitating convicts and organizing prison life, its results are unconvincing, and the question remains whether only partial remuneration for prison work is justified in the first place.

Within limits such work by prisoners is analogous to unremunerated civilian work performed by military conscripts assigned to community service.

For a long time, the family constituted a traditional, natural setting for unremunerated work. The family's vertical and authoritarian structure, based on the husband's status as head of household, both explained and justified unremunerated work by family members, whether they performed domestic chores or worked in the family farm, business or workshop. In relations between spouses, the marital obligation of mutual support was enough to justify the principle of non-remuneration. The same applied to relations between parents and their children, based on the former's obligation to feed the family, the principle of family solidarity, or a presumption of relations based on benevolence.

The decline of unremunerated work within the family[4] stems from profound changes which have affected household structure. Based on the principle of equality, the family is now structured along horizontal, egalitarian lines reflecting the advance of women's rights. As a result, domestic work or work in a family business is no longer necessarily unremunerated. Indeed, a valid employment contract can very well be drawn up between spouses, just as professional registration is now open to the spouse of someone running a business. Yet despite these developments, legal recognition of work in husband/wife partnerships is still incomplete since it does not always entail a right to remuneration. In France, this right is recognized only indirectly, through case-law, by means of ad hoc compensatory mechanisms that are not always very convincing, e.g. unjust enrichment doctrine, gifts in lieu of remuneration, or valuation of compensatory payments following divorce. Could the general right to direct remuneration not be legislated in the future?

A similar decline of unremunerated work can be observed in relations between parents and their children. Under French law, children working on the family farm are – subject to certain conditions – entitled to a "postponed wage", i.e. compensation for past unremunerated work in the event of the death of the head of the household. In other cases, the courts increasingly recognize that work in partnership, or even a particularly significant amount of help, deserves compensation by virtue of the doctrine of unjust enrichment. In other words, it is no longer taken for granted that, in principle, such work should be unremunerated. However, outside of work relationships in the usual sense, the family remains a sphere in which unremunerated work is part of the natural order. Family solidarity transcends the strict statutory obligation of family support which, in any case, applies only between direct ascendants and descendants; and the family continues to fulfil its important function of social integration.[5] Indeed, the State still relies primarily on the family for the provision and delivery of social protection.

Taking another perspective, elective political office generally appears to be shifting towards the principle of remuneration, thereby taking on features of wage employment.[6] What used to be a government of notables, in which political office was not meant to be gainful but simply honorary, has become a modern government in which public affairs are managed by people whose work is increasingly like a job in any other profession. The allowances paid to members of parliament or local government are no longer thought of as a reimbursement of expenses, but as an income accruing to an office and are treated as such for tax purposes, in particular. What is happening is in effect a professionalization of politics.

On the face of it, the most typical form of unremunerated work is voluntary work. By definition, a voluntary worker receives no direct remuneration for the service he or she provides.[7] Yet despite its distinctiveness, voluntary work is undergoing significant changes in line with the overall decline of unremunerated work.

There are many different forms of voluntary work, most of them connected with the activities of non-profit organizations. As focal points of social life, such organizations pursue a wide variety of aims (charitable, humanitarian, political, cultural), while still sharing the common characteristic of being not-for-profit. Except for a small administrative staff, the members of a non-profit organization are not actually employed when they work to further its aims and therefore receive no payment for what they do on behalf of the organization. In this respect it may even be questionable whether such activities really qualify as work. Clearly not, if work is defined exclusively in terms of the objective of producing goods and services with a measurable economic value. But the answer is less clear-cut if work is defined so as to include social activity that takes time and skill and contributes to overall social ties. Seen in this light, a community service is performed, so it is a socially useful activity.

In principle voluntary work is unremunerated, since volunteers receive no direct payment for their personal efforts. Indeed, people become volunteers precisely because they do not wish to be paid for their services. And a volunteer's personal reward from a chosen activity – i.e. satisfaction – does not in itself alter the fact that it is unremunerated, this being understood in a purely material sense.

However, closer scrutiny shows that voluntary activity is not always entirely unremunerated. It is sometimes funded indirectly and therefore carries a social cost which belies its unremunerated character. Thus, in some cases, activities that appear to be voluntary are in fact undertaken on the basis of secondments, release of employees, exceptional paid leave or time off approved by the public administrations or institutions where the voluntary workers are normally employed. Likewise, the unemployed are allowed to undertake voluntary work while continuing to receive unemployment benefits, provided that in doing so they do not take up a real job. In the sphere of social welfare in particular, such as assistance to the elderly, the lonely, the sick or the disabled, the State occasionally calls upon the services of relevant non-profit organizations, which in turn assign volunteers for the required purpose. The way voluntary work fits into such established social frameworks suggests that its unremunerated nature, though assumed in principle, is less than absolute. Recognition of the social utility of voluntary work has also prompted a search for statutory arrangements covering voluntary workers.

Traditional forms of unremunerated work are thus declining gradually. In all the cases mentioned above the process is the same: formal recognition of work, more or less broadly defined, contributes to a weakening of unremunerated work.

EMERGENCE OF NEW FORMS OF UNREMUNERATED WORK

In contrast to the decline of traditional forms of unremunerated work, new forms are now emerging.[8] They arise from responses to the protracted employment crisis, which will doubtless continue to affect the free market system for a long time to come, as globalization makes enterprises more vulnerable. Permanent wage employment is costly and therefore becoming scarcer and less secure. As a result, it can no longer be taken for granted that work and employment are assimilated. Of course, work should lead to employment. But the transition may now be slow and uncertain.

In this context, two forms of unremunerated work have become more common. Firstly, work may be integrated into vocational training. Secondly, work is subsidized in many ways, with the aim of encouraging the creation or preservation of jobs. In both cases, work is at least partly unremunerated, particularly from the point of view of the cost to the enterprises which benefit from the labour thus supplied. But work performed in such circumstances carries a social cost which should not be underestimated.

Work has virtually become an integral part of the vocational training process. This applies to almost all initial vocational training for young people, whether schoolchildren or students, in the private and public sectors alike. A period of work experience in a company or a government agency is now a requirement in many countries – a practice which will no doubt be reinforced by the deliberate vocationalization of secondary and higher education qualifications. While this trend looks set to continue, the question remains whether work undertaken for training purposes without any direct remuneration can properly be described as work, rather than as a form of training. It probably combines some of each, though their respective shares may differ significantly in practice. In any event, both the work component and its free character are undeniable.

Enterprise-based training is also frequently used in reskilling, retraining, and job placement programmes for the unemployed. Such training encompasses a wide range of schemes, and participation is often compulsory. Particularly striking in this context is the nature of work provided without charge to the enterprises that take on trainees. Indeed, the various forms of enterprise-based training could be said to contribute to a growing pool of cost-free labour. However, it is not of course completely free. The social cost of unemployment, which includes the funding of retraining and job placement programmes for the unemployed, is indeed phenomenal. This puts the offer of work by trainees into a different perspective, although the cost of trainees is borne by the community as a whole in a spirit of social solidarity which few would question. The fact remains, however, that enterprises derive an immediate advantage from taking on trainees and putting them to work without direct payment by the enterprise. This form of work can pose a competitive threat to wage employment. It is a costly paradox when such unremunerated work actually kills jobs.

The other form of indirectly remunerated work derives from subsidies to employment. Despite variations in the specific mechanisms applied, state support for the creation and preservation of employment has been a constant of public policy in Europe for many years. In practice, such support may take the form either of a reduction of, or temporary exemption from, employers' social contributions, or of direct subsidies. There seems to be a constant search for new ways of alleviating unemployment along these lines. In this case, however, the cost of work to the employer is only partially eliminated, and it might therefore be more accurate to describe it in terms of being partially free. As in the preceding case, it is an expression of collective solidarity which can pose a threat to the creation of durable jobs.

To conclude, it appears that unremunerated work continues to play a part in contemporary society, although the notion of it is changing and relative. In any case, this does not prevent such work from being acknowledged as socially useful, thus laying the basis for its formal recognition. Work is also a means of participation and social integration and as such deserves to be supported in the name of social solidarity.

Notes

[1] F. Collart Dutilleul: "Le contrat gratuit", in Alain Supiot (ed.): *Actes du Colloque "Le travail en Perspectives"*, Paris, LGDJ, 1998.

[2] Michèle Bordeaux: "La gratuité", in Supiot (ed.), op. cit. (note 1).

[3] Soizic Lorvellec: "Travail et peine", in Supiot (ed.), op. cit. (note 1).

[4] Marianne Forgit: "Le recul de la gratuité dans la sphère familiale", in Supiot (ed.), op. cit. (note 1).

[5] Henry Nogues: "Bénévolat et protection sociale", in Supiot (ed.), op. cit. (note 1).

[6] Christian Garbar: "Le travail et l'élu", in Supiot (ed.), op. cit. (note 1).

[7] Henry Nogues, op. cit. (note 5). Yves Rousseau: "Les activités des chômeurs"; Madeleine Rebérioux: "Le travail militant"; and Stéphane Carré: "Activités socialement utiles et notion d'activité professionnelle", in Supiot (ed.), op. cit. (note 1).

[8] Yves Rousseau: "Les activités des chômeurs", in Supiot (ed.), op. cit. (note 1).

BY WAY OF CONCLUSION: LABOUR LAW AND EMPLOYMENT TRANSITIONS

29

Gérard LYON-CAEN *

ON LABOUR LAW

Like any evaluation, an assessment of the state of labour law – in France or elsewhere – must consider both gains and losses. On the positive side, there has been a partial merger of training issues into those of labour – though this is not really as new as it appears. There has also been a recognition in law of the work undertaken within the family, in its broad sense – though here again, given the long history of home-based production, this is scarcely an innovation. The successful – and perhaps more unexpected – penetration of labour law into the public sector should also be counted on the positive side, even though the public service itself is still fighting to stay outside the scope of labour law. But probably the most significant gain is the assimilation or integration into labour law of numerous professions which, despite being by their very nature exercised independently, now appear in the French Labour Code (Livre VII), which contains provisions specific to particular professions. This has been an issue for over 100 years and the motives lying behind the incorporation of these professions would repay further analysis.

On the negative side, one might cite the intrusion into labour law of outside influences. For example, the educational system continues to influence the employment relationship. Leave for private (not only family) reasons is increasingly being taken, upsetting established work patterns. The full recognition of employees' constitutional rights [1] is bringing issues belonging to the political sphere into the workplace. And, finally, many employees are either choosing to operate as self-employed workers, which undermines the established legal concept of subordination in employment, or are being pushed willy-nilly into self-employment. Once wage-earners become in effect subcontractors, they are no longer subject to labour law, but to business law.

Originally published in *International Labour Review*, Vol. 135 (1996), No. 6.

* Former professor of law, University of Paris-I.

ON LABOUR

The ideology of the division of labour casts its shadow over the debates about the nature and future of work. But first one must separate the history of ideas from the historical process itself.

At the level of ideas, it is clear that before the emergence of capitalism, and especially in the City State of antiquity, work was a servile rather than a noble calling. The notion of work has been revalued since the eighteenth – even the seventeenth – century, but it is difficult to distinguish clearly the respective contributions to this rehabilitation process made by the various currents in philosophical thought. Important contributions were made in this respect through the interpretations given to science, the knowledge which enables humanity to establish dominion over nature, to crafts, which the eighteenth-century *Encyclopédistes* considered central to their work, and to the world, not as it is, but as it should be, to use the terms of the followers of Saint-Simon. Ours is a civilization which has been and remains one of producers, in the broadest sense of the word – that is, of living beings producing their own existence. Today, the concept of humanity is indissolubly linked with that of productive work.

At the level of the historical process, it is hard to avoid the conclusion that modern history starts when men were put to work, often in shocking conditions. As a result of the voyages of the great (European) explorers and the "discovery" of new worlds, the Indians of the Americas, and later black Africans, were forced in no uncertain manner into work. Later on the peasantries of Europe were expelled from the countryside and put to work in factories, and when the labour thus "freed" no longer sufficed more workers were brought from other continents. Still later, the frenzied work commitment of the peoples of Asia took over, once the European workers began to show signs of fatigue. Where once men and women migrated to meet the demand for labour, today the work itself shifts, in the "relocation" process.

Certainly today work has to become more creative, more proactive, less passive and submissive. But that apart, it is difficult to go on to argue that labour is a tradable good (or a value, which comes to the same thing); *a fortiori* it is even more difficult to argue that it is exhaustible, in the sense that a mine becomes exhausted, still less that it can be divided up into small portions so that each may have his or her share. One might equally argue that productive activity engenders activity just as sea transport stimulated the production of canvas and rigging.

THE FOUR "CONTRASTS"

There are important differences between the four pairs of contrasting concepts around which the colloquium on "perspectives on work" was organized – private- vs. public-sector work; work vs. training; remunerated vs. un-remunerated work; and wage employment vs. self-employment.

For example, work in the public sector is not primarily distinguished by the nature of the employing agency. In the final analysis, the public character of this agency (the State, local government, or a publicly owned industrial or commercial enterprise) is of little importance. What does single out public sector employment, at least in France, is that its legal underpinnings are not contractual but statutory. There is a sense, therefore, in which the contrast between private and public is merely fortuitous, and does not arise from a fundamental factor.

In future, the contrast between training or education and productive labour will diminish, in that the preservation and development of knowledge and skills will become prerequisites for employment. The laboratory is the factory of tomorrow.

It has been said that a profits-based society such as ours views volunteer or non-profit-making activity with some suspicion. But maybe things are simpler than that. On the one hand, even non-profit or unremunerated activity may elicit a reward – such as employment in some parallel activity, the prospect of future employment, benefits in kind, in this world or ... in the next. Conversely, the holding of any office – as distinct from an occupation involves some dedication to the public interest, or to a cause. Here we enter into the tangled web of the motivations of an agent: certainly these include the need to earn a living, but as soon as any other motivation comes into play, be it only the enjoyment of a calling or the desire to serve, then the simple wage employment concept no longer applies.

Hitherto the most deeply rooted and irreducible contrast has been that between wage employment and self-employment – despite the great difficulty of choosing a reliable criterion on which to base this distinction. The criterion of "subordination in employment" (which is less deeply rooted in history than is commonly thought) has become so unreliable that the courts have supplemented it with the notion of "through tasks performed regularly within an organization" (intégration dans un service organisé). Other, more pertinent, ideas also come to mind in this connection, such as the client relationship (as in the case of a lawyer who is regularly employed as an adviser but is not on the payroll) or the onus of economic risk. In view of such considerations, it is clearly time to reassess what has been known since 1930 as the condition of "economic dependence", especially in the light of its alleged compatibility with self-employment, i.e. independence in the legal sense. Since this economic dependence stems from a contractual relationship – as in the case of certain sub-contracting arrangements – it may be better to describe it in terms of legal dependence. It is impossible to say now where the line between the two will eventually be drawn.

ON TWO OTHER SITUATIONS

Two other legally contrasting situations should be considered in order to gain an understanding of where the concept of work is going.

Unemployment: the contrast between employment and unemployment is no longer what it once was, as both terms have become increasingly complex. An employed person may work only part time, even on an annual basis, which implies lengthy periods of full unemployment; that person may be laid off, or even be employed on short time with compensation over a long period;[2] or may live from one temporary contract to the next if, for example, employed on a temporary basis. This situation is not very different from that of the so-called "jobless worker" whom the French Labour Code allows to work on an "occasional or part-time" basis.

Retirement: originally, like unemployment, retirement was clearly defined as the opposite of an employment situation, but today this contrast has become blurred. Someone who is in early retirement is not retired, but rather a jobless worker who has been removed from the labour market and is prohibited from returning to it. A retired person is not absolutely forbidden from working, even if in receipt of a pension. Finally, the development of gradual retirement amounts to a transitional situation halfway between work and non-work, and thus raises many perplexing questions.

ON THE IDEA OF TRANSITION,
ON HOW THE LAW CAN HANDLE TRANSITION

Mobility is not a clear legal concept – whether in the geographical or occupational sense of the term. Yet the law does provide for transitional situations, which act as "antechambers", as staging posts between one legal situation and another; one of the major contributions of the articles in issue No. 6, Vol. 135, of the *International Labour Review* has been to bring out their importance.

The passage from education to work passes through a series of filtering stages (apprenticeship, training courses, probationary periods) and then there is a reverse passage through the situation known as continuing training, of which so-called alternating contracts are significant examples.

It is rare for a person or activity to move from the private to the public sector, less so from public to private. The privatization of a state enterprise, insofar as it entails the replacement of a statutory relationship by a contractual one, entails arrangements covering numerous transitional stages. In some cases these even preserve the statutory employment status of existing staff, whilst new staff are hired on a purely contractual basis. Thus, there may be marked differences in the employment status of people working together in the same enterprise.

A move from remunerated to volunteer work is not entirely unknown at managerial level; but the reverse is more frequent, as when a person begins by working in a volunteer capacity, and later joins the staff of an association which makes a payment for his/her contribution.

Unlike the preceding examples, the transition from self-employment to a subordinate employment relationship, and *vice versa*, raises major questions. The externalization of jobs (or outsourcing) via a shift from direct employment to various forms of sub-contracting is the preferred method used by companies seeking to reduce costs. Where a person is newly self-employed and has only one client, namely his or her former employer, this is a transitional situation. And – in addition to the ever-present possibility of retraining – one can find various support measures being provided for an initial period. Mixed situations are those where features of both self-employed and subordinate employment status are to be found. Such cases are not rare – as evidenced by the application of Article L-781.1 of the French Labour Code, which concerns the exclusive supplier relationship.[3] If a self-employed person relies on one single supplier, the relationship is very close to a contract of employment even if, in the eyes of the client, that person is an independent operator.

Multi-activity is increasingly widespread, where an individual engages in a main activity either as a salaried employee or as self-employed, and in a secondary activity in which his/her status may also be one or the other. The law has barely begun to provide for such situations.

Gradual retirement has already been mentioned as occupying an intermediate position between employment and retirement; so also have the partial unemployment and under-employment that so typify the times in which we live.

A new field of research appears to be opening up here, namely those legal acts which, because they mark the moments of a passage from one status to another, may be termed transitional acts: starting up a business; recruitment; "hiving off";[4] moving from public- to private-sector employment; the replacement of a statutory by a contractual relationship; involuntary early retirement; involuntary lay-off; departure on or return from sabbatical leave or leave for family reasons; assistance to the unemployed to start up a business; legal acts giving effect to a transformation of an employment relationship, sometimes even the creation of a new form of employment relationship. Information on this last type of case is scarce especially as regards the proper giving of consent by the parties concerned, and this suggests that provision will need to be made for a new area of dispute settlement.

PERSONAL OBSERVATIONS

Two final considerations are suggested:

(a) Labour and labour law are undergoing profound change, though there is no call to predict their decline. Wage employment is now no more than one particular case of human activity. But the labour law specialist is not in a position to conduct a full assessment of these changes, which require the contribution of all branches of law: business law, for one; the law governing non-profit-making activity; family law; the law of public finance (hiving off had hitherto figured only in legislation on fiscal matters); the law governing social security (the financing of which is currently causing a major upheaval); public law governing the professions (just as self-employment is being promoted, access to the professions is closing off or becoming increasingly restricted). Labour law alone can no longer encompass such a growing and diversifying phenomenon. These changes are due – though not exclusively – to the overwhelming globalization of markets. In all countries and sectors, unfettered competition brings with it pressures to reduce labour costs (the French Five-Year Law [5] is one example of this trend).

(b) Moreover, investment in the derivatives markets may be more profitable than that in the production of goods and services. If tax legislation were to distinguish between profits according to their nature and origin, it would doubtless help bring about a situation in which growth creates work, not reducing jobs. In conclusion, therefore, I would call for incentive systems which reward profits based on the results of work performed by human beings: in other words, given that we cannot all be entrepreneurs, capital should once again be encouraged to help people work.

Notes

[1] This is an allusion to numerous decisions of the French Constitutional Court on social legislation; and also to decisions of the Supreme Administrative Tribunal *(Conseil d'Etat)* and the Court of Appeals *(Cour de cassation)*, as a result of which the notion of subordination in employment has lost some of its significance because of considerations relating to the worker's inherent human rights (such as the use of closed-circuit cameras).

[2] This system is designed to avoid or limit the effects of dismissal for economic reasons. Under this arrangement employees who have been put on short-time work receive compensation for a period of up to 18 months, if the reduction of working hours was caused by a prolonged and widespread decline of activity.

[3] Whereby an individual sells products exclusively supplied by one company, on conditions and at prices stipulated by that company.

[4] In which an enterprise helps a redundant employee to set up on his/her own.

[5] Law of 20 Dec. 1993, governing work, employment and vocational training, in *Journal Officiel* (Paris), 21 Dec. 1993.

POST-INDUSTRIAL SOCIETY AND ECONOMIC SECURITY

Jean-Baptiste de FOUCAULD *

30

It is too easily forgotten why work, rather than being something people are just fated to do, has become a central value in society: it was the industrial revolution which brought awareness that work could be more than a means of survival. As a result of technological progress, itself the fruit of human labour, work has become a factor of progress and change, a means of transforming nature. In a word, it is work-induced development which gave work the social value it now has. Work makes possible the construction of a society capable of progress. That explains why work is valued so highly.

To put work into perspective, the question therefore needs to be asked whether the relation between paid work and development will persist, or whether it will change (or is in the process of changing). The arguments presented below assume that development will continue, since there are many needs yet to be satisfied in developed countries. But they also assume that those needs will be different, as will be the modes of production by which those needs will be met. In particular, there will be greater, more open competition or choice between paid and unpaid activities. However, while the right to paid work remains a fundamental citizenship right, it is becoming increasingly difficult to ensure that everyone can exercise that right, in France or elsewhere. This applies not only to the right to work in the strict sense, but even to the right to work the hours of one's choice which, in any event, is probably the more desirable and useful of the two. In short, emerging forms of development are making it more necessary than ever before that a right to work be written into labour law.

In order to make progress towards that objective – a field as yet largely unexplored – it must first be realized that new legal regulations have so far merely reflected social changes without any effort being made to construct

Originally published in *International Labour Review*, Vol. 135 (1996), No. 6.
* Former head of France's General Planning Commission; President of "Solidarités nouvelles face au chômage" and of "Echange et Projets".

an integrated whole. The time has come to define the objectives pursued in much more specific terms. Only then will it be possible to consider the full range of options for reconciling adaptability and economic security within the framework of a new social contract.

THE EVOLUTION OF LABOUR LAW: A DISORDERLY REFLECTION OF SOCIAL CHANGE

The new "Great Transformation" which has been taking place since the end of the "Golden Age" is a transition from a society which produced homogeneity to a civilization geared to heterogeneity.

The predominantly industrial post-war society, which achieved reconstruction, growth and full employment in Europe, was governed largely by a sort of law of increasing homogenization: Taylorist mass-production, the fragmented division of labour in which labour itself was seen as a largely fungible force or material, stereotyped consumer behaviour and lifestyles, mass- and class-based social conflicts, and the widespread development of universal rights. In retrospect, it is perhaps precisely because that law of homogenization actually worked that the period seems like an era of historic success. What is homogeneous is indeed simple and generates economies of scale.

Today, however, the pendulum seems to be swinging the other way: society is undergoing a reverse process of diversification and heterogenization, both economically and socially. Within the process of globalization, which is in a sense a continuation of the previous trend convergence, diversity is permeating the very fabric of the economy and society. This is exacerbating inequalities and making redistributive issues more complex: new jobs tend to be created in small firms, self-employment looks set to increase, working time is increasingly atypical, the boundaries between work and non-work activity are becoming blurred. Social diversity is growing because exploitation, exclusion and insecurity coexist and often overlap, making it very hard for people to form a clear idea of the desirable direction of change.[1]

Labour law has so far merely reflected these developments without seeking to control or anticipate them. Admittedly, it faces strong conflicting pressures: if labour law is used to resist change in an attempt to preserve the type of social cohesion which prevailed in the "Golden Age", it can impede economic and even social development; if it goes with the trend towards economic and social fragmentation, it will increase social vulnerability, which is already acute and precisely what it is supposed to prevent or remedy. It is difficult to find a happy medium. As is often the case in such circumstances, there is also a high risk of yielding to both temptations at once without necessarily doing the right thing, e.g. by clinging to what ought to be changed and condoning developments which ought to be countered. The result is a proliferation of statutes of limited effectiveness, coupled with a loss of bearings and sense of direction. The time thus seems to have come to innovate with a comprehensive overhaul of the social contract, specifying from the outset what its purpose is to be.

REDEFINING THE OBJECTIVES OF LABOUR LAW

At this stage, the critical examination of how major principles have changed must be left aside for a moment in order to consider what is desirable and feasible, or, to be more precise, an actual project: what is really wanted now? What can actually be achieved? How can coherence be restored between the ends and the means?

Coherence has been lost: rampant liberalism, for which no convincing arguments are available, coexists with extensive areas of inertia. There is a tendency to emphasize flexibility/insecurity – an approach which has already produced tangible outcomes in numerous spheres of economic and social life. But neither in France nor elsewhere in continental Europe is there a political or cultural consensus to turn liberalism into a coherent and efficient system, not least because the injustices it entails are not accepted. Yet it is essential to construct a system and to propose a new social contract that conforms with cultural and political traditions while meeting today's needs.

The implicit social contract of the post-war period was based on work, full employment, social security and promotion: every individual had both the right and the duty to work and, in return, was entitled to secure social security coverage and legitimate promotion. That contract has now been shaken. It must be reinforced through complementary measures so as to adapt it to new economic and social conditions. This imposes two requirements:

– the need for people and organizations to adjust continuously to ensure that employment is redistributed rapidly according to productivity gains, with a view to satisfying new needs (whether material or nonmaterial, for remunerated or unremunerated activity, for leisure time or work). This presupposes initiative, innovation, risk, change, and continuous training;

– the need to restore security to its former level, for the risks and perverse effects of the economic insecurity which has built up over the past few years are all too obvious: precautionary savings are on the increase, thwarting growth policies; there is a tendency to cling to acquired rights while rejecting changes that are necessary; and, more generally, confusion is increasing while the capacity for social innovation is declining. The faster the pace of change and the wider and more varied the areas affected (technology, but also behaviour, values, social attitudes), the more acute and legitimate the need for stability, points of reference and a sense of direction.

It is tempting to regard these two requirements as contradictory and to focus on only one or the other. Those who insist on flexibility often neglect security concerns and are prepared to foster economic insecurity in order to break resistance to change. This is a short-term economic strategy which exacerbates social injustice and puts people in the service of the economy rather than the reverse. By contrast, those who insist on security at the expense of change are liable to end up achieving the opposite of what they want. In effect, the problem lies in finding operative modes and fields for reconciling the two requirements, which are more conflictual than insurmountable. There are in fact well-documented situations where security is conducive to initiative. Those are the ones which must be given priority attention.

In short, the issue is to build up a genuine system of economic security suited to the times. From 1945 social security was based on an economy running at full capacity and offering a relatively high level of employment security. Today, economic insecurity is engendering social insecurity. This calls for the construction of a system that can provide security, continuity and stability to people who are now faced with a multiplicity of possible situations and who are continuously required to adapt. What this implies is indeed a social contract, an exchange, a quid pro quo between society and each individual: society must give support and security to people who are innovative and enterprising, those who make the effort to adjust; those who enjoy secure employment status or *de facto* security must adapt. Clearly, the same contract applies to the private, the public and the semi-public sectors alike. It is equitable and thus fully acceptable, and at all events much better than the unfortunate combination of flexibility and insecurity which often prevails. It now remains to be constructed.

EXPERIMENTING WITH NEW FORMS OF ECONOMIC SECURITY IN FRANCE

The time has come to experiment by piecing together elements which are legally coherent but as yet uncoordinated in the French system. Social policy efforts are in fact also being made – and have been under way for some time – to organize a stable structural framework for labour mobility. But these efforts are being combined with crisis-management measures to promote flexibility. The overall result is a confused muddle, as though French society had been unable to choose between two models or had failed to realize it had to choose. The explanation may be that the move to construct a flexible and stable system could not be carried through and succeeded mainly in producing fragmented and compartmentalized achievements. Indeed, a characteristic of the French system is the extraordinary fragmentation of unemployment benefit schemes, which have been built up in successive layers without proper coordination: there are three schemes, which are largely unrelated to active labour market policy measures (which are administered by government departments!) and have practically no connection with vocational training schemes, not to mention the organization of work within enterprises. To make matters worse, each of those schemes has suffered from ambiguous attempts to strike a new administrative balance between centralization, deconcentration and decentralization. It is thus not surprising that French society is finding it difficult to make collective progress in this area.

Yet there are evidently ways of interlinking different schemes. Examples include the re-employment-training benefit,[2] the secondment of qualified personnel to small and medium-sized enterprises by UNEDIC (National Inter-occupational Union for Industrial and Trade Sector Employment), the agreement on early retirement, and the "time-savings account".[3]

While much remains to be done to construct an integrated whole, there are several ways in which progress could be made.

(a)   A first option would be to build up a system based on labour law. Given that a contract of employment of indefinite duration no longer offers the stability it used to imply, an attempt could be made to design a broader and more stable type of contract applying a common set of rules not only to the various forms of contracts, but also to various types of activity (e.g. training, self-employment, establishment of enterprises, volunteer work) and even inactivity (e.g. sabbatical leave). Such a contract would do away with the problem of discontinuity between various forms of participation in economic and social life, all of which would provide the same entitlement to social protection. Such is the aim of the proposed "activity contract" outlined in the report of France's General Planning Commission,[4] the agency to which the French Government assigned the task of studying labour and employment prospects for the next 20 years. This envisages a system whereby several enterprises would get together and administer activity contracts jointly so as to allow their beneficiaries to move from one enterprise to another and from one activity status to another. The concept of career, now undermined by increasing employment insecurity, would thus gain new value and broader meaning: instead of taking place within a single large firm, a person's career would develop among various (large and small) firms and encompass various forms of activity, with moves from one to another being facilitated and, above all, organized.

This approach certainly offers an opportunity for major social innovation. But the underlying intuition still remains to be given concrete form. The required set of basic principles is taking shape, but the actual formula has yet to be worked out. In short, the idea needs to be tested experimentally, and this must be done without delay. However, this precludes the possibility of starting off from a new legal construct incorporating a set of compulsory contributions and benefits (training,

UNEDIC, in particular). It would be better to experiment on the basis of existing schemes without seeking to change them (although this obviously remains a longer-term objective). This means accepting additional costs, which are justified, however, by the medium-term advantages of better management of labour and by the savings this would generate (particularly in terms of unemployment benefits). To encourage experimentation it could be agreed that the State would match every additional franc spent by firms on non-wage labour costs, provided that the experiment is carried out in partnership with the national-level trade union organizations (which must indeed be involved in the experiment) and that it is subjected to an objective, independent evaluation.

The next question is that of the scheme's more general application, which is bound to raise the following dilemma: either a hard-and-fast (sectoral or regional) framework can be set for grouping the firms participating in the scheme – but a certain amount of flexibility and opportunity for synergy would be lost; or the activity contract can be made optional, but a likely result of this would be an "adverse risk selection" mechanism, with declining enterprises and those in depressed sectors finding it difficult to group together or doing so on more costly terms. It might therefore be preferable to make participation in the scheme mandatory, while leaving it up to firms to decide on how it should operate.

(b) These difficulties call for consideration of an alternative course of action, which would consist in constructing a system based on people, rather than enterprises, so as to allow them more control over their own situation. Assistance schemes (for setting up enterprises, for training) typically become available to people only after they have run into difficulty, when they are in a precarious position and it is more difficult for them to use assistance to best advantage. Why not organize these schemes so that people can get assistance before they end up in a situation of exclusion, precisely in order to prevent exclusion? The idea would be to give everyone an initiative credit, a time credit, a training credit which they could use whenever they wished and which would be financed by a general income tax. Thus, people who do not take initiatives (but benefit from the initiatives of others), who do not undergo training (but who benefit indirectly from other people's efforts to train), or who do not take the occasional sabbatical, would contribute to social cost-sharing instead of enjoying a free ride. This would attenuate dysfunctions. Indeed, why should people have to wait until they lose their job in order to qualify for assistance in setting up or taking over an enterprise under France's ACCRE scheme?[5] If such assistance were available to everyone there would almost certainly be fewer unemployed. Again, why do people have to be unemployed to qualify for training that even enterprises seldom provide for their own workers? It would be better to allow employed workers more scope for initiative by reviving the idea of training leave as provided for in France's 1971 Act on continuing vocational training.[6] Why not lay down the principle of sabbatical leave for all? This would be a positive way of sharing unemployment and would at least oblige everyone to finance it. And why could an unexpected period of unemployment not begin with a sabbatical to enable the worker to take stock of the situation, or with a period of independent training, before the unemployment benefit scheme comes into operation and job search begins? This would offer a dynamic, creative, "non-welfare" – i.e. non-passive – type of subsistence income designed to restore people's independence and thereby enable them to plan their life more satisfactorily, on more secure foundations. Additional costs would of course have to be accepted but, as with the preceding formula, these would generate collective savings in the long term.

(c)   The two systems, moreover, are not necessarily incompatible and may even prove complementary. The latter system would be better suited for compulsory and universal schemes. But there is nothing to prevent their administration from being entrusted, on a voluntary basis, to associations of enterprises which would derive advantages from grouping together for that purpose.

A debate on these issues must be initiated at the European level without delay, especially since the current vision of the European social model is largely defensive. Europe simply must construct a system of economic security that promotes initiative and adjustment and in order to resume the pioneering role it played in the field of social and labour law up to the 1970s. It is by taking bold steps to meet the new challenges it confronts that the European social model will best preserve its heritage.

Notes

[1] See, for example, *Echange et Projets* (Paris), No. 75 (Dec.), 1995, "Syndicalisme et exclusion" (special issue on trade unionism and social exclusion).

[2] This enables persons who have been made redundant to receive an income while they undergo retraining and, if necessary, to draw unemployment benefits thereafter. Both schemes are administered by the same authority, thus avoiding problems of transition from one to the other.

[3] Set up in 1994, this scheme enables wage-earners to convert their entitlement to profit-sharing or to wage increases into time off in lieu; the days thus accumulated can be carried forward.

[4] See Commissariat général du Plan: *Le travail dans vingt ans*, Paris, Editions Odile Jacob/La Documentation française, 1995. [Ed.: see also Jean Boissonnat: "Combating unemployment, restructuring work: Reflections on a French study", in *International Labour Review* (Geneva), Vol. 135 (1996), No. 1, pp. 5-15; and, in the same issue, "Perspectives: What is the future of work? Ideas from a French report", pp. 93-110.]

⁵ Under this scheme, unemployed persons who want to set up their own business can capitalize part of the unemployment benefit to which they are entitled and thus have approximately 30,000 French francs at their disposal for that purpose.

⁶ See *Journal Official de la République Française* (Paris), No. 164, 17 July 1971, pp. 7035 et seq. The full text of "Act No. 71-575, to organize continuing vocational training as part of life-long education" is available in English under the symbol 1971-Fr.1 in the ILO's *Legislative Series* (Geneva), Jan.-Feb. 1972.

WORK AND USEFULNESS TO THE WORLD

Robert CASTEL*

31

For reasons that will be explained below, analysis of the transformations of work from a historical perspective shows that reference to law is absolutely essential to form a clear picture of the place that work has occupied and occupies today in society. With the caution readers are entitled to expect of a non-specialist author, this article will attempt to justify the importance of law in the sense that nothing seems more urgent from the sociological point of view than the need to mobilize legal thinking to confront the current deterioration in conditions of employment.

WORK FROM A POSITION OF TOTAL DEPENDENCE

"Work and usefulness to the world": this title was inspired by a historian's record of the indictment of a vagrant by the court of the French town of Le Châtelet in the fifteenth century. The poor soul was pronounced "useless to the world, and therefore fit to die by hanging like a common thief".[1] Vagrants were "useless to the world" because they did not work and lived off society's reserves, which they had not contributed to producing. To quote another historical source, they were "the most terrible scourge ... of voracious insects that infect and desolate the countryside, devouring daily the subsistence of the farmers".[2] Vagrants have indeed always paid dearly for this uselessness, enduring various but consistently cruel forms of repression for centuries.

This leads to consideration of the relationship between work and a recognized position in society. To what extent is recognized membership of society – nowadays very loosely called "social citizenship" – based solely upon work?

Originally published in *International Labour Review*, Vol. 135 (1996), No. 6.

* Research director at the School of Advanced Studies in Social Sciences (Ecole des hautes études en sciences sociales), Paris.

Formulated in this way, however, the question is far too general because the meaning of work and the values associated with it have undergone profound transformation over time. It was only from the end of the seventeenth century and the beginning of the eighteenth that the economic value of work was fully recognized for itself, and that a "civilization of work" began to take shape. Today the above question would in many countries refer mainly to wage employment, inasmuch as this has become the dominant model of socially recognized work. The question should therefore be rephrased accordingly to ask whether, or to what extent, wage employment is the essential basis of social recognition. In fact, since today's wage employment society is in the midst of a crisis with deteriorating conditions of employment, the question needs to be even more specific: to what extent does wage employment face competition from other sources of social utility? Are there alternatives to wage employment as a source of social utility and recognition? One can try to retrace the reasons why these questions now have to be asked in those terms and thus throw some light on the options available for deciding on the place work ought to have in today's society.

To do so, it may be helpful to look back at the past for a moment and get rid of an unduly cumbersome, catch-all concept of work. It was indeed at the end of the seventeenth century and the beginning of the eighteenth that the modern concept of work began to emerge. But work was already a source of social utility in pre-industrial society, as reflected in the above-mentioned indictment of vagrancy. However, the meaning given to work in the society of that period calls for two explanatory observations. First, the economic function of work was not at that time considered as something separate. Work was caught up in a mixture of moral and religious as well as economic values. It was all at once a punishment for original sin, a means of redemption, a trial that strengthened the soul, an instrument of moralization, etc., while also being necessary for ensuring personal survival and sustaining general prosperity. This remained true up to and including the mercantilist period in the seventeenth century, despite its strong emphasis on the economic value of work.

Second, work was not an unconditional requirement for everyone. People on the upper rungs of the social ladder were not only exempt from work, but actually excluded from the order of workers. This was the legacy of the old division of society into *oratores* (clerics), *bellatores* (warriors) and *laboratores* (labourers).[3] It was only the latter who worked in the true sense of the word, that is, they toiled away in the service of others. This third order originally consisted of agricultural labourers, but it later became broader, more diverse and more complex. It came to include a growing number of occupations, trades and professions. However, within this nebulous "third estate" there remained an essential divide, which cut across manual work itself. On one side, there were the trades that conveyed a genuine "estate", i.e. both duties and privileges, weighty obligations and social recognition, often including local political responsibilities. These were the "regulated" trades, the guilds, which became known as corporations from the eighteenth century onwards. On the other side of the divide, there were tasks without quality, performed by people who were also without quality, people who counted for little, indeed people who counted for nothing. Even a thinker as progressive as Voltaire called them "the rabble", while Abbé Sieyès – the master mind of France's Declaration of the Rights of Man and of the Citizen – described them as "two-legged tools, without freedom, without morality, possessing only hands that do not earn much and deadened souls", inquiring: "Are those what you call men?" [4]

These "two-legged tools" were nevertheless socially useful because, as Sieyès also said, they were the "producers of others' enjoyment". But they enjoyed no dignity, no social recognition, no political existence (in fact they were not given the right to vote).Thus a person who was *only* a worker could be both useful and sub-human, a "scoundrel".

The point of this historical digression – one which is worthwhile even today – is that within the category of "mechanical work" itself an important distinction must be made: work brings social recognition only if it is covered by a system of regulation, if it is underpinned by some legally recognized status. In the case of France, until the industrial and political revolution at the end of the eighteenth century, jurisdiction in this matter was in the hands of the guilds and corporations, also known, appropriately, as the "regulated trades". The pre-industrial form of this jurisdiction was later brutally abolished (in France, this was done by the Le Chapelier Act in particular). But the *existence* of a jurisdiction could well be a matter of necessity, still today, to rescue work from social unworthiness.

THE TRANSFORMATION OF WORK INTO EMPLOYMENT

Of course, the establishment of a free labour market presupposed abolition of these corporatist regulations, which were both obstacles to free trade and a protection against the laws of the market. In some respects, the substitution of a contractual order for the former status of trades could well be considered a retrograde move. Indeed, from the social point of view it had destructive effects for the majority of artisans and craftsmen, who now found themselves unprotected and impoverished. Eugène Buret, for example, gives a telling account of the decline of British weavers who, from a position of self-reliance and dignity maintained through work, sank to the condition of "scoundrels" or "two-legged tools".[5] Buret does not actually use those terms, but all descriptions of poverty in the first half of the nineteenth century vividly reflect this reduction of manual workers to the condition of machines producing goods at the lowest possible cost. According to the dominant depiction at least, they became the "new barbarians", something akin to immoral and dangerous animals. The labouring classes were the dangerous classes.

A distinction must therefore be drawn between economic utility and, let us say, for want of a better expression, social recognition. Or would it be preferable to call it social citizenship? At all events the economic utility of workers in the first industrial concentrations was quite obvious. They were "useful to the world": they spearheaded industrialization and were the focus of production of the new riches. But they enjoyed no social dignity. On the contrary, they were like those "two-legged tools" depicted by Sieyès.

How did these unworthy, wretched workers acquire social dignity? To a large extent this was done through the medium of law, which freed them from total subjection to the rule of the market and set a framework for the individual transaction embodied in their contract of hire, i.e. the exchange of labour for pay. To quote a contemporary author on this point: "The workman gives his labour, and the master pays the agreed wage. That is the extent of their mutual obligations. The moment he [the master] no longer needs his [the workman's] labour, he sacks him. It is then for the workman to manage as best he can".[6] It was only after a long struggle that workers, by participating in systems of collective regulation, secured emancipation from this purely contractual order and gained a status. Thus, with the advent of collective agreements, it was no longer the isolated individual who contracted "freely"; the market transaction was underpinned by rules that both predated and transcended it.[7]

In France, the first clear indication of the introduction of a new system of work was arguably the 1910 Act on industrial and agricultural workers' pensions. While this legislation is known to have had very little impact in practice, it nevertheless recognized that part of a worker's wage eluded the market order and transcended mere economic utility. There was thus a wage for security, for protection. This recognition extended outside work situations in the strict sense, since it ensured a pension at the end of a person's working life – even though the pension itself was minute and the majority of workers died before they qualified for it.

What this suggests is that work transcended its economic utility and gained social recognition through law, the law of labour and social protection. Of course, this does not mean that law created this status for workers out of thin air. It was also necessary for the workers themselves to break out of their individual isolation and join forces in militant groups. And, more fundamentally perhaps, it was also necessary for work as such to be recognized in terms of collective production, in terms of a collective act that transcends the particular nature of the tasks carried out by individuals. This transformation was in fact concomitant with the development of an abstract notion of work, that is, recognition of working activity as a generic act of work, a social act. Work is truly a social act when it can no longer be confused with private activity, such as work in the home, or with the activity of a particular occupation, as was the case when working people's identity as wheelwrights, carpenters or weavers took precedence over their identity as workers in the generic sense. This transformation was induced by massive industrialization and the new forms of division of labour brought about by Taylorism. The outcome was recognition of the generic social function of work, in other words, its entry into the public domain. On this point, reference must be made to the views of André Gorz, particularly for his oftcited emphasis on the heteronomy of wage employment and the merits of leisure time. But he also strongly stresses the liberating character of the impersonality of wage employment. This, for example, is what rescued women from immersion in the household sphere, or farmers from confinement within local relationships beset with traditional constraints.[8]

It can therefore be argued that it is the abstract notion of work – which, incidentally, has been the target of so much criticism – that makes economic utility connect with the social function of work. Work then clearly becomes a public, collective activity, i.e. a non-domestic, non-private, even depersonalized activity. Workers – in their capacity as producers – thus take up a particular position of their own in the public domain and acquire public personality. And once the personalized character of the employment relationship has been transcended in this way, it is easy to understand how the worker can become the object or subject of law. Labour law recognizes the generic utility of a worker's activity in the same way as civil law recognizes a citizen's generic membership of the community.

Wage employment society fostered further development of that interaction between the economic, sociological and legal dimensions of work. Work was integrated in a system of rights and duties determined by collective utility, and no longer only by the economic utility of market transactions. It is no doubt these social, public and collective characteristics which explain how work became the basis of social citizenship. Just like political citizenship, social citizenship is a status comprising rights and duties based on collective membership of a community.

At the same time, however, work clearly remains a factor of alienation, subordination, heteronomy, and even exploitation. Indeed, modern wage employment rests on the dialectic tension that connects those two dimensions: work imposes constraints upon the worker, while at the same time providing a pedestal that enables the worker to be recognized as such. Throughout the period extending broadly from the end of the nineteenth century to the 1970s, the wage employment relationship continued to imply subordination. But on the one hand, that subordination was progressively mitigated by labour law which reduced and framed the arbitrary power of employers; and, on the other, it was compensated by wages above subsistence level and, more importantly, by protection and rights. There is nothing idyllic about this structure of employment relationships in a wage employment society: alienation and exploitation have not been overcome completely. At the same time, however, work is, so to say, dignified, to the extent that it has become a source of rights.

   This line of reasoning can be pursued by demonstrating that it was the consolidation of wage employment status – the strength and diversity of the attributes of work – which led to emancipation from the hegemony of work. It is when work is precarious, unprotected and entirely at the mercy of the market that the worker is completely submerged in the "order of workers". In the early stages of industrialization, for example, the proletarians who worked for a pittance under the arbitrary rule of an employer for 12 to 16 hours a day truly spent their entire lives just earning a living. Conversely, atop the pedestal of recognized and protected wage employment, a worker can engage in other pursuits, including leisure, education and participation in the activities of non-profit organizations and in social life. Collectivization of employment relationships thus allows for the development of personal interests, and it is the consolidation of conditions of employment that saves the worker from being overwhelmed by work: this is a paradox that deserves further consideration, one which should be pondered by all those who enthusiastically equate the "end of work" with the advent of freedom.

CONTEMPORARY ASPECTS OF THE RELATIONSHIP BETWEEN WORK AND SOCIAL UTILITY

The process of transforming work into legally framed employment under the impetus of wage employment society appears to have become bogged down since the mid-1970s. The link between work and protection is weakening or growing less reliable, as evidenced by mass unemployment; increasingly precarious conditions of employment; the proliferation of different types of employment contracts; and the widespread development of grey area arrangements between recognized work and non-work activity, such as odd jobs, internships, and job entry schemes.[9] Some observers have gone on to conclude that work has lost its central position in society. In other words, work is supposed to have lost much of its social utility, though it is not always clear whether those who say so think that there is less work and regret it, or that there is less need for work and welcome this as a good thing. In either case, the question is: are there alternatives to work as the source of social utility, or other legitimate grounds for social recognition?

   This raises highly complex issues that cannot be settled in a few words. Suffice it to say that if the notion of "source of utility" is taken in a broad, demanding sense – i.e. including not only the exercise of some activity for its own sake or for the sake of an income, but also whatever it takes to secure recognition and social dignity – it is difficult to imagine clear-cut alternatives to the employment-source as constructed by wage employment society. The fact that work has become scarcer or less secure does not mean that it has become less useful and less necessary. On the contrary: for evidence one need look no further than the distress experienced by most welfare recipients and most of the long-term unemployed. Inasmuch as their joblessness threatens their very place in society, they bear witness, paradoxically, to the vital importance of work. People who in earlier times would have been called "useless to the world" are thus reappearing in today's society. Unlike the vagrants of pre-industrial society, however, their plight is not imputable to the rigidity of "regulated" trades which excluded part of the available workforce from employment, but to labour market deregulation, which makes outcasts out of people incapable of adapting to the new requirements of labour mobility and competitiveness.

Some readers will find this conclusion too pessimistic. The decollectivization of employment relationships evidently translates into precarious employment and unemployment, but it also means personalization of wage employment relationships. The abstract notion of work associated with a general legal status and broad uniform categories implying standard tasks and rights is declining in favour of "specific" work, which calls for more personal skills and leads to the emergence of new types of activity and new forms of self-expression through work.

However, two remarks can be made concerning the implications of these transformations. First, people are unequally equipped to cope with them. A particular advantage is enjoyed by those who can mobilize a range of resources, good training and relationship skills to deal with increasingly competitive situations. For others, the price of this re-individualization is obsolescence of their existing skills compounded by inability to acquire new ones: they find themselves cheated by the new rules of the game. For them, individualization translates into fragmentation of tasks, weakening of collective protection, even rejection from the economic system and social isolation – that form of social uselessness currently called exclusion.

The second remark is that these transformations are again raising the issue of access to the public domain. As suggested above, the abstract notion of work offered a reliable pathway to the public domain by making collective actors out of the majority of workers. But if employment relationships are individualized, how does the worker become a "public person"? Indeed, can the worker become one? There is no doubt a deep-seated relationship though difficult to explain – between the crisis of conventional employment and the development of local-level activities, of community participation within a restricted geographical area. This would explain initiatives to base a new social citizenship on neighbourhood investments and activities recognized and valued for the tangible exchanges and range of personal contacts they generate. Hence all the talk about "untapped potential for job creation", "community services", "socially useful activities", "solidarity economy", etc. It is doubtful, however, whether such ideas will ever prove to be more than just wishful thinking unless they can also deliver a connection to law – this, at least, is the view submitted here for discussion. Indeed, what goes on at the local level is also, not to say mostly, made up of neighbourhood constraints, dependency relationships not mediated by law, such as clientship or domestic service relations. For lack of foresight perhaps, it seems impossible to conceive of a citizenship that is not linked to a general source of regulatory authority, which is precisely what law represents: not only modern political law based on the idea of a nation, but also labour law based on recognition of the worker as a collective actor whose social utility derives from the performance of a task in the collective interest in the strongest possible sense of the word. If such is the case, it would follow that one of the avenues – perhaps even the "high road" – to be explored for a creditable way out of the current employment crisis would be an overhaul of labour law. Indeed, labour law could conceivably counter the increasing precariousness of employment relationships by introducing new statutory guarantees into today's more flexible and less secure conditions of employment. The imposition of legal regulations could also ensure that "untapped potential for job creation" does not translate into a proliferation of underpaid jobs subject to the arbitrariness of employers, as was the case when – before the introduction of statutory rights – labour was just another tradable.

Notes

[1] Bronislav Geremek: *Les marginaux parisiens aux XIVe et XVe siècles,* Paris, Flammarion, 1976, p. 310.

[2] J.F. Le Trosne: *Mémoire sur les vagabonds et les mendiants*, Soissons, 1764, p. 4.

[3] Georges Duby: Les trois ordres, ou l'imaginaire du féodalisme, Paris, Gallimard, 1988.

[4] Emmanuel Joseph Sieyès: *Ecrits politiques*, Paris-Montreux, Editions des Archives contemporaines, 1985, p. 81.

[5] Eugène Buret: *De la misère des classes laborieuses en France et en Angleterre*, Paris, 1840.

[6] M.T. Duchâtel: *De la charité dans ses rapports avec l'état moral et le bien-être des classes inférieures de la société*, Paris, 1829, p. 133.

[7] Alain Supiot: *Critique du droit du travail*, Paris, PUF, 1994.

[8] André Gorz: "Revenu minimum de citoyenneté, droit au travail et droit au revenu", in *Futuribles* (Paris), Feb. 1994.

[9] See Robert Castel: *Les métamorphoses de la question sociale, une chronique du salariat*, Paris, Fayard, 1995, especially Chapter VIII.

THE TRANSFORMATION OF WORK AND THE FUTURE OF LABOUR LAW IN EUROPE: A MULTIDISCIPLINARY PERSPECTIVE

32

Alain SUPIOT *

Labour law, whether national or international, is rooted in an industrial model that is currently being undermined by technological and economic changes. This raises serious questions about the future of labour law. Must it fade away? Should it be used to resist those changes? Or should it serve to manage them, in which case labour law itself would need to change? It was against this background that, in 1996, the European Commission initiated a process of prospective, multidisciplinary reflection on the transformation of work and the future of labour law in Europe (and, more specifically, in the European Union). This article presents the salient features of the report submitted at the outcome of that process in 1998.[1] Though the aim of the exercise was legal by nature – i.e. to forecast the evolution of the legal categories underlying labour law in the European countries – it could only be attained through a multidisciplinary analysis of the changes that have occurred in practice in employment relationships. The analysis also needed to incorporate a comparative dimension and to take account of the variety of national experiences. Its objective was not to describe the present state of labour law, but rather to consider the issue from a dynamic, historical perspective. This called for a diachronic – as opposed to synchronic – approach to the issues under consideration. The challenge was therefore threefold, as will now be explained.

CAVEATS

Difficulties of a cross-national approach

Over the past 15 years or so, the building of Europe has triggered a spate of comparative research in the social and labour fields. This experience has highlighted the extreme difficulty of inter-country comparison. Thus, on

Originally published in *International Labour Review*, Vol. 138 (1999), No. 1.

* Professor, University of Nantes (France).

closer examination, what appeared to be common categories almost invariably turned out to be divergent. To give but one example: nearly 40 years after its creation, the European Community has still not managed to work out a common definition of the concept of wage employment! Given such conceptual diversity, there are two pitfalls that must be avoided. The first would be to overestimate the extent of such divergence and entertain the idea that some sort of national predestination precludes community-wide conceptualization of the issue of work today. Conversely, the second pitfall would be to underestimate divergences and to equate national cultures with a set of archaic traits destined to be swept away by economic globalization. Yet globalization is but one of the manifestations of open international markets, which also generate "re-territorialization" effects that economists have already identified. Indeed, diversification and new requirements as to the quality of goods tend to give added importance to the local-level collective resources available to enterprises (e.g. public services, transport, labour force skills, subcontracting networks).

Difficulties of a multidisciplinary approach

Legal categories cannot be reconsidered without reference to the changes that occur in practice. Hence the need for dialogue between jurists and social scientists. The fruitfulness of that dialogue, however, depends on avoidance of two pitfalls. The first is the "instrumentalization" of law. There is indeed a widespread tendency in political thinking and practice to conceive of law as a mere tool subservient to some socio-economic rationality. But that such instrumentalization leads only to dead ends has been amply demonstrated by the mishaps of the employment policies in which it has been used and abused. At the other extreme, the second pitfall would be that of self-reference, whereby law is regarded as a closed system of rules with nothing to offer the world of hard facts and nothing to learn from it. This approach would preclude any understanding of the changes that occur in law and in society. In order to steer clear of these two pitfalls, it must therefore be accepted that law is both a determinant and an expression of social relationships, and that it can just as well lag behind developments as it can anticipate them. In any case, there still remains the risk of abstraction, the risk of overlooking the extreme diversity of specific work (or unemployment) experiences. In fact, the categories framed by labour law itself – e.g. "worker" or "unemployed" – contribute to obscuring that diversity because of the way in which those categories are appropriated and then conveyed by the social sciences and their underlying statistical methods.

Difficulties of a diachronic approach

The purpose of a diachronic approach is to examine the workings of change in order to understand the direction it is taking. But here again, care must be taken to steer clear of two possible pitfalls. The first is the risk of overestimating the scale of transformation. In a changing world, it is indeed very tempting to identify that part of the world which is in motion with the whole and to overlook those forces that work to preserve the existing social system. For example, the advent of widespread unemployment does not mean "the end of work" for society as a whole. Similarly, the emergence of new forms of employment (e.g. telework) does not necessarily mean that the old forms will disappear. Of course, unemployment and today's new forms of employment are not marginal issues either. They call into question mechanisms that are central to the way our societies function. Hence the second pitfall, which would be to underestimate the significance of such changes and to cling on to constructs inherited from the industrial model on the grounds that they have continued to hold sway over labour law and still fit the situation of a very large number of workers throughout the world. Employment practices have always varied widely, and the industrial model has never been universal. Yet it was by reference to that model that the Western countries' labour law was developed. To a large extent, the same holds true of international labour law as embodied in the standards of the International Labour Organization in particular. The question, therefore, is whether and, if so, to what extent the reference model underpinning the conceptualization of an employment relationship is currently shifting.

This issue has been examined from different perspectives, each of which will now be taken up in turn – that of the scope of labour law, that of the occupational status of workers, that of working time, that of representation and collective bargaining and, lastly, that of the role of the State.

BROADENING THE SCOPE OF LABOUR LAW

Labour law is based on a concept of employment relationships that is both hierarchic and collective. Within this framework, the contract of employment is conceived of primarily in terms of the master-servant relationship (i.e. subordination) it establishes between the worker and the person using his/her services. An enterprise is conceptualized as a community wherein workers of various trades are brought together around a common economic activity and under the management of a single employer.

This concept embodies what is known as the "Fordist model" in industrial relations parlance, i.e. one in which large industrial enterprises engage in mass production based on narrow specialization of tasks and skills and on a pyramidal organization of work (hierarchic supervision of the workforce; separation of product design and manufacture). In Europe, the linchpin of this model was typical employment of indefinite duration whereby the worker conceded dependency in return for a secure livelihood. It is now commonplace to observe that this pattern is fast losing ground to other models of work organization which have developed through the interplay of three

617

factors, namely, rising skill levels (and the consequent increase in occupational autonomy independently from contractual subordination), the growing pressure of competition in increasingly open markets, and the quickening pace of technological progress (especially in the fields of information and communication).

The difficulty is that the new models are varied, that their features typically differ from one country to another (even though they may derive from the same processes of global change), and that they have not completely superseded the variety of pre-existing forms that the Fordist system of employment and benefits has spawned throughout Europe. In other words, today's economic and social situation cannot be narrowed down to the emergence of a single model of employment relationships. Indeed, it displays a variety of production environments. For example, recourse to self-employment, subcontracting or outsourcing may reflect a simple strategy of working around labour law in an attempt to reduce labour costs in traditional, low-value-added sectors of the economy. By contrast, the same forms of work organization may reflect the pursuit of innovative strategies in high-skill sectors. In the first instance, the aim is to play down the importance of human resources (in financial terms), whereas in the second it is to increase their importance (in terms of initiative, skills and qualifications). The ways in which power is redistributed or in which occupational autonomy can be balanced against protection within the employment relationship can thus have very different implications and call for equally different legal responses. This explains the growing variety of employment contract types. Somewhere in between genuinely subordinated workers and genuinely independent entrepreneurs, a third category is emerging – that of workers who are legally independent (i.e. self-employed) but economically dependent. Though workers in this position may not yet account for a substantial share of the workforce, their numbers look set to grow.

These developments are having serious consequences for worker protection under labour and social security law. The first of these is often increased insecurity for individuals, as in the case of economically dependent self-employment or in the case of workers in precarious employment who are "invited" to refrain from joining a trade union. The second consequence is an expanding grey area between wage employment and self-employment. Indeed, legally independent subcontractors – including both individuals and enterprises – can be economically dependent upon a single client or prime contractor or on a very small number of clients. Conversely, some workers who are technically in wage employment are becoming increasingly autonomous in practice. Lastly, the third consequence is that employment relationships need to be seen within the context of a network of enterprises, particularly as regards a prime contractor's liability for the safety and health of a subcontractor's workers, or the protection of contract labour, or yet the joint liability of such enterprises as may be answerable for observance of statutory working time, for example.

The report synthesized in this article lays down two principles for dealing with these developments. The first is the fundamental principle whereby determination of the legal nature of an employment relationship is not left to the discretion of the parties thereto. The second principle is that the scope of labour law be broadened to include the contracting of self-employed workers. What this foreshadows is a kind of common labour law with branches that could be adapted to cope with the variety of employment situations (e.g. conventional wage employment, economically dependent self-employment). The underlying aim is to prevent a rift from opening between workers enjoying extensive protection under a contract of employment, on the one hand, and those working under some other type of contract on account of which they enjoy less protection, on the other. Historically, one of the fundamental functions of labour law has been to provide a basis for social cohesion. And if it is to continue to fulfil this function, it must keep abreast of changes in the organization of work in today's society. In particular, it must not remain narrowly focused on those forms of work organization from which it originally derived and which are now on the decline.

TOWARDS A NEW OCCUPATIONAL STATUS FOR INDIVIDUALS

The relatively consistent and stable occupational status built up over the years by labour law and social security law was designed to suit the Fordist production model. Its archetype was a male head of household working for his family's living who, following a relatively short period of initial vocational training, held the same job or the same type of job in the same enterprise or at least in the same industry over a prolonged period, and who retired a few years before dying. The consistency of this status – in terms of both labour law and social security law – contributed to the emergence among workers of a community of interests which naturally found expression in industrial trade unionism.

That this status never applied to more than a portion of the workforce did not prevent it from becoming the reference model even among those who enjoyed none of its benefits. This is how entire categories of workers (civil servants, self-employed workers, farmers, etc.) came to claim this status for themselves either directly (by extension of the regulations applicable to wage employment) or through the transposition of all or part of those regulations into the rules governing their own status – and this includes not only individual aspects like income security and social protection but also collective aspects such as trade union rights and the right to strike and to bargain collectively. However, this central model, by reference to which all employment relationships have tended to be framed, is not so much that of the worker as

619

that of the employee – that loyal employee who devotes his/her lifetime to an enterprise in return for the assurance of a "steady job".

It is that stability which is missing from the post-Fordist models of work organization. Enterprises continue to be very demanding of their workers, perhaps even more so than in the past, in respect of skill levels, adaptability and capacity to work autonomously. Yet they no longer offer security in return. Thus, the terms of the quid pro quo that originally underpinned wage-employment status – i.e. subordination for security – have broken down, and the terms of a new quid pro quo have yet to be worked out. Workers cannot indefinitely be expected to show increasing commitment to an enterprise that offers them no prospects whatsoever, whether internally or externally. The State, which has been expected to take on the issue – and the cost – of managing the continuum of people's working lives is not in the best position to do so. Massive state intervention, which is a huge drain on public funds, can do no more than alleviate the consequences of the situation. Specifically, it does not address the central issue, i.e. the establishment of an occupational status suited to the newly dominant models of employment relationships.

Unlike the Fordist model which relied on stable, enterprise-based organization of the workforce, those new models hinge on coordination processes involving mobile individuals. Hence the necessity (and the difficulty) of designing an occupational status that can accommodate career individualization and mobility. Such mobility, should it ever become the dominant feature of the world of work, is going to raise some daunting issues under labour law. Indeed, employment stability has not been merely an effect of labour law but also one of its very aims, as a means of securing a genuine occupational status for workers. This last objective, however, has lost nothing of its relevance, so that the issue that arises today is how to adapt – not sacrifice – labour law to change.

The "employee status" that combines subordination and security needs to be superseded by a new occupational status for individuals based on a comprehensive concept of work (i.e. including non-market work), which can reconcile the requisites of freedom, security and responsibility. Today's labour law must indeed meet the requirements of equality between men and women, continuing training, involvement in public-interest assignments, family responsibilities and workers' occupational freedom. This calls for an understanding of the various forms of work based more on what they have in common than on what differentiates them. Such an approach may help to frame a new occupational status for individuals (analogous to their personal status) that would reconcile diversity and continuity in people's working lives.

This new occupational status must protect the continuity of a lifelong trajectory rather than the stability of particular jobs. First, this means protecting workers during transitional periods between jobs. Special attention must therefore be paid to re-employment rights in case of job loss; changes in status (e.g. from wage employment to self-employment); linkages between training and employment, between unemployment and training, and between school

and work; access to initial employment and prevention of long-term unemployment. Second, new legal tools need to be developed to secure the
continuity of the proposed occupational status across the entire range of
work and non-work situations. The issue at stake is none other than the end
of the linear career model. Career breaks and changes of occupation must
come to be seen as standard components of an uninterrupted occupational
status. The required continuity could be provided either by law or by collective agreement.

This occupational status must no longer be based on the restrictive concept of employment, but on the broader concept of work. Labour and social
security law can no longer afford to relegate non-market forms of work to
the background. The concept of "activity", advocated by some authors
(e.g. the "activity contract", recommended in France by the so-called Boissonnat report),[2] was discarded by the report synthesized here for being too
loose. The concept of work differs from that of "activity" in that it is linked to
some obligation undertaken voluntarily or imposed by law, which is performed for a valuable consideration or without consideration within some
statutory framework or under contract. Work invariably falls within the
scope of some legal bond. The rights accruing from wage employment (employment itself), together with the rights common to all forms of employment (health, safety, etc.) and those rights deriving from non-occupational
work (care of a dependant, voluntary work, self-training, etc.), are three clusters of rights inherent in the kind of individual occupational status envisaged
here. A fourth cluster is that comprising universal social rights, which are not
subject to any work-related requirement (health care, minimum social security, etc.) and which do not specifically fall within the scope of labour law. As
for the principle of equal treatment as between men and women, it applies in-
discriminately to all four clusters of rights.

The new occupational status thus defined carries a variety of "social
drawing rights". Recent years have witnessed the emergence of specific
labour-law rights that are innovative in two respects. First, they give workers
some freedom from employment while being linked to particular forms of
work (time off for trade union representatives, time off for training, parental
leave, etc.). Second, the exercise of such rights is discretionary and not subject to the occurrence of predetermined events. Such rights supplement traditional social and labour rights while providing individuals with a measure of
control over flexibility. The concept of social drawing rights offers a means
of reconciling the requirements of freedom, security and responsibility inherent in the new occupational status of individuals.

FROM WORKING TIME TO WORKER TIME

Being both a measure of and a limit to the amount of work done in wage employment, time is crucial to the organization of employment relationships.

Indeed, the standardization of work schedules played a central role in the organization of workforces and in the organization of time use in the public and private spheres alike – both of which have been cast in the mould of working time. The new forms of work organization – particularly flexible working time (flexible hours, annual averaging of hours of work, work on call, part-time or irregular employment) – are giving rise to a new concept of working time which is both heterogeneous (due to the emergence of a grey area between working time and free time: training, home work, work on call, time off counted as working time, etc.) and individualized. These developments raise the issue of how to preserve some "collective time" (for family life in particular) and to give people the means of managing the use of their own time. According to the report on which this synthesis is based, flexibility must be seen as a prerogative that workers are entitled to share within the limits set by the biological and social needs of human existence.

Without prejudice to the quantitative issues associated with working time – which are genuinely important and currently the subject of much debate – the said report focuses on analysing the relevant qualitative issues. Indeed, the perception of "social time" has been disrupted by three new factors. First, Fordist time was a general standard against which work was measured. Yet the adequacy of that standard is confined to the Taylorist framework of mass production. The emergence of new spheres of production calls for other instruments with which to measure not only work but also the subordination it involves and the insecurity it creates. In particular, the increasingly service-like nature of many occupations, including in the manufacturing sector, is producing a qualitative change in the way time is perceived. For example, there is paradoxically no contradiction between overworking/total job commitment and a reduction in formal working time. The maintenance of a purely quantitative standard for measuring time is thus likely to conceal diversity in the terms of involvement in work, which call for new forms of protection. Second, the growing emphasis on flexibility in the organization of work is leading to the fragmentation of time. This, in turn, needs to be examined from two distinct angles. From the point of view of the individual worker, part-time employment and flexible hours of work are just as likely to procure greater freedom as they are to increase subordination. Women are particularly exposed to this. From the collective point of view, the fragmentation of time is a source of new problems with coordination. Collective work cycles are broken, entailing disruption of the foundations of social integration. This point is illustrated by the public debate over rest on Sundays in some European countries.

Third, the trend towards individualization and heterogeneity in patterns of time use is rendering ineffective any legislation that continues to regard working time as an objective criterion or as a given in the system of employment relationships. Yet a non-interventionist policy could jeopardize the very fundamentals of workers' lives and cause still further damage to social bonds. The deregulation of working time ultimately has a disruptive effect on society. To break out of this dilemma, time must be conceived of not only in terms of working time, as a measure of the trading of labour for pay, but also as a subjective experience, i.e. as time in the life of the worker. This broader view calls for rethinking the terms on which negotiations and bargaining on time are conducted.

The issue is thus not to deregulate working time but rather to regulate it differently. To that end, the report synthesized here lays down three main guidelines:

Law needs to take a broad view of individual time and collective time. Work must be adapted to the worker who performs it – not vice versa. All the implications of this general principle must be fully grasped. Thus, at the individual level, it is important not to focus solely on the time during which work is actually performed, but to broaden the scope of reflection to include the duration of the contract as well. Indeed, this has a bearing on the conditions under which the worker learns basic safety regulations, for example. Similarly, time for life – with its various exigencies, e.g. maternity, upbringing of children, training, etc. – must be preserved as a whole. At the collective level, the law must endeavour to ensure respect for certain principles that provide the structure of societal coordination and cycles, whether those of the family or those of public life.

This view implies substantive principles. A number of general principles that underpin what amounts to subjective (personal) rights must be guaranteed, including at the community-wide level. For example, the right to a private and family life is a principle enshrined in Article 8 of the European Convention on Human Rights[3] and in the ILO's Workers with Family Responsibilities Convention, 1981 (No. 156) and its accompanying Recommendation (No. 165). This goes further than European Council Directive 93/1041EC[4] which is confined to a Fordist definition of free time and concerned only with workers' health and safety. Enjoyment of the above right presupposes the application of a principle of concordance as between the different time segments that make up every worker's life. The question of night work could thus be reappraised in the light of such principles.

This view is operationalized through collective bargaining mechanisms. Individualization of time should not be confused with individual negotiation on time. Collective bargaining offers the most appropriate framework for the regulation of time. Collective bargaining should be encouraged systematically, if necessary with penalties for non-compliance. But this would require a substantial overhaul of the terms of reference of collective bargaining – an issue which is also taken up in the report under consideration.

THE CHANGING FACE OF INDUSTRIAL RELATIONS

The collective dimension of employment relationships has always been closely linked to the forms of work organization prevailing in enterprises. Indeed, such organization determines those workforce characteristics which underpin the legal procedures for action, representation and collective bargaining. Pre-industrial work organization was based on occupational diversity and therefore induced corporative forms of action and representation. In this model, "collective bargaining" practices centred on product pricing, not wage levels. In the industrial model, crafts and trades are no longer central to the organization of work. Industry coordinates increasingly specialized tasks to meet the needs of mass production. In this new set-up, collective identities are no longer based on particular occupations but on employment within a particular enterprise or industry (the relative significance of each of these two levels of collective organization varies from one country to another). This model is still going strong though it now coexists with new forms of work organization which are reconfiguring the frameworks for action, representation and collective bargaining.

Collective bargaining has been the focus of major legal innovations over the past two decades. These innovations follow two distinct trends. First, the practice of collective bargaining is becoming generalized. In fact, it now appears as a prerequisite transitional stage in the framing of the law itself. Its rule extends beyond the scope of the law of wage employment, reaching out to those self-employed workers who, though legally independent, are economically dependent on a single client firm. Collective bargaining is also taking on new functions and pursuing new aims, thereby broadening its own scope beyond the mere distribution of productivity gains and the determination of working conditions. In cases where collective agreements are concluded within some statutory framework, these changes are altering the relationship between the law and collective bargaining. Second, collective bargaining institutions are undergoing a process of restructuring, whereby a strong trend towards enterprise-level decentralization contrasts with the emergence of new bargaining units at the sub-national and transnational levels (enterprise groups and networks, territories). Beyond its formal diversity, such restructuring introduces a degree of legal complexity hitherto unprecedented under conventional systems. Indeed, the latter are as yet devoid of any clear rules on the distribution of authority between the different levels of bargaining.

Collective representation of employers and workers has also undergone significant changes. Obviously, the restructuring of collective bargaining institutions calls into question the established structure of trade union representation. Industry-wide representation at the national level is being undermined both by the decentralization of collective bargaining to the enterprise level and by the process of consolidation into new higher-level bargaining units (groups, networks, territories, Europe). Shifts in economic organization are producing a wide variety of types of enterprise which, in turn, creates new spheres of employment relationships, e.g. enterprise clusters and groups, networks of enterprises that enable outsourcing of work and stable cooperative relationships, "dependent" enterprises (subsidiaries, subcontractors), very small enterprises, etc. Of course, decentralization of collective bargaining to the enterprise level, together with the emergence of new bargaining units that are also enterprise based (e.g. groups, networks), are strengthening the role of worker representation at those levels. Worker representation institutions elected in enterprises – i.e. works councils – are in fact the only form of elective representation that is in a position to challenge trade union representation. Works councils have consolidated their position under the dual representation systems (i.e. those combining union representation with elected staff representatives) which operate in most European countries. In some cases, there has been a tendency for them to acquire greater powers of participation and control (information and consultation) as well as some bargaining power.

At the same time the trade unions' formerly consistent human and social base – i.e. male industrial wage-earners working under a typical contract of full-time employment of indefinite duration – has been fragmented and diversified, thereby undermining the community of interests they once represented. Growing diversification, both within workforces and in the interests of individual workers, coupled with the instability of work experiences, the discontinuity of career profiles and the proliferation of arrangements for subcontracting, decentralization and relocation are all factors that contribute to weakening traditional trade union representation. As a result, the trade unions' task of representing workers has become extremely complex, prompting them to resort to methods based on representativeness. Mass unemployment has also contributed to undermining the representation capability and influence of trade unions. Fear of unemployment is indeed a strong deterrent to unionized militancy among workers. The availability of a vast pool of unemployed labour can be used to discourage those in employment from active participation in actions conducted to press union demands. Unemployment has also led to the establishment of new organizations that compete with trade unions and challenge their monopoly over representation (e.g. non-governmental organizations, organizations set up in defence of the disadvantaged and unemployed, foundations, etc.).

Generally speaking, it would be dangerous to overlook the adverse consequences that trade unionism has suffered as a result of the time factor, changes in the organization of work, routine and sheer inadequacy. The trade unions must adjust their institutional structures and their working methods to the heterogeneity of today's world of work. While such adjustment is necessary, however, it must not be allowed to overshadow the case for maintaining the system of collective representation. There are indeed a number of factors – such as the stability of trade union law, the need for trade union representation and the lack of an alternative to such representation – which make it much safer to predict some adjustment rather than an all-out overhaul of existing forms of collective worker representation.

The foregoing analysis thus rules out the possibility and the desirability of any far-reaching upheaval in the prevailing systems of collective representation. However, two models for their adjustment are emerging in the face of new forms of work organization. One of the historical functions of European trade unions has been to prevent competition within any given industry from having a depressive effect on wages (this is the basic rationale of industry-wide bargaining). In those countries where this function has been performed most successfully (in Germany, for example) it has had the beneficial effect of focusing competition between enterprises on qualitative issues and competitiveness rather than the impoverishment of workers. Today, however, the industry-level framework within which the trade unions consolidated that unifying function is being weakened by new patterns of corporate organization, especially subcontracting which enables enterprises to evade compliance with the provisions of industry-level collective agreements. Enterprises can thus play off one industry against another in order to lower their labour costs. This strengthens the case for promoting the development of bargaining units at the level of enterprise groups or networks or at the territorial level, as appropriate. This would not mean the end of centralized trade union institutions, but rather a transformation of their role. Instead of being decision-making centres, their function would be to coordinate such demands, actions and negotiations as would be undertaken in individual enterprises or in incipient bargaining units. Such a shift would constitute an effective response to the diversification of forms of employment and enterprise which makes it so much more complex to identify "workers' interests" or "employers' interests".

THE STATE AND SOCIAL CITIZENSHIP

In Western tradition, there has never been any lasting social order without laws and institutions with which society could identify. The advent of the State in the Middle Ages, followed by that of the Welfare State a century ago, thus provided the West with an institutional framework to which it could refer. But the contour of that framework is now becoming indistinct. The question is whether what is happening is yet another transformation of the State or whether the State itself is destined to give way to some other referential framework for social bonding.

Ever since the nation-State model came to dominate the world (at least formally), such States have provided the setting for the construction of what might be termed the "social estate" of individuals. The three mainstays of this construct – labour law, social security and public services – rest upon the bedrock of national institutions. Yet this fundamental role of the State is now clearly called into question by the dual forces of internationalization and regionalization. That national institutions are increasingly incapable of providing peoples with a decent standard of living is evidenced by the growing proportions of a new underclass comprising the unemployed and the working poor. Its attendant manifestations include rising poverty, violence and despair, which are now ubiquitous, most noticeably at the very heart of the market economy in the major cities of the world's richest countries.

The law and the State are insulated neither from economic forces nor from social life. They affect them and are affected by them. Any laws that fail to take account of economic and social circumstances are unenforceable. Conversely, the State sets a legal framework without which there could be no socio-economic order in today's world. In all countries, the State, the economy and society interact in complex ways that reflect history, cultural traditions and traditional political divisions. The foundations of the State's legitimacy vary from one country to another, thereby shaping a variety of economic and social expectations. Such cultural and historical diversity is what sometimes makes it so difficult to provide Europe's labour markets with a common legal framework. Understanding those markets calls for understanding how the State, the economy and society interact at the national level and for taking account of the resulting diversity of legal cultures.

In this connection, attention must be drawn to the limitations of the widespread tendency to contrast two broad views of the role of the State, namely, that of the minimalist State (or gendarme State) and that of the protector State (also known as "social State" or "Welfare State"). All of the States Members of the European Union embody a combination of these two views – which are not necessarily contradictory – and have endeavoured to ensure both freedom and security for their citizens. Accordingly, in most countries, the authority of the State derives from its capacity to protect those in the weakest position. Today's problems stem partly from the erosion of that authority due to the State's incapacity to continue to provide such protection. The question at the root of the current political/legal debate thus no longer centres on the nineteenth century dilemma between intervention and laissez-faire, but on the capacity of the State to maintain social cohesion in today's world.

The national and Keynesian State has run into a crisis. First, the underlying assumptions of state regulation no longer hold. The growing individualization of lifestyles and of citizens' expectations is incompatible with the paternalistic approach taken by the Welfare State. Besides, the opening up of the European market, coupled with budgetary constraints and the necessity of curbing inflation, have put an end to the continuous growth of public services. Second, the framework for state action is changing. As regards public services, the general trend is a shift from a manager State to a guarantor State. This implies new forms of intervention in civil society. The civil service has not been spared either. The special status enjoyed by civil servants is increasingly being replaced by ordinary contracts of employment (to varying degrees depending on the country). Third, a relative measure of state sovereignty has been transferred to the European Union.

These three developments threaten to narrow political society's scope for self-determination. It can settle neither for a minimalist State (neo-liberalism) nor for outright maintenance of the Welfare State. What needs to be sought and found is a new *modus operandi* for state intervention, especially in the socio-economic sphere.

The report synthesized in this article suggests that the required overhaul be linked to a comprehensive view of social rights based on solidarity. Such solidarity must not be conceived of merely in terms of a response to individual need. This would lead to the granting of social rights only in the event of proven individual want and hence to a shift from the Welfare State to some kind of "assistance State" or even a "charity State". Nor should the aim of the proposed solidarity be framed as a form of passive protection for individuals and enterprises based on a catalogue of specified risks. Rather, the proposal is for a form of solidarity that would ensure individual and collective security in the face of contingencies that can arise at any time anywhere, because of the inescapable increase in uncertainty.

To that end, a way must be found to provide two types of guarantee:

Procedural guarantees. Social rights presuppose that the people who are to enjoy them should participate in framing them. But such participation cannot be confined to political representation alone. It calls for a wide range of appropriate mechanisms for representation and social consultation. The law can do no more than lay down principles whose implementation then falls within the scope of the law of collective agreements. It follows that a collective agreement should no longer be seen simply as a means of adjusting the particular interests of the parties thereto, but as a legal instrument whereby those parties are joined in the pursuit of objectives laid down by the law. In this process of determining the public interest, independent agencies could also play a useful role provided that democratic debate does not become sidetracked under the influence of "experts".

Substantive guarantees. In terms of substantive content, the European Union should, as a matter of priority, strive to guarantee fundamental social rights at the European level. These basic principles are already recognized partially in the Community Charter of the Fundamental Social Rights of Workers and, more thoroughly, in the standards of the International Labour Organization, yet they could usefully be written into constitutional law at the European level. This perspective fits in naturally with the emphasis given to socio-economic issues at this stage in the construction of the European Union.

CONCLUSION

The concept of social citizenship currently appears to offer better prospects than does that of social protection for synthesizing the above aims of a re-organization of labour and social security law. Despite the diversity of national notions of citizenship, this concept could become one of the cornerstones of that entire branch of law at the European level. It has the advantage of being inclusive (it encompasses many rights besides social insurance coverage); it links social and labour rights to the notion of social integration, not only to that of work; and, most importantly, it conveys the idea of participation. Indeed, citizenship implies that the people it covers should participate in the framing and realization of their rights.

Notes

[1] This report was submitted and discussed at an ad hoc international seminar held in Madrid in June 1998. It is the product of a multidisciplinary group effort by professors Maria-Emilia Casas (Complutense University of Madrid), Jean de Munck (Thomas More College, Leuven University), Peter Hanau (Cologne University), Anders Johansson (Stockholm University), Pamela Meadows (National Institute of Economic and Social Research, London), Enzo Mingione (Padua University), Robert Salais (IDHE, CNRSIENS, Cachan), Alain Supiot (CNRS/ Nantes University), and Paul van der Heijden (Amsterdam University). Alain Supiot was the group's general rapporteur. The full text of the report has been published in French (Alain Supiot (ed.): *Au-delà de l'emploi*, Paris, Flammarion, 1999, 321 pp.) and in Spanish. German and English editions are under preparation. This article ends with a selected bibliography of the works cited in the report.

[2] See Commissariat général du Plan: *Le travail dans vingt ans* (Report of the Working Group on "Work and Employment to the Year 2015", chaired by Jean Boissonnat), Paris, Editions Odile Jacob, La Documentation française, 1995. [Ed.: For references in English, see also Jean Boissonnat: "Combating unemployment, restructuring work: Reflections on a French study" and ILO: "Perspectives: What is the future of work? Ideas from a French report", both in *International Labour Review* (Geneva), Vol. 135 (1996), No. 1, pp. 5-15 and pp. 93-110 respectively.]

[3] Paragraph 1 of this Article of the Convention provides that: "Everyone has the right to respect for his private and family life, his home and his correspondence." See Council of Europe: "Convention for the protection of human rights and fundamental freedoms", in *European treaties*, Strasbourg, Council of Europe Publishing, 1998, Vol. 1.

[4] Council Directive 93/104/EC of 23 November 1993 concerning certain aspects of the organization of working time, in *Official Journal of the European Communities* (Luxembourg), No. L.307, Vol. 36, 13 December 1993, pp. 18-24.

References

Ballestrero, Maria-Vittoria. 1987. "L'ambigua nozione di lavoro parasubordinato", in *Lavoro e diritto* (Bologna), Vol. 1, No. 1 (Jan.), pp. 41-67.

Bercusson, Brian. 1996. *European labour law*. London, Butterworths.

Beretta, C. 1995. *Il lavoro tra mutamento e reproduzione sociale*. Milano, Angeli.

Cartelier, Lysiane; Fournier, Jacques; Monnier, Lionel. 1996. *Critique de la raison communautaire. Utilité publique et concurrence dans l'Union européenne*. Paris, Economica.

Chassard, Yves. 1997. "L'avenir de la protection sociale en Europe", in *Droit social* (Paris), No. 6 (June), pp. 634-639.

Commissariat général du Plan. 1997. *Quelles politiques pour l'industrie française. Dynamiques du système productif: analyse, débats, propositions*. Report coordinated by G. Colletis et J.-L. Levet. Paris. Mar.

Coriat, Benjamin. 1994. *L'atelier et le chronomètre*. Paris, Christian Bourgeois.

Crouch, Colin; Streeck, Wolfgang. 1996. *Les capitalismes en Europe*. Paris, La Découverte.

Didry, Claude; Wagner, P.; Zimmermann, B. (eds.). 1998. *Le travail et la nation. La France et l'Allemagne à l'horizon européen*. Paris, Editions de la MSH.

Francq, Bernard. 1995. "Procéduralisation et formation", in Jean De Munck, Jacques Lenoble and M. Molitor (eds.): *L'avenir de la concertation sociale en Europe*. Leuven, Université catholique de Louvain (Centre de philosophie du droit), Vol. 2. Mar.

Freyssinet, Jacques. 1997. *Le temps de travail en miettes*. Paris, Editions de l'Atelier.

Gaudu, François. 1995. "Du statut de l'emploi au statut de l'actif", in *Droit social* (Paris), No. 6 (June), pp. 535-544.

Hanau, Peter. 1997. "Die Einwirkung des europäischen auf das nationale Arbeitsrecht – Ein Erfahrungsbericht aus Deutschland", in Juridiska Foreningen i Uppsala (ed.): *Festskrift till Stig Strömholm*. Uppsala, Iustus Förlag.

van der Heijden, Paul. 1998. *The flexibilisation of working life in the Netherlands*. Paper presented to the 15th Congress of the International Academy of Comparative Law, held at Bristol. July.

Ichino, Andrea; Ichino, Pietro. 1994. "A chi serve il diritto del lavoro. Riflessioni interdisciplinari sulla funzione economica e la giustificazione constituzionale dell'inderogabilità delle norme giuslavoristiche", in *Rivista Italiana di Diritto del Lavoro* (Milan), Vol. 13, No. 4 (Oct.-Dec.), pp. 459-505.

Leisering, Lutz; Leibfried, Stephan (eds.). 1998. *Time, life and poverty: Social assistance dynamics in the German Welfare State*. Cambridge, Cambridge University Press.

Lyon-Caen, Antoine. 1997. "Le rôle des partenaires sociaux dans la mise en œuvre du droit communautaire", in *Droit social* (Paris), No. 1 (Jan.), pp. 68-74.

Mansfield, Malcolm; Salais, Robert; Whiteside, Noel (eds.). 1994. Aux *sources du chômage. Une comparaison interdisciplinaire France-Grande-Bretagne 1880-1914*. Paris, Editions Belin.

Maruani, Margaret; Nicole, Chantal. 1989. *Au labeur des dames: métiers masculins, emplois féminins*. Paris, Syros.

Meurs, Dominique; Charpentier, Pascal. 1987. "Horaires atypiques et vie quotidienne des salariés", in *Travail et Emploi* (Paris), No. 32 (June), pp. 47-56.

Mengoni, Luigi. 1986. "La questione della subordinazione in due trattazioni recenti", in *Rivista Italiana di Diritto del Lavoro* (Milan), Vol. 5, No. 1 (Jan-Mar.), pp. 5-19.

Moreau, Yannick. 1996. *Entreprises de service public européennes et relations sociales*. Paris, ASPE.

Morin, Marie-Laure. 1996. "Sous-traitance et coactivité", in *Revue juridique Ile de France* (Paris), No. 39/40 (Jan-June), pp. 115-131.

—. 1994. "Sous-traitance et relations salariales. Aspects de droit du travail", in *Travail et Emploi* (Paris), No. 60 (3/94), pp. 23-43.

Mothé, Daniel. 1994. "Le mythe du temps libéré", in *Esprit* (Paris), No. 8-9 (Aug.-Sep), pp. 52-63.

Mückenberger, Ulrich (ed.). 1998. *Zeiten der Stadt. Reflexionen und Materialen zu einem neuen gesellschaftlichen Gestaltungsfeld*. Bremen, Temen.

Offe, Claus; Heinze, Rolf G. 1992. *Beyond employment: Time, work, and informal economy*. Cambridge, Polity Press.

Olea, Alonso. 1994. *Introducción al derecho del trabajo*. Fifth edition. Madrid, Civitas.

Priestley, Thierry. 1995. "A propos du 'contrat d'activité' proposé par le rapport Boissonnat", in *Droit social* (Paris), No. 12 (Dec.), pp. 955-960.

Rodríguez-Piflero, Miguel. 1996. "La voluntad de las partes en la calificación del contrato de trabajo", in *Relaciones Laborales* (Madrid), Vol. 12, No. 18 (23 Sep.), pp. 1-7.

—; Casas, Maria Emilia. 1996. "In support of a European Social Constitution", in P.L. Davies and Antoine Lyon-Caen (eds.): *European Community labour law: Principles and perspectives. Liber amicorum Lord Wedderburn of Charlton*. Oxford, Clarendon Press.

Sabel, Charles F.; Zeitlin, Jonathan (eds.). 1997. *World of possibilities: Flexibility and mass production in Western industrialization*. Cambridge, Cambridge University Press.

Salais, Robert; Storper, Michael. 1993. *Les mondes de production: enquête sur l'identité économique de la France*. Paris, Editions de l'EHESS.

Soskice, David. 1990. "Wage determination: The changing role of institutions in advanced industrialized countries", in *Oxford Review of Economic Policy* (Oxford), Vol. 6, No. 4 (Winter), pp. 36-61.

Storper, Michael; Salais, Robert. 1997. *Worlds of production: The action frameworks of the economy*. Cambridge, MA, Harvard University Press.

TOWARDS A NEW DEFINITION OF THE EMPLOYMENT RELATIONSHIP **33**

Ulrich MÜCKENBERGER *

This article examines the proposals advanced in the study on "Work in the year 2000" [1] from the point of view of social theory and policy. They focus mainly on labour law, hence on the individual employment relationship. They are therefore only indirectly concerned with problems of employment policy and with questions arising from collective aspects of labour or social security law. For a variety of reasons, the authors of the study consider that it has become extremely important to redefine the concept of work and the employment relationship at individual level and that ways of redefining the structures for worker representation should be explored from an interdisciplinary point of view.

OLD AND NEW CONCEPTS OF SOLIDARITY

The basic hypothesis arises from two general premises, both of them directly linked to the current modernization of the economy and both proving to be double-edged in that they open up new possibilities but also present dangers.

The process of individualization which affects wage-earners and other social actors: this holds potential for the development of identity, of self-awareness, of freedom of life choices. It could also herald the development of a new sense of social responsibility, a new work and life ethic. However, the process also involves the danger of a lessened social bond, of isolation and new forms of alienation, the risk of unbridled domination by the profit motive, of *anomie*.

Originally published in *International Labour Review*, Vol. 135 (1996), No. 6.

* Professor of Labour Law at the Institute of Economics and Political Science (Hochschule für Wirtschaft und Politik), Hamburg.

The crisis of representation affecting the world of work: the social partners managed in the past to maintain a system of self-regulation through effective representation at several levels but the danger is that they may now lose their integrating and organizing influence. This poses a threat to the trade unions above all, but also to employers' associations, since their respective monopolies of representation may be challenged by the emergence of new élites with a more individualistic power base. Conversely, the emerging movement of voluntary associations may result in a revival of the social bond, and this would be an advantage. In an optimistic scenario, there may be a chance of overcoming the traditional apathy of individuals about publicly-owned goods and the long-standing indifference of institutional representatives to the interests of society as a whole and to the external effects of their actions.

The study's proposals concerning "re-regulation" are based on a new understanding of solidarity. Traditionally, in the labour and Socialist movements, solidarity was based on and identified with equality. The workers were all in the same situation (exploited and oppressed); and their unity was founded on this equality. But this unity gave them strength and solidarity: *equality, unity, solidarity* was the old slogan.

By contrast, the new rallying call might be: *diversity, communication, solidarity*. Individuals differ from each other in many ways. Though their interests and wishes may diverge, they all accept each other as equal citizens. This formula is based on the idea not of sameness but of equal value. Citizens recognize each other as equals and equivalents, and so can communicate and coordinate their interests and wishes, according to the rules of dialogue and discourse and in a reasonable manner (communicating here meaning rallying together to create a community, through dialogue and exchanges of view). The experience of playing by these rules leads to the realization that, though they are different, workers are all confronted with the same socio-economic power structure which hinders the fulfilment of their various interests and wishes; this inclines them, despite their differences, towards a degree of mutual understanding, of social cohesion, and hence to joint action. These forms of unity and solidarity spring not from sameness but from the communication of difference.

Obviously, concepts such as "citizenship" and "dialogue and discourse" are central to this hypothesis. It is no accident, therefore, that the study's proposals concerning re-regulation of the employment relationship revolve around them. Attention should also be given to how these two concepts apply to other aspects of our lives, such as the family, relations between generations, sexes and ethnic groups, politics, culture, etc. However, this article will confine itself to the proposals regarding the world of work.

One last preliminary comment: Western countries are not all experiencing the phenomenon of individualization or the crisis of representation in the same manner. For example, despite their difficulties in recruiting members in emerging modern occupations, the German trade unions still represent a fairly solid pillar around which industrial relations in traditional industries are organized. Individualization has not yet destroyed all social and group bonds (family, church, trade unions). This examination of the new forms of solidarity has therefore occurred during a transition phase containing many paradoxes, a period in which social bonds are still fairly strong despite showing clear signs of erosion. The question is how to rethink the traditional, and currently crisis-ridden, forms of solidarity and social interaction and how to ensure their stability in the new era of individualism.

RECOMMENDATIONS

This then is the theoretical and socio-political background of the general approach adopted. The projects' recommendations are summarized below.

Modernization of workplace relations

Citizenship in the enterprise

In the German industrial sector, there should be a considerable increase in employees' rights of participation. Firstly, workers' citizenship status must be consolidated in the enterprise. Standards governing the employment relationship must be based on the principles of dialogue and equal rights, and no longer on the authority of the employer and personal dependence. A redefined employment relationship must therefore allow more room to standards and procedures based on discourse and permit the establishment of appropriate collective instruments guaranteeing individual rights.

Following from this assumption, workers' rights to organize their own lives will gain recognition at the workplace and outside it, and they will be given some opportunity to influence not only employment relations in the production process, but also the impact of that process on society and the environment, its externalities, and the goods workers produce. Workers are entitled to conditions, especially regarding working time, which enable them to exercise their rights (notably to education and training, periods of leave, communication areas, etc.). The exercise of their rights as citizens must not lead to discrimination or sanctions. They must be entitled to refuse work that might be harmful to them or to society. Ecological rights are an integral part of citizenship in the enterprise and of the new employee status.

Gender relations and the workplace

There must be changes in gender relations and in the sexual division of labour at work, in the family and in society. The study's proposals tend in two directions. Firstly, anti-discrimination laws must be made more effective and the application of existing standards reinforced. To this end, the study proposes quotas for women, affirmative action, the allocation of times and places for women to raise issues concerning their situation in the enterprise, the special representation of women workers, the right of pressure groups to file complaints with industrial tribunals on behalf of female victims of discrimination, and the application of court decisions to women who did not file a complaint but experienced the same discrimination, etc.

Secondly, ways and means must be found for both male and female workers to reconcile their roles as workers and parents, to share career and domestic responsibilities. Working time must be organized in ways that enable workers to engage in training or family-based activities. Rules governing parental leave should be improved and such leave be made more widely available. Wage compensation should be provided as an incentive to both parents to share child-rearing responsibilities, as is the case in Sweden. Finally, the person on parental leave should be guaranteed the right to training during that period, so that he or she can remain in contact with the enterprise and return fully qualified. All these measures are designed to prevent parental leave from turning into a dead-end, and to facilitate the return to work. Other proposals concern the right to day-care facilities for employees' children.

Freedom of choice on the allocation of time

A new organization of working time is proposed with a view, if not to reconciling, at least to reaching an honest compromise between three pressures: the demands of economic efficiency, the basic needs of the employees and their need to have access to various goods and services. Already some enterprises run on modern management lines allow their employees total freedom to arrange their working time. This practice involves a preliminary collective agreement on the work to be carried out by a given team, as well as rotation planning (spreading the agreed workload over the working hours of the employees in question). This system may be negotiated by the employees themselves, provided certain priorities are respected; the result is that there is no longer any need for orders to be given, for authority to be exercised. As regards any externalities arising from working-time arrangements in the enterprise, it is proposed to include concerns external to the enterprise in the internal negotiation process. Thus, for example, the interests of the unemployed would be taken into consideration in agreements on overtime, in negotiations on the reduction of working hours to safeguard jobs. Similarly, the interests of consumers would be taken into account in decisions affecting opening times of public or private services, etc. Experiments conducted in Italy as part of the operation *tempi ed orari della città* are the most advanced model in this area. However, including such concerns in the bargaining structures of enterprises is not likely to be easy, at any rate on the basis of individual labour law.

Winners and losers

A few words must also be said on the way in which a reform in labour law might contribute to the protection of workers in precarious employment and to the fight against social exclusion. The focus is on forms of employment where the risks run by the enterprise are passed on to the employees, the latter not receiving the slightest compensation or benefit in return (such as risk bonuses, the possibility of becoming self-employed, a broader range of personal options). A revision is proposed of the legal concept of "employee", which in all Western labour law is still based on the notions of personal dependence and subordination. Similarly, the threshold values specified in certain labour and social security laws should be reassessed. At present these laws discriminate particularly against workers in the "modern" employment sectors (or the ostensibly self-employed). There should be ways and means guaranteeing that atypical workers are not excluded from existing communication channels and vocational training measures in the enterprise, and that they are given the right of self-expression concerning their economic activity. It is true that such increased protection of atypical employment would have an unacceptable economic impact on small and medium-sized enterprises. The study therefore proposes establishing individual rights for the employee, which would provide employers with an incentive to group together (as in the industrial districts in Italy, for example) and thus reduce some of the risks passed on to employees.

Towards citizenship in the enterprise

The underlying aim of all these proposals is to develop in the wage employment sphere a form of dialogue based on genuine communication, on freely consented coordination and mutual trust. Clearly, such an approach does not necessarily reflect the realities of the working world we know today, with its uneven power relations, subordination and distrust. But in presenting the standard-setting model outlined here, the study sought to do two things at once: to offer a critique of traditional forms of authority and subordination as enshrined in the law, and to seek desirable alternatives, for without these the concept of citizenship in the enterprise will not be taken seriously.

Other arguments are advanced later to show that the concept of citizenship in the enterprise cannot simply be dismissed as unrealistic, interventionist and utopian. Citizenship in the enterprise was viewed as a contribution to the legalization of the concepts, procedures and projects involved in modernization which have already made some headway in Germany, but which are still far from being in widespread use. Modernization, in the broad and ambitious sense proposed here, does not occur spontaneously or automatically. Rather it comes about through a series of small advances, through the emergence of new options which only gain currency if they attract sufficient support and encouragement. One form of such support and encouragement is legal regulation.

Dialogue

The term "modern" is currently applied to a great number of situations and trends, and is used by many different social actors and organizations.

According to the definition adopted by the study, any measure or policy claiming to contribute to the modernization process should comply at least with the three criteria already mentioned in the section on working time: the first is economic in nature, the second social, the third relates to society itself.

– From an economic point of view, regulations concerning employment policy must be examined for their contribution to efficiency and productivity. This is a question of business management, which perceives the organization of labour and the labour force in purely instrumental terms.

– From a social point of view, an evaluation of such regulations should seek to establish whether they provide protection to workers and their social environment (family, neighbourhood, friends, leisure, etc.) but also opportunities for personal development, and whether they create conditions enabling plans to be made to meet the needs arising from gainful activity and those arising from other aspects of daily life. This criterion is a reflection of people's attitudes towards work, leisure and other social activities.

– Finally, regulations concerning employment policy should be examined from the point of view of society as a whole, in order to determine possible externalities with an impact on society outside the enterprise. Particular attention should be paid to any externalities detrimental to the interests of society or inflicting on the community some of the nuisances engendered by the enterprise.

Simply enumerating these three criteria indicates the conflicts between objectives, but contributes little (if anything) to their solution. However, even at this early stage of our reasoning, one observation is very important in any reflection on the legal policy to be pursued. The three criteria mentioned represent parameters which, so far, have been set by different social actors: the efficiency criterion by enterprises, the social criterion by workers and trade unions, and the criterion concerning society as a whole – in so far as it has been set at all – by public opinion in general. As regards the political strategy to be adopted this results in a well-known dilemma. The social actor evoking one of these three criteria tends to ignore or downplay the other two criteria, so that the demands and proposals put forward by that actor are considered incomprehensible and irrational by the others. Another consequence of this mutual obstructionism over criteria and policy proposals is that, in the event of conflict, the result is determined solely through a power struggle, with dialogue, good will and reason carrying little weight in the ultimate outcome.

No new form of regulation of employment relations has a chance of being applied throughout society unless these three criteria and their interaction are fully taken into account. Only on this condition can such regulation be discussed by the actors concerned, and solutions based on consensus or, failing that, on compromise be found and implemented. This does not mean that the actors on each side must first rack their own brains on these questions, and then rack each other's brains. It means that each must be able to evaluate the ever-present contradictions between these different criteria in order to understand fully any proposals deriving from them, and thus to discuss areas where consensus or compromise can be reached.

For this reason, the modern and intelligent approach to conflict resolution should rely largely on dialogue and consultation, which create the conditions for mutual comprehension and recognition of interests, motives, standpoints and aims, and include actors and concerns hitherto outside the consultation process. It is also important that a third party should be able to intervene in an advisory capacity to define areas of consensus and compromise. Such procedures are vitally important as, in situations of uncertainty, they alone can bring about fair and reasonable solutions to conflict.

The full significance of the assumptions underlying these dialogue procedures should not be underestimated. Dialogue and the rules of debate can only succeed where the balance of power is symmetrical. This means that the different sides must recognize each other as equals, must be prepared to accept the rules of debate – which is very difficult to ensure in situations where the balance of power and influence is asymmetrical, as in the employment relationship. This is why it is so important to upgrade workers' citizenship rights to the level of citizenship status. Recognition of this status is, in fact, a precondition of their status as equals, as equal partners in the dialogue. Obviously, citizenship status cannot be established simply by granting workers a *de jure* citizenship status at the workplace. But to do so could contribute by reducing the obstacles to such recognition and by encouraging employers and employees to acknowledge their equal status and their rights and obligations as citizens.

Regardless of these legal considerations, there are discernible economic trends which seem to point in the same direction. In certain secondary – and more so in tertiary – sectors, there are signs that dialogue and consultation are beginning to take root, in the context of a new organization of working life, and these will also affect individual aspects of the employment relationship. This trend is developing concurrently with a decline in traditional patterns of one-way, authoritarian transmission of instructions, and of worker subordination. The study concludes that these trends, which are outlined below, offer a real empirical basis for innovative policies in labour law.

New production patterns require new forms of regulation

In the developed countries, recent research in industrial psychology and sociology has revealed the emergence in the basic production and service sectors of a new type of employment, which Kern and Schumann[2] have called "new production models", and Piore and Sabel[3] defined as the transition from "rigid mass production" to "flexible specialization", now termed "lean production". These models are decentralized production processes, in which highly skilled workers, working in teams assigned to a given project, assume new responsibilities in respect of planning, optimization and production control. This is in keeping with developments in the United States towards what is termed "corporate identity", referred to in Germany as *neue Unternehmenskultur* (a new enterprise culture). In the organizational and operational structures of enterprises, a third set of objectives and responsibilities is gaining ground. In addition to economic efficiency and the capacity to control social conflict associated with the enterprise there is a new sense of the responsibility of industry towards the social environment, i.e. encompassing the physical environment, infrastructure, company image, regional interests, sport, art, culture, etc.

These changes affecting working life have not yet been adequately taken into account in labour law, nor have they been organized to meet modern needs. Five major developments in production and the service sector can be expected.

New forms of integrated production: with demand now focusing more on personalized goods and services and on quality, it has become vital to achieve greater flexibility in integrated manufacturing structures, in logistics. The various sectors of activity in the enterprise are being scientifically surveyed to determine their potential for optimization. Perceptions of enterprise activity and rationalization based on the distribution of tasks are increasingly giving way to a global approach: work is characterized less and less by a hierarchical organization of hermetic functions within the production unit or single enterprise, and increasingly by a synthetic approach which extends beyond the production unit. The enterprise is becoming more open to the outside world, to the environment in which it operates. There is growing acceptance of the idea of social obligation and the need for open-minded dialogue.

Controlled autonomy: organization patterns inspired not by Taylorism but by a new definition of work and skills are increasingly prevalent. Their aims are decentralization, integration and the breaking down of hierarchy. Planning can no longer be separated from execution, either in time, in space or from the human resource point of view. Unlike centralized organizational structures, which are sluggish and prone to risk, decentralized structures can react more rapidly to changing situations and new problems.

Increased personal development: workers' lifestyle preferences are becoming evident in their attitudes to work generally and in their own work. They are demanding greater participation and opportunities to exercise their creativity and achieve personal fulfilment; they are proving willing to take responsibility in the workplace and elsewhere.

"Lifetime learning": skills are now the vital link between the development of the work environment and human development. Ongoing training, the ability to make decisions and workers' ability to assume responsibility are essential both in the enterprise and in society. Generally processes such as participation, vocational training and retraining in the workplace require a new type of structure reflecting their increased importance.

Winners and losers: new production patterns can also lead to a polarization between winners and losers. Modernization does not have universally beneficial effects on workers, some of whom lose their jobs, or fail to improve their prospects through new skills or enhanced communication in the enterprise. Certain "stigmas" (associated, for example, with sex or nationality) have attracted new types of discrimination. Women are often the victims in this process, regardless of the level of their skills and qualifications. New forms of exclusion and poverty are emerging and becoming increasingly accepted.

Resistance to modernization

The modernization of manufacturing and the services does not come about automatically, it must overcome many obstacles. A *laissez-faire policy* is totally inappropriate – as is the complete deregulation of the employment relationship. Legal instruments and other forms of intervention must be used to help emerging modernization to overcome resistance, and then to spread.

The first difficulty is coping with time lags in the achievement of modernization. As regards organizational and technical progress, there are wide disparities between industries and service sectors, between regions, between small, medium and large enterprises. In many cases, there is a huge gap between public demand in respect of social responsibility, the company's external image and its employees' desire for participation, on the one hand, and the actual level of participation that companies grant their employees or that employees exercise, on the other.

Two closely related factors often prevent any real spread of a new culture of participatory management: a culture of "the leader and the led" and differences in management styles. On analysis, these factors prove to be largely cultural, not technical or organizational; in other words, they are related to perceptions, attitudes, habits and the established routines of the persons involved.

Culture of the leader and the led: sometimes, managers refuse to allow any kind of participation, even when everything points in its favour, from the technical and organizational points of view. Hierarchies in companies and government departments sometimes reveal a form of resistance born of inertia that cannot be overcome by efficiency arguments. Employees often do not dare to insist on participation, even when this might prove more productive and might be of greater advantage to society than mere subordination.

Varying management styles: even when encouraged by management, democratic behaviour patterns geared towards participation are often thwarted by internal hierarchies. Sometimes they are thwarted by resistance at lower or intermediate levels. Lean production and direct employee participation often lead, in fact, to a loss of authority at lower levels in the hierarchy, as well as to a loss of the authority exercised by worker representatives, who therefore opt for passive or active resistance, rather than trying to control developments. Indeed, new production patterns often do pose a threat to jobs lower in the hierarchy – a threat which does not necessarily involve redundancy and unemployment, but which requires role changes that are hard to accept psychologically (for example, the foreman or supervisor suddenly relegated to the function of adviser or "coach") and often associated with a loss of prestige.

The way in which information about innovation is communicated (or not) is important in breaking down passive resistance. Middle management constitutes, in a sense, a "lock" within the company's authority structure. Thus, a situation may arise in which ideas developed by higher management are not, or are only partially, communicated to the employees. Similarly, as a result of this passive resistance, employees' complaints to their immediate superiors, or their suggestions regarding improvement in work organization, "seep away" and fail to contribute to the modernization process. In part, this information lock can be attributed to a structure based on subordination and to the fact that the employees are not accorded their civil rights. These forms of resistance would undoubtedly lose their hold on company culture if individual workers were given more responsibilities and a greater right to self-expression.

Certainly, as suggested above, workers' rights to autonomy and self-determination should be interpreted as the right to the humanization of work: to this extent they represent "social" rights. But they are more than merely social in nature, they are in keeping with the progress of the "economy" and of "society", to which they may even contribute, for example in the following ways:

– Granting these rights would help put an end to obsolete cultural patterns of management and subordination, of leaders and led. Both higher management and society could be provided with information to which they would otherwise not have access – information concerning hazards and errors within the existing work organization, and also possible alternatives for the future. As well as rendering traditional forms of authority obsolete, such rights would help to release new productive and innovative forces in the workers.

– Such rights also help to restrain company practices of discrimination and exclusion, which – along with other externalities, and the social costs to employers – would sooner or later be stopped and placed under the control of a third party, such as the region or society as a whole. Such rights would act as a counterweight to the process of social disintegration and other disorders affecting society.

In short, because of their beneficial effects on the workers' personal and career development such rights can be considered truly social in nature. But they represent far more than mere social concessions by employers and society to workers (with the workers giving nothing in return); they also have positive effects on productivity both for the enterprise and for society. The idea that rights of this kind would impair the economic efficiency of the enterprise seems to be based on an interpretation of "efficiency" which dissociates microeconomic efficiency from the potential of the enterprise to influence social relations and social reality, or which even places them in opposition to one another. Such a narrow interpretation is alien to the modern approach to management and company objectives and should be considered a thing of the past.

The complementary role of modernized legislation

It would be a very serious mistake to cast doubt on the modernizing role of legislation in the social development process. Legal standards and procedures are playing an increasingly structuring role in the functioning of labour markets and the employment relationship. For this reason, any process of renewal in this sphere requires legal innovations – what Max Weber called "legal discoveries". Contrary to simplistic Marxist theories on the opposition between base and superstructure, these cannot just be taken for granted.

The relationship between individual and collective rights and the changes they are now undergoing need to be examined in greater depth. Research on the subject remains somewhat patchy. Given the current state of knowledge, therefore, the individualization process and the crisis of representation should be given very serious consideration. A mere extension of collective rights would have no effect on this process, and would certainly not contain it. For such a strategy would ignore the need for a genuine radical reappraisal of the collective community ethic, one which takes as its starting point the new civil society based on individualization and the changed role of its members. Collective association still seems essential to the advancement of individual interests, especially in situations based on asymmetrical power structures. But in cases where it is difficult to identify common interests, and hence to achieve unity, the community needs a new basis. Fundamental civil rights in employment certainly present a real challenge to traditional definitions of the ethic of collective and voluntary effort – but they may actually lead to its renewal and consolidation.

The study's proposals on legal changes are based on the three functions that such changes may assume in the actual modernization process in industry and the service sector.

The law is a basic factor in the daily life of the various actors involved. But it is naïve and simplistic to imagine that the law, as it appears in the statute book, is actually applied in practice. It is more realistic to think of the social actors as perceiving the law as a set of instruments and means to be used in their negotiations and informal discussions, which their opponents can also use if a consensual settlement to a given dispute cannot be reached. Here, paradoxically, the law functions best when it remains in the background, i.e. when it is not directly applied. In the case under consideration, therefore, it is quite unrealistic to think that increased civil rights for employees would lead to an explosion of court cases and procedures. Initially, increased rights would only give those workers who consider their opinions and convictions are constantly disregarded the possibility of formalizing the conflict, which entails additional costs to the other party, in time and in money. An employer who is aware of the possibility of such costs will be more inclined to dialogue. The fact that laws, even when they are not applied directly or do not lead to court proceedings, can encourage readiness to dialogue is borne out in practice in the day-to-day workings of the laws governing industrial relations in Germany.

One possible approach would be to examine how far existing laws actually contain positive inducements to traditional behaviour which discourage modern behaviour patterns. Such inducements can be removed so as to allow and even encourage modern forms of behaviour and conflict settlement without any loss of rights. For example, the abolition of privileges associated with traditional forms of employment relationship would not necessarily make German men readier to accept part-time work, but it would at least have the advantage of enabling those willing to take this option to do so. Similarly, a modification to the German regulations on the tax-deductible dependants' allowance, which unquestionably favour married couples where one spouse earns considerably less than the other, would remove the incentive for married women to neglect their careers.

In conclusion therefore, the law can be closely examined to determine whether it retains elements likely to have a negative effect on modernization. If these elements are eliminated, the law would no longer penalize modern forms of behaviour or approaches to the settlement of conflict – i.e. certain types of behaviour would no longer entail negative consequences under civil or criminal law. For example, the uncertain legal situation of employees who publically criticize the political or ecological attitudes of their employer may well deter workers from taking responsible action for the benefit of society as a whole. Similarly, existing labour law creates a situation in which people who are willing to withdraw temporarily or partially from economic activity (a decision that may have many positive effects on the labour market, gender relations and family responsibilities), in order, say, to work part time, become self-employed, or take on voluntary work, are reluctant to do so for fear of being permanently excluded from the labour market.

Positive legal incentives designed to preserve traditional forms of behaviour and lifestyle and negative incentives standing in the way of a more modern approach are mere relics of the patriarchal past. They are incompatible with a modern society, which sees itself as open and pluralist. The proposals discussed here reflect a determination to end such incentives by refuting their legitimacy. The intention is not to impose another lifestyle on workers, merely because it is considered "better" or "more modern". Rather, these proposals seek to create a legal situation ensuring security and individual responsibility which will permit greater diversity in lifestyles and forms of employment freely chosen by those concerned – a free choice from among different forms of employment and lifestyle, all on an equal footing, not set off against each other in terms of privileges or disadvantages. There is every reason to believe that the future of society will depend on such a pluralist system providing both protection and the possibility of individuals negotiating their own employment relationship.

Notes

[1] Hildegard Matthies; Ulrich Mückenberger; Claus Offe; Edgar Peter; Sibylle Raasch: Arbeit 2000, *Anforderungen an eine Neugestaltung der Arbeitswelt*, Reinbek bei Hamburg, Rowohlt Taschenbuch Verlag, 1994. Study conducted on behalf of the Hans Böckler Foundation.

[2] Horst Kern; Michael Schumann: *Das Ende der Arbeitsteilung?* Munich, Beck-Verlag, 1984.

[3] Michael J. Piore; Charles F. Sabel: *The second industrial divide: Possibilities for prosperity*, New York, Basic Books, 1984.

During the course of this century, the objective of guaranteeing social security has established itself worldwide as a function of the State, though the degree to which this objective has been achieved has varied. Originally, the transfer of responsibilities from private to public spheres occurred solely at national level. Since the First World War, however, growing attention has been paid to the international dimension of social security. The influence of the ILO in this respect has been particularly strong.[1] As globalization increases,[2] it is both appropriate and necessary that social security should also be seen in a global context. Social trends and perspectives can no longer be viewed and perceived in national isolation; on the contrary, analysis is possible only through the perspective of a comprehensive overview which also takes into account international aspects. The following article attempts to do this.

A brief outline of the situation will first be drawn, the key feature being that social security systems everywhere are in a state of flux – or at the very least, major issues pertaining thereto are under discussion. There is a significant need for reform and the form this takes will differ considerably according to the starting point in each country.

SOCIAL SECURITY IN A STATE OF FLUX

Throughout the world, social policy is an area in which permanent change and development are considered necessary and, indeed, do occur. This is particularly the case at the present time and it is true irrespective of the level of development and the form of government of the nation in question – though

Originally published in *International Labour Review*, Vol. 133 (1994), No. 4.

* Professor and Director of the Max-Planck-Institute for Foreign and International Social Law, Munich.

the problems do vary from country to country. All States are, nevertheless, confronted with certain common general challenges.

A wide range of problems

The full range of problems encountered in the various countries will be illustrated by means of a few examples.

Developing countries whose original economic and social structures are undergoing change continue to face the task of constructing a state social security system which will compensate for the deficiencies in social protection that development has brought in its wake. A crucial difficulty here is that such a system should cover not just the privileged classes, such as organized labour, but the population as a whole. However, in view of the economic conditions prevailing in many of these countries, such a task cannot yet be tackled.[3]

In the socialist and former socialist countries, the provision of social security occurred largely within the framework of employer-employee relations.[4] However, such an approach can function only when employment relations are stable and are expected to remain so. When unemployment or high labour turnover occur, then deficiencies begin to appear in social security arrangements – especially for long-term risks such as old age and invalidity – because of the lack of an employer responsible for this protection. This problem is even more marked in a competitive market economy with high labour mobility. Where the socialist economic system has been abandoned and employment relationships have been more or less stripped of their social protection function, then it becomes essential to set up bodies independent of the enterprise to organize protection against these contingencies. Many Central and East European countries are now going through this experience and, as a result, are attempting to model themselves on market-economy countries, including in the matter of social protection.[5] However, as the social systems of these countries are themselves very different, it is inherently difficult to base development on that foreign model.

Furthermore, even in developed, market-economy countries, questions are being asked about existing social security systems, for many and varied reasons.[6] First and foremost, there are the costs of running these systems which many believe can no longer be afforded, and their financing is considered to constrain growth. Such arguments have correspondingly greater impact during periods of economic recession. While this is not the place to enter into an assessment of such criticism of the "welfare state" it does seem appropriate here to point out the close relationship between economic and social systems and also to emphasize that the relationship is not one-sided but truly interactive.

In addition to their financial difficulties, these highly developed social systems face a series of further problems.[7] In most industrial countries, the old-age and health insurance systems need to adjust to changes brought about by an ageing population. At the same time, labour market changes mean that increasing numbers of persons no longer work in a conventional employment structure, either because they are out of work or because they are in a form of employment hitherto considered atypical. But, in nearly all cases, social security systems are based on a full-time employment relationship, with the result that, certainly where the worker is in part-time employment, a pension based on earned income is no longer sufficient to maintain living standards. This situation is even worse when the individual is doing unpaid work (usually in the home). As a result, social security systems are increasingly considering the introduction of minimum protection arrangements.[8]

Uniform trends

These few points suffice to illustrate the many different challenges facing the social sphere in individual countries. It would, of course, be possible to reduce this diversity to a few basic national trends, though some trends are also universal. Of particular significance in this context is the growing mobility of labour internationally,[9] resulting from economic cooperation between nations, and also from economic need and political persecution. This mobility casts doubt on current concepts of hermetic protection systems compartmentalized within their national boundaries.

HOW TO COPE WITH THESE DEVELOPMENTS

Thus, the problems themselves are diverse – as are the approaches to their solution. Nevertheless, a number of commonalities can be identified which ultimately derive from basic issues in social security.

Extension of coverage

The social security systems in place today developed from individual systems aimed at specific groups who were perceived to be in special need of protection and for whom an organizational structure needed to be established.[10] However, all these systems are now tending to extend coverage to new groups, the ultimate aim being universal coverage. Examples may be found in both developing and developed countries. For instance, the social insurance systems in Western Europe, which originally covered only wage-earners and salaried employees, are now gradually being opened up to self-employed persons. This is also to some extent the case in the United States, where President Clinton's health reform proposals seek to include all citizens in the health insurance programme by introducing compulsory health insurance.[11]

Extending the risks and contingencies covered

Initially, social security systems provided benefits for the standard contingencies of old age, sickness, accidents, and to survivors. However, the range of risks covered grew much broader and now includes,[12] for example, unemployment, family allowances, support during periods of training, housing assistance, income protection in the event of employer insolvency, etc. The fact that such developments continue to occur even in developed countries' social systems in spite of heavy criticism of the level of social expenditure is illustrated by the introduction in Germany of a programme of assistance to dependent persons as from January 1995.[13]

This perceived need to extend coverage to new risks and contingencies is especially noticeable in countries where the economic and social systems are in transition, as in Central and Eastern Europe where the reform progress is now under way.[14] For example, the decision to establish a market economy of necessity requires the introduction of unemployment insurance.

Respective responsibilities of the State and of the individual

Every social security system has to handle the basic issue of the distribution of responsibility for social protection between the individual and the State. This fundamental question has to be asked anew for each set of economic and social circumstances, and the answers will, of course, vary. Here, the issue is not only the responsibility of each person as an individual but also as a member of a social unit – namely the family which has always performed certain functions in society, functions which may have a legal basis – for example, responsibility for the support of dependent persons.[15]

The alternatives of leaving the responsibility for social security to the individual or entrusting it to the State may assume a variety of intermediate forms. The most important of these is social insurance, particularly as developed by Bismarck at the end of the nineteenth century and now encountered in various forms in many countries all over the world. The Bismarckian social insurance system is characterized by compulsory, individual provision based on the principle of mutual aid. This form of insurance is borne by bodies established under public law which are self-administered, not administered directly by the State.

Allocating responsibility for protection to the individual, to mutual aid associations or to the State involves issues of principle but also, significantly, raises a number of detailed problems. Three examples are presented below as illustrations.

Level of protection

Social security systems may limit themselves to guaranteeing a basic minimum; they may also guarantee the maintenance of a standard of living.

The decision as to the level which should be targeted depends on a variety of factors, including the economic capabilities of the State. However, it is also important to ask whether it is, in fact, a state function to guarantee a level of protection higher than basic minimum requirements, or whether it should be left to the individual to make his/her own private provision above this threshold.

Organization

One of the basic organizational decisions to be taken is whether the responsibility for cover should be entrusted to the State and therefore financed essentially by tax revenue, or placed with a social insurance institute separate from state administration and financed by contributions. These basic approaches are linked historically with the names of Beveridge and Bismarck. There is no general way of determining which of these approaches is suitable for all States and for all risks. An approach financed by contributions, and thus to some extent distanced from the State, does have considerable advantages. However, such an approach can be adopted only in specific circumstances, so the mutual aid solution is conceivable only where there are groups of persons with similar interests and displaying a certain degree of homogeneity. Furthermore, it must be strong enough to assume the functions of self-administration.

Privatization

One particular question of an organizational nature (in the widest sense of the term) is the extent to which social security can and should be in the hands of private insurance companies. In the case of complementary insurance, this approach is almost undisputed. It is questionable, however, whether private insurance should be adopted for basic protection. In the case of its old-age protection scheme, Chile, for example, has given a largely affirmative reply.[16] The "Chilean model" has attracted considerable attention throughout the world and is under serious discussion in many countries,[17] including those of Central and Eastern Europe, in view of the capital formation that can be expected from it. However, one of the questions that should be asked is whether such a system will guarantee the safety of long-term capital investment for old-age protection and whether it can achieve a measure of equality between the weak and the strong. Redistribution based on solidarity is a central requirement in modern social protection systems.

The international dimension of social protection

It has already been mentioned that increasing mobility worldwide is raising questions about the demarcation of national social security systems.

If social security systems continue to be strictly limited to their country of origin, then labour's freedom of movement will be considerably restricted. It is therefore significant that, wherever freedom of movement is guaranteed, as in the European Union, national social systems must urgently be coordinated in order to avoid the disadvantages that people suffer in their social rights when moving from one State to another.[18]

Furthermore, in an open world in which the hunger and misery experienced in one region cannot leave the inhabitants of other countries unaffected, there is clear international interest in the solution of social problems.[19] The globalization of the economy must go hand in hand with a globalization of social security.[20]

THE ILO AND THE FUTURE OF SOCIAL PROTECTION

Growing challenges for the ILO in social security

The developments indicated above, notably the trend towards the globalization of social problems, are bringing about a situation in which social security occupies an increasingly important position in the work of the ILO. Social security has, of course, been one of the ILO's fields of activity right from the beginning, as a number of early Conventions and Recommendations testify;[21] however, social legislation has clearly taken a back seat to labour legislation, for which many reasons may be adduced.

The ILO is founded on the principle of tripartism. Consequently, it gives pride of place to matters of concern to governments and to both social partners. In many countries, social security policy is not of vital interest to the social partners, especially to the employers' federations, and so it is not surprising that, in an international context, the latter do not take initiatives on these matters. Certainly, the social partners are more closely integrated in the system in countries with a social insurance system based on self-administration principles, such as Austria, France or the former Federal Republic of Germany. Self-administration creates a situation in which the social partners are integrated and are actively involved in an informed manner in social policy.

Social security often seems such a technical area that it is difficult to perceive its underlying general principles. But this overlooks the fact that social security is based on a number of fundamental principles whose recognition and implementation are no less important to society than, for example, the basic freedoms of working life. Certainly, it is difficult to define basic social rights for general worldwide implementation in such a way that they both retain their force and do not lock States into rigid systems inappropriate to their economic and social development.

Finally, it is clear that a social system's stage of development depends crucially, if not exclusively, on a country's economic performance. This must be taken into account in any standard-setting activity, which means a prudent approach should be adopted; otherwise the standard will obtain few if any ratifications.

The ILO's role

The ILO has a decisive role to play in designing the international dimension of social security. To this end it has available a range of instruments including standard setting and the supervisory machinery, technical assistance[22] and consultation in various forms.[23] These instruments may be employed for the further development of social protection throughout the world. In this context there are various specific tasks and objectives.[24]

Creation of internationally recognized standards

In its Conventions and Recommendations, the ILO has laid the foundations for worldwide acceptance of social standards. The ILO's norms have indeed become the model for standard setting in other international and supranational institutions. Moreover, they serve for the elaboration of general principles such as those contained in the International Covenant on Economic, Social and Cultural Rights. Certainly the ILO's special supervisory machinery[25] has contributed greatly to the effectiveness of the standards drawn up.

In future, the task will be prudently to expand these ILO standards.[26] In this process, the emphasis should be less on establishing strict compliance with standards; instead, in the social sphere, these instruments should more often simply lay down objectives.[27] In doing so, there should always be a clear connection between the standard in question and basic social rights. As may be seen from the neglect of labour standards in many economic programmes for the countries in transition, this is no foregone conclusion. The globalization of the world's economy makes it essential that social problems should also be considered and acknowledged in a global context. The ILO has a prime role to play here.[28]

Coordination of national social systems

Increasing mobility calls for the establishment of rules on the coordination of national social systems. This may be achieved by supranational regulations such as those that exist in the European Union.[29] However, in this respect too, the ILO has long-established experience. For example, as early as 1925 in its Convention No. 19 the ILO laid down provisions on equality of treatment for national and foreign workers in the event of occupational accidents. More recent approaches to the establishment of a comprehensive system of coordination have run into difficulties in their implementation, as is demonstrated by the fact that the Maintenance of Social Security Rights Convention, 1982 (No. 157), has been ratified by only two countries – Sweden and Spain. However, this does not affect the importance of this coordinating task.

Worldwide exchange of experience on social questions

In the past, social problems were discussed predominantly in a national arena. However, it is now increasingly realized that many different countries experience similar problems and that consequently one can learn from their respective experiences. Moreover, global problems must also be tackled on an appropriately international basis. The value of an international approach can be seen clearly in such problem areas as the struggle against unemployment, the overcoming of demographic difficulties in social security systems, the privatization of social protection systems, etc. More than virtually any other international institution, the ILO's mission is to provide a worldwide forum for discussion and the exchange of experience.[30] And there will be a growing need for it in the future.

Supporting the transition process

As a general rule, social systems have considerable built-in inertia. This means that changes usually take place only gradually, and on the basis of the existing system. Currently, however, the situation is different in Central and Eastern Europe and in other parts of the world which are undergoing profound change. One of the outcomes of the decision to develop market economies in Central and Eastern Europe has been the need to carry out fundamental changes in the social system as well. Expert advice can provide support in this process of reform. However, a basic condition for such support is that those giving the advice should have a comprehensive knowledge of the various approaches available, and offer their assistance in the transformation of the social system without being affected in any way by their own national interest. Here too, the ILO is particularly suited to provide such support.[31] The first task is to draw up the theoretical principles for the provision of advice in the transition process[32] and to lay down the conditions under which specific social security institutions can be introduced and operate. Here a comparison of labour and social security legislation can be useful.[33] On the basis of a comprehensive comparative analysis of the legislation, consultancy work should be carried out by experts with personal experience of as wide a range of systems as possible. The ILO itself has such experts and, moreover, can recruit consultants from national administrations and ministries.

Better coordination of activities

Many different institutions set and monitor social standards.[34] This is also true of consultancy provided in the transition process in Central and Eastern Europe. Parallel activities such as these can be highly productive if they are regulated and planned. Unfortunately, this is not usually the case, and uncoordinated parallel approaches tend to squander scarce human and financial resources. Consequently, increased efforts should be devoted to improved coordination. These efforts could be called for by individual States; however, effective coordination is conceivable only at an international level. A universal institution such as the ILO is best placed to carry out this task.

Notes

[1] For an appreciation of the work accomplished by the ILO, see the contributions to ILO: *Visions of the future of social justice: Essays on the occasion of the ILO's 75th anniversary* (Geneva, 1994).

[2] On this trend, see ILO: *Defending values, promoting change. Social justice in a global economy: An ILO agenda.* Report of the Director-General (Part I), International Labour Conference, 81st Session, Geneva, 1994.

[3] On the subject of these challenges for developing countries, see S. Guhan: "Social security options for developing countries", in *International Labour Review*, Vol. 133, 1994, No. 1, pp. 35-53; see also D. Zöllner: "Beratung beim Aufbau sozialer Sicherung in wenig industrialisierten Ländern", in Bundesministerium für Arbeit und Sozialordnung/Bundesvereinigung der deutschen Arbeitgeberverbände (BDA)/Deutscher Gewerkschaftsbund (DGB): *Weltfriede durch soziale Gerechtigkeit. 75 Jahre Internationale Arbeitsorganisation* (Baden-Baden, Nomos Verlag, 1994), pp. 122-129.

[4] In the case of the former German Democratic Republic, see U. Lohmann : "Sozialrecht der ehemaligen DDR", in B. von Maydell (ed.): *Lexikon des Rechts* (Neuwied, Luchterhand, 1993), p. 565.

[5] See M. Zukowski: "Transformation of the economic system and social security in Central and Eastern Europe", in B. von Maydell and E. M. Hohnerlein (eds.): *The transformation of social security systems in Central and Eastern Europe* (Louvain, Peeters, 1994), p. 61.

[6] For fundamental criticism of this type see, for example, the essays collected in Ludwig-Erhard-Stiftung: *Umbau des Sozialsystems* (Krefeld, Sinus, 1994).

[7] In the case of Germany, see Bundesministerium für Arbeit und Sozialordnung (ed.): *Sozialstaat in Wandel* (Bonn, Economica, 1994).

[8] On the subject of old-age insurance, see B. Schulte: "Perspektiven der Alterssicherung in der Europäischen Union", in *Zeitschrift für ausländisches und internationales Arbeits- und Sozialrecht* (ZIAS) (Heidelberg), Vol. 8, No. 3, 1994, pp. 240-253.

[9] See B. von Maydell: "75 Jahre internationale Arbeitsorganisation", in *Soziale Sicherheit* (Vienna), Vol. 43, No. 5, 1994, pp. 180-184.

[10] See P. Trenk-Hinterberger: "The range of persons covered by social security schemes", in von Maydell and Hohnerlein, 1994, op. cit., p. 105.

[11] See J. Kruse: "Eckpunkte des jüngsten Reformversuchs im Gesundheitssystem der USA", in *ZIAS*, Vol. 8, No. 3, 1994, pp. 203-212.

[12] See G. Igl: "The contingencies covered by social security systems", in von Maydell and Hohnerlein, 1994, op. cit., p. 73.

[13] On this point, see K. Jung: "Die fünfte Säule – Über den langen Weg zur sozialen Pflegeversicherung", in Bundesministerium für Arbeit und Sozialordnung, BDA, DGB, 1994, op. cit., p. 197ff.

[14] See Gesellschaft für Versicherungswissenschaft und -Gestaltung (GVG): *Neue Aufgaben für die Systeme der sozialen Sicherung in der Bundesrepublik Deutschland durch die Öffnung Mittel- und Osteuropas*, Schriftenreihe, Vol. 24 (Cologne, GVG, 1992).

[15] See B. von Maydell: "Unterhaltsrecht und Sozialrecht", in Deutscher Familiengerichtstag e.V. (ed.): *Zehnter Deutscher Familiengerichtstag 1993, Brühler Schriften zum Familienrecht*, Vol. 8 (Bielefeld, Gieseking, 1994), p. 23ff.

[16] See C. Gillion and A. Bonilla: "Analysis of a national private pension scheme: The case of Chile", in *International Labour Review*, Vol. 131, 1992, No. 2, pp. 171-195.

[17] See "Privatization of pensions in Latin America", in *International Labour Review*, Vol. 133, 1994, No. 1, pp. 134-141.

[18] On the subject of the European Union's coordination system, see B. Schulte: "Allgemeine Regeln des internationalen Sozialrechts – supranationales Recht", in B. von Maydell and F. Ruland (eds.): *Sozialrechts-Handbuch* (Neuwied, Luchterhand, 1988), p. 1195ff.

[19] The link between social protection and world peace has been appreciated and stressed – though with varying degrees of emphasis – since the creation of the ILO; more recently, see K. Maier: "Internationale Sicherheit durch Sozialpolitik – Eine neue Perspektive", in *Sozialer Fortschritt* (Bonn and Berlin), Vol. 42, 1993, p. 133ff.

[20] See von Maydell, 1994, op. cit.

[21] See A. Otting: "International labour standards: A framework for social security", in *International Labour Review*, Vol. 132, 1993, No. 2, pp. 163-171.

[22] To appreciate all the various functions, see C. Hess: "Internationale Arbeitsnormen und Technische Zusammenarbeit", in Bundesministerium für Arbeit und Sozialordnung, BDA, DGB, 1994, op. cit., pp. 109-121.

[23] See ILO: *Defending values, promoting change…*, 1994, op. cit.; and ILO: *International labour standards*. Report of the Director-General, International Labour Conference, 70th Session, Geneva, 1984.

[24] For the future work of the ILO, see N. Valticos: "The ILO is 75 years old: The objectives, structure and measures of the ILO in facing the future", in *Visions of the future of social justice*, 1994, op. cit., pp. 297-301.

[25] On this function, see K. Lörcher: "Die Normenkontrolle in der IAO – aktueller Stand und neue Entwicklung", in Bundesministerium für Arbeit und Sozialordnung, BDA, DGB, 1994, op. cit., pp. 77-86.

[26] See B. von Maydell: "Das Sozialrecht in der Normensetzung der IAO", ibid., pp. 47-54.

[27] See M. Weiss: "Zur künftigen Rolle der internationalen Arbeitsorganisation", ibid., pp. 243-254.

[28] See ILO: *Defending values, promoting change…*, 1994, op. cit., pp. 56-66.

[29] See Schulte, 1988, op. cit.

[30] Note also the Director-General's statements on the ILO as a forum for debate in ILO: *Defending values, promoting change…*, 1994, op. cit., p. 75.

[31] See V. Klotz: "Die soziale Flankierung des Reformprozesses in den Staaten Mittel- und Osteuropas", in Bundesministerium für Arbeit und Sozialordnung, BDA, DGB, 1994, op. cit., pp. 217-224.

[32] This approach was taken by the Symposium organized by the Max-Planck-Institute on Foreign and International Social Law, held in Tutzing in spring 1993. See von Maydell and Hohnerlein, 1994, op. cit.

[33] The comparison of labour legislation is also very important in the drafting of standards. See J. Schregle: "Internationale Sozialrechtsvergleichung in der normenschaffenden Tätigkeit der internationalen Arbeitsorganisation", in H.F. Zacher (ed.): *Sozialrechtsvergleich im Bezugsrahmen internationalen und supranationalen Rechts*, Vol. 2, Schriftenreihe für internationales und vergleichendes Sozialrecht (Berlin, Duncker und Humblot, 1978), p. 133ff.

[34] On the protection of social rights by the European Union, for example, see M. Zuleeg: "Der Schutz sozialer Rechte in der Rechtsordnung der Europäischen Gemeinschaft", in *Europäische Grundrechte Zeitschrift* (Kehl), Vol. 19, 1992, p. 329ff; and, on the activities of the United Nations, B. Simma and S. Bennigsen: "Wirtschaftliche, soziale und kulturelle Rechte im Völkerrecht. Der internationale Pakt von 1966 und sein Kontrollverfahren", in J. Baur; K. Hopt; and P. Mailänder (eds.): *Festschrift für Ernst Steindorff zum 70. Geburtstag am 13. März 1990* (Berlin, de Gruyter, 1990), p. 1477ff.

TOWARDS A POLICY FRAMEWORK FOR DECENT WORK

35

Philippe EGGER *

REFOCUSING ILO ACTIVITIES

Over recent years, the ILO has striven to refocus its activities on the central unifying concept of "decent work". Decent work is enshrined in the original principles and values of the ILO, namely, the promotion of social justice and humane conditions of work. The ILO's Constitution emphasizes the situation of working people, particularly the need for conditions that enable all human beings "to pursue both their material well-being and their spiritual development in conditions of freedom and dignity, of economic security and equal opportunity" (Declaration of Philadelphia, II (a)). These principles inspired the Report of the Director-General to the 87th Session of the International Labour Conference, 1999, in which he sought to restate the purpose and objectives of the ILO focusing on the primary role of securing decent and productive work for women and men everywhere.

This concern to refocus is a response to the growing diversity of ILO activities as a result of the changing demands of the Organization's constituents, funding opportunities and technical capacity. It is also a response to growing public concern over rights at work, employment opportunities and working conditions which rapid developments in technology, trade and communications in the globalized economy have failed to address adequately. The marked contrast between the economic success of the few and the social

Originally published in *International Labour Review*, Vol. 141 (2002), No. 1-2, in the "Perspectives" section.

* Policy Integration Department, ILO, Geneva. This perspective was compiled from the contributions to a conference on Decent Work Issues and Policies, held in Turin, 30 Sep.-2 Oct. 2001. Attended by some 60 mainly ILO staff from different units and offices, the conference addressed substantive policy areas, and sought to consider both technical issues and operational policy concerns, focusing on the issue of collaboration. The ILO Director-General addressed the conference in a substantive session on decent work as an ILO policy framework. This perspective draws its inspiration from the presentations made and discussions of the conference, elaborating on the main themes. It is in no way a summary or transcript thereof. For the conference papers, see http://training.itcilo.it/decentwork.

stagnation of the many in the globalization process, so frequently evoked in the debate on the benefits of globalization, goes to the heart of the ILO's purpose and mission. Indeed, it justifies the ILO's seeking to play a more proactive role in shaping the global agenda.

For this refocusing to occur, and for the ILO to become more proactive on the global stage in this respect, there must be better integration of the various strands of ILO policy, hence the elaboration of a "Decent Work Agenda". The ILO's constituents fully support this approach and requested the Office to assist them in implementing decent work policies and programmes at the country level. In response, in his Report to the 89th Session of the International Labour Conference, 2001, the Director-General spelt out the challenges facing the ILO, which must inter alia:

- raise [its] capacity to work with ILO constituents to put in place an integrated approach to decent work at the national level; and

- build support for a balanced and integrated approach to sustainable development and growth in the global economy in which economic, social and environmental goals can be achieved together (ILO, 2001, p. 14).

INTERNATIONAL LABOUR STANDARDS AND JOBS

The ILO was established in order to improve conditions of work by adopting Conventions and Recommendations which set out universal minimum labour standards, and by monitoring their application. The ILO's adoption of a large number of Conventions and Recommendations undoubtedly associates it with a regulatory approach to labour matters, but it would be wrong to overlook the flexibility afforded by many of these instruments.

The orthodox school[1] holds that international labour instruments seeking to establish minimum standards inevitably raise the cost of labour above its market-determined price, with detrimental consequences on the level of labour demand. At the heart of this debate lies a supposed trade-off between more employment and less regulation, or more protection and less employment.[2] Such views are concerned less with freedom of association or the prohibition of forced labour than with employment protection and social security. The fact that international labour standards mostly provide guidelines and policy directions rather than specifying levels of wages or benefits is of little concern to defenders of these views. However, the inherent flexibility of labour standards needs to be recalled here. International labour standards call for different means of action, including national legislation but also policy guidelines, collective bargaining, and best practice at national or enterprise levels; in any event, when they are ratified, the ratifying country's national circumstances are taken into account.[3] Moreover, standards encourage consultation with and the active participation of employers' and workers' organizations, which are grounded in workplace realities. Nevertheless, international labour standards are perceived by some as raising the labour costs and hence reducing the level of employment. The ILO's response to this criticism should therefore not only refute the argument, but also demonstrate that decent work, the various components of which are covered in the relevant ILO international labour standards, is a positive factor of production.[4] A decent work framework can thus provide instruments with which to raise both the level of productivity and of employment, contributing to higher and more sustained levels of economic growth. The role of labour standards in balancing competition by preventing any one party, employers or workers, from using their full market power to the detriment of the other has already been examined by Sengenberger and Campbell (1994).

GOOD JOBS, BAD JOBS, MORE JOBS

The discussion of the Director-General's Report *Reducing the decent work deficit: A global challenge* at the 89th Session of the International Labour Conference in 2001 revealed diverging views on the main concepts involved, notably over whether priority should first be given to job creation and only then to decent work.[5] Very similar concerns have been expressed by researchers.[6] This dilemma is not new to the ILO. In the early 1970s, the ILO focused on the concept of the working poor, thus raising both poverty and employment policy issues, and sought to promote a productive and protective approach to workers in the informal sector (safeguarding that sector's capacity to create jobs whilst also raising its levels of productivity and of protection). This is reflected in the Employment Policy (Supplementary Provisions) Recommendation No. 169, adopted in 1984, that seeks to balance job creation and regulation.[7] In many low- and middle-income countries, however, the informal sector remains a reservoir of bad jobs with very low levels of productivity, and one in which demand is basically determined by supply, with little application of labour standards.

The ILO has never held that a job is a job, irrespective of its characteristics. Some jobs will always be bad jobs wherever they are found, for instance forced labour, child labour, and low-productivity informal-sector jobs. Some such bad jobs are universally deemed contrary to basic social values, and hence are unacceptable. International labour standards establish principles banning such forms of labour. Other jobs perceived as bad and only barely acceptable in one country (because of the long hours, dangerous working conditions or low wages involved) may be considered a worthwhile option in another country. Such jobs will tend to evolve and improve as a result of economic and social developments, labour standards and people's changing perceptions of what is acceptable and reasonable. Individuals' perception of their jobs measured in terms of their job satisfaction can be an important intrinsic job characteristic. However, individual and collective preferences inevitably mesh with exogenous aspects of the job though here, too, everything remains relative. Job satisfaction is not simply a function of the wages paid, nor is the distribution of varying degrees of job satisfaction entirely random (Hamermesh, 1999). Variations in job satisfaction tend to be explained by one dominant factor: features such as good pay, safety and job security are likely to be found together and to characterize good jobs.

Thus, international labour standards as well as individual perceptions and preferences set the criteria determining what characterizes an acceptable job. The issue at stake then, is the conditions needed to move gradually from bad to better jobs without jeopardizing either the existence of the jobs or the improvements achieved. To achieve this, a phased strategy is needed combining macroeconomic policies promoting growth and employment and social policies enhancing protection and productivity, and the extended practice of social dialogue to link the two. The challenge to the ILO is to produce just that.

GLOBALIZATION AND THE ILO

Reflections on the future of the ILO, sparked by the celebration of its 75th anniversary in 1994, led to the establishment of the Governing Body Working Party on the Social Dimensions of Liberalization of International Trade (later the Working Party on the Social Dimensions of Globalization) and, four years later, to the adoption of the ILO Declaration of Fundamental Principles and Rights at Work (ILO, 1998a). The Declaration was designed as a response to the debate on the link between trade and labour standards (i.e. the promotion and application of core labour standards rather than trade-based sanctions), as well as to the unbalanced developments that globalization has either spurred or failed to redress. In addition to campaigns launched to promote ratification of the eight Conventions considered to be fundamental by the international community,[8] there is now a regular procedure with which to highlight the situation in countries which have ratified the fundamental Conventions as well as in those which have not. Within the on-going debate over the benefits of free trade, the Declaration has been widely recognized as a useful tool; for some, however, it has also reinforced the regulatory image of the ILO. In most countries, alongside issues of basic rights at work, there is widespread concern about matters pertaining to employment, wages, skills and poverty alleviation, related directly or indirectly to trade and globalization. Clearly, these concerns, as well as those about rights at work, lie at the heart of the controversy over globalization. Decent work, including rights at work, employment, social protection and social dialogue based on freedom of association, must be the ILO's answer to these concerns.

The challenge is two-fold: to design and promote a global set of policies that promote core labour standards as well as employment and social protection; and to design and promote national policies with the same objectives.

Poverty alleviation and employment are as much national as global concerns, and the ILO Declaration, trade liberalization and macroeconomic policies are the tools for their achievement. An initial answer proposed is based on the "social pillars" of globalization (education and training, social safety nets, labour law and industrial relations, and core labour standards) (Torres, 2001). Further research is needed into the potential contributions of these policy areas and, notably, into the way they interact.

INTERNATIONAL LABOUR STANDARDS AS GLOBAL PUBLIC GOODS

National public goods cannot be privately appropriated, nor can they be used by some at the expense of others. The same is true at the international level. The full exercise of freedom of association in one country does not in any way reduce its actual or potential exercise in another country. It can only contribute to a broader exercise of freedom of association globally. The same rationale can be applied to the body of international labour standards. However, global public "bads", in the form of poverty, ill-health or poor working conditions, do spill over on to other countries, as is recognized by the ILO's Constitution.[9] This has become dramatically evident in recent times.

Globalization has spurred interest in the development of global regulations applicable in most countries, and certainly in those trading goods and services on the global market. From prudential regulations for banks to the defence of rights of property-, patent- and shareholders, to safety standards on food items and specifications for pressure valves or telecommunications equipment, the marked increase in the share of traded goods and services calls for such regulations. Scarcely anyone questions this, indeed such regulations are actively sought. The situation is less clearcut for labour standards, although support for them from international financial institutions and other quarters has lately become quite explicit. However, it scarcely amounts to a common framework for addressing employment, rights and growth, economic and social policies.

A connected and more general issue is a universal "floor of rights" – a set of minimum rights to which everyone is entitled, regardless of status in employment. Arthur Okun observed that rights could not and should not be bought and sold (Okun, 1975). Rights can be exercised, or their exercise limited through legislation, national practice or constraining conditions, but they cannot be amassed or transacted for private benefit. It was Karl Polanyi who first said that a market economy should be "embedded" in society, as opposed to a market society (Polanyi, 1944, p. 60), and Okun echoed this when he observed, "The market needs a place and the market needs to be kept in its place" (Okun, 1975, p. 119). It is a small step from there to suggest that the global market itself needs to be embedded in a rules-based global society, with the rights and duties of all parties defined as a counterbalance to market power. When international labour standards ban certain forms of market transaction, they seek to uphold basic rights against the power of the market. The banning of forced labour, of related forms of labour trafficking, or of the worst forms of child labour reflect this stance. Such labour must be ruled out, through national legislation, enforcement measures, changes in economic conditions and greater public awareness. The most likely net effect on the labour market, if any, is a marginal reduction in labour supply. But the signal to the market and to society is that certain forms of labour at very low levels of productivity and at the cost of human dignity do not satisfy the basic principles and rights by which society seeks to limit unbridled market power. International labour standards translate such universal principles into policy instruments.

A DEVELOPMENTAL APPROACH

The life of an animal is misery and slavery: that is the plain truth. But is this simply part of the order of nature? Is it because this land of ours is so poor that it cannot afford a decent life to those who dwell upon it? (George Orwell, *Animal farm*, p. 8).

In fact there are numerous linkages between international labour standards, the alleviation of poverty, employment and social protection. Illustrative examples include child labour and poverty; but links also exist for the achievement of decent work within enterprises.

Child labour

In many ways, child labour is a consequence of the poverty experienced by families who cannot afford to send their children to school and need the net additional income their children provide in order to meet the family's basic needs. This situation calls for measures to improve the employment conditions of parents and older children and thus incidentally to eradicate the need for child labour. This is the aim of the Minimum Age Convention, 1973 (No. 138), which inter alia calls on national authorities to pursue policies designed to ensure the effective abolition of child labour (Article 1). However, child labour is also recognized to be a cause of poverty, as it deprives children of the education, skills and health they need to find suitable employment at the appropriate age, thus lifting themselves out of poverty. The absence of policies actively discouraging child labour, or ensuring effective school attendance of all children up to the specified age, directly and indirectly encourages conditions in which child labour can exist, thereby undermining future skills formation and economic growth. In some parts of Brazil, school attendance of children from low-income families is encouraged through an income subsidy to mothers conditional upon the children's enrolment and attendance. The positive results of this approach are being closely examined with a view to its wider adoption, both within Brazil and in other countries. There is no guarantee that basic education and effective school attendance will reduce poverty, but lessons from many countries suggest that such policies form a major part of the response to poverty.

Certain forms of child labour should not be tolerated in any circumstances, as underscored by the unanimously adopted Worst Forms of Child Labour Convention, 1999 (No. 182). The appropriate response to the worst forms of child labour is prohibition. The appropriate response to poor jobs is a set of policies that will affect both the supply of labour (more children at school and fewer on the labour market, and a better educated and skilled workforce) and the demand for labour (higher demand for more productive labour). Both sets of policies are addressed by international labour standards.[10]

Poverty

Very similar arguments can be made with regard to poverty. No international labour standard has the single aim or indeed the power to ban poverty but, apart from those that seek to ban unacceptable forms of work and employment, many other standards address basic aspects of poverty. The incidence and severity of poverty are very much functions of the level and pattern of economic growth. But labour standards provide a host of principles and guidelines for a fair distribution of the benefits of growth and for sustaining a rising level of labour productivity. The right to form, join or choose an organization representing the collective interests of workers and providing them with the means to voice their concerns and press their claims, often against the more powerful segments of society, represents a major means of combating poverty. Although the benefits of trade union organization are often felt within an urban enterprise setting, freedom of association applies generally.[11] Whether organizations represent the rural poor, poor urban women, or wage workers, they remain workers' organizations. Measures aiming to improve occupational safety and health, particularly in the sectors most likely to employ low-skilled labour, e.g. agriculture, construction, and small-scale manufacturing, can help considerably in raising the productivity of workers, and hence their value, motivation and self-esteem. Social policy is critical to the alleviation of poverty because it enhances workers' productivity by giving them access to health and education, and also because it provides income protection for them in old age and in case of disability. Likewise, when appropriately designed and implemented, a minimum wage policy can provide the required protection to low-wage workers without serious consequences for labour demand. It can also help achieve equal remuneration. The gender sensitivity of poverty alleviation policies and measures is key to their effectiveness. Targeting women has been shown to produce numerous positive developments, from lower fertility rates to higher school attendance, better housing and nutrition. In all these areas, international labour standards seek to promote basic principles, not fixed standards or levels for wages, benefits or compensation. The flexibility required to adapt to national conditions is an in-built feature of these labour standards, which seek to enable workers and employers to interact in a mutually productive way.

Decent work in enterprises

In general, working conditions depend very much on policies and practices at the workplace, which are influenced by national and international regulations. In the small enterprise sphere, the ILO has started documenting the conditions in which better relative job quality can translate into positive returns to business. A range of issues is involved, from use of brushes rather than fingers to paste glue, proper storage and equipment when handling dangerous substances, better organization of the working week or childcare for working mothers. Such issues are likely to imply substantial costs for small enterprises. However, they are just as likely to imply better-quality work, or greater output for the same number of hours worked. Hence, job quality can pay off, even in small enterprises. The management training tools widely used by the ILO to train entrepreneurs in small businesses should therefore adequately reflect these trade-offs. Although the methods and contexts may vary, much the same issues arise in medium and large enterprises. High-performance workplaces seem to apply a successful combination of some employment security, social protection, adequate working conditions and motivation through participation – an example which is widely studied and applied. There is increasing recognition of the value to enterprises of human capital and of workers in general. However, when the value of shares soars in the stock market as a result of enterprise restructuring resulting in sizeable lay-offs, it is unclear whether what is gained (higher share value at that moment) compensates for what is lost (workers and human capital). Again, the ILO needs to spell out these trade-offs and their costs much more forcefully.

POLICIES FOR GROWTH AND EMPLOYMENT

The Copenhagen Declaration on Social Development, adopted by the World Summit for Social Development (Copenhagen, 1995), committed its signatories to "promoting the goal of full employment as a basic priority of our economic and social policies, and to enabling all men and women to attain secure and sustainable livelihoods through freely chosen productive employment and work" (United Nations, 1995, Part 6, Commitment 3). The ILO was requested to monitor the application of this last principle, one which echoes very closely the Employment Policy Convention, 1964 (No. 122), where it calls on States to "declare and pursue, as a major goal, an active policy designed to promote full, productive and freely chosen employment" (Article 1). Both texts emphasize the centrality of employment policies and suggest that such employment should be of a certain standard. Yet the exact nature of an "active policy" to promote full employment is not specified in detail. The level of employment is basically a macroeconomic issue, dependent on the rate and composition of growth. This calls for monetary, fiscal and exchange rate policies that can sustain the highest level of demand for labour compatible with the highest level of labour or total productivity, within agreed parameters of macroeconomic stability. For some countries, globalization (in the form of foreign direct investment and international trade) has been the opportunity to achieve precisely that objective. Many countries in East Asia have followed such a strategy, first by raising the level of output in agriculture, then gradually shifting towards labour-intensive exports, and moving on to higher-value-added activities. Such countries have significantly reduced poverty by raising the level of productivity of the poor, through both supply and demand policies. On the supply side, better education, training and health, some forms of social protection, better occupational safety and health, work organization and the like gradually raise the quality and productivity of the workforce. On the demand side, shifting the composition of output towards more productive and efficient activities in those sectors more dependent on the labour of the poor tends to raise the aggregate level of productivity, with positive returns for employment and wage levels. A striking feature of such policies is their capacity to sustain high rates of growth in conditions of relative macroeconomic stability. Another is the gradual opening of these economies to international trade, with selective use of export promotion measures accompanied by selective measures protecting some industries and sectors for a limited period. The economic crisis of 1997 dramatically revealed major shortcomings in the social protection systems; these are gradually being redressed and strengthened. In employment and other fields, the management of change becomes a critical factor in the overall sustainability of policies.

Decent work policies crucially rely on sound macroeconomic policy for employment generation and poverty alleviation. To implement its strategy, the ILO must identify the employment implications of different combinations of macroeconomic policy options, as well as the macroeconomic implications of a full productive employment strategy. Particularly important are fiscal policy and the level and composition of public spending on essential infrastructure projects seeking to reduce transaction costs and attract private investment, as well as on social policies to ensure access to basic services. In this respect, the ILO must engage in an ongoing debate with the IMF and the World Bank on these and related issues. It must be in a position to ensure that employment issues are placed squarely on the global agenda shaping economic and social policies, so as to be able to advise countries and constituents on how to implement their commitment to full employment and secure and sustainable livelihoods.

The ILO's influence is often greatest when effective social dialogue is combined with sound technical work. The two exist independently, but are far more effective in tandem. This apparently banal observation has profound socio-economic and socio-political implications. For, it is well established that motivating workers to participate, whether in safety measures or work organization at the workplace, or through negotiations at enterprise, branch or national levels, leads to far more productive outcomes than not doing so. The participation of employers' and workers' organizations in shaping social and labour policies is essential to the design, implementation and sustainability of sound policy. There are many, well-known reasons for this. For one, labour ministers are in far more volatile positions than are the captains of industry and union leaders. Furthermore, legitimacy brings a major contribution to policy effectiveness. It is well known that policies negotiated with employers and workers, or between them, are more legitimate and effective. Such legitimacy is a cornerstone (though never a guarantee) of democracy, and of social and economic stability.

POLICY INTEGRATION

The issues just described point naturally to policy integration. First, because the problems in which the ILO is active (poverty alleviation, development, the social dimensions of globalization, among many others) are complex and cut across several distinct policy fields. Second, because the effectiveness of the ILO's response is greatly heightened if more than one school of thought is taken into account and a variety of instruments are applied. Health and safety issues cannot be ignored in the promotion of small enterprises; nor can employment and labour market issues be set aside when the extension of social protection is being discussed; nor can effective social dialogue be engaged in without sound preliminary technical work. These different aspects of policy integration can be addressed in various ways. Clearly, more analytical work is needed to spell out the complementarities and trade-offs of different contributions of social and economic policies at different levels of per capita GDP. For instance, in low-income countries, which systems and levels of social protection are viable and can help improve the health of the work force, remove from the labour market anyone outside the usual active lifecycle (15-64 years), and come as near as possible to providing universal basic education for the young (6-14 years)? Within a poverty reduction strategy, what is the right balance between social protection policies and employment policies, between income transfers and training? Such social policies should be made compatible with a set of macroeconomic policies ensuring an acceptable rate of output growth, based on a composition of output generating employment levels proportionate to anticipated labour force growth. There may be trade-offs between social, labour and economic policies, but there are also many complementarities. A better definition is urgently needed of the trade-offs and synergies involved in different policy combinations, in order to achieve the results that families and communities wish for.

DELIVERING DECENT WORK

The concept of decent work and its agenda have been well received. The ILO's task now is to demonstrate that it is a useful developmental agenda carrying the promise of improved policies and programmes delivering better results. A number of operational considerations follow from these observations. These are now considered in turn.

Measuring decent work

For the concept of decent work to become a useful policy framework, the ILO must be able to measure it and to monitor change over time. Precise quantitative information is essential for constituents and for public information purposes. Indicators of decent work need to be designed, possibly on two levels: one set of internationally comparable indicators; and another, more detailed set, for use in national contexts. Basic indicators of rights, employment, social protection and social dialogue are required, using internationally comparable definitions, if possible. Choices will obviously have to be made as to coverage of countries and areas in terms of what is desirable and what is available. A phased approach may be necessary, initially using available indicators and data, gradually refining definitions and expanding on existing regular surveys or conducting new ones. Obviously, existing ILO databases would be fully used, complemented where necessary by other national or international data sources, and by ad hoc surveys, where deemed possible.

Decent work country programmes

Decent work requires policies that are effective at national level. One way to contribute to their effectiveness is to reorganize the ILO's work at country level on the basis of a coherent decent work programme. As yet no blue print for such programmes exists; at this stage more information and learning from existing experience may be more necessary than seeking to evolve one single approach. Initial experience in the ILO's decent work pilot programme suggests the following road map for developing national decent work programmes. A four-pronged approach is suggested, allowing for different combinations and stages of implementation, as follows:

(i)   an in-depth decent work analysis reviewing a given country's situation as regards rights, employment, social protection and social dialogue, and reviewing different policy options to achieve a higher level of decent work;

(ii) regular opportunities for tripartite and bipartite social dialogue to consider and discuss major policy issues arising in the achievement of decent work in that country, where possible on the basis of technical work by the ILO;

(iii) exploration of synergies and complementarities between ongoing and planned ILO technical cooperation activities, with a view to enhancing understanding of and approaches to common and integrated problems and issues;

(iv) design and implementation of integrated activities relating, for example, to poverty alleviation, urban informal employment, globalization and competitiveness.

Innovative approaches need to be elaborated and tested, documented and disseminated in order to build up a genuine knowledge base on decent work policies. This will require strong internal partnerships to be built up between the ILO's geographical and technical units. It will also necessitate closer and more effective collaboration between the international and financial and technical agencies, possibly in the context of the recently adopted international development goals.

Notes

[1] For a critical review, see Wilkinson (1994).

[2] Jeffrey Sachs, the development economist, spoke to such concerns in a lecture given at the ILO in 1996 "[T]he greatest damage to growth is in across-the-board labour standards that dictate either minimum standards or minimum conditions for higher and fairer wages or, worse still, provide for the extension of wages across the economy; in short, the German system applied to South Africa or some other developing country" (Sachs, 1996, p. 14).

[3] "A widespread misconception (...) is the belief that international labour standards can be given effect only through legislative action. It is true of course that standards do establish legal rules and that no social policy can be effective unless it is based on the rule of law. However, ILO standards do not necessarily require the adoption of specific, formal legislation at the national level. Often, they simply provide guidelines which States are invited to follow in pursuit of an objective which may never be fully attained as such" (Valticos, 1996, p. 475).

[4] "The burden of proof of the merits of labour standards rests on the ILO" (Larsson, 2001, p. 8).

[5] As illustrated in the following three excerpts from the general discussion: "As far as the issues related to achieving decent work in Japan are concerned, our foremost priority is employment creation" (Employer, Japan); "... we must demand policies giving us access to decent work, not just any type of work" (Worker, Argentina); "The ILO constituents cannot, and must not, believe that [achieving decent work] can be divided into two separate steps, work first, conditions for decency later" (Worker, Italy).

[6] "[B]ad jobs at bad wages are better than no jobs at all" (Paul Krugman, quoted in Kimberly and Freeman, 2001, p. 25); "It is a dilemma faced by women – whether it is better to have a poor quality job than no job at all" (Anker, 1998, p. 9).

[7] "Members should take into account that integration of the informal sector into the formal sector may reduce its ability to absorb labour and generate income. Nevertheless, they should seek progressively to extend measures of regulation to the informal sector" (Recommendation No. 169, paragraph 29 (2)).

[8] The Freedom of Association and Protection of the Right to Organise Convention, 1948 (No. 87), and Right to Organise and Collective Bargaining Convention, 1949 (No. 98); the Forced Labour Convention, 1930 (No. 29), and Abolition of Forced Labour Convention, 1957 (No. 105); the Minimum Age Convention, 1973 (No. 138), and Worst Forms of Child Labour Convention, 1999 (No. 182); and the Equal Remuneration Convention, 1951 (No. 100), and Discrimination (Employment and Occupation) Convention, 1958 (No. 111).

[9] "[T]he failure of any nation to adopt humane conditions of labour is an obstacle in the way of other nations which desire to improve the conditions in their own countries" (ILO, 1998b, Preamble).

[10] The World Bank argues similarly against linking trade sanctions to labour standards and for development: "Child labor, widespread in many developing countries, is concentrated overwhelmingly in agriculture, not in export industries, and it signals poverty, not exploitation. Children's labor force participation drops rapidly as GNP per capita rises. So the best way to reduce child labor is to raise incomes and schooling opportunities. This will not be accomplished by trade sanctions." (World Bank, 2000, p. 311).

[11] "Trade union activities can be conducive to higher efficiency and productivity. Unions provide their members with important services. At the plant level, unions provide workers with a collective voice. By balancing the power relationship between workers and management, unions limit employer behaviour that is arbitrary, exploitative, or retaliatory. By establishing grievance and arbitration procedures, unions reduce turnover and promote stability in the work force — conditions which, when combined with an overall improvement in industrial relations, enhance workers' productivity." (World Bank, 1995, p. 80).

References

Anker, Richard. 1998. *Gender and jobs: Sex segregation of occupations in the world.* Geneva, ILO.

Hamermesh, Daniel. 1999. *The changing distribution of job satisfaction.* NBER Working Paper No. 7332. Cambridge, MA, National Bureau of Economic Research.

ILO. 2001. *Reducing the decent work deficit: A global challenge.* International Labour Conference, 89th Session. Report of the Director-General. Geneva.

—.1999. *Decent work.* International Labour Conference, 87th Session. Report of the Director-General. Geneva.

—.1998a. *ILO Declaration on Fundamental Principles and Rights at Work.* Geneva.

—.1998b. *Constitution of the International Labour Organisation and Standing Orders of the International Labour Conference.* Geneva. Feb.

Kimberly, Ann Elliott; Freeman, Richard B. 2001. *White hats or Don Quixotes? Human rights vigilantes in the global economy.* NBER Working Paper No. 8102. Cambridge, MA, National Bureau of Economic Research.

Larsson, Allan. 2001. *Perspective on the ILO decent work agenda: Policies, policy-making and actors.* Paper presented to the conference on Decent Work Issues and Policies, held in Turin, 30 Sep.-2 Oct. 2001. Available on the conference web site at: http://training. itcilo.it/decentwork/ (last visited on 17 May 2002).

Okun, Arthur. 1975. *Equality and efficiency: The big tradeoff.* Washington, DC, Brookings Institution.

Orwell, George. 1951. *Animal farm.* London, Penguin.

Polanyi, Karl. 1944. *The Great Transformation: The political and economic origins of our time.* Boston, MA, Beacon Press.

Sachs, Jeffrey. 1996. *Globalization and employment.* Public lecture given on 13 Mar., Geneva. Geneva, International Institute for Labour Studies.

Sengenberger, Werner; Campbell, Duncan. 1994. *Creating economic opportunities: The role of labour standards in industrial restructuring.* Geneva, International Institute for Labour Studies.

Torres, Raymond. 2001. *Towards a socially sustainable world economy: An analysis of the social pillars of globalization.* Geneva, ILO.

United Nations. 1995. *Copenhagen Declaration on Social Development.* World Summit for Social Development 1995. New York.

Valticos, Nicolas. 1996. "The ILO: A retrospective and future view", in *International Labour Review* (Geneva), Vol. 135, No. 3-4, pp. 473-480.

Wilkinson, Frank. 1994. "Equality, efficiency and economic progress: The case for universally applied equitable standards for wages and conditions of work", in Sengenberger and Campbell, pp. 61-86.

World Bank. 2000. *World Development Indicators 2000.* Washington, DC.

—.1995. *World Development Report 1995: Workers in an integrating world.* Washington, DC, World Bank/Oxford University Press.

GLOBALIZATION AND DECENT WORK POLICY: REFLECTIONS UPON A NEW LEGAL APPROACH

36

Jean-Michel SERVAIS *

From the ongoing debate on the future of work, it is becoming increasingly clear that social policies and related legislation need adapting to more open and competitive markets and to more complex, segmented and technology-driven ways of organizing production and services. Indeed, that labour law needs remodelling to adjust to the "new economy" in the broadest sense of the term can hardly be disputed. It is no longer a question of whether, but how the remodelling process will take place.

The modernization of social and labour policies calls for reconsideration of the optimum balance to be struck between workers' protection, job creation and competitiveness – i.e. the balance between economic development and nationally or internationally recognized values and rights.

The primary goal of the ILO today is to promote opportunities for women and men to obtain decent and productive work, in conditions of freedom, equity, security and human dignity. This is the main purpose of the Organization today. Decent work is the converging focus of all its four strategic objectives: the promotion of rights at work; employment; social protection; and social dialogue. It must guide its policies and define its international role in the near future (ILO, 1999, p. 3).

The concept of decent work thus embodies the expression of the ILO's resolve to bring together all the components of harmonious economic and social development, of which regulations for the protection of labour are a key feature.

The goal is not just the creation of jobs, but the creation of jobs of acceptable quality. The quantity of employment cannot be divorced from its quality. All societies have a notion of decent work, but the quality of employment can mean many things. It could relate to different forms of work, and also to different conditions of work, as well as feelings of value and satisfaction. The need today is to devise social and economic systems which

---

Originally published in *International Labour Review*, Vol. 143 (2004), No. 1-2.

* International Labour Office – email: servais@ilo.org. This article is based on the address made on behalf of the ILO at the XVIIth World Congress on Labour Law and Social Security (Montevideo, 2-5 September 2003).

ensure basic security and employment while remaining capable of adaptation to rapidly changing circumstances in a highly competitive global market (ILO, 1999, p. 4; see also ILO, 2003, pp. 77-80, 91-92 and 117-119).

Hence also the need to determine the most effective ways of implementing the chosen policy, i.e. how to translate the above policy mix into outcomes that will make a real difference in workers' daily lives. Not all options involve legislation. Indeed, the potential of approaches based on political agreements, economic measures, training and information, technical "standards" and practical guidelines should not be underestimated, though their effects do tend to be circumstantial. The legal approach, by contrast, presupposes a longer-term vision. It implies a decision to make policy more durable by grounding it in legislation and, if necessary, to resort to penalties – a distinctive feature of law.

The purpose of this article is to consider the most effective ways of legislating. Though the role of judicial decision-making in the concrete application of law will not be discussed in depth here, it should be borne in mind that the judiciary plays a key part in the implementation of social policy at the micro-economic level (Servais, 2002).

From the perspective of standard-setting, the aim of the ILO's decent work policy is to satisfy all the prerequisites for ensuring that labour regulations are actually applied. In this respect, the obstacles encountered typically stem from socio-economic resistance – a problem compounded by the difficulty of measuring the cost of applying labour standards.

The very concept of "decency" suggests possible responses to these concerns. To begin with, it implies the capability of women and men at work to practise solidarity instead of seeking mutual domination. The concept thus suggests dialogue, calling for the support of the social partners in the design, drafting and implementation of labour laws; after all, the social partners would seem to be well placed to assess the consequences of such laws, including their financial implications. The concept of decent work also suggests that human relationships cannot be reduced to some utilitarian ideology: they need to embody an ethical dimension.

These prerequisites – i.e. recognition of ethical values and emphasis on social dialogue – highlight the desirability of grouping international labour standards into three categories. The first comprises fundamental rights at work; the second consists of standards concerned with more technical provisions of labour and social security laws; and the third covers rules of a programmatic nature, which typically stress the role of employers' organizations and trade unions, and indeed of other organizations.

The first section of this article examines the principal modes of social regulation. The question here is whether some are preferable to others or whether there are alternatives to legislation. We will then seek to identify the extent to which a hierarchy can be established among labour standards and the values they embody, in order to draw conclusions with respect to legislative action to be taken. Finally, we will consider the methods to be preferred in adapting labour standards to present realities, before concluding with a new vision of the State based on the outcome of this discussion.

AUTONOMOUS STANDARDS, HETERONOMOUS STANDARDS AND ALTERNATIVES TO SOCIAL REGULATION[1]

In practice, the balance between the legal option and other means of achieving social policy objectives will depend on the level of political commitment to coercive action. This second course, which relies chiefly on persuasion and rationality, may involve the conclusion of political agreements, the adoption of economic measures, the launching of training initiatives and information campaigns, as well as the setting of "technical" (as opposed to "legal") standards and practical guidelines. All such initiatives can be taken without recourse to measures that are binding in the legal sense, hence the ambiguity of referring to them as "soft law". However, this in no way detracts from their usefulness, as advocated, say, by the countries of the European Union in connection with their coordinated efforts to promote employment.[2]

Implementing social policy: Choosing the right options

The concept of law – particularly in regard to social rights – is nevertheless ambiguous and calls for some clarification. It refers primarily to a means of implementing policy, a means of enforcing a particular line of conduct subject to the threat of punishment. Of course, both policy and conduct may sometimes seem repugnant (for example, if they are imposed by a brutal dictator), but this does not necessarily affect the binding force of the legal rules in which they find expression.

This positivist conception of law is overlaid with another, whereby a specific objective is assigned to the law itself – rather than to the authority that enacts it – i.e. the pursuit of certain values, such as social justice, based on ethical or religious precepts, or on a particular conceptualization of society and relations between its members.

It may seem eminently reasonable and often highly desirable to invoke principles and set social objectives when designing and implementing policy. Yet the affirmation, in this context, of moral "rights" that everyone should enjoy does not automatically turn them into actual rights that they *do* enjoy. To proclaim, say, the right to work without an accompanying penalty for its non-realization is tantamount to expressing a wish or a political message which is certainly important but devoid of legal force.

Again, these remarks do not in any way detract from the usefulness or persuasive power of such proclamations. Indeed, socio-economic conditions often preclude the adjunction of the legal dimension that would give them permanence and coercive effect. But when they are given the force of law – and only then – the lawmaker's intent may be discerned from the specific legislation adopted and the latter may be interpreted in the light of that intent.

If the legal option is chosen as the sole means, or as one of the means, of implementing social policy, a decision must then be taken on the most appropriate form of regulation. Regulation can be left to voluntary private initiative (self-regulation); or it may be enforced by the State, thereby giving it permanence (see, however, Perrocheau, 2000, pp. 11-27), transparency and binding force; or it may result from an agreement negotiated by the social actors concerned. Achieving a satisfactory mix of these three approaches will depend on national circumstances and, particularly in a democratic society, on the degree of social consensus that can be attained. In considering these different options for implementing a social policy, it should be borne in mind that the preference given to one or more legal instruments over others will ultimately depend on each country's socio-political context.

A crucial first step is to decide which regulatory functions concerning employment and work are to remain in the hands of the State and which are to be devolved to the private sector. In particular, this question arises in respect of employment services and agencies; social protection (i.e. social security, social insurance, social welfare); the settlement of labour disputes (individual or collective; conflicts of law or of interest); and even inspection of working conditions. As will be seen below, the state authorities may prefer to focus on poverty reduction and the promotion of employment, while leaving the regulation of working conditions largely up to the main social stakeholders.

Another option is to distinguish, in those areas left to private regulation, between the sphere falling to commercial actors (e.g. the multinationals) and the sphere devolved to actors that are not directly profit-seeking (e.g. employers' associations, trade unions, etc.). The first would include company-level collective agreements and codes of conduct adopted unilaterally by management; in the case of such unilateral initiatives, the legal status and duration of the employer's commitment need to be ascertained – not necessarily an easy matter – together with the procedure for checking its effective implementation. The second sphere comprises, in particular, regulation by collective agreement at levels higher than the enterprise. A supplemental option here centres on whether or not to include new actors in the bargaining process: e.g. global, regional or local institutions; other organizations representing civil society, etc.

This raises yet another issue: while there have been many appeals for the conclusion of a new "social pact", few of the advocates of this course have stated clearly or realistically who would be the parties thereto. The natural way to seek consensus would seem to lie in a return to the principles of freedom and democracy on which modern societies were built. Indeed, freedom of association, expression and assembly afford people confronting common problems the opportunity to set up institutions to act as intermediaries between citizens and the State. In France, there has been talk of an "explosion" in the number of non-governmental social organizations (Malaurie, 1999, pp. 22 et seq.). In effect, three types of organization have taken on a significant role in the design and implementation of social policy, namely: employers' and workers' organizations, social and labour groups that do not fit into the previous category, and other NGOs pursuing social aims (ILO, 1997, pp. 51 et seq.).

Social organizations, social partners

The expression "employers' and workers' organizations" is standard ILO terminology that refers to professional organizations whose aims are to promote and defend the interests of employers and workers, respectively.[3] The concept is a broad one. On the workers' side, it covers trade unions and, whatever the actual terms used, any associations of wage earners or self-employed workers pursuing similar aims. Associations representing the most underprivileged sections of the population – particularly informal-sector organizations in developing countries – now also seem to have gained widespread acceptance alongside traditional trade unions (ICFTU, 1996, p. 81).

The second type of organization that plays a part in social policy-making consists of associations established to pursue more narrowly focused social objectives, such as the promotion and defence of women, consumers, the environment, small business, civil liberties, local or neighbourhood interests, students, school children's parents, specific communities or ethnic minorities. Some of these groups take the form of cooperatives. Like workers' and employers' organizations, such associations act as intermediaries between their members and the public authorities or intergovernmental institutions. They have several characteristics in common with professional organizations. For example, they are democratically created (by the association of their members) and take decisions through democratic processes. This usually ensures transparency and facilitates verification of their representativeness, objectives, the provenance of their financial resources and the accountability of their leaders. It also provides a basis for building trust both in relations among the various groups and in their relations with trade union federations. There are in fact countless examples of alliances formed for specific industrial-action campaigns or for wider purposes.

The socially-oriented non-governmental organizations (NGOs) that make up the third category do not, strictly speaking, function like associations. They range from churches, charitable organizations and mutual assistance networks (particularly for the unemployed) to projects for technical cooperation, development assistance or occupational safety and health. Their staff typically includes experienced professionals who devote themselves, in a personal capacity, to training, placing and rehabilitating people at risk of social exclusion (e.g. the long-term unemployed, the homeless, welfare recipients, over-indebted households, illegal immigrants, drug addicts or, simply, the destitute). These institutions often work together with local authorities and their social workers. But compared with the second type of organization outlined above, they tend to lack transparency in terms of representativeness and resources. This can make it more awkward to deal with them, though they have at times proved to be useful partners.

Organizations in the second and third categories – particularly those with supranational, regional or global outreach – have recently had a visible impact on national and international policy-making. Yet their operations are often erratic or unpredictable because they are subject to the vicissitudes of media coverage and financial sponsorship. This stands in sharp contrast to the permanence and genuine representativeness of professional organizations whose institutionalization makes them a force to be reckoned with in the field of social policy. Indeed, even when union members account for only 10 to 15 per cent of a country's working population, trade unions usually have a membership base that is proportionally much stronger than that of other organizations.

Against this background, a few general questions need to be addressed. In particular: how much scope for action do these "civil society organizations" really have? What can they contribute to social policy and on what terms can they do so? These questions have already generated an abundant literature.[4] Other issues that arise in this connection could be summed up as follows:

(a) Can a better match be found between the applicable legal framework and the work of these organizations? Those that operate primarily "in the field" have occasionally taken part in genuine negotiations (e.g. in South Africa, Ireland, Italy and Latin America), with outcomes which may be purely political but which can also have legal implications, i.e. provision for sanctions;

(b) Could labour regulations not be reframed – along more programmatic lines – so as to promote recognition of social actors and give them a freer hand, while channelling their efforts towards objectives predetermined by the public authorities?

Returning to the subject of state regulation, the first step is to decide who is going to make the rules: parliament, government, the judiciary, some administration (centralized or otherwise), local authorities, etc. Then, consideration also needs to be given to the extent – in terms of criteria, means and institutions – to which the public authorities should proceed, either in laying down binding rules or in encouraging or assisting citizens and civil society organizations to work out their own self-regulatory solutions, in which case legislation would essentially provide a framework for private initiative.

The appeal of these various options will depend on the kind of policy chosen by the State, ranging from a "hands-off" approach to centralization of decision-making power. Dialogue can take on an almost infinite variety of forms. There is hardly any need to elaborate on this point, except perhaps to stress the need for broadening the basis of social consensus to encompass all social actors, including organizations representing the most underprivileged.[5]

FUNDAMENTAL, TECHNICAL AND PROMOTIONAL STANDARDS

Analytically, the labour standards adopted by the ILO and the values they embody can be classified into three categories (Servais, 1991, pp. 449 et seq.; but see also Jenks, 1963, p. 103). The proposed classification is based not only on their fundamental aims and, therefore, prioritization of their provisions, but also on the type of obligations they entail. The first category concerns the fundamental rights of men and women at work; the second relates to the more technical provisions of labour and social security legislation; and the third comprises standards of a programmatic nature. This classification may also provide a useful framework for broader discussions on the future of labour regulation not only internationally, but also at the national and regional levels. In particular, more frequent recourse to programmatic standards could result in fewer deadlocked situations.

Fundamental standards

The provisions of standards in the first category may be either technical or programmatic. What distinguishes them is the pre-eminence which they are clearly accorded by the ILO's executive bodies. In most countries, they find expression in basic constitutional principles concerning public freedoms or social rights. They are concerned with the right of freedom of association and collective bargaining, the abolition of child labour and forced labour, and equal opportunities and treatment in employment. Their fundamental nature is almost universally recognized, and they are reflected in a number of instruments, including the United Nations International Covenant on Civil and Political Rights and, in particular, its International Covenant on Economic, Social and Cultural Rights. Other examples are the ILO's Constitution, several of its Conventions, and the Declaration on Fundamental Principles and Rights at Work and its Follow-up, adopted by the International Labour Conference in June 1998. These succinctly worded instruments embody general principles that can be applied in a number of different ways. As a result, they sometimes give rise to the same difficulties of interpretation as do national constitutional provisions, because of the need to steer a middle course between extremes of laxity and prescriptiveness.

Of all the international instruments mentioned above, however, the ILO Declaration (ILO, 1998) is the one with the greatest potential for transcending the strictly inter-governmental framework, even though it is primarily directed at ILO member States. Indeed, while covering the entire range of workers' fundamental rights, it spells them out without detailing any specific implementation procedures. Its binding force is thus limited, and its follow-up procedures are considerably less demanding than those of the ILO's traditional supervisory machinery. Although it is aimed primarily at the Organization's member States, inviting them to adopt appropriate implementing measures, the general terms in which it is worded make it a framework of reference that can readily be used by the new global actors as well. In particular, it can serve to define the common rules to be observed by the ILO and the major international financial institutions in the actions they take at country level. Its provisions can be transposed into the social charters adopted by regional bodies, such as the European Union, the Council of Europe, NAFTA and MERCOSUR. In most cases, in fact, such regional instruments are already strongly influenced by the ILO's fundamental standards. The ILO Declaration can also be invoked by NGOs advocating the establishment of a list of basic principles to be respected in the making of social policy. Multinational corporations, too, can turn to the Declaration for inspiration in drawing up their codes of conduct or in determining the criteria to be observed in their industrial relations or social audits. Private initiative can thus supplement national legislation on such issues or – as is more often the case – ensure better compliance.

Drawing on notions of freedom and democracy, fundamental labour standards embody basic principles of public policy which give workers themselves an opportunity "to claim freely and on the basis of equality of opportunity their fair share of the wealth which they have helped to generate, and to achieve fully their human potential" (ILO, 1998, p. 6). Incorporating these standards into constitutional instruments affirms their pre-eminence; transposing them into legislation can make their infringement subject to penalties. Without prejudice to the usefulness of such other, non-legal measures as may be adopted to promote the application of standards in specific socio-economic circumstances, the significance of legal measures appears to be both unquestioned and unquestionable.

Technical standards

Most labour standards belong in this second category, which is characterized by its more specifically technical content. They deal with conditions of work and employment in a broad sense, labour administration and social security.[6] They are the focus of most of today's debate over the future of statutory protection for labour. Here, lawmakers, both national and international, are sometimes faced with conflicting interests, with tensions between the divergent concerns of employers and wage earners – not to mention other interest groups – and with the need to reconcile them with the public interest. Choices have to be made. Sometimes those choices are the fruit of more or less formal negotiations involving reciprocal concessions; at other times, they are the result of a delicate process of arbitration. In democratic societies, the legislative authorities typically endeavour to secure some basic consensus as a means of guaranteeing that the standard will be effective.

It is easier to reach agreement on a subject like, say, occupational safety and health than on many of the other issues on the social agenda. This is indeed an area where employers and workers broadly share the same concerns – often centring on technological change – though their views may well differ on practical aspects of application or on the pace of planned reforms. It is much harder to achieve consensus on issues over which the parties stand divided between proponents of regulatory rigour and advocates of flexibility. Working time is a case in point, with heated debate on how to adapt the old rules on hours of work to new technical constraints and contemporary social aspirations. Such deadlocks as do occur, however, owe less to bureaucratic wrangling or lack of flexibility in national procedures than to the sheer difficulty of reconciling varied and divergent points of view on substantive issues.

Often lacking today is basic agreement on the underlying principles of regulation. As a result, entire sections of labour law are being laid open to question. The difficulty of working out compromise solutions is compounded by the fact that trade union federations and even employers' federations find it more difficult than in the past to speak out on behalf of all those they are supposed to represent. Technical standards tend to focus discussions on how to strike the best possible balance between economic considerations and the protection of labour. Hence the value of investigating the significance and potential of a third category of standard whose binding force may be less immediate.

Programmatic standards

The standards in this category are designed to organize and prompt action: they set goals to be achieved through promotional action. Their implementation requires the adoption of a variety of measures, not necessarily of a legal nature, such as political projects, economic measures, information and training campaigns, non-legal "regulation", etc. In brief, programmatic standards seek to regulate by setting objectives in the way that modern human resource management methods do. Such standards tend to be worded in general and flexible terms. They place no immediate obligation on the employer or any other party to achieve a particular result, but rather they lay down an obligation of means, as the case may be, on the part of States themselves, to adopt measures, to carry out certain activities, to design or implement certain projects, to promote certain approaches, etc.

These standards apply primarily to employment, vocational training and discrimination. By way of illustration, excerpts from two ILO Conventions are given in boxes 1 and 2, respectively the Employment Policy Convention,

---

Box 1. Employment Policy Convention, 1964 (No. 122) (excerpts)

Article 1

1.   With a view to stimulating economic growth and development, raising levels of living, meeting manpower requirements and overcoming unemployment and underemployment, each Member shall declare and pursue, as a major goal, an active policy designed to promote full, productive and freely chosen employment.

2.   The said policy shall aim at ensuring that –

(a)   there is work for all who are available for and seeking work;

(b)   such work is as productive as possible;

(c)   there is freedom of choice of employment and the fullest possible opportunity for each worker to qualify for, and to use his skills and endowments in, a job for which he is well suited, irrespective of race, colour, sex, religion, political opinion, national extraction or social origin.

3.   The said policy shall take due account of the stage and level of economic development and the mutual relationships between employment objectives and other economic and social objectives, and shall be pursued by methods that are appropriate to national conditions and practices.

Article 2

Each Member shall, by such methods and to such extent as may be appropriate under national conditions –

(a)   decide on and keep under review, within the framework of a co-coordinated economic and social policy, the measures to be adopted for attaining the objectives specified in Article 1;

(b)   take such steps as may be needed, including when appropriate the establishment of programmes, for the application of these measures.

1964 (No. 122), and the Discrimination (Employment and Occupation) Convention, 1958 (No. 111).

These standards seek to make the public authorities' action more consistent and systematic on the issues they address. To that end, they establish such procedures and machinery as will enable a given programme to be implemented, occasionally specifying concrete labour market policy measures and means of evaluating their effectiveness. With regard to employment, for example, some of the specified measures appear to be aimed at achieving immediate results – e.g. exemption from social security contributions to boost recruitment of young people at a particular time – whereas others aim to lay the foundations of a strategy to combat unemployment (e.g. reform of the vocational training system or, more simply, incentives for geographical or occupational mobility).

Again, a single legal instrument may contain both directly binding provisions and programmatic standards. Legislation on equal opportunity and equal pay provides a good illustration of this point as it typically combines provisions for promotional measures with rules that invalidate acts of discrimination falling within its particular scope. Furthermore, programmatic and technical standards on a given subject like, say, occupational health can be interrelated, as in the case of so-called framework legislation and regula-

Box 2.   Discrimination (Employment and Occupation) Convention,
1958 (No. 111) (excerpts)

Article 2

Each Member for which this Convention is in force undertakes to declare and pursue a national policy designed to promote, by methods appropriate to national conditions and practice, equality of opportunity and treatment in respect of employment and occupation, with a view to eliminating any discrimination in respect thereof.

Article 3

Each Member for which this Convention is in force undertakes, by methods appropriate to national conditions and practice:

(a)   to seek the co-operation of employers' and workers' organisations and other appropriate bodies in promoting the acceptance and observance of this policy;

(b)   to enact such legislation and to promote such educational programmes as may be calcu- lated to secure the acceptance and observance of the policy;

(c)   to repeal any statutory provisions and modify any administrative instructions or practices which are inconsistent with the policy;

(d)   to pursue the policy in respect of employment under the direct control of a national authority;

(e)   to ensure observance of the policy in the activities of vocational guidance, vocational train- ing and placement services under the direction of a national authority;

(f)   to indicate in its annual reports on the application of the Convention the action taken in pur- suance of the policy and the results secured by such action.

tions made hereunder. Here, the basic principles laid down in the legislation are supplemented by specific provisions in its implementing regulations. This, incidentally, suggests a possible way of modernizing the ILO's stand- ard-setting activities.

The concept of programmatic standards also extends to provisions aimed a facilitating communication between social groups and institutions so as to help them work out their own solutions to problems that have been identified (Hepple, 1986, p. 10; Habermas, 1986; Treu, 1994, pp. 461 et seq.; Barnard and Deakin, 2000, pp. 340 et seq. and 2002, p. 139). They have been described in terms of "coaching a process". Many of the provisions concern- ing industrial relations fall into this category. Programmatic standards thus clearly combine features of both regulation and prescriptiveness.

Supervision of the application of such standards raises specific issues because it needs to focus on the deployment of means rather than the attain- ment of end results. As a legislative option, however, the adoption of a programmatic standard does not amount to "deregulation". Nor can it be equated with a strictly "voluntarist" approach that would leave it entirely up to individuals and the social partners to determine their industrial relations (Wedderburn, 1991, pp. 3-4; de Munck, Lenoble, Molitor, 1995, pp. 20 et seq.; Antoine Lyon-Caen, 1995, pp. 176 et seq.). On the contrary, the parties are required to interact within a given framework and in pursuit of given objectives that are specified by legal rules, i.e. with provision for penalties in the event of any breach. Nevertheless, when such rules do call upon workers' and employers' organizations to play a part, they presuppose a reasonable balance of bargaining power between them – i.e. that they be capable of acting on a relatively equal footing – lest they should exacerbate inequalities between the parties. This is why States also need to equip themselves with a firm base of fundamental standards such as those described above (Barnard and Deakin, 2002, p. 146).

In European and international law, promotional standards appear to be commonly used as a means of influencing state action. European Union directives are a good example of this approach, though further illustrations can also be found in national legislation. Japanese law, for instance, lays down obligations "to do one's best" to adopt particular measures instead of a downright obligation to adopt them. It is then up to the administrative authorities – usually the Ministry of Labour, often acting in collaboration with the trade unions and employers' organizations – to convince enterprises to do all they can to translate the spirit of the law into action. In 1986, for example, an amendment to Japan's Old Persons' Employment Stability Act required employers "to do everything within their power" to postpone the mandatory retirement age to 60 years or later (it was previously well below 60). Pursuant to a further amendment introduced in 1990, employers came under an obligation "to do their best" to re-employ retired workers who so wished until they reached the age of 65. The Ministry of Labour ordered action programmes to be drawn up accordingly. Nevertheless, the Government subsequently found it necessary to increase the impact of the measures that had been taken and, in 1994, legislated a compulsory retirement age of 60 years. The law thus enacted also provided for stronger incentives to encourage employers to keep their workers until the age of 65 (ILO, 1995, pp. 91-92). While the policy of raising the age of retirement may well change because of momentary economic difficulties, the regulatory approach taken by the Government seems to be deeply rooted in Japan's legal tradition.

The adoption of promotional standards tends to cause little controversy. They are generally well accepted, except when they increase the burden of administrative constraints on enterprises. Yet their potential for reconciling workers' protection with today's overriding economic considerations has so far not received the consideration it deserves. More so than fundamental standards, they allow for regulations – on, say, occupational health – to be updated to keep pace with scientific and technological developments (Servais, 1997, pp. 87 et seq.).

Such standards also give the parties directly concerned, at all levels, the responsibility both for adjusting their conditions of work in the light of their day-to-day experience and for finding the most appropriate balance between economic efficiency and safeguards for workers. Admittedly, the transfer of these responsibilities to actors at the grassroots level should not be taken too far: a sense of the general interest should be retained. Yet there appear to be many labour and employment regulations that could be adapted to changing economic conditions in this way.

LABOUR STANDARDS FOR A GLOBALIZING ECONOMY

The point of the foregoing discussion is to facilitate the search for the most appropriate way of addressing recurrent questions on the relationship between the quality of work and the quantity of employment in any given society and at any given time in its history. In particular, labour standards should not hamper change from one production system to another. Rather, their purpose should be to minimize the adverse human consequences of such change, to ensure that the transition from the old system to the new is as harmonious as possible in social terms.

The diversification of work

Most research on labour and its regulation has been based on the labour market model or paradigm. This conceptual framework has certainly been appropriate for explaining the exchange between work and wages that takes place within the employment relationship, particularly when the latter is characterized by some stability over time. But this model becomes less effective if more precarious forms of employment – which have recently proliferated – and self-employment are factored in. It is similarly ill-suited to analysis of other activities such as voluntary work or very low-paid work, whether it is done individually (e.g. childcare or care of the elderly or disabled) or within an institution or association; training and retraining; or leave taken for family reasons (maternity leave, parental leave, etc.) or to perform civic duties (e.g. military service). Although many of these activities are socially useful, they do not really fit into the paradigm of exchange for profit.

Efforts have been made to take fuller account of these contingencies in socio-economic analysis. Examining labour market flexibilization, some researchers (e.g. Schmid and Auer, 1998; Gautié, 2003) have observed that new institutional arrangements increasingly take account of the need for ongoing training, that the diversity of individual needs requires greater flexibility in the organization of work, and that atypical forms of employment call for reconsideration of the relationship between paid work and other socially useful activities. These researchers have put forward the concept of "transitional labour markets" as a framework for identifying the main features of the implementation of these new arrangements (in terms of organization, income policy, social and labour policy and their tax implications).

Some take a very pessimistic view of the future of the labour market – stressing its rapid "informalization" in the industrialized and developing countries alike – in order to justify, inter alia, the payment of a guaranteed citizenship income (Standing, 1999).

Others, particularly from the French school of thought (e.g. Supiot, 1998 and 1999), have more clearly distanced themselves from the labour market framework. They stress the wide variety of occupations that can be pursued in the course of a working life: employment, self-employment or entrepreneurship; voluntary and paid work; work in the public service or in the private sector; training courses, internships or retraining; private pursuits (e.g. housekeeping) or public duties (military service, political activities). These researchers highlight the ambiguity of the legal criterion of subordination, a crucial feature of the employment relationship.

Taking this perspective, they have come up with ideas that envisage working-life scenarios based on "modules" to be coordinated, whereby work would alternate with retraining and leave, e.g. maternity or parental leave, leave for military service, etc. (Commissariat général du Plan, 1995; Valli, 1988, pp. 13-38 and pp. 177-197; Ladear, 1995, p. 143).

Improved qualifications and greater independence – the two being inextricably linked – would not only ensure more satisfactory coordination between the various individual activities (e.g. professional work, training and retraining, leave for specific reasons, voluntary or poorly paid but socially valuable work, like childcare or care of the elderly, assistance for the victims of abuse, etc.), but they would also make it possible to plan for those activities over an entire lifespan. Such arrangements would help to resolve conflicts of interests, both those experienced by workers personally and those arising in their relations at work, and thereby help to strike a satisfactory balance between private (family) life and professional activities.

These proposals offer a fresh perspective on the fragmentation of people's working lives observed in the industrialized countries. They also provide a better framework for understanding the various occupations people pursue in developing countries, particularly in the informal sector. Admittedly, they could serve to justify payment of a minimum income, or even the granting of some limited credit for certain purposes (e.g. training, care for people in need, social work within an organization, etc.).

In practice, however, the application of those proposals would come up against a number of serious obstacles. First, labour force statistics indicate that traditional wage employment is far from being a thing of the past; in fact, it still offers the best possible guarantee of income security (Castel, 1999, pp. 438-442; Jacobs, 2000, pp. 55 et seq.). Second, it would be difficult to separate income from work and reach a consensus on how to finance a subsistence allowance in the absence of paid employment (through income tax? turnover tax? VAT?). Besides, would it truly be practicable to map out a person's "career" in this way? The answer may lie in the difference between insecurity and uncertainty. Indeed, social protection aims to alleviate the *insecurity* experienced by those who work or want to work in that it covers contingencies that may jeopardize their lives, their health, their livelihoods and those of their dependents. It is certainly not intended – how could it be? – to provide for every single event or to organize people's lives down to the last detail. In short, it was never meant to eliminate *uncertainty*. In fact, uncertainty is one of the incentives that drive achievers to create, to innovate, to be enterprising, and is therefore a factor of progress.

Innovative approaches

As these observations suggest, it might be preferable to consider a more down-to-earth approach – one in which every effort is made to ensure a closer match between the social guarantees envisaged and the workings of today's economy. Earlier in the discussion, it was suggested that programmatic standards should be used more often to encourage individual and collective players – who *are* familiar with day-to-day realities – to assume greater responsibility for the implementation of labour policies whenever they have not already done so. But outside this category of standards, there are also new forms of security that are more compatible with the increased instability of employment. Here again, the challenge is to identify or design the most appropriate structures and institutions. This point will be illustrated with a few examples.

First, let us consider cases where programmatic standards appear to have been implemented with success. One such case concerns the reform of the Dutch system of sickness benefits: the amounts are determined by law, but it is up to individual employers to decide how the benefits are provided, e.g. by acting as their own insurance company, by taking out individual insurance, by setting up a joint scheme with other employers, etc. (Auer, 2000, p. 63).

In the United States – to give another example – social insurance is mostly company-based and, in principle, forfeited if workers leave their job (hence the question of the portability of acquired rights). In Silicon Valley, the showcase of the "new economy", Amy Dean, the local representative of the AFL-CIO, has been pleading for her organization to provide health insurance, unemployment insurance and ongoing training to workers who have become freelancers so as to offer a substitute for the single-employer link that firms have severed (*Le Monde*, 2000, p. 15). Significantly, the trade unions in several northern European countries continue to manage the payment of unemployment benefits – either alone or jointly (ILO, 1997, p. 26-27).[7]

The explanation for this practice is historical: trade unions were the first to help the jobless, long before the State took over this responsibility. The history of social security offers plenty of examples of institutions in Western countries that developed from private initiatives to meet the new and urgent needs arising from the industrial revolution and its social consequences.

Something similar is happening today: in many cases private organizations are stepping in to fill a social policy vacuum in order to meet an unsatisfied collective need.

The diversification of employment situations has led lawmakers in countries such as Belgium, France and Italy to authorize derogations from labour law on issues – particularly working time flexibility – to be settled by collective agreement (Gérard Lyon-Caen, 1995, pp. 41 et seq.; Revet, 1996, pp. 61 et seq.). In such cases, the law merely sets a framework and the limits of flexibilization, i.e. conditions, possible compensation, and the extent of the exceptions permitted. Along the same lines, the law can specify the circumstances – and limits – within which the public authorities may allow labour disputes to be settled by private conciliation, mediation or arbitration.

There is another subject that the social actors and public authorities could usefully reflect upon, namely, official recognition of socially useful activities and of those who engage in them. Such activities include assistance to the most disadvantaged, but they should be understood in a broader sense too. Obviously, the point is not merely to delegate public service responsibilities to private organizations;[8] this might simply open up a new market for commercial interests or result in a bureaucratic mire. Socially useful activities also include schemes such as Italy's "time bank" or France's "SELs" (local exchange schemes), i.e. networks of private individuals who exchange services, e.g. babysitting for minor house repairs. Clearly, many of these activities strengthen the social cohesion of local communities. Their official recognition ought to be accompanied by payment of a decent wage provided by the beneficiaries or by government agencies, as is already the case in the arts and in scientific research. Incidentally, this would also lead to reconsideration of the analytical frameworks traditionally applied to the informal sector and, again, to inclusion of the activities of private organizations.

The idea behind this latter proposition is ultimately to broaden the scope of operative legislation so as to provide for new forms of security compatible with even the most precarious forms of employment. With self-employment and precarious forms of wage employment on the increase, workers' protection can hardly remain conditional upon a permanent employment relationship. Indeed, the right to health care and to a basic pension should be extended to all, irrespective of employment status. In poor countries, this should be a top priority. But in the industrialized countries too, there is an urgent need to set up or revive institutions that can serve as anchor points in today's context of increased occupational mobility (from one company, employment relationship or activity to another). That the idea is not purely speculative or unrealistic is illustrated by the following two examples.

The first of these is the Netherlands' system of so-called "flexicurity", which seeks to reconcile job flexibility with income security. Following broad consultations among the parties concerned, a law was passed on 1 January

1999 to set up a new scheme for temporary workers: after working for an employment agency for a certain period of time (basically 26 weeks, subject to extension by collective agreement), workers are deemed to have an employment contract with the agency (Heerma van Voss, 1999, pp. 419-430). This "anchors" their entitlement to more comprehensive protection under labour and social security laws, while maintaining their employment mobility. This scheme seems to have found acceptance among all those concerned.

The second example is from France, where a principal and a subcontractor may be held jointly liable for ensuring that wages are paid and that the "obligation to provide security" is discharged in respect of their workers. A similar arrangement is also in operation in Canada.

CONCLUDING REMARKS: THE ROLES OF THE STATE AND LABOUR COURTS

Government authorities have a social duty to implement "decent work" policies which not only mitigate the adverse human consequences of economic change, but which also strengthen its positive outcomes for peoples' lives and their work. In some cases, such policies may involve no more than slowing down the pace of change to the point where it becomes humanly tolerable (Polanyi, 1957, pp. 33 et seq.).

States continue – and should continue – to have recourse to legal means of implementing their social policies. However, there is scope for change in the way States view their role and legislative capacity. As the foregoing discussion suggests, they could give the social actors – as defined above – a more significant part to play in the regulatory process. This, in turn, calls for programmatic rather than purely prescriptive standards.

In every concrete situation, the key role of the State – or, more specifically, of the national, regional and local authorities – should consist in identifying and recognizing the social actors, promoting their development and access to information (by removing obstacles such as anti-union practices), recognizing the institutions they set up (for example, by taking part in their establishment) and facilitating relations between them. In short, the State should be not so much a "tutor" as a source of inspiration and a mediator in creating an environment conducive to dialogue. Its aim should be to set up such communication mechanisms as may be needed to facilitate concerted action (Supiot, 1999, pp. 270-271; Durán López, 1998, pp. 869-888; Evans, 1997, pp. 62-87). The various representative actors must also be invited to take part in the work of the agencies that implement policies in the areas of vocational training, credit, social security, etc. The scope of their autonomous negotiations should be broadened; or they may be called upon to participate systematically in the making of social policies and in the drafting of laws that translate them into long-term and (more or less) binding measures. The same applies to inter-governmental institutions.

The State's role needs to be specially focused when it comes to certain kinds of activities, such as those of the informal sector or small and medium-sized enterprises, where social dialogue is more difficult to get going. Here too, however, there have been successful attempts to set up a conducive framework. For example, the achievements of the districts of Emilia Romagna in Italy have been the subject of numerous case studies on this point (Pyke, Becattini and Sengenberger, 1990; Cossentino, Pyke and Sengenberger, 1996). The informal sector also has its success stories (see ILO, 1997, pp. 187 et seq.).

Strengthening the capabilities of social negotiators should, if the process is properly managed, lead to a consolidation of the State's own position in today's globalized world. To that end, the State should not only promote these new forms of participative decision-making, but also ensure smooth coordination between the different levels involved.

Many countries have long given a special role to the social partners in the judicial settlement of labour disputes. Indeed, labour tribunals appear, more than any other social institution, to be above controversy. There are exceptions, of course, but they are rare (Blouin, 1996). It may therefore be useful to consider what it is that has so far enabled labour jurisdictions, minor incidents notwithstanding, to steer clear of the social crisis marking the start of the new millennium. The answer probably lies in their capacity to come up with workable means of reconciling the two key dimensions of progress, namely, productivity and human welfare. Of course, they are not always successful, but they never stop trying. At all events, no better system appears to have been found to work out the delicate compromises that need to be reached in that respect. That the labour jurisdictions have been so successful no doubt owes much to the contributions of representatives of the parties concerned, i.e. workers' and employers' organizations. Another factor in their success is the balance they have managed to strike between the dispassionate administration of justice, on the one hand, and relative informality coupled with speedy decision-making, on the other hand. Yet another lies in the system's provisions for ensuring genuine equality between litigants, including legal aid, the ease with which professional associations can institute proceedings and the flexibility of the rules on evidence. And lastly, there is of course also the very way in which labour courts are organized and the efforts made to improve the way they are managed. These factors also help explain their success.

In today's difficult circumstances, these distinctive features of labour courts give their judges a renewed role in the implementation of social policies. Indeed, the extent to which those policies are meaningful ultimately depends on the effect they are given at the grass-roots level – i.e. in respect of each and every enterprise, of each and every individual. As a result of the quiet diligence with which judges perform their duties, however, their fundamental role often tends to get overlooked in public debate. This may be yet another advantage they enjoy.

Current changes in the world of work could well upset this equanimity because of the reduction in the number of workers in regular (wage) employment as compared with the number of those working under precarious contracts – workers who are legally independent but economically fragile or "parasubordinate". Yet it is the latter's status that raises the most questions about the relevance of labour law and, sometimes unintentionally on their part, about the representativeness of workers' organizations – often the very ones that sit on labour courts. Admittedly, there are a few cases in which labour court officers have been elected by self-employed workers (as in Belgium, with respect to social security litigation), but such cases remain exceptions. The way in which the courts adapt to these changes is bound to have a huge impact on their future.

Finally, the ultimate aim of any social policy and its implementation remains unchanged: it is to help men and women cope with the contingencies of the market economy. Spinoza once wrote that fear made people weak of mind. The democratic States of the world have established procedures whereby their citizens are represented in decision-making processes. These include not only parliamentary systems, but also the workings of social dialogue in the broad sense. But more open borders and the accelerated internationalization of economic exchanges have reduced the capacity of all nation States – and of their participatory bodies – to control economic and social policy. The greatest challenge for the twenty-first century – and at the same time the most pressing need – is thus to make good the resulting democratic deficit (ILO, 2001, pp. 81-83; Mazur, 2000, pp. 79-93), to invent new institutions offering all those concerned a chance to participate, at any level whatsoever, in designing and implementing policies and programmes that will provide them with decent work, i.e. jobs performed in conditions that respect human dignity, with social protection covering work-related risks.

Notes

[1] On this subject, see also Servais (2001).

[2] See Borstlap, 1999, pp. 365-382; Pedersen, 1999, pp. 383-401; Chozas Pedrero, 1999, pp. 403-418; Biagi, 2000, pp. 155-173; Sciarra, 2000, pp. 209-229; Goetschy, 2003, pp. 281-301.

[3] Particularly in terms of the Freedom of Association and Protection of the Right to Organise Convention, 1948 (No. 87), the Right to Organise and Collective Bargaining Convention, 1949 (No. 98), and the Rural Workers' Organisations Convention, 1975 (No. 141).

[4] See, for example, the special issue of *Esprit* (March-April 1998), entitled "A quoi sert le travail social?" ("What is the point of social work?").

[5] Another issue – essential to the credibility of any system – centres on the manner in which the regulations adopted are implemented. Specifically, this concerns the role of the labour judiciary and how the administration of justice is viewed.

[6] Examples include the Weekly Rest (Industry) Convention, 1921 (No. 14); the Medical Examination of Young Persons (Underground Work) Convention, 1965 (No. 124); the Part-Time Work Convention, 1994 (No. 175); the Protection of Workers' Claims (Employer's Insolvency) Convention, 1992 (No. 173); and the Seafarers' Hours of Work and the Manning of Ships Convention, 1996 (No. 180).

[7] These countries – namely, Belgium, Denmark, Finland, Iceland and Sweden – are also among those with the highest rates of unionization.

[8] See the March-April 1998 issue of *Esprit*, pp. 108 et seq. (see note 4 supra).

References

Auer, Peter. 2000. *Employment revival in Europe: Labour market success in Austria, Denmark, Ireland and the Netherlands*. Geneva, ILO.

Barnard, Catherine; Deakin, Simon. 2002. "Corporate governance, European governance and social rights", in Bob Hepple (ed.): *Social and labour rights in a global context: International and comparative perspectives*. Cambridge, Cambridge University Press, pp. 122-150.

—; —.2000. "In search of coherence: Social policy, the single market and fundamental rights", in *Industrial Relations Journal* (Oxford), Vol. 31, No. 4 (Oct.-Nov.), pp. 331-345.

Biagi, Marco. 2000. "The impact of European Employment Strategy on the role of labour law and industrial relations", in *International Journal of Comparative Labour Law and Industrial Relations* (The Hague), Vol. 16, No. 2 (Summer), pp. 155-173.

Blouin, Rodrigue. 1996. *La juridiciarisation de l'arbitrage de grief.* Cowansville (Québec), Yvon Blais.

Borstlap, Hans. 1999. "Modernised industrial relations: A condition for European employment growth. A Dutch view", in *International Journal of Comparative Labour Law and Industrial Relations* (The Hague), Vol. 15, No. 4 (Winter), pp. 365-382.

Castel, Robert. 1999. "Droit du travail: Redéploiement ou refondation", in *Droit social* (Paris), No. 5 (May), pp. 431-437.

Chozas Pedrero, Juan. 1999. "The Luxembourg Process and the Spanish experience", in *International Journal of Comparative Labour Law and Industrial Relations* (The Hague), Vol. 15, No. 4 (Winter), pp. 403-418.

Commissariat général du Plan. 1995. *Le travail dans vingt ans.* Paris, La Documentation française/Odile Jacob.

Cossentino, Francesco; Pyke, Frank; Sengenberger, Werner. 1996. *Local and regional responses to global pressure: The case of Italy and its industrial districts.* Research Series, No. 103. Geneva, ILO International Institute for Labour Studies.

Durán López, F. 1998. "Globalización y relaciones de trabajo", *Civitas* (Madrid), No. 32, Nov.-Dec.

Evans, Peter. 1997. "The eclipse of the State? Reflections on stateness in an era of globalization", in *World Politics* (Princeton, NJ), Vol. 50, No. 1 (Oct.), pp. 62-87.

Gautié, Jérôme. 2003. "Marché du travail et protection sociale: quelles voies pour l'après-fordisme?", in *Esprit* (Paris), No. 299, Nov., pp. 78-115.

Goetschy, Janine. 2003. "The European Employment Strategy and the open method of coordination: Lessons and perspectives", in *Transfer* (Brussels), Vol. 9, No. 2 (Summer), pp. 281-301.

Habermas, Jürgen. 1986. "Law as medium and law as institution", in G. Teubner (ed.): *Dilemmas of law in the Welfare State.* Berlin, W. de Gruyter.

Heerma van Voss, Gustav J.J. 1999. "The 'tulip model' and the new legislation on temporary work in the Netherlands", in *International Journal of Comparative Labour Law and Industrial Relations* (The Hague), Vol. 15, No. 4 (Winter), pp. 419-430.

Hepple, Bob (ed.). 1986. *The making of labour law in Europe. A comparative study of 9 countries up to 1945*. London, Mansell.

ICFTU. 1996. *The global market: Trade unionism's greatest challenge*. Sixteenth World Congress of the International Confederation of Free Trade Unions, Brussels, 25-29 June. Brussels.

ILO. 2003. *Working out of poverty*. International Labour Conference, 91st Session, Report of the Director-General. Geneva.

—.2001. *Reducing the decent work deficit: A global challenge*. International Labour Conference, 89th Session, Report of the Director-General. Geneva.

—.1999. *Decent work*. International Labour Conference, 87th Session, Report of the Director-General. Geneva.

—.1998. *ILO Declaration on Fundamental Principles and Rights at Work and its Follow-up*. Geneva.

—.1997. *World Labour Report 1997-98: Industrial relations, democracy and social stability*. Geneva.

—.1995. *World Labour Report 1995*. Geneva.

Jacobs, A. 2000. "Critique du rapport du Groupe de Madrid sur la transformation du travail", in *Semaine sociale Lamy* (Paris), Supplement No. 997, 2 Oct.

Jenks, C. Wilfred. 1963. *Law, freeedom and welfare*. London, Stevens & Sons.

Ladear, K.L. 1995. "Social risks, welfare rights and the paradigms of proceduralisation: The combining of the liberal constitutional State and the social State", in de Munck, Lenoble and Molitor, Vol. 1.

Le Monde (Paris). 2000. "Amy Dean et la 'job machine'", 25 Jan., p. 15.

Lyon-Caen, Antoine. 1995. "Droit du travail et procéduralisation", in de Munck, Lenoble and Molitor, Vol. 2.

Lyon-Caen, Gérard. 1995. *Le droit du travail: Une technique réversible*. Paris, Dalloz.

Malaurie, Guillaume. 1999. "Le boom des associations", in *Problèmes économiques* (Paris), No. 2605, 24 Feb., pp. 22-26.

Mazur, Jay. 2000. "Labor's new internationalism", in *Foreign Affairs* (New York), Vol. 79, No. 1 (Feb.), pp. 79-93.

de Munck, J.; Lenoble, J.; Molitor, M. (eds.). 1995. *L'avenir de la concertation sociale en Europe*. Vol. 1. Louvain, Centre de philosophie du droit, Université catholique de Louvain.

Pedersen, Jesper Hartvig. 1999. "Mainlines in Danish labour market policy as presented in the Danish National Action Plan 1999", in *International Journal of Comparative Labour Law and Industrial Relations* (The Hague), Vol. 15, No. 4 (Winter), pp. 383-401.

Perrocheau, Vanessa. 2000. "L'expérimentation, un nouveau mode de création législative", in *Revue française des affaires sociales* (Paris), No. 1 (Jan.-Mar.), pp. 11-27.

Polanyi, Karl. 1957. *The great transformation: The political and economic origins of our time*. Boston, MA, Beacon Press.

Pyke, Frank; Becattini, Giacomo; Sengenberger, Werner (eds.). 1990. *Industrial districts and inter-firm cooperation in Italy*. Geneva, ILO International Institute for Labour Studies.

Revet, Thierry. 1996. "L'ordre public dans les relations de travail", in Thierry Revet (ed.): *L'ordre public à la fin du XXIᵉ siècle*. Paris, Dalloz.

Schmid, Günther; Auer, Peter. 1998. "Transitional labour markets: Concepts and examples in Europe", in European Academy of the Urban Environment (ed.): *New institutional arrangements in the labour market: Transitional labour markets as a new full employment concept*. Berlin, EAUE, pp. 11-28.

Sciarra, Silvana. 2000. "Integration through coordination: The employment title in the Amsterdam Treaty", in *Columbia Journal of European Law* (New York, NY), Vol. 6, No. 2 (Spring).

Servais, Jean-Michel. 2002. "Labour conflicts, courts and social policy: Reflections based on ILO deliberations on decent work", in Roger Blanpain (ed.): *Labour law, human rights and social justice: Liber Amicorum in honour of Professor Ruth Ben-Israël*. The Hague, Kluwer Law International, pp. 75-86.

—.2001 "Working conditions and globalization", in Roger Blanpain and Chris Engels (eds.): *Comparative labour law and industrial relations in industrialized market economies*. Seventh edition. The Hague, Kluwer Law International, pp. 339-364.

—.1997. *Droits en synergie sur le travail. Eléments de droit international et comparé du travail*. Brussels, Bruylant.

—.1991. "Le droit international en mouvement: déploiement et approches nouvelles", in *Droit social* (Paris), No. 5 (May), pp. 447-452.

Standing, Guy. 1999. *Global labour flexibility: Seeking distributive justice*. London, MacMillan.

Supiot, Alain. 1999. *Au-delà de l'emploi. Transformation du travail et devenir du droit du travail en Europe*. Report of the European Commission. Paris, Flammarion.

— (ed.). 1998. *Le travail en perspective*. Paris, LGDJ.

Treu, Tiziano. 1994. "Strikes in essential services in Italy: An extreme case of pluralistic regulation", in *Comparative Labor Law Journal* (Philadelphia, PA), Vol. 15, No. 4 (Summer).

Valli, A. (ed.). 1988. *Tempo di lavoro e occupazione. Il caso italiano*. Rome, La Nuova Italia Scientifica.

Wedderburn of Charlton, Lord. 1991. "The Social Charter in Britain: Labour law and labour courts", in *Modern Law Review* (Oxford), Vol. 54, No. 1 (Jan.).

GLOBAL UNIONISM: A POTENTIAL PLAYER

Andreas BREITENFELLNER *

37

The loss of freedom by workers anywhere in the world is a definite threat to the freedom of workers everywhere. [1]

Trade unions are typically omitted from studies on international political economy, and apparently for good reason. At first glance, labour simply does not feature as a front line player in international relations. In the post Second World War order, they acted predominately within states, sheltered by international arrangements like the Bretton Woods system or the Marshall Plan, and by national consensus based on Fordism, Keynesianism and protectionism. A climate of cooperation, both within and between states, was triggered by vivid memories of the Great Depression and its consequences, and by the imperatives of the Cold War. Closer examination, however, reveals that trade unions did play an important role in forging what, from today's point of view, is called the "Golden Age" (Marglin and Schor, 1990). They were acutely aware of the desirability of achieving a stable external environment that fostered economic growth and thus bolstered their domestic bargaining position. Although they were to some extent coordinated internationally, they acted as silent lobbyists to their governments, which remained the chief arbiters of foreign policy.

The situation changed substantially after the collapse of the fixed exchange rate system and the first oil shock in 1973. The new forces of structural change and globalization swept away earlier mainstays of stability. On the international scene, financial markets became far more important as a result of currency volatility, debt crises, reduced transaction costs and deregulation; and multinational corporations (MNCs) became more powerful as a result of increasing capital mobility and declining transport and communication costs (Strange, 1995). Global money and global business gained greater influence on access to technology and resources which, in turn, gave them

Originally published in *International Labour Review*, Vol. 136 (1997), No. 4 (Winter).

* Austrian Federation of Trade Unions (ÖGB).

enormous bargaining power against territory-bound states and trade unions. Governments certainly lost some measure of their sovereignty, and, to the extent that unions relied on governments, they also were negatively affected. Meanwhile, trade unions had already been shaken by structural adjustment and new production management methods that favoured a diversified and flexible, non-unionized workforce. On the domestic front, the diversification of the exit-options of business, the deflationary pressure exerted by financial markets on governments, and the diminished clout of labour combined to erode or change the tripartite consensus where it existed. Furthermore, unions found themselves in a more hostile climate as public authorities turned their inability to guarantee full employment into an affirmative stance of radical free-market liberalism. Reagan- and Thatcher-style de-unionization strategies set standards which even social democratic governments could not effectively oppose.[2]

It would appear to be self-evident that if business and capital go global, then government and labour should follow suit. However, the seductive short-term benefits promised by competition hamper such a process. Trade unions, like nation-states, may be reluctant to cooperate. Despite their professed ideals and internationalist traditions, they tend to vie with each other in the worldwide bid for scarce resources such as technology and capital. Unlike states, however, such behaviour jeopardizes the very existence of unions. Thus, the imperative of global unionism follows from the rationale of unionism itself.

Since global unionism *per se* apparently does not yet exist, the following discussion has to resort to some speculation, though consistent and logical conclusions may be inferred from an analysis of the present. Global unionism is not an end in itself, but a means of resolving problems that arise in the world economy. First, unions could be instrumental in spurring governments to cooperate with each other. Second, they may reproduce their national function at the worldwide level by instigating tripartite agreements between global labour, global business and the international community of states in order to bring global financial markets – i.e. the fourth player – under control.

This approach of course focuses on the institutional dimension of the international political economy. Institutionalism is a fourth option, alongside laissez-faire, protectionism and residual structuralism. The issue is not a purely academic consideration, nor is it a matter merely of long-term economic efficiency; what is at stake ultimately is the pursuit of social justice and global security. Structuralist approaches have been invalidated, for the most part, by the end of the Cold War. Radical liberalism tends to ignore inequality and its potential for causing social unrest and civil war. Mercantilist responses may trigger irrational nationalism and trade wars. Only the establishment of reliable institutions and a commitment to cooperate two aims of global unionism can contribute to achieving stable international relations.

This article sketches the effects of international trade and investment on welfare and on working conditions, and then discusses the impact on social policies of the globalization of financial markets. It subsequently describes the dilemma of labour organizations and makes a theoretical case for global unionism, before examining the disparate foundations of global unionism within the international labour movement and enlarging upon strategic alternatives. It closes with a summary and an attempt to counter some anticipated criticisms.

LABOUR IN THE GLOBAL ECONOMY

In fact, the real *problématique* of globalization is, arguably, the growing disparity between the mobility of labour and of capital *(Campbell, 1994, p. 187)*.

Globalization has generated considerable excitement among the rank and file of workers in industrialized countries. Economists, businessmen and journalists have been quick to reassure: "Rather than damaging wages and throwing people out of work in advanced countries, globalization has been a force for prosperity in much of the world" (Wolf, 1997, p. 14). Others, including not only trade unionists, but also social and political scientists, draw a somewhat bleaker picture of the current economic process. "The global economy is a great leveller – but it levels downwards" (Gallin, 1994, p. 111). "It undermines every nation's ability to maintain social cohesion" (Greider, 1997, p. 7). However, common sense and comparative observation suggest that some stand to win and others stand to lose from the ongoing process. This analysis seeks to go beyond sensationalism by comparing theory and evidence.

The IMF describes globalization as "the growing economic interdependence of countries worldwide through the increasing volume and variety of cross-border transactions in goods and services and of international capital flows, and also through the more rapid and widespread diffusion of technology" (1997, p. 45). Globalization rests upon improved technologies that reduce transport and communications costs, as well as on organizational innovations, both of which expand the range of tradeable goods and services. It is driven by the liberalization of trade and investment and the deregulation of financial markets, and it is underpinned by a radical shift towards neo-classical economic policies. The latter, in turn, were recommended on account of the perceived success of export promotion in East Asia, the failure of import substitution elsewhere in the South, the collapse of centrally planned economies and the problems experienced by Keynesian regulation in the West.

At the same time, evidence exists of a global employment crisis and of growing inequality between and within countries. Over the past two decades, the employment situation has deteriorated in most parts of the world. Many advanced economies, particularly in Europe, suffer from persistently high unemployment. While employment levels are much higher in the United States, the real wages of its manufacturing workers have dropped substantially. This implies the existence of a "diabolical dilemma" (ICFTU, 1996, p. 25) which obliges industrialized countries to choose between mass unemployment and the presence of "working poor".[3] Most countries of Africa, Latin America and South Asia are experiencing sharp declines in real wages, high unemployment and expansion of the informal sector. Unemployment rates in excess of 10 per cent are now common in Central and Eastern Europe. In the world as a whole, the World Bank estimates that some 120 million people are unemployed and at least 800 million underemployed (World Bank, 1995). The only exceptions are Japan – where unemployment is disguised – and, still, the fast-growing economies of East Asia. Thus, there appear to be grounds for the apprehension that globalization results in job losses and income inequality.

The concern regarding the impact of trade on labour in industrialized countries is theoretically supported by the Stolper-Samuelson theorem which predicts that increasing imports from low-wage economies will lead to a fall in the relative price of labour-intensive goods competing with those imports, and in the relative wages of low-skilled workers. If labour market rigidities impede the downward adjustment of wages, then unemployment among these workers will increase. Foreign direct investment (FDI) will lead to the relocation of low-skilled jobs to low-wage countries, thereby exacerbating the effects of import competition.

A lively debate has arisen among economists as to whether theoretical predictions have been borne out by experience and whether the magnitudes are significant. Adrian Wood (1994) presented a sound theoretical framework and extensive empirical evidence.[4] He argued that the cumulative effects of North-South trade expansion in the 30 years up to 1990 caused a 20 per cent reduction in the demand for unskilled labour in the North, which was equivalent to its rate of unemployment arid of wage dispersion. Lawrence and Slaughter (1993) considered trade to be only a minor explanatory factor and could not confirm the decline in the relative prices of labour-intensive products predicted by the Stolper-Samuelson theorem. In contrast, Sachs and Shatz (1996) were able to identify such relative price changes. The differences in the results of these studies indicate that the problem is, in part, one of data.[5] It is also one of conception.[6] Standard (Heckscher-Ohlin) trade theory, from which the Stolper-Samuelson theorem derives, is not the only framework to infer that integration might have a negative impact on equity. A number of different methods produce similar results, even without changes in relative prices,[7] but these seem to be simply ignored by many studies (e.g. IMF, 1997, p. 53).

Many economists express reservations regarding the magnitude of trade and investment effects. In 1992, the share of developing countries' manufactured exports in the OECD market was just 3.1 per cent, up from 0.4 per cent in 1970 (UNCTAD, 1995, p. 137). This sort of ratio, however, understates the impact of trade on labour markets, for two reasons. The first relates to the huge wage differential between North and South whereby imports from low-wage countries contain a far larger labour component than the same value of goods in the import-competing industry.[8] The second reason is the introduction of defensive process-rationalizing technologies in response to Southern competition. Although such business strategies have kept import penetration low, the demand for low-skilled labour in the North has none the less been reduced (Wood, 1994).

Similarly, FDI outflows are said to represent no more than 0.5 per cent of GDP in the industrialized countries (Lee, 1996, p. 488, citing Krugman, 1994a). But this does not include investment financed by the profits of foreign subsidiaries, which might double that figure. Nor does it take account of the leverage effect on FDI of modern management methods, such as joint ventures, franchising and outsourcing. The purpose of much of this cross-border investment is, however, to gain access to new markets, which is why anecdotal evidence of the substitution of capital investment for high-wage labour should not be interpreted at face value as a general trend. At all events, such FDI-to-GDP or trade-to-GDP ratios do not reflect the weakened bargaining position of labour as its demand curve becomes more elastic because of the sheer potential for substituting foreign for domestic labour. The situation is in no way mitigated by the fact that, on occasion at least, managers merely allege such exit-options in order to bring pressure to bear on workers and their representatives; it just illustrates the seriousness of the problem confronting labour.

Many authors seek to allay concern by drawing attention to the mutual benefits of economic integration (Lee, 1996). Theory and evidence support this view, simultaneously demonstrating that these benefits are unequally distributed. Industrialized countries' exports have benefited mainly highly-skilled workers, "symbolic analysts" in Reich's (1991) terminology, while FDI has obviously favoured owners of capital. Both developments emphasize the patterns of growing income disparity. The sizeable share of factor service sector incomes in the United States and the United Kingdom may already denote a shift towards a "rentier economy" (Sachs and Shatz, 1996, p. 12). Much of the increase in demand for low-productivity and low-paid services in those countries clearly originates from those individuals whose position has improved as a result of globalization (UNCTAD, 1995, pp. 205-208).

Another prediction of the Stolper-Samuelson theorem is that the relative wages of low-skilled workers in developing countries will rise as industrialized economies dismantle their trade barriers. Indeed, the southeast and east Asian economies succeeded in combining rapid economic growth with comparatively low inequality, though in contrast to several Latin American countries where income disparity increased in the aftermath of trade liberalization. Various factors could account for this seeming inconsistency, among them labour market deregulation and an increased demand for highly-skilled workers due to the introduction of new technology, or a shift of comparative advantages in middle-income economies (World Bank, 1995). Meanwhile, booming exports from large low-wage countries, such as China, India and Indonesia, may have worsened the terms of trade of labour-intensive products, thereby depressing the wages of low-skilled workers in the South. Finally, the Heckscher-Ohlin model itself can be modified by allowing for outsourcing when explaining wage dispersion in both the North and the South (Feenstra and Hanson, 1996).

Some commentators go so far as to proclaim the emergence of a "global labour market" comprising 2.5 billion people today (World Bank, 1995, pp. 9 and 50). In this process, international migration has not necessarily played an important role since trade in goods and services, in conjunction with capital flows, are substitutes for labour mobility. The advent of the transition economies and the growing participation of the populous developing countries in the world market system have significantly increased the supply of labour competing for investment and employment opportunities. In 1990, the developing countries' share in worldwide manufacturing employment already exceeded 50 per cent (Lee, 1996). Yet the high wage discrepancy between developing and industrialized economies can only partly be attributed to a productivity gap. Unit cost differentials between North and South range between 30 and 60 per cent in various industries (Bloom and Brender, 1993, p. 19). Over and above differences in product quality, the existence of trade barriers and the lower overall level of labour productivity in developing economies, this disparity may indicate the existence of labour oppression by authoritarian regimes.[9] Consequently, trade unionists fear that "European, North American, Japanese or Australian labour is in direct competition with the labour force of countries where wages are kept ten to twenty times lower, with both rising unemployment and falling wage levels in the old industrialized countries" (Gallin, 1994, p. 109). Such statements should not be taken literally, however. Over two-thirds of the workforce in the industrialized economies is employed in the predominantly non-tradeable service sector (Krugman, 1994b). In low-income economies, by contrast, the bulk of employment is still in the rural subsistence and urban informal sectors. On average, only 12 to 15 per cent of jobs in these economies are in tradeable, modern-sector activities (Lee, 1996, p. 492). Indeed, labour markets retain a predominantly domestic focus. None the less, services are becoming increasingly tradeable, and are attracting more substantial FDI. Even where this is not occurring, services constitute important inputs for export and import-competing industries.

The perception of globalization as an exclusively North-South phenomenon is inaccurate, since the bulk of trade and investment occurs within the advanced OECD area. Growing competition between the three dominant industrialized trading blocs is proving to be at least equally important. Over the last three decades, the shares in world economic activity of the United States and Western Europe (except Germany) declined, while that of Japan and the Asian NICs increased. The old industrialized areas thus appear to be vulnerable not only to competition from low-wage economies, but also to competition from producers with high levels of quality, flexibility and productivity. Clearly, intra-industry trade also opens the door for new markets, but strategic trade and investment policies can lead to a welfare-decreasing "prisoners' dilemma".

This short and unavoidably incomplete presentation of the subject demonstrates that it is too early to pronounce the conjectured havoc of globalization to be "largely mythical" (Wolf, 1997). An element of exaggeration may be present and doubts may never be fully resolved. "But if exaggeration is unwarranted then so too is complacency" (Lee, 1996, p. 493). Globalization clearly bestows net benefits on advanced economies, but it should also be acknowledged that low-skilled labour is subject to at least some harmful effects. Of course, other factors may share responsibility for the emerging polarization, such as sluggish growth, technological change, female participation in the labour market, and deregulation and de-unionization, but it does not make sense to isolate these phenomena from each other. Many of these determinants could be endogenized in a model – which would admittedly be difficult to construct – of structural shift towards a "global post-industrial economy" (Zamagni, 1996). In such a dynamic framework, the combined effects of the uncertainties of global financial markets, "hyper-competition", uncooperative state behaviour and increasing inequality *per se* might slow down worldwide economic growth. A vicious circle would be set in motion, before which even the most pessimistic trade unionists would quail.

LIMITS TO NATIONAL SOVEREIGNTY

[M]arkets are going to become the policemen of politics.[10]

While competitiveness has been described as a "dangerous obsession" (Krugman, 1994b), growing inequality should also give cause for concern, whether it derives from globalization alone or in combination with technology, structural shifts or anything else. References to the transitory character of skill mismatches are not very helpful, since "transitory" can mean a whole generation or more. Education and training are already broadly accepted as a useful answer (Wood, 1994). Yet, it will take time for the desired results to become visible. It will take even longer for the strategies targeting the cutting edge of high-value-added production and involving intensified research and development to produce results. Senior low-skilled production workers who have lost their jobs will hardly be consoled by recommendations for lifelong learning. At least in the short run, they should be compensated by those who are benefitting from globalization. Under normal circumstances, this would be an easy task, since the gains of the winners are likely to exceed by far the detriment suffered by the losers. But the circumstances are not normal.

While trends in trade and cross-border investment are following "normal" integration patterns which were already taking shape at the end of the nineteenth century, the globalization of financial markets constitutes a genuinely new process. Money has gradually been uprooted from its functions in the productive economy – i.e. barter, storage and *numéraire* – and a sort of "casino capitalism" has emerged. During the course of the past two decades, the ratio of global financial transactions to world output has increased from 15:1 to 78:1 (Hoffmann and Hoffmann, 1997, p. 11). This process, in which the "real" economy is increasingly supplanted by a "fictitious" economy, was sparked off by the collapse of the Bretton Woods system of fixed exchange rates. Subsequently, the trend was reinforced by the emergence of Eurodollar markets inflated by petrodollar surpluses; debt crises and the establishment of offshore banks; speculative bubbles and the creation of derivative markets; high interest rates generated by the increasing risks assumed by the banking system; relatively low private investment causing economic growth to slacken which, in turn, resulted in higher public deficits (Schulmeister, 1995).[11]

In the production sphere, the explosion of liquid international funds has produced a shift in firm culture towards a rather short-term-oriented, so-called Anglo-Saxon model of capitalism. The proliferation of "shareholder values" has prompted efforts to reduce variable costs, notably wages (Hoffmann and Hoffmann, 1997). Although not yet totally "footloose", MNCs are playing a pioneering role in adapting investment strategies to the new paradigm via lean production, global sourcing, offshore funding and other such means. The consequent labour shedding and tax evasion exacerbates the problems to which labour markets and budgets are subject. In turn, the proliferation of methods whereby firms may remove themselves from domestic jurisdiction has pushed governments gradually to eliminate capital controls in order to remain competitive, thus surrendering even more of their sovereignty to short-term capital flows (Goodman and Pauly, 1995).

States – and even regions, such as the European Union – are increasingly competing for that financial capital as well as for FDI, which is also becoming decisive in terms of access to knowledge and technology (Drucker, 1996). Under the triple pressure of sluggish growth, high debt and high interest rates, countries find themselves in a "strait-jacket of international financial markets" which threatens their national autonomy (ICFTU, 1996, p. 32). Monetary, fiscal and social policies are today more sensitive to the judgements of global financial markets. The discretion of governments, including central banks, over interest and exchange rates has been reduced, and the scope for deficit spending has been curtailed. "Soothing the speculators has meant deflationary policies" (ICFTU, 1996, p. 32). Greater capital mobility hampers governments' capacity to tax and regulate, at a time when the need for active labour market programmes and redistribution is greater than ever. "Lean government" is, in turn, laying additional burdens on the crisis-ridden labour markets. "Th[e] golden age of egalitarian policy is apparently over" (Bowles and Gintis, 1995, p. 559).

This does not mean, however, that financial market globalization generates a unique "best practice" of policies and institutions to which all countries are obliged to conform. Labour and capital markets are still organized differently in such similarly successful economies as the United States, Japan and Germany. National policies still have their place in employment policy and labour standards. "However, a basic paradox in the current phase of globalization is that, at the same time as the social dislocations caused by increasing international competition are rising, the capacity, and even perhaps the will, of governments to take such compensatory or ameliorative action is weakening" (Lee, 1996, p. 496).

In short, the impact of financial market globalization on macroeconomic policies is a much less controversial issue than that of production and long-term investment. Differences may, however, emerge in the attitude towards this process, which ultimately depends on distinct value systems. An affirmative stance welcomes the new discipline imposed on governments: "The forces of globalization increase both the benefits of good policies and the cost of failure. Although no group of workers can rely on the forces of convergence to raise their wages automatically, neither need they fear that such forces will unavoidably pull their wages down. Whether a new golden age arrives for all depends mostly on the responses of individual countries to the new opportunities offered by this increasingly global economy" (World Bank, 1995, p. 54). From a more structuralist point of view, and in trade union parlance, a new "global feudalism" may be viewed more pessimistically: "If national laws are rendered impotent, then so are a nation's citizens" (Greider, 1996, p. 336). Such scepticism is not without foundation, according to Greider: first, competition can destroy invested capital as even viable factories have to close; second, production overcapacity depresses wage levels worldwide; third, wage depression and unsteady capital investment perpetuate insufficient demand (1996, p. 335).[12] Both views depart somewhat from an institutionalist perspective which focuses mainly on the "evil of uncertainties" precipitated by unregulated globalization. The fact that American trade unionists, in particular, tend to put forward more radical interpretations might have to do with their own, less-than-rosy outlook.[13]

THE CHALLENGE TO TRADE UNIONS

The slogan 'Think global; act local' needs to be reversed. It is global action that is now needed *(MacShane, 1996, p. 3)*.

While the negative impact of globalization on workers may still be open to question, there can be no doubt that unions are the great losers of growing interdependence. International union leaders perceive that "our movement is now under attack on a global scale and with an intensity never before experienced in its history. Unions at the national level are seeing much of what they have achieved being undermined by global financial and industrial decisions" (ICFTU, 1996, p. 5). But to what extent are such perceptions founded in fact?

Trade union membership has certainly plummeted – down by one-quarter in the past two decades, from 36 to 27 per cent of the total workforce in the OECD area (Ariza Rico, 1995, p. 3). And it is striking that this should occur just as globalization trends were emerging, but could it not be mere coincidence? The disaggregation of international, unweighted average union density, however, exhibits only small changes within different sectors, thus suggesting that the main pressure derives from sectoral shifts in employment. Yet a so-called shift-share analysis on a cross-country basis shows that, with the exception of the United Kingdom, the "structural drag" between sectors accounts for little of the decline. The average share of public sector trade union membership has risen with employment and, except in France and the United States, the gap between public and private sector union density has not increased. "All of this seems to indicate that changes in aggregate unionization rates generally result mainly from movements within individual industries" (OECD, 1991, p. 115). Within services, for example, the downward trend in unionization of expanding and highly productive, strategic producer services – compared to low-wage personal services, where union membership is already low – points to the pattern of polarization associated with increasing individualization of labour relations. Other aspects of structural change, such as a shift from blue-collar to white-collar occupations, from full-time to temporary and part-time work, from male to female employment and from large to small and medium firms, also have an impact (OECD, 1991, pp. 112-115). The substantial disparities between countries demonstrate, none the less, that institutional factors still make a decisive contribution to the relative stability of trade union density. On a microeconomic level, the new forms of business organization and the division of internal labour markets into core and periphery, closer ties between workers and management, or successive waves of corporate restructuring have contributed to the decline of unions. Finally, the part played by unemployment in discouraging workers from joining unions should not be underestimated. Many of these developments can be attributed to globalization, although its impact on unionization and equity can hardly be isolated from that of other factors, such as new technology and workforce diversity. "This range of experience would seem to suggest that economic interdependence *per se* is not synonymous with the decline of trade unions" (Campbell, 1991, p. 39).

Unions now appear to be on the defensive. It is "ironic that just as trade unions in many countries around the world have been forfeiting influence and membership the need for a strong employee voice in corporate decision-making, industry-level interactions and national policy-making is growing" (Locke, Kochan and Piore, 1995, p. 156). In comparing the situation in industrialized countries, researchers observe a fundamental transformation of labour relations where differences between national systems become blurred and systematic variations within countries appear. These common patterns of synchronized social polarization in terms of income and working conditions underline the influence of growing economic interdependence, interrelated with other phenomena (op. cit., p. 159).

In theory, economic integration and increasing competition can be expected to erode the bargaining power of trade unions. If wages and employment conditions are to be taken out of competition, labour organizations "must cover the extent of product markets" (Campbell, 1991, p. 43). But while product markets have expanded, the scope of union organization has failed to follow suit. In addition, the existence of a broader range of exit-options makes global businesses more reluctant to commit to bilateral or tripartite agreements with labour and government for the provision of public goods. By the same token, union strategies to influence the regulatory framework tend to fail because government policies themselves are becoming ineffectual. Furthermore, while MNCs select their managers carefully in keeping with their global corporate culture, unions are at a disadvantage as regards the skill structure of their officers (in terms of languages, communication skills, etc.). It is not by accident that trade unions interact with their clients and their negotiating parties mainly within national boundaries: it is part of their function as labour market organizers to stake out a clearly-defined area of protection. And such labour market protection has always tended to involve protectionist measures. Today, however, the increasing mobility of goods and capital allows such obstacles to be readily circumvented, thereby prompting the trade union movement to adopt a global approach. Under the present circumstances, however, it is not possible to contemplate any organizational form of global labour market.[14] Thus, global unionism would not make national strategies obsolete. Rather, the main objective – and difficulty – is to provide labour protection without protectionism.

Before making a theoretical case for global unionism, the general economic rationale for unionism should be clarified. Trade unions provide workers with a collective voice with which to communicate their preferences and proposals. Those proposals go well beyond their direct interests and often bring benefits for society as a whole. Unions usually oppose injustice and discrimination and promote equality (though at the risk of possibly inefficient wage compression).[15] Improvements in working conditions (e.g. job safety) and restraints on employers' arbitrary actions are also to the public good. However, it can be argued that the monopolistic behaviour of unions can have negative effects on non-unionized workers (World Bank, 1995, p. 81). Yet monopolistic bargaining structures may be more efficient than decentralized forms, if one is to judge from the small wage premium of unionized workers in Europe (half) compared to that in the United States. One might then suspect that labour markets would be characterized simultaneously by monopolies on the supply side and monopsonies on the demand side. When labour and management are organized at the industry and national levels, collective bargaining will tend to reconcile higher employment and higher wages, enhancing the efficiency of the economy as a whole (Frank, 1994, p. 590).[16] Centralized socio-economic agents with the power to impose penalties on free-riders are usually inclined to exercise social responsibility and thereby assure positive externalities, like stability. Moreover, experience with the introduction of innovative modes of work organization and new technologies in Germany suggests that the presence of strong social partners can foster beneficial solutions in the trade-off between stability and flexibility (Locke, Kochan and Piore, 1995). Countries with corporatist and non-adversarial industrial relations systems – such as those of Austria, Germany, the Netherlands or the Scandinavian countries, which generally enjoy high productivity and wages – offer telling examples of the unexpected virtue of "monopolistic" labour organization.[17] In addition to their economic function of balancing production and distribution, trade unions also have a democratic function, in that they give people a say in their working life, and a social function in combating unemployment, poverty and exclusion (ILO, 1997, p. 27).

Such reasoning may be applied beyond the national level as employers, and particularly MNCs, become global monopsonies. Trade unions have four types of strategic options to cope with globalization. The first involves raising wages and labour standards – this is global unionism in the narrow sense. The second relates to restricting capital mobility with a view to reducing the capacity of business to shop for cheaper labour (e.g. consultation rights and codetermination). The third seeks to facilitate labour market adjustment to competition in high-wage and high-performance industries (Campbell, 1991, p. 44). The last focuses on economic policy coordination and institutional arrangements to promote stability and prosperity. All these objectives can be pursued through the dual channels of private agreements with employers and the legislative system which, in conjunction, constitute the basis for a tripartite system of industrial relations. But is it realistic to seek to replicate such a social partnership system on a global level? An assessment of the feasibility of these strategies calls for an analysis of historical developments and of the current situation.

THE FRAGMENTARY FOUNDATIONS OF GLOBAL UNIONISM

The working men have no country *(Marx and Engels, 1848, p. 142)*.

From its very inception, the labour movement has endeavoured to reach out beyond national borders. In contrast to the early craft or "bread and butter" unions in the United Kingdom and the United States, the political unionism of continental Europe was largely shaped by franchise restriction. Slower industrial development, church hostility[18] and state prosecution triggered the emergence of conflicting political currents of a socialist, anarcho-syndicalist or confessional nature, among others. It might further be argued that the suppression of an internationally-coordinated reaction gave impetus to both labour internationalism and nationalism. However, this conflict between nationalism and internationalism, which led to the schism of the labour movement during the First World War and the Russian Revolution, persists today. After the Second World War, an attempt to unite the two tendencies by creating the World Federation of Trade Unions came to nothing after it was misused as an instrument of the Cold War; anticommunist unions walked out and formed the International Confederation of Free Trade Unions (ICFTU) and Christian unions went their own way and founded the World Confederation of Labour. But even within the ICFTU, ideological battles continued regarding United States influence, developing countries and the growing interest in *détente*. Finally, the rise of "Eurounionism" culminated in the foundation of the European Trade Union Confederation which linked socialist, communist and Christian centres (Busch, 1980).

With the Cold War at an end, the ICFTU, with its 127 million members,[19] is now by far the most important worldwide labour organization. Since their creation at the turn of the century, the industry-based and more pragmatic International Trade Secretariats (ITSs) developed a successful response to MNCs by organizing worldwide works councils.[20] In contrast to the labour diplomacy conducted by the political factions, the constructive activity of the ITSs in coordinating national strategies may have paved the way for global unionism. Trade unions are already represented in several international organizations or institutions, such as the Organization for Economic Cooperation and Development (OECD) and the International Labour Organization (ILO). The latter is unique in that it is tripartite, including governments, employers and workers, offering an example of how a future "global social partnership" might function. If the ILO were strengthened, it could take its place beside the World Trade Organization (WTO), the International Monetary Fund (IMF) and the World Bank in the concert of world economic organizations.

More recently, trade unions have strengthened their position in regional free trade areas, notably under the North American Free Trade Agreement (NAFTA),[21] in which trade is already linked to basic workers' rights, and in the European Union. In 1994, the efforts of the European Trade Union Confederation (ETUC) to develop a European system of industrial relations were rewarded by the EU Directive on European Works Councils (EWC).[22] Some 1,150 companies are affected by its implementation. However, the significance of the Councils goes far beyond Europe, since almost 200 United States-based MNCs are also covered (Danis, 1996,

p. 90).[23] Another major breakthrough in European collective bargaining was the agreement on parental leave signed by the social partners in 1995 (Hoffmann, 1996, p. 12).[24] In general, the aim of social cohesion in terms of living and working conditions is set out in the social chapter of the Maastricht Treaty, which prepared the ground for economic and monetary union. Europe promises to become the chief laboratory for experiments in global unionism.

One of the organizations nearest to being a global trade union is the International Transport Workers' Federation (ITF), whose affiliates total some five million members in 120 countries. In international shipping, "the ITF has come close to imposing a worldwide minimum wage ten times higher than some local rates" (*The Economist*, 1997, p. 85). Even vessels under a flag of convenience are guaranteed safe passage only if they pay the stipulated remuneration, together with a donation to the Federation's welfare fund; 100 ITF inspectors around the world hand out union seals of approval without which the ship-owners risk strikes, boycotts and the perishing of cargo. However, it is unclear whether the Federation can serve as a model for other unions, since seamen are physically concentrated and are consequently much easier to organize than other workers.[25]

But other organizations can also successfully fight international labour campaigns, as was demonstrated by the telecommunications unions in the case of Sprint, an American MNC which fired Hispanic workers who wanted to organize a subsidiary.[26] Subsequently, members of German, French, Mexican and Nicaraguan unions, in turn, put pressure on their respective employers to include labour standard clauses in cooperation contracts with that company (MacShane, 1996, p. 25). Codes of conduct are of course a relatively weak instrument, since they generally deal, in a unilateral manner, with matters relating to third parties.[27] Prompted by a tragic fire in a Chinese toy factory where 87 women were locked in, such a code was recently agreed by Artsana, an Italian-based toy multinational, and the three Italian national trade union centres. Artsana's subcontractors worldwide are now required to ensure that the trade union rights and other core labour standards enshrined in ILO Conventions are observed, and to offer "decent pay and working conditions". Any breach will result in the cancellation of contracts. Compliance is monitored through independent on-site inspections, and is subject to annual assessment (see ICFTU, 1997b). But, even with appropriate monitoring procedures, codes of conduct serve at best as complements to direct agreements which include subcontractors so as to deal with "chameleon corporations" that behave responsibly only where national regulation or union ascendancy leaves them no choice.

Two recent cases of cross-border industrial action merit closer attention. The first "Euro-strike" (ILO, 1997, p. 41) was sparked off in early 1997 when the partly State-owned French car manufacturer Renault announced the closure of its plant in Vilvorde, Belgium. This decision, which involved the loss of 3,000 jobs, precipitated stoppages coordinated by the European Metalworkers' Federation in Belgium, France, Spain, Portugal and Slovenia. In Belgium, workers throughout the automobile industry and in some other sectors went out on strike. The World Confederation of Labour called on its members to refuse work transferred from Vilvorde to other sites. Several hundred Belgian "flying pickets" concentrated on mobilizing French workers. Belgian newspapers called for a consumer boycott, and public orders were cancelled. About 70,000 workers from all over Europe participated in demonstrations in Brussels and Paris. The company was twice convicted, in France and Belgium, for disregarding two EU Directives relating respectively to European Works Councils and to collective redundancies. This gave the ETUC the occasion to lobby for amendments to these regulations.[28] The affair became a major issue in the French parliamentary election campaign. Yet, despite the Socialist victory, a government enquiry supported the redundancy plans subject to a negotiated "social plan" providing for early retirement, retraining and re-employment at other Renault sites (Ewing, 1997, pp. 6-7; *Labour Research*, 1997, p. 9). These events served to demonstrate the potential of transnational labour unity and to quote Marc Blondel, the leader of France's Force Ouvrière (FO) – marked "the birth of a more reactive and less technical European unionism" (*Libération*, 1997, p. 2).

A satisfactory settlement was likewise reached in another key trade union dispute, against the Japanese tyre producing group, Bridgestone/Firestone, Inc. Some 2,300 workers who were striking against announced pay cuts and reduced working conditions were laid off and replaced. Following a two-year stand-off, the International Federation of Chemical, Energy, Mine and General Workers' Unions (ICEM), helped the United Steelworkers of America to launch a "cyberstrike", by providing a list of addresses on its web site to facilitate the unauthorized occupation of the sites and electronic mail boxes of the company's management, as well as of those of car makers and distributors, tyre retailers, banks and other bodies with a stake in Bridgestone (Peter, 1997). Finally, the multinational was forced to back down and re-hire the dismissed workers.

Economic globalization has also created opportunities for trade unions. New and inexpensive technologies have swept away communications barriers and opened the way for joint efforts in research and bargaining. Cross-border interaction between workplaces is now possible. In this sense, the Internet is not only a medium but also a message.[29] Although its impact should not be overstated, it can play a part in democratizing unions and empowering members,[30] although the fact that Internet access varies within and between countries may create a new hierarchy. Just-in-time production and subcontracting procedures make businesses vulnerable to strikes affecting the production of essential components without which the entire production network can be brought to a standstill. Employers may seek to protect themselves by adopting the counter-strategy of parallel sourcing, but this is costly (Van Liemt, 1992, p. 466). Unions may also make global consumers a new source of power, through "social labelling",[31] and address their campaigns to shareholder groups. Multinational offenders could be embarrassed by complaints to the ILO, or they may be brought to justice through international legal proceedings before the European Court of Justice (MacShane, 1996, p. 26).

None the less, the problems that beset cross-border solidarity are by no means negligible. The legal basis for transnational industrial action is circumscribed by the different national legislations and labour relations systems. Solidarity action is usually subject to strict requirements, such as the ability to demonstrate a valid interest in supporting the primary action. In some countries, notably in the United Kingdom, sympathy action not related to the narrowly-defined employer is not accepted even within national boundaries. However, trade unions have traditionally acted as instigators of legislative change. The Renault case has eloquently demonstrated that the possibility of enforcing European collective agreements by striking is less "futuristic" than it may have seemed (ETUC, 1997). In addition, global unionism must cope with a communications problem. The fact that multinationals generally use English as the first company language means that the same tends to occur in the labour movement. While this puts non-native speakers and their system of industrial relations at a disadvantage, it does facilitate the exchange of information and ideas; cultural diversity is a luxury that trade unions cannot always afford. Of far greater import than the above-mentioned technical difficulties, however, are the material benefits that can be gained from locational competition. At worst, this leads to conscious social dumping and, at the very least, to a squandering of resources.

Globalization offers organized labour the alternative of collaborating with employers to enhance productivity, adaptability and product or service quality, in exchange for job security and higher wages (MacShane, 1996, p. 26). One particular organization affiliated to the British Trade Union Congress (TUC) is currently demonstrating in a quite extraordinary manner just how far such "productivity partnerships" can go. The Amalgamated Engineering and Electrical Union (AEEU) has published a colourful booklet in several languages, including Korean and Japanese, which directly invites potential foreign investors to establish plants in the United Kingdom (AEEU, 1996). The union offers its human resource services, contacts with local authorities, links to production networks and the promise of industrial peace, in return for which it requests exclusive recognition (single union agreement). This is not to criticize the union for violating internationalist principles, but it exemplifies how industrial relations themselves are becoming a factor in global competition. But productivity pacts may be counterproductive if the macroeconomic environment is unfavourable to growth. Unions can avoid one-sided choices and diversify their strategies to include elements of international solidarity and national adaptationism. Economic integration may lead either to nationalism or to internationalism, the "twin tendencies of working class organisation" (Wills, 1997, p. 1). It is a natural reaction to retract into the national shell, but union leadership must "react logically, not instinctively" (Gallin, 1997, p. 5). Strategic thinking must be global in nature.

Should the international proclivity gain ascendancy, a new system of international industrial relations would become essential – one in which the International Trade Secretariats might truly act as front-line industrial organizations. They can indeed play a crucial part in shifting the power relationship within multinational corporations – the "real decision networks of the world economy" (ICEM, 1995, p. 4). These secretariats should already be involved in the action planning stage, as opposed to serving as a last resort when action has failed locally. They may become discussion fora, information nodes, service centres, assistance pools and rallying points for solidarity. Their databases could provide effective support for collective bargaining. An evaluation of "best practice" experiences in negotiation strategies could facilitate agreements involving works councils throughout the world. Such agreements could in turn serve as a basis for further organization. Decentralization of decision-making processes contributes to democratization, but it must not degenerate into "competitive regionalization". In view of the advanced stage of integration in Europe, regional trade secretaries there are required also – though not exclusively – to function as political lobbyists.

Choosing the appropriate strategy is not an easy task, and the different strategic approaches may even clash. Potential sources of contradiction should be identified in connection with the current mergers of International Trade Secretariats, such as that of chemical workers and miners into the ICEM. Such mergers may be undertaken with a view to strengthening international labour unity or to fostering synergies generated by cross-sectoral links or by vertical organization by product chains. Alternatively, they may simply be motivated by the fact that individual organizations' revenues are shrinking. A possible culmination of this process towards a "rational" structure of International Trade Secretariats aimed at avoiding "wasteful duplication of effort and expertise" might be to merge the current 15 branches into five: industry; public services; commercial and professional services; transport and communications; media and cultural services (ICEM, 1995, p. 7). Such an approach is countered by the argument that general purpose unions lose grass-roots links and span excessively diverse interests (ILO, 1997, p. 22). Yet, mergers respond to the reality of the current situation in which employers ignore sectoral divides and employees are losing their professional ethos. If the sectoral, industrial and regional structures within the unions are retained, the right balance may more readily be struck between centralization and democratization, thus ensuring that global power is locally based.

The relationship between unions in industrialized and developing countries is also a delicate matter. Since both Northern and Southern workers have a growing interest in strengthening the unions of low-wage regions, unilateral aid for union development becomes more attractive (Ross, 1995, p. 87). However, given fears of renewed "trade union imperialism", the "aid model" could be replaced by a "solidarity model" of mutual cooperation (Wills, 1997, p. 13). The International Metalworkers' Federation, for example, sees no clash between mutual support and traditional assistance by the stronger union to the weaker. This Federation is urging home country unions to help non-organized labour to organize in MNC host countries. In the same vein, it is experimentally including representatives from MNC subsidiaries as observers in the collective bargaining process (International Metalworkers' Federation, 1997, p. 34).

The former consensus regarding the *modus vivendi* with the official unions of countries which systematically violate labour and human rights appears to be vanishing. While the IUF continues to pursue a policy of strict exclusion of such official unions in order to encourage independent movements – albeit sporadic – to emerge, the International Metalworkers' Federation pursues a variable strategy of cautious approach and acceptance at the first signs of democratization.[32] Midway between these two positions, the policy of the Chemical Workers' International seeks to establish contact with any workers and plant-level representatives who attempt to "move the official labour apparatus onto a more independent line" (ICEM, 1997, p. 14). The ambitions of the ICFTU's Asian and Pacific Regional Organization to establish closer links with official Chinese and Indonesian unions were dampened when the regional secretary of the IUF was expelled from Indonesia for seeking to attend the most recent Congress of the non-recognized Indonesian Worker Prosperity Union (SBSI).

Factional differences within the international labour movement also arise on how to deal with the Bretton Woods institutions and other organizations. In contrast to the International Metalworkers' Federation which wants NGO status in the World Trade Organization and the World Bank, the ICEM refuses "loyal opposition" within institutions it deems fundamentally unjust. Similarly, the World Federation of Trade Unions (WFTU) is opposed to the OECD's proposed Multilateral Agreement on Investment which it considers to represent a threat to national sovereignty (see WFTU, 1997, p. 3), while the Trade Unions Advisory Committee to the OECD (TUAC) advocates the incorporation in the proposed Agreement of the OECD Guidelines for Multinational Enterprises and binding labour clauses. However, to over-emphasize such differences would be to misrepresent the international labour movement, since views do not effectively diverge on the overwhelming majority of issues. Moreover, a measure of diversification may even strengthen the effectiveness of global unionism by making it accessible from different angles and offering greater flexibility in its responses to new challenges.

Trade unions have a genuine interest in a "Global New Deal" (Collings-worth, Goold and Harvey, 1996). Despite repeated postponement, the question of incorporating so-called social clauses in the framework of the new WTO still heads the international union agenda. The ICFTU proposes a procedure whereby compliance with basic labour standards – to which many countries are already committed under ratified ILO Conventions – is made a precondition of trade concessions under the GATT/WTO. The objective is to prevent "social dumping" through child labour, forced labour or union suppression. The proposal continues to be dismissed by the governments of some developing countries as "social imperialism".[33] Controversy likewise surrounds the proposal to expand the autonomy of national monetary policies by a tax on speculation, as put forward by James Tobin: "Transactions taxes are one way, a quite innocuous way, to throw some sand in the wheels of super-efficient financial vehicles" (TUAC, 1995, p. 14). In addition, the International Metalworkers' Federation has called for tighter financial market regulation and worker control over pension funds, which are often used in a manner that is contrary to their best interests (1997, p. 37). It argues that international monetary and macroeconomic policy coordination should be encouraged in the interests of promoting economic growth, if the "diabolic dilemma" of unemployment and income inequality is to be tackled. A case can also be made for a sort of a "global Marshall Plan" for developing and transition economies, which would favour workers and trade unions in the advanced economies as well. In line with this, the ICFTU is demanding increased IMF lending quotas and Special Drawing Rights. However, the international labour movement is reluctant to call for the introduction of a global minimum wage as suggested by Greider (1996). Certainly, such a minimum wage would be hard put to accommodate the enormous disparities in productivity and living standards between countries. Nevertheless, procedures to secure the gradual convergence of employment conditions and remuneration are worth considering. Global bargaining could only make sense if it were underpinned by commitment to a solidarity principle as regards compensation matters.[34]

In many of these areas, trade unions may well find allies among other workers' organizations, social associations and NGOs (ILO, 1997, p. 47), provided they do not succumb to the temptation to see themselves as "privileged bearers of internationalism" (Wills, 1997, p. 3, citing Waterman, forthcoming). Opportunities for new partnerships are also generated by the pressure the International Metalworkers' Federation is putting on creditor countries' unions for reducing the debt of developing countries and for introducing environmental clauses.

"Global organization is not the same thing as international organization" (ICEM, 1995, p. 3). It includes an awareness of workers' interdependence along with a shared vision of social progress. Such an approach would envisage the control of enterprises by the stakeholders rather than by the shareholders (ICEM, 1995, p. 12). Innovative and proactive international manpower policies may prove effective in overcoming the negative image of unions as mere clubs for privileged wage-earners (ILO, 1997, p. 23) and may attenuate excessive concentration of power in corporate hands.

SUMMARY AND CONCLUSIONS

Global markets need global rules backing coordinated policies *(ICFTU, 1996, p. 47)*.

While economic integration is typically beneficial overall, it may well have undesirable distributional consequences. Little doubt remains that globalization – in the form of increasing international trade and investment – has had some negative impact on the wages and/or job security of low-skilled workers in advanced economies. In developing countries, its generally positive effects on the corresponding labour market segment depend on various institutional conditions. The crucial problem, however, is that the negative judgements of the fast-growing international financial markets tend to frustrate governments' efforts to redistribute. The outcomes of closer attention to education and infrastructure may be experienced by blue-collar workers only in the long run, and the scope for such "good policies" is limited by budget constraints. Hence, the reservations expressed by workers' representatives and politicians regarding globalization cannot be attributed – or at least not exclusively – to a lack of information, as is frequently alleged. This neither concludes the debate nor understates the opportunities offered by economic integration.

Like states, trade unions have lost some of their room for manoeuvre against global business and finance, which has triggered further depression of wages, working conditions and collective bargaining. Of course, other factors, such as structural change and technological and organizational innovations have also contributed to the decline of labour's bargaining power and to social polarization. However, the outlook is not unrelievedly bleak. States remain the "key unit" in responding to global change (Grunberg, 1996, p. 355), and in this framework national trade unions continue to strive to protect workers without resorting to protectionism. But, as the balance between economic and socio-political forces becomes skewed, states and unions must be complemented by some type of transnational element along the lines of inter-governmental cooperation.

This article has emphasized the significance of global unionism as a further desirable element in restoring the socio-economic balance of power. It has been argued that global unionism can draw on the tradition of labour internationalism. The organizational framework of the international labour movement as it has developed over time can serve as a basis, but requires a new lease of life. Indeed, global unionism goes beyond congress diplomacy, information exchange and policy coordination. It involves the ability to develop strategies, to operate and to bargain on an international level. What is needed is global action based on local experience. New and cheaper communication technologies facilitate the closer links between all levels of the labour movement. Trade unions should perceive themselves as being part of a global civil society, and forge strategic alliances with governmental and civil organizations. The ultimate aim of global unionism would be to institutionalize a system of tripartite social partnership for the purpose of regulating the global economy in the interest of greater equality, prosperity and stability. All this would no doubt entail a radical change in the attitudes of conservative and inward-looking labour organizations. "Globalization opens as many doors as it shuts" (Wills, 1997, p. 25, citing Agnew and Corbridge, 1995, p. 219). The real challenge of globalization is to take advantage of the new opportunities if international solidarity is to embrace more than traditional worker anthems.

Some possible criticisms have been anticipated, although many others have not been mentioned. It might be claimed that global unionism would transpose the insider/outsider problem to the world level.[35] Yet if the potential dangers of irresponsible or rent-seeking behaviour are to be minimized, broad categories of industries and occupations should be included within organizational units. At the opposite extreme, union pluralism might be advocated to prevent the appearance of a corporatist Leviathan – an unjustified concern in the light of contemporary patterns of "de-unionization". This article has suggested that labour market monopolies or wage cartels are a pillar of efficient industrial relations. However, this is not to deny the usefulness of some degree of competition in maintaining a high quality of service and in avoiding opposition to necessary change. The co-existence of competitive product markets and a form of global unionism in the nature of a non-hierarchical network might go some way to ensuring the necessary flexibility.

Notes

[1] George Meany, former President of the American Federation of Labor – Congress of Industrial Organizations (AFL-CIO), quoted in Gershman (1975, p. 2).

[2] It would, however, be excessive to play off the ideological phenomenon of a "global hegemony of neoliberalism" (Arbeitsgemeinschaft für Wissenschaftliche Wirtschaftspolitik, 1997) against the material phenomenon of globalization. Increasingly, fierce competition and neoliberalism are allies, reinforcing each other while eroding labour's bargaining strength "from above" and "from below" (Wills, 1997, p. 2, quoting Peck, 1996, p. 233).

[3] The situation is of course far more complicated. The fact that there are "working poor" has to do with the low productivity of many of the new jobs created in the United States ("hamburger economy"). While the labour productivity of the United States economy as a whole is low, that of manufacturing, and of producer services in particular, surpasses the bulk of OECD countries. The problem with such statistics is that productivity in the public and service sectors is basically measured by wages, with the result that Europe's higher overall productivity reflects the greater relative size of its public sector and its higher wage level in services, achieved through collective bargaining. But the dilemma remains that there appears to be a trade-off between a labour market dualism induced by

deregulation and privatization, on the one hand, and higher wages and unemployment, on the other. Hence, under the conditions of slow economic growth, the only remaining choice is whether or not to introduce the insider/outsider problem into internal or external labour markets.

[4] Wood (1994) used a framework of comparative advantages based on different skill levels within the workforce, thus circumventing the Leontiev paradox. (Leontiev found that the United States imported predominantly capital-intensive goods and exported relatively labour-intensive goods.)

[5] Sachs and Shatz (1996, p. 39), for example, exclude the computer industry from their sample, which they believe to be an exception on account of its outstanding productivity growth. They also use relatively high estimates for the "magnification effect" linking the behaviour of relative prices and wages. Furthermore, the scant availability of reliable statistics has led to the glaring omission of services, which already account for one-third of world trade, and for half of FDI.

[6] Lawrence and Slaughter (1993) discovered that the ratio of non-production to production workers has been increasing in US manufacturing, contrary to the Stolper-Samuelson predictions. This supports the interpretation of technological progress as being "biased" against unskilled labour, and constituting an additional source of the growing income disparities. Yet, such technological change has been evident for almost a century and was associated until the early 1970s with a narrowing rather than a widening wage gap (Sachs and Shatz 1994, p. 41). Moreover, there is reason to question whether occupational distinctions are an accurate proxy for skill differences since, in modern manufacturing, blue-collar workers frequently need a much higher level of education and experience than many back-office clerks.

[7] Krugman and Venables (1995, pp. 860-875) present a simple model with interaction between scale economies and continuously falling transport costs which, at a certain critical level, would entail the convergence of wage rates between the core and the periphery region. Sachs and Shatz (1996) developed alternative approaches including highly realistic assumptions of capital mobility or monopolistic competition where low-skilled workers are forced to seek jobs in low-paid, non-tradeable sectors. Additionally, they offer a model of global markets, in which the division of labour is increased by technological change, therefore favouring high-skilled workers.

[8] Such factor intensity reversals are disregarded by theorems in the nature of Stolper-Samuelson.

[9] For example, 1996 is reported to have been the "worst year ever for union repression". Violations of trade union rights occurred in 108 countries, including 264 murders, 2,000 injuries, 4,264 arrested activists and 153,494 dismissals for being union members *(Fiet Info,* 1997, p. 6; ICFTU, 1997a).

[10] Hans Tietmeyer, Governor of the Bundesbank, at the World Economic Forum in Davos, 1996, quoted in Yuste Ramos, Foden and Vogel (1996, p. 5).

[11] There are, of course, alternative interpretations. Most prominently, the IMF (1995) traces the slow-down of growth back to public deficits themselves. While allowing for some additional impact of financial markets, liberalization and decreasing returns on productive capacity, it makes government dissaving responsible for high interest rates and their adverse effect on growth. Although this explanation coincides with the crowding-out effect of text book economics, it lacks the appeal of the present argument, which characterizes government behaviour as a response to macroeconomic difficulties arising from monetary uncertainties.

[12] In response to the first, typically Marxist assumption, it might be countered that much of this obsolete capital is already written off. Furthermore, it can be auctioned and, at the low transport costs of today, easily transferred even from one continent to another, as happens with whole steel plants shipped from Europe to Asia. The second argument is underpinned by anecdotal evidence which, although difficult to generalize, should be taken seriously. For example, the labour costs per hour for a worker in the Mexican export processing zone *(maquiladora)* decreased from 1.12 to 0.56 dollar between 1981 and 1989. The example given to support the third argument, however, is striking. The worldwide capacity of automobile factories would be sufficient to produce 45 million cars a year, but demand does not exceed 35 million (Greider, 1996, p. 335).

[13] Another explanation might lie in the United States' more adversarial system of industrial relations.

[14] By analogy with the theory of an "optimal currency area" something like an "optimal area of labour market organization" might be considered.

[15] As illustrated by the cases of Austria and Japan, this need not lead to compression of wage differentials.

[16] Here the analysis of a monopsonistic labour market is applied to minimum wage law, but could be easily extended to monopolistic labour supply.

[17] As long as product markets remain competitive, the rent-seeking behaviour of unions will be constrained.

[18] At least until the papal encyclical Rerum Novarum of 1891.

[19] This figure has only been prevented from declining by the affiliation of new organizations, like South Africa's COSATU.

[20] The ITSs' membership comprises some 200 million. With current union density estimated at 5 to 10 per cent of the global workforce, the aim of global labour market organization appears to be unattainable.

[21] The social clauses in the NAFTA keep legislation and jurisdiction in the hands of national authorities, allowing for bilateral arbitration procedures.

[22] An example of EWC compatibility with international human resource management is provided by the Norwegian Kvarner Group, which employs about 23,000 people in 50 countries. By 1992, the company had come to view itself as an "international company", making English the language of meetings, communication and training, and establishing a committee in each of its operational divisions. Two years later, a working party was created to reconcile different industrial relations cultures with a view to the establishment of a future European Works Council (*European Industrial Relations Review*, 1994, pp. 21-23).

[23] The EWC Directive has been criticized for including only information and consultation rights and, hence, possibly weakening national codetermination rights. Indeed, a General Motors chief executive expressed the hope that the EWC might be used to "limit the power of German unions" (ICEM, 1995, p. 5). Unless the EWC is seen as a means to the end of multinational works councils – entirely independent of any region or nation – it "will be more of a hindrance than a help to the workers" (op. cit., p. 6).

[24] Other breakthroughs in international collective bargaining were negotiated as early as the 1980s, such as the contracts between Danone (the former BSN) and the IUF (International Union of Food, Agriculture, Hotel, Restaurant, Catering, Tobacco and Allied Workers' Associations).

[25] After the successful strike against United Parcel Service (UPS) in the United States, ITF is attempting to organize the company's worldwide workforce of over 200,000 workers. The same is planned with the staff of deregulated airlines.

[26] Other examples are the IUF's historic campaigns against Nestlé in 1973 and Coca Cola in 1980 and 1984.

[27] A pioneering agreement on codes of conduct between two international partners, the food workers' international (IUF) and the French-based multinational Danone, was signed in 1994. One year later, the same International Trade Secretariat achieved agreement with the Accor hotel group which, for the first time, included franchisers.

[28] The rulings of the French courts demonstrated the EWC directive to be a sound basis for transnational labour law, while urging its transposition with effective sanctions into national legislation. Therefore, calls by Members of the European Parliament for further European codes of conducts should be viewed with scepticism (Lorber, 1997).

[29] Meanwhile, a plethora of union homepages are now on-line, providing international labour news, propelling labour campaigns via strike pages, boycott lists, corporate watch and government pages; they give access to industrial relations libraries, research databanks and online publications. See, for example, http://www. igc.org./labornet/index.html.

[30] Freedom of communication is still limited. For example, "sending an e-mail to a trade union activist in China or Burma is likely to do him or her more harm than good" (*Trade Union World*, 1997, p. 9).

[31] As in the case of codes of conduct, the credibility of social labels hinges on effective verification procedures laid down in formal agreements (ILO, 1997, p. 43).

[32] Attempts by some member organizations to secure the expulsion of the official Indonesian Metal Workers' Union from the International Metalworkers' Federation have so far failed, but it is likely that an independent Indonesian union will join the Federation as well.

[33] The WFTU notes, in connection with this debate, that MNCs and their subcontractors, who are "the actual entities responsible for the non-implementation of international labour standards managed to escape criticism" (1997, p. 2).

[34] A first step in this direction is to provide information which makes the different remuneration systems comparable (see, for example, International Metalworkers' Federation, 1996).

[35] Experience in Europe, where unions have recently pursued a policy of real pay restraint in exchange for job protection, precludes the general application of the insider/outsider model (Fajertag, 1996).

References

AEEU. 1996. *Partners in success: How the AEEU can help you to establish a profitable enterprise in the UK.* Kent, AEEU.

Agnew, J. ; Corbridge, S. 1995. *Mastering space: Hegemony, territory and international political economy.* London, Routledge.

Aithaner, Karl S.; Hanappi, H. (eds.). 1995. *Die Geburt der Weltwirtschaft?* Vienna, Sonderzahl.

Arbeitsgemeinschaft für Wissenschaftliche Wirtschaftspolitik (ed.). 1997. *Wirtschaftspolitisch Alternativen zur globalen Hegemonie des Neoliberalismus.* Vienna, Verlag des ÖGB.

Ariza Rico, Julián. 1995. "La afiliación a los sindicatos", in *Cinco Días* (Madrid), 19 Jan., p. 3.

Balaam, David N.; Veseth, Michael (eds.). 1996a. *Readings in international political economy.* Upper Saddle River, NJ, Prentice Hall.

—; —. 1996b. *Introduction to international political economy.* Upper Saddle River, NJ, Prentice Hall.

Bloom, David E.; Brender, Adi. 1993. "Labor and the emerging world economy", in *Population Bulletin* (Washington, DC), Vol. 42, No. 2, pp. 2-38.

Bowles, Samuel; Gintis, Herbert. 1995. "Productivity-enhancing egalitarian policies", in International Labour Review (Geneva), Vol. 134, No. 4-5, pp. 559-585.

Busch, G.K. 1980. *Political currents in the international trade union movement.* EIU Special Report No. 75. Two volumes. London, The Economist Intelligence Unit.

Campbell, Duncan. 1994. "Foreign investment, labour immobility and the quality of employment", in *International Labour Review* (Geneva), Vol. 133, No. 2, pp. 186-204.

—. 1991. *Globalization and strategic choices in tripartite perspective: An agenda for research and policy issues.* New Industrial Organization Programme, Discussion Paper DP/46/1991. Geneva, ILO-IILS.

Collingsworth, Terry; Goold, J. William; Harvey, Pharis J. 1996. "Time for a global new deal", in Balaam and Veseth, 1996a, pp. 226-230.

Danis, Jean-Jacques. 1996. "European Works Council", in Gabaglio and Hoffmann, pp. 77-94.

Drucker, Peter F. 1996. "Trade lessons from the world economy", in Balaam and Veseth, 1996a, pp. 90-96.

The Economist (London). 1997. "Follow the flag of convenience", in Vol. 342, No. 8005, 22 Feb., pp. 85-86.

ETUC. 1997. *Replies to the ETUC NETLEX questionnaire on transnational trade union rights.* Mimeo. Brussels.

European Industrial Relations Review (London). 1994. "Going global – a case study of Kvarner Group", in No. 246 (July), pp. 21-23.

Ewing, K. 1997. "Social Europe versus the free market", in *International Union Rights* (London), Vol. 4, No. 7, pp. 6-7.

Fajertag, Giuseppe. 1996. "Current trends in collective bargaining in Europe: An overview of the 1995 collective bargaining round", in Gabaglio and Hoffmann, pp. 109-120.

Feenstra, Robert C.; Hanson, Gordon R. 1996. *Globalization, outsourcing and wage inequality.* NBER Working Paper No. 5424. Cambridge, MA, National Bureau of Economic Research.

Fiet Info (Geneva). 1997. "1996 – Worst-ever year for union repression", in No. 4/97, p. 6.

Frank, Robert H. 1994. *Microeconomics and behavior.* Second edition. New York, NY, McGraw-Hill.

Frieden, Jeffrey A.; Lake, David A. (eds.). 1995. *International political economy: Perspectives on global power and wealth.* London, Routledge.

Gabaglio, Emilio; Hoffmann, Reiner (eds.). 1996. *European Trade Union Yearbook.* Brussels, ETUI.

Gallin, Dan. 1997. *Address to the Global Labour Summit*, Copenhagen, May 31-June 1. Geneva, Global Labour Institute.

—.1994. "Inside the new world order: Drawing the battle lines", in *New Politics* (Brooklyn, NY), Vol. 5, No. 1 (Summer), pp. 107-132.

Gershman, Carl. 1975. *The foreign policy of American labour.* Washington Papers Series, Vol. 3, No. 29. Beverly Hills, Sage.

Goodman, John B.; Pauly, Louis W. 1995. "The obsolence of capital controls? Economic management in an age of global markets", in Frieden and Lake, pp. 299-317.

Greider, William. 1997. *One world, ready or not: The manic logic of global capitalism.* New York, Simon & Schuster.

—.1996. "The global marketplace: A closet dictator", in Balaam and Veseth, 1996a, pp. 323-338.

Grunberg, Leon. 1996. "The IPE of multinational corporations", in Balaam and Veseth 1996b, pp. 338-359.

Hoffmann, Jurgen; Hoffmann, Reiner. 1997. *Globalization – Risks and opportunities for policy in Europe.* Brussels, ETUI.

Hoffmann, Reiner. 1996. "Editorial", in Gabaglio and Hoffmann, pp. 7-16.

ICEM. 1997. "Change in China's unions?", in *ICEM Info* (Brussels), Vol. 1, p. 14.

—.1995. *Unite and organise: The way ahead for world labour.* http://www.icem.org/docs/unite.html [visited 17 Dec. 1997].

ICFTU (International Confederation of Free Trade Unions). 1997a. *Annual survey of violations of trade union rights 1997.* Brussels.

—.1997b. "Italian trade unions strike major deal with toy multinational", in ICFTU *On-line archive* (www.icftu.org), 5 Nov. [visited 3 Feb. 1998].

—.1996. *The global market – trade unionism's greatest challenge.* Report to the 16th World Congress of the ICFTU, Brussels, 25-29 June. Brussels.

ILO. 1997. *World Labour Report 1997-98: Industrial relations, democracy and social stability.* Geneva.

IMF. 1997. *World Economic Outlook, May 1997.* Washington, DC.

—.1995. *World Economic Outlook, May 1995.* Washington, DC.

International Metalworkers' Federation. 1997. *Action Programme 1997-2001.* Geneva.

—.1996. *The purchasing power of working time: An international comparison 1994-95.* Geneva.

Krugman, Paul. 1994a. "Does third world growth hurt first world prosperity?" in *Harvard Business Review* (Boston, MA), Vol. 72, No. 4, pp. 113-121.

—.1994b. "Competitiveness: A dangerous obsession", in *Foreign Affairs*, (New York, NY), Vol. 73, No. 2 (Mar-Apr.), pp. 28-44.

—; Venables, Anthony J. 1995. "Globalization and the inequality of nations", in *Quarterly Journal of Economics* (Cambridge, MA), Vol. 110, No. 4 (Nov.), pp. 857-880.

Labour Research (London). 1997. "Renault dispute finally ends", in Vol. 86, No. 9 (Sep.), p. 9.

Lawrence, Robert Z.; Slaughter Matthew J. 1993. "International trade and American wages in the 1980s: Giant sucking sound or small hiccup?", in *Brookings Papers on Economic Activity* (Washington, DC), Microeconomics, No. 2, pp. 161-210.

Lee, Eddy. 1996. "Globalization and employment: Is anxiety justified?", in *International Labour Review* (Geneva), Vol. 135, No. 5, pp. 485-497.

Libération (Paris). 1997. "Une marche pour faire vivre l'Europe sociale: Mobilisation contre les licenciements à l'usine de Vilvorde", 17 Mar., p. 2.

Locke, Richard; Kochan, Thomas; Piore, Michael. 1995. "Reconceptualizing comparative industrial relations: Lessons from international research", in *International Labour Review* (Geneva), Vol. 134, No. 2, pp. 139-161.

Lorber, Pascale 1997. "The Renault case: The European Works Council put to the test", in *International Journal of Comparative Labour Law and Industrial Relations* (The Hague), Summer, pp. 135-142.

MacShane, D. 1996. *Global business: Global rights.* Fabian Pamphlet 575. London, Fabian Society.

Marglin, Stephen; Schor, Juliet B. (eds.). 1990. *The golden age of capitalism: Reinterpreting the postwar experience.* Oxford, Clarendon Press.

Marx, Karl; Engels, Fredrich. 1848. "Manifesto of the Communist Party", in J.H. Laski (ed.): *Communist manifesto: Socialist landmark.* London, George Allen and Unwin Ltd., 1948.

OECD. 1991. *Employment Outlook 1991.* Paris. July.

Peck, Jamie. 1996. *Work-place: The social regulation of social labour markets.* London, Guildford.

Peter, Kristyne. 1997. "Labor on the Internet", in *Working USA* (Armonk, NY), May-June, pp. 82-87.

Reich, Robert B. 1991. *The work of nations: Preparing ourselves for 21st century capitalism.* New York, Alfred A. Knopf.

Ross, Robert J. S. 1995. "Global capital, global unions: Speculations on the future of global unionism", in Althaner and Hanappi, pp. 83-92.

Sachs, Jeffrey D.; Shatz, Howard J. 1996. *International trade and wage inequality in the United States: Some new results.* Development Discussion Paper No. 524. Cambridge, MA, Harvard Institute for International Development.

—; —.1994. "Trade and jobs in U.S. manufacturing", in *Brookings Papers on Economic Activity* (Washington, DC), No. 1, pp. 1-84.

Schulmeister, Stephen. 1995. "The double role of the dollar as world currency and as national currency and the international economy since Bretton Woods", in Althaner and Hanappi, pp. 36-63.

Strange, Susan. 1995. "States, firms and diplomacy", in Frieden and Lake, pp. 61-68.

Trade Union World (Brussels). 1997. " 'Cyber-pros' versus 'cyber-proles'!", in Vol. 2, p. 9.

TUAC. 1995. *International financial markets and employment and social policy.* Report of a Round-Table Discussion, Ottawa – 29 May 1995. Paris.

UNCTAD. 1995. *Trade and Development Report 1995.* New York, United Nations.

Van Liemt, Gijsbert. 1992. "Economic globalization: Labour options and business strategies in high labour cost countries", in *International Labour Review* (Geneva), Vol. 131, No.4-5, pp. 453-470.

Waterman, Peter. Forthcoming. *From labour internationalism to global solidarity.* London, Cassell.

WFTU. 1997. "WFTU memorandum to the international meeting of workers confronting neoliberalism and globalization (Havana, 6-8 August 1997)", in *Flashes from the Trade Unions* (Prague), No. 14, pp. 1-5.

Wills, Jane. 1997. *Taking on the cosmo corps? Experiments in trans-national labour organization.* Re-scaling British industrial relations, Working Paper 1. University of Southampton.

Wolf, Martin. 1997. "Global opportunities", in *Financial Times* (London), 6 May, p. 14.

Wood, Adrian. 1994, *North-South trade, employment and inequality: Changing fortunes in a skill-driven world.* Oxford, Clarendon Press.

World Bank. 1995. *World Development Report 1995: Workers in an integrating world.* Washington, DC.

Yuste Ramos, Antonia; Foden, David; Vogel, Laurent. 1996. *Globalization, deregulation and employment: A contribution to the debate.* Discussion and Working Paper 96.08.2 (E). Brussels, European Trade Union Institute.

Zamagni, Stefano. 1996. *Globalization as a specificity of the post-industrial economy: Economic implications and ethic options.* Mimeo. University of Bologna. Nov.